# THINK SOCIAL PSYCHOLOGY

Canadian Edition

Kimberly J. Duff
Cerritos College
Kristine A. Peace
Grant MacEwan University

PEARSON
Toronto

*Vice-President, Editorial Director:* Gary Bennett
*Editor-in-Chief:* Michelle Sartor
*Acquisitions Editor:* Matthew Christian
*Marketing Manager:* Lisa Gillis
*Senior Developmental Editor:* Darryl Kamo
*Project Manager:* Marissa Lok
*Manufacturing Manager:* Susan Johnson
*Production Editor:* Cindy Miller, Element
*Copy Editor:* Tara Tovell
*Proofreader:* Catherine Wilson
*Compositor:* Element
*Photo and Permissions Researcher:* Tara Smith
*Art Director:* Julia Hall
*Cover Interior Designer:* Anthony Leung
*Cover Image:* iStockphoto/Thinkstock

To all of my current and past students: You continue to influence my thinking and my teaching. Finally, to my husband who helped me to "sway in the breeze" while chaos reigned.

*Kimberly J. Duff*

To my students and colleagues: You have continued to inspire me in both the science and art of teaching. To my parents and fiancé: Thank you for your encouragement and "calm blue ocean" during the storm of writing this text.

*Kristine A. Peace*



10 9 8 7 6 5 4 3 2 1 CKV

**Library and Archives Canada Cataloguing in Publication**

Duff, Kimberley, 1969-
Think social psychology / Kimberley J. Duff and Kristine A. Peace.
Includes bibliographical references and index.
ISBN 978-0-205-23589-6
1. Social psychology. I. Peace, Kristine A. (Kristine Anne), 1977- II. Title.

HM1033.D84 2012 302 C2012-901076-6 ISBN 978-0-205-23589-6

# BRIEF CONTENTS

# CONTENTS

## THE POWER OF PERSUASION 116



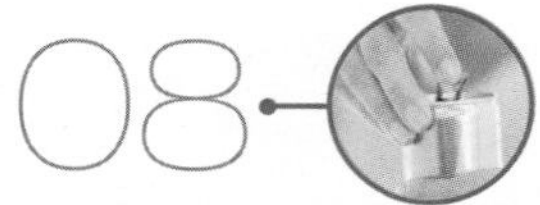

## SOCIAL INFLUENCE: SHOULD WE RESIST? 138

## THE POWER OF THE GROUP 156



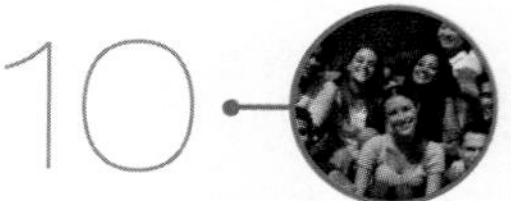

## STEREOTYPES, PREJUDICE, AND DISCRIMINATION: CAUSES AND CONSEQUENCES 176

11 

## AGGRESSION 202



12 

## ATTRACTION AND CLOSE RELATIONSHIPS 228



13 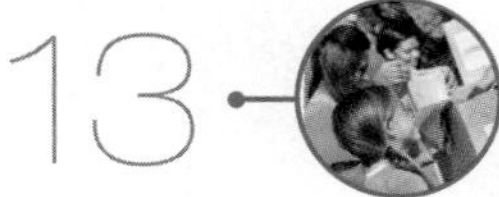

## PROSOCIAL BEHAVIOUR: WHY WE HELP, AND WHY WE DON'T 252

# ACKNOWLEDGMENTS

Thank you to Matthew Christian for diligently establishing the need for this text in the Canadian educational market and working to make this book a reality. To Darryl Kamo—your faithful emails, reminders, patience, and humour have been much appreciated and have helped in the completion of this book. To my production team—you have been so encouraging and dedicated to designing this book according to our vision: Marissa Lok (Pearson Project Manager), Cindy Miller and Heidi Allgair (Production Editors), and Tara Tovell (Editor). I appreciate the honesty and sincerity of each of you, and thank you for making this book a success.

I would also like to thank the reviewers for this book: Michael Boisvert, Fanshawe College; Paul Dupuis, Algoma University; Jill Esmonde, Georgian College; Patrice Esson, Fanshawe College; Francis Ho, Cégep Vanier College; Sara Mormul, Sir Sandford Fleming College; Jason Morris, St. Clair College; Kavita Prakash, Heritage College; and Greg Tyndall, College of New Caledonia. Your comments were helpful and provided excellent feedback and guidance for this and future editions of this text. Additional thanks go to the Marketing Team at Pearson for their dedication to this project.

Finally, to those in my life that stood along side me for the duration of this project, I owe you the largest thanks. To my parents—your encouragement, support, and task reminders were always needed and welcome. Thank you for always standing by me, and for being my faithful rocks during the storms. To my fiancé Casey—thank you for being patient and understanding of our limited time together, for being my shoulder to lean on, and the smile that got me through each day. To my "second Mom" Lynda—thank you for the encouragement, breakfast's and coffee's to get me going in the mornings, and cocktails to reward a day of hard work! To Tanya, Danille, Brianna, Allison, and Jellybean—thanks for your laughter breaks, anti-procrastination efforts, and being willing to listen to my endless textbook-related chatter. To my friends and colleagues at MacEwan—your support, "clicks", advice, and ideas have been invaluable, as have the de-stressing pints. Thank you all so much!

# ABOUT THE AUTHORS

KIMBERLEY J. DUFF received her PhD in Social Psychology at the University of Illinois at Chicago. She is currently a professor of psychology at Cerritos Community College in California, where she is passionate about teaching and helping her students succeed. Every year, she teaches over 600 students in Social Psychology, Introductory Psychology (both online and in traditional classrooms) and a Research Methods laboratory course. At Cerritos College, she has twice been recognized for her teaching and mentoring of students with the Outstanding Faculty Award and the Outstanding Advisor of the Year Award. More recently, the American Psychological Association's Society for the Teaching of Psychology honored her with the Wayne Weiten Teaching Excellence Award. She has given presentations on teaching methods at the American Psychological Association, NITOP (National Institute for the Teaching of Psychology) and Western Psychological Association annual conventions.

Kimberley has conducted research on spontaneous attributions, racial and social stereotypes, the benefits of tutorials on learning, and the impact of podcasting in the classroom. She also mentors her students in original psychological research that many of them present at psychological conferences, and she serves as a mentor for graduate students in the Teaching Assistant Program. To capture the success of her students' accomplishments, Kimberley developed a mentoring Web site for psychology students found at www.cerritos.edu/kduff/map. She serves as a co-advisor for the Cerritos College Psychology Club and Psi Beta chapter, which has been recognized three times with the national Outstanding Chapter of the Year Award under her guidance. Additionally, she has authored and developed multimedia content for a top-selling Introductory Psychology textbook.

KRISTINE A. PEACE received her PhD in Experimental Forensic Psychology from Dalhousie University in Halifax, Nova Scotia in 2006. She is currently an Assistant Professor at Grant MacEwan University, and teaches several different classes including Social Psychology, Introductory Psychology, Forensic Psychology, Human Memory, and various Topics in Forensic Psychology seminars. She has received awards in Teaching Excellence from both student societies and at a University level, as well as research funding and conference presentation grants. She has given several public lectures on topics as diverse as false memories, the social science of alcohol, and credibility assessment, and works as a consultant on legal cases. In addition, she is involved in MacEwan's "Forensic Days" where she hosts sessions for high-school students to demonstrate forensic and applied social psychological issues.

Kristine has conducted research on deception and its detection, judgments of victim/witness credibility, social decision making, trauma and memory in forensic settings, malingering traumatic disorders, and the influence of psychopathy on emotion processing. She also works with several honours and independent study students each year, collectively designing research and writing projects, as well as conference presentations (see her website at: http://academic.macewan.ca/peacek/). Kristine currently serves as the Honours Advisor for the Psychology Department, and is working to mentor students to maximize their undergraduate education. She also conducts Study Skills sessions each term to enhance student success, time management, and exam preparation. Finally, she has designed and developed multimedia and testbank supplements for many top-selling Introductory and Social Psychology texts.

THINK
SOCIAL PSYCHOLOGY
Canadian Edition

# WHAT IS SOCIAL PSYCHOLOGY?

*<<< Can people be discriminated against for superficial distinctions such as what group or team they are assigned to in class or at summer camp?*

**WHAT** IS SOCIAL PSYCHOLOGY?
**WHAT** ARE THE DIFFERENT PERSPECTIVES OF SOCIAL PSYCHOLOGY?
**IS** SOCIAL PSYCHOLOGY JUST COMMON SENSE?
**WHAT** ARE THE ROOTS OF SOCIAL PSYCHOLOGY?

At some point in their lives, most people have been divided into groups and have engaged in competitive actions against other groups. Think about classroom groups for school games, sports teams, or cabin groups at summer camp that you may have experienced. You likely bonded with members of your own group and wanted your team to win any games or prizes. The authors of your text had similar experiences. In fact, one of the authors of this text (KP) was a camp counsellor and remembers witnessing the campers from her cabin become a tight-knit group as they worked together to win "cabin cleaning" prizes against other cabins. Interestingly, this led to the exclusion of members of other cabins in activities that involved all campers. In fact, campers from each cabin tended to gravitate toward their own groups even when there were no competitive activities (e.g., they would sit together around campfires).

Can these superficial groupings lead to discrimination? In your reflections on your experiences, did you ever act negatively toward members of other groups or teams? The answer is likely yes. In fact, we are no strangers to treating people differently based on group membership. In the classic 1954 Robbers Cave Experiment, social psychologist Muzafer Sherif and his colleagues (1961/1988) demonstrated how easily discrimination can occur. During Phase 1 of his experiment, 22 boys of similar backgrounds were randomly divided into two groups. During the first week of "camp," the boys bonded with the members of their own group, engaged in common activities, and decided on a name and flag for their group. Neither the Eagles nor the Rattlers were aware of the presence of the other group until Phase 2 of the experiment began, in which the groups were introduced to each other and performed a series of competitive activities (e.g., tug-of-war, baseball) designed to generate frustration and competition between the groups. As the competitions continued, the boys began verbally expressing negative attitudes toward members of the other group (e.g., name-calling), which progressed to direct discriminatory acts against one another (the Eagles burned the Rattlers' flag, and the Rattlers raided and stole items from the Eagles' cabin). The results of this study have been fundamental to our understanding of how competition can lead to prejudice and discrimination.

How much of a role do prejudice and discrimination play in your life? Have you ever been the victim of prejudice or discrimination, or have you ever been the perpetrator of this behaviour? As a society, we are programmed to assume that the divide that instigates prejudice between minority and majority groups is based on race, gender, or other socially significant factors, such as white versus Aboriginal, men versus women, gay versus straight, or able-bodied versus disabled. Our social norms support this idea, but social psychologists argue that discrimination can also be based on factors that are purely arbitrary and meaningless, such as height, hair colour, or even shoe size.

# CHAPTER 01

**SOCIAL PSYCHOLOGY** the scientific study of the nature and causes of individual behaviour and thought in social situations

**SOCIAL PERCEPTION** the process through which individuals form impressions of others and interpret information about them

**SOCIAL INFLUENCE** the process through which other people affect an individual's thoughts or actions

**SOCIAL INTERACTION** relationships between two or more individuals that affect our perceptions of others and our behaviours

^^^ Social factors can influence many different types of behaviour, **including stem cell research into disorders that have widespread social consequences. For example, Dr. Nagy at Mount Sinai Hospital has conducted influential research on multiple sclerosis.**

## What Is Social Psychology?

What possessed explorers hundreds of years ago to leave their home countries to sail across virtually unknown seas? Why have doctors dedicated much of their time and effort to creating and utilizing stem cells to study genetic disorders? If you were a psychologist, you might say that the possibility of locating new resources and the novelty of being the first to discover something or cure disease was the motivation. If you were a sociologist, you might say that humans are curious by nature and that their interest in the unknown drove them to seek out uncharted territories. If you were a *social psychologist*, however, you might say that the motivation came from the individual cultures of the explorers and how the people around them expected them to behave. Christopher Columbus set out on his expedition because the people of Spain desired to gain political and economic power in Europe by discovering new trade routes. Canadian doctors and researchers are driven in the quest to battle genetic and autoimmune diseases (e.g., Alzheimer's, diabetes, Parkinson's, multiple sclerosis) and establish their place in the scientific world of medical investigation (e.g., Carlson, 2009). No explanation is right or wrong; they simply emerge from different schools of thought.

Psychology, sociology, and social psychology can be viewed as existing on a continuum, with psychology at one end, sociology at the other, and social psychology somewhere in between. Sociologists focus on the entire group, or the societal level, while social psychologists are interested in the interaction of the individual person and the given situation. **Social psychology** can be generally defined as the scientific study of the nature and causes of individual behaviour and thought in social situations. In other words, it involves understanding how and why people think and act the way they do within a social context. The focus of social psychology can be described as having three main facets: *social perception*, *social influence*, and *social interaction* (see Table 1.1). In addition, social psychologists apply their research to help understand and address issues in other fields such as law, business, and health (see the Applying Social Psychology sections throughout your text).

**Social perception** is the process through which individuals form impressions of others and interpret information about them. For example, when we see a person driving a flashy sports car, we may think that the driver has a lot of money and is successful in life. **Social influence** is the process through which other people affect an individual's thoughts or actions. A person may experience social influence when deciding what profession to pursue. For example, an individual may choose to become a doctor not just because she is interested in medicine, but also because her parent is a doctor. Or, the choice could be influenced by the fact that in our society medicine is viewed as a noble profession, and the individual wishes to be respected by others. Social influence results from social interaction. **Social interaction** refers to the relationship between two or more individuals and how those relations change not only our perceptions of others but our behaviour as well. This is the basis of analysis for social psychologists, who strive to understand and explain how the thoughts, feelings, and behaviours of individuals are influenced by the actual, imagined, or implied presence of others (Allport, 1954).

<<< **Social perception causes us to think that people who** wear glasses are more intelligent than those who don't.

Social psychologists study behaviour using two different types of research methods. **Basic research methods** refer to "pure" research that is driven by curiosity or obtaining scientific knowledge about a phenomenon. **Applied research methods** involve the application of basic research to solve practical problems in the real world. For example, a social psychologist examining the way in which we use heuristics (or mental shortcuts) to make judgments about the cause of others' behaviour is studying a basic process. An applied social psychologist may investigate how situational and social factors can contribute to and affect mental health or decision making in the legal system (i.e., juries), how businesses can increase the effectiveness of their employees, and whether group work in school is advantageous or detrimental to social relationships and learning. As you can see, social psychology is a broad field, with many applications and many different ways of examining social behaviour.

**BASIC RESEARCH METHODS (IN SOCIAL PSYCHOLOGY)** "pure" research that is driven by curiosity or obtaining scientific knowledge about a phenomenon

**APPLIED RESEARCH METHODS (IN SOCIAL PSYCHOLOGY)** the application of basic research to solve practical problems in the real world

## What Are the Different Perspectives of Social Psychology?

All psychologists use the scientific method in their research, but since there is no one single perspective that can explain all human behaviour or thinking, they may use several different theoretical approaches when testing

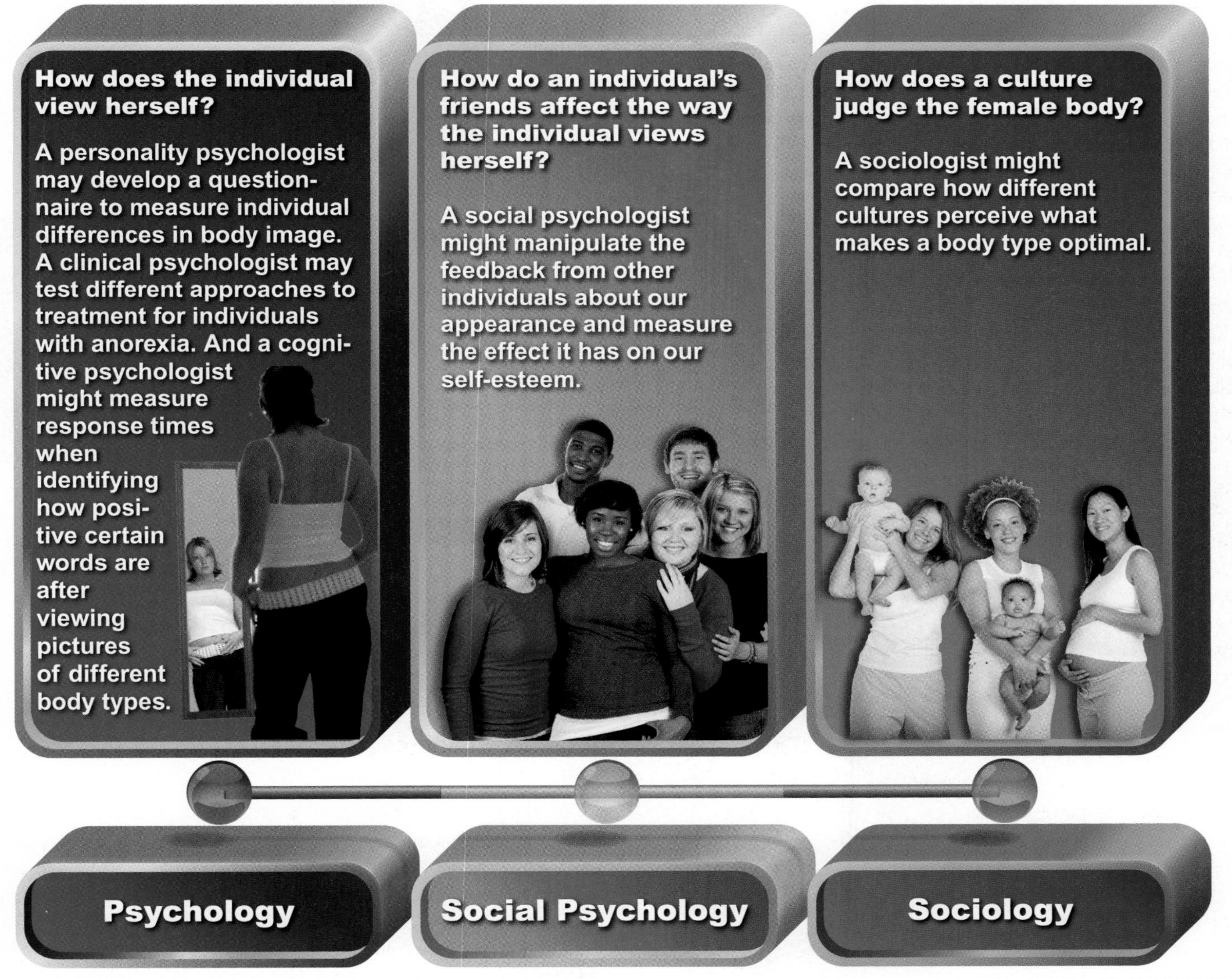

How does the individual view herself?
A personality psychologist may develop a questionnaire to measure individual differences in body image. A clinical psychologist may test different approaches to treatment for individuals with anorexia. And a cognitive psychologist might measure response times when identifying how positive certain words are after viewing pictures of different body types.
How do an individual's friends affect the way the individual views herself?
A social psychologist might manipulate the feedback from other individuals about our appearance and measure the effect it has on our self-esteem.
How does a culture judge the female body?
A sociologist might compare how different cultures perceive what makes a body type optimal.
Psychology
Social Psychology
Sociology


**Teen Body Image Issues on the Method of Thinking Spectrum.** Psychology, sociology, and social psychology can be viewed as existing on a continuum, **with psychology at one end, sociology at the other, and social psychology somewhere in between.** But it doesn't have to be one or the other; **an interdisciplinary approach merging two or all three can be taken as well.**

**SOCIOCULTURAL PERSPECTIVE** a perspective that focuses on the relationship between social behaviour and culture

**EVOLUTIONARY PERSPECTIVE** a perspective that focuses on the physical and biological predispositions that result in human survival

**NATURAL SELECTION** the process whereby individuals with certain characteristics are more frequently represented in subsequent generations as a result of being better adapted for their environment

**SOCIAL COGNITIVE PERSPECTIVE** a perspective that builds on behavioural theories and demonstrates that an individual's cognitive process influences and is influenced by behavioural associations

**SOCIAL LEARNING PERSPECTIVE** a perspective that stresses the particular power of learning through social reinforcements and punishments

hypotheses. Modern social psychological perspectives maintain that prior learning experiences and intrapsychic forces (e.g., the unconscious), as well as social and cultural context, shape human behaviour and mental processes. The **sociocultural perspective** focuses on the relationship between social behaviour and culture. This perspective is important because it highlights the fact that human behaviour is influenced not only by an individual's close companions but also by the culture in which the individual lives. For example, the children in the Robbers Cave Experiment described in the chapter opener showed signs of prejudice, even though all were from similar racial, socio-economic, and religious backgrounds. What do you think would have happened if this study were conducted in a different culture that emphasized group relationships over competitive activities?

The **evolutionary perspective** takes a slightly different approach by focusing on the biological bases for universal mental characteristics that all humans share. Psychologists who follow the evolutionary perspective are interested in explaining general mental strategies and characteristics, such as how we attract members of the opposite sex, why we lie, why we like to play sports, and other similar concepts. The evolutionary perspective involves principles that are derived from evolutionary biology and Charles Darwin's principle of natural selection, and it focuses on the physical and biological predispositions that result in human survival (Boyd & Richerson, 1985). **Natural selection** is the process by which individuals with certain characteristics are more frequently represented in subsequent generations as a result of being better adapted to their environments. The evolutionary perspective would answer the question "Why do we lie?" by claiming that lying somehow aided in our ancestors' survival, and over time, the characteristic of lying became so widely represented that it is now common in our society.

The **social cognitive perspective** and the **social learning perspective** accept and expand on conditioning principles, which assume

**Evolutionary Perspective:** People steal because gaining certain objects, even if through stealing, improves a person's ability to survive.

**Sociocultural Perspective:** People steal because our culture appreciates objects more than people.

**Social Learning Perspective:** A person steals because he learned through example that stealing is an acceptable behaviour.

**Social Cognitive Perspective:** A person steals because he simply doesn't believe it is wrong.

**Modern Social Perspectives on Why People Steal.** While each perspective takes a different approach, **all four can work together to address the same issues.**

An evolutionary psychologist might say that we find taller, muscular men and young-looking females to be attractive because these are signs associated with virility, **and humans have a natural desire to reproduce.**

direct correlations between learning and behaviour. The social cognitive perspective builds on behavioural theories and demonstrates that an individual's cognitive process influences and is influenced by behavioural associations. For example, imagine that you offend a friend by telling him or her your opinion about his or her new dating partner. Your friend may feel you should apologize for your rude behaviour; however, you do not believe you were in the wrong to tell the truth, and you interpret your behaviour as that of a true friend.

The social learning perspective stresses the particular power of learning through social rewards and punishments. A key theory to many of social psychology's core concepts, Albert Bandura's (1977) social learning theory, argues that in addition to learning through consequences in our environment, people also learn from each other. This is called *observational learning*, when people are influenced by watching the modeled behaviours of others. For example, children who witness aggressive behaviour to obtain a desired object (e.g., a new toy) may engage in this behaviour themselves as they may learn that aggression is a strategy for getting what you want.

## SOCIAL PSYCHOLOGY AND OTHER DISCIPLINES

Social psychologists do not work alone in their field. Economists, business leaders, and even neuroscientists help to guide and also benefit from the work of social psychologists. Because social psychologists are interested in what motivates particular behaviour, such as purchasing items, economists may team up with social psychologists to better understand the spending habits of certain populations. Similarly,

"Social psychologists do not work alone in their field. Economists, business leaders, and even neuroscientists help to guide and also benefit from the work of social psychologists."

business leaders may enlist the help of social psychologists to better understand and manage the behaviour of their employees. Social loafing, for example, may be a problem that a company hopes to minimize. Social psychologists can help the company change how it assesses the accountability of employees. Conversely, individuals from these various disciplines can assist social psychologists by creating tools and platforms for research.

Neuroscientists have helped social psychologists literally look into the minds of humans through the development of magnetic resonance imaging (MRI) and positron emission tomography (PET) scans (Adolphs, 2003). These tools allow neuroscientists and social psychologists to observe brain activity when a study participant thinks about or engages in certain behaviour, such as solving a problem, stereotyping, or the social implications of childhood brain injuries (e.g., Yeates et al., 2007). An emerging field called

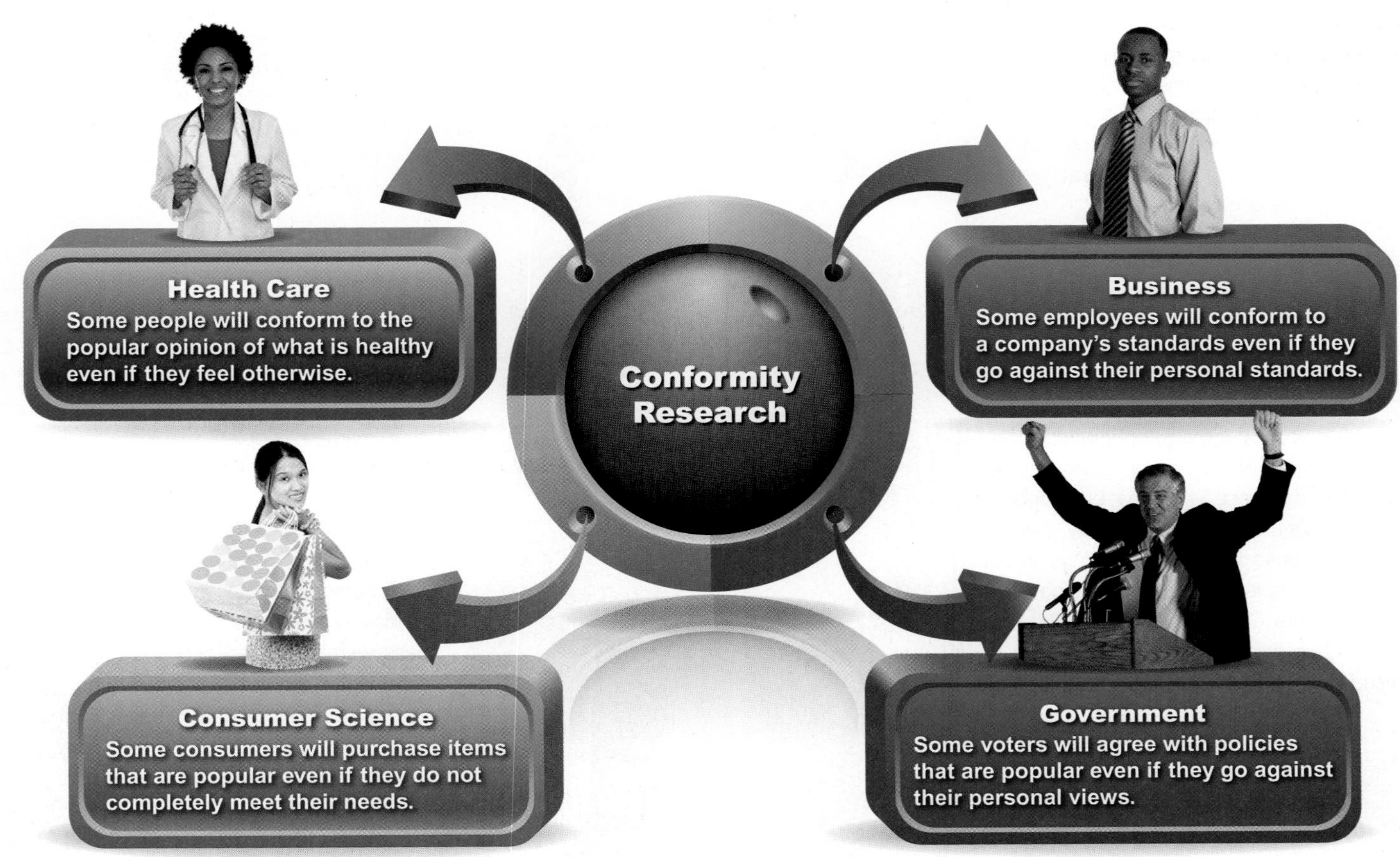

Health Care
Some people will conform to the popular opinion of what is healthy even if they feel otherwise.
Conformity Research
Business
Some employees will conform to a company's standards even if they go against their personal standards.
Consumer Science
Some consumers will purchase items that are popular even if they do not completely meet their needs.
Government
Some voters will agree with policies that are popular even if they go against their personal views.


**Social Psychology and Other Fields. Social psychologists can work with individuals from** other disciplines to perform research that is mutually beneficial.

## Table 1.1: Topics in Social Psychology

| | |
|---|---|
| **Social Perception:** Understanding How We View Ourselves and Others | • Why do we worry more about having safe flights than having safe car rides? (See Chapter 3)<br>• What impact does culture have on the way you see yourself? (See Chapter 4)<br>• How can you tell when someone is lying to you? (See Chapter 5) |
| **Social Influence:** Understanding How We Influence One Another | • Why do your attitudes sometimes disagree with your actions? (See Chapter 6)<br>• Why are we more likely to say yes when we are already in a good mood? (See Chapter 7)<br>• How far would you go to obey someone? (See Chapter 8)<br>• How does competition affect performance? (See Chapter 9) |
| **Social Interaction:** Understanding Why We Interact the Way We Do with Others | • Is racial prejudice on the decline? (See Chapter 10)<br>• What impact does testosterone have on aggression? (See Chapter 11)<br>• Do opposites really attract? (See Chapter 12)<br>• Why does helping someone make you feel good? (See Chapter 13) |

*social neuroscience* integrates the study of physiological mechanisms with social psychological perspectives (Cacioppo et al., 2007). For example, recent social neuroscience research has found specific parts of the brain that are responsible for our affective responses to other people and our ability to interpret and empathize with the emotions of others (Decety & Jackson, 2006). The possibilities for social psychology to interact with other fields and industries are endless.

## Is Social Psychology Just Common Sense?

So now that you have read about what social psychology is and the types of topics people study within this field, you may be wondering whether or not this area merely reflects our commonsense beliefs and feelings about events. For example, as you were reading about Sherif's Robbers Cave Experiment in the introduction to this chapter, you may not have been surprised that the children demonstrated prejudiced behaviour. In fact, you may have even predicted the outcome. Consider the following statements and answer whether you think each is true or false:

1. Individuals who are mentally ill are frequently involved in criminal behaviour because they are dangerous and unpredictable.
2. Even though we have a strong justification for lying to someone (e.g., to protect them from harm), we feel worse about this than when we have no excuse for lying.
3. Groups are more effective and less biased in the decision-making process than any one individual.
4. Opposites attract. Partners who are opposites form long-lasting romantic relationships because they help to balance each other out.
5. The greater the number of people who witness an accident or see someone in need of help, the more people there are who are willing to provide assistance.

Does the truth of these assertions seem obvious to you? You may have answered "true" in all instances because you feel you are already aware of these facts and have seen them in your everyday life—they are common sense! But if common sense tells us all the answers to questions such as these, what need is there for social psychology? While each of these statements seems to reflect our common-sense ideas or beliefs about the world, research in social psychology has found that they all are false. For example, people often falsely assume that a relationship between two things (e.g., mental illness and crime) exists because of the *availability heuristic*. This mental shortcut leads us to make judgments based on how easily information comes to mind; in our example, rare and dramatic cases of mentally ill individuals engaging in criminal acts (e.g., the Greyhound bus murder in 2008) are reported more often in the news and tend to stick out in our minds. As a result, we make errors in our social judgments about the frequency of certain events.

Don't feel bad if you believed the statements above to be correct. Most people do! Common sense is our natural way of understanding things. We sometimes assume that social psychology is common sense because the subject matter is often personal and familiar. We believe that we are naturally knowledgeable about human behaviour, but many of our common beliefs have been disproved by social psychologists. For example, the idea that opposites attract is believed by many, but social research has concluded that married couples are more likely to be similar in terms of religious beliefs, political attitudes, and values than randomly paired couples (de Vries, 2005). The same researcher also found that married couples who showed similar personality traits in terms of anxiety and avoidance, agreeableness, and conscientiousness were more satisfied and happy in their marriages than the couples who did not show similar personality traits. Further, the similarity–attraction relationship extends to our preference for dating partners of the same culture as ourselves (e.g., Osbeck, Moghaddam, & Perreault, 1997). These findings support the old adage that "birds of a feather flock together" rather than "opposites attract."

>>> **In love, do "opposites attract"** or do "birds of a feather flock together"?

Psychologists cannot rely on common sense because they must base their conclusions on evidence that is acquired through careful and deliberate study. Through such studies, psychologists form theories that predict behaviour *before* it occurs. When people use their common sense, they make "predictions" *after* the behaviour occurs. This type of prediction occurs due to a phenomenon that psychologists call **hindsight bias**, or the tendency to think that you knew that something would occur all along. For instance, did you find yourself saying after the fact that you knew the Conservative Party of Canada would achieve a majority government in the May 2011 federal election, especially if you had been planning all along to vote for that party? After the Stanley Cup 2011 riots in Vancouver, did you say to your friends that you knew all along that Canucks fans would react badly if their team lost?

Although beliefs developed through common sense are often the result of good judgment, they can also generate ambiguous and conflicting explanations for behaviour. Let's say you have a friend who is madly in love with her boyfriend. As she prepares to leave for a study-abroad program in Paris, she becomes worried about her ability to maintain her relationship with her boyfriend, who will be waiting for her at home. You reassure her that her relationship will overcome the distance because you believe that "absence makes the heart grow fonder." After two months abroad, however, your friend tells you that she's fallen in love with an artist named Pierre and wants to stay in France. You think, "I knew this was going to happen. After all, Paris is a romantic city, and when a person is out of sight, he is out of mind." If your friend's relationship survived the separation, then you probably would have said, "I told you so" and never doubted your original judgment. As you can see, the hindsight bias influences many of our interpretations of others' behaviour and our self-evaluations.

## DON'T WE ALL HAVE COMMON SENSE?

Have you ever judged someone by claiming she has no common sense? As in, "Emma is book smart, but she has no common sense." As a child, your parents may have questioned your common sense after you did something foolish, such as crossing the street without looking. You didn't ignore your common sense when engaging in this behaviour; at the time, you and your parents had different senses of danger. Common sense is a subjective concept, which makes it problematic to rely on common sense to explain behaviour. What one person believes to be common sense might not fall in line with another person's belief. This is because common sense assumptions are usually based on personal observation and experience rather than solid evidence, and therefore bias becomes a factor.

For example, it's common knowledge that men are more authoritative than women, right? You might believe that if you grew up in a male-dominated household, but you might think quite differently if women were the authority figures in your upbringing. A person's values, principles, and tendencies can create bias in his or her perception of how broadly these beliefs are held (Ross, Greene, & House, 1977). Similarly, if you grew up in a household where prejudiced beliefs about particular minority groups were expressed, you are likely to believe that these opinions are more widespread among others than they are (e.g., Watt & Larkin, 2010).

> "Common sense is a subjective concept, which makes it problematic to rely on common sense to explain behaviour."

**HINDSIGHT BIAS** the tendency to think that one knew that something would occur all along

**FALSE CONSENSUS EFFECT** a phenomenon that causes individuals to assume that everyone shares the same opinion they do

**DIFFERENTIAL CONSTRUAL** the act of judging circumstances differently

**CONFIRMATION BIAS** the tendency to notice information that confirms one's beliefs and to ignore information that disconfirms one's beliefs

**SCIENTIFIC METHOD** an approach to thinking that involves using systematic observations, measurements, and experiments to assess information

The assumption that everyone shares the same opinion as oneself occurs as the result of the **false consensus effect.** The false consensus effect increases when situations permit **differential construal,** or the act of judging circumstances differently (Gilovich, 1990). For example, you may think that everyone knows it is unprofessional to wear flip-flops in the workplace, but that is in reality a matter of opinion, not a matter of fact. Multiple parties can construe the idea of what is considered "professional" differently. False consensus can be problematic in activities such as creating public policy. If elected officials or committees assume that the majority of constituents are in favour of strong regulations on issues such as gun control, abortion, dangerous offender designations, or stem cell research and health care, they could pass legislation that does not actually represent the desires of the public.

## HOW DO YOU MINIMIZE BIAS?

*Hindsight bias* and the *false consensus effect* are two ways in which false conclusions can be derived through biased actions or thoughts. But sometimes, the conclusion itself can create biased actions or thoughts. Let's say you just moved to a new town and are looking to make new friends. You read a recent article in a major newspaper that cited a study that concluded that people who wear colourful clothing tend to be friendlier than people who wear neutral tones. As you mingle with people at a local event, you realize that the study was right—the people you met who were wearing colourful clothing were significantly friendlier than those in muted clothing. What you might not have realized is that by reading only the conclusion of the study, you created a bias that may have subconsciously caused you to demonstrate behaviour that helped to confirm your thoughts. For example, you may have been more relaxed around the people who were wearing colourful clothing because you assumed that they were sociable, thereby making it easier to have a friendly conversation. This tendency to notice information that confirms one's beliefs and to ignore information that disconfirms one's beliefs is called **confirmation bias**.

How do social psychologists eliminate these biases when conducting their research? The answer to this question is complex because there is no way to completely remove bias from processes that humans administer. But social psychologists strive to minimize bias through the use of the scientific method. The **scientific method** is an approach to thinking that uses systematic observations, measurements, and experiments to assess information. It is used by other members of the scientific community such as chemists, physicists, biologists, and other psychologists to minimize bias and reduce errors. As you move forward in this course, you will need to apply the scientific method to your everyday thinking. We will discuss the scientific method in more detail in Chapter 2.

Social psychology is not just of interest to neuroscientists, other scientists, and people in the medical field. Understanding human behaviour, and particularly how it relates to social and cultural aspects, can be beneficial to almost any field. So it is safe to say that the field of social psychology will continue to grow and mature as it becomes increasingly useful and relevant to our modern world. As we carry on with our journey into learning about social psychology, we will explore many of these ideas in detail. But first, let's take a look at where the field of social psychology had its beginnings.

## What Are the Roots of Social Psychology?

Social psychology is a fairly young discipline that did not distinguish itself within the broader field of psychology until the 20th century. While the activities that define concepts such as social interaction and social influence have been present for as long as there have been humans on Earth, a strong platform on which to study these concepts did not exist until the development of Western culture. In fact, Gordon Allport (1954) stated that "the roots of social psychology lie in the intellectual soil of the whole Western tradition" (see Farr, 1996). While researchers from the United States were among the first to embrace this new discipline, it is now an area of focus for researchers worldwide.

One of the earliest formal studies in social psychology occurred at the end of the 19th century. In 1898, researcher Norman Triplett conducted a study that asked the question, "What happens when individuals join together with other individuals?" As a fan of bicycling, Triplett noticed that competitive cyclists performed better during races than during solo rides. He timed their unpaced solo rides, when cyclists were only trying to beat their own established times, and compared them to paced rides against other contestants (Triplett, 1898). To understand how pace keeping and competition among others affect an individual's performance, Triplett arranged a study that measured the performance of 40 children while playing a simple game that involved winding up a fishing line on a reel (Triplett, 1898). The results of the study suggested that the children performed better when playing in pairs than when playing alone. This study, considered to be the first published study in social

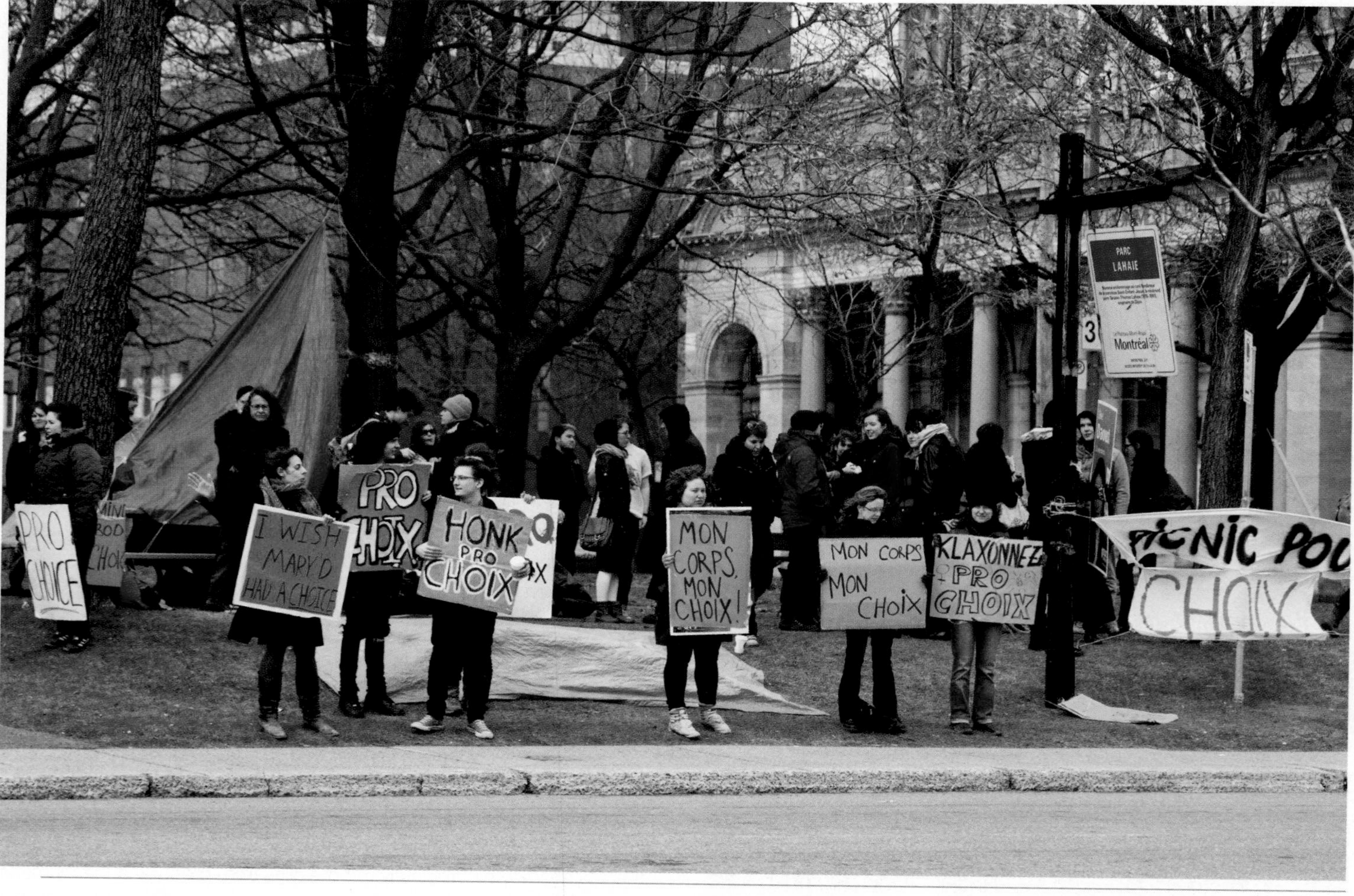


If you believe in women's right to an abortion, then you may assume that most people share your position. And if you are pro-life (like these demonstrators at the Morgentaler abortion clinic in Montreal), you may overestimate how many people hold this belief as well.

**SOCIAL FACILITATION** the enhancement of a well-learned performance when another person is present

**SOCIAL LOAFING** a phenomenon that occurs when individuals make less effort when attempting to achieve a particular goal as a group than they would if they were attempting to achieve the goal on their own

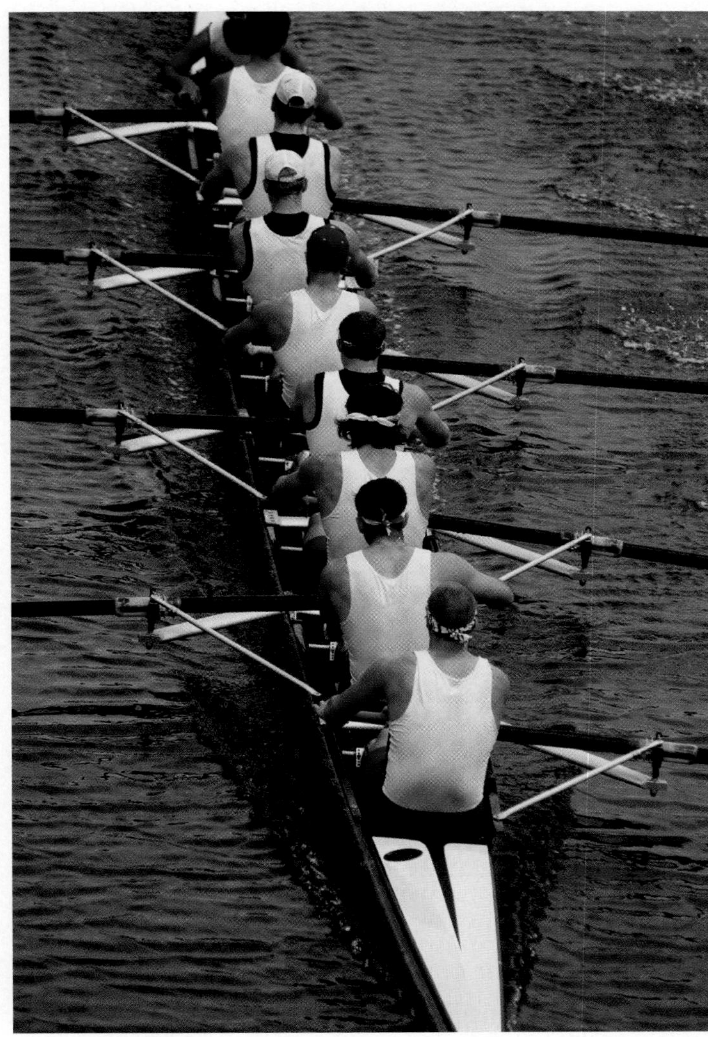

According to the concept of social loafing, the presence of others may cause these rowers **to put forth less effort when working as a team than they would if they were working individually.**

psychology, documented the concept of **social facilitation**, or the enhancement of performance when other people are present. You may feel the effects of social facilitation in your academic life. For example, if your professor asks you to complete a task that you are well skilled at, such as reading a paragraph in a foreign language, you likely would perform better in class than if you were alone.

While the concept of social facilitation has been supported in many studies on both humans and animals (e.g., Lambert et al., 2003; Tolman, 1965; Zajonc, Heingartner, & Herman, 1969), these results were contrary to earlier research on performance evaluation. In 1883, French professor Max Ringelmann conducted a study (not published until 1913) in which he asked a group of individuals to tug on a rope both individually and as a team. He found that the participants pulled harder when working as individuals than as a team. In fact, he found that the larger the group, the weaker the individual effort. He concluded that an individual's performance actually gets worse in the presence of others (Ringelmann, 1913). Ringlemann's study illustrated the concept of **social loafing**, a phenomenon that occurs when individuals make less of an effort when attempting to achieve a goal as a group than they would if they were attempting to achieve the goal on their own. You may have had firsthand experience with social loafing if you have worked on a group project for class and one member of the group hasn't pulled his or her weight. You might refer to this type of social loafer as a slacker.

While these conclusions may seem at odds, if we examine them closely we can see that the results actually highlight two different patterns of human behaviour. In the bicycle study, the contribution of each individual member could be identified, but in the rope study, each individual's contribution was not discernible, meaning that each individual's effort, or lack thereof, would not be noticed by the spectators. Another explanation for these conflicting results is that social performance depends upon the complexity of the task (Bond & Titus, 1983). Specifically, performance on a task that is simple or

**The phenomenon of social facilitation** would cause this athlete to lift more weight in front of a crowd than he would alone.

**Social Loafing Versus Social Facilitation.** Accountability is a major factor in determining **whether a person will be a loafer or a facilitator, as illustrated here.** But if the task is important, loafing is diminished, and if we are good at it, we will likely perform well. **These factors can eclipse accountability.**



well-learned for you (e.g., sorting shapes) will be enhanced in the presence of others. That is, you will experience *social facilitation*. However, if you are engaging in a complex or unlearned task, such as calculating difficult physics formulas, the presence of others would result in decreased performance, or *social inhibition* (e.g., Zajonc, 1965). As you can see, the social influences on our behaviour are multi-faceted and complex—and these discoveries were made while social psychology as a discipline was still in its infancy!

## SOCIAL PSYCHOLOGY IN THE 20TH CENTURY

By the start of the 20th century, social psychology had begun to establish itself as an independent discipline through the development of a separate curriculum and the formation of a specialized organization. A major milestone in the development of social psychology curriculum was the publishing of textbooks. The first two textbooks on the subject of social psychology were published in 1908, one by sociologist Edward Ross and the other by psychologist William McDougall, titled *Social Psychology* and *Introduction to Social Psychology*, respectively. These two works laid the groundwork for further study in the field. In 1924, psychologist Floyd Allport created a second version of *Social Psychology* that was heavily based on experimental research studies and focused on external influences on behaviour (Katz, 1979). This was followed in 1935 by the publication of *The Handbook of Social Psychology* (now in its fifth edition), which is considered the quintessential reference guide for the field of social psychology (Fiske, Gilbert, & Lindzey, 2009).

In 1936, Gordon Allport, Floyd's younger brother, and other social psychologists formed the Society for the Psychological Study of Social Issues (SPSSI) in an effort to bring together a national group of socially minded psychologists to address social and economic issues, applying social psychological research to social issues and public policy. Since its formation, the SPSSI has had a significant impact on the discipline of psychology and on society as a whole. Its publication, the *Journal of Social Issues*, has published research that has changed the way psychologists and other concerned members of society understand human behaviour. The organization strives to inform public policy and encourages public education through its research and advocacy efforts. Today, SPSSI has grown into an international group of more than 3,000 psychologists, allied scientists, students, and other academics who share a common interest in research on the psychological facets of important social issues (Society for the Psychological Study of Social Issues, 2010). Journals in social psychology include *Basic and Applied Social Psychology, Journal of Applied Social Psychology, Journal of Experimental Social Psychology, Journal of Personality, Journal of Personality and Social Psychology, Journal of Social Psychology, Personality and Social Psychology Bulletin, Social Cognition, Social Psychology Quarterly*, and many others in which social psychologists publish research on a vast area of topics such as those noted in Table 1.1.

Other early social psychologists had profound impacts on the field. When people began to recognize social prejudice in the 1930s, researchers found that participants had developed ideas about different racial and ethnic groups even without having contact with members of these groups (Katz & Braly, 1933). This gave shape to the idea of stereotypes as social psychologists study them now. Further, LaPiere (1934) found that individuals often displayed discrepancies between their attitudes and behaviours about racial groups. LaPiere travelled around the United States with a Chinese couple and visited over 350 restaurants and hotels. During this time, the couple was rejected entry just once. When surveyed after the trip, however, 92 percent of the businesses who answered the questions reported they would not accept Chinese individuals as patrons (LaPiere, 1934; see Chapter 6 for a more detailed description of this study). The topic of the relationship between attitudes and behaviours became a mainstay among the areas that social psychologists continue to study (e.g., Dovidio, Glick, & Rudman, 2005; Esses, Dovidio, & Hodson, 2002; Markus, 2008).

## The Impact of World War II

As social psychology moved into a more modern form during the mid-20th century, global events began to have a major influence on the development of the academic discipline. World War I had a significant impact on the social and political climate of the world, but it was World War II and the Nazis' occupation of Europe that completely changed the structure and direction of social psychology. In fact, Cartwright stated, "If I were required to name the one person who has had the greatest impact upon the field, it would have to be Adolf Hitler" (Cartwright, 1979).

How could one person have such a significant impact on an entire academic field? The rise of fascism brought about by Hitler and the Nazi regime created a strong anti-Semitic and anti-intellectual environment in several of Europe's academic institutions. This forced several of the continent's leading social scientists, such as Kurt Lewin, Fritz Heider, and Solomon Asch, to migrate to North America to escape persecution. As the Western world watched countries and cultures willingly convert to a fascist form of thinking,

^^^ Social psychologists address important social issues such as examining the positive and negative consequences **of long-term helping on those who need help and those who volunteer to provide it.**

government officials looked to social psychology to answer their questions about human behaviour and the power of political propaganda. Social psychologists in the United States used their knowledge and results from government-funded research to develop several wartime programs, including the selection of officers for the Office of Strategic Services—precursor to the Central Intelligence Agency (CIA)—and the manipulation of enemy confidence and morale.

The budding respect for the science behind social psychology and its useful application in solving real-world problems that occurred during World War II confirmed the beliefs of influential social psychologist Kurt Lewin, who is credited with the adage "No research without action, and no action without research" (Ash, 1992). Lewin pioneered what is today called the *interactionist perspective*, combining internal factors (from personality psychology) and external factors (from social psychology). Lewin and his colleagues conducted research on leadership style, and found that when groups of boys worked under three different types of leaders (autocratic, democratic, or laissez-faire), they performed the best when they had a democratic leader (Lewin, Lippitt, & White, 1939). These findings were significant to our understanding of how political policy can influence group behaviour.

> "No research without action, and no action without research."
> —Kurt Lewin

Adolf Hitler's ability to manipulate the values of thousands of Germans **generated many questions about human behaviour and the power of propaganda.**



In the postwar era, social psychology research became an integral part of understanding how certain social changes could take place, specifically the widespread acceptance of Nazi ideology by Germans and other European citizens. Following World War II, there was an explosion of many of the theories that now make up the core of social psychology. For instance, Solomon Asch (1951) showed that people were readily willing to agree to a clearly wrong answer provided by the majority. Later, Stanley Milgram (1963) illustrated how people would compromise their personal values in the interest of obedience. The powerful concept of social influence will be discussed in greater detail in Chapter 8.

Leon Festinger took these ideas about conformity further and developed his theory of cognitive dissonance (1957), the idea that our attitudes are often at odds with our behaviours (see Chapter 6). He also developed social comparison theory (1954), a theory to explain how people perceive themselves in terms of others (see Chapter 4). Another building block of social psychology, attribution theory, developed by Fritz Heider (1958), examined how and why people explain their own behaviours and the behaviours of others (further discussed in Chapter 5). Using these basic theories of Asch, Milgram, Festinger, and Heider, social psychologists today continue to expound upon these ideas and generate new questions and theories from them.

From the mid-1950s through the 1960s, research turned to topics dealing with social relations and interactions such as stereotyping and prejudice. The foundation of social psychology was further built upon by psychologists including Gordon Allport (see Chapter 10), who developed the Scale of Prejudice (1954); Latane and Darley (see Chapter 13), who researched altruism and prosocial behaviour (1969); and Clark and Clark (1947), whose work later impacted court decisions to desegregate schools in the United States and Canada. Aggression and attraction also took a front seat during this period in social psychology, and these topics will be covered in Chapters 11 and 12, respectively.

During the 1970s and 1980s, a cognitive revolution impacted psychology as a whole, and this included social psychology. Festinger's theory of cognitive dissonance (1957) was central to this, and researchers Kahneman and Tversky (1973, 1974, 1982) developed the idea of different *heuristics*, or mental shortcuts, that people unintentionally take to make sense of the world around them. Kahneman and Tversky's findings will be covered in Chapter 3. These ideas changed the approach researchers took to studying topics such as stereotyping, personal relationships, and helping behaviours, among other ideas. Today, many researchers take a social-cognitive approach to understanding behaviour.

It is important to remember that social psychology is primarily considered to be a Western-dominated discipline. In fact, 75–90 percent of social psychologists live in North America (Smith & Bond, 1993). However,

# ACTION LEARNING

## Practising What We Preach

Kurt Lewin, the father of modern social psychology, coined the term *action research* a half-century ago to describe research that is conducted with the goal of solving social problems. Lewin was interested in discovering how to get individuals to act in ways that are beneficial both to them and to society as a whole. Unlike the majority of his professional peers, Lewin was less interested in "pure research" that has no implication for practical application than he was in research that encourages action learning (i.e., applied research methods), which he felt would lead to a better understanding of human behaviour and a more considerate and peaceful world. He is credited with stating, "Research that produces nothing but books will not suffice" (Lewin, 1948).

Lewin found that the encouragement of actions is more effective when people make public commitments to them. For example, in one of his experiments on the power of public commitment, Lewin attempted to convince people to switch from eating white bread to eating wheat bread. When participants were asked to make a public commitment, such as raising their hands or verbally announcing that they intended to serve only wheat bread in their homes, they displayed a stronger commitment to the change.

Lewin's idea of action learning inspired a new generation of social psychologists who aim to make the world a better place through research. Several researchers in Canada have taken a participatory action research (PAR) approach to assist in both community and public health improvements (e.g., Brydon-Miller, 1997; Khanlou & Peter, 2005; Park, Brydon-Miller, Hall, & Jackson, 1993). For example, social psychologists have been involved in action research on diabetes prevention projects among the Mohawk community in Canada and nutrition education for low-income populations in Halifax, Nova Scotia (Macauley et al., 1999). Similarly, in the United States, researchers have developed the website GreaterGood.com, designed to promote the study and development of human happiness, compassion, and prosocial behaviour through the delivery of scientific and educational resources. GreaterGood.com translates social psychology research on compassion and cooperation for a broad audience of educators, health care providers, government officials, and concerned citizens by offering resources that can help people learn how to forgive, apologize, and express gratitude, along with several other behaviours.

Participatory action research and related websites demonstrate that experimental findings from social psychology are powerful tools for promoting a more compassionate and cooperative society because its resources, which are derived from research, can benefit the individual user as well as society as a whole. For example, a review of research on forgiveness encourages individuals to consider how the new field of remedial justice offers an alternative to the traditional legal justice system (Social Psychology Network, 2010). Lewin's concept of action learning has inspired other projects that use research to promote activities, such as reconciliation between conflicting nations and the reduction of youth violence.

Now that you know how social psychology can benefit the individual and society: take action! Think about the issues that affect the students on your campus—for example, campus safety. Create a program that can decrease crime on your campus based on social psychological principles concerning aggression, prosocial behaviour, social psychology and the law.

What will you learn from this action project?

1. Learn what makes students on your campus feel unsafe and identify elements that can help deter crime on campus. Think about existing programs such as Safewalk and emergency response plans at many colleges and universities across Canada.
2. Understand the motivation behind the crimes that occur on campus.
3. Get firsthand knowledge of the benefits of applying the concepts of social psychology.

during the 1990s, research by social psychologists in other cultures began to take on more prominence, and the impact of culture became a closely investigated subject (Triandis, 1994). For instance, social psychology is greatly impacted by the idea of *individualistic cultures*, or those that focus on independent individuals, such as the cultures of Canada and the United States; and the idea of *collectivist cultures*, or those that emphasize the individual in relation to his or her connectedness to those surrounding him or her, such as the cultures of Japan and India. You will learn more about individualism and collectivism at the cultural level in Chapter 4.

While social psychology in Canada has developed out of U.S. traditions, the focus of Canadian social psychologists also has included evaluation of the multicultural nature of our society and how this influences group and social processes. In fact, several research groups in Canada approach social psychological issues from a cultural perspective, such as Darrin Lehman and Steven Heine at the University of British Columbia, and John Berry at Queen's University. In addition, the Canadian Psychological Association (CPA) designated social and personality psychology as a separate sub-discipline in 1986. Since this time, social psychologists in Canada have become well recognized for both basic and applied research on topics such as organizational behaviour, aggression (including bullying and cyber-bullying), decision making concerning risky sexual behaviours, and prejudice and discrimination. As you explore this textbook, you'll see how social psychology applies to your everyday life and experiences, and learn about research that is ongoing in your own province or territory.

# CHAPTER 01 Review

## Summary

### WHAT IS SOCIAL PSYCHOLOGY? p. 4

• Psychology is the study of an individual's behaviour, and sociology is the study of cultural behaviours; social psychology combines the two. Social psychology approaches discussing individual behaviours within the context of the individual's environment and culture, as well as many other factors. Concepts that are integral to the study of social psychology include social perception, social influence, and social interaction.

### WHAT ARE THE DIFFERENT PERSPECTIVES OF SOCIAL PSYCHOLOGY? p. 5

• The four main perspectives that social psychologists may take are the sociocultural perspective, the evolutionary perspective, the social learning perspective, and the social cognitive perspective.
• The sociocultural perspective focuses on the relationship between social behaviour and culture. The evolutionary perspective emphasizes the biological bases for universal mental characteristics that all humans share. The social cognitive perspective builds on behavioural theories and demonstrates how an individual's cognitive process influences and is influenced by behavioural associations. And the social learning perspective stresses that social rewards and punishments are responsible for the way people act.

### IS SOCIAL PSYCHOLOGY JUST COMMON SENSE? p. 8

• Common sense is our natural understanding of things. We sometimes assume that social psychology is common sense because the subject matter is often personal and familiar. We believe that we are naturally knowledgeable about human behaviour, but many of our common beliefs have been disproved by social psychologists.
• Social psychologists cannot rely on common sense because they must base their conclusions on evidence that is achieved through careful and deliberate study. In these studies, social psychologists form theories that predict behaviour before it occurs. Avoiding relying on common sense helps researchers avoid bias.

### WHAT ARE THE ROOTS OF SOCIAL PSYCHOLOGY? p. 10

• Social psychology is a relatively new discipline within the larger field of general psychology. Two of the earliest formal studies in social psychology were Norman Triplett's social facilitation experiment and Max Ringelmann's social loafing study.
• Soon after, social psychology textbooks began to be published, and the Society for the Psychological Study of Social Issues (SPSSI) was established. Social psychology studies became particularly prominent in the wake of World War II, when people questioned how someone like Adolf Hitler was able to exert his influence over so many.



## Key Terms

**applied research methods (in social psychology)** the application of basic research to solve practical problems in the real world *5*

**basic research methods (in social psychology)** "pure" research that is driven by curiosity or obtaining scientific knowledge about a phenomenon *5*

**confirmation bias** the tendency to notice information that confirms one's beliefs and to ignore information that disconfirms one's beliefs *9*

**differential construal** the act of judging circumstances differently *9*

**evolutionary perspective** a perspective that focuses on the physical and biological predispositions that result in human survival *6*

**false consensus effect** a phenomenon that causes individuals to assume that everyone shares the same opinion they do *9*

**hindsight bias** the tendency to think that one knew that something would occur all along *9*

**natural selection** the process whereby individuals with certain characteristics are more frequently represented in subsequent generations as a result of being better adapted for their environment *6*

**scientific method** an approach to thinking that involves using systematic observations, measurements, and experiments to assess information *9*

**social cognitive perspective** a perspective that builds on behavioural theories and demonstrates that an individual's cognitive process influences and is influenced by behavioural associations *6*

**social facilitation** the enhancement of a well-learned performance when another person is present *11*

**social influence** the process through which other people affect an individual's thoughts or actions *4*

**social interaction** relationships between two or more individuals that affect our perceptions of others and our behaviours *4*

**social learning perspective** a perspective that stresses the particular power of learning through social reinforcements and punishments *6*

**social loafing** a phenomenon that occurs when individuals make less effort when attempting to achieve a particular goal as a group than they would if they were attempting to achieve the goal on their own *11*

**social perception** the process through which individuals form impressions of others and interpret information about them *4*

**social psychology** the scientific study of the nature and causes of individual behaviour and thought in social situations *4*

**sociocultural perspective** a perspective that focuses on the relationship between social behaviour and culture *6*

# Test Your Understanding

## MULTIPLE CHOICE

1. Which individuals are interested in the interaction of the person and situation?
   - **a.** behavioural psychologists
   - **b.** sociologists
   - **c.** social psychologists
   - **d.** social workers
2. Which is an example of social influence?
   - **a.** seeing a person in a military uniform and assuming he is trustworthy
   - **b.** eating only seafood that is sustainable to help the environment
   - **c.** taking a fashion design class in an attempt to meet girls
   - **d.** buying the same cellphone as your friend
3. What historic event was a precursor to the development of social psychology?
   - **a.** the damage done by the Nazis during World War II
   - **b.** the Industrial Revolution
   - **c.** the end of the Medieval period in Britain
   - **d.** the start of the Golden Age in Europe
4. Which is an example of social loafing?
   - **a.** finishing a race with a personal best time
   - **b.** doing extra credit to raise your grade in class
   - **c.** forgetting to turn in a research paper
   - **d.** putting forth a minimal effort on a group project, in which every student will receive the same grade
5. What was a major milestone in the development of social psychology?
   - **a.** the formation of organizations
   - **b.** the development of field-specific textbooks
   - **c.** the migration of psychologists to Europe
   - **d.** the invention of the radio
6. Who do some think is the individual who had the greatest influence on social psychology?
   - **a.** John B. Watson
   - **b.** Pierre Trudeau
   - **c.** Adolf Hitler
   - **d.** Sigmund Freud
7. Which social psychologist developed the theory of cognitive dissonance?
   - **a.** Milgram
   - **b.** Festinger
   - **c.** Asch
   - **d.** LaPiere
8. Which of the following is NOT a reason why common sense is unreliable?
   - **a.** It is a subjective concept.
   - **b.** It can be obstructed by hindsight bias.
   - **c.** It is used to make predictions before events occur.
   - **d.** It is not based on scientific research.
9. Which social psychology perspective focuses on the relationship between social behaviour and culture?
   - **a.** evolutionary perspective
   - **b.** sociocultural perspective
   - **c.** cognitive learning perspective
   - **d.** social learning perspective
10. How might a member of Parliament use social psychology to improve his or her political campaign?
    - **a.** impressing constituents with a large vocabulary
    - **b.** using common sense to figure out what the people want
    - **c.** making the voting process easier
    - **d.** using research to find out what makes a candidate likable

**ANSWERS:** 1. c; 2. d; 3. a; 4. d; 5. b; 6. c; 7. b; 8. c; 9. b; 10. d

## ESSAY RESPONSE

1. Explain how a psychologist, a sociologist, and a social psychologist might approach an explanation of the various mass school shootings that have occurred in both Canada and the United States in recent years.
2. Have you ever been guilty of social loafing? Explain how you rationalized your lack of effort.
3. Explain why social psychology can apply to areas not involving science or psychology. Use an example from your own life where social psychology may apply.
4. Think about Sherif's Robbers Cave Experiment. How might this relate to both basic and applied research methods?
5. Examine the problem of student debt from a sociocultural perspective. How does the relationship between social behaviour and culture affect students' finances?

## APPLY IT!

Based on what you have learned about social psychology as a discipline, think about why it would be important to educate your campus or community about social psychological research. Prepare a two-page argument in which you try to convince students of the importance of taking a social psychology class and what they could learn from it that would impact their daily lives.

**Remember to check www.thethinkspot.ca for additional information, downloadable flashcards, and other helpful resources.**

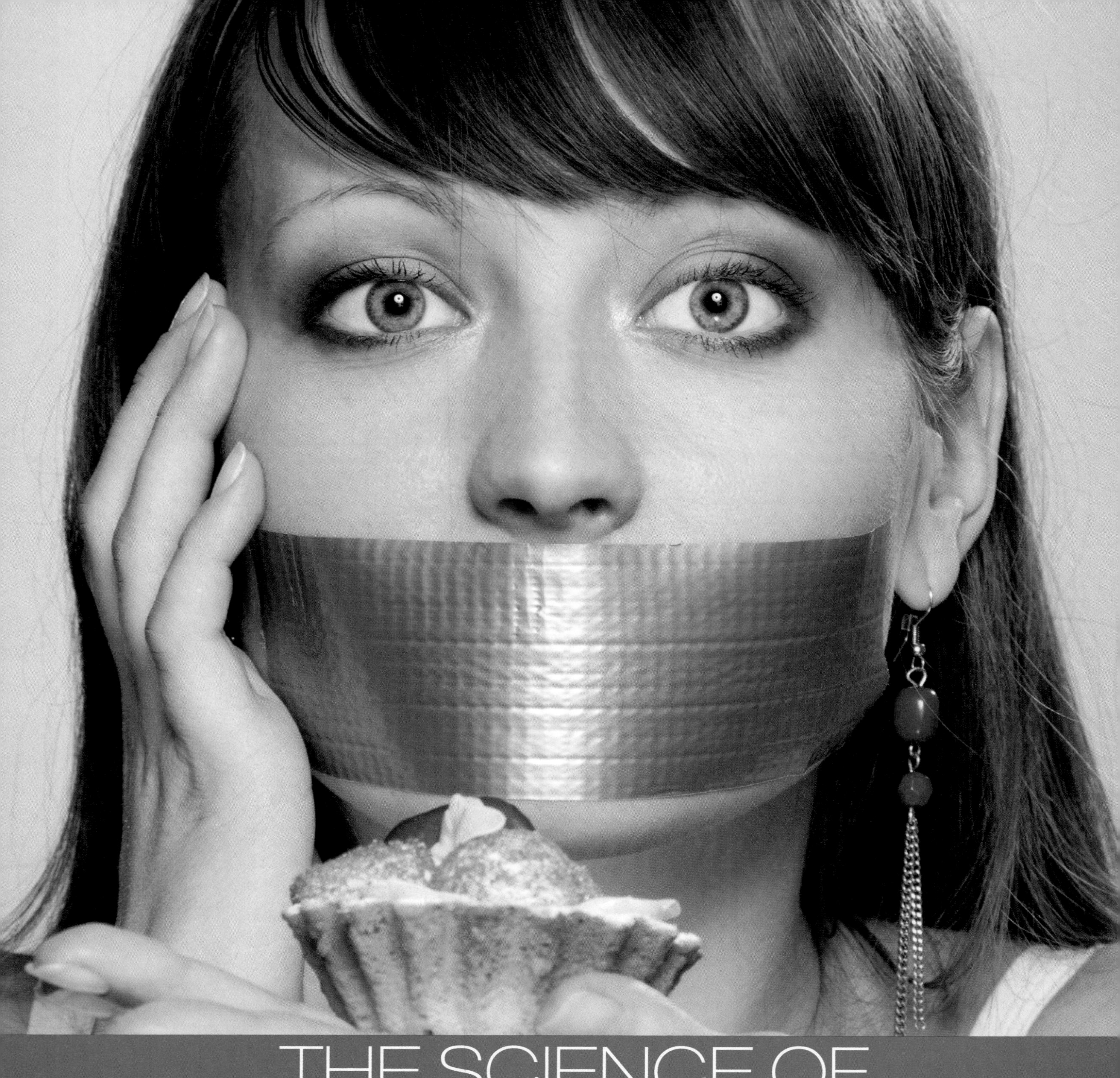

# THE SCIENCE OF SOCIAL PSYCHOLOGY

<<< *Imagine you are on a diet and a friend brings over this dessert. You try hard not to think about it, but does that really work?*

**HOW** CAN RESEARCH METHODS IMPACT YOU EVERY DAY?
**HOW** DO SOCIAL PSYCHOLOGISTS FIND THE TRUTH?
**WHAT** CAN DESCRIPTIVE METHODS SHOW US?
**WHAT** DO CORRELATIONS TELL US ABOUT RELATIONSHIPS?
**WHAT** DO EXPERIMENTAL METHODS HAVE TO SAY?
**HOW** DO WE CONDUCT ETHICAL RESEARCH?

# Have you

ever wondered why you think about things the way you do? It seems as if thoughts float in and out of our heads effortlessly. But are they ever easy to control? When your stomach is tied up in knots days before an important exam, what do you tell yourself? "Just try not to think about it." When you're in a restaurant and all the diners around you have desserts, but you're trying to lose a few pounds, what do you tell yourself? "Just try not to think about it." Everyone has tried to shut out certain thoughts at some point. However, is there any merit to this strategy? Sometimes, it seems trying to block out thoughts of those desserts is not only futile but also counterproductive. Why?

This is where research comes in. It helps us more accurately evaluate and attempt to explain our thought processes. For instance, when it comes to *thought suppression*, social psychologists have applied research methods to examine these and other questions. In general, researchers have found that being told not to think of something means your mind becomes inundated with thoughts of that particular thing (Wenzlaff & Wegner, 2000). The "something" can be almost anything. In one investigation, a researcher found that participants were likely to eat more chocolate if they had been actively trying not to think about it (Erskine, 2008). In another study, failures in thought suppression were found to be linked to the persistence of obsessive thoughts present in obsessive-compulsive disorder (Purdon, Rowa, & Antony, 2005).

What this tells us is that the science of social psychology helps us objectively examine our thoughts and behaviours, and this is done through research. This chapter will help you recognize the importance of psychological research, understand the research process and techniques, and learn how to apply research results to your daily life.



CHAPTER 02

## How Can Research Methods Impact You Every Day?

Thought suppression is just one area that social psychological research can attempt to explain and understand. Why do you like what you like? Why do you dislike other things? Why do you make the decisions you do? These are examples of questions social psychologists may try to answer. Understanding research can help you critically evaluate information that is presented to you and make well-informed decisions in all aspects of your life. Every day, we struggle to make the right choices. Although this process is difficult, in general we would all like to think that we choose the best option, given the circumstances. However, that is not always the case, and *we are often not aware of the social processes influencing our behaviour*. When you go to a restaurant for dinner and are deciding on the tip to leave your server, you may be aware of several obvious characteristics of the server that influence your decision, such as attractiveness, attentiveness, and friendliness. However, those things held constant, are you also aware that if a server compliments your meal selection, you are more likely to leave a higher tip? Research on complimentary and non-complimentary servers has revealed just that (Seiter, 2007). So how does research in social psychology influence our everyday lives? Consider the following concepts and how they may apply to your own life.

^^^ Advertisements for temporary price cuts **create a false sense of value for consumers.**

### SOCIAL JUDGMENTS AND "GOOD" DECISIONS

Social processes operate in our everyday lives through the judgments we make, particularly about what will make us happy. In his book *Stumbling on Happiness*, Gilbert (2006) explains that people often think they can accurately determine the outcome of their actions, guaranteeing a positive result. His theories point to one main flaw in human decision making: *we underestimate the odds of our current gains (or losses) and overestimate our future value* (Gilbert, 2006). By learning to interpret information with facts rather than feelings, people can avoid this pitfall and, in turn, make better decisions in their personal, professional, and academic lives. Imagine you want to purchase a new car. Wouldn't it be best if that decision were influenced by objective data rather than flashy media messages? Or imagine you are stuck on a multiple-choice test question in one of your classes. Wouldn't you be most likely to get the question right if you analyzed each option using facts rather than being influenced by gut feelings?

Interestingly, most people are terrible at estimating when something is of "good value" or knowing what factors they should consider when making decisions. For instance, a consumer may see a bottle of maple syrup marked down from $15 to $7.99 and one with an original price of $7.99. She may assume the marked-down maple syrup is a better quality simply because at one time it held a higher price. Gilbert (2006) explains that people are often preoccupied with past value rather than

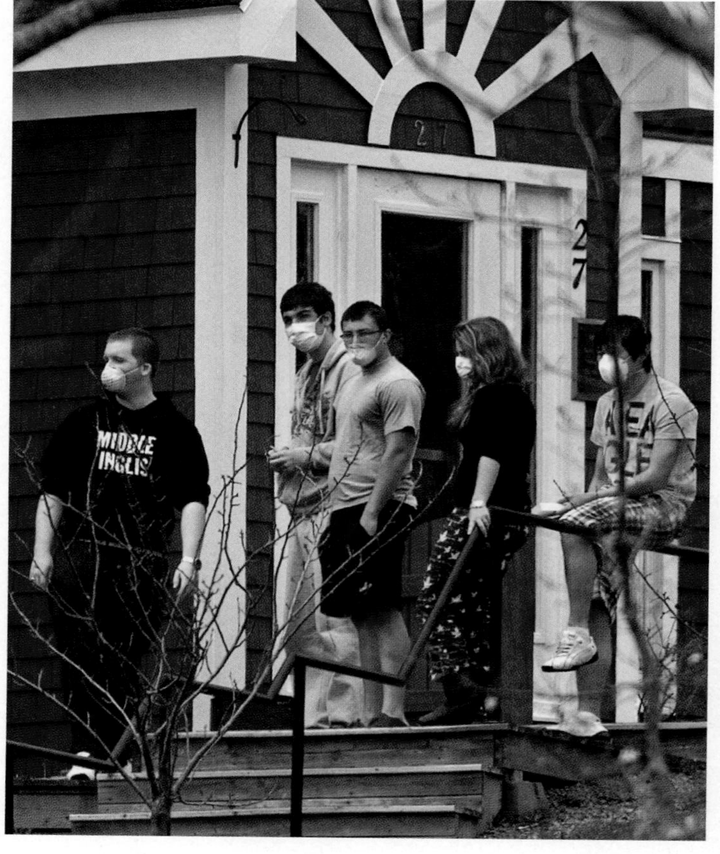

>>> **Thinking Critically About H1N1.** To attract readers and viewers, **the media often use misleading sensationalism (headlines and images), as in the case of 2009's H1N1 virus outbreak. These students in Windsor, Nova Scotia, wore masks after four students from their school contracted swine flu while on an exchange trip to Mexico. Although people feared the worst, Health Canada quickly approved and set up immunization programs for vulnerable populations; only approximately 10 percent of Canadians were infected with the virus, and the majority of cases were non-fatal (Public Health Agency of Canada, 2010).**

focusing on actual value. In another example, think about your beliefs and actions concerning your likelihood of getting the flu each year. Do you get the flu shot? What influences your estimates that you will get the flu? If a person was asked to estimate the odds of contracting the H1N1 virus, the "swine flu" that reached pandemic status in 2009, and he or she recently watched a news program that featured a report on an outbreak at a local school, then that person might guess the odds are three in five. Conversely, a person who has read or heard very little about the H1N1 virus might estimate the odds to be one in 50. According to the Public Health Agency of Canada and the Canadian Pandemic Influenza Plan, the actual odds of contracting the H1N1 virus are approximately three in 10 (Picard, 2009). As you can see, our social environments (including what we watch on television or how many of our Facebook friends are posting that they are sick) can dramatically influence our beliefs and subsequent actions!

## COMMON SENSE BIASES

Research in social psychology is focused on determining how our social contexts influence our thoughts, feelings, and behaviours. As discussed in Chapter 1, much of what we believe comes from our past experiences and our "common sense" notions about behaviour. Even when we fail to stop an unfavourable event from happening, we tend to think the events were inevitable. For example, when Vancouver Canucks fans began rioting following the team's loss in the Stanley Cup playoffs on June 15, 2011, many Canadian citizens said they had seen it coming and had predicted it based on previous riot behaviour in 1994 ("A Tale," 2011). This tendency gives way to the classic adage "Hindsight is 20/20," meaning the warning signs that were blurred before an occurrence seem crystal clear after it. Most people have experienced this phenomenon at some time in their lives.

If you knew it was going to rain, **why didn't you bring your umbrella?**

While it is common sense that wearing seatbelts and driving sober save lives, people neglect to consider the role of distractions in causing accidents. **The Canadian government has launched a public safety campaign hoping to make it common knowledge that paying attention and remaining free from distractions (e.g., cellphones, music players) while driving saves lives.**

After a teacher issues a pop quiz to your class, have you ever thought to yourself, "I knew this was going to happen?" You suddenly remember your teacher mentioning that certain information would be helpful in the "future." Your hindsight bias has led you to believe that you predicted the quiz, but if you actually had known that it was going to happen, you would have been able to prepare yourself. Have you ever gotten stranded in the rain, kicking yourself for not bringing an umbrella when you just *knew* it would rain?

A phenomenon such as *hindsight bias* can cause errors in the way we recall and explain information. This is not because what we believe to be common knowledge is necessarily wrong but because it is always easier to describe what *has* happened than what *will* happen (e.g., Musch, 2003). Psychological research is our most adequate resource for predicting what will happen, but even the most thorough research cannot guarantee that certain events or behaviours will occur (e.g., Cannon & Quinsey, 1995; Slovic & Fischhoff, 1977). The Nobel Prize–winning physicist Niels Bohr once quipped, "Prediction is very difficult, especially if it's about the future." This statement is true for even the most intuitive or well-informed people. To avoid this, social psychologists state their predictions before they put them to the test.

Another cause of failed assumptions is the *false consensus effect* (introduced in Chapter 1), which is the tendency to overestimate the extent to which others share our beliefs and behaviours. In addition, we tend to overestimate the number of others who like the same

**THEORY** a general framework for understanding a concept that allows us to describe, explain, and predict behaviour

things as we do more so than for our dislikes (Gershoff, Mukherjee, & Mukhopadhyay, 2008). This usually occurs in contained environments, which can range from a small group of friends to an entire country. If you lived in Calgary, Alberta, during the 2011 federal election, you probably assumed that Prime Minister Stephen Harper would win by a landslide. After all, advertisements and signs supporting his campaign were everywhere, local news programs followed his every move, and the majority of people around you planned to vote for him. However, if you lived in Halifax, Nova Scotia, you probably thought that NDP leader Jack Layton had a good shot at winning the election for similar reasons. A similar type of thinking also happened during the 1992 Canadian Referendum, where students' voting preferences dictated their beliefs concerning others' voting behaviour (Koestner, Losier, Worren, Baker, & Vallerand, 1995). The false consensus effect can potentially have dangerous consequences, as it can lead individuals to think certain actions are "normal," when in fact they can be abnormal and potentially harmful to their health or well-being.

So, how does one avoid hindsight bias and the false consensus effect? Because these are common results of human behaviour, it is difficult to avoid these ways of thinking completely, but understanding the value of research is the first step toward becoming a critical thinker who uses scientifically supported facts rather than intuition to make a decision. Consider what the chapter opener illustrated about the shortcomings of thought suppression. This information could prompt you to think of another technique to keep a diet on track or to stop thinking about your reading week holiday during midterm exams! As we explore the steps of the research process in the next section, think about other ways you can apply research to your everyday life.



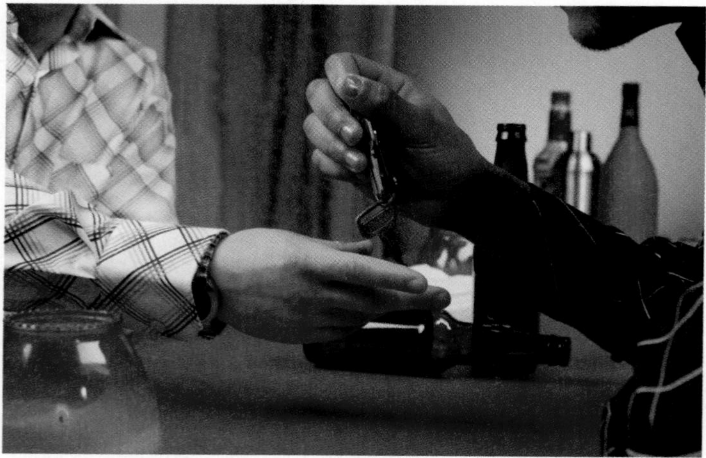

**A person who comes from a family that consumes alcohol regularly may be under the false assumption that it takes more alcoholic drinks to impair their driving.** In reality, blood alcohol concentration depends on the type of alcohol consumed and an individual's body mass more than frequency of drinking.

**To be good researchers,** psychologists have to put their detective skills to use.

## How Do Social Psychologists Find the Truth?

To understand how social psychologists test their ideas, you should think less like Sigmund Freud and more like Sherlock Holmes. Social psychologists gather evidence to answer a question just as detectives gather evidence to solve crimes. To be confident in their conclusions, good detectives want to collect as much evidence as possible. Usually, the strongest evidence takes the form of physical support, such as DNA and fingerprints and testimonies such as eyewitness accounts and alibis. Similarly, to confidently answer a question about behaviour and mental processes, psychological researchers collect information from many different sources and using multiple methods, such as self-report measures, naturalistic observation, surveys, correlations, and experimental design. Each type of method is able to answer a different type of question, and each has advantages and limitations. Therefore, like a detective, a researcher must collect as much evidence as possible to best understand behaviour.

### STEPS IN THE RESEARCH PROCESS

So, what prompts a psychologist to start the research process? Again, like a detective, a psychologist may wonder why or how an event, a trend, or a behaviour in society happened. He may ponder questions both simple and complicated, from "Why do companies use celebrities to market products?" to "How do others' expectations of us change our own behaviours?" Before a psychologist begins looking for evidence,

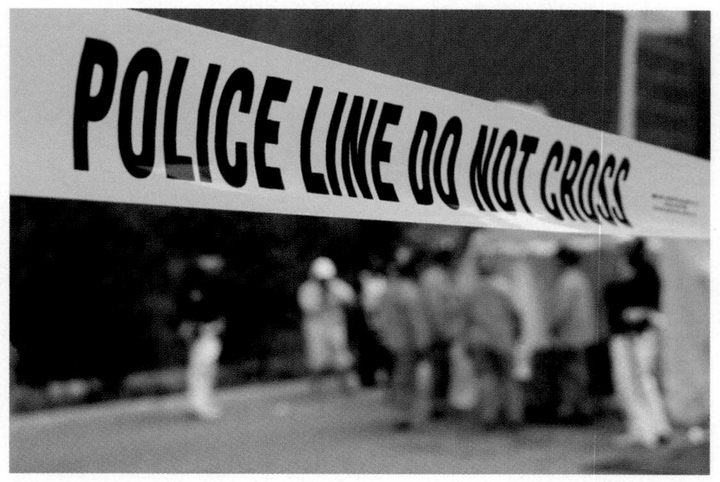


^^^ **Psychologists refer to the lack of help people** provide when witnessing a crime as "bystander apathy."

she may already have developed a **theory**, or a general framework for understanding a concept that allows us to describe, explain, and predict behaviour. A theory is a framework that ties together existing ideas from which we can make and test predictions about future events or behaviours. It explains a set of observations and is considered to be better as more data are collected to support its predictions. Good theories will attempt to explain behaviour, generate a testable model, and use multiple methods. For instance, social learning theory suggests that aggression is learned from observing aggressive role models (Bandura, 1977). Researchers can expand upon this theory to attempt to explain other behavioural patterns (e.g., does playing violent video games lead to aggressive behaviour?), and these ideas can be tested in a multitude of ways (e.g., Anderson et al., 2010; Tremblay & Nagin, 2005).

**STEP 1**: What question or theory do you have about human behaviour? Your query can be crafted into a **research question**, the first step in the research process. Anything from firsthand observations to recent news stories may inspire research questions. For example, in April 2010, 79-year-old Yusef Hizel was robbed aboard the Toronto subway by two young "thugs" while an estimated two dozen people watched (O'Toole, 2010). The bystanders failed to intervene, even though the victim called for help and actively pursued the perpetrators (Roberts, 2010). In fact, no witnesses even came forward and reported the crime, although the police pleaded for assistance from the public. Many Torontonians and the broader Canadian public wondered why. For psychologists, the resulting research question in such a situation is "How does the presence of others influence an individual's reaction to a crime?"

**STEP 2:** Once a research question is formed, the next step in the research process is to scour the pre-existing, relevant research literature. Doing so provides background information on the topic, giving an understanding of the broader context of the research as well as the limits of the topic. Before starting a search, scientists identify the relevant key words. For example, in the instance of the behaviour during the Toronto robbery, useful key words might include "group," "influence," "helping behaviour," and "crime." Looking for these key words in journal articles and books published by other scientists can yield useful materials. Remember, although Wikipedia and personal blogs and websites may be easy to use, the information is not always accurate, nor has it undergone **peer review** (the process by which experts in the field review and comment on each other's work), so it is therefore not considered reliable.

**RESEARCH QUESTION** the query that is the first step in the research process

**PEER REVIEW** a process by which experts in the field review and comment on each other's work

**HYPOTHESIS** a proposed explanation that can be either supported or disproven with statistics or observations

**VARIABLES** stimuli or characteristics that can take on different values, such as level of attraction or age

**OPERATIONAL DEFINITION** a definition that assigns one or more specific operational conditions to an event and then identifies how those conditions should be measured

**STEP 3:** Gathered material can be used to form a testable **hypothesis**. A hypothesis is a proposed explanation that can be either supported or disproven with statistics. It must be testable with **variables**, stimuli or characteristics that can take on different values, and must be capable of being falsified. This doesn't mean that it is false, but rather that the data don't support it. For instance, a psychic may not actually be able to read your mind. But unless she admits to those shortcomings, you have no way of disproving her claim. One of the problems with research in social psychology is that scholars often address broad concepts (such as aggression or love) and need a way to measure specific behaviours in order to test their hypotheses. Further, hypotheses may be too vague to be able to test scientifically. An example of a hypothesis in need of tweaking would be "Positive people are more successful in business." Because "positive people" and "more successful" are vague and abstract terms, it is impossible to empirically support or deny that success in business is solely due to one's positive attitude.

So how do you define variables in such a way that you can measure them accurately? Applying an **operational definition**, or a definition that assigns one or more specific operational conditions to an event and then identifies how those conditions should be measured, can make a variable specific. A better version of the hypothesis above would be "Individuals

^^^ **What is considered** attractive in one culture may not be seen as attractive in another culture.

**VALID** when a variable measures what it is supposed to measure

**RELIABLE** consistent measurement

**SAMPLE** selection of who or what will be tested in the research process

**REPLICATION** the process of repeating a study to verify effects, usually with a different sample of participants

with positive attitudes toward work are more likely to receive promotions than are persons with negative attitudes." In this example, a researcher may identify "success" as an operational condition and use the number of promotions or positive evaluations an employee receives to measure quantitatively what defines "success" in this particular work environment (e.g., Cliff, 1998; Morton & Allen, 2001). In addition, the researcher may use a standardized scale to measure positive and negative dispositions in order to test for differences between groups (e.g., Lyubomirsky, King, & Diener, 2005).

It is important that operational definitions are **valid**, meaning they measure what they are supposed to measure, and **reliable**, meaning the results are consistent measurements (Robinson, 2007). Validity and reliability are vital in a hypothesis so that one's desire to support a theory does not lead to manipulation of the facts of research. For example, well-known Canadian scientist Wilder Penfield theorized that our memories function similarly to a video camera: they record experiences as they happen and then replay them in their original form. He misinterpreted evidence from epileptic patients to support this (incorrect) view (Lewis, 1983).

^^^ It is difficult to build testable hypotheses around vague ideas **like "positive people" or "attractiveness" because such concepts are subjective, not objective.**

**STEP 4:** Once a testable hypothesis is formed, it is time to propose a study. To do this, the researcher must determine the best method to collect data for the hypothesis. This includes choosing the **sample**, or who or what subjects will be tested, and describing the reasons for testing this particular group. Every year, *People Magazine* puts out its list of the sexiest men alive. Similarly, *Esquire* publishes its list of sexiest women alive. Past recipients of this title, such as Canada's Ryan Reynolds and Rachel McAdams, are generally viewed as attractive, but "sexi*est*" man or woman alive? Says who? The opinion of a few magazine editors is probably not the same as that of every person in the world, especially because studies have shown that what people view as attractive varies across cultures. For example, Dion, Pak, and Dion (1990) proposed that attractiveness is moderated not only by cultural preferences (e.g., shapely figures are preferred by black and Hispanic populations, whereas slim figures are preferred by whites and Asians; Fox, 1997), but also by the extent to which one's culture is individualistic or collectivistic. In cultures that emphasize the importance of the individual, physical attractiveness may be more valued in relationships than it is in more communal and group-oriented cultures.

This highlights the fact that for an experiment to be valid, it is imperative that researchers take into consideration cultural variables and examine whether they hold up across different cultures (e.g., Berry, Poortinga, Segall, & Dasen, 2002). However, many cultural differences found in research also may be explained by the different relationships the participants have with their respective cultural groups, both within the same country and across countries (i.e., the reference-group effect; Heine, Lehman, Peng, & Greenholtz, 2002). The subtle impacts of culture cannot be ignored. See the THINK Reading after this chapter for further discussion on this topic.

**STEP 5:** Once data are collected, the results can be analyzed and developed into a conclusion. The conclusion of a study must answer the initial research question and support or deny a hypothesis. While analyzing results, researchers must note areas where further research may be necessary or convey the limitations of the process. If results indicate major flaws in the original hypothesis or theory, the researcher may choose to revise it and begin the research process again.

**STEP 6:** So now that you know the first five steps of the research process, you may ask yourself why different researchers seem to be studying the same topics or doing the same type of research. When it comes to research processes, replication can be used to apply the basic findings of one study to another. **Replication** describes the process of

<<< **In more individualistic cultures, there tends to be** more emphasis on physical attractiveness than in collectivistic cultures.

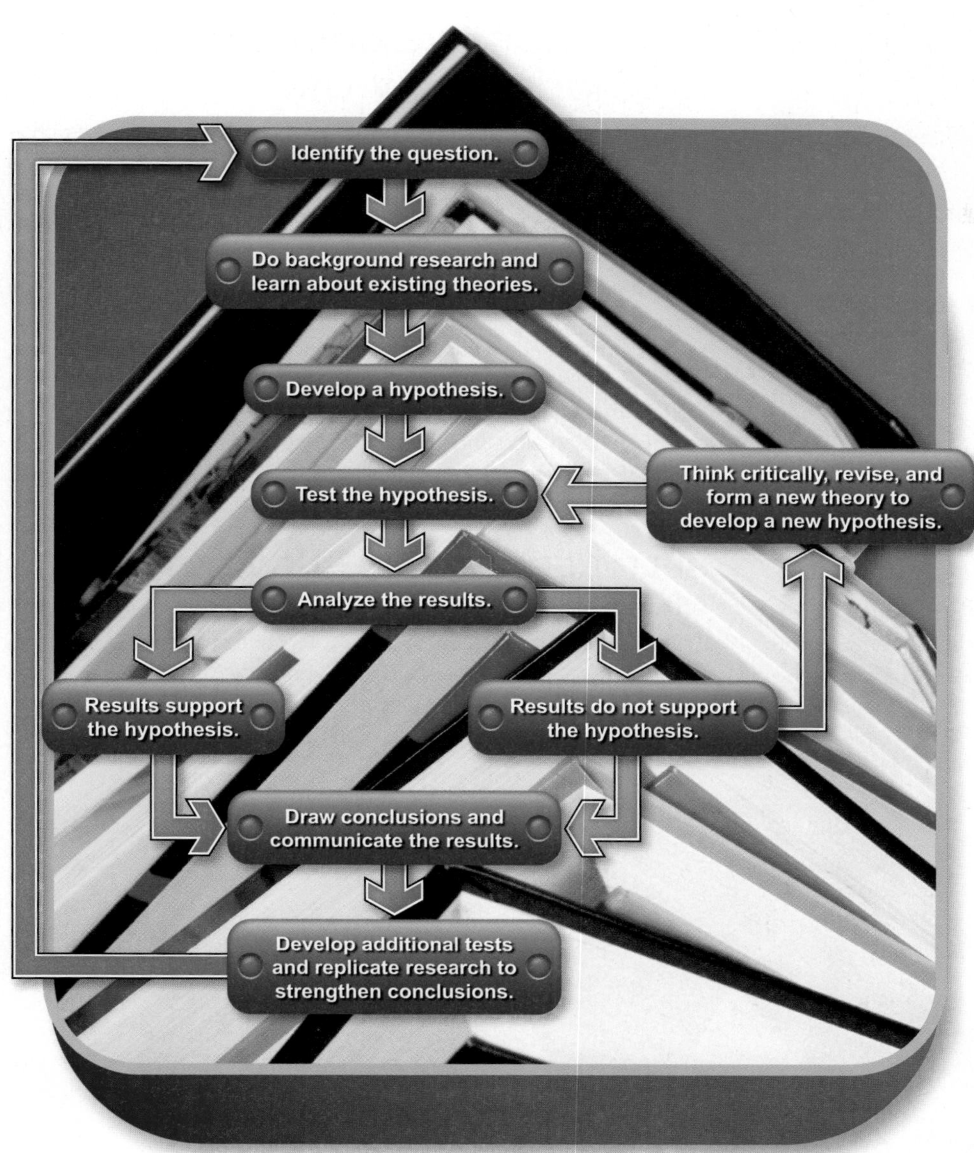
Identify the question.
Do background research and learn about existing theories.
Develop a hypothesis.
Test the hypothesis.
Think critically, revise, and form a new theory to develop a new hypothesis.
Analyze the results.
Results support the hypothesis.
Results do not support the hypothesis.
Draw conclusions and communicate the results.
Develop additional tests and replicate research to strengthen conclusions.

repeating a study to verify effects, usually with a different sample of participants to determine whether the findings of the original are applicable to other variables. For example, researchers who want to study the effects of violent cartoons on school-aged girls might use the same operational definitions and data collection methods as a previous study on the effects of violent cartoons on school-aged boys (e.g., Josephson, 1995; Pepler, & Sedighdeilami, 1998). In some cases, researchers may perform an exact replication of a previous experiment to strengthen the reliability of the original findings (Kirsch, 2006). While this is not a requirement of conducting research, replication of studies with contradictory or unexpected findings is beneficial to make sure your results are accurate.

Anyone can use the scientific method to solve a problem (Landry, Amara, & Laamary, 2001). For example, in the book *The Scientist in the Crib: What Early Learning Tells Us About the Mind*, Gopnik and her colleagues describe research showing how infants generate and test theories about their environments (Gopnik, Meltzoff, & Kuhl, 1999). You probably do this, too, without even realizing it (Neuman, 2008). You might try different ways to start your car if it's being difficult on a cold morning. Or think about if you received a C on an important exam. If you used the scientific method as

<<< **The Scientific Method.** The scientific research process is cyclical.

## ACTION LEARNING

### Research, Replication, and Recycling

Social psychologists cannot just rely on common sense; they must put their ideas to the test. You might think that littering in public places is a rare occurrence or that only certain types of people litter. Previous research has suggested, however, that the situation may have a powerful impact on our behaviour. Our environment can impact our likelihood of engaging in destructive acts (Zimbardo, 1969) or littering (for a review, see Cialdini, 2003).

One study showed that when participants find a flier on their cars, 38 percent litter by throwing it on the ground, and individuals are more likely to do so when their current environment is already littered. However, when a member of the research team, a confederate, models the desirable behaviour of throwing away the trash or putting recyclables in their appropriate receptacles, only 4 percent of the observed subjects litter (Cialdini, Reno, & Kallgren, 1990).

Replication is key to validating your research findings. Would you find the same type of results in your campus environment? Select a public environment to observe littering behaviour and take note of the individuals' behaviours. Model throwing away or recycling the trash, and monitor how that affects the subjects you're observing. Are your observations similar to or different from past research? How could you develop this project into a true experiment? Share your findings and the overall experience with your classmates and friends. Once you see the impact that your behaviour can have on others, you should be more aware of your own recycling and littering behaviour.

What will you learn from this action project?

1. Discover how to develop a research project.
2. Learn the importance of replication in scientific research.
3. Prevent littering and encourage eco-friendly behaviour.

**DESCRIPTIVE RESEARCH** research used to obtain information regarding the current status of a population or phenomena to describe the who, what, when, where, and how questions with respect to variables or conditions in a situation

a way of thinking, you would try to generate explanations for why you received this grade. You may hypothesize that you didn't study enough. But what if you studied every day for the last two weeks? You would revise your hypothesis. Maybe the exam did not address what you studied, maybe you spent too much time reading and not enough time self-testing, maybe it wasn't graded accurately, or maybe you were anxious. You might test your hypothesis by visiting your instructor during office hours to determine what factors led to your unsatisfactory grade.

In this chapter, we have described the standard steps in the research process, but it is important to remember that there is not just one methodology. Techniques used in research can vary depending on the research question, on how feasible it is to study a particular behaviour, and even on potential resources. No method is perfect; each has advantages and limitations. However, if multiple studies using a wide range of methodologies all generate similar results, we can be more confident in our conclusions and develop a better understanding of the behaviour we are studying.

## What Can Descriptive Methods Show Us?

Using descriptive methods of research is a common practice in psychology. **Descriptive research** is used to obtain information regarding the current status of a population or phenomena to describe the who, what, when, where, and how questions with respect to variables or conditions in a situation. For example, descriptive research can help psychologists determine whether boys are more susceptible to peer pressure than girls (e.g., Santor, Messervey, & Kusumakar, 2000) or to learn about adults' most common reactions to work-related stress (e.g., Bernier, 1998; Lee, Carswell, & Allen, 2000). Descriptive research involves a range of methods from observations to case studies (Key, 1997). The common thread among all descriptive methods is that their purpose is to *describe* a phenomenon. In this section, we will discuss the different descriptive methods researchers use to test their hypotheses.

### SELF-REPORT AND SURVEY MEASURES

After purchasing an item online, have you ever received a survey asking you to evaluate your online shopping experience? Or has a server at a

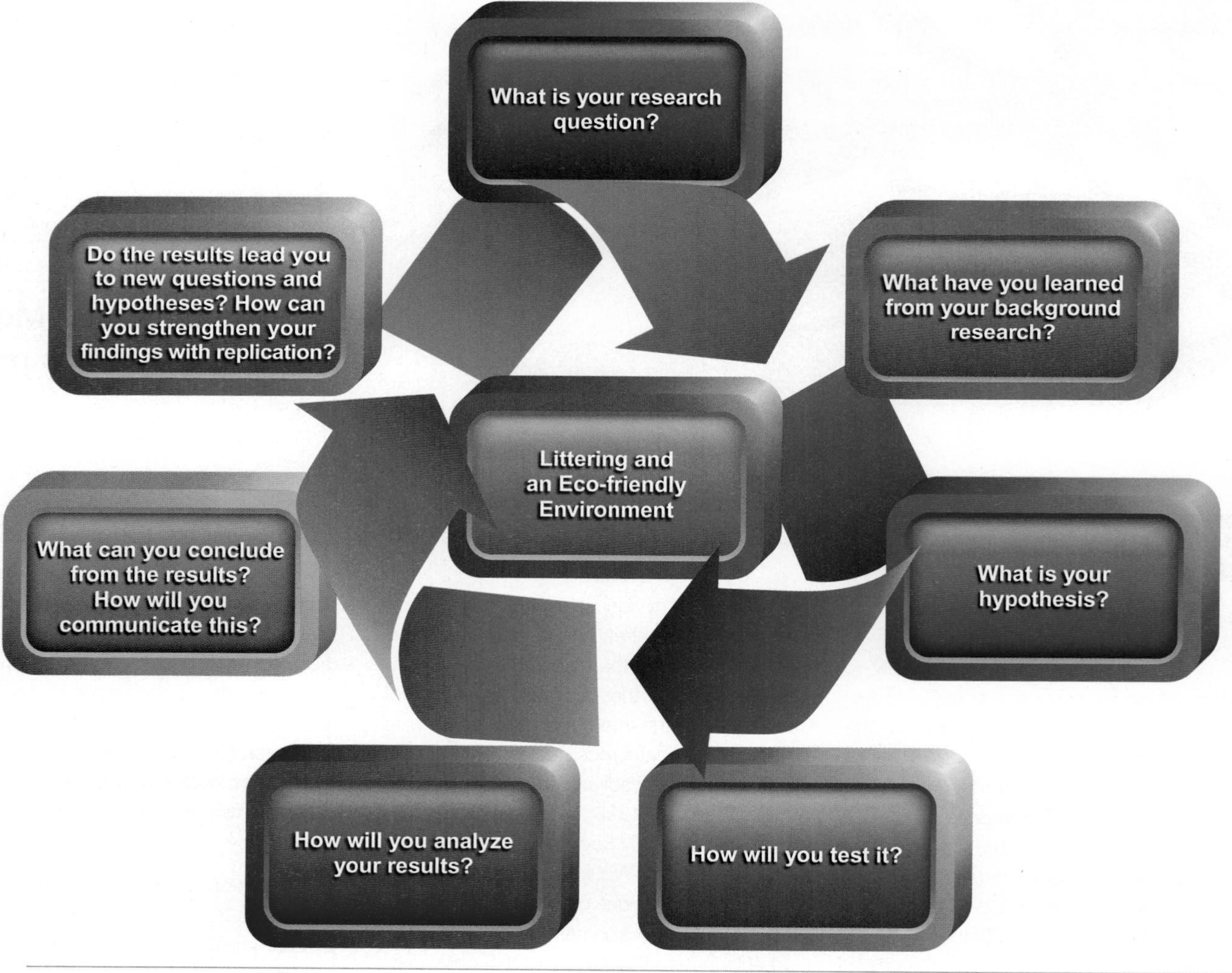


**Your Recycling Experiment.** Use this visual to **organize your ideas** about your action learning project.

restaurant offered a comment card along with your dinner bill? If you have filled out these documents or similar forms, then you have participated in a method of research referred to as the self-report method. The **self-report** or **survey method** is a form of data collection in which participants are asked to rate or describe their own behaviours or mental states (e.g., I am satisfied, I am unsatisfied, I have no opinion). This type of method is typically conducted in the form of interviews or questionnaires.

However, sometimes this method may not be appropriate for studying behaviours that people tend to lie about (e.g., how aggressive they are). Let's say you want to learn about the social impact of bullying behaviour. How often do people engage in bullying? Are certain groups (i.e., males versus females, children versus adolescents versus adults) more likely to be bullies or to be bullied? What makes people bully others? You could answer these questions by administering a survey that asks about bullying to 75 people. Although this method might offer some interesting answers, it may not provide the most accurate data. The individuals who fill out the survey may be unaware of their own aggressive behaviour, or they may not be willing to admit they bully others or have been bullied, or the people selected for the survey may not fall into either group. Survey data are useful for getting a self-report of what individuals think; however, survey data may not accurately reflect the behaviour that are taking place. Observation may be a more appropriate research method for this particular subject (and other sensitive topics) because it allows researchers to use their own eyes and ears to gather information instead of relying on the opinions of participants, which can be skewed by bias.

## OBSERVATIONAL RESEARCH

Observation can occur in a contained environment or in the real world. A contained environment, like a laboratory, is useful when certain variables must be consistent (Evans & Rooney, 2008). For instance, a researcher may put child participants in a contrived playground setting to examine the extent to which bullying behaviour occurs. But even if the atmosphere is realistic, some elements of the manufactured situation could alter the way the participants feel and behave (e.g., they are aware they are being watched, school peers are not present), thus damaging the validity of the study. In this situation, a naturalistic observation might be most appropriate.

**Naturalistic observation** involves watching behaviour in a real-world setting. Observations can be collected with video or audio recordings or with old-fashioned paper and pencil. To observe the bullying behaviours of a group of children, one could observe kids at various schools during recess and lunches (both on and off the playground) and take note of the relevant whos, whats, wheres, and whys. In a naturalistic study, sometimes it is not the people but the environment that can give researchers valuable results. One study sought to determine whether bullying in Canadian schools was more prevalent on the playground or in the classroom. Craig, Pepler, and Atlas (2000) used both video and audio recordings of children in class and on the playground, and coded behaviour according to multiple bullying criteria (including whether a child was the bully, victim, or a participating peer). While the researchers determined that playground bullying was more common, they also noted that there were more opportunities for children to engage in aggressive behaviour outside the classroom, especially in the presence of their peers. In addition, they found that indirect bullying (e.g., gossip, exclusionary behaviours) occurred more often in the classroom and direct aggression occurred more frequently on the playground. This type of naturalistic observation allows researchers to gather an extensive amount of data in a short amount of time.

**SELF-REPORT/SURVEY METHOD** a form of data collection in which participants are asked to rate or describe their own behaviour or mental state

**NATURALISTIC OBSERVATION** research that involves watching behaviour in a real-world setting

**FIELD STUDIES** studies involving data or information that is collected in naturally occurring settings

**ARCHIVAL STUDIES** research that entails culling information from existing records ranging from magazine articles to website analytics

**CASE STUDIES** in-depth analyses of an individual, group, or event

## FIELD, ARCHIVAL, AND CASE STUDIES

Apart from observing behaviour, sometimes researchers may conduct a study in an applied setting. **Field studies** refer to data or information that is collected in naturally occurring settings (i.e., not within the laboratory), and may involve purely descriptive or experimental elements (we will discuss these shortly). For example, a researcher who studies the influence of multiple eyewitnesses to a real crime, and the group decision-making processes that may influence correct eyewitness memory and identification, is conducting a field study (e.g., Cutshall & Yuille, 1989). In general, field studies capitalize on naturally occurring events (e.g., disasters) and study social reactions or processes involved in the aftermath. They are sometimes preferable when studying "real-world" phenomena that are difficult to replicate in laboratory settings.

**Archival studies** entail culling information from existing records ranging from magazine articles to website analytics. The appeal of archival research is that researchers can look at data from an extended period, knowing that they will not inadvertently influence the implications. For example, several researchers have examined Canadian court documents to determine the rate of historical abuse and recovered memory claims, the prevalence of expert witnesses in such trials, and whether recovered memory cases differ across jury or judge-only trials (e.g., Connolly, Price, & Read, 2006; Connolly & Read, 2006; Read, Connolly, & Welsh, 2006).

Researchers also may use case studies to describe and interpret behaviour. **Case studies** are in-depth analyses of an individual, group, or event. The goal of this method is to discover principles of behaviour that may apply to other situations. In the case of Yusef Hizel presented earlier in this chapter, researchers might examine what led to the apathetic

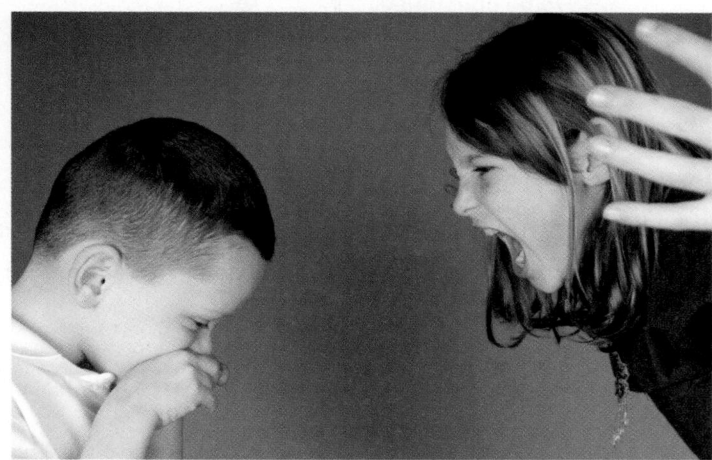

**As with animals, it is sometimes best to** observe human beings in their natural environment.

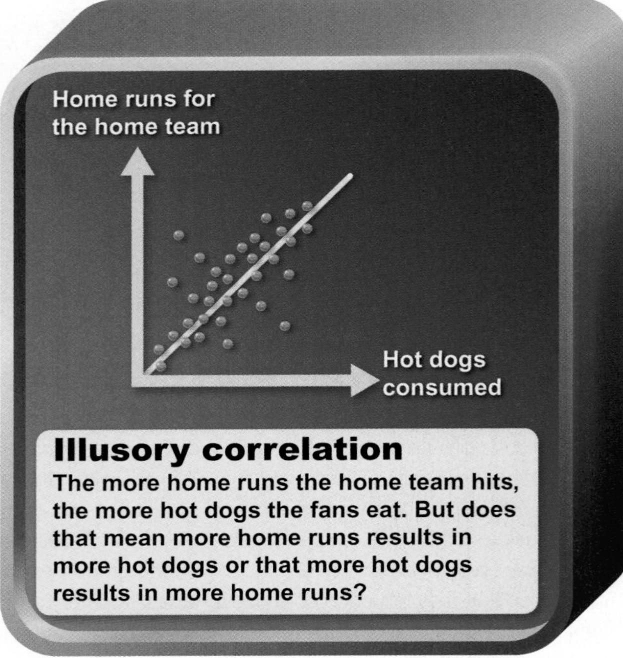

Home runs for the home team
Hot dogs consumed
Illusory correlation
The more home runs the home team hits, the more hot dogs the fans eat. But does that mean more home runs results in more hot dogs or that more hot dogs results in more home runs?


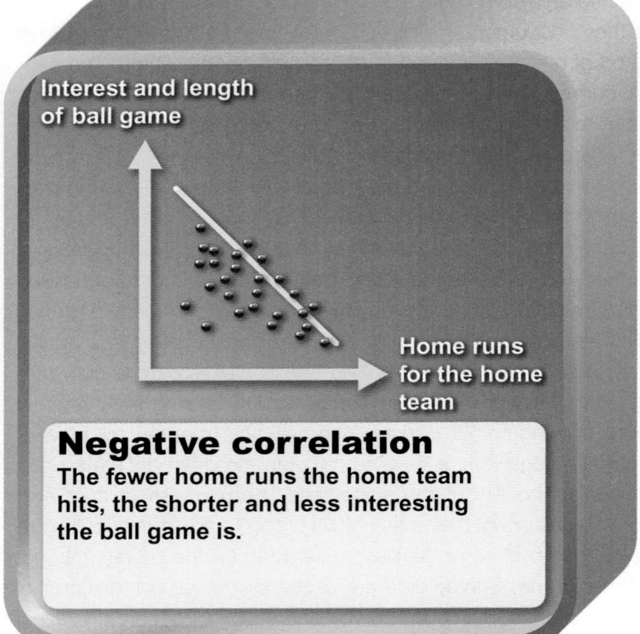

Interest and length of ball game
Home runs for the home team
Negative correlation
The fewer home runs the home team hits, the shorter and less interesting the ball game is.


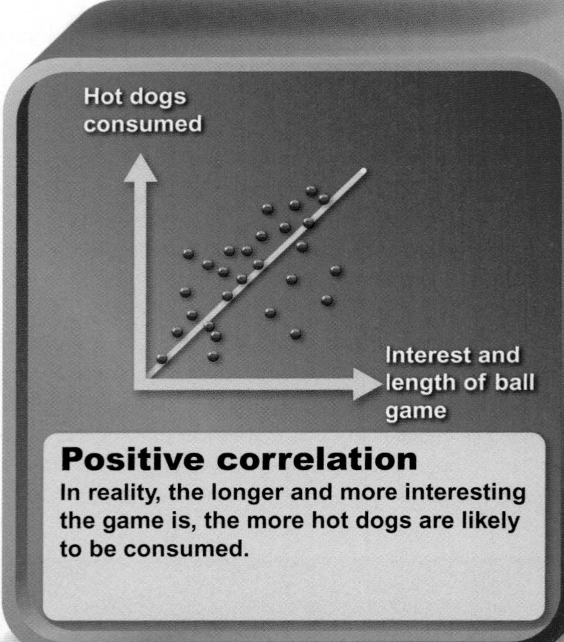

Hot dogs consumed
Interest and length of ball game
Positive correlation
In reality, the longer and more interesting the game is, the more hot dogs are likely to be consumed.


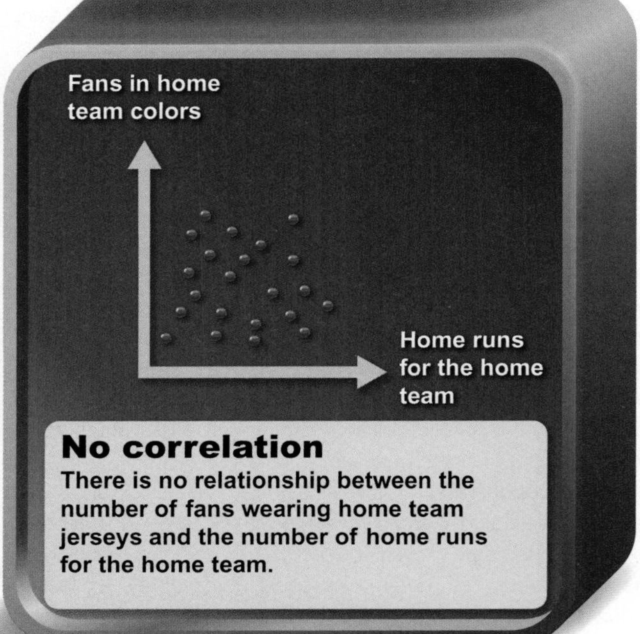




**Types of Correlations.** Did hot dog sales cause more home runs or vice versa? **Or, more likely, is there a third variable that affects each of the other two?** A correlation indicates a relationship between two variables, but it's not necessarily a causal one.

behaviour of the bystanders. They might ask questions such as the following: Why did no one help? Do features of the group or social setting dictate helping behaviour? Are certain methods more effective in soliciting help from strangers in emergency situations? Much has been learned about helping behaviour from consideration of case studies, which often leads to further correlational or experimental research (e.g., Levine, Prosser, Evans, & Reicher, 2005).

## What Do Correlations Tell Us About Relationships?

Have you ever wondered if your bad luck with finding a date is related to your poor fashion sense, or if your unsatisfactory grades are connected to your lack of sleep? Data from descriptive studies may lead researchers to notice correlations. **Correlational research**, often the second level of investigation, aims to determine whether there is a relationship between two variables. Researchers may collect descriptive data using one of the methods above and then form a hypothesis to test whether the variables they measured are related.

Examples of correlational research conducted without the manipulation of any variables are studies on the role of the hormone oxytocin in mother–infant bonding (e.g., Chen & Johnson, in press; Feldman, Weller, Zagoory-Sharon, & Levine, 2007). The researchers found a positive correlation between oxytocin levels in the mothers and their bonding behaviours, like affectionate touch and attachment-related thoughts. These findings, combined with others, have encouraged some individuals to name oxytocin the "love drug" or "liquid trust." The fact that there is an established relationship between oxytocin and the desire to love or trust may change the way the hormone is used for therapeutic measures in the medical field and in social situations (Childs, 2008). However, such research may fail to consider that other variables (e.g., temperament or cultural norms) may influence both oxytocin levels and attachment bonding (e.g., Kim et al., in press). For example, a correlational study might find that there is a relationship between poor sleeping habits and lower grades, but that doesn't mean that poor sleeping habits necessarily *cause* unsatisfactory grades.

## LIMITATIONS AND ADVANTAGES OF CORRELATIONS

Correlations can be very useful for determining whether two or more variables are connected, but there are definitive limitations to the conclusions that can be drawn from the findings of a correlational study. One of the most common errant conclusions of a correlational study is that one element of the relationship causes the other (e.g., oxytocin causes a person to trust another more easily). But *correlation does not automatically indicate causation*. Two variables can be connected without having a cause-and-effect relationship. For example, there may be a correlation between men who wear blue socks and men who hold high-paying jobs, but that does not mean that wearing blue socks will earn a man a higher salary. In the correlation between sleeping habits and grades mentioned earlier, there is no manipulation of variables, so it is impossible to conclude that one thing indeed caused the other. People who neglect their sleep may also neglect their studies because they are busy playing video games, chatting on MSN or Facebook, or hanging out with friends, and those may be the actual culprits to blame for the poor grades.

Distinguishing correlation from causation can be difficult, and the news media only makes it harder by reinforcing the blurry line with misleading headlines. Consider the headline "Mom killed and ate her daughter," which is immediately followed by mention that the mother had schizophrenia and was found Not Criminally Responsible due to Mental Disorder (NCRMD) in November 2002 (Walton, 2003). In another example, one headline regarding the Allan Schoenborn case read "Father was insane when he killed 3 children, judge finds" ("Schoenborn 'Not Criminally Responsible,'" 2010). These and other sensational media stories tend to suggest that mental illness *causes* crime, and mental illness is frequently associated with dangerousness and a negative tone in news media (e.g., Chopra & Doody, 2007; Wahl, Wood, & Richards, 2002). In fact, research by the Canadian Mental Health Association (2011) indicates that individuals with a major mental illness are more likely to be *victims* of violence and no more likely to commit crimes than those who are not mentally ill. Further, police often are not properly trained on dealing with persons with mental illness, as evidenced by higher rates of fatal shootings of those with Axis I disorders (e.g., schizophrenia, psychosis) by police (Kesic, Thomas, & Ogloff, 2010). That said, a recent report released by the Vancouver Police Department called for greater collaboration between police and mental health professionals, including more training on dealing effectively with mentally ill persons and reduced police strain (Thompson, 2010).

**CORRELATIONAL RESEARCH** research in which researchers do not manipulate variables but observe whether there is a relationship between two variables

**THIRD VARIABLE** any additional factor that could be responsible for an observed effect

**MATCHED SAMPLES DESIGN** a research design in which two or more groups of individuals are identical, or matching, in terms of the third variable

There are multiple factors involved in the causes of crime, and correlational designs do not allow us to isolate what these causal factors are, but the headline "Correlations do not allow us to isolate causal factors of crime" doesn't grab you like the ones presented above do. Next time you see a headline that claims or suggests a relationship between two variables, read with caution and think critically. If the study is based only on correlational data, then you'll know that the headline is simply implying a relationship. In fact, consider the suggested relationship with respect to the following problems associated with correlations that limit our ability to draw causal conclusions.

### The Third Variable Problem

Conclusions drawn from correlational studies may be misleading because of an presence of a **third variable**, any additional factor that could be responsible for an observed effect. For example, when we hear that there is a correlation between aggression and watching television, a possible third variable might be the presence of aggressive role models. When children observe aggression exhibited by individuals they look up to, they are more likely to interpret that behaviour as "normal," and this increases their own aggressive behaviour (Orue et al., 2011).

To avoid the third variable, researchers might choose study participants through the use of matched samples. A **matched samples design** is a research design in which two or more groups of individuals

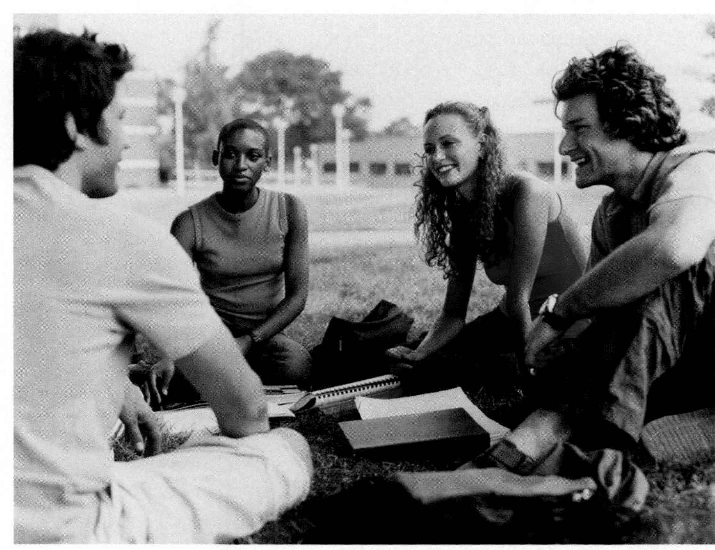

Matching individuals on their age, gender, and ethnicity **may be important to the outcome of research studies.**

**BI-DIRECTIONAL CAUSALITY** a situation in which variable X could cause variable Y or vice versa

**EXPERIMENTAL RESEARCH** research that attempts to control all the factors (like a potential third variable) that may affect the results of an experiment

**INDEPENDENT VARIABLE** the variable an experimenter has control over and can alter

**DEPENDENT VARIABLE** the variable an experimenter does not control that is used to measure whether the change in the independent variable has an effect

are identical, or matching, in terms of the third variable. For example, in a study linking sleep to academic success, researchers may want to choose subjects who commit a similar amount of time to their academic studies. It wouldn't make sense to compare a person who studies 40 hours a week to a person who only studies five hours a week. This is just one of the scientific safeguards that researchers can use to try to ensure their research is valid and objective.

### The Problem of Directionality

The problem of directionality is like the chicken and the egg riddle: How do we know which came first? In a correlation, it is unknown which variable preceded the other. **Bi-directional causality** refers to a situation in which variable X (e.g., warm parenting style) could cause variable Y (e.g., well-adjusted kids) or vice versa (i.e., are parents warmer when their kids behave better?). Consider another example: does watching a lot of violent cartoons lead to aggressive behaviour? Or was the child already aggressive, leading her to choose to watch aggressive television as an outlet or escape? Unfortunately, using this research method can never determine whether one factor caused the other.

But just because correlational research doesn't identify the exact cause of an event or behaviour, this doesn't mean that it can't offer useful and interesting information. We can still make predictions based around the strength of a correlation. For example, if credit score has a positive correlation with a person's job performance, then by checking potential employees' credit histories, we would be able to predict which candidates will perform best in a given job. Still, it is important to remember that because the relationship between credit scores and job performance isn't necessarily a cause-and-effect one, it should not be the sole consideration of what causes job performance.

## What Do Experimental Methods Have to Say?

Although descriptive and correlational methods of research often provide valuable data, many studies benefit from experimental methods. **Experimental research** attempts to control all the factors (e.g., a potential third variable) that may affect the results of an experiment. Controlling these factors allows a researcher to identify the exact cause of an event or behaviour and, therefore, predict future events or behaviours. As a child, you may have built a mini-volcano in elementary school and been asked if more vinegar or more baking soda would get you the better "eruption." You might hypothesize that twice as much baking soda as vinegar gets you the best reaction, and you'd go about experimenting with different amounts of baking soda. You might conclude that more baking soda gives you the best eruption.

This ability to identify cause and effect is what separates experimental methods from descriptive and correlational research. Once researcher Paul Zak established a relationship between oxytocin and trust in data found from measuring oxytocin levels after monetary transfers (Zak, Kurzban, & Matzner, 2005), he proceeded with experimental research to isolate the cause. To identify the actual causation of the trusting feeling that people get from oxytocin, Zak has conducted experiments in which he controlled the amount of oxytocin participants were given and measured their generosity to strangers. In general, it appears that artificial increases in oxytocin hormone levels in participants cause increased generosity and feelings of trust (Zak, 2008). Similarly, these results stimulated other studies that have found lower oxytocin levels in abused versus non-abused women (e.g., Heim et al., 2009) and enhanced processing of positive relative to negative emotions when oxytocin levels are higher in healthy adult (e.g., Simplicio, Massey-Chase, Cowen, & Harmer, 2009) and dementia populations (e.g., Finger, in press). Because these researchers were able to control oxytocin levels, they were able to take their conclusions beyond correlational relationships and have established that oxytocin is a potential cause for increased feelings of trust. Taken together, correlational and experimental research can complement one another and strengthen the conclusions about the role of oxytocin in bonding.

We often use the word *experiment* casually. You might say you are conducting an experiment when you hold off mentioning that your anniversary is coming up because you want to see if your significant other remembers the date. In psychology, an experiment has very specific components: the manipulation of the variable hypothesized to be the cause, the independent variable, and random assignment of participants to experimental conditions.

## INDEPENDENT AND DEPENDENT VARIABLES

A study cannot be an experiment without the manipulation of an **independent variable**. An independent variable is the variable an experimenter has control over and can alter. A **dependent variable** is the variable an experimenter does not control, and it is used to measure whether the change in the independent variable has had an effect. In Zak's (2008) experiments, the independent variable was the level of oxytocin given to participants. Therefore, the dependent variable was the participants' subsequent levels of generosity to strangers. The group that gets the

Study says depression can lead to violence

Media **headlines can** falsely **imply causation.**

main treatment or manipulation—in this case, the oxytocin—is called the **experimental group**. The group that doesn't, and can be used for comparisons, is called the **control group**.

You may conduct experiments with dependent and independent variables in your everyday life. When cooking, you may experiment by adding crushed garlic to your pasta sauce to see if it improves the taste. In this example, the amount of garlic is the independent variable, and the dependent variable is the level of taste in the sauce after you are finished cooking. An easy way to remember the difference between these two variables is to remember that the dependent variable relies (or depends) on the level of the independent variable, or what was manipulated. Or think of the independent variable as the cause and the dependent variable as the effect.

> "An easy way to remember the difference between these two variables is to remember that **the dependent variable relies (or depends) on the level of independent variable, or what was manipulated.**"

**EXPERIMENTAL GROUP** in an experiment, the group that gets the main treatment or manipulation

**CONTROL GROUP** the group that does not get the main treatment in an experiment, but is used as a baseline to compare results with the experimental group

**RANDOM ASSIGNMENT** a required technique in an experiment to be able to infer cause and effect; every participant has any equal chance of being assigned to any group in the experiment

**EXTERNAL VALIDITY** the extent to which results apply to a general population

**INTERNAL VALIDITY** the ability to infer cause and effect; that the variable was manipulated was the only factor to change across conditions and so was what led to the observed effect

## RANDOM ASSIGNMENT

The second component of a true experiment is **random assignment**. Random assignment is a required technique in an experiment to be able to infer cause and effect; every participant has any equal chance of being assigned to any group in the experiment. The Stanford Prison Experiment, a simulated study of the psychological impacts of incarceration, is a classic example of the importance of random assignment (Zimbardo, 1971). To conduct this study, experimenters gathered a group of 24 voluntary male college students from the Stanford area. After preliminary examinations, all participants were deemed healthy, intelligent, and with normal dispositions. Half of the group was randomly labelled guards, while the rest were prisoners. The prisoners were brought in police cars to a simulated but realistic jail. They were handcuffed and blindfolded at the time of arrival. Each prisoner was systematically searched, stripped naked, and sprayed with a liquid that seemed to be a disinfectant, simulating the humiliation that real prisoners experience in real prisons. Prisoners were also assigned uniforms and placed in chains.

The guards were given no specific training on how to perform their duties. They were free, within limits, to do whatever they believed was necessary to maintain order in the prison system. They received clubs, uniforms, and special sunglasses to create a "tough guy" image. Standard prison activities such as roll call, punishment with push-ups, and set eating, drinking, chores, and bathroom use times were enforced. Less than 36 hours into the experiment, the first prisoner began to suffer from acute emotional disturbance, disorganized thinking, and uncontrollable crying. Similar emotional breakdowns occurred with other prisoners, as well as some aggressive and defiant behaviour. While the ethics of this experiment have been questioned (see later in this chapter), the results of this experiment highlighted the emotional strain that imprisonment has on an individual (see Zimbardo, 2008, for further discussion). The fact that this group was picked through random assignment shows that imprisonment can have adverse effects on average individuals, not just hardened criminals.

Random assignment made it so that each group contained the same types of individuals, making the results more reliable. Had the groups been sorted according to particular traits, the results could have been skewed.

## THE VALIDITY OF EXPERIMENTS

In social psychology, experiments can take place in the laboratory and also in the field. Field experiments, similar to naturalistic observation, are considered to be high in **external validity**, which is the extent to which results apply to a general population. Lab experiments cater more toward **internal validity**, which is focused on a particular experiment and, therefore, better for examining potential cause-and-effect relationships. There is usually a trade-off with internal and external validity; if you increase one, you usually decrease the other. For example, imagine participating in a study that asks you to watch a video of an eyewitness event and report what you remember. Contrast this with witnessing an actual crime and then being interviewed by police and/or researchers (e.g., Cutshall & Yuille, 1989). The

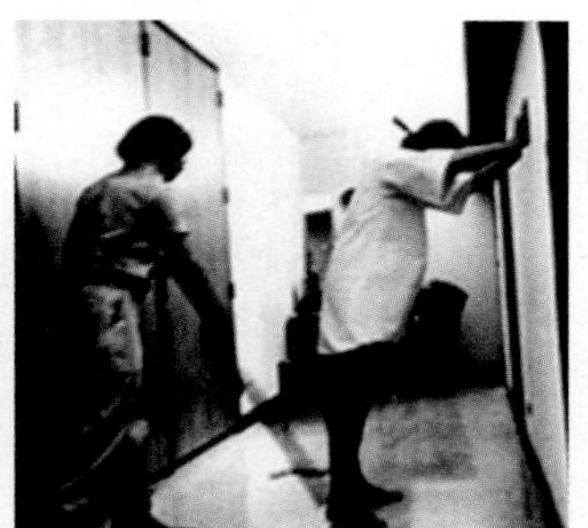

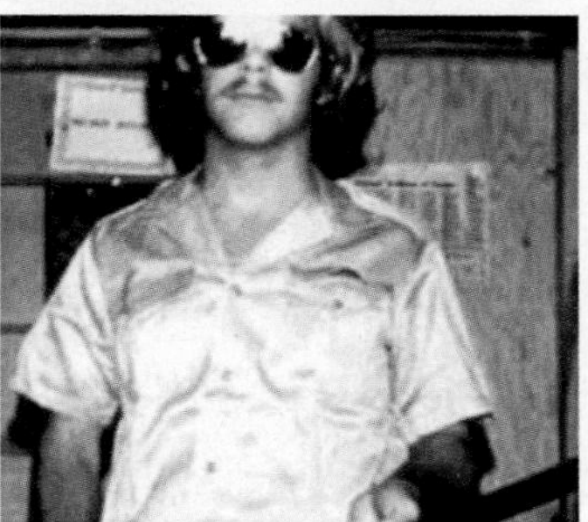

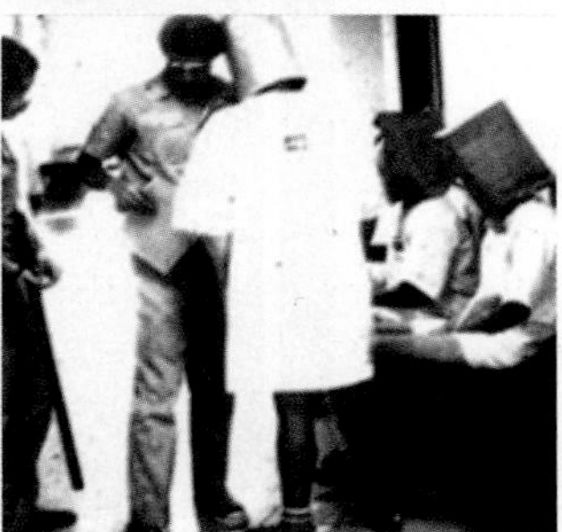

**Experiments involve** manipulating variables to test hypotheses and must use random assignment to determine cause and effect.

| | Type of Method | What Is It? | Advantages and Limitations | Type of Question |
|---|---|---|---|---|
| Descriptive Methods | Self-Report/ Survey | Data collection in which participants are asked to rate or describe their own behaviour or mental state | • Rich source of data from the individual<br>• Individuals may not be fully honest in responses | How do people think about their own attitudes, beliefs, and behaviours? |
| | Naturalistic Observation | Watching behaviour in an actual, real-world setting | • Able to generalize findings (external validity)<br>• Difficult to draw cause-and-effect inferences (internal validity) | How do individuals behave in their naturally occurring environment? |
| | Archival Studies | Examining what existing materials over time imply | • Researchers have no effect on collection of data<br>• Available data may be incomplete | What do historical trends tell us? |
| | Case Studies | In-depth analysis of individuals, groups, or events | • Allow for study of rare phenomena and challenge existing knowledge<br>• Cases may be atypical, data not generalizable | How do studies examining social reactions to natural disasters inform us about prosocial behaviour? |
| | Field Studies | Experiments with controlled variables in an uncontrolled environment. Field studies can be both descriptive and experimental depending on the design of the research | • Allows cause-and-effect conclusions, and behaviour may be more natural<br>• Less control than in a laboratory experiment | Did the variable that was manipulated cause a change in the measured behaviour? |
| Correlational Methods | Correlation Research | The measurement of naturally occurring variables and the relationship between them | • Identify relationships for follow-up studies, helps predict behaviour<br>• Cannot make casual conclusions, and relationships may be superficial | Is there a relationship between changes in one variable (e.g., oxytocin levels) and changes in another variable (e.g., bonding behaviours)? |
| Experimental Methods | Laboratory Experiments | Experiments with controlled variables in a controlled environment | • Ability to identify cause of behaviour<br>• May be artificial, and researchers unable to manipulate all variables | Did the variable that was manipulated cause a change in the measured behaviour? |

**Research Methodologies at a Glance.** Social psychologists use multiple methodologies to support or deny their findings. **Each method has advantages and limitations, so the more methods used, the better.**

results may be quite different. Lab experiments can be high in internal validity because the researcher has more control, but because the lab setting may be artificial, the external validity is lower. In contrast, studies conducted in natural settings are higher in external validity, but once you leave the lab, you may compromise internal validity.

**CONFOUND** any difference other than the levels of the independent variable between the experimental group and the control group

**PARTICIPANT BIAS** bias that occurs when a participant's suspicions, expectations, or assumptions about the study influence the result

## CONFOUNDS

In order for an experiment to be considered valid, the independent variable must be the *only* differentiating factor in the experimental group and the control group. If there is an additional difference in the groups, then it is impossible to know whether it was the independent variable that forced an effect on the dependent variable. Psychologists refer to any difference other than the levels of the independent variable between the experimental group and the control group to be a confounding variable, or **confound**. For example, imagine you are conducting a study on consumption of Tim Hortons coffee and sleep habits. You manipulate the number of cups of coffee participants consume over a period of a week (independent variable) and measure the number of hours they sleep per night and self-rated sleep quality (dependent variables). However, if you have failed to measure levels of pre-existing caffeine consumption and sleep patterns, these would be confounding variables in your study. In particular, if an individual regularly consumes a lot of coffee, she may have developed a tolerance to caffeine so that caffeine does not influence her sleep, compared to an individual who does not drink coffee at all or limits his consumption to one small double-double per day.

### Participant Bias

Researchers can do their best to control every aspect of an experiment, but when dealing with human beings, it can be difficult to control everything, so researchers must plan for some things to go wrong. **Participant bias** occurs when a participant's suspicions, expectations, or assumptions about the study influence the results. For instance, if participants in a thought-suppression study suspect that the researchers are

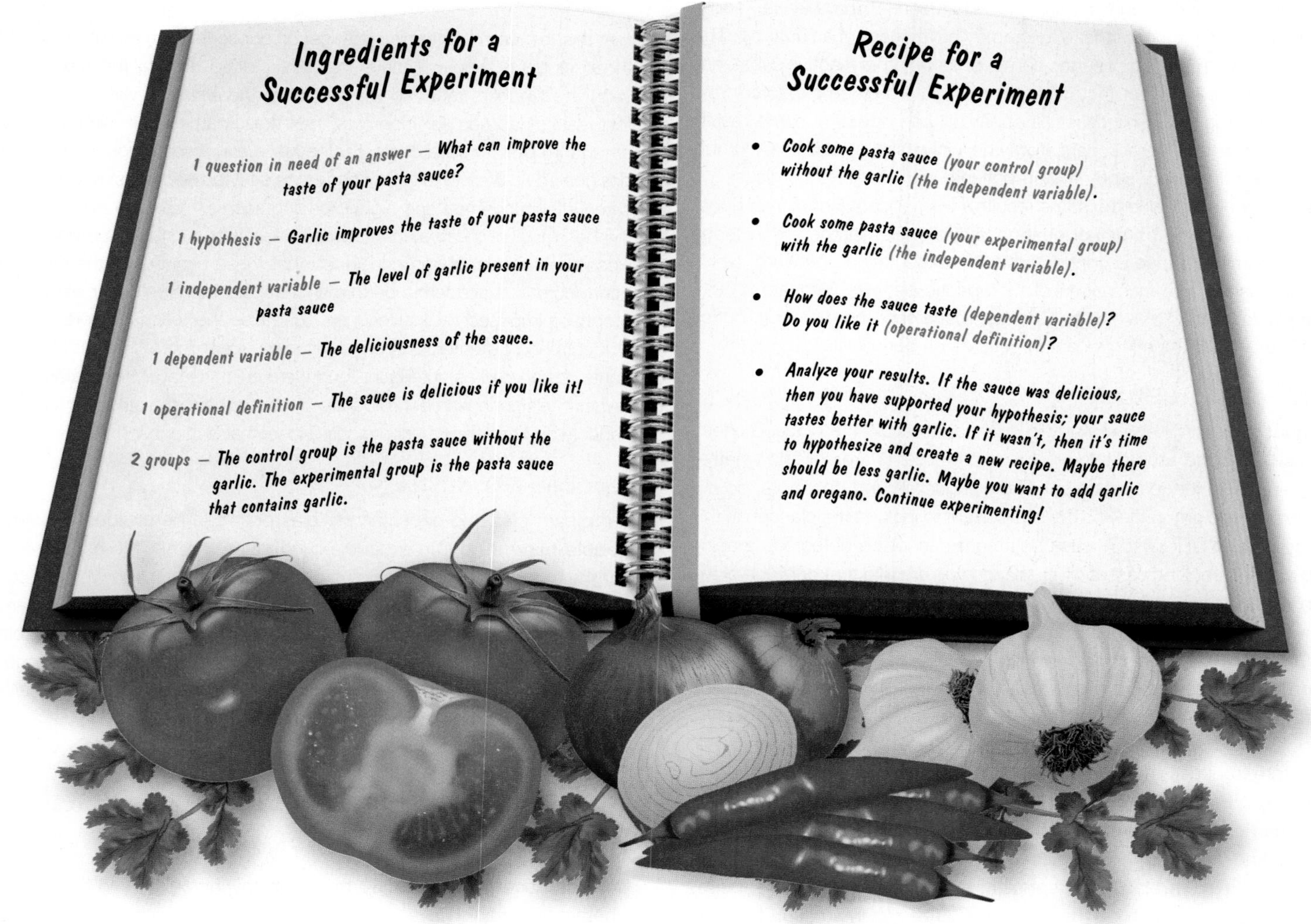

Ingredients for a Successful Experiment
1 question in need of an answer – What can improve the taste of your pasta sauce?
1 hypothesis – Garlic improves the taste of your pasta sauce
1 independent variable – The level of garlic present in your pasta sauce
1 dependent variable – The deliciousness of the sauce.
1 operational definition – The sauce is delicious if you like it!
2 groups – The control group is the pasta sauce without the garlic. The experimental group is the pasta sauce that contains garlic.
Recipe for a Successful Experiment
Cook some pasta sauce (your control group) without the garlic (the independent variable).
Cook some pasta sauce (your experimental group) with the garlic (the independent variable).
How does the sauce taste (dependent variable)? Do you like it (operational definition)?
Analyze your results. If the sauce was delicious, then you have supported your hypothesis; your sauce tastes better with garlic. If it wasn't, then it's time to hypothesize and create a new recipe. Maybe there should be less garlic. Maybe you want to add garlic and oregano. Continue experimenting!


**The Experimental Method.** Experiments **can be compared to** cooking. **Is your pasta sauce bland?** Change up the recipe!

**PLACEBO EFFECT** a measurable or observable improvement in health or behaviour that is not attributed to medication or any other treatment given

**SINGLE-BLIND STUDY** study in which two groups of participants are not told whether they are given the real treatment or the placebo and, therefore, do not know which group they are in

**EXPERIMENTER BIAS** bias exhibited by the experiment administrator in inadvertently but subtly changing his behaviour toward participants because of knowledge of which group is control and which group is experimental; this also occurs when the researcher subconsciously shows bias in his or her evaluation of results in an effort to reach the desired conclusion

**DOUBLE-BLIND STUDY** study in which neither the experimenter nor the participant knows which group is experimental and which is control

**DECEPTION** providing participants with false or incomplete information

measuring the amount of chocolate or dessert they will eat after being told not to think about desserts, they may try to control their behaviour to avoid "falling for the trick." These participants can skew the results of a study and create unreliable results.

Another issue that complicates the interpretation of the results is the **placebo effect**. The placebo effect refers to a measurable or observable improvement in health or behaviour that is not attributed to medication or any other treatment given. In Latin, *placebo* means "I shall please," and in layman's terms, it means "fake." You may have heard of a sugar pill. This is a type of pill made up of sugar, saline, or some other inactive substance that produces an effect that is similar to what would be expected from an active drug. In some cases, a sugar pill can have the same results as an active pill. Researchers from the University of British Columbia discovered through a study that in patients with Parkinson's disease, a placebo could produce the same results—a significant increase in dopamine in the brain—as actual pharmaceuticals. Researchers concluded that dopamine release is connected to the expectation of reward, which in this case is the anticipation of therapeutic benefits (Graham, 2001). The placebo effect makes the job of the researcher more difficult, but as in this example, the effects can sometimes be beneficial.



### Single-Blind Study

Conducting a single-blind study is one way to avoid the placebo effect. In a **single-blind study**, two groups of participants are not told whether they are given the real treatment or the sugar pill, and, therefore, do not know in which group they are. It is important to include the placebo in this study so that lack of the active treatment cannot be detected. Imagine you are in a smoking cessation study and you are told that only one of the two study groups is going to be given a pill that is supposed to suppress cravings. If your group takes a pill while the other group receives nothing, there is no question as to which group is getting active treatment. But with one group taking the actual pill and the other the sugar pill, the participants are "blind" to whether they are receiving actual treatment.

A single-blind study reduces the participant's expectations and, therefore, reduces the placebo effect, but it still leaves room for bias—from the individual administering the study in this instance. Administrators may inadvertently but subtly change their behaviours toward participants if they know who is receiving the real treatment, which may affect a participant's interpretation of treatment. Or the researcher may subconsciously show bias in his or her evaluation of results in an effort to reach the desired conclusion.

This potential confound is referred to as **experimenter bias**, and it was the subject of a classic study conducted by Rosenthal and Jacobson in 1968. The study team asked a group of teachers to administer an intelligence test called "The Harvard Test of Inflected Acquisitions" and told them

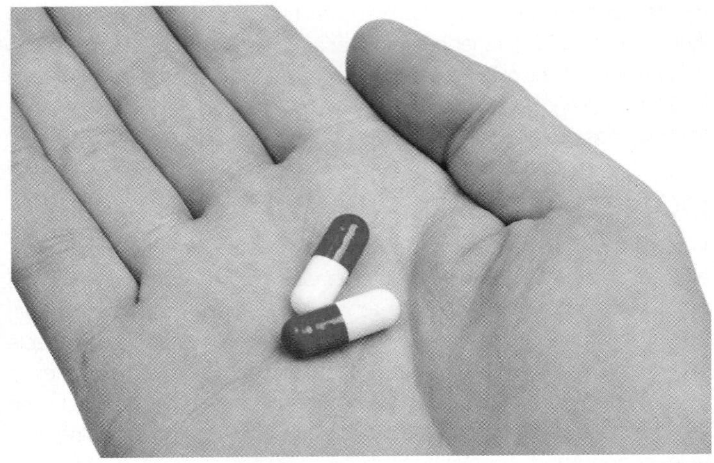

**Can you tell which pill contains active ingredients and which is the placebo? A placebo effect indicates the** importance of perception and the brain's role in maintaining health.

that this test could determine intelligence quotients (IQs) as well as identify those students who will thrive in future grades. Before the next school year, the teachers received the names of the students with the "highest test results" labelled as "bloomers," but these names were simply chosen at random by the researchers. By the next year, those students who were designated as likely to excel in academics showed better test results on the same intelligence test and higher reading scores. Teachers even believed the behaviour of these students was better than during the previous year. Rosenthal and Jacobson concluded that these changes in the students' behaviours and academic performances were the result of a self-fulfilling prophecy imposed by the teachers. Because the teachers were told the students had potential, they unintentionally spent more time with the students designated as "intelligent" and were even friendlier than before. As a result of this change in behaviour from the teachers, the students felt more capable and performed accordingly (Rosenthal & Jacobson, 1968).

### Double-Blind Study

Participant bias and experimenter bias both can be avoided through a **double-blind study**. In a double-blind study, neither the experimenter nor the participant knows which group is experimental and which is control. The double-blind study is considered the gold standard in research because it supplies the most reliable results without the threat of bias from either party. However, it might not always be possible to conduct a researchers may be able to employ this technique to guard against unintentionally tampering with the results.

## How Do We Conduct Ethical Research?

Consider research conducted by social psychologists and think about whether you would have wanted to participate: participants have been asked to sing the national anthem out loud, to steal money from an office drawer, to write statements about politicians with whom they don't agree, to lie, and to be involved in many other peculiar situations. In 1963, Dr. Stanley Milgram conducted what is now a classic study of obedience, using **deception**, or providing participants with false or incomplete information. Participants were told that they were studying the effect of punishment on learning and were focused on the relationship between the "teacher" (themselves) and the "learner," who was a confederate of the experimenters. This directed their attention away from the real purpose of the study, which was measuring obedience to a perceived authority figure. Milgram gave study participants what they believed to be a machine designed to give electric shocks to someone they couldn't see, but could hear, on the other side of a wall. Every time the person on the other side of the wall answered a question incorrectly, the participant was instructed to administer increasingly dangerous shocks. The participants could hear cries of pain on the other side, and eventually silence, but the majority of participants persisted in obeying the researcher and giving shocks—even at the maximum levels—to the person on the other side (Milgram, 1963). The person on the other side wasn't actually receiving shocks, and the participants had a **debriefing** following the experiment—that is, they were given a full explanation of the hypothesis being tested, procedures used to deceive participants, and the reasons for the deception. Would you have "shocked" the learner if you knew the shocks were not real or that the study was really about whether or not you would obey the experimenter? Probably not!

> "An understanding of research methods will assist you **as you explore different topics that social psychologists study.**"

That said, given the guidelines we have in place today, would it be likely that Milgram's obedience study would be allowed? How would you feel if you had participated? Was the study ethical? Researchers continue to disagree on the value of past research that has violated human ethics. For example, would we know what we know about conformity and obedience if Zimbardo and Milgram had not conducted their respective studies? Some research "in the name of science" has clearly been unethical (e.g., Nazi experiments on prisoners, LSD experiments on mind control, aversion shock therapy to "cure" homosexuality). While we are comforted by the fact that these violations don't seem to occur in "our backyard," we are incorrect in this assumption. For example, between 1929 and 1972, the Alberta Eugenics Board sterilized nearly three thousand residents of the province classified as "feeble-minded" to prevent passing on mentally "defective" traits. Many more individuals were forced to be sterilized across the country, although most provinces abandoned these eugenics programs by the 1950s and 1960s (Grekul, Krahn, & Odynak, 2004). Significant ethical safeguards are now required to conduct any medical or psychological research with human or animal participants.

Basic ethical principles in research are mandated by the *Tri-Council Policy Statement: Ethical Conduct for Research Involving Humans* (Canadian Institutes of Health Research et al., 2010) and have been influenced by the Canadian Psychological Association's *Code of Ethics for Psychologists* (Canadian Psychological Association, 2000). The core principles that Canadian ethical policies are based on are respect for persons, concern for welfare, and justice. *Respect for persons* refers to recognizing that humans deserve respect and consideration and should be valued as participants in all aspects of research, including moral obligations to respect freedom of choice (i.e., autonomy) and not interfere with those who have impaired decision-making abilities. At the beginning of a study, researchers should provide participants with enough detail about the study, including risks and benefits, so that they can decide with their eyes open whether they would like to participate (i.e., informed consent). *Concern for welfare* refers to providing safeguards to protect against any negative effects of research on participants' physical and mental health, as well as their life circumstances. Finally, *justice* demands that the benefits and burdens of the research be fairly distributed (TCPS 2, 2010).

Institutions in which scientific research is conducted are required to have **research ethics boards (REBs)** that evaluate proposed research to ensure that research meets the three ethical guidelines for both human and nonhuman participation. To maintain the integrity of a research study, though, it is sometimes necessary to deceive study participants. For instance, Milgram used deception in his obedience study by allowing participants to believe they were physically harming another person when in reality they weren't. When deception is used, participants must be told at the beginning of a study as much information as possible about the participation in the study to determine if they would like to be involved. This is called **informed consent**. Participants do not need to know which information is omitted or changed—just that 100 percent of the details involved in the study are not disclosed. Participants will be debriefed on the complete details of the study after the study is complete.

An understanding of research methods will assist you as you explore different topics that social psychologists study. Importantly, taking this course and gaining knowledge of research methodology will help you become a better consumer of information in your everyday decisions, ability to think critically, and capability to evaluate real-world problems (VanderStoep & Shaughnessy, 1997).

**DEBRIEFING** a procedure that involves giving participants a full explanation of the hypothesis being tested, procedures used to deceive participants, and the reasons for the deception

**RESEARCH ETHICS BOARD (REB)** a committee that has been established to approve and oversee research that involves human and nonhuman animal subjects

**INFORMED CONSENT** consent given when subjects are told at the beginning of a study as much information as possible about the participation in the study to determine if they would like to be involved

<<< Researchers do not have to divulge every detail of a study, **but they do need to inform participants that they may not be given complete information.**

CHAPTER

# 02 Review

## Summary

### HOW CAN RESEARCH METHODS IMPACT YOU EVERY DAY? p. 20

- Research methods can help us better understand why we think and behave the way we do. This helps us think more effectively and critically evaluate and process the information we confront every day.
- The ability to think critically is the first step in making better decisions about everything from which products to buy to how to answer a question on an exam. Separating common sense, hindsight bias, and the false consensus effect from a scientific way of thinking can lead you to make the most effective choices.

### HOW DO SOCIAL PSYCHOLOGISTS FIND THE TRUTH? p. 22

- Like detectives, social psychologists gather evidence to answer questions, test theories, and come to conclusions. To do this, a researcher poses a question, researches theories, develops a hypothesis, and tests the hypothesis using variables with operational definitions, samples, and replication. Once the researcher draws a conclusion, the cycle begins again.
- When conducting research, social psychologists must consider ethics and culture. Because study participants are often human beings, informed consent and debriefing must be a part of the process.

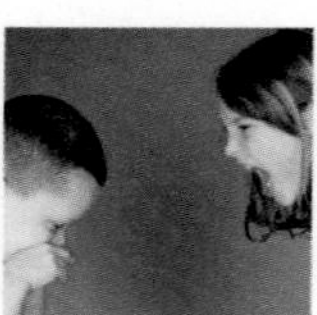

### WHAT CAN DESCRIPTIVE METHODS SHOW US? p. 26

- Descriptive methods answer the who, what, when, where, and how questions about a particular phenomenon. They describe patterns and trends but do not evaluate cause-and-effect relationships.
- These methods include naturalistic observation, self-report or survey data, and other methods such as archival, case, and field studies.

### WHAT DO CORRELATIONS TELL US ABOUT RELATIONSHIPS? p. 28

- Correlations help us to examine the relationship between two variables, and what patterns the associations form (e.g., positive, negative, illusory correlations).
- Correlational research cannot lead to causal conclusions. Correlations have several limitations such as the third variable and bi-directional causality problems, but can be beneficial for helping us predict behaviour.

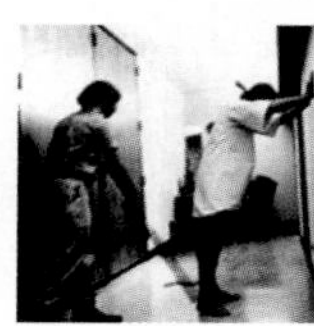

### WHAT DO EXPERIMENTAL METHODS HAVE TO SAY? p. 30

- Experimental methods differ from descriptive ones in that researchers attempt to control all factors that may affect the results. These methods can support or deny an existence of a cause-and-effect relationship.
- Independent and dependent variables are used to conduct experimental methods. Researchers will take measures like random assignment, single- and double-blind studies, and the use of placebos to take into account confounds and participant and experimenter bias that could alter the results.

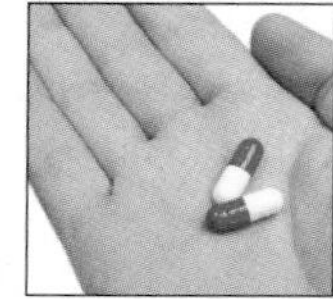

### HOW DO WE CONDUCT ETHICAL RESEARCH? p. 34

- Experiments with questionable ethics have brought about the development of specific ethics guidelines that regulate human research.
- While deception is still permitted in experiments, participants must provide their informed consent to participate and be fully debriefed as to the true nature of the study at its conclusion.

## Key Terms

**archival studies** research that entails culling information from existing records ranging from magazine articles to website analytics *27*

**bi-directional causality** a situation in which variable X could cause variable Y or vice versa *30*

**case studies** in-depth analyses of an individual, group, or event *27*

**confound** any difference other than the levels of the independent variable between the experimental group and the control group *33*

**control group** the group that does not get the main treatment in an experiment, but is used as a baseline to compare results with the experimental group *31*

**correlational research** research in which researchers do not manipulate variables but observe whether there is a relationship between two variables *29*

**debriefing** a procedure that involves giving participants a full explanation of the hypothesis being tested, procedures used to deceive participants, and the reasons for the deception *35*

**deception** providing participants with false or incomplete information *34*

**dependent variable** the variable an experimenter does not control that is used to measure whether the change in the independent variable has an effect *30*

**descriptive research** research used to obtain information regarding the current status of a population or phenomena to describe the who, what, when, where, and how questions with respect to variables or conditions in a situation *26*

**double-blind study** study in which neither the experimenter nor the participant knows which group is experimental and which is control *34*

**experimental group** in an experiment, the group that gets the main treatment or manipulation *31*

**experimental research** research that attempts to control all the factors (like a potential third variable) that may affect the results of an experiment *30*

**experimenter bias** bias exhibited by the experiment administrator in inadvertently but subtly changing his behaviour toward participants because of knowledge of which group is control and which group is experimental; this also occurs when the researcher subconsciously shows bias in his or her evaluation of results in an effort to reach the desired conclusion *34*

**external validity** the extent to which results apply to a general population *31*

**field studies** studies involving data or information that is collected in naturally occurring settings *27*

**hypothesis** a proposed explanation that can be either supported or disproven with statistics or observations *23*

**independent variable** the variable an experimenter has control over and can alter *30*

**informed consent** consent given when subjects are told at the beginning of a study as much information as possible about the participation in the study to determine if they would like to be involved 35

**internal validity** the ability to infer cause and effect; that the variable was manipulated was the only factor to change across conditions and so was what led to the observed effect 31

**matched samples design** a research design in which two or more groups of individuals are identical, or matching, in terms of the third variable 29

**naturalistic observation** research that involves watching behaviour in a real-world setting 27

**operational definition** a definition that assigns one or more specific operational conditions to an event and then identifies how those conditions should be measured 23

**participant bias** bias that occurs when a participant's suspicions, expectations, or assumptions about the study influence the result 33

**peer review** a process by which experts in the field review and comment on each other's work 23

**placebo effect** a measurable or observable improvement in health or behaviour that is not attributed to medication or any other treatment given 34

**random assignment** a required technique in an experiment to be able to infer cause and effect; every participant has any equal chance of being assigned to any group in the experiment 31

**reliable** consistent measurement 24

**replication** the process of repeating a study to verify effects, usually with a different sample of participants 24

**research ethics board (REB)** a committee that has been established to approve and oversee research that involves human and nonhuman animal subjects 35

**research question** the query that is the first step in the research process 23

**sample** selection of who or what will be tested in the research process 24

**self-report/survey method** a form of data collection in which participants are asked to rate or describe their own behaviour or mental state 27

**single-blind study** study in which two groups of participants are not told whether they are given the real treatment or the placebo and, therefore, do not know in which group they are in 34

**theory** a general framework for understanding a concept that allows us to describe, explain, and predict behaviour 22

**third variable** any additional factor that could be responsible for an observed effect 29

**valid** when a variable measures what it is supposed to measure 24

**variables** stimuli or characteristics that can take on different values, such as level of attraction or age 23

# Test Your Understanding

## MULTIPLE CHOICE

**1.** Which psychological researcher is responsible for a controversial study on obedience?
- **a.** Sigmund Freud
- **b.** Paul Zak
- **c.** Stanley Milgram
- **d.** Daniel Gilbert

**2.** Which is an example of hindsight bias?
- **a.** knowing that putting a candle near a loose set of curtains is dangerous
- **b.** thinking you knew it was going to rain after it did
- **c.** assuming more expensive wine tastes better than cheaper wine
- **d.** overestimating the number of people who shared your belief that the Conservative Party of Canada would win the 2011 federal election

**3.** Which key word is unlikely to help you if you are researching bystander apathy?
- **a.** obedience
- **b.** group
- **c.** crime
- **d.** influence

**4.** What makes a hypothesis untestable?
- **a.** a variable that has an operational definition
- **b.** a variable that is reliable and valid
- **c.** a variable that is subjective
- **d.** a variable that is objective

**5.** Which is not one of the three basic ethical principles established in the Tri-Council Policy Ethics Statement?
- **a.** justice
- **b.** integrity
- **c.** respect for persons
- **d.** concern for welfare

**6.** Which would not be an example of a good source for doing research?
- **a.** an encyclopaedia
- **b.** an online peer-reviewed journal
- **c.** a newspaper
- **d.** Wikipedia

**7.** What is an example of a cause-and-effect relationship wrongly assumed from a correlation?
- **a.** The more home runs a home team hits at a ball game, the more hot dogs are consumed.
- **b.** The more home runs a home team hits at a ball game, the longer the game lasts.
- **c.** The longer a ball game lasts, the more hot dogs fans eat.
- **d.** The more exciting a ball game is, the likelier people are to attend and stay.

**8.** Which group of participants receives the main manipulation or treatment?
- **a.** the control group
- **b.** the matched sample group
- **c.** the experimental group
- **d.** none of the above

**9.** What aspect of an experiment is considered a confound?
- **a.** the independent variable
- **b.** matched samples
- **c.** a third variable
- **d.** external validity

**10.** Which technique eliminates experimenter bias?
- **a.** placebo effect
- **b.** single-blind study
- **c.** correlational study
- **d.** double-blind study

**ANSWERS:** 1. c; 2. b; 3. a; 4. c; 5. b; 6. d; 7. a; 8. c; 9. c; 10. d

## ESSAY RESPONSE

1. Using Paul Zak's work on oxytocin and trust as an example, explain the differences between descriptive research and experimental research.
2. Why is the false consensus effect potentially dangerous? Give an example of when this could be the case.
3. Provide an example of a hypothesis in need of improvement. Alter it to make it testable and explain the difference.
4. Describe the role of a research ethics board.
5. Explain the differences between naturalistic observation and the observation that takes place in a laboratory. What are the advantages and disadvantages of each?

## APPLY IT!

Find a newspaper article that implies causation from a correlational study. What does the study actually explain? How is the article misleading?

**Remember to check www.thethinkspot.ca for additional information, downloadable flashcards, and other helpful resources.**

# THINK READINGS

NATURE

## Most People Are Not WEIRD

By JOSEPH HENRICH, STEVEN J. HEINE and ARA NORENZAYAN

Published: July 1, 2010

Much research on human behaviour and psychology assumes that everyone shares most fundamental cognitive and affective processes and that findings from one population apply across the board. A growing body of evidence suggests that this is not the case.

Experimental findings from several disciplines indicate considerable variation among human populations in diverse domains, such as visual perception, analytic reasoning, fairness, cooperation, memory and the heritability of IQ.[1,2] This is in line with what anthropologists have long suggested: that people from Western, educated, industrialized, rich, and democratic (WEIRD) societies—and particularly American undergraduates—are some of the most psychologically unusual people on Earth.[1]

So the fact that the vast majority of studies use WEIRD participants presents a challenge to the understanding of human psychology and behaviour. A 2008 survey of the top psychology journals found that 96% of subjects were from Western industrialized countries—which house just 12% of the world's population.[3] Strange, then, that research articles routinely assume that their results are broadly representative, rarely adding even a cautionary footnote on how far their findings can be generalized.

The evidence that basic cognitive and motivational processes vary across populations has become increasingly difficult to ignore. For example, many studies have shown that Americans, Canadians and western Europeans rely on analytical reasoning strategies—which separate objects from their contexts and rely on rules to explain and predict behaviour—substantially more than non-Westerners. Research also indicates that Americans use analytical thinking more than, say, Europeans. By contrast, Asians tend to reason holistically, for example by considering people's behaviour in terms of their situation.[1] Yet many long-standing theories of how humans perceive, categorize and remember emphasize the centrality of analytical thought.

It is a similar story with social behaviour related to fairness and equality. Here, researchers often use one-shot economic experiments such as the ultimatum game, in which a player decides how much of a fixed amount to offer a second player, who can then accept or reject this proposal. If the second player rejects it, neither player gets anything. Participants from industrialized societies tend to divide the money equally, and reject low offers. People from non-industrialized societies behave differently, especially in the smallest-scale nonmarket

[1]Henrich, J., Heine, S. J. & Norenzayan, A. *Behav. Brain Sci.* doi:10.1017/ S0140525X0999152X (2010).
[2]Henrich, J., Heine, S. J. & Norenzayan, A. *Behav. Brain Sci.* doi: 10.1017/ S0140525X10000725 (2010).
[3]Arnett, J. Am. Psychol. **63**, 602–614 (2008).



*From what you learned in Chapters 1 and 2 about the development of social psychology and the process of setting up experiments, why do you think people from "WEIRD" societies are the most commonly used participants?*

*Throughout this book, you will learn about the differences between individualist and collectivist cultures. Individualist cultures, like the United States or Canada, approach each person in the context of himself or herself, unconnected to anyone else. Collectivist cultures, like that of many Asian countries, approach each person in the context of his or her relationships to those surrounding him or her.*

societies such as foragers in Africa and horticulturalists in South America, where people are neither inclined to make equal offers nor to punish those who make low offers.[4]

Recent developments in evolutionary biology, neuroscience, and related fields suggest that these differences stem from the way in which populations have adapted to diverse culturally constructed environments. Amazonian groups, such as the Piraha, whose languages do not include numerals above three, are worse at distinguishing large quantities digitally than groups using extensive counting systems, but are similar in their ability to approximate quantities. This suggests the kind of counting system people grow up with influences how they think about integers.[1]

## Costly generalizations

Using study participants from one unusual population could have important practical consequences. For example, economists have been developing theories of decision making incorporating insights from psychology and social science—such as how to set wages—and examining how these might translate into policy.[5] Researchers and policy-makers should recognize that populations vary considerably in the extent to which they display certain biases, patterns and preferences in economic decisions, such as those related to optimism.[1] Such differences can, for example, affect the way that experienced investors make decisions about the stock market.[6]

We offer four suggestions to help put theories of human behaviour and psychology on a firmer empirical footing. First, editors and reviewers should push researchers to support any generalizations with evidence. Second, granting agencies, reviewers and editors should give researchers credit for comparing diverse and inconvenient subject pools. Third, granting agencies should prioritize cross-disciplinary, cross-cultural research. Fourth, researchers must strive to evaluate how their findings apply to other populations. There are several low-cost ways to approach this in the short term: one is to select a few judiciously chosen populations that provide a "tough test" of universality in some domain, such as societies with limited counting systems for testing theories about numerical cognition.[1,2]

A crucial longer-term goal is to establish a set of principles that researchers can use to distinguish variable from universal aspects of psychology. Establishing such principles will remain difficult until behavioural scientists develop interdisciplinary, international research networks for long-term studies on diverse populations using an array of methods, from experimental techniques and ethnography to brain-imaging and biomarkers.

Recognizing the full extent of human diversity does not mean giving up on the quest to understand human nature. To the contrary, this recognition illuminates a journey into human nature that is more exciting, more complex, and ultimately more consequential than has previously been suspected ■

**Joseph Henrich, Steven J. Heine** and **Ara Norenzayan** are in the Department of Psychology, University of British Columbia, Vancouver, British Columbia V6T 1Z4, Canada. Joseph Henrich is also in the Department of Economics.
email: joseph.henrich@gmail.com

[4]Henrich, J. et al. *Science* **327**, 1480–1484 (2010).
[5]Foote, C. L., Goette, L. & Meier, S. *Policymaking Insights from Behavioral Economics* (Federal Reserve Bank of Boston, 2009).
[6]Ji, L. J., Zhang, Z. Y. & Guo, T. Y. *J. Behav. Decis. Making* **21**, 399–413 (2008).

*This statement is an illustration of why the concept of random sampling that you learned about in Chapter 2 is so vital to our analysis of the results of any experiment. Think about what would happen if the federal government made all its decisions based on the cognitive processes of only people from Quebec. Then think about how such a process could affect the world on a global scale.*

*How would you ensure a diverse participant sample when utilizing each of the methods discussed in Chapter 2?*

*Evaluate these four suggestions. Do you think they w[...] solve the problem discussed in this article? Do you ha[...] any suggestions to add based on what you learned in Chapter 2?*

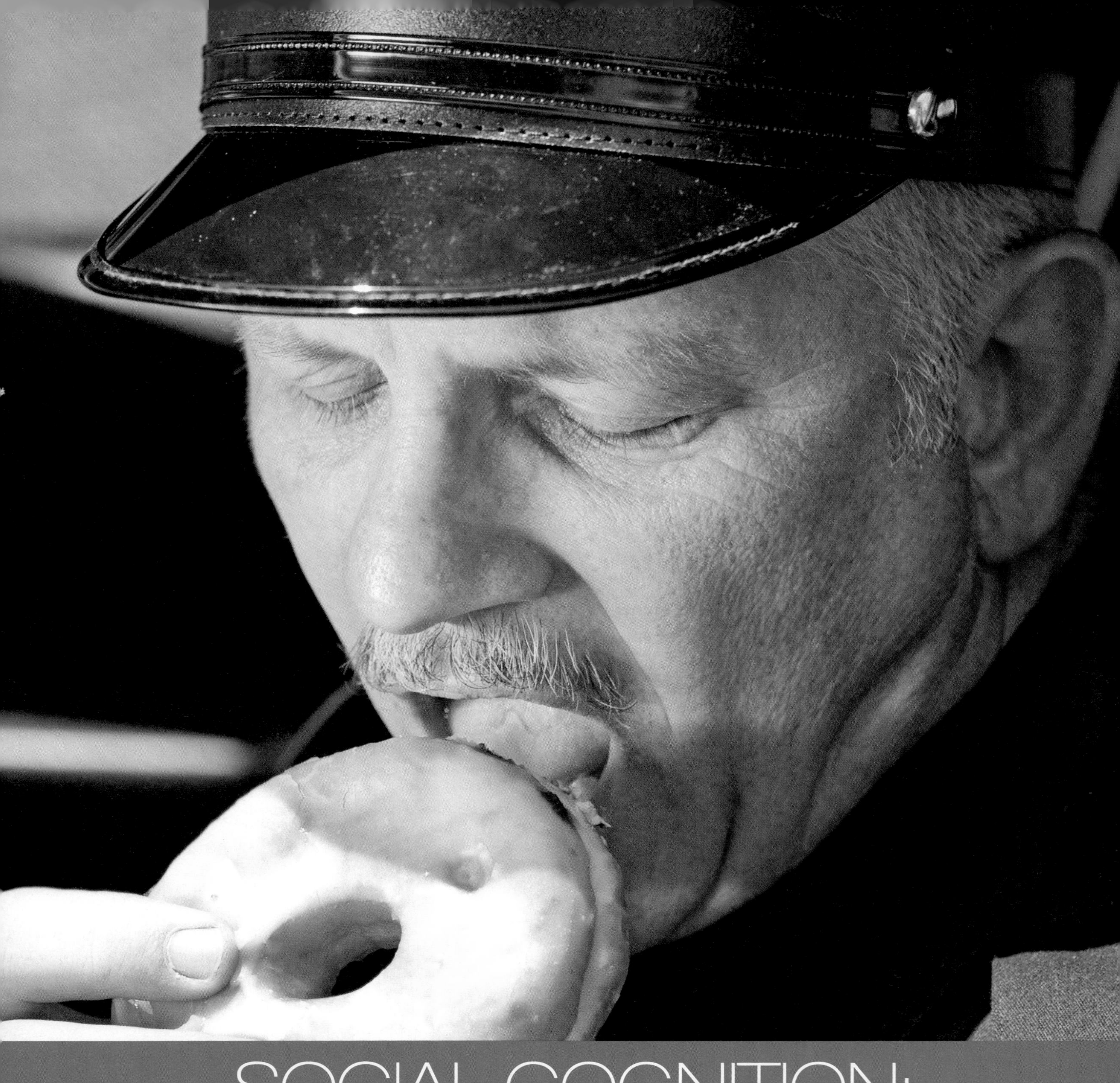

# SOCIAL COGNITION: THINKING ABOUT THE SOCIAL WORLD

<<< *Why do we all seem to associate police officers with doughnuts? What causes this connection?*

**HOW** DO SCHEMAS GUIDE THE WAY YOU THINK ABOUT THE WORLD AROUND YOU?
**HOW** EFFECTIVE ARE MENTAL SHORTCUTS?
**WHAT** ARE OTHER SOURCES OF BIAS IN SOCIAL COGNITION?

Having just pulled off a successful heist, three black-clad bank robbers hop into the getaway car. "Move it!" their leader yells to the woman behind the wheel, and she floors it, peeling out of the parking lot. She drives faster and faster down Bay Street, shocked that there are no cops in sight. Nervously, the two robbers in the back look over their shoulders. The police officers must be onto them! Any second, they'll hear the sirens and see the flashing lights.

As the car picks up speed, the law-breaking foursome blows past a Tim Hortons. They can barely make out a figure sitting at the counter. It's a police officer. With a steaming cup of coffee at his elbow, he tears into a frosted doughnut, completely oblivious to the gang of bad guys speeding their way to freedom.

In the darkened movie theatre, the audience erupts into laughter. It's inevitable, really. Think of all the times you've seen a similar scenario played out on TV or in a movie. It always gets at least a chuckle, doesn't it? Somehow, we've all collectively come to associate police officers with doughnuts and coffee.

In fact, you can probably think of a time you've noticed (and maybe even pointed out to your friends) police officers eating doughnuts. Have you paid the same attention to the times you've seen a police officer without a doughnut in his hand? Probably not, because looking for these instances takes more controlled and effortful cognitive processing.

Our brains don't always have the resources to devote to such a level of processing. To help save time and mental energy, we rely on mental shortcuts such as this police officer–doughnut connection. Sometimes this results in accurate judgments, but often it leads us to biased thoughts. These collections of information, including our knowledge and expectations for a particular stimulus, are called schemas, and they are just one of the ways your brain attempts to bring order to and understand the world around you and your place in it.

**SCHEMA** an automatically created cognitive framework that helps guide the way we think about and understand the society around us

**PRIME** to activate a schema through a stimulus

## How Do Schemas Guide the Way You Think About the World Around You?

**Schemas** are automatically created cognitive frameworks that help guide the way we think about and understand the world around us. Think of a schema as all of the information that you have about a particular concept. This schema continues to help guide your processing of future information efficiently.

Consider what happens when you go to the movies. You buy your ticket at the counter (or take one look at the long line and decide to buy a ticket using your BlackBerry instead). You buy popcorn and a drink at a separate concessions counter, and before you can go to your seat in the theatre, you hand your ticket to a theatre employee who tears it in half and waves you on. You know once you're in the theatre, you'll sit through some commercials and then some movie trailers before watching the movie you came to see. If you went to the movies in a new city that you had never been to before, you would still know exactly what to do, because you have a schema that guides the experience of going to the movies.

Schemas can exist for people, places, events, or any other stimulus that you might encounter in the social world. Of course, as helpful as schemas are for organizing information accurately and efficiently, they can also result in errors in thinking or in remembering information. Schemas affect what we notice, seek out, and remember; when you encounter something that doesn't fit a schema, it could lead to such a processing error. Have you ever gone to the movies and noticed a long line at the ticket counter, while several of those automated ticket kiosks sat unused? Many people fail to notice them, even though using the kiosks could save them 10 minutes in line, simply because they haven't yet been fully incorporated into their schema for going to the movies.

> "The recent use of a stereotype, even in an unrelated situation, **can actually carry over to influence a person's interpretation of behaviours and interactions.**"

Schemas are created through experience. As you encounter similar experiences, people, social roles, and so on, you develop schemas for those things. After going to the movies a few times, you have the process down and have a pretty robust schema for that experience. Think about the doughnut-eating police officer from the beginning of this chapter. What kind of effect do you think the media have on the creation of schemas?

Once they are in place, schemas are activated through a stimulus. You go to the movies and the schema for going to the movies is activated, or **primed**. You go to the doctor's office, and your expectations for the experience and for the behaviour of your doctor are activated. Most of the time, these behaviours are carried out more or less involuntarily. Higgins, Rholes, and Jones (1977) first demonstrated the impact of priming on how we form impressions of other individuals. As part of a first task, participants read word lists such as "brave, adventurous, independent" or "reckless, foolish, careless." In what participants thought was a separate experiment, they were then asked to read about an individual who climbed mountains and sailed across the Atlantic Ocean. The types of words that participants had previously been exposed to coloured their perceptions of this individual. All the participants read the same description, but if they had read the list of positive words, they formed a more positive impression of the target individual than if they had read the list of negative words. Further, schemas can influence your decisions *even if you are unaware that you have been primed*. Researchers at McGill University demonstrated that subliminal positive or negative primes altered participants' reports of the social support and coping strategies they would use in relation to a hypothetical unplanned pregnancy scenario (Pierce & Lydon, 1998). Schemas can dramatically affect our thinking, even when we're removed from the initial stimuli that activated them. For example, having liberal or conservative value schemas activated can change our later endorsement of political policies (e.g., Bryan, Dweck, Ross, Kay, & Mislavsky, 2009).

According to the *confirmation bias*, activated schemas affect how we process incoming information. A schema stays activated until there is an opportunity for expression of the behaviours associated with that schema. How do you feel after going to see a horror movie? Maybe you look over your shoulder a few times as you go to your car. Maybe the road seems just a little darker, and you wouldn't be surprised if someone jumped out in front of the car. Maybe you turn on every light in your home as you get ready for bed. You feel nervous, no matter how many times you tell yourself, "It was only a movie."

Once a schema has been activated, it will colour how subsequent information is interpreted. If you just had an experience that activated your schema for being in a dangerous situation or feeling fearful, you're more likely to perceive the experiences that follow that one in a similar way. In fact, one of the authors of this text (KP) had such an experience after watching the original *Halloween* movie. Upon arriving home, the power went out in her university residence, she could hear breathing, and she was convinced villain Michael Myers was after her. Note: the breathing she heard was her own, which was magnified by her fear in the pitch black.

Activated schemas affect what we notice, actively seek out, and remember. We often notice and remember information that is in line with the schema that has already been developed. However, information that is highly inconsistent with our schemas (e.g., getting popcorn dumped on you by the concession vendor) is likely to stand out in our memories (e.g., Ensslen & Peace, 2010). Reliance on schemas makes it easier for us to organize information, but it can also invite a few problems. For example, research has found that both schema-consistent and schema-inconsistent information may be susceptible to false recall (e.g., Nemeth & Belli, 2006).

### THE TROUBLE WITH SCHEMAS

If we encounter something that doesn't match up with the schema for a particular stimulus, we either filter it out or mentally file it away as the "exception that proves the rule." Your brain wants sensory information within your schemas to be consistent, because this makes it much easier for your brain to process and retrieve the information. Of course, this filtering out of valid information simply because it's not consistent with a developed schema is just one of the ways in which schemas can distort the way we view the world.

## Stereotyping

Once it's been formed, a schema can be hard to change. The tendency for a schema to remain intact even when it comes up against discrediting information is called the **perseverance effect**. This plays a large role in one type of schema—the **stereotype**, in which the characteristics of someone or something are generalized according to preconceived notions about the group to which that person or thing seems to belong.

Imagine your friend was set up on a blind date. You meet her for coffee the next day to get the lowdown on how it went. She simply can't stop gushing about him. He was funny, charming, and athletic. "I thought this date was going to be snoozeville," she admits, "but he's really not like all of those other dull math majors!" Rather than acknowledge that her schema for math majors may be incomplete or incorrect, your friend has, instead, filed this example as a subcategory of "math major," the previously mentioned exception that proves her stereotype. She continues thinking that all other math majors are dull, whereas this particular one is just different. We will revisit the idea of schemas when we discuss stereotypes and subtyping in Chapter 10.

The recent use of a stereotype, even in an unrelated situation, can actually carry over to influence a person's interpretation of behaviours and interactions. This activation of stereotypes can affect the behaviour of the individual holding the view, sometimes in unexpected ways. For example, one study found that after being primed on words associated with stereotypes of elderly persons (e.g., *careful*, *wise*, *helpless*), participants actually demonstrated some of these traits themselves. In fact, participants whose stereotypes had been activated walked more slowly down the hallway than those who had not had the stereotype primed (Bargh, Chen, & Burrows, 1996).

**PERSEVERANCE EFFECT** the tendency for a schema to remain intact, even when it comes up against discrediting information

**STEREOTYPE** a type of schema in which we apply generalized information to an individual based on the group to which he or she belongs

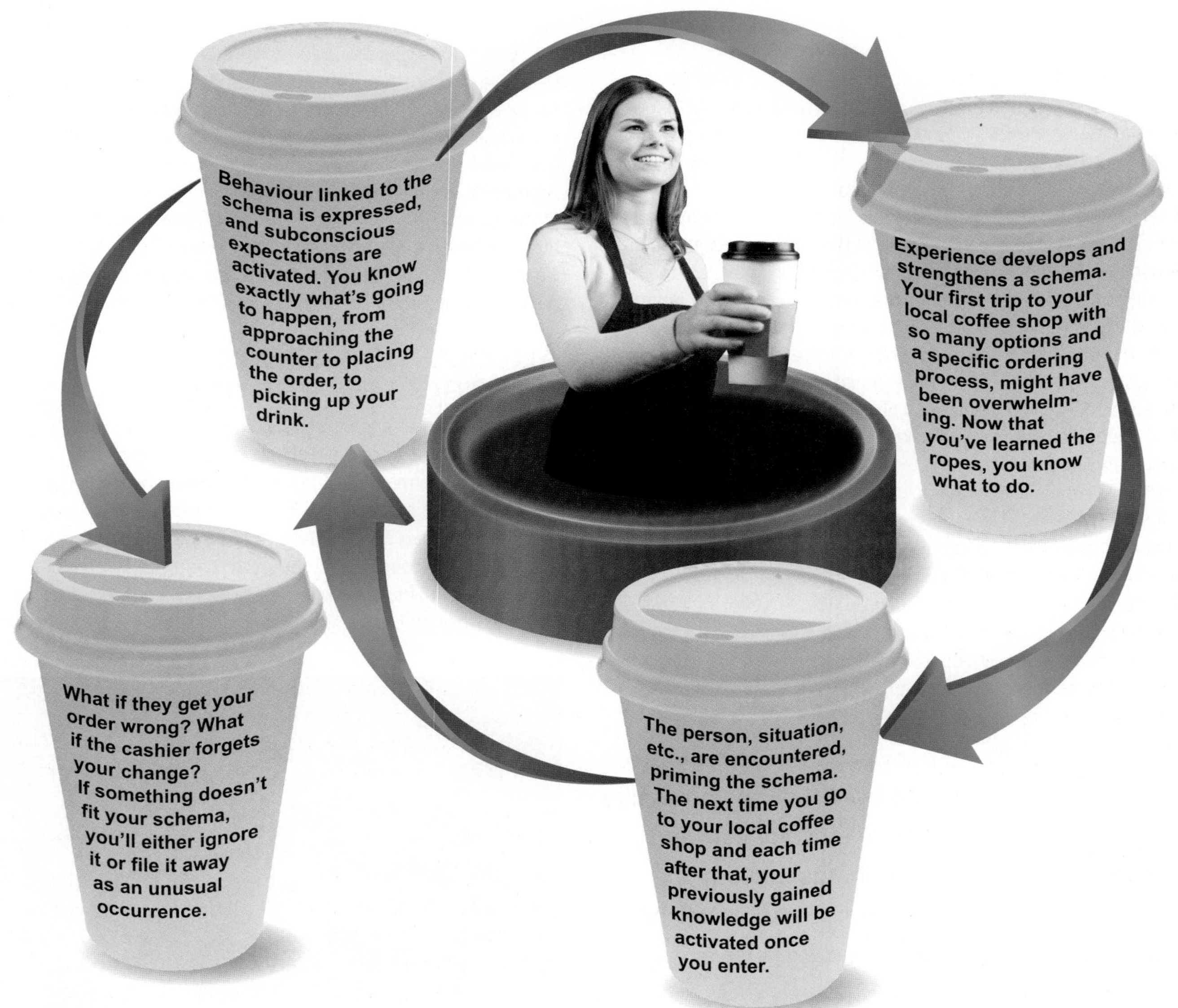

Experience develops and strengthens a schema. Your first trip to your local coffee shop with so many options and a specific ordering process, might have been overwhelming. Now that you've learned the ropes, you know what to do.
The person, situation, etc., are encountered, priming the schema. The next time you go to your local coffee shop and each time after that, your previously gained knowledge will be activated once you enter.
What if they get your order wrong? What if the cashier forgets your change? If something doesn't fit your schema, you'll either ignore it or file it away as an unusual occurrence.
Behaviour linked to the schema is expressed, and subconscious expectations are activated. You know exactly what's going to happen, from approaching the counter to placing the order, to picking up your drink.


**A Schema for Your Local Coffee Shop.** Schemas are developed and verified through experience.

**SELF-FULFILLING PROPHECY** a prediction that causes itself to come true

**SELECTIVE FILTERING** paying more attention to sensory information that fits a given schema, at the same time filtering out information that is inconsistent

**AUTOMATIC PROCESSING** the processing of information "on the fly," using schemas as shortcuts

**CONTROLLED PROCESSING** a type of mental processing that takes purposeful thought and effort as decisions or courses of action are weighed carefully

### Self-Fulfilling Prophecy

Related to the issue of stereotyping is the fact that schemas can also lead to what Merton (1948) termed **self-fulfilling prophecies**, predictions that cause themselves to come true. Numerous studies have found that the stronger and more developed the schema is, the more attention we pay to sensory information and traits that fit that schema. At the same time, our minds automatically filter out traits and information that are not consistent with the schema (Allen, Sherman, Conrey, & Stroessner, 2009). In paying more attention to information that fits a given schema, it seems that the schema is confirmed as correct (no matter how much discrediting information we have to filter out to make that confirmation!).

This **selective filtering** can lead to self-fulfilling prophecies in another way. Because schemas include set expectations for experiences, we tend to unconsciously mould our behaviour to those expectations. Imagine you have to go into a store you hate. Your schema for that store includes expectations that it is crowded and that the employees there are unhelpful and rude. Because of this, you dread going in, but it's the only local place that carries your favourite brand of ice cream. Before you even set foot in the door, you have set yourself up to have a terrible experience in the store. Your nerves might already be on edge, a small amount of clutter at the end of an aisle could lead you to break out in a cold sweat, and you're more likely to judge a store employee as being rude if she does so much as fail to smile as soon as you approach her. You might even behave in the way you criticize the employees for behaving. Your own attitude going in, guided by your schema for this store, has helped ensure that you have the terrible experience you anticipated. Can you override this experience by controlling your schemata?

Self-fulfilling prophecies can have pretty serious consequences, as demonstrated by the classic study discussed in Chapter 2 on randomly identifying children as "bloomers" in the classroom and evaluating subsequent IQ scores (Rosenthal & Jacobson, 1968). A review of literature on teacher expectations found that groups subject to social stigmas are most likely to experience the effects of self-fulfilling prophecies (Jussim & Harber, 2005). Further, recent evidence suggests that *negative* self-fulfilling prophecies exert stronger effects on our behaviour than positive ones (e.g., Madon, Guyll, Spoth, & Willard, 2004). These can be particularly problematic in romantic relationships in which partners may be sensitive to rejection (rejection expectancies), which can, in turn, lead them to behave in ways that lead to rejection from romantic partners and interpret their partner's actions negatively (e.g., Downey, Freitas, Michaelis, & Khouri, 1998). On the other hand, expectations of acceptance during interactions with new individuals leads to warmer behaviour, and subsequently greater acceptance, than relationships resulting from expectations of rejection (Stinson, Cameron, Wood, Gaucher, & Holmes, 2009). Try to think of other ways in which self-fulfilling prophecies influence your everyday life.

This same concept of self-fulfilling prophecies can also be easily applied to real-world events. Think of a stock-market crash. News starts trickling in that things are getting bad, people panic and start selling off their stocks, and what happens? It *does* get bad, and depositors don't even realize that it's their own panicked withdrawals and sales that cause the collapse. In addition, our reliance on social media (e.g., Twitter) and the internet can play a major role in these panic-driven, self-fulfilling prophecies. In 2008, an online rumour claimed that Apple CEO Steve Jobs had suffered a massive heart attack. As word spread, a curious thing happened—Apple's stock dropped more than 2 percent to hit a 17-month low. Why? Jobs was perceived to be irreplaceable as the head of Apple. People assumed that, without him, the company would suffer greatly. After seeing what happened after the false story, though, it appears some of the harm to the company may have resulted from a self-fulfilling prophecy created out of panic (Thomasch & Paul, 2008). Interestingly, people seemed to learn from this initial experience, and after the announcement of Steve Jobs' death on October 5, 2011, Apple stock changed little and has maintained a strong place in the market ("Apple Co-Founder," 2011; Cruz, 2011). Whether the market will see gradual declines over time may depend on investors' confidence in Apple's current CEO Tim Cook.

## AUTOMATIC VERSUS CONTROLLED PROCESSING

The problems that arise from relying on schemas to organize the social world often come from the distinction between automatic and controlled processing (Sherman et al., 2008). **Automatic processing** is just what it sounds like. We process information "on the fly," effortlessly making use of those schemas and mental shortcuts without conscious awareness. **Controlled processing**, on the other hand, takes careful thought and effort. It comes into play when decisions or courses of action must be carefully weighed before a judgment is reached.

>>> **Imagine your friend convinces you to go to a club with her. You agree to go even though you dislike clubs and "fist-pumping." Before arriving, you've already decided that the cover charge is too high, the club will be crowded and hot, the people will be annoying, and the drinks will be too expensive.** This could lead to a self-fulfilling prophecy, as you'll tend to ignore anything that doesn't fit your negative schema for "clubbing."

Scientists have discovered that these two types of processing, though they might be used during the same experiences, seem to be housed in different areas of the brain. Researchers think that automatic processing, which is more emotion driven, occurs for the most part in the **limbic system**, which is thought to be critical to emotional processing. One of the key structures in the limbic system is the **amygdala**, which is located in the medial temporal lobe and is responsible for automatic processing of emotions. Specifically, this structure has been linked to emotional learning and fear conditioning—both of which, as you might assume, are strongly related to automatic processing. Consider automatic processes we make, such as implicit race or gender biases—unconscious judgments made on a basis of perceived race or gender. In studies on these biases using subliminal display of photographs, behavioural measures associated with such biases are correlated with amygdala activation (e.g., Cunningham et al., 2004; Knutson, Mah, Manly, & Grafman, 2007). That said, the amygdala does not seem to play a role in controlled processing. People with damage to the amygdala show problems with automatic responses in fear conditioning but are able to successfully demonstrate controlled processing (Cunningham, Johnson, Gatenby, Gore, & Banaji, 2003). Activation of the limbic system, in general, has been seen in studies that have presented unconscious fear-related stimuli (e.g., Bayle, Henaff, & Krolak-Salmon, 2009), immediate reward choices (e.g., Cohen, 2005), and affective facial expressions important in social behaviour (e.g., Beall & Herbert, 2008).

> "Scientists have discovered that these two types of processing, though they might be used during the same experiences, **seem to be housed in different areas of the brain.**"

Controlled processing, which calls for much more mental work than does automatic processing, appears to involve parts of the **prefrontal cortex**. The prefrontal cortex plays a role in higher-order thinking and evaluation. Patients with damage to the prefrontal cortex demonstrate difficulty in controlled processing. Though it plays a major role in controlled processing, the prefrontal cortex also plays somewhat of a part in automatic processing (e.g., Cunningham et al., 2003; Sherman et al., 2008).

Because of the enormous amount of information with which we come into contact every day, we must rely on automatic processing much of the time. If we didn't, we might not get past picking out what to wear or choosing what to have for breakfast in the morning! If a situation fits into a schema, the schema is used even when evaluating new situations (e.g., Holmes, 2000). For example, if you meet someone new, you might rely on a schema for that "type" of person in making a quick decision as to whether or not you like him or her. Most of the time we are on "automatic pilot," but we can engage in effortful, conscious processing when necessary.

Sometimes, though, we are forced out of this automatic processing. If a new experience doesn't fit into any of our schemas, we must think more carefully and logically. Consider that your schema for buying or downloading a music album likely involves being told how much money you are expected to pay for each disc or song. However, in 2007, British rock band Radiohead released its album *In Rainbows* online, allowing fans to pay as much—or as little—as

**LIMBIC SYSTEM** the area of the brain thought to be crucial to emotional processing and memory

**AMYGDALA** a small structure found in the medial temporal lobe of the brain's limbic system that is involved in automatic processing and emotion

**PREFRONTAL CORTEX** the part of the brain that plays a role in higher-order thinking, including judgment, decision making, and evaluation

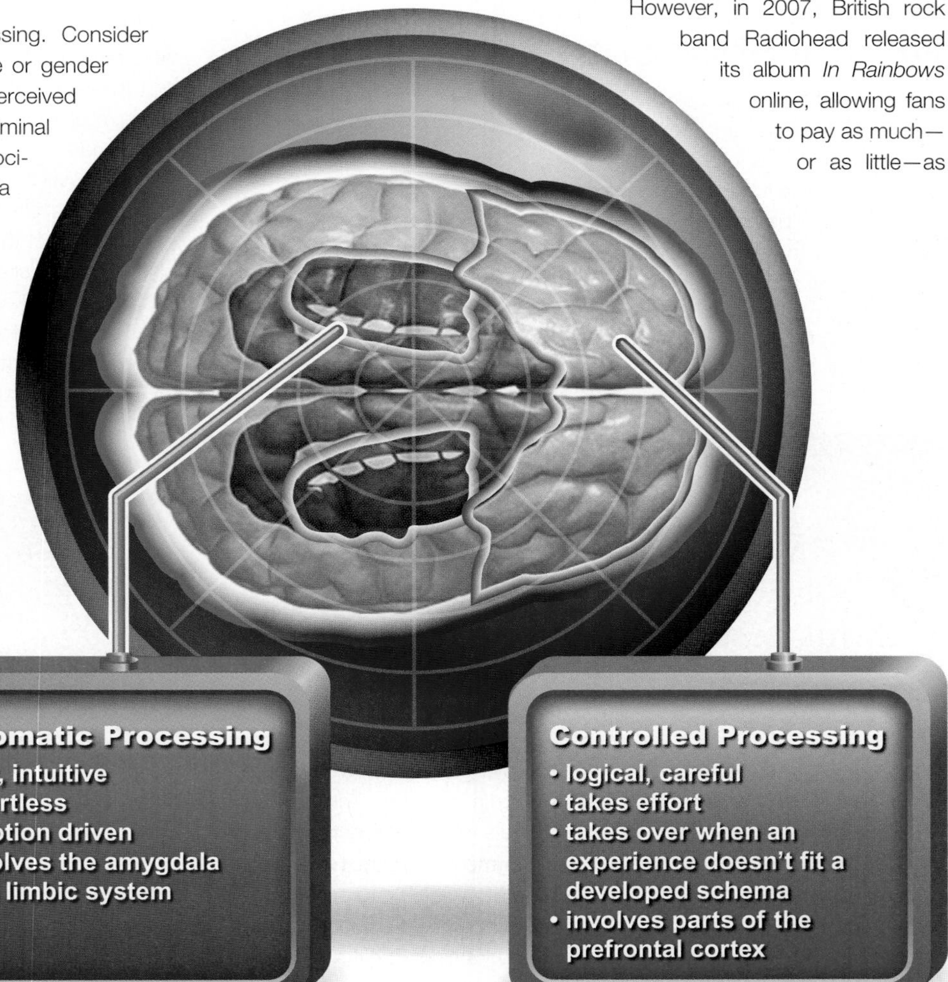
Automatic Processing
• fast, intuitive
• effortless
• emotion driven
• involves the amygdala and limbic system
Controlled Processing
• logical, careful
• takes effort
• takes over when an experience doesn't fit a developed schema
• involves parts of the prefrontal cortex

**Automatic Versus Controlled Processing.** Automatic processing is effortless, **while controlled processing takes mental work.**

**HEURISTICS** simple rules that reduce mental effort and allow us to make decisions or judgments quickly

**AVAILABILITY HEURISTIC** a rule used to estimate the likelihood of a given occurrence based on how easily one can recall an example of that occurrence

they wished to download the album. Of course, it created a huge buzz, especially once it was revealed that many fans were still willing to pay "normal" prices for the music (Geist, 2007). How might this model of buying music force you out of automatic processing and into controlled processing? Rather than having someone tell you how much you owe and handing over cash or your credit card, you actually have to think about how much you will pay. Will you pay the suggested price? More? Less? Could this lead to a shift in our schemas for buying music? This may be possible given that other bands, such as Oasis and Jamiroquai, have announced that they will use similar models for upcoming albums (Wallop & Cockcroft, 2007). In addition, this model has been applied to other aspects of our lives, such as restaurants that apply a pay-what-you-will premise with suggested price ranges but no obligation (Volkman, 2010).

## How Effective Are Mental Shortcuts?

Imagine your friend has asked you to drive him to the airport. After you help him unload his bags from the car, you give him a hug and say, "Have a safe flight!" Why is it so common for people to wish others a safe flight? If you ask people if they are more likely to be in an airplane crash or a car accident, most people are likely to pick the former, even though you are far more likely to be in a car accident. Statistically speaking, there's about a 1,000 times greater chance of a person being killed in a car accident than in an airplane crash (Bailey, 2006). In fact, it would be more fitting for your friend to wish you a safe drive home from the airport than for you to wish him a safe flight!

> "Though the statistics tell us otherwise, **we continue to worry more about getting on a plane than about getting in our cars.**"

Though the statistics tell us otherwise, we continue to worry more about getting on a plane than about getting in our cars. This can be explained by taking a look at **heuristics**, simple rules that reduce mental effort and allow us to make decisions or judgments quickly. Here, we'll discuss four of the heuristics, first described by well-known psychologists Amos Tversky and Daniel Kahneman in the 1970s: availability, representativeness, anchoring and adjusting, and framing. They're definitely useful in cutting down on decision-making time, but each invites bias that can affect the outcomes of those decisions.

### THE AVAILABILITY HEURISTIC

Consider the letter *R* and all the words in which it appears. Do you think the letter *R* most often holds the first position within those words or the third position? What do you think is the ratio for those two options? Tversky and Kahneman (1973) used this question in a study to illustrate the availability heuristic. Participants were given the same question about five consonants in the English language: *K, L, N, R,* and *V.* Among 152 subjects, 105 answered that these consonants were more often found in the first position, while only 47 answered that they were more often found in the third position. Overall, participants estimated that the ratio of first-position appearances to third-position appearances was two to one. In fact, all of the consonants listed appear more frequently as third letters than as first letters within words.

Tversky and Kahneman (1973) described the **availability heuristic** as the rule used to estimate the likelihood of a given occurrence based on how easily one can recall an example of that occurrence. What does that have to do with all of those people wrongly determining that those five consonants are more often the first rather than the third letter in words? It's far easier to think of a list of words that begin with *K* or *N* than it is to think of a list of words that have one of those letters in the third position within the word. Using the shortcut of the availability heuristic, the participants followed this easy recall to the conclusion that more words must start with these letters.

We often use the availability heuristic in efforts to protect ourselves. After the terrorist attacks of September 11, 2001, air travel drastically declined all over the world. Even though terrorist attacks in Canada were rare, the constant media coverage of the events of September 11 and the fact that the attacks were fresh in people's minds made this example of a terrorist attack very easy to recall. The situation, therefore, presented a prime example of the use of the availability heuristic. People avoided travel by air because it *seemed* more likely that a terrorist attack could occur. Unfortunately, this led to more people travelling by car despite the fact that it is far more likely that one will die in a car accident than in a terrorist attack (Gigerenzer, 2004a).

Once you know about the availability heuristic, it's actually pretty easy to use it to influence decision making. In their book *Nudge*, Thaler and Sunstein (2008) point out that people can be "nudged" toward a particular decision using this heuristic. If you want to increase the fear of a bad outcome, remind them of a related scenario

At a restaurant where patrons decide **how much to pay for a meal,** controlled processing might have to **take over for the usual automatic processing.**

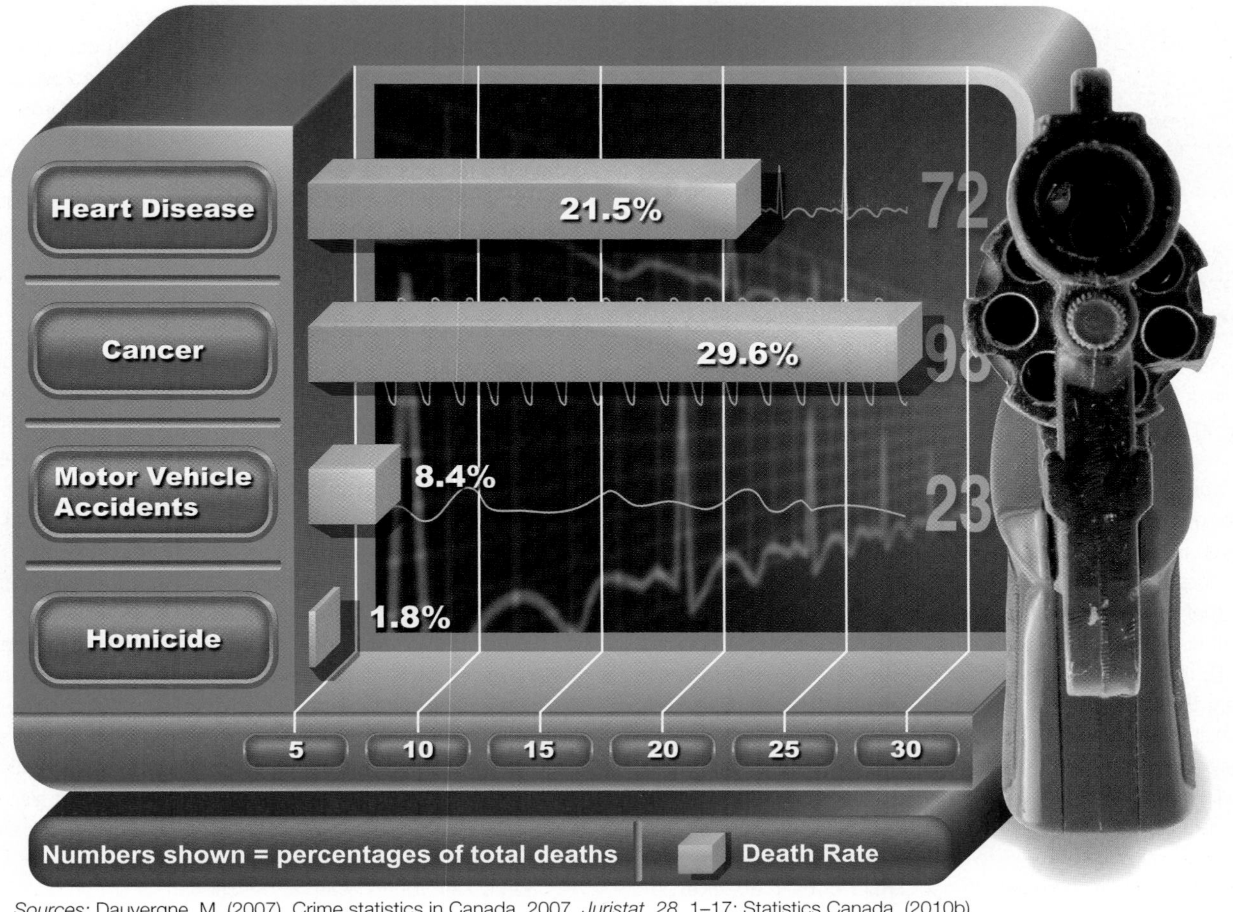


*Sources:* Dauvergne, M. (2007). Crime statistics in Canada, 2007. *Juristat, 28*, 1–17; Statistics Canada. (2010b).

<<< **Death and the Availability Heuristic. Even though people are more likely to die** of cancer or heart disease than homicide, the availability heuristic creates **a far greater fear of the latter cause.**

in which everything went wrong. If you want to make people feel more confident about a decision, remind them of a related scenario in which things went well.

Let's say you're at a convenience store with your sister, and she mentions she might buy a scratch-and-win ticket. Here's where this exercise comes into play. Remind her of the last three times she bought one and didn't win a thing—that she spent the whole rest of the evening complaining about throwing away money. With this on her mind, she is more likely to decide that she'll skip buying a ticket this time. What if, however, you remind her of the one time she won $50 and how excited she was? With this more positive scenario called up, she is more willing to hand over the price of the ticket, confident that she might get lucky again. Making use of the availability heuristic involves the ease with which we can call various events or outcomes to mind. Of course, your new-found powers of the availability heuristic should be used only for good!

>>> Whether or not you hand over money **to purchase the ticket could depend on what kind of outcome**—positive or negative—comes more easily to mind.

**REPRESENTATIVENESS HEURISTIC** a rule used to estimate the likelihood of an event based on how well it fits with your expectations of a model for that event

**BASE RATE FALLACY** an erroneous conclusion reached when the representativeness heuristic is used to draw a conclusion without considering the base rate

## THE REPRESENTATIVENESS HEURISTIC

Imagine you've received a text message from your friend Sarah. The text simply says "Go out Friday night?" Sarah's always been really quiet and mellow. In school, she could be found in the library with a book between classes, and she's never been big on crowds. So what do you think Sarah wants to do—check out a singer/songwriter at a coffee shop downtown or go out to a nightclub and dance all night?

When you use the **representativeness heuristic**, you estimate the likelihood of an event based on how well it fits with your expectations of a model for that event (often, a stereotype). As Tversky and Kahneman (1974) described it, you're deciding the probability that object A belongs to category B, that event A is a result of process B, that process A will result in event B—all based on how closely A seems to represent B. In the above example, Sarah's personality (A) more closely fits going to a coffee shop (B). So, when you open the email, you might be pretty surprised to find Sarah asking if you want to join her in dancing the night away. The representativeness heuristic can be useful in sizing up new situations, but it's most certainly susceptible to error. This heuristic may lead to discriminatory biases present in decisions we make about experiences associated with particular ethnicities, gender, or sexual orientations. For example, Triplett (1992) reported that participants involved in a hypothetical medical decision task were more likely to label homosexual patients as having AIDS (independent of their symptoms) relative to heterosexual patients. As such, the representativeness heuristic can reflect our biases and prejudices.

While useful, the representativeness heuristic also can cause misperceptions when we believe that random events or sequences are ordered. Given a sequence of coin tosses, people expect the string of heads and tails to match what they conceive of as "random." On the other hand, given an actual random string of events, people often seek to find patterns where there are none. Flip a loonie three times. If it comes up heads every time, you might be surprised or think that something is up with the coin. If you flip a loonie many times, though, it wouldn't be odd to see three heads in a row; however, isolating those three flips and coming up heads every time does not match up with our notion of what is random, and so we feel it cannot *be* random. Another example is the "hot hand" phenomenon seen in basketball games. Fans tend to believe that a player is "on fire"—that he is more likely to make a basket following a hit rather than a miss on the previous shot. Of course, when the records are analyzed, it's shown that streaks are a misperception and that sequences of hit shots really are random (Gilovich, Vallone, & Tversky, 1985). The differences in these two heuristics are summarized in Table 3.1.

### Base Rate Fallacy

Suppose you meet your friend's new girlfriend, Erin, for the first time. You strike up a conversation with her and find she's very passionate about feminist issues and politics. Now, suppose you had to guess Erin's major. Is she more likely to be a gender studies major or a math major? Based on your brief encounter with Erin, you might guess that she is a gender studies major. That might fit, but you would be forgetting an important part of the puzzle. There are far more math majors than gender studies majors at your university, so it is actually more likely that Erin is a math major.

*Base rate* refers to how common a behaviour or characteristic is. When we use the representativeness heuristic to draw a conclusion without considering the base rate, this is an example of **base rate fallacy**. When deciding whether Erin is more likely to be a gender studies major or a math major, you cannot take into account only how similar she is to other members of the available categories. You must also consider the base rate, and there is a very low base rate for gender studies majors at your school.

Let's say you're given a description of a person. This person is either an engineer or a lawyer. You're told that there are 100 descriptions in total, half of which are of engineers and half of which are for lawyers. Based on this information, what would you say is the likelihood that the description you've been given is of a lawyer? Would the content of the description affect your judgment? The answer seems kind of obvious, right? There is a 50 percent chance that the description you have is of a lawyer.

Tversky and Kahneman (1974) put the representativeness heuristic (and its drawbacks) to the test in a study using the same setup. They gave subjects personality descriptions of several individuals, supposedly sampled from 100 engineers and lawyers. Divided into two groups, the subjects were asked to assign the label "lawyer" or "engineer" to each description. In the first group, subjects were told that there were 70 engineers and 30 lawyers. In the second, they were told that there were 70 lawyers and 30 engineers. The odds that any one description is



### Table 3.1: The Availability and Representativeness Heuristics

| Heuristic | Definition | Example | Downside |
|---|---|---|---|
| Availability | A rule used to estimate the likelihood of a given occurrence based on how easily one can recall an example of that occurrence | Fearing air travel more after hearing the news about a major airplane crash | Giving more weight to the scarier, more vivid occurrences (i.e., plane crashes) without fearing other, more likely instances (i.e., car accidents) |
| Representativeness | A rule used to estimate the likelihood of an event based on how well it fits with your expectations of a model for that event | Thinking that Jen is a librarian because she wears glasses and is considered to be an introvert | Ignoring other important information |

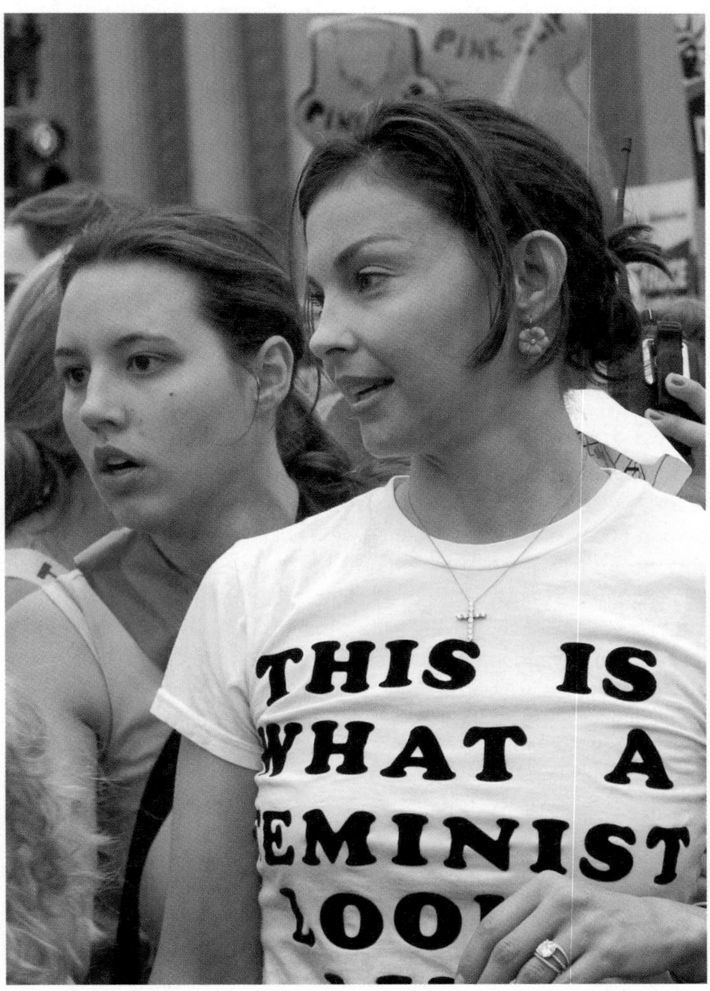


**Gender studies major or math major?** When we fail to take into account how common a behaviour or characteristic is, **we run the risk of committing the *base rate fallacy*.**

of a lawyer would be much higher in the second group, right? For every seven lawyers, there should be three engineers—and the reverse would be true for the first group. So, did the subjects take their knowledge of these ratios into account when categorizing the descriptions?

Surprisingly, no. Both groups of subjects produced the very same probability judgments. Rather than pay attention to the base rate of engineers and lawyers in the sample, they evaluated the descriptions based on the degree to which they fit their stereotypes of engineers and lawyers. They did, however, use the base rates correctly when they weren't provided with descriptions. For example, the first group of subjects correctly determined the probability that a random person was an engineer to be 70 percent (Tversky & Kahneman, 1974). When the researchers added a description—even one with absolutely no guiding information—this logical thinking went out the window. For example, Tversky and Kahneman gave subjects the following description: "Dick is a 30-year-old man. He is married with no children. A man of high ability and high motivation, he promises to be quite successful in his field. He is well liked by his colleagues."

**ANCHORING AND ADJUSTMENT HEURISTIC** a heuristic in which we use a number as a starting point on which to anchor our judgment

Tversky and Kahneman (1974) intended for this description to contain no information relative to the lawyer or engineer question. The probability that Dick is an engineer should be equal to the given proportion of engineers in the group (70 percent or 30 percent, depending upon the group to which the subject belonged), right? Subjects ignored this fact and judged that there was a 50/50 chance of Dick being an engineer, thereby committing a base rate fallacy. Unfortunately, errors in judgment caused by the base rate fallacy can lead to much more serious consequences than misjudging a person's occupation, such as medical or psychiatric misdiagnoses (Barbey & Sloman, 2007) or wrongful convictions. For example, we may estimate that persons of a particular ethnicity are more likely to commit criminal acts even though base rates suggest otherwise (e.g., Davis & Follette, 2002).

## THE ANCHORING AND ADJUSTMENT HEURISTIC

It's your big chance. You got tickets to a taping of the game show *The Price Is Right*. You are jumping up and down, trying to attract the attention of Drew Carey and the announcers—and your excitement has paid off! You have finally heard the words you want to hear: "Come on down!" Soon, you find yourself face-to-face with one of your favourite games from the show: the "Dice Game." The prize? A new car!! The first number in the price of the car is revealed, and you now have to determine the price of the car by rolling the die four times and indicating whether the next number in the price of the car is higher or lower than the number rolled. As you begin to play, do you just start blindly guessing, hoping you'll end up with a correct answer? Of course not. There's a system to playing this game. The number displayed on the die gives you a point from which to start your estimation of the actual price. Mentally, you take the information you do know (the rolled number) and adjust until you've reached a satisfactory answer. When you do this, you are using the **anchoring and adjustment heuristic**, in which known information is

**Higher or lower? Contestants on *The Price Is Right* must make use of the** anchoring and adjustment heuristic to win.

**FRAMING HEURISTIC** a rule that guides decision making based on the framework in which a situation or item is presented

used as a starting point from which revisions are made until an answer is reached (Tversky & Kahneman, 1974).

This heuristic does, of course, have its problems. For one, there is the problem of insufficient adjustment. In one study, when people used self-generated anchor values, they tended to stop adjusting once a reasonable value was reached. Basically, once they reached an answer that was "good enough," they stopped working toward finding a more accurate answer (Epley & Gilovich, 2006). In another study, Tversky and Kahneman (1974) asked subjects to estimate percentages such as that of African countries in the United Nations (UN). For each question, a number between zero and 100 was determined by spinning a wheel (this, of course, became the anchor). The subjects were asked to decide whether the percentage of countries was higher or lower than the anchor and then to estimate the percentage by moving upward or downward from the anchor. Participants with an anchor of 10 estimated that 25 percent of countries in the UN were African, relative to the 45 percent estimate following an anchor of 65. The researchers determined that anchors, even when they are arbitrary, have major impact on the final adjusted answer. However, sometimes anchors are not arbitrary. For example, your resumé is an anchor that influences subsequent interpretations of your skills and personality during a job interview (e.g., Kataoka, Latham, & Whyte, 1997).

Anchors can also affect your mood or your outlook in life. In a study by Thaler and Sunstein (2008), college students were asked a two-part question: How happy are you? How often are you dating? Asked in that order, the questions didn't seem to correlate to one another (the correlation was .11). When the researchers switched the questions, though, it was a different story. Suddenly, the correlation rose to .62. With the dating question as an anchor, the answer to the question about students' happiness was adjusted accordingly. Students were suddenly given a frame of reference for their happiness. They might have thought "I'm not dating . . . and I'm not happy" (or the reverse). Given an anchor for the question of their happiness, their emotional states became dependent upon that anchor.

We also rely on our own feelings and experiences (the anchor) when making judgments (and changes to our judgments) about others. In fact, our stereotypes often serve as anchors for our opinions about other people. For example, research by MacKinnon, Hall, and MacIntyre (2007) at Cape Breton University found that personal experiences of temporary stuttering serve as an anchor in our judgments about the traits associated with individuals who regularly stutter. Further, we tend to see ourselves as "above average" relative to other groups (especially when making cross-cultural comparisons) and often fail to take into account their skill level (Kruger, 1999). Think about the 2010 Olympic Games in Vancouver, British Columbia. Canadian athletes were the "favoured choice" to win in many sports, such as skiing, curling, and figure skating. In women's curling, the Canadian team won the silver medal, and the gold went to Sweden. However, many people feel that Canada is the "anchor" for the best curlers, and they fail to make sufficient adjustments to consider the skill of athletes from other countries.

## THE FRAMING HEURISTIC

Imagine your doctor wants you to try a new medication. He says there is a 75 percent success rate. You decide that it sounds like it's worth a try and accept the prescription. Now, imagine the same scenario, only your doctor tells you that the drug has a 25 percent failure rate. Would this change the decision you make? Looking at both scenarios together like this, you might say, "No, it's the same thing." Consider this, though: researchers have found on several occasions that the presentation of a product can greatly influence your decision about that product. There's a reason that ground beef is labelled "75 percent lean" instead of "25 percent fat." Presenting a negative attribute of a consumer product invites negative associations.

Subjects asked to evaluate beef reacted more favourably to that which was labelled in terms of percent-lean and more unfavourably to beef labelled in terms of percent-fat, even though the two percentages refer to the very same ratio between lean and fat (Levin & Gaeth, 1988). When you base a conclusion about a situation or item on the framework in which it is presented, you are using the **framing heuristic**.

# What Are Other Sources of Bias in Social Cognition?

We like to think that we are incredibly logical beings. When we think about making decisions, we picture ourselves carefully weighing all aspects of a situation and making informed decisions, but that's not always the case, is it?

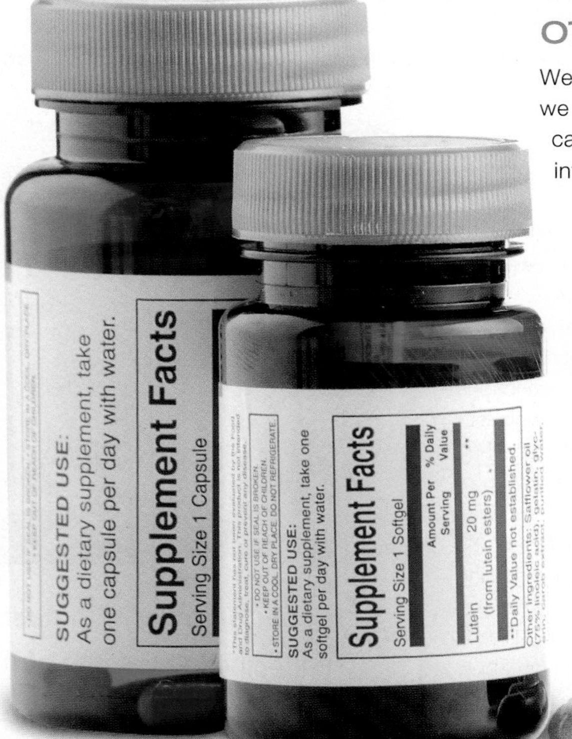


<<< **You might be less likely to buy a bottle of dietary supplements or vitamins if they are advertised as being 10 percent ineffective relative to 90 percent effective.** Think about the framing effect next time you are in the grocery store.

Think about the mental energy that must be devoted to making such careful decisions. Now, think about using that mental energy for every single decision you make throughout your daily life. It would be exhausting, not to mention completely inefficient! Of course, the fact that we can't make every decision according to a perfect model and must instead rely on shortcuts such as schemas and heuristics can sometimes cause trouble. Using these shortcuts invites bias. This results in certain "tilts" in social cognition that can lead us to serious error as we depart from rational thought in favour of easily accessed shortcuts.

One of these possible tilts is the **illusion of control** (e.g., Langer, 1982; Thompson, 1999). This is the perception that uncontrollable events are somehow controllable and that one can influence events that actually depend upon chance. This error in social cognition can lead to better coping skills and fewer depressive symptoms following negative life events (Alloy & Clements, 1992). However, it also helps to explain negative behaviours such as gambling. In one study, people were either assigned a lottery number or were invited to choose a number. Then, participants were asked if they would sell their tickets and for what price. Those who chose their own numbers demanded four times as much money as those who had been assigned random numbers (Langer, 1975). Similarly, when participants in another study were provided with a stopping device on video lottery terminals, they played for longer periods of time and believed they would win more money due to the illusion that they could control the outcome (Ladouceur & Sévigny, 2005). Even though the outcome of these games depended entirely upon chance, people found ways to feel they had control.

## NEGATIVITY BIAS

Imagine you're taking a date to a new restaurant for the first time. Everything is going wonderfully. The food is fantastic, the servers have been attentive, and the conversation has been flowing easily. Then something happens. Perhaps the server is a little late coming with the bill, or the couple one table over starts arguing loudly enough for other patrons to hear. It's just one thing, but it's enough to ruin the whole experience and make you feel unpleasant. This is an illustration of **negativity bias** (e.g., Fiske, 1980; Rozin & Royzman, 2001).

Negative information tends to stick out in our minds. We focus on it and are sensitive to it. We are more likely to notice and remember negative information than positive information. Research shows that negative information has a stronger influence over our evaluation of people and situations than does positive information. This is most evident in impression formation. One study, in which participants evaluated positive and negative descriptions of people, showed that negative traits are given greater weight than positive ones (Ito, Larsen, Smith, & Cacioppo, 1998).

Is there any value to (often subconsciously) focusing on the negative? Some say yes. From an evolutionary point of view, this negativity bias makes perfect sense. If we are wired to protect ourselves from danger, it follows that we would pay more attention to potential warning signs than to positive information. For example, did you know that we seem to be much faster and better at identifying negative facial expressions than we are at identifying positive facial expressions? This research supports the idea that we must be able to respond to negative stimuli, and so we are more likely to filter out the positive (Ohman, Lundqvist, & Karolinska, 2001). That said, this effect also depends on the extent to which negative and positive information is arousing (e.g., Schimmack, 2005), personally relevant (e.g., Tomaszczyk, Fernandes, & MacLeod, 2008), or associated with uncertainty (e.g., Hirsh & Inzlicht, 2008), where higher levels are associated with greater attention. Researchers at the University of Waterloo also have found that the negativity bias is more prevalent in young adults, whereas older adults tend to show a positivity bias (Tomaszczyk et al., 2008).

**ILLUSION OF CONTROL** the perception of uncontrollable events as being controllable

**NEGATIVITY BIAS** the tendency for people to be more sensitive to and more likely to notice and remember negative information, which then influences the evaluation of people and situations

## OPTIMISTIC BIAS

It's a sunny day in May or June, and just about every member of the college/university community has gathered for the graduation ceremony. Those years of hard work, of endless papers, and tough exams, have finally paid off. The graduating students are surrounded by beaming family members. Onstage, one of the most popular professors is positioned behind the podium and is speaking about how proud she is of all the students in front of her. As they listen, are the graduates thinking about the discouraging job market and the difficulty of finding a job? Are they thinking about the potential struggle of paying off student loans? Of course not! They are caught up in the excitement of the day and the promise of future possibilities.

In our lives, we generally expect things to turn out well for us, despite any statistics or figures that might demonstrate the likelihood of the contrary. We expect that bad things are more likely to happen to other people and that we will experience mostly good things. This

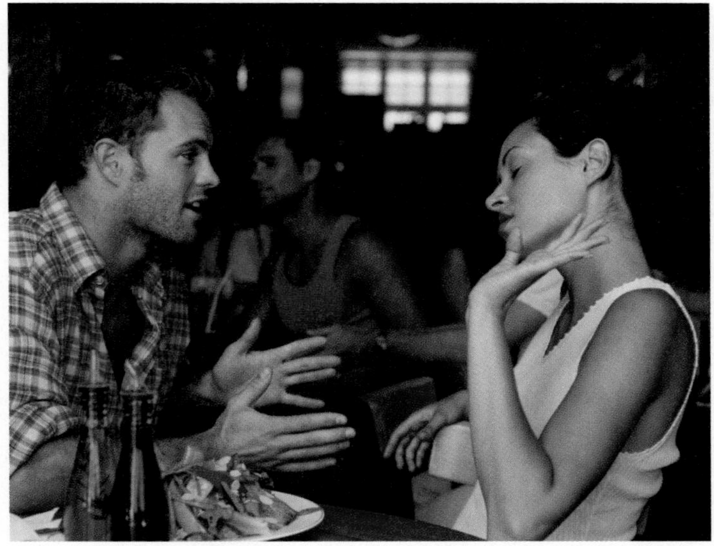

^^^ **You've had a great meal at a new restaurant,** but then a couple at a nearby table starts arguing, making everyone uncomfortable, and suddenly your pleasant evening out is ruined. **This attitude may be a downer,** but is there an evolutionary reason for it?

**OPTIMISTIC BIAS** the belief that bad things will happen to other people and that an individual is more likely to experience good things in life

**OVERCONFIDENCE BARRIER** a state of having more confidence in one's judgment or control over a situation than is really justified

**COUNTERFACTUAL THINKING** the tendency to imagine alternative outcomes for an event

"rose-coloured glasses" view is the flipside of the negativity bias and is called the **optimistic bias** (Armor & Taylor, 2002). Research has shown that most people believe they are less likely than others to experience negative events and more likely to experience positive ones. When you think about the future, you probably think about what will make you happy—about the plans and goals you have for your life.

It doesn't really sound bad, does it? You'd think it would be considered healthy to assume positive outcomes in your life. Of course, in many ways it is, but the optimistic bias does have drawbacks. One of these is the **overconfidence barrier**, which describes a state of having more confidence in our judgments or control over a situation than is really justified. In fact, the optimistic bias is often more evident in people who have high self-esteem, confidence, and defensiveness (e.g., Harris, Griffin, & Murray, 2008).

Sure, it's good to be confident, but this overconfidence barrier can lead to some pretty serious consequences. Have you ever underestimated the time it would take you to write a term paper for one of your classes? We are often overly optimistic about our ability to complete academic tasks. This leads to procrastination (because it won't take us "that long" to write that paper!) and to potential mark deductions when things don't progress as planned (e.g., Buehler & Griffin, 2003). Another area related to overconfidence is one's financial situation. Overconfidence may lead a person to take on more debt than he can handle, believing that he'll be able to pay it off in the future but not accounting for illness, lost jobs, or depressed economies. In Chapter 4, we will further discuss some of the downsides of overconfidence in social interactions.

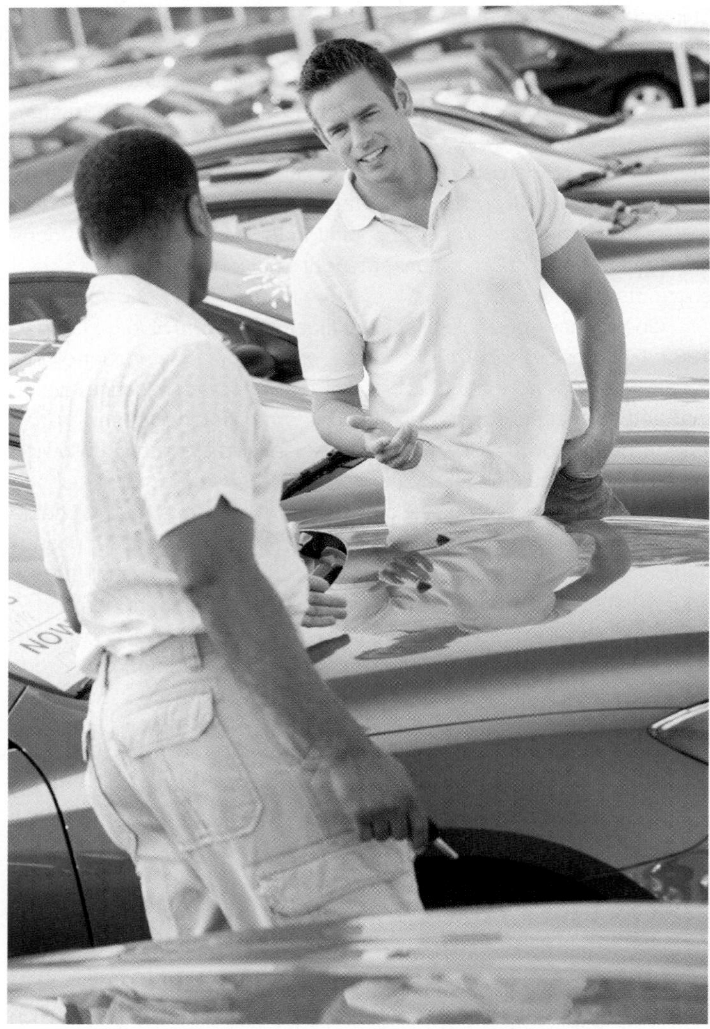

**Is he thinking about the possibility of losing his job or one of his children being ill?** Chances are, he's hit the overconfidence barrier and believes his financial situation will always be secure enough that he can make the car payments.

## COUNTERFACTUAL THINKING

It's the moment you've been dreading. Exam grades are coming back, and you don't think you're going to like what you see. Unfortunately, it turns out that you're right. As you stare at the "72 percent" in front of you, the very first thought that pops into your head is "If only I had spent more time studying, I would have gotten a much higher grade." This kind of thinking, called **counterfactual thinking**, happens automatically. It is defined as the tendency to imagine alternative outcomes for an event and comes into play especially when something bad has happened (Gavanski & Wells, 1989). Counterfactual thinking can have a dramatic effect on a person's emotional reaction to an event or a situation (Mandel, Hilton, & Catellani, 2005).

Many times, counterfactual thinking has a negative effect on your mood. If you imagined a better outcome for an event (like getting a 97 on that exam instead of a 72), you could end up feeling pretty bad about your performance or envious of classmates who got better grades. Circumstances in which you imagine better outcomes than you achieved are called *upward counterfactuals* (Roese, 1997). And when do you think you are more likely to be upset—when you receive a 75 percent or a 79 percent? Although you might expect that you would be most upset by the lower score, Medvec and Savitsky (1997) found that individuals on the borderline of a grade (e.g., 84 percent) report being more upset because it is easier to imagine getting an A– (i.e., 85 percent) if they get an 84 percent rather than an 80 percent.

Sometimes, though, counterfactual thinking can actually help you feel *more positive* about a situation. If you compare a real-life outcome with something less desirable, then counterfactual thinking can actually lighten your mood. Picture seeing that 72 percent on your exam again. Only this time, imagine that you felt completely confused when you were taking the test and thought you were going to completely bomb it. In this situation, you'd engage in counterfactual thinking more along the lines of "it could have been worse," which might actually make you feel better about the real event. This imagined worse alternative is called a *downward counterfactual* (Roese, 1997).

Researchers have demonstrated the dramatic emotional difference between upward and downward counterfactuals, using Olympic medalists as their participants. For any given event, do you think the bronze or silver medalist is happier with the outcome? You might think it would be the silver medalist, because he or she reached a higher level of achievement. However, it turns out that the opposite is generally the case. For silver medalists, the most convincing counterfactual scenario is having won gold. This upward counterfactual leads them to feel less satisfied than bronze medalists, for whom the easiest alternative to picture is usually finishing without a medal (Husted, Madey, & Gilovich, 1995).

Counterfactual thinking is often used to assign blame in a situation. If Karen was supposed to take care of buying flood insurance for her family business but dropped the ball, what happens when the building floods? Is it Karen's fault that the flood occurred? Sometimes, that's where our minds automatically go. We see a causal relationship where there is none. Focusing on "what could have been" can lead to self-blame and feelings of guilt. For example, when prisoners were asked to focus on counterfactuals (alternatives) to being caught for their current offence, they reported higher feelings of blame and guilt over being caught, but not more shame (Mandel & Dhami, 2005).

The phenomenon of counterfactual thinking also explains why we get so upset when we hear stories in which people are in the "wrong place at the wrong time." We've all heard stories of situations like the flight attendant who switches schedules with a friend, only to end up on a plane that crashes, or the man who leaves for work an hour earlier than usual, only to be involved in a car accident. Here, the imagined alternatives in which the subject of the story never goes through his or her ordeal are even easier to call up, since they are what was "supposed to happen."

It might not be immediately obvious, but counterfactual thinking can actually be useful. Imagining what could have been can help us better plan and prepare for similar experiences in the future. Maybe getting that 72 percent, but feeling you could have gotten an A if you had devoted more time to studying, leads you to set aside more time to prepare for the next test. By imagining what could have been, you can picture achieving it and, therefore, set a plan to make it happen.

<<< **Between the bronze and silver medalists,** who is happier? The answer might actually surprise you—**it's due to the difference between upward and downward counterfactuals. Take, for example, the gratitude and happiness expressed by Joannie Rochette after winning a bronze medal for Canada in the 2010 Olympic Games in Vancouver. Given that her mother had just passed away unexpectedly, she could have performed much worse under the circumstances (downward counterfactual). Therefore, she was elated she performed as well as she did.**

**MOOD CONGRUENCE EFFECT** the fact that we are more likely to remember positive information when in a positive mood and negative information when in a negative mood

## Marketing and Counterfactual Thinking

It's a hot summer day. "Mom! We're bored!" comes the call from two miserable-looking kids slumped on the living room couch. The day seems to drag on, Mom is getting irritated, and she just doesn't know what to do. As she yells at the kids to get out of the house and find something to do, a helpful, booming voice comes from nowhere, reminding Mom that she could have easily combated the mid-summer blues. All she had to do was take the kids to the circus! Suddenly, there's a fake flashback in which we see how different things could have been. The kids are laughing, Mom's smiling, and, in the background, an elephant pulls off a clown's hat. See how much happier the family could have been, if only they'd bought tickets to the circus?

Watch television for a half hour, and you'll see plenty of examples of counterfactual thinking being used to sell you things. You'd get a date so easily, if only you'd use the right deodorant. Your dinner guests would have had so much fun, if only you'd served them the right brand of pasta. Advertising seems to have been built on how easy it is for us to picture alternative outcomes, as well as on harnessing our emotional responses to counterfactual thinking.

## The Effect of Mood on Cognition

The way we use heuristics—and even the way we think—has much to do with mood. When you're in a good mood, annoying little things just don't bother you as much, do they? Negative experiences just roll off, you're more willing to give people the benefit of the doubt, and the day seems to go pretty well. This is explained by **mood congruence effects**—the fact that we are more likely to remember positive information when in a positive mood, and negative information when in a negative mood (e.g., Bower, 1987; Myers, 2000; Forgas, Bower, & Kranitz, 1984).

This isn't the only way in which mood affects the way we think. It can also influence what specific information is retrieved from memory,

**MOOD-DEPENDENT MEMORY** the fact that the mood that we are in when we learn information may serve as a retrieval cue when we try to remember that information

due to an effect called **mood-dependent memory** (e.g., Eich, 1995). This refers to the fact that what we remember when in a given mood is influenced in part by what was learned when previously in that mood. Do you get nervous when you take exams? Do you feel like you forget everything, only to remember it all hours later when you're just relaxing? Think about your state of mind when you study—if you are calm when you study, the principle of mood-dependent memory tells us you're more likely to recall the information you studied when you're feeling calm. If you are a person who gets nervous when you take a test, you might actually remember more of the test material if you study when you're feeling nervous! That said, if you study when you are nervous and try to "fake" being nervous while writing an exam, it is unlikely that you will experience mood-dependent effect on memory (Eich & Macaulay, 2000).

Is a good mood always a good thing? That's a ridiculous question, right? Of course it must be! This isn't always the case, though. It turns out that when you're in a good mood, you're more likely to rely on heuristics, more likely to use stereotypes, and (as we'll explore in Chapter 7) more easily persuaded. It might sound strange, but it makes sense. Think back to what you learned about automatic versus controlled processing. When we are faced with a difficult task or something unfamiliar, our brains work harder. Otherwise, we tend to rely on the autopilot setting of automatic processing. When you are in a good mood, you're just not motivated to use effort to evaluate incoming information. Instead, the tendency is to rely on heuristics and other shortcuts so as not to distract from our mood state (Wegener & Petty, 1994).

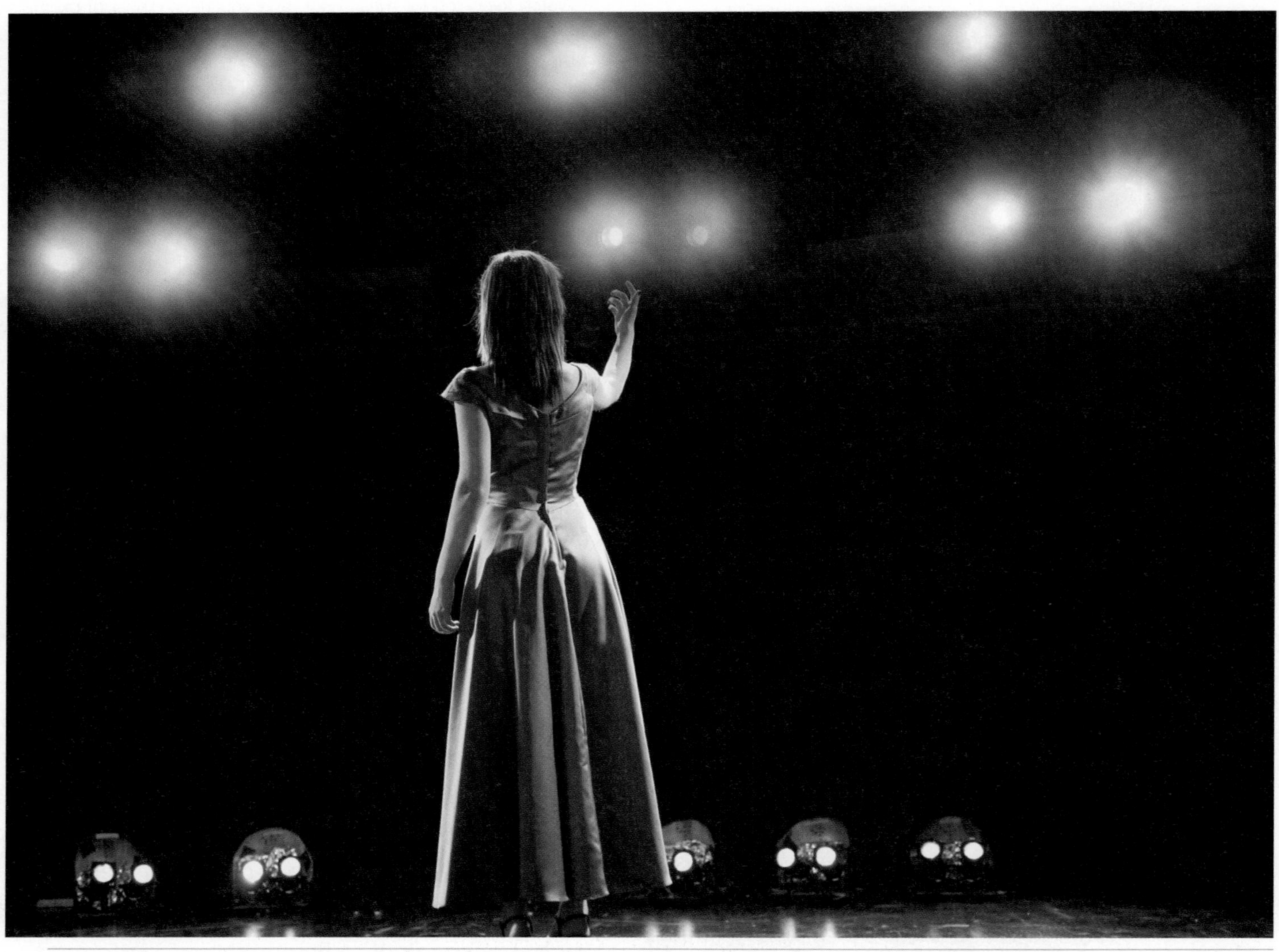

**If she doesn't get the part,** she'll probably engage in counterfactual thinking, imagining how things could have been different—**if only she hadn't stumbled over that line or had been more confident shaking hands with the director.** This thinking actually can end up being good for her, **if she uses it to prepare herself for her next audition.**

## ACTION LEARNING

### Hyping It Up

Social cognition isn't just about our own social experiences. The same biases that affect our personal interactions also play a major role in the way we learn about events around the world. Turn on the news, and you're likely to hear plenty of sensational reports about negative subjects, but how much of it is an accurate portrayal of what's going on in the world? One researcher found that, in a one-week period, 66 percent of headlining stories on major news networks' websites were about negative subjects (Caldwell, 2005). This might lead people to believe that their country is not a safe place to live, especially when the media's focus does not match up with the actual rates of violent crime. For example, in 2009 the homicide rate in Canada was 1.8 per 100,000 people (Statistics Canada, 2010a), yet the media frequently reports on murder and violence. So why are we inundated with stories of horrible crimes? What is at play here?

For years, researchers have studied how bias affects the way stories are reported and the ways in which the public responds. Arguing that the public depends on news media for reliable information, researchers have pressed for more responsible reporting. In one study, it was found that the news media significantly distorts the prevalence of and risk factors for the leading causes of death (e.g., Frost, Frank, & Maibach, 1997). Some causes—such as tobacco use—were underrepresented, while others—including car accidents—were vastly overrepresented. For example, homicides often receive the same amount of news coverage as the leading causes of death: cancer and heart disease. So what's the big deal? Well, think about the availability heuristic. If we see something popping up on the news frequently, we believe that it's a reflection of what's going on in the real world. If homicide gets just as much attention as heart disease, our view of how likely we are to be murdered starts to become distorted. Statistically, you are far less likely to be a victim of homicide than of heart disease, but watching the news, you might become fearful that you could easily become a victim. In addition, causes of death such as cancer, when mentioned, are often associated with messages of fear and inevitability (e.g., Clarke & Everest, 2006).

Throughout this chapter, you've considered how heuristics and other sources of bias influence our social interactions. Now, you will discover how they affect our relationship with media. Think about a news story that is currently creating controversy. Find two different media outlets in which the story is being reported but described differently. Using what you have learned in this chapter, identify the ways in which bias shows up in the reporting. What effect does the bias in each of the two reports have? Who or what does the bias seem to benefit?

Then rewrite the story so that it is more objective. Share what you have learned with your classmates and friends. Discuss the possible effects of heuristics and other sources of bias on our perception. How does an awareness of these sources of bias make you a better consumer of information?

**You** may not value your own life, but what about your child's life?
**Smoking is not only suicide, it's murder.**

What will you learn from this action project?

1. Identify heuristics and other sources of bias used in the media.
2. Isolate the objective facts from a news story.
3. Encourage more responsible consumption of media.

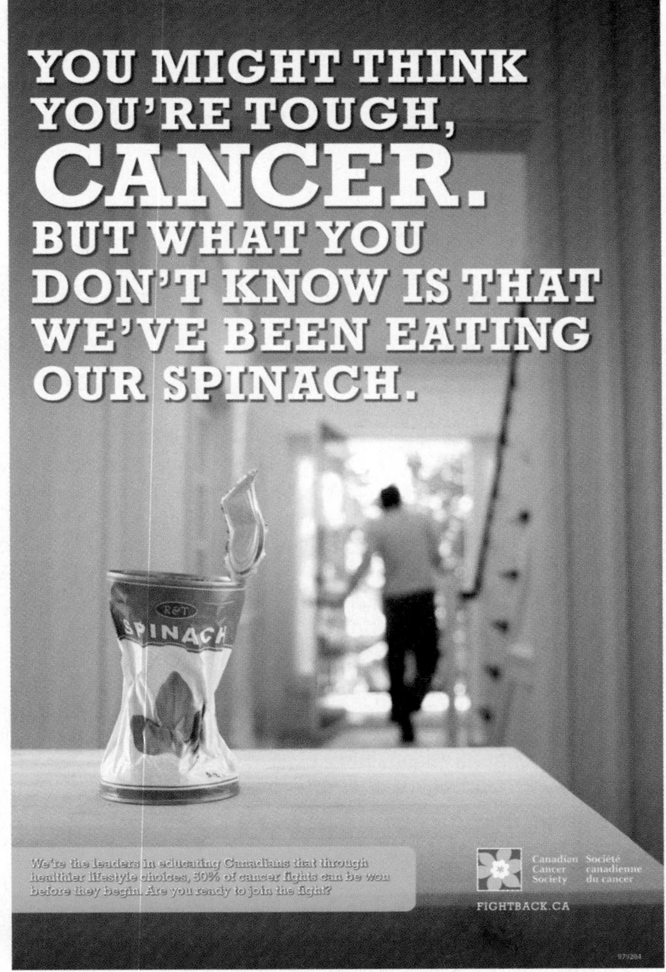

YOU MIGHT THINK YOU'RE TOUGH,
CANCER.
BUT WHAT YOU DON'T KNOW IS THAT WE'VE BEEN EATING OUR SPINACH.
SPINACH
We're the leaders in educating Canadians that through healthier lifestyle choices, 50% of cancer fights can be won before they begin. Are you ready to join the fight?
Canadian Cancer Society
Société canadienne du cancer
FIGHTBACK.CA


<<< **Coverage of Cancer in the Media. Cancer is one of the leading causes of death in Canada, but how is it portrayed in the news? Not only are stories of murder and violence more common, but cancer messages are often associated with fear and uncertainty.** Which type of message do you think has a more significant effect on the public? What biases are revealed in the media?

# CHAPTER 03 Review

## Summary

### HOW DO SCHEMAS GUIDE THE WAY YOU THINK ABOUT THE WORLD AROUND YOU? p. 42

• Schemas are automatically created cognitive frameworks that help guide the way we think about and understand the world around us. They are created through experience as you encounter similar people, processes, social roles, occupations, and so on. Once in place, they are activated through a stimulus and trigger behaviour and expectations.

• The tendency to ignore sensory information that doesn't fit with a schema is just one of the problems associated with schemas. Stereotypes, which are a form of schema, can lead to bias in our social interactions. Selective filtering can lead to self-fulfilling prophecies, in which we unconsciously mould our behaviours to fit expectations. These problems come from the brain's tendency to favour automatic over controlled processing.

### HOW EFFECTIVE ARE MENTAL SHORTCUTS? p. 46

• Heuristics reduce mental effort and allow us to make quick decisions. The availability heuristic allows us to estimate the likelihood that something will happen based on how easily we can recall examples of that event. The anchoring and adjustment heuristic involves starting with a supposed given and working toward a solution from there. Basing a decision on the framework in which it is presented is referred to as using the framing heuristic.

• We use the representativeness heuristic to determine how well a given person or event will fit into a certain category. This heuristic is subject to base rate fallacy, which occurs when we draw a conclusion without taking into account how common a behaviour or event truly is.

### WHAT ARE OTHER SOURCES OF BIAS IN SOCIAL COGNITION? p. 50

• Though we like to think we are logical beings, this isn't really the case. Our minds favour automatic shortcuts, and this can lead to bias. Negative information tends to have stronger influence than does positive information, leading to a negativity bias in social cognition. On the flip side, the optimistic bias can lead us to believe we are unlikely to experience bad events in life.

• Counterfactual thinking, in which we imagine alternative outcomes for events, can have a strong effect on your emotional reaction to given events. Depending on whether the imagined alternative is better or worse than the real-life event, counterfactual thinking can darken or lighten your mood. Advertisers use this strong emotional connection to the "what-if" to influence our decisions as consumers.



## Key Terms

**amygdala** a small structure found in the medial temporal lobe of the brain's limbic system that is involved in automatic processing and emotion *45*

**anchoring and adjustment heuristic** a heuristic in which we use a number as a starting point on which to anchor our judgment *49*

**automatic processing** the processing of information "on the fly," using schemas as shortcuts *44*

**availability heuristic** a rule used to estimate the likelihood of a given occurrence based on how easily one can recall an example of that occurrence *46*

**base rate fallacy** an erroneous conclusion reached when the representativeness heuristic is used to draw a conclusion without considering the base rate *48*

**controlled processing** a type of mental processing that takes purposeful thought and effort as decisions or courses of action are weighed carefully *44*

**counterfactual thinking** the tendency to imagine alternative outcomes for an event *52*

**framing heuristic** a rule that guides decision making based on the framework in which a situation or item is presented *50*

**heuristics** simple rules that reduce mental effort and allow us to make decisions or judgments quickly *46*

**illusion of control** the perception of uncontrollable events as being controllable *51*

**limbic system** the area of the brain thought to be crucial to emotional processing and memory *45*

**mood congruence effect** the fact that we are more likely to remember positive information when in a positive mood, and negative information when in a negative mood *53*

**mood-dependent memory** the fact that the mood that we are in when we learn information may serve as a retrieval cue when we try to remember that information *54*

**negativity bias** the tendency for people to be more sensitive to and more likely to notice and remember negative information, which then influences the evaluation of people and situations *51*

**optimistic bias** the belief that bad things will happen to other people and that an individual is more likely to experience good things in life *52*

**overconfidence barrier** a state of having more confidence in one's judgment or control over a situation than is really justified *52*

**perseverance effect** the tendency for a schema to remain intact, even when it comes up against discrediting information *43*

**prefrontal cortex** the part of the brain that plays a role in higher-order thinking, including judgment, decision making, and evaluation *45*

**prime** to activate a schema through a stimulus *42*

**representativeness heuristic** a rule used to estimate the likelihood of an event based on how well it fits with your expectations of a model for that event *48*

**schema** an automatically created cognitive framework that helps guide the way we think about and understand the society around us *42*

**selective filtering** paying more attention to sensory information that fits a given schema, at the same time filtering out information that is inconsistent *44*

**self-fulfilling prophecy** a prediction that causes itself to come true *44*

**stereotype** a type of schema in which we apply generalized information to an individual based on the group to which he or she belongs *43*

# Test Your Understanding

## MULTIPLE CHOICE

1. Schemas exist for
   - a. people.
   - b. processes.
   - c. situations.
   - d. all of the above.
2. The tendency for a schema to remain intact even when it comes up against discrediting information is called
   - a. a stereotype.
   - b. priming.
   - c. the perseverance effect.
   - d. selective filtering.
3. Scientists believe automatic processing involves the
   - a. amygdala only.
   - b. prefrontal cortex only.
   - c. prefrontal cortex and amygdala.
   - d. limbic system and amygdala.
4. Controlled processing is activated when
   - a. you must make a decision quickly.
   - b. a new experience doesn't fit an existing schema.
   - c. your brain is tired.
   - d. None of these is correct.
5. The concept of heuristics was first described by
   - a. Tversky and Kahneman.
   - b. Gerd Gigerenzer.
   - c. Thaler and Sunstein.
   - d. Sparrow and Wegner.
6. Which is an example of the availability heuristic?
   - a. choosing a different route to work because yesterday your friend got a flat tire on your usual route
   - b. guessing that your friend's new boyfriend isn't very intelligent because he works at Burger King
   - c. forgetting the year your parents got married, but figuring it out using your birth date as a starting point
   - d. being thrown off by an automated ticket machine at the movies because you weren't expecting it to be there
7. Which is an example of the representativeness heuristic?
   - a. assuming that Oliver is from the Maritimes because he goes sailing often and loves seafood
   - b. thinking that Janice could be a librarian because she is female
   - c. deciding that Dan is a good student because he has a GPA of 3.85
   - d. thinking about Charlene because you just saw her walk by
8. Upward counterfactuals tend to have a _____ effect on mood.
   - a. positive
   - b. negative
   - c. negligible
   - d. short-term
9. Which is an example of a downward counterfactual?
   - a. getting an 88 percent on a test and imagining how you could have gotten an A
   - b. being more likely to buy ice cream that is labelled "90 percent fat free" than ice cream that is labelled "10 percent fat"
   - c. being passed up for a promotion at work and imagining that you could be without a job
   - d. having a terrible time at a party in part because you expected it would be a negative experience
10. Research on bias in the news media has found that
    - a. news outlets tend to emphasize negative stories.
    - b. headline stories contain factual errors 40 percent of the time.
    - c. the media is biased strongly toward Liberals.
    - d. heart disease is emphasized as the leading cause of death.

**ANSWERS:** 1. d; 2. c; 3. d; 4. b; 5. a; 6. a; 7. b; 8. b; 9. c; 10. a

## ESSAY RESPONSE

1. Explain how schemas are developed and how they affect how we process incoming information. Include an example in your response.
2. Provide an example of a self-fulfilling prophecy. How do you think the outcome could be altered? What kind of processing would that require?
3. Choose one of the heuristics. Define it and provide an example of a situation demonstrating the use of that heuristic.
4. Describe how base rate fallacy leads to cognitive error.
5. What is the difference between upward and downward counterfactuals? What effect does each have on a person's emotional response to an event?

## APPLY IT!

Make a point of watching several television commercials. Identify where upward and downward counterfactuals are being used. What do you think is the intended emotional effect of each instance?

**Remember to check www.thethinkspot.ca for additional information, downloadable flashcards, and other helpful resources.**

# THE SELF: WHO AM I AND HOW DO OTHER INDIVIDUALS SEE ME?

*<<< Who am I? Sometimes it is more difficult to understand the self than it is to understand others. Where do our ideas about our own identities come from?*

**WHAT** IS SELF-CONCEPT, AND WHERE DOES IT COME FROM?
**IN WHAT** WAYS DOES OUR NEED FOR SELF-ESTEEM MOTIVATE OUR ACTIONS?
**HOW** DO WE REPRESENT OURSELVES TO OTHERS?

# Imagine

being asked to explain who you are—that is, how you define yourself—while engaging in the following activities: responding to questions at a job interview, completing an online dating or social media profile (e.g., on Facebook), eating dinner with your significant other's parents for the first time, or having a heart-to-heart conversation with your parents or best friends. Think about four or five things you would say in each situation to describe who you are. Don't consider the question for too long; just respond with whatever comes to mind.

There are many ways to answer the question about your identity, and the way you respond will probably depend on the situation, who's asking the question, and even life circumstances that are influencing you at the time. For example, one of the authors of this text (KP) was born and raised in Saskatchewan and later Alberta. However, she moved to Nova Scotia to complete her graduate studies and quickly recognized the Eastern culture as being very distinct from the Western culture she was used to. Upon first moving to Halifax, when people asked where she was from she would say Alberta. However, after a time, she began to identify as a Maritimer and even picked up some of the speech patterns of Canadians from Eastern provinces. When she moved back to Alberta, she became known as the transplanted Maritimer with an accent, even though she had originally lived in Alberta. She had not realized that she had adopted a new cultural identity until she moved back west. Among her Western friends, she was now from "out East," and this influenced the music she liked, the foods she ate, what she drank, her approaches to problems, and how she spoke. Having now lived in Alberta again for five years, she identifies herself as both Albertan and Nova Scotian, as these are formative parts of her self-identity. However, sometimes one's self-concept will vary depending on the situation and with whom one is interacting. For example, KP's expression of her background will differ if she is out for pints with friends or conversing with a colleague at a professional conference.

Think about the ways your own self-description changes based on the scenarios above. How much do your responses differ from one another? What factors do you think play the strongest roles in your self-descriptions? Which description of yourself do you think is the most accurate? This chapter may help you begin to answer some of these questions. It will guide you to discovering the various factors that impact your sense of identity and the way you present yourself to others. You will learn how sometimes these presentations and perceptions can be deceiving, and how certain things about you might be more revealing than you would guess.

CHAPTER 04

**SELF-CONCEPT** your mental representation or overall sense of "you"

**SELF-SCHEMA** beliefs about aspects of your identity that organize the processing of information related to the self

**SELF-EFFICACY** a person's belief in one's ability to achieve certain goals

## What Is Self-Concept, and Where Does It Come From?

For each of us, our sense of self is affected by culture, by personal factors (such as gender or motivations), and by social factors (the way we see ourselves in relation to others) that we will explore in this chapter. If you play several sports well and like to be physically active, you may think of yourself as an athlete. If you are the only one among your family members or friends who plays sports, you are even more likely to include "athlete" as part of your sense of identity because your athleticism is something that sets you apart from the people around you.

Your **self-concept**, your mental representation or overall sense of "you," is made up of all the various beliefs you hold about yourself. When asked to describe yourself, you can probably identify traits like "outgoing," "smart," and "funny" that describe you and even identify roles that make up part of your self-concept like "student," "big brother," "best friend," or "musician." Each of these beliefs about an aspect of your identity is a **self-schema** that helps organize the processing of information related to yourself. Self-schemata are like puzzle pieces that fit together to create your overall self-concept (Markus, 1977).

Of course, certain schemata will be more significant to you than others, just as different schemata take on different levels of importance for different people. For example, fashion is an important self-schema for some people. They think of themselves, and like others to think of them, as stylish dressers. For fashion schematics, everyday situations involving clothing, such as walking past a row of clothing boutiques, watching an episode of *What Not to Wear* on TV, or even noticing how other people around them are dressed, will trigger thoughts about the self. They may think, "Am I wearing the right clothes for the occasion? Are other people here better dressed than I am? Is there a fashion trend I'm missing out on?" On the other hand, there are many people for whom this is not the case; fashion doesn't play an important role in their lives, and they don't connect it with their thoughts about themselves.

Our individual schemata also take on different levels of importance in different situations. We all have private selves and public selves. For example, you probably find that you have certain traits that become more pronounced when you're among close friends or family than when you're in the company of casual acquaintances. Our self-concepts are complicated and somewhat fluid. They evolve with life experience and can change in relation to environment, circumstances, mood, and social situation.

Sometimes major events, such as relationship breakups, can alter self-concepts. Researchers have found that romantic partners come to shape one another's identities through the sharing of activities, social groups, and goals (Slotter, Gardner, & Finkel, 2009). After a breakup, individuals tend to report a disrupted self-concept, leading to confusion and emotional distress (e.g., Lewandowski, Aron, Bassis, & Kunak, 2006). Researchers at McGill University have reported that we tend to display a positive bias in our evaluations of relationships, which can lead to later disappointment and negative effects on self-esteem when we realize that our idealistic views of our partners are distorted (Gagné & Lydon, 2004). Along the same lines, we tend to seek out and are more committed to relationships that confirm our self-concepts, whether they are positive or negative (Swann, Hixon, & De La Ronde, 1992).

Whether you realize it or not, much of your self-concept is shaped by your relationships with other people. Sociologist Charles Cooley (1902) coined the term *looking-glass self* for the way other people act as a mirror in which we perceive ourselves. To expand on this idea, George Herbert Mead (1934) argued that our self-concept is not based on how others actually see us but on how we *imagine* they do. Researchers also have theorized that the self is relational, and that relationships with important people in our lives significantly impact the way we act and how we evaluate/define ourselves (e.g., Andersen & Chen, 2002; Murray, Holmes, & Griffin, 1996).

In fact, the way we believe others see us, which impacts the way we see ourselves, can have an important effect on our ability to succeed. One recent study found that when children saw their future selves as being in careers dependent on college/university education (law or medicine, for instance), rather than being in degree-independent careers (like pop music or sports), they performed better in school, an area consistent with their future selves (Destin & Oyserman, 2010). Having a well-developed sense of self can lead to stronger **self-efficacy**. Self-efficacy refers to a person's belief in her ability to overcome challenges and achieve certain goals. The concept of self-efficacy was central to Canadian-born psychologist Albert Bandura's research (1977), in which he found that people with high levels of self-efficacy approach difficult tasks as challenges they can master rather than as threats they should avoid. Other studies have confirmed that when we have a positive sense of self-efficacy, we are more likely to achieve our goals (e.g., Chemers, Hu, & Garcia, 2001; Judge, Erez, & Bono, 1998; Pajares, 1996; Schunk, 1995; Zimmerman, Bandura, & Martinez-Pons, 1992). For example, teens with higher perceived self-efficacy were more likely to achieve personal health goals, like regular exercise, than teens with poor perceived self-efficacy (Luszczynska et al., 2010).

### PHYSIOLOGICAL INFLUENCES

So where do our self-concepts come from? While our self-concepts can be shaped by a variety of outside factors, our abilities to form self-concepts are rooted in the brain itself. When people experience major brain

<<< **We all have different selves that we project in different situations.** Celebrity gossip magazines and tabloids attract readers by promising to deliver glimpses **into both the public and private lives of today's big stars.**

injuries, their self-concepts may be altered or completely destroyed (e.g., Miller et al., 2001). Take the case of Clive Wearing, who, in 1985, contracted herpes encephalitis, an infection of the brain that not only erased nearly all of his past memories but also prevented him from forming new memories that lasted beyond several seconds (Sacks, 2007). The disease almost completely destroyed the hippocampus, a structure of the brain implicated in memory (Squire, 1992). Before the infection, Wearing had been a professional musician with a detailed knowledge of composers and musical scores. However, after the infection, he couldn't name more than a handful of composers and didn't recognize the names of songs he had once knew. He also couldn't remember the names of his wife or daughter, the places he had travelled, or most of the things he had once cared about. Surprisingly, however, he was still able to play music, he could recognize his wife by sight, and he could perform many everyday tasks. But, without memory to give these things a meaningful context, Wearing had completely lost his sense of self.

As we learn new information or skills, the synapses in our brains record and store information. If the synapses become unable to record information, as in Wearing's case, we no longer have a biological method of forming memories (Baddeley, Eysenck, & Anderson, 2009). The way we think about ourselves, our beliefs about what others think of us, and our knowledge about how we respond to different situations are mostly learned through experience and stored in memory. In his 2002 book *Synaptic Self: How Our Brains Become Who We Are*, Joseph LeDoux posits that memory is the glue that enables each of us to have a coherent self-concept.

"The way we think about ourselves, our beliefs about what others think of us, and our knowledge about how we respond to different situations are mostly learned through experience and stored in memory."

Brain imaging technologies have shown that certain parts of our brains are activated when we're thinking about ourselves (e.g., Craik et al., 1999; Gusnard, Akbudak, Shulman, & Raichle, 2001; Miller et al., 2001; Sebastian, Burnett, & Blakemore, 2008). For instance, researchers have found that certain portions of the brain (i.e., medial prefrontal cortex) become active when participants are making judgments about themselves relative to either familiar or unfamiliar others (e.g., Kelley et al., 2002; Heatherton et al., 2006; Morita et al., 2008). Though research is continuing to develop in this area, it is becoming clear that the self occupies a unique part of the brain and that trauma to the brain can transform who we are. (Note: Look up the classic case of Phineas Gage for an example of how brain injury can change who we are.)

Although the roots of self-concept are housed in the brain, many psychologists believe that self-recognition—the ability, when standing in front of a mirror, to recognize the reflection as one's own—shows the influence of social relations in developing the self-concept (e.g., Boysen & Himes, 1999; Iacoboni, 2009). In one classic experiment, a full-length mirror was placed outside chimpanzee cages to determine whether the chimps were able to recognize themselves in the reflection (Gallup, 1977). At first, they displayed social behaviours, reacting as if the reflection was another chimpanzee, but after several days, they began to respond in self-oriented ways, such as using the mirror for grooming.

More recent research with orangutans, dolphins, elephants, and humans has suggested that self-concept develops at differing rates and may be dependent on our social environments (e.g., Anderson & Gallup, 1999; Barth, Povinelli, & Cant, 2004). For example, infants placed in front of a mirror with a red dot on their forehead will typically try to remove it from their mirror image (the "other baby") up until around two years of age (Courage, Edison, & Howe, 2004). Similar studies with chimpanzees have shown recognition of a red dot placed on their foreheads only in chimps raised in social environments (see Anderson & Gallup, 1999). This demonstrates that our self-concepts begin to form once we perceive ourselves as distinct from, and yet connected to, others in our environments (Jeannerod, 2003).

## SOCIAL INFLUENCES

The chapter opener highlights how at different times and in different contexts, our self-perceptions shift. Some ways of thinking about yourself may even seem to contradict others. So which "you" is the truest you,

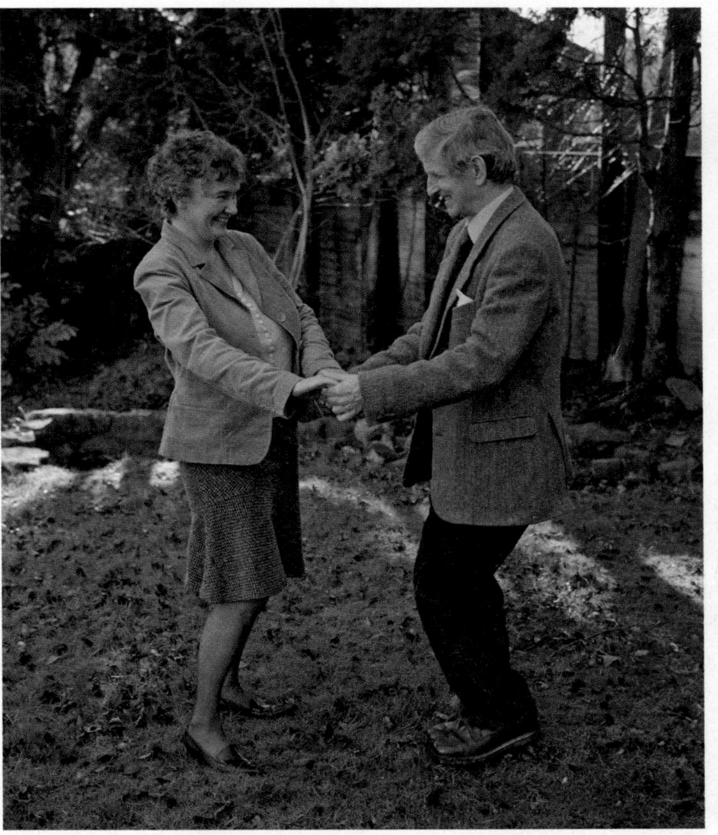

^^^ Clive Wearing keeps journals in which he records his thoughts about himself. **Without memory as "glue," these thoughts consist only of statements like "I am awake" and "fully conscious."**

**SOCIAL IDENTITY THEORY** a theory in which we develop our identity from our group memberships

and how do you know? In fact, there isn't one self-concept that defines you more accurately than others. Each of our selves reflects a part of who we are.

Our sense of self is connected to others (Chen, Boucher, & Tapias, 2006). According to **social identity theory**, the development of our identities is connected to particular social groups (Tajfel & Turner, 1986). On the continuum between personal identity and social identity, we may, at one extreme, focus only on the attributes of *personal identity* that set us apart from other members in a social group. For instance, you may characterize yourself as adventurous or artistic because you see yourself as being more adventurous or more artistic than some of your friends and acquaintances. Of course, these perceptions will change depending on the group to which you are comparing yourself. Within your family, you might see yourself as "the chef" because you are a better cook than anyone else. However, if you started going to culinary school, you might view yourself as an amateur cook relative to your instructors and peers. Group membership results in a categorization of an in-group—a group that we consider ourselves to be a part of—and an out-group—a group that we do not belong to that is separate from our in-group (Tajfel & Turner, 1986). As soon as we categorize groups into an in-group and an out-group, we engage in an "us versus them" mentality, favouring the in-group as one way to bolster our self-concept (Brown, 2000).

**Experiments with chimpanzees and humans suggest** that self-concept begins with self-recognition.

**Our significant relationships shape** our self-concepts to a large degree.

At the other extreme of the identity continuum, our *social identity* involves viewing ourselves in relation to traits we share with certain groups that are different from other groups. Think, for instance, of example in the chapter opener, when I said that I initially thought of myself as "Albertan" when I moved to Nova Scotia because I shared traits with other Albertans that set me apart from my Nova Scotian friends. However, after living in Halifax for so long, my in-group expanded to include other Maritimers, as I assimilated to my new Eastern culture. According to social identity theory, we can develop different group identities and associate with new groups (Brown, 2000).

## Gender and Identity

Gender is another social identity. If you identify yourself as male, you will likely think of yourself in terms of the characteristics you see yourself sharing with other men, in contrast to more feminine traits. Further, recent Canadian research has found that self-concepts for men and women differ according to their level of interdependence (e.g., Anthony, Holmes, & Wood, 2007). Women tend to define themselves in more relational terms (i.e., in terms of close relationships such as being a partner, child, friend, mother), whereas men define themselves in more collectivist terms (i.e., in terms of social groups such as business associations and sports teams) (e.g., Cross, Bacon, & Morris, 2000; Guimond, Chatard, Martinot, Crisp, & Redersdorff, 2006).

Gender influences not only how we identify ourselves but our sense of self-esteem. For example, researchers from McGill University and the University of Winnipeg have conducted several studies examining how social evaluations (i.e., feedback that is rejecting or accepting) influence self-esteem across genders (e.g., Baldwin, Granzberg, Pippus, & Pritchard, 2003). These researchers found that women responded to rejection with increased self-criticism, and that acceptance was associated with decreased self-criticism. Interestingly, the pattern for men was opposite. They expressed the highest positive ratings of self-esteem associated with negative feedback. The authors suggest that men engage in more defensive strategies by attempting to boost their self-esteem to compensate for perceived rejection. In contrast, self-esteem was lower in any sort of evaluative condition for women. This, and other research, suggests that women's interdependent self-concepts can be undermined by negative feedback and rejection, whereas men have a more independent self-concept and derive less of their self-esteem from interpersonal relations (e.g., Baldwin et al., 2003; Baldwin & Sinclair, 1996).

## Culture and Identity

Where you place yourself on the personal-versus-social identity continuum may at times be situational. However, a large body of research also suggests that culture largely dictates a tendency toward one or the other end of the spectrum. In Western cultures like those of Canada and the United States, people tend to emphasize **individualism**, focusing on the self as *independent* of others and placing more importance on individual, rather than collective, goals. People are encouraged to "stand out from the crowd" and to discover and embrace the attributes that make them unique. In particular, Canadians are more likely to describe themselves in terms of individual traits such as "exciting," "attractive," "interesting," and "intelligent" than are people from Asian cultures (Anthony et al., 2007). On the other hand, many non-Western cultures emphasize **collectivism** and focus on the self as *interdependent* and defined by the connectedness of people to one another. In particular, connectedness to people close to ourselves (i.e., family, friends) factors heavily into self-definitions such as being a brother, son, father, and role model (e.g., Brewer & Chen, 2007; Kitayama & Uchida, 2005). In such collectivist cultures, an individual's talents and opinions are considered to be of secondary importance to his or her membership to various groups. A common expression in Japan is "the nail that sticks up gets pounded down" (Markus & Kitayama, 1991).

**INDIVIDUALISM** at the cultural level, a focus on the self as independent from others and a valuing of individual goals over the collective

**COLLECTIVISM** a cultural focus on the self as interdependent and defined by the connectedness of people to one another—in particular, the people closest to them

The stability and consistency of our sense of self across contexts is often assessed using the Self-Concept Clarity Scale (Campbell et al., 1996), which asks individuals to rate a series of statements about their self-beliefs (e.g., "Sometimes I feel I am not really the person that I appear to be"). These researchers found that Japanese students appeared to have lower self-concept clarity relative to Canadian students (Campbell et al., 1996). Similarly, responding to the question "Who am I?" on the Twenty Statements Test (Kuhn & McPartland, 1954) has been associated with cultural differences in self-perception. Specifically, American students were more likely to respond with trait descriptions, whereas

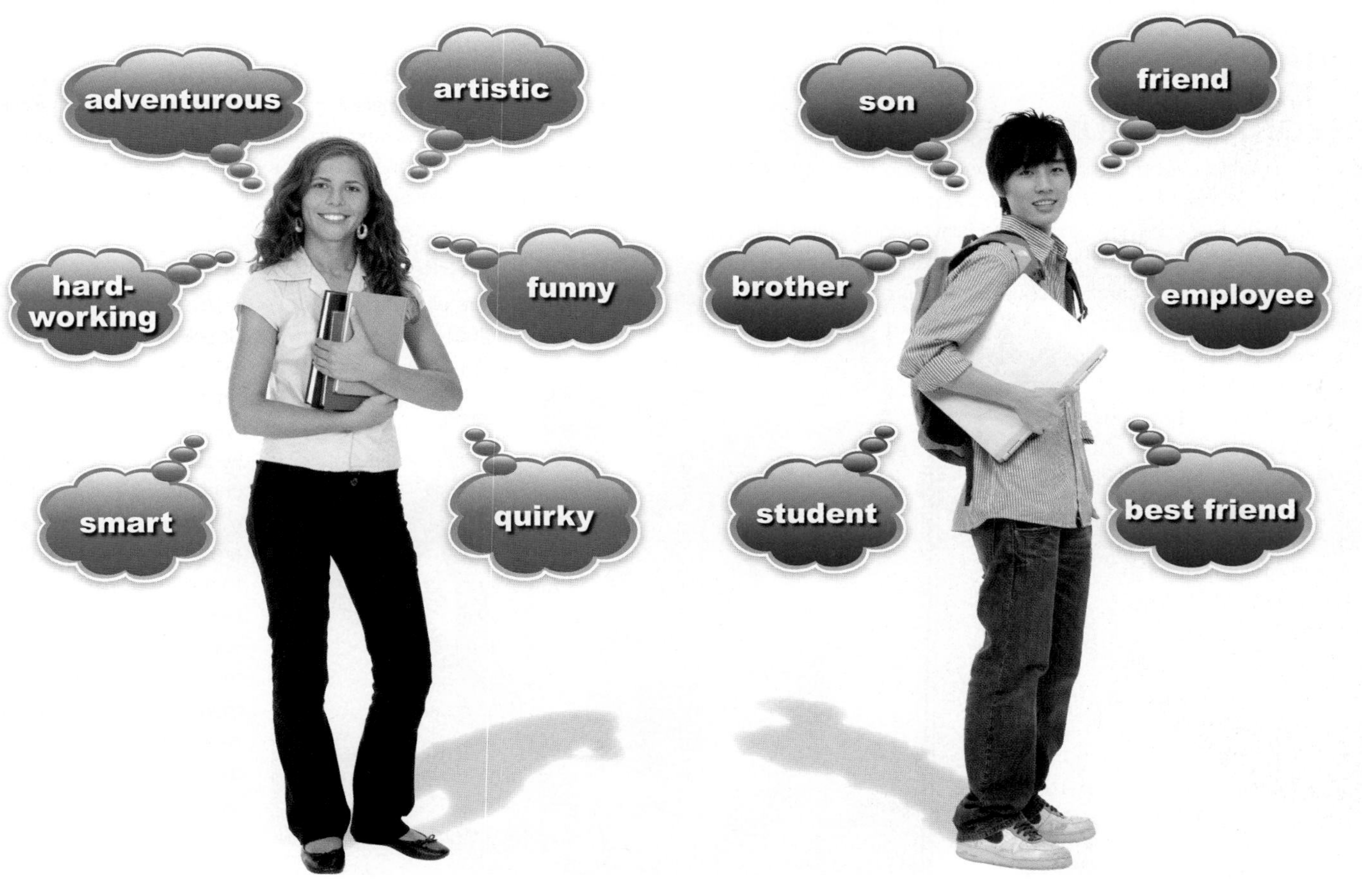


**Independent and Interdependent View of Self.** Western cultures emphasize the independent self, **which focuses on individuals' unique attributes, while** non-Western cultures tend to emphasize the interdependent self, **placing value on each person's connectedness to others (Anthony et al., 2007).**

**INTRODUCTION** the process of thinking about your own thoughts

**AFFECTIVE FORECASTING** the process of predicting the impact future events will have on our overall emotional states

**SELF-DISCREPANCY THEORY** a theory in which our concepts of self are influenced by how close our actual selves are to the selves we would like to be

Chinese students were more likely to indicate group affiliations (Trafimow, Triandis, & Goto, 1991). But just as no issue is black and white, no culture is homogeneously individualist or collectivist. Instead, there are varying degrees of both qualities among every culture's members (Oyserman et al., 2002).

Further, in multicultural societies such as Canada, less distinction between independent and interdependent views of self is evident as contact between cultures increases (Higgins & Bhatt, 2001). That said, recent research with Canadian populations of anglophone Quebecers, as well as with First Nations, Inuit, and Métis Aboriginal groups, has found that understanding and clarifying one's *cultural* identity leads to a greater sense of *personal* identity, which enhances well-being and self-esteem (e.g., Taylor & Usborne, 2010; Usborne & Taylor, 2010). In fact, these authors use the statement "When I know who 'we' are, I can be 'me'" to express this relationship (Taylor & Usborne, 2010, p. 93). While these studies demonstrate that social groups and cultural identity play a powerful role in shaping our self-concepts, research has shown that personal influences play an important part as well.

## PERSONAL INFLUENCES

What was the last decision you made? How did you make it? Whether it was something major (*Should I accept this summer internship, or look for a summer job that pays?*) or something fairly insignificant (*Do I want sushi or a sandwich for lunch?*), you probably had a process for making your choice. Did you carefully consider the pros and cons, or did you "go with your gut"? How did you feel after you made your decision? Were you satisfied with your choice? It may surprise you to know that research has shown that when we make choices based on our gut instincts, rather than on careful reflection about our preferences, we are generally happier with the outcome (Gilbert & Ebert, 2002). This has to do with the process of introspection, the results of which are not always as accurate as we'd like to believe. In this next section, we will consider how this and other personal factors influence our self-concepts.

### Introspection

Self-help books often advise us to look inward when facing a challenge or difficult decision, concentrating on our thoughts and feelings until we understand our inner states. After all, no one knows you as well as you know yourself, right? The process of **introspection**, or thinking about your own thoughts, is not as helpful as conventional wisdom would lead us to believe. In fact, some research suggests this process can lead us astray more often than not. In a number of studies, when people were asked to analyze their reasons for holding particular attitudes, their stated attitudes were *less* likely to match up with their actual behaviours. For example, pretend your friend Jesse holds a strong attitude against drunk driving, but yet drives home after consuming several alcoholic beverages on occasion. This shows that we are not always good at predicting or understanding our feelings (e.g., Wilson, 1990; Wilson & Schooler, 2008). This also is why we are likely to make better decisions based on instinct than when we engage in analysis.

We are also less in touch with our "inner selves" when it comes to predicting the impacts that certain events will have on our feelings and attitudes. Think about your dream job, car, and house. If someone suddenly handed you all of those things today, how do you think you would feel five years from now? Chances are pretty good that you wouldn't feel as happy then as you might guess right now. This is because our attempts at **affective forecasting**, predicting the impact future events will have on our overall emotional states, are usually inaccurate. We tend to overestimate the intensity and duration of our emotional responses (e.g., Buehler & McFarland, 2001; Dunn & Ashton-James, 2008; Wilson & Gilbert, 2005). For example, we might predict we would feel a greater degree of unhappiness following a relationship breakup than we actually do (Gilbert et al., 1998). However, recent research at the University of British Columbia has revealed that high levels of emotional intelligence were associated with greater affective forecasting accuracy across political, academic, and sports scenarios (Dunn, Brackett, Ashton-James, Schneiderman, & Salovey, 2007).

### When Our Selves Don't Match

At some point, we all have wished we could act differently or be different than we actually are; we all have *ideal selves* that don't correspond exactly to our *actual selves* (e.g., Higgins, 1987; Markus & Nurius, 1986). For instance, maybe you wish you were more confident, more physically fit, or better at telling jokes. According to **self-discrepancy theory**, our concepts of self are influenced by how close our actual selves are to the selves we would like to be (Higgins, 1987). If you perceive a large gap between your actual and ideal selves, then you will generally have a more negative self-image. For example, if you think of yourself as an A student, and then you get a C grade on an exam or a paper, you are likely to feel worse about it than a student who already perceives himself as a C student and receives the same grade.

However, some researchers argue that we are not always aware of the discrepancy between our actual and ideal

**The well-known song "If I had $1000000" by Canadian band The Barenaked Ladies relates to affective forecasting.** Would you be able to accurately predict how you would feel or what you would do if you won a million dollars?

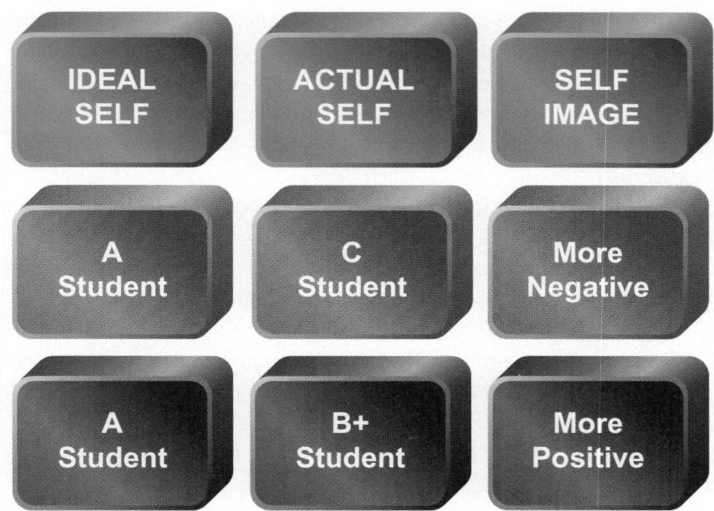


**Self-Discrepancy Theory.** When we perceive our actual selves to be closer to our ideal selves, **we have a more *positive self-concept* than when we perceive a large gap between the actual and the ideal.**

selves, but if we experience heightened **self-awareness**, we will be motivated to change our behaviours to match our personal standards (Moretti & Higgins, 1999). Have you ever seen a video of yourself giving a speech, performance, or presentation? Did it reveal tics or other flaws of which you hadn't been aware? Often, people record themselves in these situations so that they will be able to improve their performance in the future. Looking in a mirror, standing in front of a crowd, and listening to a recording of your voice are all ways to increase self-awareness. In a classic study, a bowl of candy was left on a researcher's front porch on Halloween with a request that each trick-or-treater take just one piece (Beaman et al., 1979). Results showed that when a full-length mirror was placed behind the bowl, only 12 percent of children took more than one piece of candy, as opposed to the 34 percent who took more than one piece without the mirror in which to see themselves (Beaman et al., 1979). In a more recent study, researchers found that employees chipped in more cash for coffee in an office break room when a picture of a pair of eyes was placed over the donations box than when the box had other images over it (Bateson, Nettle, & Roberts, 2006).

An increase in self-awareness can lead people to match their behaviours to their attitudes. Conversely, it can result in an individual's desire to escape self-awareness. In fact, individuals may engage in a variety of self-destructive behaviours as a method of decreasing self-awareness, including alcohol consumption (e.g., Hull & Young, 1983), binge eating (e.g., Heatherton & Baumeister, 1991), masochism (e.g., Baumeister, 1988), risky sexual behaviour (e.g., Hynie, MacDonald, & Marques, 2006), and even suicide (Baumeister, 1990). While these may seem extreme to you, even behaviours associated with procrastination, such as partying, sleeping, and watching TV, can occur as an escape from self-awareness. For example, Moskalenko and Heine (2003) manipulated the type of feedback individuals would receive about their level of intelligence. After measuring participants' actual and ideal selves, they found that individuals who received negative feedback about an IQ test they had taken spent more time watching television in the laboratory than those who received positive feedback.

**SELF-AWARENESS** when attention is brought about on the self; for example, looking in a mirror, standing in front of a crowd, and listening to a recording of your voice

**SELF-PERCEPTION THEORY** a theory in which, if we are unsure of the attitudes we hold, we look to our behaviour and use that to make inferences about our attitudes, much like an outside observer

**FACIAL FEEDBACK HYPOTHESIS** a hypothesis that states that a change in our facial expressions can lead to a subsequent emotional change

## What Does Our Behaviour Say About Ourselves?

Have you ever noticed that you make assumptions about other people's attitudes and preferences based on the behaviour patterns you notice? If your roommate turns you down every time you invite him to go get pizza with you, you might assume that he doesn't like pizza. On the other hand, if he turns you down every time you ask him to do anything with you, you might assume he doesn't like *you*. According to Daryl Bem's **self-perception theory**, we make the same kinds of judgments about ourselves based on our own behaviour (Bem, 1972). Specifically, if we are unsure of the attitudes we hold, we look to our behaviour and use that to make inferences about our attitudes, much like an outside observer. For example, growing up, you may never have been exposed to folk music, and as a result, a dislike of "folksy" things has become a part of your self-concept. However, if a friend convinced you to attend the Edmonton folk festival, you may find that you actually really enjoy the music and that your previous opinion of folk music was founded on a lack of exposure. This positive experience can shift your own self-perception and turn you into a lifelong fan of the music.

Are we happy because we smile, or do we smile because we are happy? Similar to self-perception theory, the **facial feedback hypothesis** states that our facial movements can impact the emotions we experience. According to this hypothesis, smiling, even when you don't feel like it, can help improve your mood. So there is some truth in the common advice to "just smile—you'll feel better," as smiling can lead to more positive emotions. In the first study to test this, James Laird (1974) attached electrodes to individuals' faces and gave them instructions to either smile or frown while they were watching cartoons. When people were instructed to smile, they rated the cartoons as funnier than when they viewed cartoons while frowning. Similarly, Strack, Martin, and Stepper (1988) had participants hold a pencil or pen with either their lips (activating frowns) or their teeth (activating smiles) and then rate cartoons. Their results were in line with the facial feedback hypothesis. Try this technique yourself (refer to image) and see if changing your expression from a smile to a frown affects how you feel.

What if we could not change our facial expressions? Would we still experience a change in emotion? Recent research suggests that impairment of facial movement may be an obstacle (Havas et al., 2010). When individuals were given Botox treatments that impaired their abilities to frown, it actually took them longer to emotionally process a series of angry and sad statements they were asked to read. However, other studies have found that individuals with facial paralysis can still experience and discriminate emotional expressions in others (e.g., Keillor, Barrett, Crucian, Kortenkamp, & Heilman, 2002). So, what is the mechanism behind the facial feedback hypothesis?

Some researchers, including Laird, argue that it works as a form of self-perception, and that we infer our mood state from our behaviour (i.e., if I'm smiling, it must be because I am happy). Other researchers (e.g., Izard, 1990; Zajonc, 1993) argue that facial expressions bring about a

**INTRINSIC MOTIVATION** the drive to perform an action because we enjoy it and are likely to engage in it more fully and with greater curiosity and pleasure

**EXTRINSIC MOTIVATION** the drive to perform an action in response to an external pressure or obligation, to avoid punishment, or to achieve some outside benefit

**SELF-ESTEEM** a person's evaluation of his or her self-worth

physiological change in the brain and that is responsible for the change in emotion. The facial feedback hypothesis even extends to other nonverbal gestures, such as a shrug of the shoulder, furrowing the brow, or a nod of the heads. In fact, Briñol and Petty (2003) found that if you can get audience members to shake their heads affirmatively, then they will be more likely to agree with the message the speaker is presenting.

### Motivation

Think about the subject area you have chosen to study. What were your reasons for choosing this major or concentration? Motivation—the force that drives us to complete a task or achieve a goal—plays a part in self-perceptions. If you enjoy your classes and are generally interested in your academic major, this is probably because your choice to pursue this major was an **intrinsically motivated** one. When we take a certain action because we enjoy it, we are likely to engage more fully and with greater curiosity and pleasure. In addition, we may be less susceptible to the influences of conformity and self-handicapping when intrinsically motivated (e.g., Arndt, Schimel, Greenberg, & Pyszczynski, 2002).

By the same token, **extrinsically motivated** actions—those that we perform in response to an external pressure or obligation, to avoid punishment, or to achieve some outside benefit (e.g., money, success, recognition)—can have negative consequences for our overall sense of well-being and happiness if they dominate our experience (Sheldon, 2005). For example, say your parents really want you to go to university to become an accountant. However, your real interests involve acting or becoming an artist. From a practical perspective, they may argue that your passions may not be associated with financial stability in the future relative to accounting. That said, you would have much higher intrinsic motivation for art-related projects or activities than accounting classes or placements. In fact, much literature suggests that placing "conditions of worth" on someone (e.g., your partner will love you more if you lose 30 pounds) is detrimental to that person's sense of self-worth (e.g., Baldwin & Sinclair, 1996; Rogers, 1959). This supports the idea that we prefer to engage in activities when our reasons for doing so are internally triggered.

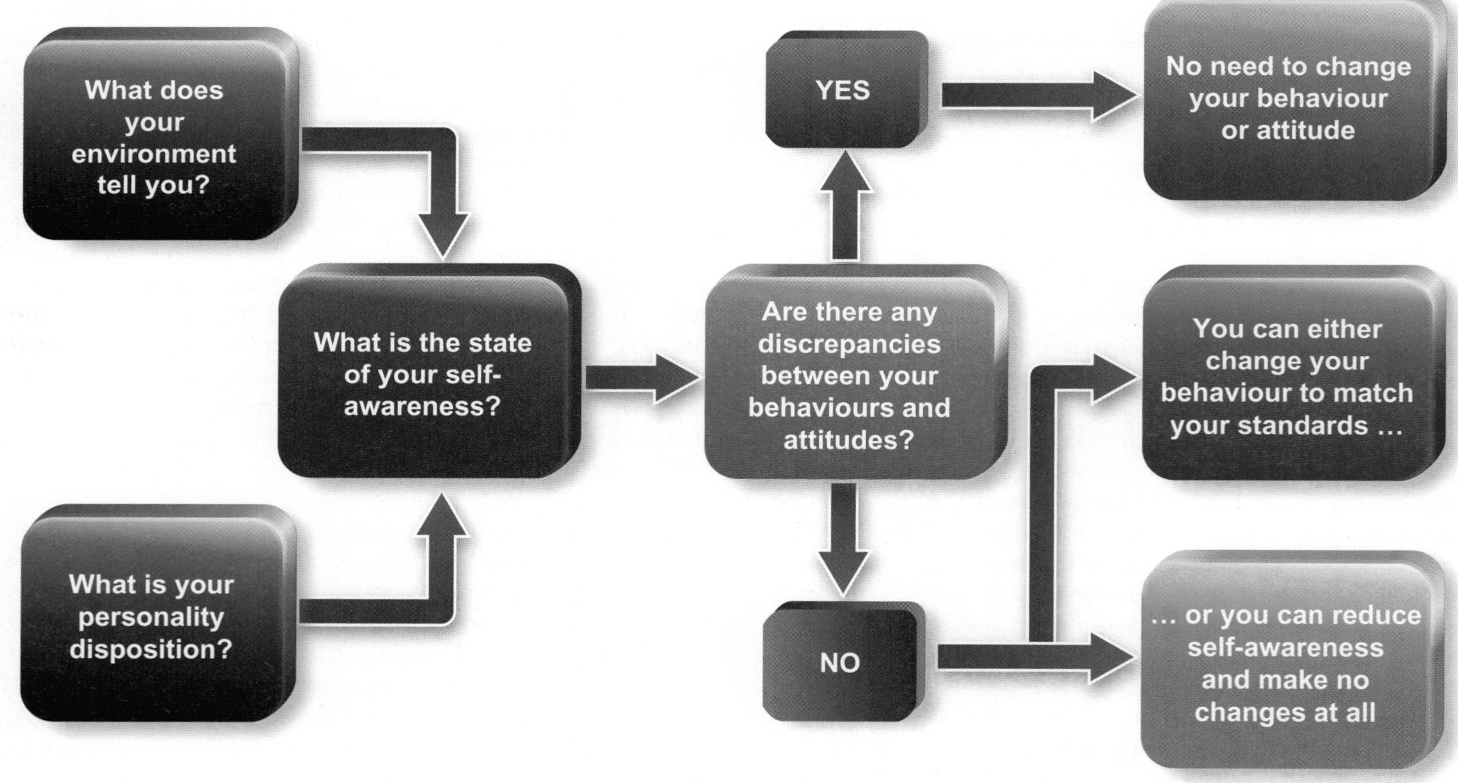


**Self-Awareness Theory and Discrepancies.** Increased self-awareness makes people conscious of the gap between their actual and ideal selves, **which in turn may cause them to modify their behaviour to bring it more in line with their ideals. On the other hand, the situation might also lead people to try to escape self-awareness.**

<<< Try holding a pencil in your lips and then watching a funny video clip. Now try holding a pencil in your teeth and watching a funny video clip. **Which did you find funnier? According to the *facial feedback hypothesis,* when holding the pencil in your teeth, you are activating the muscles associated with smiling, thus facilitating more happy emotions (e.g., Strack et al., 1988)**

In one study of the impact of motivation on behaviour, University of Western Ontario researchers Pretty and Seligman (1984) had undergraduate students complete a series of puzzles, an activity for which they expected to receive an award (i.e., lottery tickets), received an unexpected reward, or received no reward. The researchers found that participants who received no reward or an unexpected reward were more intrinsically motivated to work on the puzzles in their "free" time within the experiment than were those who knew they would get a reward regardless. Further, when people engaged in the task knowing they would receive a reward, they experienced more negative affect and were unmotivated to work on the puzzles (Pretty & Seligman, 1984). This phenomenon, known as *overjustification*, causes people to lose interest in a task when the motivation is apparently extrinsic. If compensation for a task is a surprise, people are more likely to derive satisfaction from it because they still believe they are engaging in the task for its own sake.

"If compensation for a task is a surprise, people are more likely to derive satisfaction from it because they still believe they are engaging in the task for its own sake."

Motivations can also be influenced by culture and society (Maehr, 1974). For example, Huang and Van de Vliert (2003) found that intrinsic job satisfaction (i.e., being motivated by intrinsic job factors such as recognition and accomplishment instead of pay and benefits) was higher in countries that promoted social welfare and were individualistic and richer (e.g., Canada, New Zealand, Sweden, Germany) than in more collectivistic countries (e.g., India, Philippines, Thailand, Hong Kong).

## In What Ways Does Our Need for Self-Esteem Motivate Our Actions?

How do you feel about yourself? Your **self-esteem** encompasses your own attitudes about yourself, from the way you look, to your intelligence, to your physical abilities and more. Although self-esteem is a mostly stable construct, it can fluctuate on a moment's notice in response to our social environment. What remains present, however, is an innate human need to feel good about ourselves. One of the most widely used assessments of our self-esteem is the Rosenberg Self-Esteem Scale (Rosenberg, 1965), which asks individuals to rate their level of agreement with a series of statements about how they feel about themselves overall. Because the need for high self-esteem is such a powerful and inherent factor in our lives, it seems to have a direct effect on our overall happiness, relationships, and perhaps our successes throughout life.

However, Baumeister and his colleagues (2003) found that while positive self-esteem is correlated with positive performance in school and work, high degrees of popularity, and good physical health, it's just that—a correlation. A cause cannot necessarily be inferred, as explained in Chapter 2's discussion of correlations. Previous explanations also fail to take into account variations in self-esteem across individualistic and collective cultures (e.g., Cheng et al., 2011). Further, researchers have shown that there can be a downside to pursuing an increase in self-esteem (e.g., Crocker & Park, 2004; Taylor & Brown, 1988). They argued that trying hard to maintain and boost self-esteem can cause anxiety and can cause people to avoid activities that may end in failure, to neglect others, and to struggle with stress-induced health problems.

The relentless need for positive self-esteem can cause us to sometimes ignore criticism or to justify our actions when we might condemn the same actions in other people. Moreover, in many cases, we aren't even aware of our biased thinking about ourselves in relation to others. Of course, there are times when we *do* feel inferior to others, when we think someone else is smarter, better-liked, or more attractive than we are (e.g., Leary, 1998, 2004, 2007; Zuckerman & Jost, 2001). And there are some individuals who do legitimately struggle with self-esteem. However, in general, self-esteem as a motivating factor behind our actions is more prevalent than most people realize (e.g., Leary, 2004, 2007; Tesser, 1988).

>>>Based on the relationship *between motivation and culture,* someone from a Canadian or American culture might apologize if she orders the same menu item as others in her group because choosing from a menu is motivated by one's concept of individuality and uniqueness. **By contrast, in Asian cultures, ordering from the menu could be a group decision motivated by a desire to show belongingness and collective unity (e.g., Iyengar & Lepper, 2000).**

## ACTION LEARNING

### Maintaining a Positive Self-Concept

Maintaining a positive self-concept is the key to succeeding at our goals and experiencing overall well-being throughout our lives. Individuals who have stable, high self-esteem experience positive emotions more consistently than those with poor self-concepts. In addition, they have a lower chance of depression (Tennen & Affleck, 1993). Where goals are concerned, it should come as no surprise that people who believe in themselves and their abilities have a higher chance of accomplishing what they set out to do (Parker et al., 2010), whether it be personal goals or relationships (Murray et al., 1996). On the other hand, when we experience self-doubt and think poorly of our attributes and abilities, we are likely to fail (e.g., Crocker, 2002; Crocker & Luhtanen, 2003; Kernis, 2003).

Self-concepts can be influenced by others' preconceived images of ourselves, which can lead to the self-fulfilling prophecy. For example, a student whose teacher thinks she is a poor performer will come to share this belief, and as a result, the student is more likely to fail (e.g., Choi, 2005; Jussim, 1986; Marsh & Craven, 2006). On the other hand, if we have a positive self-view, we are likely to live up to our expectations. Researchers found that if an individual thinks of himself or herself as a likeable person, others are apt to like him or her. For example, in their study of undergraduates at a large university, Stinson et al. (2009) found that students with positive self-concepts were more likely to behave warmly when meeting a group of new acquaintances, and the group, in turn, was more likely to accept those students who behaved this way.

With this in mind, you can appreciate why it is important for people to take steps to maintain a positive self-concept. Try to find an advertisement or commercial on television that promotes positive self-concepts. Use social psychological principles to demonstrate how this advertisement attempts to promote positivity. Think about how your self-concept is defined and how television and the media influence your self-concept. Now how would *you* create a public service announcement or advertisement to promote a positive self-concept? Select two ideas from this chapter and show how they impact the self-concept. Finally, share at least one technique that can be used to improve an individual's self-concept.

What will you learn from this action project?

1. Identify ways social psychologists think about the self.
2. Discover the real impacts our behaviours, attitudes, and biases have on self-concept.
3. Learn how to develop and help others develop a positive self-concept.

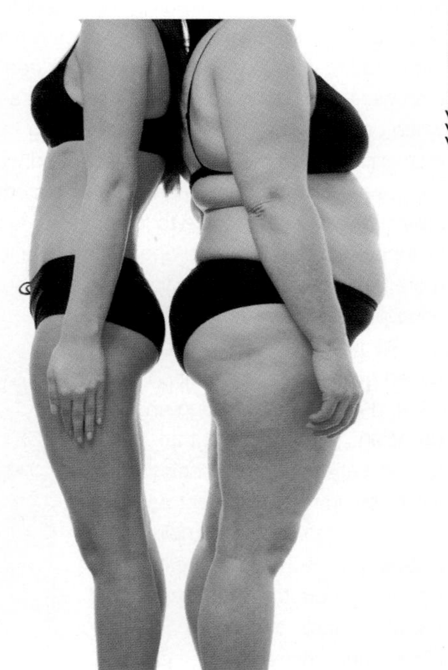

Female body image has become the focus of many public service announcements **in response to increases in teenage and young adult eating disorders as** young women aspire to look like supermodels.

## MEMORY BIAS

Have you ever had the experience of discussing a common memory with a family member only to find out that she remembers the event differently? Maybe you were certain that it snowed on your birthday two years ago, but your mother insists that it didn't snow at all that year. It is no secret that memory is unreliable (Loftus, 2005). In fact, distorting some memories to come out slightly in your favour is one trick your brain may play on you to help maintain a positive self-esteem. Multiple studies have found that when remembering past choices, we tend to attribute positive features to options we selected and negative features to options we decided against (e.g., Mather, Shafir, & Johnson, 2000; Henkel & Mather, 2007). For example, when individuals were asked to make a choice between two different job candidates, each of whom had about the same number of positive and negative attributes, participants were more likely later on to remember more positive qualities about the candidate they selected and to assign more negative qualities to the one they rejected (Mather & Johnson, 2000).

## SELF-SERVING BIASES

Apart from distortions in memory, we also engage in several types of self-serving biases in order to protect our self-esteem (i.e., attributions, false consensus, and unrealistic optimism). These tend to serve both motivational and cognitive functions. Specifically, self-serving biases are used to protect or enhance our self-esteem (motivational), and because we have an inherent expectancy to succeed, we need to explain why we may not (cognitive). For example, individuals tend to vary on whether they feel their intelligence is fixed or fluid, and as a result, may take on more or fewer challenges depending on predicted success/failure (e.g., Dweck, 1999). In one study, researchers praised children's high performance on test questions by linking the children's success to their intelligence (i.e., "You must be smart at these problems"; Mueller & Dweck, 1998, p. 36). When this happened, the children were more likely to respond negatively to setbacks because they believed that confusion or failure was due to an uncontrollable lack of intelligence. By the same token, children with a fixed view of their intelligence were less motivated to take on challenges because they were afraid that failure would invalidate their abilities and confirm their deficiencies. However, children who were praised for their effort (i.e., "You must have worked hard at these problems") rather than their intelligence were more likely to recover quickly after failure because they attributed setbacks to a temporary lapse in effort rather than a failure of intelligence. Because they attributed their success to variable factors, these children were also more likely to enjoy and seek out challenging tasks.

> "Our bias leads us to choose an explanation that will make us feel better about ourselves."

### Self-Serving Attribution

**Attribution**, or deciding who or what is responsible for the outcome of a situation, is another way we cope with failure and respond to success in order to maintain self-esteem (Heider, 1958). Sometimes it is clear whether the outcome of a situation is due to a person's innate abilities or whether it can be attributed to her level of effort. For instance, if you fail an exam because you did not attend class or study the material, it is clear that your level of effort is responsible for your test grade rather than the test being too hard. In many cases, however, the causes of an event are unclear. Heider (1958) explained that in ambiguous situations, "the person's own needs or wishes determine the attribution." In other words, our bias leads us to choose an explanation that will make us feel better about ourselves. For example, imagine you meet up with a friend after class on the day he is expecting to get his graded psychology exam back. When you ask him how he did, he tells you that he got a D but quickly goes on to explain that the professor graded some of the questions unfairly. Also, he was feeling sick on the day he took the test, *and* he had just had a fight with his girlfriend before going to class that day. Ultimately, your friend indicated he was not in the right frame of mind to perform well.

**ATTRIBUTION** deciding who or what is responsible for the outcome of a situation; another way we cope with failure and respond to success in order to maintain self-esteem

**SELF-SERVING ATTRIBUTION** a self-protection strategy in which we are likely to believe that external factors are responsible for situations in which we perform poorly

You may have heard similar explanations—or offered similar explanations—for poor test results in the past. The **self-serving attribution**, a tendency to see ourselves in a favourable way leads us to make attributions for our behaviour that favour the self. A self-serving attribution is a self-protection strategy in which we are likely to believe that *external* factors like unfair grading or a difficult environment are responsible for situations in which we perform poorly (Campbell & Sedikides, 1999). By the same token, in situations when we succeed, we tend to attribute the outcome to *internal* qualities, like intelligence or skill. If your friend did well on the test, he might be likely to tell you he tends to be a good test taker or that psychology is his best subject.

There are many examples of how the self-serving attribution operates in everyday life. When group projects turn out well, individual group members are likely to cite their own efforts as a factor, whereas when projects turn out poorly, they are likely to blame others in the group (Fast & Tiedens, 2010). Studies of marital behaviour have found that when a relationship ends, individuals often appraise the relationship failure in an egocentric and self-enhancing manner, such as "He wasn't the right person for me" or "She didn't understand me," rather than examining how their own behaviour may have contributed to the breakup (e.g., Gray & Silver, 1990). Interestingly, self-serving attributions are dependent on a person's individual perspective. Drivers involved in car accidents tend to attribute the accident to external factors (like road conditions), while observers and passengers tend to attribute the accident to both internal and external factors such as someone driving too fast for the road conditions (Bordel et al., 2007). In addition, causal explanations for our behaviour also are dictated to some degree by culture. Specifically, collectivistic cultures tend to use contextual factors as explanatory frameworks for life events more so than individualistic cultures (Higgins & Bhatt, 2001).

### False Consensus

When we do something we feel guilty about or when we fail at a task, we often choose to protect our self-esteem or justify our actions by assuming that others have done the same thing. For example, when young adult smokers were asked to estimate the percentage of those in their

**UNREALISTIC OPTIMISM** optimism that occurs when we tend to imagine that the outcomes of situations will be better for us than for other people

**SOCIAL COMPARISON THEORY** a theory wherein we compare ourselves to others in different situations because there is no given standard against which to measure our abilities and opinions

age group who also smoked, the respondents overestimated the proportion of others who smoked by an average of 20 percent (Cunningham & Selby, 2007). In another study conducted during a water conservation crisis, when a shower ban was put in place for several days, those who ignored the ban and showered anyway were highly likely to overestimate the number of others who also disregarded the ban (Monin & Norton, 2003). We also are likely to overestimate consensus when it comes to our opinions, especially those opinions we hold on controversial issues. For instance, research has shown that when we hold prejudiced attitudes, we are more likely to assume that a significant number of people share these feelings, so we therefore do not appear to ourselves to be prejudiced in relation to others (Watt & Larkin, 2010).

According to Dawes (1990), the false consensus effect may, in part, be the result of the fact that we tend to spend time with people who are similar to us. People who have a lot in common with us are more likely to engage in the same behaviours and hold similar views, so our perceptions of what is the "majority opinion" are influenced by exposure to a limited sample of the people we associate with. A number of studies have supported this possibility (e.g., Krueger & Clement, 1994; Marks & Miller, 1987; Ross, Greene, & House, 1977). For instance, when members of extremist groups expressed their opinions regularly in online communities of like-minded people, they tended to overestimate the number of others who shared their views (e.g., Wang, Walther, & Hancock, 2009; Wojcieszak, 2008).



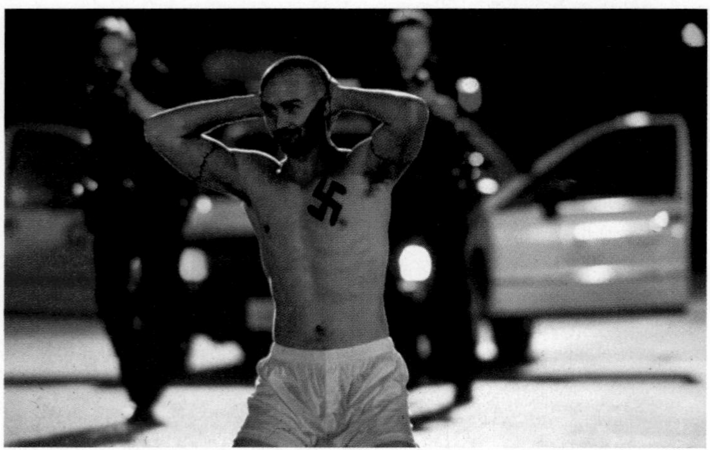

Individuals who hold prejudiced attitudes **(such as the White Power group portrayed in the movie *American History X*)** often justify their actions by believing that others would act the same way if they let out their true feelings. **This helps protect their self-esteem and is an example of the false consensus effect. Does this also affect the company we keep?**

### Unrealistic Optimism

Optimism, the tendency to see events and situations in a positive light, also may bias us to see *ourselves* in a more positive light. **Unrealistic optimism** is when we tend to imagine that the outcomes of situations will be better for us than for others. For instance, a college or university student may imagine that he or she is more likely to get a job following graduation than are his or her friends or classmates. In fact, research has found that college students tend to see themselves as more likely than their fellow students to get good jobs and become financially successful, despite having similar educations (Hoorens et al., 2008). This demonstrates that people tend to have unrealistically optimistic predictions about their own futures relative to others in the same circumstances. Unrealistic optimism also may explain why people buy lottery tickets or place bets in hockey playoff pools—they believe that they are more likely to win than others. Apart from positive experiences, this phenomenon relates to our tendency to think we are less likely to encounter negative events than our peers. For example, Lochhead and Tipper (2008) found that individuals estimate there is only a 10 percent chance of their own marriage failing, despite a rate of 40 percent of first marriages in Canada resulting in divorce ("Four in 10," 2010). That said, unrealistic optimism also is moderated by culture. Canadian students tend to show significantly more unrealistic optimism relative to Japanese students, and especially for events involving communal efforts (Heine & Lehman, 1995).

While a greater degree of optimism promotes self-efficacy and may lead people to recover more quickly from setbacks and experience lowered rates of depression, there are a number of potential hazards to unrealistic optimism as well. One problem with unrealistic optimism is that it can lead us to under-prepare for future events. For example, students who are overconfident tend to study less for tests and to receive lower grades than students who have similar abilities but are more pessimistic about those abilities (Norem & Cantor, 1986). The "it won't happen to me" attitude applies to the optimistic bias as well. For instance, college students tend to predict that life-threatening problems and severe illnesses will not affect them. This, in turn, makes students less likely to take precautions against a number of potential hazards to health and life (Weinstein, 1982). For example, students are more likely to engage in risky sexual behaviour when they believe they are unlikely to contract sexually transmitted diseases (e.g., MacDonald & Hynie, 2008; Thompson, Anderson, Freedman, & Swan, 1996). Another study found that unrealistic optimism makes people more likely to drive after they have been drinking because they believe they are less likely than others to lose control of their vehicles (Causse et al., 2004). Similarly, students underestimate their likelihood of experiencing severe problems due to binge drinking, when this increases risk of alcohol-related problems later in life (Dillard et al., 2009). That said, individuals who have previously been victimized are less optimistic (i.e., they believe they are more vulnerable) about the likelihood of recurrences of negative life events (Higgins, St. Amand, & Poole, 1997).

## COMPARISON TO OTHERS

When you were in high school, you probably compared your experiences and performance in school with those of your classmates. For example, if you were feeling bad about your performance on a particularly challenging pop quiz, you may have checked with others in the class to see if they also had a hard time. Knowing that your classmates found the quiz as difficult as you did probably made you feel better about your own performance. Regardless of the grade that you actually received, it felt good to know that the quiz was difficult for everyone and that you were not falling behind your peers.

This method of evaluation is described by **social comparison theory**; according to this theory, we compare ourselves to others who are similar to us on the dimension in question because there is no given standard against which to measure our abilities and opinions (Festinger, 1954). However, while other people can serve as a useful frame of reference, we are not always objective in our comparisons. The desire to feel good about ourselves overwhelms the desire to accurately assess our achievements and abilities (Sedikides & Gregg, 2003).

### Downward Social Comparison

One clear way to feel better about the self through social comparison is to compare yourself to someone who is less capable or worse off than you are. This process, known as **downward social comparison**, may, for instance, be why television talk shows and reality TV are so popular (e.g., Frisby, 1999; Nelson, 2003). Seeing people with broken relationships or dysfunctional families is likely to make you feel better about your own situation. And seeing people make fools of themselves or treat each other badly is likely to make you feel better about your own behaviour. In marriages and dating relationships, couples who engage in downward social comparison with other couples are more likely to feel satisfied about the state of their own relationships (Buunk et al., 2001). And college students who have experienced recent academic setbacks will feel better about themselves when they are exposed to downward comparison information about other students' performances (Aspinwall & Taylor, 1993). For example, an A student may feel better about her B grade on an exam when she finds out most of her classmates got a C.

### BIRGing and CORFing

After winning the gold medal in the 1988 Olympic Games, Ben Johnson, a Jamaican-born Canadian sprinter, was disqualified for steroid use. Interestingly, Stelzl and her colleagues (2008) noticed that when the Canadian media first reported on Johnson's win, they identified him as Canadian, but when they later covered news about his disqualification, they began to label him as Jamaican. Intrigued by these findings, they created a study in which they gave Canadian research participants information about a fictional athlete with a Canadian-American identity. They found that in cases where they told participants the fictional athlete had lost, people were more likely to identify him as an American, but when participants believed he had won, they identified him as a Canadian (Stelzl et al., 2008). These research findings are an example of what psychologists call **BIRGing**, or "basking in reflected glory," a strategy by which we reinforce our positive self-concepts by identifying ourselves with successful others. You'll probably, for instance, be more likely to wear clothing with the name of your favourite hockey team on it the day after your team has won a game than on a day after the team has lost. You might even say "We won!" when discussing the victory with other fans. BIRGing also occurs in situations when we can make ethnic, religious, or appearance-based connections to others who have succeeded (Cialdini et al., 1976).

We also engage in the opposite of BIRGing, **CORFing** ("cutting off reflective failure"), when we try to disassociate ourselves from others who have failed or behaved poorly. For example, if your favourite sports teams (e.g., Edmonton Oilers, Toronto Blue Jays, Saskatchewan Roughriders) are on a losing streak, you may decide not to cheer for them or watch the games as they are not worth your time. BIRGing and CORFing are often associated with sports figures and teams, but they can also occur in a number of other situations, such as politics. For instance, you may have noticed that after the recent Conservative majority vote in the 2011 federal election, individuals who supported the Conservative Party of Canada were more likely to leave endorsement signs up on their lawns than were those who supported the badly defeated Liberal Party (also see Miller, 2009). That said, some recent research suggests that we also may engage in "basking in spite of reflected failure" (BIRFing) to help explain why teams with low winning percentages (e.g., Toronto Maple Leafs) continue to maintain a strong fan base, and "cutting off reflected success" (CORSing) to explain why we don't "jump ship" and cheer for teams with higher success rates (e.g., Vancouver Canucks) (Campbell, Aiken, & Kent, 2004).

**DOWNWARD SOCIAL COMPARISON** the process of comparing yourself to someone who is less capable or worse off than you are

**BIRGING** "basking in reflected glory," a strategy by which we reinforce our positive self-concepts by identifying ourselves with successful others

**CORFING** "cutting off reflective failure," a strategy by which we try to disassociate ourselves from others who have failed or behaved poorly

**SELF-HANDICAPPING** a process that involves setting up an obstacle before engaging in a task as a way to give ourselves a ready-made excuse in case we don't perform well

### Self-Handicapping

If you have ever procrastinated on a term paper or decided to go out with your friends the night before taking an important exam, you may have been engaging in **self-handicapping** behaviour. Self-handicapping involves setting up an obstacle before engaging in a task as a way to give ourselves a ready-made excuse in case we don't perform well. We are especially likely to self-handicap when we feel nervous or uncertain about an important performance. For instance, a child feeling nervous about an upcoming piano recital might decide to stop practising so that if he plays poorly, he can tell people that it was due to lack of practise. Similarly, studies have found that students may self-handicap by listening to distracting music while working, by taking drugs or alcohol before engaging in an academic task, or by avoiding studying altogether (e.g., Leonardi & Gonida, 2007; McCrea, 2008).

> "Be yourself; everyone else is already taken.—Oscar Wilde"

## Impression Management: How Do We Represent Ourselves to Others?

How do you want others to perceive you? Which of your characteristics do you value more than others? How does the context affect how you want to be viewed? To some degree, we can control others' impressions of ourselves by emphasizing the information that highlights certain character traits. For instance, if you want people to think you're a hard worker, you might mention the number of hours you spend at your job or the amount of research you've been doing on a paper. If you want people to think you're laid back, you might make sure they can tell that you're calm in stressful situations, or make it clear that you aren't concerned with keeping to a strict schedule. Of course, the way you present yourself will change depending on the situation and the people in it. When you go to a job interview, you will probably choose to emphasize personal qualities like responsibility, organization, and motivation. When you go on a first date, you may play up your charm or sense of humour.

When we want others to think well of us in general, we may use a different form of impression management. Individuals in a work

**INGRATIATION** a way of controlling others' impressions of us through flattery

**SPOTLIGHT EFFECT** the belief that our behaviour, our appearance, and even our internal states are obvious to others

**SELF-VERIFICATION THEORY** a theory wherein we want others to see us as we see ourselves—even when our self-concepts are negative

**SELF-MONITORING** the process through which people regulate their behaviour to be perceived well by others; low self-monitors act consistently across situations, acting according to their personal views, while high self-monitors are constantly monitoring their behaviour and adjusting their reactions to fit the situation they are in

environment may try to increase their influence or likeability with management by complimenting them, agreeing with their opinions, or performing favours for them (Appelbaum & Hughes, 1998). This process, known as **ingratiation**, is a way of controlling others' impressions of us either through *flattery* (e.g., "You're looking really great! Have you been working out?") or calling attention to *incidental similarities* (e.g., "We have the same glasses! We must both have good taste!"). For example, job applicants who employ ingratiation tactics are rated more highly and are more likely to be successful candidates (Varma, Toh, & Pichler, 2006). Similarly, a study found that waiters who complimented couples on their dinner selections received significantly higher tips than those who did not (Seiter, 2007).

Of course, because we want to maintain our self-esteem, we want to believe the complimentary things people say about us, which is why ingratiation can be so effective. Generally in these situations, when there is an additional person present, the person receiving the compliment is much more likely to form a favourable impression of the compliment giver than is the person who is not receiving the compliment (Vonk, 2002). However, there is a catch to ingratiation. If people believe we are not sincere in our attempts to win their approval, the tactic may backfire (Vonk, 2002).

Although we tend to devote a good deal of time and mental energy to the way we present ourselves to others, it may help to know that other people aren't often paying as much attention to us as we think they are. For instance, when giving a presentation, you might start to feel more nervous because you're worried that other people can tell that you're nervous. But chances are your audience doesn't notice that your palms are sweaty or that your hands are shaking a little. The belief that our behaviour, our appearance, and even our internal states are obvious to others is known as the **spotlight effect**.

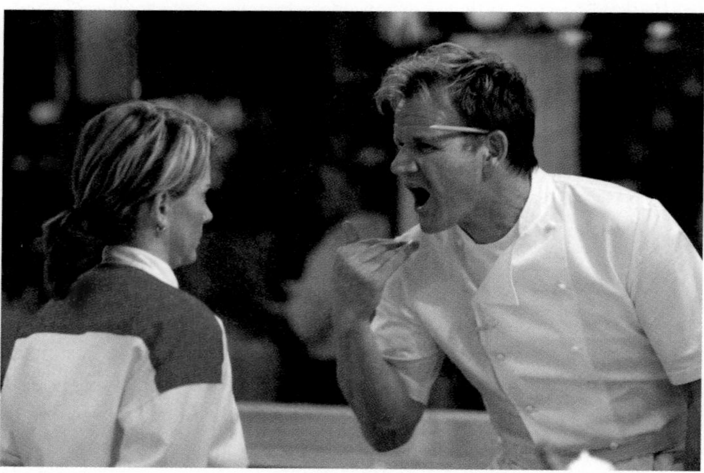

^ Is our love of reality TV and TV talk shows ^ inspired **by the self-esteem boost we get from favourably comparing ourselves with others?**

How do you feel when you aren't comfortable in your clothes? Chances are, you feel less confident and more exposed—under a proverbial spotlight. Gilovich, Medvec, and Savitsky (2000) demonstrated the spotlight effect by asking college students to walk into a room filled with other people while wearing a flattering or potentially embarrassing image (i.e., a picture of Barry Manilow) on their T-shirt. Consumed with their own embarrassment and self-consciousness, participants significantly overestimated the number of other people who actually noticed the embarrassing or flattering shirt (Gilovich et al., 2000). Similarly, when we are associated with individuals who behave embarrassingly or act inappropriately, we also erroneously believe that other observers are paying more attention to us than they are (Fortune & Newby-Clark, 2008).

What about self-presentation when it comes to interacting online? If you have a Facebook or MySpace page, you probably realize that it is much easier to control what people think of us when we build an online profile because people only see the information we want them to see. A recent study supports the idea that many people prefer text messages and online interaction (like email and instant messaging) to face-to-face interactions or phone calls (Madel & Muncer, 2007). This is because in situations where the interaction is less immediate, it is easier for us to control other people's perceptions of us. Later on in this section, you will read about self-presentation in the context of online dating.

## SELF-VERIFICATION

If you consider yourself to be an honest person and someone you know has the false impression that you are dishonest, you will probably try to get her to see you as an honest person. But what if you think you are lazy? If someone you know sees you as a hard worker, will you try to change his favourable perception to a less favourable one? Some studies suggest that yes, you will (e.g., Evans & Stukas, 2007; North & Swann, 2009). According to **self-verification theory**, we want others to see us as we see ourselves; even when our self-concepts are negative, we still prefer that others perceive our self-concepts as accurate (Swann, Stein-Seroussi, & Gieslder, 1992). Self-verification, even of negative traits, gives us the illusion of having control or ensuring some level of predictability, which is reassuring. In long-term relationships with significant others, we need to self-verify in order to feel secure and develop intimacy (Kraus & Chen, 2009). Because self-verification reduces anxiety and leads to greater harmony in interactions, we are likely to be involved with groups and social organizations that reinforce our perceptions of ourselves (Seyle & Swann, 2007).

## SELF-MONITORING

While self-presentation is a general human concern, some people are more likely than others to adapt their self-presentation depending on the situation and social group. Some people try to match the types of people they are with the situations they are in (Snyder, Berscheid, & Glick, 1985). These individuals, known as high **self-monitors**, are more likely to

^^^ **When someone asks your opinion about their clothing,** do you manage the impression you want to make **or are you completely honest?**

change their opinions or behaviours to fit the context. Self-monitoring scales measure this tendency in people via true/false statements, like "At parties and social gatherings, I do not attempt to do or say things that others will like" and "I laugh more when I watch a comedy with others than when alone" (e.g., Lennox & Wolfe, 1984; Snyder, 1974). Although this conceptualization of self-monitoring does not fully encompass our strategies in self-presentation (e.g., Briggs & Cheek, 1988), situational and social contexts are highly relevant in determining how we choose to act.

Assuming that high self-monitors would be more concerned than others with having an attractive dating partner, Snyder et al. (1985) performed a study in which they asked male college students to choose one of two women to take on a date. The first woman was highly unattractive (rated 1.87/7 on an attractiveness scale), but participants were told that she was open and outgoing, listened well to others, and had a great sense of humour. The other woman was quite attractive (5.75/7) but was described as being shy, self-centred, and moody. As expected, the participants identified as *low* self-monitors were more likely to choose the first woman, demonstrating that physical appearance was not of primary concern in their choice of dating partners. The *high* self-monitors, on the other hand, mostly chose the woman who was more attractive.

Self-monitoring may also play a role in online dating scenarios (e.g., Toma & Hancock, in press). As discussed earlier, we can be more selective about how we present ourselves when creating an online profile. It should come as no great surprise that people tend to lie about things like age, salary, and weight—components of our level of attractiveness to potential mates—when creating profiles for a dating website (e.g., Toma & Hancock, 2010). Is there a pattern to the way people lie on dating sites? Hancock, Toma, and Ellison (2007) guessed that members of dating websites would engage in self-monitoring practices when creating their personal profiles. Noting that men tend to look for physical attractiveness and youth in a dating partner, whereas women are more concerned with social status (education and career), the researchers proposed that women would be more likely to lie about factors like age and weight, whereas men would be more likely to lie about height—a characteristic often associated with status and power. Their findings confirmed that such self-monitoring does occur; women consistently under-reported their weight, while men consistently over-reported their height, though the magnitude of deception was small (Hancock et al., 2007).

"Who are you?" may seem like a simple question, but it is clear that our identities are complex and multilayered. Often, they are strongly influenced by external factors and situations, and an inherent need to feel good about ourselves can sometimes make self-understanding challenging and unclear. What has this chapter taught you about yourself? In the next chapter, we'll turn the tables on other individuals and look at how we perceive people in our social environment.

^^^ Who is telling the truth on dating websites? Research shows that almost nine out of 10 people **lie about themselves in their online dating profiles (Hancock et al., 2007).**

CHAPTER

# 04 Review

## Summary

### WHAT IS SELF-CONCEPT, AND WHERE DOES IT COME FROM? p. 60

• Our self-concepts are made up of all the various beliefs we hold about ourselves. They develop as we mature, and they are apt to change depending on circumstances and context.
• According to social identity theory, we develop our identity from our group memberships. Culture may impact the influence of the social groups we belong to.
• Our self-concepts are influenced by our behaviour (self-perception theory) and our awareness of how close our ideal selves are to our actual selves. Our self-concepts are tied to our motivation too; if we believe we are doing something for its own sake (intrinsic motivation), we are more likely to enjoy it.

### IN WHAT WAYS DOES OUR NEED FOR SELF-ESTEEM MOTIVATE OUR ACTIONS? p. 67

• To maintain a high self-esteem, people often engage in biased thinking when assigning responsibility for the causes of events or outcomes. High self-esteem can lead to more happiness and success, but it can also cause stress and anxiety in attempts to attain it. We also engage in biased, self-serving thinking in the ways we compare ourselves to others.

### HOW DO WE REPRESENT OURSELVES TO OTHERS? p. 71

• Because the self occupies an important place in our thoughts, we often believe that we occupy an important place in other people's thoughts, and, as a result, we go to great lengths to control the way others perceive us.
• We may modify our behaviour so that our opinions and attitudes seem to match those of the people we are around, or we may use flattery to get others to like us. We feel most comfortable when we are around people who see us as we see ourselves.

## Key Terms

**affective forecasting** the process of predicting the impact future events will have on our overall emotional states *64*

**attribution** deciding who or what is responsible for the outcome of a situation; another way we cope with failure and respond to success in order to maintain self-esteem *69*

**BIRGing** "basking in reflected glory," a strategy by which we reinforce our positive self-concepts by identifying ourselves with successful others *71*

**collectivism** a cultural focus on the self as interdependent and defined by the connectedness of people to one another—in particular, the people closest to them *63*

**CORFing** "cutting off reflective failure," a strategy by which we try to disassociate ourselves from others who have failed or behaved poorly *71*

**downward social comparison** the process of comparing yourself to someone who is less capable or worse off than you are *71*

**extrinsic motivation** the drive to perform an action in response to an external pressure or obligation, to avoid punishment, or to achieve some outside benefit *66*

**facial feedback hypothesis** a hypothesis that states that a change in our facial expressions can lead to a subsequent emotional change *65*

**individualism** at the cultural level, a focus on the self as independent from others and a valuing of individual goals over the collective *63*

**ingratiation** a way of controlling others' impressions of us through flattery *72*

**intrinsic motivation** the drive to perform an action because we enjoy it and are likely to engage in it more fully and with greater curiosity and pleasure *66*

**introspection** the process of thinking about your own thoughts *64*

**self-awareness** when attention is brought about on the self; for example, looking in a mirror, standing in front of a crowd, and listening to a recording of your voice *65*

**self-concept** your mental representation or overall sense of "you" *60*

**self-discrepancy theory** a theory in which our concepts of self are influenced by how close our actual selves are to the selves we would like to be *64*

**self-efficacy** a person's belief in his or her ability to achieve certain goals *60*

**self-esteem** a person's evaluation of his or her self-worth *66*

**self-handicapping** a process that involves setting up an obstacle before engaging in a task as a way to give ourselves a ready-made excuse in case we don't perform well *71*

**self-monitoring** the process through which people regulate their behaviour to be perceived well by others; low self-monitors act consistently across situations, acting according to their personal views, while high self-monitors are constantly monitoring their behaviour and adjusting their reactions to fit the situation they are in *72*

**self-perception theory** a theory in which, if we are unsure of the attitudes we hold, we look to our behaviour and use that to make inferences about our attitudes, much like an outside observer *65*

**self-schema** beliefs about aspects of your identity that organize the processing of information related to the self *60*

**self-serving attribution** a self-protection strategy in which we are likely to believe that external factors are responsible for situations in which we perform poorly *69*

**self-verification theory** a theory wherein we want others to see us as we see ourselves—even when our self-concepts are negative *72*

**social comparison theory** a theory wherein we compare ourselves to others in different situations because there is no given standard against which to measure our abilities and opinions *70*

**social identity theory** a theory in which we develop our identity from our group memberships *62*

**spotlight effect** the belief that our behaviour, our appearance, and even our internal states are obvious to others *72*

**unrealistic optimism** optimism that occurs when we tend to imagine that the outcomes of situations will be better for us than for other people *70*

## Test Your Understanding

### MULTIPLE CHOICE

1. Why does research show that you are more likely to be happy with the outcome of a decision when you "go with your gut"?
   - **a.** because if we hesitate, we may lose an opportunity
   - **b.** because we are not always in touch with our true feelings and motivations
   - **c.** because we often make decisions to please others
   - **d.** because most decisions don't really matter anyway

2. Because Clive Wearing's memory was severely impaired,
   - **a.** he had low self-esteem.
   - **b.** he was unable to remember how to play music.
   - **c.** he had no frame of reference on which to construct his self-concept.
   - **d.** he was highly self-aware.

3. According to self-discrepancy theory,
   - **a.** when others have a poor opinion of us, we are likely to confirm that opinion.
   - **b.** we are more motivated to do things that challenge the way other people see us.
   - **c.** we present different selves in different situations.
   - **d.** if you perceive a large gap between your actual and ideal selves, then you will generally have a more negative self-image.

4. In which situation(s) might you engage in BIRGing?
   - **a.** when your school's football team wins a game
   - **b.** when a family member loses a job
   - **c.** when a friend gets his name in the paper for an accomplishment
   - **d.** when you win a race

5. Which is a hazard of unrealistic optimism?
   - **a.** It may lead you to under-prepare for an event.
   - **b.** You may disappoint someone who was counting on you.
   - **c.** It may lead you to perceive others in a more positive light.
   - **d.** You might make others feel insecure about their own abilities.

6. As opposed to Western cultures, Asian cultures tend to
   - **a.** emphasize the connectedness of people to one another.
   - **b.** emphasize the individual's achievements.
   - **c.** emphasize the individual's identity as distinct from his or her social group.
   - **d.** make choices that will set them apart from others in a group.

7. In which situation(s) might you engage in the false consensus bias?
   - **a.** when you hold a prejudiced view about someone
   - **b.** when you binge after trying to keep yourself to a strict diet
   - **c.** when you think that you are better than everyone else
   - **d.** when your friend tells you that he stole something from a convenience store

8. People with high self-efficacy
   - **a.** are more likely than others to achieve their goals.
   - **b.** are more likely than others to change their behaviour in response to a situation.
   - **c.** have an overall positive feeling about themselves.
   - **d.** are engaging in biased behaviour.

9. Mueller and Dweck (1998) found that when children were praised for their high intelligence after completing a task that they initially found fun,
   - **a.** they developed strong self-concepts.
   - **b.** they were less likely to take risks that could result in failure on future tasks.
   - **c.** they were likely to tell their friends.
   - **d.** they were likely to help others after they had finished future tasks.

10. If you believe your motivation for performing a certain action is extrinsic, what are you likely to do?
    - **a.** work harder to achieve your goals
    - **b.** spend more time at the task
    - **c.** find other, similar tasks to undertake
    - **d.** lose interest in the task

**ANSWERS:** 1. b; 2. c; 3. d; 4. a; 5. a; 6. a; 7. a; 8. a; 9. b; 10. d

### ESSAY RESPONSE

1. Use your own experience to define and explain social identity theory. In which situations do you find yourself more likely to identify with a group? When are you most likely to see yourself as an individual? In what ways might this be culturally influenced?
2. Based on what you've learned about motivation, make a case for a hypothetical community service program you could implement at your university. What would you do to ensure that students were highly motivated to engage in the work, both now and in their futures?
3. Develop a hypothetical experiment in which you could test the false consensus bias as it applies to cheating on college or university exams. How would you develop and implement the study?
4. Describe three situations in which social comparison could be a useful tactic, contributing to a healthy self-concept.
5. A number of studies have shown that self-verification reduces anxiety levels. Based on what you now know about self-verification theory and self-concept in general, why might this be the case?

### APPLY IT!

Browse a number of online profiles for a social networking site to which you belong (Facebook, MySpace, LinkedIn, Match.com, etc.). Do you notice any self-serving biases in the way people present themselves? Which self-schemata seem to be the most important for people? If you know the people personally, how closely do their profiles match what you know about them? Explain your observations in terms of the concepts you've learned in this chapter.

**Remember to check www.thethinkspot.ca for additional information, downloadable flashcards, and other helpful resources.**

# SOCIAL PERCEPTION: HOW DO WE PERCEIVE OTHERS?

***<<< How do we decide what causes other people's behaviour?***

**NONVERBAL COMMUNICATION:** HOW DO WE COMMUNICATE WITHOUT WORDS?

**TO WHAT** DO WE ATTRIBUTE PEOPLE'S BEHAVIOURS?

**HOW** DO WE DECIDE WHAT OTHER PEOPLE ARE LIKE?

Canadian country pop superstar Shania Twain had kept her personal life and marriage to music producer Robert John "Mutt" Lange private. That is, until it was discovered that her husband had an affair with her former best friend, Marie-Anne Thiebaud in 2008. Their highly public divorce was made official in June 2010, but this country legend had withdrawn from the public eye even before that time. Rumours about what happened, why he cheated on her, and why Shania was not speaking out about her ordeal became a common topic of conversation. Why did he cheat on her? Why did he have an affair with a comparatively unattractive woman? Why the betrayal with her best friend? What was Thiebaud's role in the affair?

You probably asked yourself these questions, but what did you think at the time regarding the reasons why? Did Robert Lange cheat on his wife because something was so internally wrong with him that he literally couldn't control himself? Could it be considered an illness? Or did you think he did it because, at his core, he is simply a selfish person who cares more about his own needs than those of his loved ones? Did you consider the possibility of situational factors? Maybe the relationship was already on the rocks when Lange chose infidelity. Maybe the pressures of the celebrity spotlight and life with a famous country star caused him to act in ways he wouldn't have otherwise.

It was not until 2011 that Shania Twain announced her return to the music scene and began to speak publicly about her personal trials and future aspirations. In an interview on *Oprah*, Twain stated that she was devastated by the breakup of her marriage but that it had led to a sense of empowerment and a new perspective on life (Shenfeld, 2011). Further, after a five-year music hiatus and being diagnosed with dysphonia (musculature squeezing of the voice box), she is more determined than ever to reclaim her musical career. In fact, this songbird seems back on track. She remarried, and was recently inducted into the Canadian Music Hall of Fame at the 2011 Juno Awards. She also received a star on the Hollywood Walk of Fame the same year (Paloucek, 2011).

What causes people to act as they do, and how do we decide to *believe* why people behave the way they do? Why is it that one of your friends thinks "Mutt" Lange is an inherently horrible person while another feels bad for him? This chapter will take a look at the many ways we perceive others and the psychological theories behind them. But first, it is necessary to consider nonverbal behaviour, given that this is the first thing we frequently use to form our first impressions.

# CHAPTER 05

**NONVERBAL CUES** behaviours, gestures, and expressions that convey thought or emotion without words

## Nonverbal Communication: How Do We Communicate Without Words?

Part of navigating our social environments is deciphering others' true thoughts, feelings, and intentions. This is crucial precisely because they have a powerful impact on us. When we first meet someone, we often observe the person's behaviour in order to determine his or her intentions. If a person makes us a promise, we must decide whether or not we trust that person to keep it. If someone compliments us, we must decide if we believe that the individual is being genuine or if there is some underlying motive for the compliment. If we need a favour, we are most likely to get what we need if we can determine who the best person is to ask. Who is most likely to help? Who has the skill set most appropriate for assisting? These decisions are difficult to make because the inner lives of others are invisible to us—but that does not stop us from inferring the content of those inner lives (i.e., making dispositional attributions). We regularly infer the thoughts and feelings of others to try to come to understand them. On what do we base these inferences?

Given that people often do not disclose their true motives, thoughts, and feelings, we must use **nonverbal cues** to try to decipher them. But this is not the whole story. Our automatic tendency to make inferences about others and categorize information persists even when we are not trying to learn about others or even actively attending to their behaviours. In both of these cases, nonverbal cues are paramount. The basic methods of nonverbal communication will lead to inferences by others, whether conscious or not.

"These decisions are difficult to make because the inner lives of others are invisible to us—**but that does not stop us from inferring the content of those inner lives**."



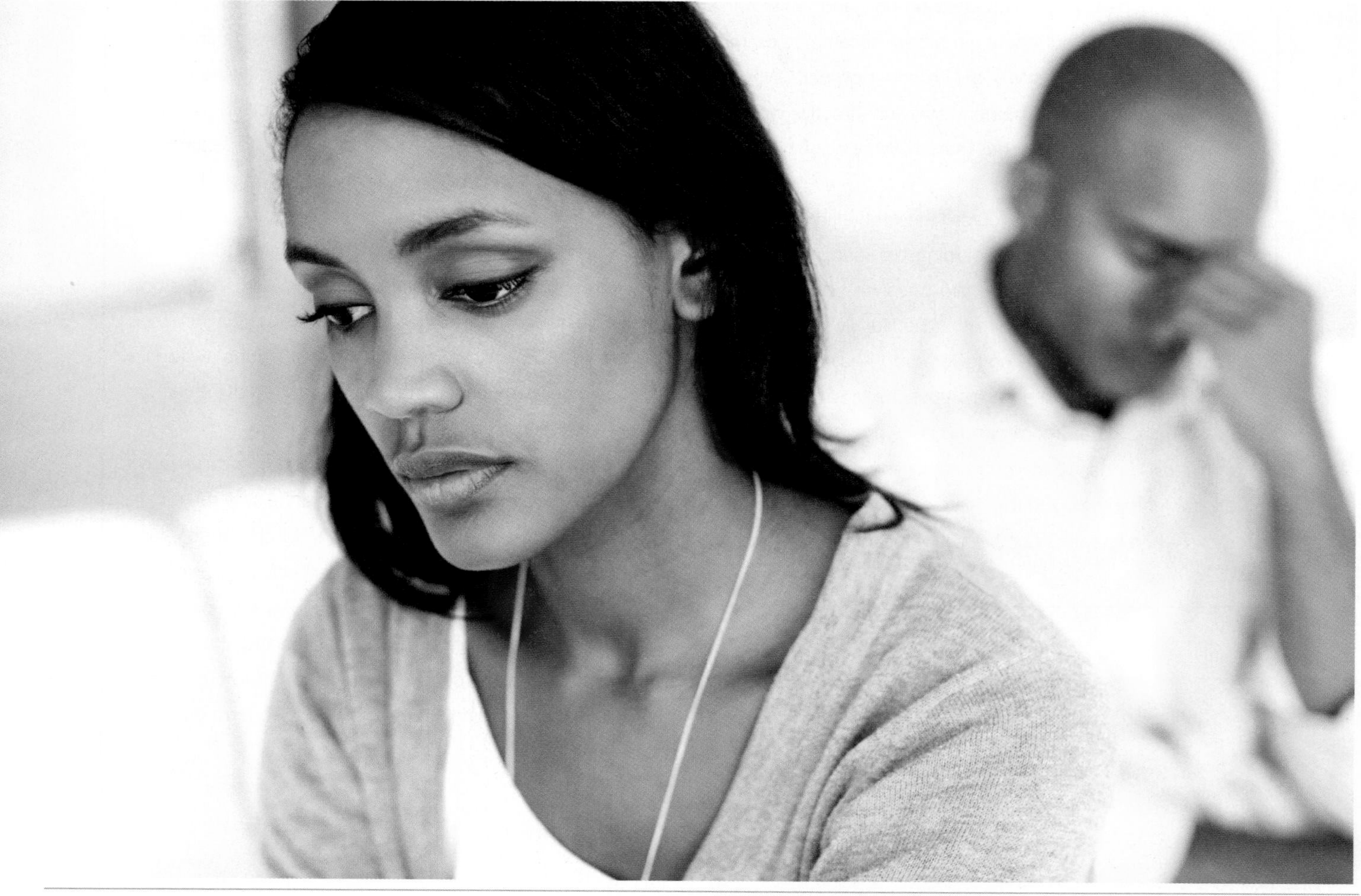

"Just go. It's fine." **People's nonverbal behaviours can communicate a wealth of information** that may be contradictory to their words.

## EMOTIONAL EXPRESSION

There are many sorts of nonverbal behaviours that people tend to use, which fall into five basic channels of nonverbal behaviour: facial expressions, eye contact, body movements, posture, and touching (Knapp & Hall, 2006). Facial expressions, for one, are so fundamental to communication that six basic emotions are conveyed with the same expressions across cultures: happiness, fear, sadness, anger, surprise, and disgust (Ekman, 1994). For example, people in both Western and Eastern cultures will identify a furrowed brow and pursed lips as anger. Recent evidence from University of British Columbia researcher Jessica Tracy indicates that pride and shame may be additional basic emotions that are recognized by others across cultures (e.g., Tracy & Matsumoto, 2008; Tracy & Robins, 2008). Further, each of these emotions can be readily identified using standardized facial emotion coding systems (e.g., Tracy, Robins, & Schriber, 2009).

Some argue that this constancy reflects the fact that these are the core emotions upon which all other emotions are built. For example, frustration could be seen as a combination of anger and disgust.

**Emotions Across Cultures.** These faces are recognized as reflecting the same emotions across different cultures.

**MICROEXPRESSIONS** involuntary expressions of facial emotion that only last a fraction of a second

However, the tendency of people around the globe to use the same expressions to reflect these basic emotions suggests the primacy of facial expression in nonverbal communication, no matter the language spoken. The varied muscles in the face all play a role—a crooked smile can convey mischief, while a raised eyebrow can convey doubt or surprise. These expressions can be *automatically* evoked. For example, when reminded of someone you love dearly, you will likely automatically exhibit positive facial expressions (e.g., Andersen & Berk, 1998). Although we may attempt to conceal our emotions, we actually reveal **microexpressions**—very brief and involuntary facial expressions that reflect our underlying emotions (Ekman, 2007). Independent of whether we intend to display our emotions or not, we automatically do through microexpressions. Luckily, such fleeting expressions are often undetected by the untrained eye. However, trained professionals (such as the character Dr. Cal Lightman in the hit television series *Lie to Me*) have used analysis of microexpressions to detect concealed emotion and deception (e.g., Ekman, 2009).

One especially notable aspect of facial expression is eye gaze and movement. Without the eyes, interpreting the emotions of others can be a frustrating endeavour. If a person makes eye contact, her intentions seem more genuine, and she seems more confident. In fact, continued eye contact is usually a sign of positive regard and attention. Despite that, an unwavering stare can even be intimidating. Darting eyes may suggest anxiety, while a lowered gaze may suggest shame or guilt. Simply changing one's gaze direction or intensity can powerfully impact what is communicated to others. For example, recent research suggests that we can communicate the presence of environmental danger simply by a displaying a directed gaze with a fearful expression; this combination then activates fear-processing and "fight-or-flight" areas in the brains of other individuals (Hadjikhani, Hoge, Snyder, & de Gelder, 2008). Further, culture may partially determine the types of gazes we display. In a study of "thinking" behaviour, McCarthy, Lee, Itakura, and Muir (2006) found that Canadian, Trinidadian, and Japanese participants all had varied gaze displays (i.e., up/down, direct contact) for thinking exercises associated with known or unknown answers.

The rest of the body, too, conveys information to others about intentions and feelings. Research has shown that gesturing works together with speech to create meaning (McNeill, Cassell, & McCullough, 1994). One fairly straightforward form of body language involves the speed of one's motions. If someone is fidgeting, rubbing his or her arms rapidly, or engaging in some other repeated, quick motion, it is easy to infer that the person is aroused, whether in a positive or negative way. Gestures can range from small movements, like a roll of the eyes, to large movements, such as an entire body posture. Importantly, what is communicated by one part of the body may not map onto what is communicated by another part—this is likely due to some part being monitored and regulated by the actor to appear a certain way, while other parts reflect underlying feelings. These inconsistencies are often called *interchannel discrepancies* and may be useful for detecting deception and concealed emotions (e.g., Vrij, Granhag, & Porter, 2010).

It is important to note that differences in situational context can result in the exact same nonverbal behaviour being interpreted in very different ways. Imagine your friend is sitting next to you reading a book. You ask her what she wants to order for dinner, and she shrugs. How would you interpret that behaviour? Probably as ambivalent but calm. Now imagine she is instead your girlfriend, and you asked her if she minded if you went out with your friends instead of staying with her, and she shrugged. How would you interpret that behaviour? It would probably be taken as more hostile than in the former example. The gestures were identical, but the interpretation of them hinged on the context. The actions and their subsequent interpretations can also depend on *who* uses them. For example, if a child cries, people will usually infer that she is sad. If a man cries, many people will (unfortunately!) consider that he is weak or overly sensitive. Much of social psychology rests on this notion—that our understanding of the world is an intricate interaction of person and situation factors.

## DETECTING DECEPTION

Imagine it is summer, and you're living with your parents again until the fall semester begins. You got used to going where you wanted to, when you wanted to, but now your parents want to know everything you do. You really want to go to a concert, but you don't have anyone to go with, and your parents would never let you go alone. The night of the concert comes, and your parents ask you with whom you're going. What do you do? How will you convince them that your friend really *is* coming with you?

Given all the methods of communication that occur without awareness, one might expect that we would be fairly good at detecting lies in others. However, this is not the case (Vrij, 2008). We are only slightly better than 50 percent accurate at detecting lies—that is, only slightly above chance, or as accurate as we'd be if we flipped a coin. This is in part because we tend to assume that people are generally honest (i.e., we have a truth bias; Peace & Sinclair, 2012), and as such don't attend to possible clues that they might be being dishonest.

This faulty belief is especially incredible considering that we tend to lie—and often. People tell at least one lie every day, though we don't lie equally to everyone; we mostly lie to strangers, and we lie much less often to family and friends (DePaulo & Kashy, 1998). Why might that

<<< **Facial expressions of *pride* may be** another basic emotion that is recognized by others across cultures.

be? We lie for many reasons. One reason is self-presentation—we lie so that others will see us how we want to be seen. However, once we know someone well, that person knows us well, too, and it is thus harder to tell a convincing lie to that person.

Moreover, **self-verification** needs may take over (Swann & Read, 1981)—we want others to see us as we see ourselves—and as such, we are less likely to be intentionally dishonest (we were first introduced to this concept in Chapter 4). In addition, we may be somewhat more likely to feel guilty about manipulating a loved one with lies. However, that does not suggest that we do not still lie to loved ones, but that we may do so to spare their feelings or to avoid the repercussions of some misbehaviour (Cole, 2001).

**SELF-VERIFICATION** the motivation of an individual for others to know him or her accurately, including his or her negative features

## How to Detect Deception

There are several nonverbal behaviours that have been identified as being indicative of deception. For one, the briefly exhibited facial expressions mentioned earlier (microexpressions) may be indicative of deception if they differ from the subsequently expressed, intentional facial posturing (Ekman, 2007). Another possibility is that the emotion exhibited by one body part or gesture may vary from another part or gesture (i.e., interchannel discrepancies; Vrij, 2008). If a person smiles broadly at you but shifts uncomfortably on her feet, she is likely to not be as calm as she may have initially appeared.

What we say is also an indicator of whether or not we are lying. For example, people will use different words, recall fewer details, fail to recount conversations or describe visual images, and tend not to be as consistent in the content of their speech when lying relative to telling the truth (e.g., Peace & Porter, 2011; Vrij, Evans, Akehurst, & Mann, 2004). Further, truth-tellers provide more coherent reports, engage in more spontaneous corrections (i.e., "Oh, oops, I meant it happened on a Friday"), and recall events in a more unstructured fashion (Peace, Brower, & Shudra, in press). In fact, verbal cues tend to be better indicators of deception than nonverbal cues (DePaulo et al., 2003). While nonverbal cues do exist and can indicate lying, they are not as good as predicting lies in real-life interactions.

Moreover, the nonverbal cues that are typically thought to indicate lying do not always indicate deception. Research by Mann, Vrij, and Bull (2004) showed that police officers who were considered experts at lie detection and had experience in it were only accurate 65 percent of the time in detecting lies. Notably, their use of nonverbal behaviours such as gaze aversion or fidgeting, which are often thought to be indicative of deception, was negatively correlated with accuracy; it *decreased* their rate of accuracy. Such nonverbal behaviours may be associated more with arousal rather than deception and may vary widely across culture. For example, one of the authors of this text (KP) once had a conversation with a police officer who indicated that he believed Aboriginal suspects lie frequently because they do not look him in the eye. However, what he failed to acknowledge was that in traditional Aboriginal cultures, it is a sign of disrespect to make direct eye contact, as it is considered confrontational (also see Porter & ten Brinke, 2009). Those who tend to demonstrate enhanced accuracy in detecting lies are more likely to report using cues from the story itself, such as the number of details provided to describe it (e.g., Peace et al., in press; Vrij et al., 2010).

Detecting deception remains equally important in online environments, in which many people spend most of their days. However, it is increasingly difficult. Despite the importance of the words we use, the absence of nonverbal cues creates a deficit in the ability to detect deceit. Liars in an Internet setting used more words, fewer first-person pronouns (e.g., "I"), more third-person pronouns (e.g., "she"), and more terms that referenced the senses (e.g., "saw") (e.g., Hancock, Curry, Goorha, & Woodworth, 2008). The increase in words may seem to contrast with liars' tendency to provide less detail, but it may be that liars will embellish under normal conditions but hesitate to do so when a suspect in a crime for fear of saying something that would reveal the lie. Despite this, the recipient of the lies communicated online, in most cases, was unable to use these cues to detect the lie (e.g., Hancock, Woodworth, & Goorha, 2010).

As you can see, our evaluations of nonverbal behaviour have important consequences for how we feel about others and how we interpret

>>> How do we know **when someone is lying?**

**DISPOSITIONAL ATTRIBUTION** inferring that a person's traits, something internal, caused his or her behaviour

**SITUATIONAL ATTRIBUTION** inferring that the situation a person is in—something external to the person—caused his or her behaviour

**CORRESPONDENT INFERENCE THEORY** the theory that people base their inferences regarding the source of others' behaviours on whether or not the behaviour was freely chosen, if the consequences are distinctive, and if the behaviour was socially desirable

**COVARIATION THEORY** the theory that people base their inferences regarding the source of others' behaviours on whether or not there is a consensus regarding the way one ought to respond, the distinctiveness of the response, and the consistency of the person's response across situations

their behaviour. That said, nonverbal behaviour is not the only component we consider in our social perceptions.

# To What Do We Attribute People's Behaviours?

Think back to the chapter opener describing Shania Twain's situation and the actions of her ex-husband. Two of your friends have vastly different opinions on why Lange chose to behave the way he did. On one hand, Evan thinks that men who cheat on their wives are simply bad people. Why? He says they are selfish and insincere. That sort of explanation is a **dispositional attribution**. Evan thinks their hurtful decisions are the results of inherent parts of their personalities. However, your other friend Natasha gives them the benefit of the doubt. She thinks that men who cheat may be motivated by already failing relationships. She makes a **situational attribution**. This distinction can also be seen as an internal versus external attribution for behaviour; a person engages in some act because of something intrinsic (dispositional) to him or her or because of something extrinsic (situational). Internal attributions are made when behaviours are believed to be caused by personal or dispositional attributes (i.e., stable personality traits), whereas external attributions are made when behaviours are believed to result from the situation (i.e., temporary or contextual factors).



## CORRESPONDENT INFERENCE THEORY

Why do people make one type of inference over another? Several theories have been developed to explain this process. One such theory is **correspondent inference theory** (Jones & Davis, 1965). This theory suggests that people are more likely to attribute behaviour to others' personalities based on three factors. The first is *whether or not the behaviour was freely chosen*. If someone is forced into an action, people will generally not make an attribution to the person's traits. However, if the person chose to act in that way, and could have acted in any other way instead if he or she so desired, a dispositional attribution will be made. For example, if a cashier at your local Superstore smiles at customers because the store has imposed a rule that cashiers must smile, that behaviour does not say anything about the cashier's personality because she has to do it. However, if there was no such rule, the cashier might be judged as being a friendly person.

The second factor is *whether or not the behaviour is what would be expected given the situation*. For example, if someone acts nicely and respectfully to an old person, one might infer that it is not that the actor is a particularly nice person, but instead that acting in such a way is what one is supposed to do. By contrast, if that same person yells at the old person, completely unprovoked, one would instead consider the actor to be mean. Behaviour in accordance with situational expectations doesn't tell us much about the person himself or herself.

The third factor is *what the consequences of a given action are*. If there are multiple positive consequences of an action, it is difficult to isolate which of them may have caused the action. By contrast, if there is only one positive consequence of an action, it can generally be assumed to be the cause. For example, if a frozen microwavable dinner tastes terrible but is low in calories, it can be assumed that the consumer may be dieting and bought it because of its low calories. After all, why else would one intentionally choose a food that tastes bad? However, if it is also delicious, it is unclear what prompted the purchase, and nothing can be inferred about the buyer.

## COVARIATION THEORY

Another theory designed to explain the attributions people make is covariation theory. **Covariation theory** (e.g., Kelley, 1972; Kelley & Michela, 1980) focuses on the factors that are present when a particular behaviour does or does not occur—that is, what *covaries* with the behaviour. While this depends somewhat on which information in the surrounding context people pay attention to when making their attributions, we generally rely on three specific types of information when making judgments of others.

The first is the *consensus* regarding a behaviour. That is, if most people would behave in a certain way in a given situation, the behaviour does not reflect anything unique about the actor. For example, as in the example at the beginning of the chapter, if most people in our society are unfaithful to their spouses, then nothing is notable about the behaviour of Shania Twain's ex-husband. However, since cheating isn't widely accepted, the behaviour reflects something personal. The second consideration is *distinctiveness*. This refers to the distinctiveness of the individual's behaviour in the given situation as compared with all other situations. If Lange only cheated once or with one woman, then it is likely a situational factor that evoked an isolated behaviour from him (i.e., an infidelity while intoxicated). However, if he regularly cheated when given the opportunity, it is probably indicative of his personality. The third and final consideration is *consistency*. Consistency refers to the reaction of the individual to a particular stimulus over repeated experiences with the stimulus in different situations. If the person always responds in the same way to the stimulus across all contexts, then that behaviour can be given a dispositional attribution. If the person does not, then that variation in behaviour can be attributed to the context. For example, if every time Lange encounters a potential mistress, he cheats, he may have a disloyal personality. By contrast, if he only cheated after a fight with Shania, then regardless of whether he is right or wrong, the situation had an influence on his choice.

Research on covariation theory has demonstrated that people may rely on consensus, distinctiveness, and consistency information differently depending on whether or not they are aware of their own attributional process. For example, a study conducted at the University of Western Ontario by Hazlewood and Olson (1986) found that when participants were exposed to covariation information that implied either a personal or a situational attribution, their ratings concerning an interaction with an impolite confederate followed in line with the information they were given. Specifically, if participants were told that the confederate was the only one who refused to answer personal questions in an interview (*low consensus*), and that she did the same thing in a previous interview (*high consistency*), and that she refused to answer other questions (*low distinctiveness*), participants inferred that it was likely the confederate had a rude and impolite disposition. The same pattern was evidenced when participants were given information that suggested the confederate's behaviour was something to do with the situation (i.e., the questions being asked of the confederate were inappropriate and made people uncomfortable). However, if participants were asked questions about their attributions following their exposure to the impolite confederate (and the personal or situational covariation information), they seemed less certain about the cause of the confederate's behaviour (Hazlewood & Olson, 1986).

Another factor that influences covariation is emotion. Eyre (2000) found that when participants were given scenarios about emotion-eliciting events that varied according to the type of emotion (i.e., anger, anxiety, depression, happiness), participants were much less likely to make situational attributions when the scenario depicted a depressed individual relative to all the other emotions. These findings suggest that when certain emotions or traits are unlikely to be caused by the situation (such as depression), we tend to automatically interpret these as features of one's disposition or personality. Further, positive emotions such as happiness appear to be more variable in our attributions relative to negative emotions (Eyre, 2000). That is, when people are happy, we tend to make situational and dispositional attributions based on information available. Conversely, when confronted with negative emotions, we tend to err on the side of personal attributions, which were perhaps advantageous in evolutionary history to avoid threats (e.g., Ekman, 2007; Green & Phillips, 2004).

## HOW DO BIASES COME INTO PLAY?

The two theories just discussed both assume that people are logical and rational in their tendency to attribute causes to behaviour. However, as with any social psychological phenomenon, there is a rational as well as a biased side to human behaviour and cognition. When deciding whether a behaviour is due to an individual's disposition or to the *situation*, people are biased first and foremost by their own perspectives. When we perform an action, we aren't looking at ourselves; we're looking out at our world, our environment. Therefore, the situation we are in is most salient. By contrast, when we are observing another person's actions, *that person* is what is most salient to us. We may not even be aware of the entire situation that person is in. For example, imagine you are standing in line waiting for your morning coffee and a man who was not in line walks right up to the till in front of everyone else. Your initial reaction is that the man is rude and inconsiderate (dispositional traits), but what you are not aware of is that he had already waited in line as a customer but the cream in his coffee was curdled, so he was bringing it back. As such, when we are the actor, we tend to make situational attributions for our behaviour, and when we are the observer, we tend to make dispositional attributions for the behaviour of others. This is referred to as the **correspondence bias**, or more commonly known as the **fundamental attribution error** (Ross, 1977), and it is common in individualistic cultures.

This bias can be to the benefit or detriment of the people being judged. For example, when we watch the news, newscasters such as Peter Mansbridge or Dawna Friesen usually appear to be quite intelligent and informed, and as such, we consider them intelligent people, making a dispositional attribution. However, we neglect to remember that newscasters in general are in prescribed roles and are reading off of cue cards. Although they may, in fact, be intelligent (such as the examples above), they are simply performing their roles. Newscasters, just as with any other group of people, vary considerably in intelligence despite appearances. For example, a longitudinal study of news commentators from both CNN and Fox News found that they were not more accurate in predicting major events such as elections or the future of the economy

**CORRESPONDENCE BIAS** the tendency of people to make dispositional attributions for others' behaviours

**FUNDAMENTAL ATTRIBUTION ERROR** a more commonly known name for the correspondence bias (see previous). The scientific community now leans toward using *correspondence bias* so as not to suggest that these inferences are inherently in "error."

(Tetlock, 2005). Consider another example: how intelligent do you think *Jeopardy* host Alex Trebek is relative to the show's contestants? Research on the fundamental attribution error (e.g., Ross, Amabile, & Steinmetz, 1977) found that individuals who were randomly assigned to be "questioners" were perceived as being more intelligent relative to those assigned to be "respondents" on a series of general knowledge questions—even though they were equally knowledgeable in general!

The fundamental attribution error was first revealed in research wherein volunteers were asked to read an essay about Cuba under Fidel Castro's communist regime and to indicate their impressions of the essayist's attitudes toward Cuba (Jones & Harris, 1967). The essay was either pro- or anti-Castro, and, importantly, the essay was written either freely (i.e., the opinion advocated chosen by the student) or under constraint (i.e., the opinion advocated assigned by an instructor). Independent of whether the attitude expressed in the essay was written freely or assigned, participants reported that the writers held the opinion they advocated in the essay. Most importantly, dispositional attributions were made even when the essayists had been assigned their positions, indicating a situational factor.

This process of attributing traits to others and ignoring the situation occurs quite automatically. Even if we are not asked to form an impression

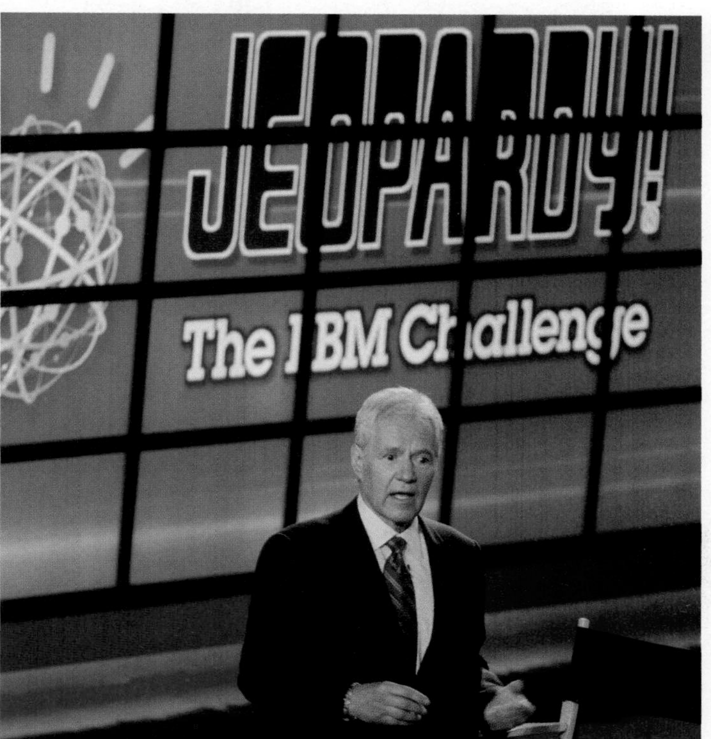


We assume that people in roles in which they are required to appear intelligent **are actually more informed than others**—which is not always true.

**SPONTANEOUS TRAIT INFERENCE** the process of automatically inferring traits from another person's behaviour

of others and have no particular motivation to do so, we will infer traits about even briefly encountered others (e.g., Uleman, 1989; Uleman, Newman, & Moskowitz, 1996). This phenomenon is called **spontaneous trait inferences**. Uleman, Saribay, and Gonzales (2008) asked students to remember information about target persons—statements reflecting specific behaviours the people exhibited. An example of such a sentence might be, "He pushed the woman out of the way to get onto the train." These students immediately and unintentionally inferred traits about these people—for example, "selfish" or "mean" rather than recalling situational aspects of their behaviour such as "commuter" or "subway."

### Culture

Can an individual's culture affect the type of attributions that are made? In individualistic cultures (first discussed in Chapter 1), such as those in Canada, the United States, and England, people tend to focus on the needs and desires of the individual, emphasizing competition between individuals for success, and reliance on the self for that success and happiness. By contrast, collectivistic cultures, such as those in Japan and India, focus on the needs and desires of the group, prioritizing group goals over personal goals. While some research suggests there are no cultural differences in use of the correspondence bias (e.g., Krull et al., 1999), other studies have reported that collectivistic cultures are more likely to use situational attributions and individualistic cultures are more likely to attribute behaviour to a person's disposition (e.g., An, Hui, & Leung, 2001; Higgins & Bhatt, 2001; Miller, 1984; Morris & Peng, 1994; Oyserman, Coon, & Kemmelmeier, 2002).

Notably, these cultural differences become more evident with age, suggesting that increased exposure to the culture and its norms creates these differences in how behaviour is explained (Miller, 1984). Additional research has shown that those with a collectivistic orientation will automatically infer situational causes for behaviour and will *not* make spontaneous trait inferences, as those who are more individualistic do (e.g.,

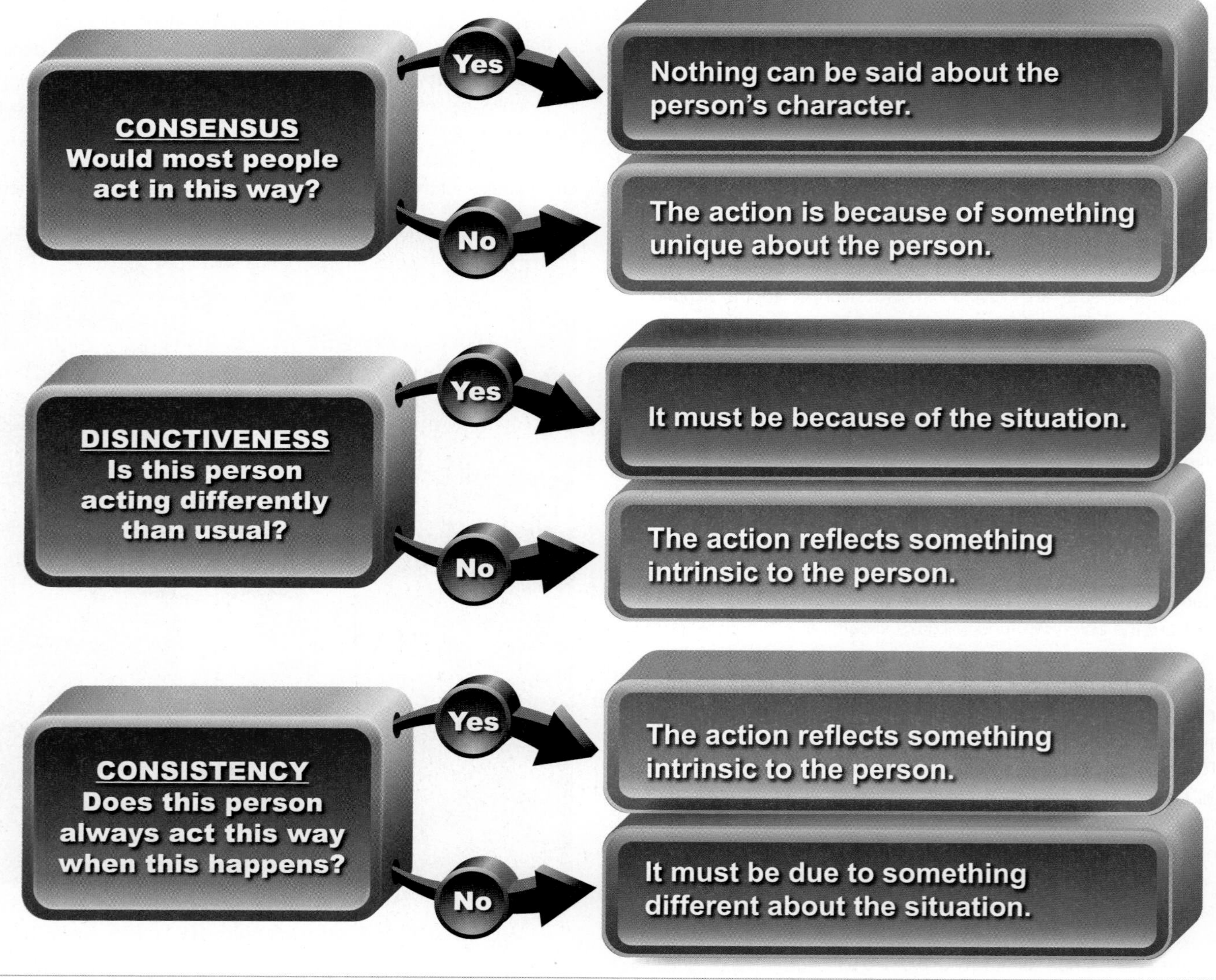
CONSENSUS
Would most people act in this way?
Yes
Nothing can be said about the person's character.
No
The action is because of something unique about the person.
DISINCTIVENESS
Is this person acting differently than usual?
Yes
It must be because of the situation.
No
The action reflects something intrinsic to the person.
CONSISTENCY
Does this person always act this way when this happens?
Yes
The action reflects something intrinsic to the person.
No
It must be due to something different about the situation.

**Decision Making in Covariation Theory.** Consensus, distinctiveness, and consistency all factor into deciding on the source of a behaviour.

Duff & Newman, 1997; Newman, 1993). Thus these cultural differences exist, even when the individual is not asked to directly make a judgment.

## Cognitive Capacity

Does it follow, then, that if you were raised in an individualistic culture, it would be automatic and natural for you to make snap dispositional judgments? If this is the case, then why do Evan and Natasha disagree over attributions about men who cheat on their wives despite having grown up in the same neighbourhood? What about growing up in a multicultural society such as you likely have? Does where you live in Canada and your own cultural background relative to the broader Canadian culture make a difference in your attributions? Say your cultural heritage is Japanese, and your parents still endorse the traditional values they grew up with. The extent to which you are assimilated into the broader individualistic culture or identify more with traditional Japanese collectivistic values will influence your attributions (e.g., Carpenter, 2000; Nisbett, Peng, Choi, & Norenzayan, 2001). In fact, you may endorse both universal and culture-specific features in making causal attributions of behaviour (Higgins & Bhatt, 2001).

> "Does it follow, then, that if you were raised in an individualistic culture, **it would be automatic and natural for you to make snap dispositional judgments?**"

Differences in attributions also may be, in part, explained by our cognitions. In the **three-stage model of attribution**, an observer automatically characterizes a behaviour, automatically makes a dispositional inference, and then uses conscious effort to correct for situational constraints if the observer has the cognitive capacity to do so (Gilbert, Pelham, & Krull, 1988). We often revert solely to automatic judgments because we are experiencing cognitive load (i.e., stress, distraction, preoccupied). However, if we have the time, energy, and motivation to think through our judgments we are more likely to account for situational factors (e.g., Gilbert & Malone, 1995).

For example, you may read a news story about a teenager who was arrested for holding up a local convenience store. A paragraph in, you're thinking about how selfish and violent the teen is. Stealing is always wrong, isn't it? And if he needs money, maybe he should get a job waiting tables like you did in high school. Maybe you toss the paper in the trash. After all, you've automatically characterized the teen's behaviour, and you've made your dispositional inference.

But what if you keep reading? You find out that the teen does have a job, but in addition to being a full-time student, he only has pocket money. And that's not enough, since his father is too sick to work and his mother was just laid off. With two other siblings to support, the teen made a misguided decision in order to help his parents make ends meet. Now what do you think? You have probably changed your opinion and now believe that the teen is not violent, but dealing with unfortunate circumstances. You have gained new knowledge, and it gives you the cognitive capacity to adjust your evaluation of the situation. This is how the third stage of the three-stage model of attribution comes into play.

**THREE-STAGE MODEL OF ATTRIBUTION** a model in which an observer automatically characterizes a behaviour, automatically makes a dispositional inference, and then uses conscious effort to correct for situational constraints if the observer has the cognitive capacity to do so

**NEED FOR COGNITION** the need that some individuals have to think, solve problems, and understand their world accurately

**BELIEF IN A JUST WORLD** people have to believe the world is fair and adjust their other beliefs to maintain that stance by concluding that bad things happen to bad people and good things happen to good people

## The Need for Cognition

One might argue that "errors" such as the correspondence bias might be due to people's lack of effort in understanding the real reasons behind others' behaviour. Some people have what is known as the **need for cognition**, a drive to solve problems; they enjoy thinking, like to analyze everything carefully, and seek to understand their world accurately (Cacioppo et al., 1996). Might these people be less susceptible to the correspondence bias?

Participants in a study examining this question were asked to read a speech either favouring or opposing legal abortion (D'Agostino & Fincher-Kiefer, 1992). In all cases, participants were told that the speechwriter was assigned to the position and as such had no choice. Those low in need for cognition exhibited the traditional correspondence bias: they believed the speech reflected the writer's true attitude. However, those participants high in cognition considered the situational factors in their attributions. Building on the original correspondence bias research (Jones & Harris, 1967), this study demonstrated that this bias can be overcome if one is sufficiently motivated to critically examine ideas and uncover the truth. For example, researchers Ungar and Sev'er (1989) studied the public disbelief and reactions to Canadian athlete Ben Johnson being stripped of his world record and gold medal at the Seoul 1988 Olympic Games. They found that while Canadians initially made dispositional attributions, they noticed a shift toward situational causes as more information and base rate knowledge about use of anabolic steroids was reported in the media.

It is not only effort and motivation to be accurate that can impact one's attributions. Our values and ideology can also alter the types of attributions we make when trying to explain social issues (e.g., poverty, abortion, euthanasia). For example, we all tend to make dispositional attributions when initially assessing behaviour. However, when these attributions differ from our ideological beliefs (i.e., liberal versus conservative), we tend to engage in motivational corrections of our attributions that are in line with our beliefs about the world (e.g., Morgan, Mullen, & Skitka, 2010). For instance, when thinking about AIDS patients, conservatives were more likely to make dispositional attributions for the patients' predicaments, while liberals would initially make dispositional attributions but then adjust to situational attributions (Skitka et al., 2002). Likewise, while liberals tend to make more situational attributions for social problems, conservatives make more situational attributions for military and police misconduct (Morgan et al., 2010).

## Belief in a Just World

It is to our psychological benefit to believe that others are to blame for their own misfortunes; after all, if it were a situation they could not control, those misfortunes could befall us as well. As such, we are motivated to believe that things happen for a just reason—good things happen to good people, and bad things happen to bad people. That is, we have **belief in a just world** (Lerner, 1980). Therefore, since we are evidently

**ACTOR-OBSERVER EFFECT** the tendency people have to make dispositional inferences for others' behaviour but situational attributions for their own

good people (in our own opinions), only good things will happen to us, and, thus, we are safe from harm and need not continually fear the future (Hafer & Bègue, 2005).

Having read that last statement, you are likely to have realized that the extent to which people believe in a just world varies from person to person. Some people, notably those with anxiety or depressive disorders, do fear the future (though belief in a just world is one way of coping with anxiety about the future). However, most people do, to some degree, believe that the world is fair as a self-protective mechanism. The more strongly one holds this belief, the more one will think that people who have fallen on hard times are responsible for their plights. For example, beliefs about certain types of crimes, such as sexual assault, tend to lead to the misconception that victims were "asking for it" or were responsible for being victimized. Also known as *blame attributions* (e.g., Loza & Clements, 1991), such misconceptions in turn lead to judges' and juries' disbelief of a victim's testimony and to less punitive measures being taken against perpetrators (e.g., Hafer, 2000). Further, these attributions may vary by gender, as male victims are often seen as more responsible for their actions than are female victims (Rye, Greatrix, & Enright, 2006).

Belief in a just world causes us to infer that those who have had bad things happen to them must be bad themselves—**and that we, being good people, will never suffer such a fate.**

> "It is to our psychological benefit to believe that others are to blame for their own misfortunes; **after all, if it were a situation they could not control, those misfortunes could befall us as well.**"



Whether we attribute the source of people's behaviour to disposition or situation is not only important because of what it leads us to believe about others; it also has very serious practical implications. If we blame others for their problems, we are less likely to offer them help, with our hands, wallets, or votes. By contrast, if we blame the situation, we do provide help. This, as mentioned earlier, can to some extent be predicted by political ideology—liberals are more likely to attribute the source of social problems such as poverty to the situation and thus are more likely to support aid programs such as welfare, whereas conservatives are more likely to attribute it to the person and thus are against forms of welfare (e.g., Morgan et al., 2010).

### Biases and the Self

There is, even in individualistic cultures, two major exceptions to the correspondence bias. First, the **actor-observer effect** (Jones & Nisbett, 1971) occurs when we make causal attributions about our own behaviour relative to other people's behaviour. When we are the actor, we are privy to knowledge about everything that impacted the decision, including the environment in which we were. But when we are the observer, we are focused on the other person himself or herself and not only have less access to, but also pay less attention to, the environmental factors that may be influencing the other person. That is, we attribute our own behaviour to situational causes and others' behaviour to dispositional causes. Further, if the actor is a member of our in-group, we are more likely to make a situational attribution. But if he or she is in the out-group, we'll probably make a dispositional attribution. For example, imagine you are sitting in one of your classes and another student is being very disruptive. If this student is a close friend, you are likely to interpret their behaviour according to situational causes. However, if the student is not a friend of yours, you will likely believe their disruptiveness is a result of their being rude and disrespectful (e.g., see Higgins & Bryant, 1982).

The second exception to the correspondence bias relates to the interpretation of our own positive and negative outcomes. As discussed in Chapter 4, the self-serving attribution (Miller & Ross, 1975) occurs when we believe that positive outcomes stem from our own abilities (i.e., dispositional causes), whereas negative outcomes are believed to occur due to situational factors. For example, if you get an A+ on an exam that you hardly studied for, you are more likely to attribute your grade to your own intelligence rather than believe that the exam must have been easy. If, however, the outcome was negative and you failed the same exam, you are more likely to believe that the exam was way too hard (situational) rather than admit you didn't study hard enough (dispositional). That said, these biases may be influenced by our cultural background. In a study comparing Japanese and Canadian student samples, Heine and Lehman (1997) found that the cultural background of the participant was important in making attributions that maintained a positive cultural identity for Canadian students. On the other hand, Japanese students

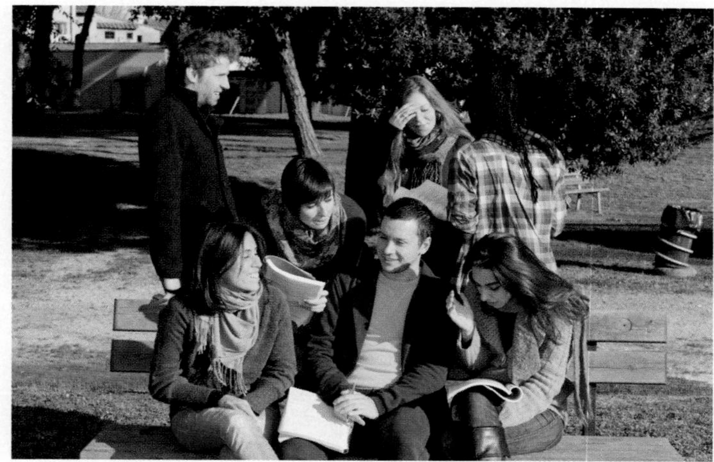

^^^ You might be procrastinating on your schoolwork because you've had a rough week and you're tired, but your classmate might conclude that it's because you're lazy. **The actor-observer effect is the fact that we attribute others' behaviours to dispositions but our own behaviours to the situations.**

evaluated negative behaviours on behalf of members of their own culture as dispositional and part of an "out-group." As a result, some researchers have classified the self-serving bias as more of a "Western" phenomenon and less prevalent in collectivistic cultures (Kitayama, Takagi, & Matsumoto, 1995).

## How Do We Decide What Other People Are Like?

While we would like to believe that our impressions of others are formed deliberately and after careful consideration of a person's behaviour, we would be denying that our impressions are formed nearly instantaneously (see Uleman, Newman, & Moskowitz, 1996 for a review). In fact, research suggests that it takes less than 50 milliseconds to form first impressions of our visual world and the people we meet (e.g., Lindgaard, Fernandes, Dudek, & Brown, 2006; Willis & Todorov, 2006). To see for yourself how rapidly an entire personality is inferred for another person based on very little information, try this exercise: think for a minute how you would picture a person described as being intelligent, skilful, industrious, warm, determined, practical, and cautious. Write down for yourself some immediate thoughts about this person—how you're picturing him. Would you want to work with him? Now consider a different person. This person is described as being intelligent, skilful, industrious, cold, determined, practical, and cautious. Again, quickly write down some thoughts about the person and how you picture him. Would you want to work with him?

Your overall image of these two people is probably quite different. And yet the only difference between the two was that the first was described as being "warm," while the second was described as being "cold." The reason for the influence of these two traits above the others was their *centrality* to personality; the other traits provided were specific ones that describe particular features of a person, whereas warmth is considered to be a more global trait that can encapsulate an entire personality in one word. Thus, even a one-adjective difference in information provided about another person can create profound differences in the overall image formed of that person. This is exactly what Solomon Asch (1946) found in his classic study on impression formation. By altering the adjectives provided about a person to include *cold* instead of *warm*, he dramatically changed the description participants provided about that person (Asch, 1946).

**PRIMACY EFFECT** the phenomenon whereby the first pieces of information to which we are exposed have the most impact on our judgments

**RECENCY EFFECT** the phenomenon whereby the last pieces of information to which we are exposed have heightened impact on our judgments, relative to information received in the middle

Why might this be important? Consider the evaluations you make of your professors when you start a course at the beginning of the semester. Do you think that your first impression influences your interpretation of the professor? Research suggests that it absolutely does! For example, based on the work of Kelley (1950), Widmeyer and Loy (1988) had a visiting professor come in to provide a "neutral" lecture, where half of the class was told beforehand that he was a warm person and the other half was instructed that he was cold and distant. Following the lecture, the students rated the effectiveness of the lecturer and his personality characteristics. Ratings tended to be in accordance with the first impression they were given of the professor, even though both groups saw the same lecture! Further, students' end-of-term evaluations of their professors also tend to be heavily influenced by first impressions (see Ambady & Skowronski, 2008).

In addition, even within the first few minutes of coming to know a person, the very first features of the person hold extreme importance. In one of Asch's early studies, some participants were asked to rate a person described as envious, stubborn, critical, impulsive, industrious, and intelligent. Other participants were asked to rate a person described as intelligent, industrious, impulsive, critical, stubborn, and envious. Note that the lists contain exactly the same information, only in opposite order. The second group, which learned about the person's positive qualities first, rated the person more highly than the first group, which learned about the person's negative qualities first. Moreover, when he examined the relative impact of each individual word, Asch discovered that the first word on the list was of utmost importance in the impressions formed about the person; this is termed the **primacy effect** (Asch, 1946).

Notably, there is another phenomenon termed the **recency effect**, which states that the information presented last will also dominate in memory and have an effect on impressions (Thorndike, 1935). This may lead one to believe that the primacy effect can be undone, but this is not so. The effect of recent information dominates our impressions immediately after the information is presented. However, it does not have the long-term impact on impressions that the primacy effect does. Imagine you went on a blind date and your first impression of your date was that they were rude and inconsiderate. Independent of the fact they may pay for your meal at the end of the date (recency), their rude behaviour will likely have more influence on your decision not to date this individual again (primacy). Recently provided information can affect how others see you right now, but the first impression will affect how they see you later.

These impressions are crucial when trying to navigate one's social world; being aware of the initial impression one conveys to others can have a profound impact. It can also be extremely difficult to monitor the impression others develop of us, because it is not simply contingent upon our own behaviour. For example, social roles play a large part in

**WHAT IS BEAUTIFUL IS GOOD EFFECT** the phenomenon wherein beautiful things are imbued with positivity and activate positive things in the mind

identifying what traits are considered positive for a given person. This is not always a bad thing. We want our mothers to be warm and caring, whereas it is less important for our electricians to act that way; we may simply want them to be professional. However, sometimes these expectations can lead to discrimination when people don't fit in with their prescribed social role. For example, gender-typed roles of women dictate they should be gentle, nurturing, and submissive. As a result, career-driven professional females are often considered to be aggressive, unkind, domineering, and unwomanly, and are promoted less often to managerial level positions (see Heilman, 2001).

Such rapid impressions are thus important in many day-to-day encounters. Consider in your own life how often this is and will be relevant. In a very short time, employers must decide if they will hire you—and you must decide if you want to work for that employer. Do you think that classmate across the room is someone you want to approach for help? And after a first date, do you want to continue to a second? At these times, we know very little about the people we are evaluating, and they know very little about us—but nonetheless, we and they must make character judgments based on this minuscule amount of information.

So what type of information do we have available to us when first meeting someone? One of the first and foremost things we evaluate is the physicality of others. How attractive a person is creates a powerful bias in our behaviour, in what is termed the **what is beautiful is good effect** (Dion, Berscheid, & Walster, 1972). While most people do

## ACTION LEARNING

### Dispositional or Situational?

Consider the attribution biases discussed in the chapter—that is, our tendency to attribute others' actions to their dispositions but our own actions to the relevant situations. Focus on the correspondence bias—the idea that, at least in individualistic cultures, we are more likely to focus on dispositional explanations for behaviour and not take into account the situational constraints. Take one 24-hour period to note all the times you make judgments about another person's behaviour (someone that you don't already know). Record the individual's behaviour and your initial reaction to it (i.e., did you focus on a dispositional or situational explanation?). Take time to consider alternative explanations for why the individuals behaved the way they did and record these as well.

In a separate 24-hour period, record all the occurrences during which you believe others are making judgments about *your* behaviour. Do you think they are making dispositional or situational judgments about your behaviour? Think about how your and others' judgments have been affected by attributional biases. Consider what role culture plays in attributions, such as if a person is from an individualistic or collectivistic culture. Consider what steps you could identify to reduce your own biased impressions in the future. Share your findings with your classmates. What will you learn from this action learning project?

1. You will see how often we all engage in these biases.
2. Research suggests that by becoming aware of when you engage in these biases, you may be more motivated to avoid them in future interactions (e.g., Lilienfeld, Ammirati, & Landfield, 2009; Gergen, 1973).
3. You will gain some insight into why others may react to your behaviours as they do.

Target exhibits a behaviour, like eating fast food.
Individualistic culture
Collectivistic culture
Infer a dispositional cause for behaviour: "He must eat fast food every day and live an unhealthy lifestyle!"
Infer a situational cause for behaviour: "Maybe he was in a rush when he decided to get fast food for lunch."

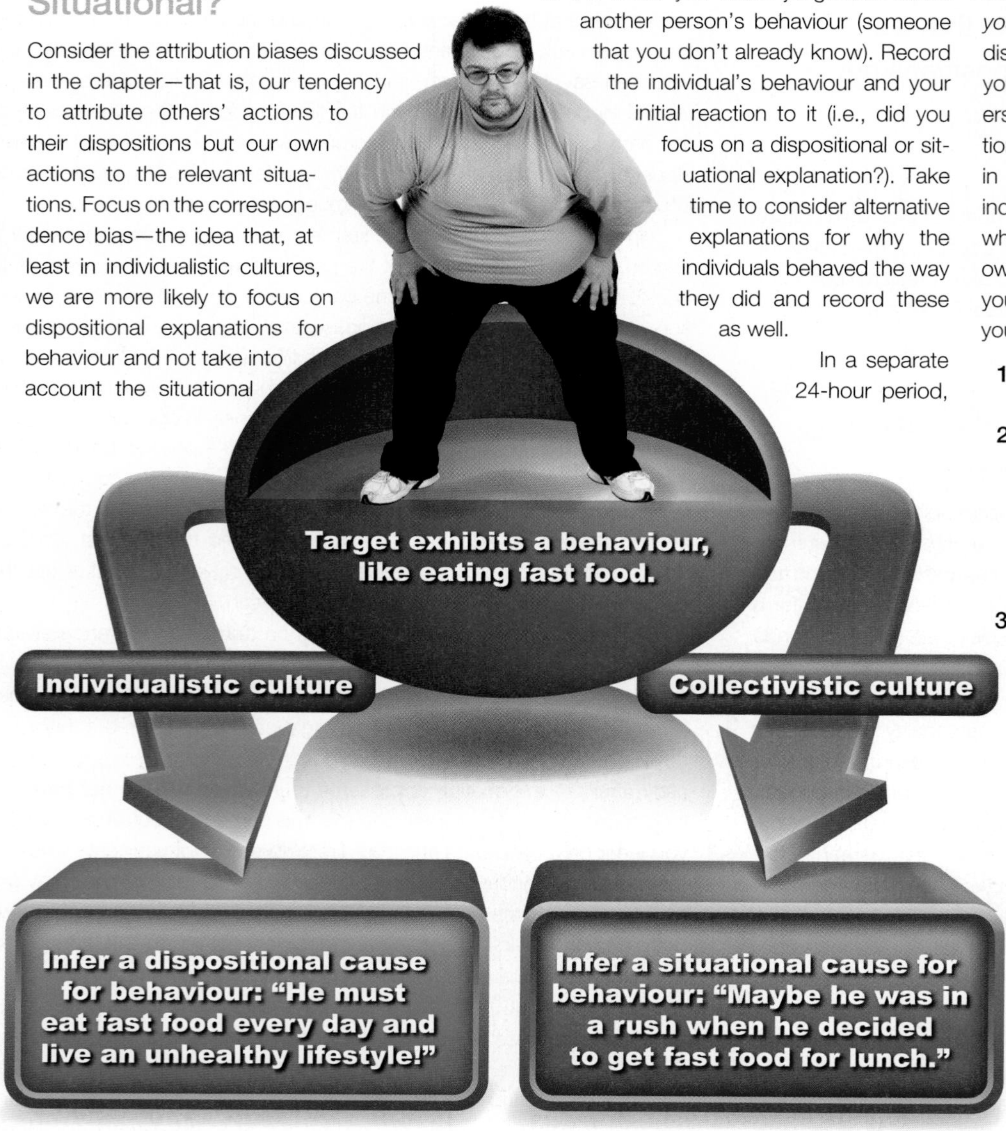

<<< **Cultural Differences in Attribution.** While we all automatically infer causes for behaviour, **the types of causes inferred vary dramatically by culture.**

> "It can also be extremely difficult to monitor the impression others develop of us **because it is not simply contingent upon our own behaviour.**"

**HALO EFFECT** when one positive thing is known or believed about a target person, we tend to infer that the individual is positive overall and thus has other positive features

not intend to infer that beautiful equates to good and ugly equates to bad, these associations are, to some extent, automatic in our brains. Consider the popularity of television shows such as *The Biggest Loser* and *What Not to Wear*; these are geared toward changing the external appearance of individuals due to negative appearance stereotypes. Exposure to pictures of beautiful faces leads to faster categorization of positive traits relative to exposure to unattractive faces (e.g., Olson & Marshuetz, 2005). For example, think of Canadian celebrity Rachel McAdams from the popular movie *The Notebook*. Do you automatically get the impression that she is a mean and vengeful person, or that she is kind, compassionate, and genuine? More likely than not, you would choose the latter interpretation. This is because seeing beautiful faces makes positive things more accessible, or ready to come to mind, and as such, they are identified more quickly. By contrast, this effect has not been found to occur when people are exposed to pictures of beautiful homes instead of faces, suggesting that there is something particularly powerful, important, and positive about faces.

The effects of our facial features do not stop with beauty. The size and shape of particular facial features impact whether people are perceived to be kind-hearted or mean-spirited. We tend to perceive someone as more kind-hearted if he has a full, round face; curly hair; long eyelashes; large eyes; a short nose; full lips; and an upturned mouth (Hassin & Trope, 2000). In addition, the more "baby faced" a person is, the more likely people are to give that person the benefit of the doubt but also to judge the person as weak, naive, and submissive (Berry & Zebrowitz-McArthur, 1988). We will revisit the relationship between beauty, physicality, and positive biases in Chapter 12, and we will explore additional research about how sometimes being too attractive can be detrimental in Chapter 14.

While the effect of beauty on impressions may be particularly profound, other seemingly irrelevant aspects trigger impressions. Our opinions regarding the music on a person's iPod (e.g., Rentfrow & Gosling, 2006) or name (e.g., Young et al., 1993) can have an impact on our judgment of that person. Imagine you love the band Nickelback and you find out a new date loves them too. This is going to lead to a positive impression. However, imagine you had a negative past relationship with a partner named Harold or Carrie. If you meet a new person with that name, the person already has one strike against him or her! Further, people with names associated with older generations (i.e., Edith) or unattractive/negative individuals (i.e., Lucifer, Adolf) are considered less popular and intelligent than those with more "modern" names (e.g., Harari & McDavid, 1973). People's belongings, Facebook page profiles, and dorm rooms are used to form sweeping impressions of them (e.g., Gosling, 2008). Even the pitch of a person's voice is used to infer the masculinity or femininity of the person (e.g., Ko, Judd, & Blair, 2006). These examples demonstrate that impressions also are contingent upon our experiences and personal associations with a person's features. In summary, people readily make snap judgments about others based on a variety and wealth of potentially irrelevant factors.

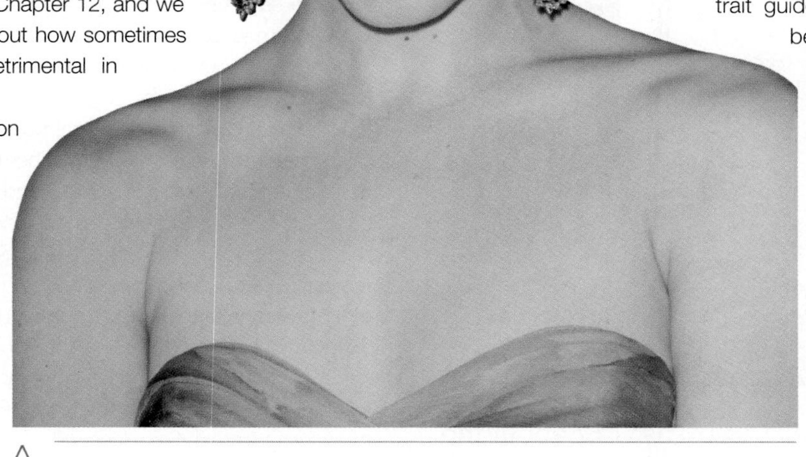

Beautiful faces **have a powerful effect on behaviour.**

## HALO EFFECTS

Once we form these sweeping impressions of others, we use them to guide our interpretation of subsequent behaviours. If we form an overall positive impression of another person, then we have what is termed a *positive implicit personality theory*, a theory centred on the idea of the **halo effect**, about that person. The theory is then applied to whatever the person does thereafter. If we have witnessed behaviour that we think implies one positive trait in a person, we are more likely to infer that the person possesses myriad other positive traits as well (Nisbett & Wilson, 1977). People will fail to distinguish among various behaviours exhibited by a person and assume that they are all positive—for instance, if that person has been judged to be a good worker, her projects and assignments will be uniformly evaluated more positively, even if one slips through the cracks. That worker will be seen as positive on many dimensions of work, such as initiative, creativity, and diligence, even if she is not necessarily as creative as she is diligent.

That said, we can also form negative implicit personality theory about an individual. This is considered the *reverse halo effect*, where a single undesirable trait guides inferences about a person or behaviour, resulting in a negative impression (Nisbett & Wilson, 1977). For example, imagine your new co-worker is late for his first day of work and is rude once he arrives. You are likely to interpret the rest of his behaviour throughout the day as supporting your negative impression.

These effects apply not only to people but are also heavily associated with advertising and the media (Klein & Dawar, 2004). For example, advertising campaigns based on

**BELIEF PERSEVERANCE** holding on to one's beliefs, even in the face of contradictory evidence

**SELF-FULFILLING PROPHECY** expecting that something will happen and acting in ways that may unintentionally elicit exactly what we expected

comedy (e.g., Mac versus PC) or cute animals (e.g., Telus) are very effective for recognition and promoting a halo effect. Marketing managers want consumers to believe that if the advertisements are good, the products also are good. For example, the launches of the iPad and iPhone have increased sales of Mac desktop computers, as people extend their positive associations to all Apple products (Maisto, 2010).

## CONFIRMATION BIAS

Imagine you are a staunch supporter of the "law and order" mentality, which holds that criminals should be more harshly punished for their crimes. Amendments to the Criminal Code of Canada in 2008 specify that offenders convicted of three or more violent and/or sex crimes must prove that they are not a danger to society; otherwise, they will be labelled as "dangerous offenders" and imprisoned indefinitely (CBC News, 2011c). Imagine now that you have read a research article that shows, quite powerfully, that a new form of treatment has been successful in "curing" violence, making such offenders unlikely to commit further crime. Would this change your opinion and would you decide that the dangerous offender designations for serious criminals should be abolished? Or would you decide that the research must be flawed?

If you said that you would decide that the research is flawed, this is most likely what would happen. People defend their existing beliefs even against overwhelming evidence to the contrary. How? By selectively attending to information that supports their opinions and discounting information that does not. This is called the confirmation bias, as we saw in Chapter 1.

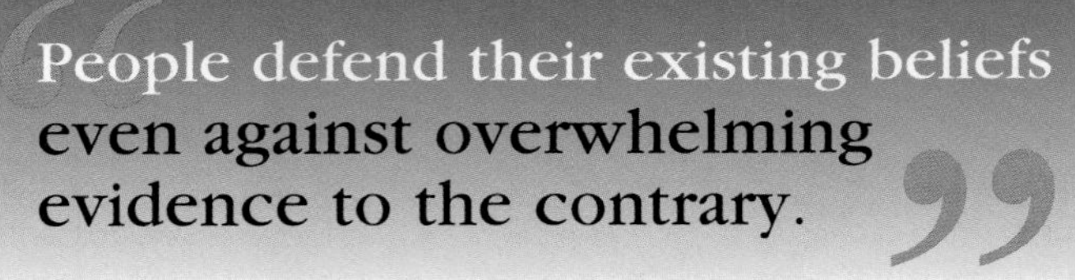
People defend their existing beliefs even against overwhelming evidence to the contrary.

What assumptions are you making **about the person who lives here?**

Research has repeatedly demonstrated the presence of the confirmation bias (Nickerson, 1998). If we are given information about a person's background (e.g., socioeconomic status, personality, sexual history, criminal history), we are likely to interpret all other information we receive about that person in accordance with our impression and ignore facts that don't support our view (e.g., Darley & Gross, 1983; Snyder & Swann, 1978). For example, some clinicians and members of the public still strongly hold on to the belief that traumatic memories can be repressed and later recovered as an unaltered record of reality (e.g., Porter, Peace, Douglas, & Doucette, in press; Read & Desmarais, 2009). These individuals tend to take anecdotal cases as evidence as well as research cited in self-help books such as *The Courage to Heal* (Bass & Davis, 1988) or *Secret Survivors* (Blume, 1990), while ignoring the wealth of scientific evidence that has refuted such claims (e.g., Loftus & Davis, 2006). In fact, empirical studies have found that trauma, while not immune to distortion, is more often than not remembered *better* than other types of neutral and emotional experiences (e.g., Porter & Peace, 2007). This biased examination of the evidence is termed *confirmatory hypothesis testing* (Snyder & Swann, 1978). In this way, we both passively and actively engage in **belief perseverance**, maintaining our original beliefs in the face of countervailing evidence (Ross, Lepper, & Hubbard, 1975).

## SELF-FULFILLING PROPHECY

Once impressions are formed, confirmation bias suggests that our expectations will influence the way others' behaviour is perceived and understood. This has effects not only on our impressions of others but also on *how we act toward those others*. Importantly, by acting in ways based upon our expectations of the other person, we may unintentionally elicit exactly the behaviour we expected, whether or not the person would have acted that way otherwise. For example, if you are paired with a classmate who you expect to be lazy, you may treat her contributions as less valuable and take more of the work on yourself. And whether or not the classmate is actually lazy, she might see that you're taking most of the responsibility, and she'll take a backseat. This is the premise behind the **self-fulfilling prophecy**, which says that if we expect that something will happen, we will act in ways that elicit exactly what we expected.

We have cognitive constructs that guide our understanding of the world, termed *schemas*. Schemas, discussed in Chapter 3, organize information about something and provide meaning and structure. For instance, rather than thinking of an object as bright, made of glass, and small, we can just think of a light bulb, and all of those features come to mind in one package. We form schemas for what things are "like," such as what a good student is "like," and we use these to infer information about others. These schemas are part of what causes the self-fulfilling prophecy to occur. Therefore, if teachers expect good students to attend regularly, ask questions in class, and be inquisitive, they may inadvertently give more attention and nurturing to students who conform to these expectations, in turn making them better students (e.g., Rosenthal & Jacobson, 1968). Even though teachers' expectations can be self-fulfilling, for the most part the expectations they have are accurate, and a teacher's expectation alone will not cause a student to fail. Nor will the expectation cause a student to rise to the top of the class (e.g., Jussim & Harber, 2005). Whatever the reason, this finding suggests that the

**The Self-Fulfilling Prophecy: How It Happens.** We cause our own expectations to come true **by acting in ways that elicit expected behaviour from others.**

self-fulfilling prophecy may not be written in stone in all circumstances (Jussim, Eccles, & Madon, 1996).

## HOW WE CAN BE ACCURATE

This chapter attempts to illuminate many of the ways in which people are imperfect when perceiving others. On some level, it may lead you to believe that perceiving another person accurately is hopeless, but that is not the case. For example, we are generally more accurate in perceiving people with whom we are familiar (e.g., Kenny, 2000) and even for those people who we believe are similar to ourselves (e.g., Kenny & Acitelli, 2001).

In addition, motivation to be accurate can influence our impressions (e.g., Kruglanski & Webster, 1996). The *theory of social hypothesis testing* claims that a high motivation for accuracy will lead people to engage in extensive diagnostic testing, to generate alternative hypotheses, and to take those hypotheses into account as they make decisions (Trope & Liberman, 1996). As such, they are more likely to consider multiple possible sources for others' behaviours before arriving at a decision. Further, research on empathic accuracy (i.e., the ability to discern the thoughts and feelings of others) has shown that motivation (e.g., Ickes & Simpson, 2004) and feedback from targets about their true thoughts and feelings (e.g., Marangoni, Garcia, Ickes, & Teng, 1995) can increase such judgments. That said, both emotion and motivation can sometimes impair accurate decision making, such as in studies of deception detection (e.g., Peace & Sinclair, 2012; Porter, McCabe, Woodworth, & Peace, 2007).

Accuracy in social perception is thus its own area of research, with an abundance of findings examining what facilitates accuracy in understanding others. And in terms of overcoming bias, while it cannot be fully overcome—and in some cases, leads to accuracy—what you have learned in this chapter may enable you to be more aware of these processes occurring in yourself and thereby allow you to correct for them, improving your social perception skills. Teaching people about the biases they have in social perception may enable them to make changes in their ways of perceiving others (e.g., Lilienfeld, Ammirati, & Landfield, 2009; Nisbett, Fong, Lehman, & Cheng, 1987).

CHAPTER 05 **Review**

## Summary

### NONVERBAL COMMUNICATION: HOW DO WE COMMUNICATE WITHOUT WORDS? p. 78

• Communication occurs via many parts of the body, from one's gaze to one's posture. Facial expressions are such a primary method of communication that six basic emotions are identifiable by the exact same expressions across cultures. These expressions can be evoked either consciously or automatically.

• These communications can give an indication of when someone is lying—for example, if one body part suggests one thing is true, but another body part suggests another. Despite the belief that most people are generally honest, people tend to lie at least once per day, though are more likely to do so to strangers than to close friends or family.

• Lacking nonverbal cues can impede people's abilities to detect deception. That said, verbal cues tend to be effective indicators in real-world situations, though people still generally perform poorly at detecting lies in others.

### TO WHAT DO WE ATTRIBUTE PEOPLE'S BEHAVIOURS? p. 82

• Behaviours can be attributed to a person's disposition (traits) or situation. There are both rational processes that go into making these decisions and biased ones. Rational processes include whether or not the action was freely chosen and how distinctive the action is compared to what would be expected in the situation. Biased processes include one's perspective—the fundamental attribution error is when we attribute others' behaviours to their dispositions, but our own to the situation.

• People in individualistic cultures tend to make dispositional attributions quite automatically—termed *spontaneous trait inferences*. By contrast, those in collectivist cultures will make attributions equally as automatically and unintentionally, but the inferences they make will be situational. Thus, in all cultures, people have the tendency to immediately determine the cause of a given behaviour—perhaps reflecting an innate need to understand our world.

### HOW DO WE DECIDE WHAT OTHER PEOPLE ARE LIKE? p. 87

• The content of information we are provided about a person is not the only thing that impacts our impressions; the centrality of the trait to personality as well as its order of presentation impact the extent to which it influences your impressions. Notably, first impressions are key. The primacy effect suggests that the very first thing to which we are exposed has a lot of weight in our evaluations of a person.

• The role that we are in can also influence how our behaviours are understood, as can having beauty or a baby-faced quality. Once we form an opinion of someone else, we are loath to change it—so much so that we seek out information that confirms our original beliefs. Moreover, with our own behaviour, we elicit behaviour from others that is consistent with our beliefs.

## Key Terms

**actor-observer effect** the tendency people have to make dispositional inferences for others' behaviour but situational attributions for their own *86*

**belief in a just world** people have to believe the world is fair and adjust their other beliefs to maintain that stance by concluding that bad things happen to bad people and good things happen to good people *85*

**belief perseverance** holding on to one's beliefs, even in the face of contradictory evidence *90*

**correspondence bias** the tendency of people to make dispositional attributions for others' behaviours *83*

**correspondent inference theory** the theory that people base their inferences regarding the source of others' behaviours on whether or not the behaviour was freely chosen, if the consequences are distinctive, and if the behaviour was socially desirable *82*

**covariation theory** the theory that people base their inferences regarding the source of others' behaviours on whether or not there is a consensus regarding the way one ought to respond, the distinctiveness of the response, and the consistency of the person's response across situations *82*

**dispositional attribution** inferring that a person's traits, something internal, caused his or her behaviour *82*

**fundamental attribution error** a more commonly known name for the correspondence bias. The scientific community now leans toward using *correspondence bias* so as not to suggest that these inferences are inherently in "error." *83*

**halo effect** when one positive thing is known or believed about a target person, we tend to infer that the individual is positive overall and thus has other positive features *89*

**microexpressions** involuntary expressions of facial emotion that only last a fraction of a second *80*

**need for cognition** the need that some individuals have to think, solve problems, and understand their world accurately *85*

**nonverbal cues** behaviours, gestures, and expressions that convey thought or emotion without words *78*

**primacy effect** the phenomenon whereby the first pieces of information to which we are exposed have the most impact on our judgments *87*

**recency effect** the phenomenon whereby the last pieces of information to which we are exposed have heightened impact on our judgments, relative to information received in the middle *87*

**self-fulfilling prophecy** expecting that something will happen and acting in ways that may unintentionally elicit exactly what we expected *90*

**self-verification** the motivation of an individual for others to know him or her accurately, including his or her negative features *81*

**situational attribution** inferring that the situation a person is in—something external to the person—caused his or her behaviour *82*

**spontaneous trait inference** the process of automatically inferring traits from another person's behaviour *84*

**three-stage model of attribution** a model in which an observer automatically characterizes a behaviour, automatically makes a dispositional inference, and then uses conscious effort to correct for situational constraints if the observer has the cognitive capacity to do so *85*

**what is beautiful is good effect** the phenomenon wherein beautiful things are imbued with positivity and activate positive things in the mind *88*

# Test Your Understanding

## MULTIPLE CHOICE

1. Which of these emotions is not one of the core six, recognizable by the same facial expressions across cultures?
   **a.** fear
   **b.** anger
   **c.** sympathy
   **d.** disgust

2. Why are we bad at detecting deception?
   **a.** We assume people are honest.
   **b.** We don't attend to cues that would reveal deception.
   **c.** We aren't lied to very often so we don't have much experience with it.
   **d.** We endorse stereotypes about what nonverbal behaviours mean.

3. When are we most likely to make a dispositional attribution?
   **a.** if we are from a collectivistic culture
   **b.** when we are judging our own behaviour
   **c.** when we have a high need for cognition
   **d.** when we are judging others' behaviour

4. Which of the following factors influences impressions the least?
   **a.** primacy
   **b.** concentration
   **c.** recency
   **d.** centrality of the trait to personality

5. Belief in a just world does not arise from:
   **a.** a desire to believe that things happen for a reason.
   **b.** a belief that we are good, so good things should happen to us.
   **c.** efforts to ameliorate anxiety about our futures.
   **d.** depressive disorders.

6. Which of the following factors does not strongly influence our first impressions of others?
   **a.** their physical appearance
   **b.** our political beliefs
   **c.** our own personal experiences
   **d.** their name

7. Why did changing a person's description from including "warm" to including "cold" have such a profound effect on impressions of that person in Asch's (1946) study?
   **a.** because it was presented last
   **b.** because it was central to personality
   **c.** because people were asked to form impressions based on all the words
   **d.** because people focus on visceral words

8. Exposure to a beautiful face can do all of the following except
   **a.** activate other positive things in memory.
   **b.** make you more helpful toward that person.
   **c.** make you more helpful in general.
   **d.** make women want to change their appearance.

9. You meet an employee in your company who is described as "diligent." You later remember him or her as being hardworking. This is an example of
   **a.** the halo effect.
   **b.** confirmation bias.
   **c.** correspondence bias.
   **d.** the primacy effect.

10. If we believe someone is introverted, which of the following situations best demonstrates the confirmation bias?
    **a.** We only ask them questions about introverted activities.
    **b.** We ask them questions about extroverted activities.
    **c.** We make them participate in social activities.
    **d.** We take them to a social skills workshop.

**ANSWERS:** 1. c; 2. a; 3. d; 4. b; 5. d; 6. b; 7. b; 8. c; 9. a; 10. a

## ESSAY RESPONSE

1. What sorts of cues can we use to detect deception? Discuss the strengths and weaknesses of each.
2. Define the halo and reverse halo effects and relate each to the concept of implicit personality theories. Now apply these definitions to two specific examples in advertising where halo and reverse halo effects have occurred in your life.
3. Discuss the part social roles play in how behaviours are interpreted by perceivers. Use a concrete example, such as behaviour in the workplace, newscasting, or behaviour in any position where a person's role impacts what others infer about him or her.
4. Think about the difficulties inherent in finding middle ground on any contentious issue due to the confirmation bias. Discuss what the confirmation bias is and how it can serve to divide people with opposing opinions.
5. Explain what the self-fulfilling prophecy is and the negative impact it can have on social perception. Use the example of teacher expectations for students in your answer.

## APPLY IT!

Think about a celebrity you admire. Why do you admire this person? To what extent has his or her position/role contributed to your positive thoughts about him or her? Would you still admire this person if he or she were not famous and instead lived next door to you?

**Remember to check www.thethinkspot.ca for additional information, downloadable flashcards, and other helpful resources.**

## APPLYING SOCIAL PSYCHOLOGY

### Business

Imagine working for a company that provides free gourmet meals during your lunch break; offers you custom-made milkshakes when you are in the mood for a sugar fix; features an on-site gym, laundry room, hairdresser, and games room; and even provides you with inexpensive massages should you find your working environment too stressful. Throw in a comprehensive health care plan, generous salary and benefits, and the opportunity to bring your pet to work with you every day, and you are probably wondering about the inevitable catch. For once, it seems there isn't one. Google has consistently been named one of *Fortune Magazine*'s top employers because of the numerous perks it offers its employees. In exchange, the company is inundated with more than 3,000 job applications every day, has its pick of the world's brightest and most talented prospective employees, and is able to cultivate a loyal, hardworking workforce. As Google cofounder Larry Page puts it, "It's common sense: Happy people are more productive" (Lashinsky, 2008).

Page's philosophy incorporates some of the principles of industrial-organizational (IO) psychology, a specialized area of psychology that focuses on workplace productivity and related issues, such as the physical and mental well-being of employees. Social psychologists also may focus on similar issues in the workplace in collaboration with IO psychologists. For example, they may perform research to answer questions such as the following: How are applicants selected for jobs? What makes an effective leader? What factors motivate people to work hard, and what influences levels of job satisfaction?

Two common issues that fall under the realm of IO psychology are *personnel selection and evaluation*. In particular, recommendations have been made by IO psychologists in Canada that intersect with the field of social psychology, such as recruitment procedures that enhance attitudes of fairness and selection/evaluation procedures that are free from bias (Latham & Sue-Chan, 1998).

Imagine you are taking part in a job interview with the managing director of a company. During a particularly enthusiastic response, you sweep a cup of coffee across the table, and it lands in the managing director's lap. Is it possible to redeem yourself, or will you (assuming that you are still in the running for the position) be forever remembered as a clumsy, ham-fisted oaf who should never be entrusted with wining and dining prospective clients? Unfortunately, as you learned in Chapter 5, it appears that we never get a second chance to create a first impression; when meeting new people, we make relatively accurate and persistent evaluations about them based on less than 30 seconds of observation (Ambady & Rosenthal, 1993). A recent study identified the neural processes responsible for these snap judgments. During a social encounter, two key regions in the brain sort information based on its personal and subjective significance, essentially formulating a first impression (Schiller et al., 2009). These impressions are often based on nonverbal clues or physical appearance. When observers viewed full-body photographs of 123 strangers in a naturally expressed pose (e.g., a smiling expression or an energetic stance), they were able to accurately assess nine out of 10 personality traits, ranging from agreeableness and emotional stability to religiosity and political orientation (Naumann, Vazire, Rentfrow, & Gosling, 2009). First impressions of personality features may be used not only in the selection of employees but also in their placement in certain groups or divisions of a company. Given the recent movements of organizations in Canada to emphasize team building and management structures, IO psychologists have attempted to address what strategies can be applied

"First impressions of personality features may be used not only in the selection of employees but also in their placement in certain groups or divisions of a company.

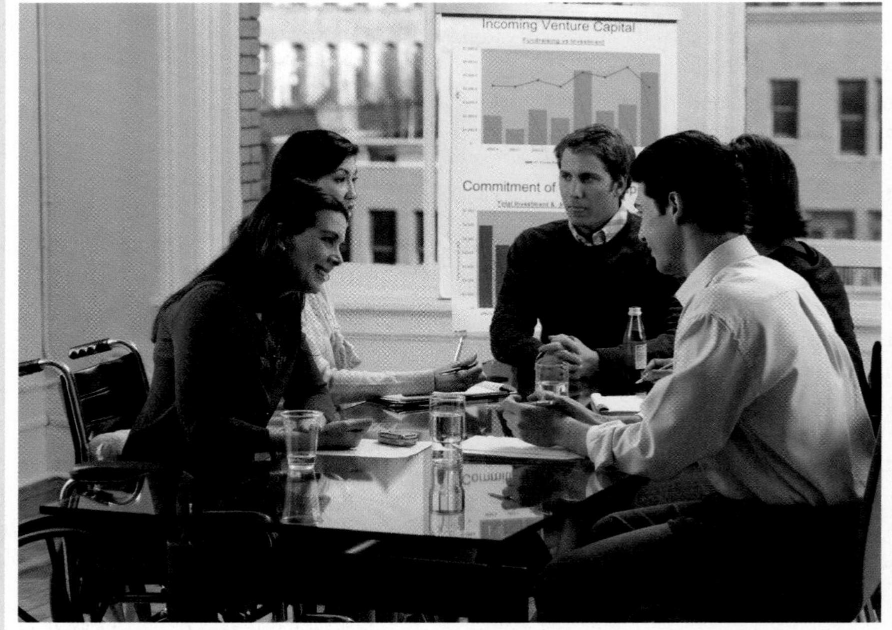


**Many companies are embracing the principles of industrial-organizational psychology to make the workplace a better social environment for their employees.**

that increase effectiveness and decrease social loafing. For example, Kichuk and Wiesner (1998) found that equivalent levels of conscientiousness and higher levels of extroversion extraversion across group members were related more to successful than to unsuccessful teams. Further, the Big Five personality traits appear to be more related to specific job criteria and tasks than to overall job performance (Hogan & Holland, 2003). As such, employers should consider whether potential employees have the personality to fit the specific tasks they will be performing.

However, first impressions are not always accurate, and supervisors and evaluators often fall prey to the social perception biases discussed in Chapter 5. In the workplace, such social and cognitive bias may work in an employee's favour or may hinder his career progress. For example, research shows that appraisers are more likely to rate an employee favourably if he or she took part in the initial appraisal or hiring process, even when provided with negative information about that employee (Bazerman, Beekun, & Schoorman, 1982). Appraisers are also likely to fall victim to the *halo effect*—a failure to differentiate between different aspects of an employee's performance (Cooper, 1981). As a result of the halo effect, employers are prone to assuming that a worker who is friendly and warm is also likely to be efficient and a strong team player, whereas an employee who is antisocial often rates lower on unrelated measures of performance (see Chapter 12 for more information about the halo effect). Researchers have found that the halo effect is particularly prevalent when evaluators rate someone they don't know well, or when a time delay has affected their recollection of an employee's performance (e.g., Kozlowski, Kirsch, & Chao, 1986; Murphy & Balzer, 1986).

Once a first impression has been made, it is difficult to shake off because we have a natural tendency to pay attention to information that supports preconceived stereotypes and ignore information that contradicts them, a phenomenon known as *confirmation bias* (see Chapter 10 for further discussion of the confirmation bias). Thus, once an employer has pigeonholed an employee as lazy, bright, intelligent, useful, or inept, the employer will only be conscious of the employee's actions if those actions support the employer's previous opinion. Recent trends in IO psychology in Canada have recommended performance assessments based on a concept called *360-degree feedback*—meaning that performance evaluations are collected from numerous sources, including co-workers, customers, managers, supervisors, subordinates, and self-appraisals (Sulsky & Keown, 1998). This type of feedback is believed to eliminate some of the social biases that we engage in, even without our awareness.

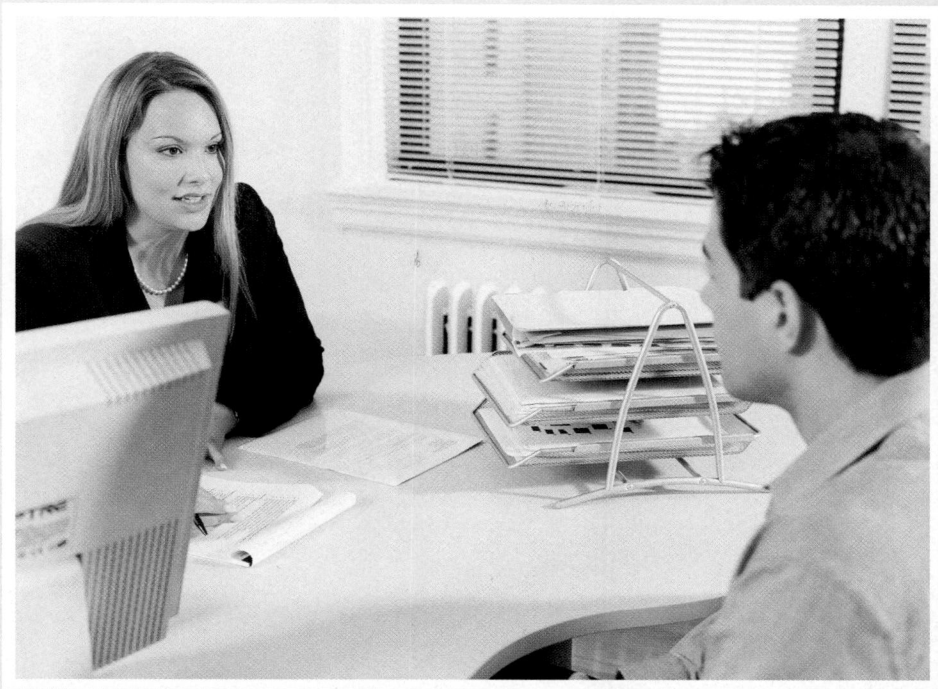

**Studies indicate that whether you are in a business environment or a social setting, first impressions last a long time.**

In addition to these two areas, IO psychologists also study other aspects of organizational behaviour. For example, Nancy Langton at University of British Columbia offers seminars to organizations concerning employee productivity; workplace relationships; and attracting, retaining, and developing employees (also see Langton, Robbins, & Judge, 2010). By making employers and employees aware of biases and influences on interpersonal behaviour in the workplace, social psychology can help increase our knowledge of how to be productive, effective, and happy in the work force.

> "Once a first impression has been made, it is difficult to shake off because we have a natural tendency to pay attention to information that supports preconceived stereotypes and ignore information that contradicts them."

# ATTITUDES: MAKING EVALUATIONS ABOUT THE WORLD

*<<< What makes us care about some issues, such as the outcome of the trial for Greyhound Bus killer Vince Li, while we remain apathetic toward others (e.g., recycling, global warming)?*

**HOW** DO ATTITUDES DEVELOP?
**DO** ATTITUDES INFLUENCE BEHAVIOUR?
**WHEN** DOES BEHAVIOUR INFLUENCE ATTITUDES?

On July 30, 2008, Canadians turned on the news to hear of one of the most grotesque, bizarre, and horrific crimes in our country's history. Vince Weiguang Li stabbed, beheaded, and cannibalized 22-year-old Tim McLean aboard a Greyhound bus just west of Portage La Prairie, Manitoba. Police received a report of the event around 8:30 p.m. and responded to the scene, where other passengers had fled the bus and were waiting on the side of the road. Police were unable to get Li to leave the bus for approximately five hours, during which time he severed McLean's head and additional body parts and began eating parts of his body. Li was charged with second-degree murder, pleaded not criminally responsible on account of mental disorder (NCRMD), and was diagnosed with paranoid schizophrenia following assessment by a psychiatrist for the defence counsel (CTV News, 2009). On March 5, 2009, Li was found not criminally responsible and was remanded to a secure forensic psychiatric facility, where he remains to this day (CBC News, 2009b).

Many Canadians were outraged by this crime and the outcome of Vince Li's trial, arguing that his disposition was a miscarriage of justice. They believed that Li was not being punished for his gruesome acts and was "getting away with murder." Witnesses to the incident say he acted like a cold robot and believed his actions to be premeditated (CityTV News, 2009). The media reported that Li had no history of mental illness, which caused the public to doubt his defence. That said, psychiatrists stated that Li suffered a major psychotic break and believed that God ordered him to kill his seatmate because he was plotting to harm Li (McIntyre, 2009). The public vocally criticized Greyhound policies and the police for their actions in not preventing or resolving the situation while it was occurring, and several witnesses to the crime have launched law suits (Winnipeg Free Press, 2011). Although the trial is over and Li is in a psychiatric facility, many individuals are still contesting Li's right to take walks outside the facility and the possibility that he could be released should he respond to treatment (Canadian Press, 2011). For other people, though, this crime and its aftermath were just another story on the news; and they may have thought "Oh, that's an awful event" or "That doesn't seem fair" but not considered it much further.

In many cases, this crime prompted a change in attitude. People who had neutral feelings concerning how mentally ill offenders are treated started feeling negatively toward the criminal justice system. Does that mean they joined letter writing campaigns, petitions, or sought out more knowledge on NCRMD defences? Not necessarily. As you have likely seen many times in your life, how you feel about something doesn't always correspond to the way you act. In this chapter, we will look at the factors that affect the development of attitudes, including what factors predict attitudes, how attitudes change, and whether attitudes predict subsequent behaviour.

**ATTITUDES** having an evaluative component toward a stimulus that is made up of affective, behavioural, and cognitive information

**AMBIVALENCE** simultaneously experiencing strong contradictory emotions or motivations

**IMPLICIT ATTITUDES** attitudes that are automatically formed and activated without our even being aware of it

**EXPLICIT ATTITUDES** attitudes of which one is aware and that one can control

### Table 6.1: How Do You Categorize Your Attitudes?

| Attitude | Positive Reaction | Negative Reaction | Example |
|---|---|---|---|
| Positive | High | Low | "I love guacamole! It's my favourite dip." |
| Negative | Low | High | "I despise guacamole! I'll never eat a bite." |
| Indifferent | Low | Low | "I've never tried guacamole, so I really have no opinion." |
| Ambivalent | High | High | "I love guacamole, but avocados make me sick to my stomach!" |

*Source:* Adapted from: Cacioppo, J. T., Gardner, W. L., & Berntson, G. G. (1997). Beyond bipolar conceptualizations and measures: The case of attitudes and evaluative space. *Personality and Social Psychology Review, 1*, 3–25.

## How Do Attitudes Develop?

Social psychologists have defined **attitudes** in many different ways; however, we will stick with one definition—having an evaluative component toward a stimulus that is comprised of affective, behavioural, and cognitive factors (e.g., Schwarz & Bohner, 2001; Zanna & Rempel, 1988). As you saw in Chapter 5, it takes only a split second to form an impression about someone or something. In fact, you may not even realize that you've formed an attitude because your mind is constantly and unconsciously judging and analyzing the environment. Once an attitude is formed, it can vary greatly in strength or intensity. Maybe, like one of the authors of this text, you have a strong aversion to olives and can't even stand the smell of them. There might be a political or relationship issue that gets your blood boiling (e.g., abortion or infidelity). At the other end of the spectrum, there might be a particular actor you don't really like, but you're not going to refuse to see one of his movies if your friends want to go. This latter example reflects a *weak* attitude toward disliking an actor, whereas if you detest a particular actor and refuse to see his or her movies, you would be expressing a *strong* attitude.

Attitudes also might also be ambivalent. This word might be unfamiliar, but it is a safe bet you know *exactly* what this feels like. Let's say you were accepted to a school several hundred kilometres away from your hometown. You think it could be an exciting new adventure to live so far away from home. At the same time, maybe many of your friends are planning to go to schools in your home province. You are torn—you want new experiences, but you don't want to leave your friends. An **ambivalent** attitude is defined as simultaneously experiencing strong contradictory emotions or motivations.

Think again about the Vince Li trial. While most people acknowledged that Li's actions were bizarre and indicative of a mental illness, many were uncertain where to place the blame and what the right disposition for his crimes should be. How did you feel? Did you think Li should have gone to jail and been held accountable for his actions? Did you think that the judge made the right decision in finding Li not criminally responsible? Did you blame the police for not putting an end to this horrific crime sooner? Maybe you blamed Greyhound for not having more stringent policies regarding weapons and the safety of their passengers (modifications that they have since made). Maybe your attitude was ambivalent and you experienced conflicting feelings of who was responsible, how the crime and the trial should have been handled, and how the courts should have treated Vince Li. As the story developed, you may have cycled through several different attitudes toward the crime and the outcome of Li's trial. Some people, overwhelmed by media coverage, may have even decided not to care at all about the issue and turned their attention away from it. This, too, is a kind of attitude where people decide to be *indifferent* to the issue. Weak or strong, positive or negative, indifferent or ambivalent—we all have attitudes on everything that comes across our "radars," as Table 6.1 illustrates.

We often don't have to think too hard to know **what our attitude about something is.**

### ATTITUDE FORMATION

Many times, attitudes are automatically formed and activated without our even being aware of them: these are called **implicit attitudes** (e.g., Fazio & Olson, 2003). Such attitudes are outside of our conscious control. Think about the attitudes you had as a child, and how they have changed. For example, let's say as a child, Tasha was afraid of dogs, despite never having had a negative experience with one. She simply felt afraid when she saw a dog. As she grew up, though, she was able to override that attitude. Tasha told herself that her fear was irrational and sought out interactions with dogs in an effort to overcome her fear. Now, Tasha loves dogs. This is an example of an **explicit attitude**—an attitude that one recognizes and can control (e.g., Gawronski & Bodenhausen, 2006; Nosek, 2007).

There are four factors that differentiate between implicit and explicit attitudes: early experiences, affective experiences, cultural biases, and cognitive consistency principles (Rudman, 2004). Many social psychologists argue that implicit attitudes stem from early, even forgotten, experiences, while explicit attitudes are formed in reaction to more recent experiences. Affective experiences also may have more effect on implicit attitudes because they have to do with automatic emotional reactions, while explicit attitudes come from a more cognitively controlled mindset. For the same reason, cultural biases have more influence over implicit rather than explicit attitudes. You may feel uncomfortable around someone of a particular cultural background (implicit) but not consciously know why (explicit). Finally, cognitive consistency principles affect attitudes through a formula that can be expressed as "I like X, and Y is X, so I must like Y." For example, if you like *Will & Grace* star Eric McCormack (X), and he is starring in a new sitcom (Y), you'll probably have a positive attitude about watching the new show.

Although attitudes are primarily evaluative, both implicit and explicit attitudes comprise three separate components: *affect*, *behaviour*, and *cognition* (Eagly & Chaiken, 1993). An *affective* response is based on your emotions, such as feeling badly for the victim and witnesses to the Greyhound bus killing. You may also find yourself joining a campaign for weapon screening and metal detectors to be placed aboard all forms of public transport, which is a *behaviour* that demonstrates your attitude toward the crime. Finally, the negative thoughts you may have had about the RCMP and Greyhound for not preventing or responding quickly to the incident reflected the *cognition* underlying your attitude, as you weighed what they *could* have done against what they *did* do.

When you are evaluating a person, an object, an event, or an idea, your mind weighs both positive and negative information in its analysis. However, research indicates that negative information makes much more of an impact on your attitudes (Vaish, Grossmann, & Woodward, 2008). Put another way, you remember the bad things more than you do the good things when you are forming an attitude about something. This is called the *negativity bias* (e.g., Kunda, 1999; for a review of the negativity bias, see Rozin & Royzman, 2001). It has been suggested that this bias stems from our evolutionary history, when it was more important for our survival that we attend to the dangers we encountered than to positive information (Schaller, 2008). We may in fact be hardwired to avoid danger, and as a result have developed systems to remember hazardous situations or objects in order to avoid them in the future.

To determine whether this tendency is truly hardwired, researchers have measured the electrical activity in people's brains when they viewed positive photos (e.g., a Ferrari, a pizza), neutral photos, and negative photos (e.g., a mutilated face, a dead cat). The measurements reflected the responsiveness of the brain to the valence of the stimulus—that is, its response the moment the brain recognizes a stimulus as being positive, negative, or neutral. The results showed that there were larger brain waves, reflecting a dramatic increase in brain activity, when participants viewed the negative photos as opposed to when they viewed the positive or neutral photos (e.g., Delplanque, Lavoie, Hot, Silvert, & Sequeira, 2004; Ito et al., 1998). Thus, the brain reacts much more strongly to negative information than to positive or neutral information as soon as the brain recognizes the valence of what its owner is seeing. Recent research suggests that the level of arousal we receive from negative information is a greater predictor of attention and bias relative to threat or negativity alone (Schimmack, 2005). However, both age (i.e., younger individuals are more sensitive to negative information; Tomaszczyk, Fernandes, & MacLeod, 2008) and gender (i.e., men show a greater negativity bias and greater arousal to negative information relative to women; Grabe & Kamhawi, 2006) also moderate the expression of this bias.

The negativity bias might be why politicians these days rely on "negative advertising," making accusations that an opponent will cut health care and educational spending and won't look out for you (e.g., the anti–Michael Ignatieff/Liberal

Your Attitude:
The Greyhound bus killing was a negative occurrence.
Affect:
You felt bad for the victim and witnesses.
Behaviour:
You joined a campaign to increase safety aboard public transportation systems.
Cognition:
You thought the police and Greyhound should dealt with the crime more effectively.

**The ABCs of the Greyhound Bus Killing.** Our attitudes are expressed by and composed of **the affect, behaviour, and cognition that reflect them.**

**CLASSICAL CONDITIONING** a type of learning by which a neutral stimulus gets paired with a stimulus (UCS) that elicits a response (UCR). Through repeated pairings, the neutral stimulus (CS) by itself elicits the response (CR) of the second stimulus

**UNCONDITIONED STIMULUS (UCS)** a stimulus that elicits a response automatically, without learning taking place

**UNCONDITIONED RESPONSE (UCR)** a response that occurs automatically in reaction to some stimulus, without learning taking place

**CONDITIONED STIMULUS (CS)** a stimulus that, only by repeated association with a particular unconditioned stimulus, comes to evoke the response associated with the unconditioned stimulus

**CONDITIONED RESPONSE (CR)** a learned response to the conditioned stimulus that was previously a neutral stimulus

**MERE EXPOSURE EFFECT** the phenomenon whereby objects become better liked with exposure—we like things as they become more familiar to us

Party commercials that dominated the last federal election in 2011). Those weaknesses will stick in viewers' brains and possibly draw attention away from the opposing candidate's positive features. We all know from experience that it can go too far and that nobody likes a bully. Particularly vicious attacks on another person may backfire and cast a negative light on the attacker, and that too will be remembered. These examples illustrate how attitudes are based on evaluation, but let's take a closer look at how it happens.

## Classical Conditioning

One example of how attitudes, both negative and positive, develop is in the case of **classical conditioning** (for a review of this concept, see Jones, Olson, & Fazio, 2010). Classical conditioning is a type of learning in which a neutral stimulus gets paired with a stimulus that automatically elicits a response. Once conditioning has occurred through repeated pairings, the neutral stimulus by itself already elicits the response of the second stimulus.



Ivan Pavlov (1927) uncovered this type of conditioning in his famous experiment with dogs. Each time the dogs were given meat, they would salivate. The meat is the **unconditioned stimulus (UCS)** and the salivation is the **unconditioned response (UCR)**, because it occurs automatically without learning. Then Pavlov added a second stimulus—each time the dogs were given meat, he would ring a bell (neutral stimulus). Sure enough, after repeated trials, the dogs began to salivate when they heard the bell—even if there was no meat to be found! By association with the unconditioned stimulus, the bell became the **conditioned stimulus (CS)** and the salivation at the sound of the bell (without presentation of the food) became the **conditioned response (CR)**.

Similarly, our attitudes can be formed by associations. For example, you might associate the smell of a certain cologne or perfume with your boyfriend or girlfriend, so whenever you smell that scent you become filled with positive and romantic thoughts and feelings, or even sexual arousal (e.g., Hoffman, Janssen, & Turner, 2004). This reaction happens because, over the time you have been dating your partner, you have smelled the cologne repeatedly while simultaneously receiving your partner's positive and loving attention. On the contrary, you could also associate certain smells with negative experiences, such that the smell of a particular cologne worn by an ex-boyfriend or ex-girlfriend elicits a negative emotional reaction and feelings of anger or sadness. You do not have to put any conscious effort into evoking either of these reactions—they happen quite automatically.

So how can classical conditioning impact attitudes? In the previous example, the positive associations with your romantic partner are likely to make you feel positively about his or her cologne, too. Notably, these associations need not be purposeful—they can involve two things that occur together completely incidentally. For example, researchers at McGill University paired self-related words with images of smiling faces, and found that they could increase participants' automatic attitude about themselves (Baccus, Baldwin, & Packer, 2004). These principles have been applied not only to attitudes about ourselves or others but also in advertising campaigns (e.g., Janiszewski & Warlop, 1993; Laroche, Kim, & Zhou, 1996). Recently, Gibson (2008) paired images that were positive (i.e., flowers, a mother and child) or negative (i.e., a graveyard, the word *terrifying*) with either Coke or Pepsi. Participants who were previously neutral in terms of which pop they preferred were more likely to select the type of pop that had been associated with positive images relative to negative images (Gibson, 2008). Of course, these sorts of things happen in everyday life, too. For example, if Jack is eating sushi when he learns that his mother has been in a car accident, he may develop a negative attitude toward sushi. Even if he's not entirely aware of it, for him, eating sushi may now be linked with fearful and negative feelings. Associations can come to impact our attitudes toward even the soda we drink and food we eat.

Associations need not be between two objects—there is an inherent association between things with which we are familiar and positive effect, as well as between the unfamiliar and negative affect (Whittlesea & Price, 2001). This, too, may have arisen due to a need to protect ourselves from the unknown. This is called the **mere exposure effect**, which states that simply having been exposed to something increases our liking for it (Zajonc, 1968). Things and people that originally invoke a *neutral* response grow on us the more we are exposed to them (Mita, Dermer, & Knight, 1977). That said, the mere exposure effect can certainly backfire. If our initial response to a stimuli is *highly negative* (i.e., you hate a song the first time you hear it), no amount of continued exposure will make you like the stimulus (e.g., Szpunar, Schellenberg, & Pliner, 2004). However, we may experience a reduction in negative affect if our initial

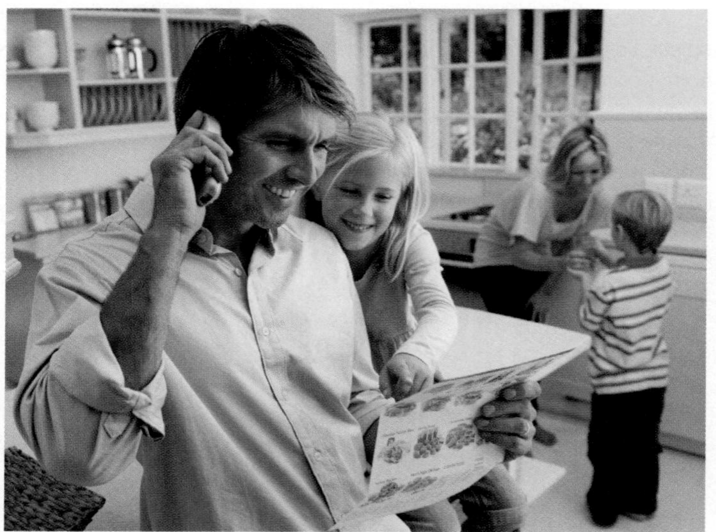

^^^ If something is paired with food often enough, it might just make you salivate on its own—**such as the feeling of increased hunger and salivation after placing a delivery order.**

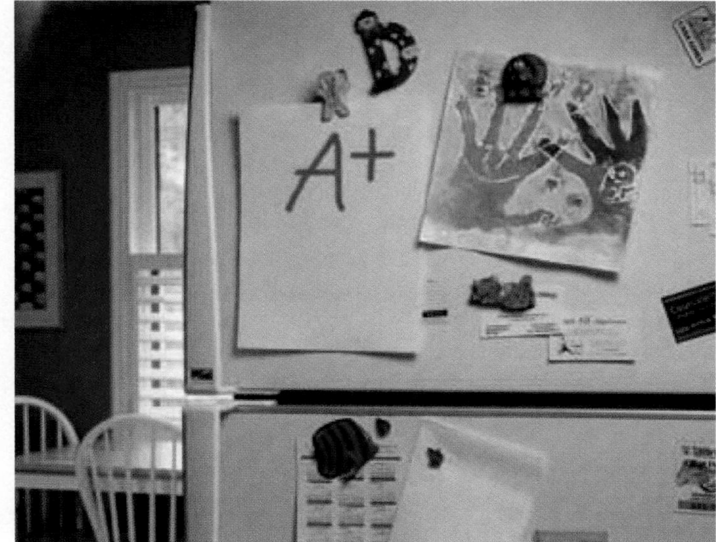


Rewards for good behaviour **make people want to practise those good behaviours more often.**

response to a stimulus is only *mildly negative* (Robinson & Elias, 2005). Sometimes, though, you may be exposed to a stimulus so often that it becomes annoying (i.e., seeing the same commercial so many times that it begins to grate on your nerves), you will likely develop negative feelings toward it. You will learn more about the mere exposure effect in Chapter 12.

One recent finding that powerfully demonstrates that exposure increases positive regard is called the **name–letter effect** (e.g., Nelson & Simmons, 2007). Research has uncovered that we have a preference for our own names and initials; in fact, we have a tendency to prefer our own initials over any other letters in the alphabet and even seek them out unconsciously. This can have both positive and negative impacts, however. If your initial matches a positive performance label (such as getting an A or B grade in class), you are more likely to perform better. For instance, researchers found that individuals with names like Chris or Derek tended to have lower grades than students with names like Allison or Bob (Nelson & Simmons, 2007). In addition, your first initial may also determine the products that you buy and places you live (e.g., Jones et al., 2004; Brendl, Chattopadhyay, Pelham, & Carvall, 2005). Tanya is more likely to live in Toronto and drive a Toyota than Sarah, but Sarah may choose to live in Saskatoon and drive a Subaru. It is important to keep in mind, however, that even though this research shows that initials are linked to some outcomes, these studies are correlational only. Remember from Chapter 2 that we learned we cannot infer that our name *causes* these consequences, as this type of study design only permits conclusions about *relationships* among variables. Of course, classical conditioning is just one theory of how attitudes are developed. Let's examine another theory.

## Operant Conditioning

If each time you earned an A on a paper or exam, you received an expensive gift like a Blackberry, an iPad, or a $100 Future Shop gift card, you might be inclined to try to rack up as many A's as possible, right? However, if each time you received a C or lower you were punished by

**NAME–LETTER EFFECT** the tendency to show a preference for letters in our own name and prefer stimuli that contain those letters

**OPERANT CONDITIONING** a type of learning in which the frequency of a behaviour is determined by reinforcement and punishment

**OBSERVATIONAL LEARNING** acquiring an attitude or behaviour due to the observation of others exhibiting that attitude or behaviour

having your cellphone or laptop taken away, you would also likely try hard to keep your grades high. This is an example of **operant conditioning,** a method of learning that occurs through rewarding desirable behaviour and punishing undesirable behaviour. It is a method that is used as a measure of implicit self-esteem—if we think well of ourselves, we was first discovered by Edward Thorndike and elaborated on by the psychologist B.F. Skinner (1938).

Operant conditioning occurs through the mechanisms of reinforcement and punishment, of which there are two types, positive and negative. *Positive reinforcement* refers to the addition of a desirable item in order to reinforce or increase the likelihood or repetition of a behaviour. For example, your parents might offer you money for every A on your report card. *Negative reinforcement*, by contrast, refers to the removal of something unpleasant in order to increase the likelihood of repetition of a behaviour—if you improve your grades, you don't have to go to boring tutoring sessions. *Positive punishment* refers to the addition of an undesirable stimulus in order to reduce a behaviour. Spanking is an example of this. *Negative punishment* refers to the removal of something pleasurable in order to decrease the frequency of a behaviour (e.g., if your parents take away your car because your semester grades were too low).

Operant conditioning can influence attitudes as well. If a behaviour is reinforced, our attitudes toward it are likely to become more positive, and if it is punished, our attitudes are likely to become more negative. This can even extend to the way we feel about other people. For example, couples who provide each other with reinforcements such as favours, running errands, giving gifts, and so forth, are more likely to be together for longer durations than those who do not provide many rewards (e.g., Berg & McQuinn, 1986). Therefore, if you want your relationships to last longer, make sure to give your friends and dating partners reinforcement!

## Observational Learning

**Observational learning** (Bandura, 1977), or modeling, is yet another way in which attitudes can be formed. People develop attitudes about things or other people based on how they see others act. In doing so, they take on the same views of those they observe. For instance, if a girl grows up watching her father act distrustful of a particular racial or ethnic group, she may very likely adopt those same views. That said, attitudes developed in this way can be reversed. In a classic experiment, Bandura, Grusec, and Menlove (1966) exposed children who were initially afraid of dogs to a little boy playing in a dog playpen for 20 minutes each day for four days. After the four days, 67 percent of the dog-phobic children were comfortable enough to climb inside the playpen and play with the dog, even when all others left the room. Just seeing another child playing with the dog helped the children learn not to fear dogs.

Another more recent study demonstrated the potent effect of observational learning. Grade 9 students were exposed to scenes in movies where people were either smoking or not (i.e., the smoking was edited out; Pechmann & Shih, 1999). Those who watched smokers tended to look favourably upon the smokers' social stature, had an increased sense of positive arousal and had more intention to smoke compared to those who did not watch smokers. While this is a powerful

**Implicit Association Test (IAT)** a test that measures how easily we associate categories with positive or negative attitudes, including measures in categories ranging from racial and religious attitudes to attitudes about presidents. See implicit.harvard.edu/implicit/demo/.

statement in support of observational learning, these deleterious effects were overcome if the students were shown an anti-smoking advertisement before watching the movie. Therefore, while observational learning can directly impact attitudes toward objects and behaviours, it can be countered with educational techniques that create healthy attitudes before the unhealthy stimulus is encountered (e.g., Hollands, Prestwich, & Marteau, 2011).

## ASSESSING ATTITUDES

You can usually tell what your friends and acquaintances think about certain people or social objects. You know Dave dislikes Tim's girlfriend because he rolls his eyes almost every time she speaks. It is obvious that Megan really likes Sean because she gives him a warm hug as soon as he walks into a room. These indicators let you know what Dave's and Megan's *explicit* attitudes are. Explicit attitudes are, again, attitudes of which we are aware and that are often obvious to an outsider. In the beginning of this chapter, we talked about attitudes toward the Greyhound bus killing. People's actions and words let us know their attitudes about the event. You could tell people felt strongly when they joined a campaign for increased security, refused to ride on Greyhound buses, or wrote letters to the police or Greyhound. Explicit attitudes can be assessed by *self-report measures* (discussed in Chapter 2)—questionnaires where participants are asked what they think or how they feel. This method relies on participants willingly and honestly revealing the way they feel about someone or something.



On the flipside, it is impossible to perceive all the attitudes people have about the world around them. In fact, they may not even know what some of their own attitudes are! These *implicit* attitudes require a more precise method of assessment. If you don't even know how you feel about something, how would a researcher be able to find out? The answer is that researchers have to go undercover, so to speak, and use covert measures to ascertain what your underlying attitudes are about something.

One possibility is *unobtrusive observation*. Observation (also discussed in Chapter 2) can provide insight into both explicit and implicit attitudes. For example, if Mark is at a party and splits the last piece of pizza with his friend, an observer might think Mark values sharing. Does Mark really value sharing, though, or does he just want people to *think* he does? That is, is Mark's selflessness an implicit, automatically activated reaction toward seeing his friend's desire for that last piece of pizza, or must he activate it with conscious effort to impress others? However, if the same thing happened while Mark and his friend were dining one-on-one, it would suggest that sharing is more likely to be an implicit attitude. One could argue though, that any behaviour is, in part, an effort to convince *ourselves* that we are who we want to believe we are.

Of course, measuring such things is incredibly difficult (Gawronski, 2009). There are a few ways researchers try to tap into implicit attitudes using self-report data. You may be wondering how self-reported data on attitudes can be useful—after all, won't people just lie to make themselves look better? To control for this and increase accuracy of self-report data, researchers use the "bogus pipeline" (Roese & Jamieson, 1993). Basically, participants in a study are led to believe that a non-functioning (of course, they do not know it is non-functioning) machine can predict their responses. The researchers conduct a sample trial to show the participant how it works. In studies using this method, individuals are less likely to answer in a socially desirable fashion and instead are more truthful, even when truthful responses are indicative of negative behaviours (e.g., Gannon, Keown, Polaschek, 2007; Jones & Sigall, 1971; Peace & Brower, 2011).

Another method used to assess implicit attitudes is a self-report test called the **Implicit Association Test**, or the **IAT**. (To review additional measures of implicit attitudes, see Fazio & Olson, 2003.) The IAT measures how easily we associate categories with positive or negative descriptions. For instance, a person may associate Canadians with open-mindedness, Americans with arrogance, Japanese persons with intelligence, or French people with snobbishness. These attitudes may not even be conscious to the person who holds them, and the IAT is one tool that may allow us to gain insight into these implicit attitudes

**We learn how to act by observing others' behaviours. In this way, children sometimes** pick up undesirable behaviours from their parents that can impact **the way they approach situations and other people for the rest of their lives.**

*Source*: Adapted from: Jelenec, P., & Steffens, M. C. (2002). Implicit attitudes toward elderly women and men. *Current Research in Social Psychology, 7*, 275–293.

**Implicit Attitudes. If you have implicit knowledge of the stereotypes that "young" is positive and "elderly" is negative,** your reaction time will be faster to words that are congruent with your stereotype and slower to those that are not.

(Hofmann, Gawronski, Gschwendner, Le, & Schmitt, 2005). In other cases, our implicit attitudes may be ones we consciously deny. For example, research with imprisoned child molesters in Ontario has begun to utilize the IAT to assess what offenders' cognitions are concerning child sexual abuse and how this relates to their criminal offence patterns and recidivism (e.g., Nunes, Firestone, & Baldwin, 2007).

If you're brave enough and interested in self-discovery, you can take the test online and find out not only what your implicit attitudes may be toward different ethnic and racial groups, but also other attitudes such as those you have toward recent presidents of the United States. The test can be found at https://implicit.harvard.edu/implicit/.

In general, the IAT asks you to categorize words, faces, or images presented on a screen. For instance, in one trial assessing bias against senior citizens, you may be asked to click the A key if a word is positive or a face is "young" and click the L key if a word is negative or a face is "old" (e.g., Jelenec & Steffens, 2002). This pairing, if you possess the implicit attitude that "old" is negative and "young" is positive, should be easy and you would press the correct keys quickly. However, if you held the same attitude but the pairing presentations were "old"-positive words and "young"-negative words, you would have a more difficult time and respond more slowly. It is important to note that the reaction times are measured in terms of milliseconds; these are reactions that occur quickly, without conscious control. Remember, these implicit attitudes reflect associations between concepts—that when the category is encountered, the associated concepts are activated in unconscious memory (see *accessibility*). That does not mean that those associations are endorsed by the person but simply that they have been created by repeated exposure.

As such, the IAT is not without controversy. Opponents of the test claim that since it simply measures a person's subconscious association of adjectives with specific social groups, but does not necessarily reflect what the person actually believes, it isn't meaningful. In fact, studies tend to indicate low correlations between measures of implicit and explicit attitudes (Hofmann et al., 2005). As described in Chapter 5, the person will not know that his or her stereotypes are guiding decision making because they are not actively endorsed, but they have a deleterious effect nonetheless. In this and many other ways, associations between groups of people and constructs in memory matter, even if they are not believed to be true.

## Do Attitudes Influence Behaviour?

We have a surplus of attitudes about almost everything, and it seems as though, if we believed in something, we would necessarily act in accordance. But do we? Let's say your best friend is having a birthday bash on Saturday night, but you have a paper due on Monday, and you have not even started writing. It is going to require a lot of research and time. Even though education is one of your top priorities, do you stay home on Saturday night and skip the party? The likely answer is no. Despite your positive attitude about your education, that attitude does not come into play in every decision you make. In this case, it is likely because of the competing, stronger positive attitude toward your friend. Likewise, some individuals might be strongly opposed to gay marriage and want to stop it from happening. However, this doesn't necessarily mean that they will hop on a plane to join a protest on Capitol Hill in Ottawa, or claim before the Supreme Court of Canada that their Charter Rights have been violated, or that they will even make a call to their premier to express their disapproval.

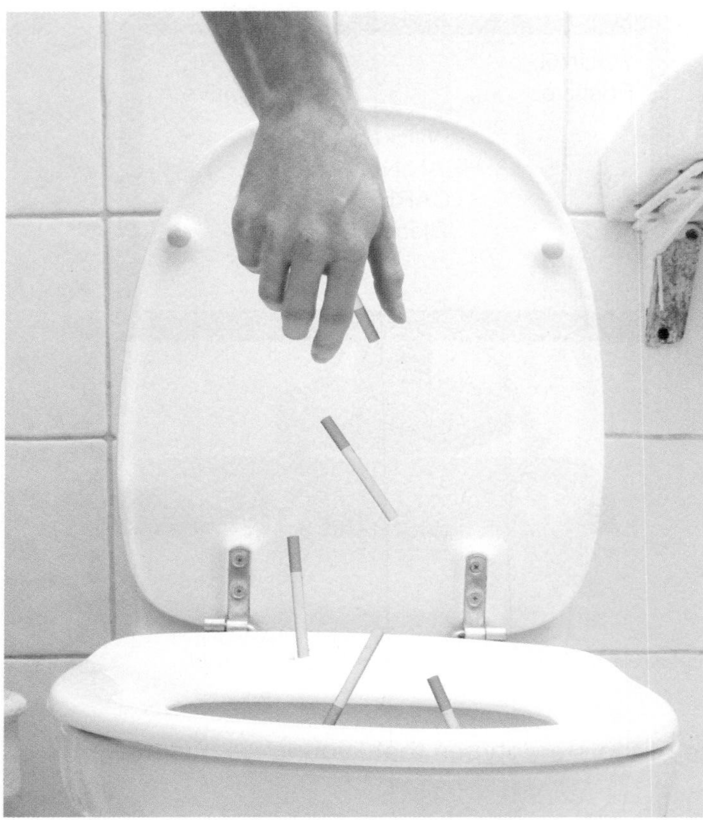

**Whether or not our attitudes influence our behaviour can depend on a number of factors,** just as all those who want to stop smoking do not necessarily do so, even if they hold the attitude that smoking is bad.




## WHEN ATTITUDES DO NOT PREDICT BEHAVIOUR

The disconnect between attitude and behaviour was demonstrated by a classic study conducted by a researcher named LaPiere in 1934 (we mentioned this briefly in Chapter 1). LaPiere was struck by the existence of racial prejudice against the Chinese in the United States and wanted to investigate this attitude further. He happened to be travelling with a young Chinese student and his wife when he realized that they were able to find rooms in hotels with no trouble, even in hotels in very prejudiced areas. He travelled all over the United States with the young Chinese couple and remained hidden while the couple went into a variety of restaurants and hotels. LaPiere found that the couple was denied entry to only one establishment out of 66 hotels and 184 restaurants. Six months later, LaPiere sent questionnaires to those same hotels and restaurants asking if they would be willing to accommodate a Chinese couple. The vast majority of the businesses responded "no" (92 percent of restaurants and 91 percent of hotels), despite having accommodated the Chinese couple earlier. Ultimately, the attitudes of the restaurant and hotel operators did not necessarily predict their behaviours. However, one of the flaws of this research is that we don't know if the employees who completed the survey were the same ones who had displayed the non-discriminatory behaviour (LaPiere, 1934).

In another classic study demonstrating this disconnect, Corey (1937) tested university students in an educational psychology class. He first administered a questionnaire to the students to ascertain their attitudes toward cheating. On average, many of them displayed attitudes that indicated moderate disapproval of cheating. Next, every week for five weeks, the students were given a fivequestion true-or-false test. The students gave the test to the researcher, who secretly graded the exams so he or she would know the students' true scores and then returned the exams to the students so that they could grade the exams themselves. Such a scenario allowed the students to cheat by covertly changing their answers to improve their scores while grading. Shockingly, students cheated on 76 percent of the tests, regardless of their previously stated attitudes toward cheating. In fact, their attitudes toward cheating were *completely unrelated* to whether or not they actually did so; rather, the best predictor of cheating was the difficulty of the exam. It seems that these students could talk the talk, but most of them could not walk the walk when it came to being consistent with their attitudes against cheating.

"In fact, their attitudes toward cheating were *completely unrelated* to whether or not they actually did so; rather, the best predictor of **cheating was the difficulty of the exam.**"

## HOW ATTITUDES DO INFLUENCE BEHAVIOUR

It is not always the case that attitudes do not impact behaviour; certainly, it is easy to think of examples from our lives when they have. More notably, there have been studies showing the dramatic effects our attitudes can have on our lives. For example, optimism has been shown to improve immune system functioning and treatment outcomes (i.e., longer life) in both student and cancer patient populations (e.g., Novotny et al., 2010; Segerstrom & Sephton, 2010). However, attitudes also influence our behaviour in negative ways. For example, if you believe that aggression is a good way to get what you want, or that you must be perfect to be attractive, you may be more likely to engage in bullying or disordered eating behaviours, respectively (e.g., Hewitt, Flett, & Ediger, 1995; Salmivalli & Voeten, 2004). Similarly, people may engage in risky health behaviours or fail to seek treatment for medical issues because they have an "it won't happen to me" attitude toward negative outcomes (e.g., MacDonald & Martineau, 2002; Myers Godin, Lambert, Calzavara, & Locker, 1996).

It is evident that our attitudes can impact our behaviour in significant ways, but does this always occur without our awareness? Have you ever made a decision after a long period of thoughtful deliberation? Let's take the example of a young woman in an emotionally abusive relationship with a boyfriend. She is seriously contemplating leaving him. Perhaps she writes a list of pros and cons about leaving him, and her list of pros—reasons why she should leave him—is much longer than the cons—reasons why she should stay with him. She then develops a positive attitude about the prospect of leaving him. She imagines what those who care about her would think if she left him, and how happy they would be for her. This makes the young woman certain that she can leave her boyfriend, so she sets the intention to do so. The very next day she breaks off the relationship. The young woman breathes a sigh of relief. The deed is done.

The underlying structure of this rational process is what social psychologists refer to as the **theory of planned behaviour** (Ajzen & Fishbein, 1977, 1980). This theory suggests that attitudes, social norms, and the perceived control of the individual lead to behaviour. Behavioural options are considered, the consequences of each are weighed, and a decision on how to act is made. The theory of planned behaviour, in addition, postulates that people will also consider the feasibility of performing the action before committing to it.

According to this theory, an intention to form a behaviour will arise from reasoned thinking and involves three considerations: (1) one's own attitudes toward the behaviour, (2) the attitudes of others toward that behaviour (subjective norms), and (3) the perceived feasibility of the behaviour (the perceived behavioural control). The decision the young woman in the above example made was based on those three considerations—her own favourable attitude toward breaking up, the favourable attitudes of people she cared about regarding breaking up, and her belief that she could actually perform the behaviour. In combination, these three factors tended to promote the occurrence of the behaviour. Conversely, behaviour may be prevented if any one of these factors is not supportive of behavioural change. For example, imagine you would like to quit smoking and think that you could be successful in doing so; however, all of your friends smoke (the subjective norm) and have said they will not quit smoking around you. Do you think changing this behaviour will be more difficult?

### Why Attitudes Matter

Attitudes provide us with scaffolding with which to organize our world. For example, if you hold a particularly strong attitude about legalizing marijuana, and are presented with information that supports this attitude, you would tend to consider that information to be more reliable than information that argues against your attitude (e.g., Munro & Ditto, 1997). Recall the discussion of the *confirmation* bias in Chapter 1—we tend to seek out and notice information that is consistent with the

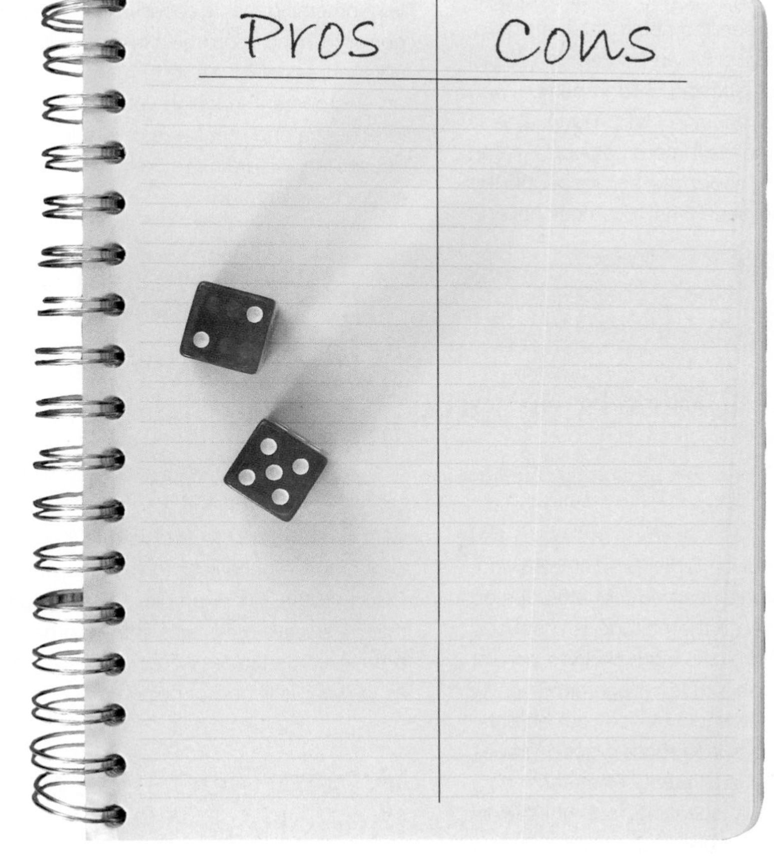


Sometimes, we truly do base our **actions on reasoned, thoughtful decisions, rather than chance.**

**THEORY OF PLANNED BEHAVIOUR** the theory that attitudes, social norms, and the perceived control of an individual lead to behaviour

attitudes or beliefs that we hold. The attitudes that we hold and that we publicly express impact our social interactions and how others form impressions of us. Attitudes, therefore, can be context-dependent, meaning that how strongly we appear to hold an attitude or whether or not we express an attitude may depend on the social environment that we are in (Schwarz & Bohner, 2001). For example, if you were being interviewed in a room with several individuals who had a very favourable attitude toward the Conservative Party of Canada, and you had a negative attitude toward that same political party, you might not express your attitude in that setting.

## FACTORS TO CONSIDER WHEN EVALUATING BEHAVIOURS

We've discussed the ways in which attitudes contribute to planned behaviours, and why attitude is important in considering behaviours. However, there are several other factors we need to consider when evaluating whether our attitudes will correspond to our actual behaviours—strength of attitude, specificity, and accessibility.

### Strength of Attitude

You have many different attitudes, and they inevitably vary with regard to how important they are to you. For instance, if you have a particularly strong attitude about the environment, you are more likely to act on that attitude as opposed to a weaker one. Why might this be? There are two reasons—the *importance of the attitude to you personally* and the extent to which these attitudes are formed based on *direct experience*.

Imagine you had to volunteer time to a social cause. What type of organization would you choose to work for? Most likely, you would volunteer to help out a cause that is personally relevant to your life. For example, you may have friends or loved ones who have chronic diseases such as diabetes or multiple sclerosis and may therefore choose organizations that support research into these diseases. Alternatively, you may have been in an abusive relationship in the past and may choose to help others by volunteering your time to a distress line. In each of these cases, if something is personally important to you, it is going to have more of an impact on your behaviour (e.g., Crano, 1997; Visser, Krosnick, & Simmons, 2003).

**ACCESSIBILITY** the degree to which a concept is active in our consciousness

**CHRONIC ACCESSIBILITY** accessibility arising from frequent and recent exposure to a construct that has permanence—i.e., it is accessible all the time

Join
William Shatner
in supporting
March of Dimes
View PSA

**Similar to us, celebrity spokespersons for charities often lend their assistance to a cause because of personal relevance and/or direct experience.**

As another example, you may decide to offer your support to an aid program such as UNICEF or Plan Canada to help children who are starving in other countries. Unfortunately, many of us don't think about donating or providing help to these programs until we are directly exposed to images of starving children or see the detrimental effects of poverty on childhood development either in our own country or abroad during our travels. If you have ever seen a starving child in person, you are much more likely to act in support of ending child poverty. This is because direct experience with an issue makes it more palpable—it can no longer be ignored. For instance, think about the spokespeople for various disease-related charities that you see. What do most have in common? Either they or a loved one have dealt with that disease. In this latter example, the issue is now *both* personal and one with which they have direct experience, and as such, these spokespeople are some of the most passionate, active supporters of their causes you will find.

> "Direct experience with an issue makes it more palpable—it can no longer be ignored."

## Specificity

Another factor that affects how strongly our attitudes predict behaviour is how specific an attitude is. We have already learned that attitudes do not necessarily predict behaviour. However, if the attitude is a specific one, tailored to you and a specific situation, it is more likely to predict your behaviour. If you are asked, "How important is college or university to you?" you might give a stock answer that would please your parents. Instead, if you are asked, "How important is it to receive good grades this semester?" your answer may be quite different. Post-secondary education may be important to you, broadly speaking, but whether or not you are motivated to translate that into good grades right now is a very different issue. Similarly, asking participants about their attitudes toward donating money to a homeless shelter is a better indicator of the attitude–behaviour link than asking how an individual feels about homeless people in general (e.g., Schwarz & Bohner, 2001).

In demonstration of this effect, several studies have asked students how they feel about using condoms and about their intentions to engage in sexually "risky" behaviour. In general, students indicate positive attitudes toward using condoms and engaging in safe sex. That said, in many cases, their behaviour did not correlate with their responses (e.g., MacDonald, MacDonald, Zanna, & Fong, 2000; MacDonald & Martineau, 2002). However, when asked more specific questions such as "How do you feel about using condoms every time you have sex in the next month when you are with a new partner?" participants' responses tend to be much more consistent with their behaviours (e.g., Sheeran, Abraham, & Orbell, 1999). As such, when forced to think about specific behaviours at particular moments in time, people are much more likely to report attitudes that are consistent with their eventual behaviours.

## Accessibility

Another factor that influences the tendency of our attitudes to impact our behaviour is **accessibility** (Fazio, Chen, McDonel, & Sherman, 1982). Accessibility refers to the degree with which a concept is active in our consciousness (Higgins, Rholes, & Jones, 1977). Constructs are made accessible by frequent and/or recent exposure (see Fazio, 1995 for a review of this concept). Fazio, Ledbetter, and Towles-Schwen (2000) suggest that some attitudes we hold may be more accessible than others.

Let's say you've been caring for a friend's pet snake while he is away on vacation for a week. After seeing the snake every day for a week and a half, you might be more likely to think you saw a snake on the ground if you encounter a strangely shaped stick. This is due to the concept of "snake" being **chronically accessible** in your mind. Not only will something that is accessible come to mind more often, but it will also come to mind more quickly and easily. As a student, you might often categorize individuals in terms of their intelligence, because you are in an environment in which you are constantly exposed to the concept of intelligence and measures of intelligence. When a concept is chronically accessible, we are more likely to describe others in terms of that concept (Higgins & King, 1981).

Accessibility of an attitude can directly impact its strength. Recent research demonstrated that when an attitude is made transiently accessible by repeated expression of it, people will report more commitment to the attitude (e.g., Holland, Verplanken, & van Knippenberg, 2003). By increasing the strength of the attitude, as mentioned earlier, it will be more likely to translate to behaviour. More directly, accessibility can increase behaviour toward the object of the attitude (e.g., Roese & Olson, 1994). For example, Clark, Wegener, and Fabrigar (2008) found that persuasive messages shown to participants that are in line with their pre-existing attitudes about a topic increase accessibility of the attitude as well as likelihood of being persuaded by the message.

# When Does Behaviour Influence Attitudes?

Attitudes are complex, and sometimes we may be unaware of them. We may even disagree with our own attitudes. But that doesn't necessarily mean that they're so deeply ingrained that we can't change them. In this section, we will discuss changes in attitudes due to self-persuasion. In

Read the following statements and rate how much you agree or disagree with them.
**1** = strongly disagree, **2** = disagree, **3** = no opinion, **4** = agree, **5** = strongly agree

1. People talking on cellphones while driving can cause accidents.
2. Children are our future.
3. It is important to save our planet.
4. It is important to study hard.

**Answer the following questions:**

1. Do you drive while talking on your cellphone?
2. Do you personally spend time mentoring or working with children?
3. Do you engage in environmentally friendly behaviour, like recycling?
4. Do you study hard for all of your classes, all of the time?

Are your attitudes consistent with your behaviour? How does it make you feel? When you consider your actual behaviour, does it make you reconsider how you feel about these issues?

*Source:* Carkenord, D. M., & Bullington, J. (1993). Bringing cognitive dissonance to the classroom. *Teaching of Psychology, 20,* 41–43.

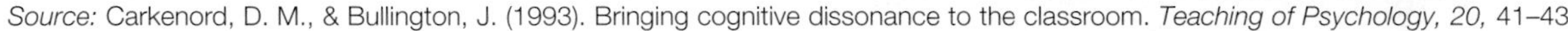

**Awareness of Behaviour and Attitude Change.** Being aware of one's own behaviour will often cause a person to modify his or her attitudes to accommodate that behaviour as permissible (Carkenoid & Bullington, 1993). What will you do in the above situations?

**COGNITIVE DISSONANCE** the anxiety that arises from acting in a way discordant with your attitudes. This anxiety is resolved by adjusting one's attitudes to be in line with the behaviour

Chapter 7, we'll explore the influence of other persuasion—when other individuals bring about a change in our attitudes or behaviours.

## COGNITIVE DISSONANCE

Did you ever think that if you were paid a lot of money for a task, you might actually like it less than somebody who is paid less money for the same task? It sounds backward but turns out to be true. Researchers asked college student participants to complete a very boring task that was supposed to be so boring as to verge on unpleasant. Then they paid the participants either $20 or $1 to tell a lie to the next participant awaiting her turn at the study—that the task was actually enjoyable. Afterward, in a confidential interview, the participants who were paid $20 admitted that the task was actually boring. But, interestingly enough, the participants who were paid $1 claimed that the task was somewhat enjoyable (Festinger & Carlsmith, 1959).

Can you guess why the participants who were paid $20 to lie admitted to being bored while the ones who were paid $1 to lie said that they enjoyed the task? The answer has to do with a concept called **cognitive dissonance**. Cognitive dissonance theory states that people want their behaviour to be consistent with their beliefs and feel uncomfortable with any inconsistency between the two. After all, if you believe something to be true, it would feel strange for you to act in a manner inconsistent with that truth. If people's behaviours are inconsistent (or dissonant), they feel the need to justify or rationalize their behaviour. The people who were paid the $20 to lie had the payment as justification for lying. On the contrary, those who were paid $1 did not have a high payment as justification for the lie. Therefore, they had insufficient justification for telling the lie, so they experienced more discomfort (dissonance) and were more likely to adjust their attitudes to match their behaviours. In situations in which external justification for behaviour (receiving $20) is not enough, insufficient justification calls for one to internally justify his or her behaviour ("Hey, that wasn't so bad, after all!") to reduce dissonance.

People do not want to think of themselves as inherently deceitful, so these participants justified the lie by deciding that they *actually enjoyed the task*. It is worth noting that no participant cited what is perhaps the truest justification for the lie—that he or she was in the role of "participant" and felt compelled to do what the experimenter asked. Thus, people can be ignorant of the true reasons for their behaviour, and in the absence of such information will fill in the blanks with what they *need* to believe is true.

These findings on cognitive dissonance have been used to attempt to promote healthy behaviours in young people by making them aware of the inconsistency between their attitudes and behaviours. In one study, sexually active college students who gave speeches in which they advocated condom use by others were more likely to make some effort toward condom use, either through discreet purchase or by taking home information pamphlets (Stone, Aronson, Crain, Winslow, & Fried, 1994). Recent research has demonstrated that students often hold ambivalent attitudes about condom use, and may feel simultaneously positive and negative about purchasing condoms (e.g., Dahl, Darke, Gorn, & Weinberg, 2005). When such a conflict occurs, individuals may try to reduce the dissonance of their conflicting feelings by focusing on instances where their behaviour (i.e., condom use) matched their current attitude concerning purchasing condoms. In another line of research, Schumacher and Smith Slep (2004) found that cognitive dissonance experienced by high school students who expressed attitudes toward dating violence that were inconsistent with their behaviour led to greater behavioural change (i.e., less aggressive actions towards dating partners) over time.

One of the key factors in cognitive dissonance leading to behavioural change is individuals' mindfulness or awareness of their own behaviour and attitudes. For example, Dickerson, Thibodeau, Aronson, and Miller (1992) attempted to change participants' behaviour by inducing feelings of hypocrisy (i.e., that you say one thing and do another) to make them aware of their actions. These researchers first asked people who were environmentally conscious about their water usage in the shower. Those who were reminded of their own excessive water usage and asked to make a public commitment to take shorter showers, and thus made to feel hypocritical if they took long showers, later took significantly shorter showers than those either not reminded of their usage or not asked to make a commitment. The participants who took shorter showers wanted to rid themselves of the cognitive dissonance they felt between their own environmentally conscious beliefs and the fact that they took long showers.

Sometimes, all it takes is effort to make something seem worthwhile. When we spend a lot of time and energy making something happen, we more often than not see value in that accomplishment—even if we

<<< **We look for explanations for our behaviour—**and why would we do something for only a dollar versus $100.00?

^^^ Cognitive dissonance can actually help people **act more in line with their attitudes, such as the importance of safe sex.**

shouldn't. Why? Because working hard to achieve something and then finding it wasn't worth the effort is a sure source of cognitive dissonance. To combat this, we justify effort that was spent. This is referred to as *effort justification*. An illustration of this concept comes in the form of a study concerning people who were trying to lose weight. Participants were asked to complete high- or low-effort cognitive tasks, none of which were actually proven to help with weight loss. People who completed the high-effort tasks lost an average of over eight pounds, while those who spent less time on low-effort tasks didn't lose weight (Axsom & Cooper, 1985).

In addition to altering our behaviours, dissonance plays a role in affecting our attitudes toward the choices we have already made, as described earlier. Imagine you have been asked to make a choice between two posters to decorate your dorm room. You like both posters equally, but you only have enough space for one. After you've made your decision, you may find that you now like your selected poster better and have a lower opinion of the rejected one. **Post-decision dissonance** results from having to reject one appealing choice in favour of another. To combat this, we enhance our opinions of what we've chosen to justify our choice cognitively. In a recent study, researchers had participants rate a series of photographs, then choose between pairs of them, and then rate them again. Those who were chosen experienced an increase in rating from the first rating to the second, and those who were not chosen experienced a decrease in rating. Notably, this effect occurred even in persons with amnesia who could not remember which items they chose and which they did not. As such, the change in evaluation that occurs when we make a choice occurs relatively unconsciously (e.g., Lieberman, Ochsner, Gilbert, & Schacter, 2001).

The photo on page 110 shows an image of one of Aesop's famous fables. If you are not familiar with it, the story is about a fox who looks longingly at a bunch of grapes and tries repeatedly to reach them. After several attempts, he gives up and says, "They must have been sour anyway." Cognitive dissonance operates in this way—making us believe that we wanted all along what we have and did not want what we do not have. Cognitive dissonance enables our attitudes to shift so that we are more content with our lot in life than we might otherwise be (Tavris & Aronson, 2007). In addition, it can compel behavioural change that makes people act more in line with how they wish to behave.

**POST-DECISION DISSONANCE** cognitive dissonance that results from having to reject one appealing choice in favour of another

Interestingly, though, dissonance effects are limited in collectivist cultures. Indeed, Japanese participants were found to engage in dissonance-reducing attitude changes only after being asked to consider the preferences of a self-relevant other person (e.g., Kitayama, Snibbe, Markus, & Suzuki, 2004). That is, they engaged in dissonance-reducing techniques to please others and therefore justify their collectivist ideals. In this way, people from such cultures can believe that what they want is truly what the group wants. Further, dissonance-reduction strategies may not be utilized in collectivistic cultures to the same degree as in individualistic cultures because personal discomfort does not threaten their sense of interdependent self (e.g., Heine & Lehman, 1997). Culture moderates the extent to which individuals experience dissonance, and in what contexts (i.e., interdependent or independent) they will change their attitudes or behaviour to reduce dissonance (Hoshino-Browne et al., 2005).

> "Cognitive dissonance enables our attitudes to shift so **that we are more content with our lot in life than we might otherwise be.**"

Since the inception of the theory of cognitive dissonance, some modifications to the theory have been provided. One notable modification postulated a four-step model by which attitude change occurs (Cooper & Fazio, 1984):

1. The individual must realize that the attitude-discrepant action has negative consequences.
2. The individual must take personal responsibility for the action.
3. The individual must experience physiological arousal.
4. The individual must attribute the arousal to the action.

So how are these steps involved in the arousal and reduction of cognitive dissonance? First, a behaviour that doesn't match an attitude must cause *negative consequences*. (Remember those study participants who were offered money to lie about the experiment being interesting?) Then, there must be a feeling of *personal responsibility* for the negative outcome of the behaviour. For this to happen, the person must feel that he or she had a choice in the matter and that the consequences were to some degree foreseeable. The people who were given $1 to lie about the experiment felt guilty about lying—they were given the choice to lie and knew there would be negative consequences. The third step in the new model is physiological *arousal*. Cognitive dissonance causes physical discomfort and tension—of course you want to reduce it. Finally, there must be an *attribution* of the arousal to the behaviour (Cooper & Fazio, 1984). The people who got $1 for lying to the next participant knew they felt bad because of what they had done.

**SELF-AFFIRMATION THEORY** the theory that we are more open to attitudinal change when we have recently been given an opportunity to affirm our core values and identity

**IMPRESSION MANAGEMENT** the process by which people either consciously or unconsciously attempt to monitor how they appear to others by regulating the information conveyed about themselves in a social interaction, and thus attitude change is more likely when counter-attitudinal behaviour occurs in public

All four of these factors must be in place for attitude change to occur. Yet, this theory does not take into account the ability of cognitive dissonance to change behaviour instead of attitudes. One possible factor may be the extent to which the behaviour *can* be changed. While some choices are unalterable, others can be changed, as can our behaviour. Future research, perhaps, can more precisely delineate when each one will change and when each one will not.

## Alternative Methods of Self-Persuasion

Cognitive dissonance is just one theory of attitude change. Other researchers have proposed theories to address how behaviour may lead to attitude change. *Self-perception theory* (to which you were first exposed in Chapter 4) suggests that we infer our own attitudes by observing our own behaviours (Bem, 1967, 1972). For instance, if we see ourselves opening the cover of a book we've already read, we may then infer that we really like that book. This theory originated from the idea that we can infer the true thoughts of others in many cases simply by observing their behaviour, without access to their internal states; therefore we should not need access to our own either. Also, emotions often follow rather than precede behaviours, arising as a result of interpreting our behaviours. In a classic study, Valins (1966) exposed male students to "centrefolds" while they were hooked up to electrodes they believed were measuring heart rate. In fact, the researcher controlled the heartbeat reading output, leading participants to believe they experienced a greater response to one particular (randomly selected) photo. When they were invited to take one of the photos home, which do you think they chose? Of course, the vast majority of the men chose the photo they thought got their heart rates revved up, believing this was the photo they liked the most (Valins, 1966). More recently, studies have found that if people are made to smile while watching something, they will report liking it more than if they are made to frown (e.g., Laird, 2007). Thus, under self-perception theory, attitudes can be adjusted by altering one's behaviour.

LE RENARD ET LES RAISINS. Fable LIII.
J. Punt del. et sculps. 1761.


^ When something is unattainable, **we tend to devalue it.**

Once we establish a sense of self, we are motivated to maintain it and reaffirm it. **Self-affirmation theory** (Steele, 1988) states that, in the face of threat, people will try to restore their self-worth by reaffirming their values. But how does this relate to shifting attitudes? Under normal circumstances, people are motivated to maintain existing beliefs as a way of affirming their understanding of themselves. However, if people are allowed to affirm their sense of self in some other way—for instance, by the acquisition of a value symbol such as a degree if they place value on their intelligence, or even by thinking or talking about an important part of their identity—they are more open to others' ideas and will process those ideas in less biased ways, opening themselves up to attitude change (e.g., Correll, Spencer, & Zanna, 2004).

We are not only concerned with understanding ourselves but also with how others perceive us. People must create and maintain impressions of themselves that match how they want others to understand them, as described by the theory of **impression management** (e.g., Piwinger & Ebert, 2001). Impression management states that people either consciously or unconsciously attempt to monitor how they appear to others by regulating the information conveyed about themselves in a social interaction. Even social media such as Facebook, messenger programs, blogs, and Twitter are designed to allow individuals to control the impression they make on others, a quality that serves as a major motivation for use of such media (e.g., Krämer & Winter, 2008). Research suggests that attitudinal shift as a result of cognitive dissonance is much more likely to occur when the counter-attitudinal behaviour is conducted publicly (e.g., Gaes, Kalle, & Tedeschi, 1978). As a result, we are more concerned with appearing consistent with our attitudes to others than we are with actually being consistent, and that concern can drive attitude change.

In many ways, our attitudes define who we are. Attitudes, behaviour, and cognition have a reciprocal relationship with one another—it's safe to say you can't study one without studying the others. Research on attitudes helps us to understand our behaviours and interactions with one another. In fact, you might see attitudes as the root of social interactions. Everything we say and do starts with an attitude, whether negative, positive, or somewhere in between. Research allows us to not only understand how attitudes, behaviours, and cognition interact with each other, it also allows an opportunity for change. The more we know about our attitudes and how they are linked (or not linked) to our behaviours, the more resources we will have for ensuring that our attitudes and subsequent behaviours reflect ourselves.

## ACTION LEARNING

### Cognitive Dissonance

Cognitive dissonance is a theory of self-persuasion. When your attitude is inconsistent with your behaviour, you are likely to experience an unpleasant feeling (dissonance) and will try to bring your attitude more in line with your behaviour. Consider a current behaviour that you have that you would like to change (because it is inconsistent with your attitude). For example, maybe your attitude is that you would like to be healthier, but you eat a lot of fast food meals or you don't exercise. Or maybe your attitude is that you care about the environment, but you currently do not recycle. You could just change your attitude, but for this project we want to bring about a behavioural change. For one week, change your behaviour. Plan a healthy diet, exercise daily, or recycle all your plastics. This may be difficult to do, so pick a simple behaviour and stick to it. Make a public commitment by writing down the steps you will take to change your behaviour. When you feel tempted to return to old behaviours, think about times in the past you've engaged in those behaviours and how you felt when you realized that they were inconsistent with your attitude.

At the end of the week, note your attitude toward the behaviour. Now that you have modified your behaviour, how do you feel? Did the attitude grow stronger or stay the same strength? Did you make cognitive dissonance work for you?

What you will learn from this action learning project:

1. How to bring about a change in your behaviour
2. How powerful self-persuasion can be
3. How being aware of discrepancies between actions and attitudes can help you to act more in line with your attitudes

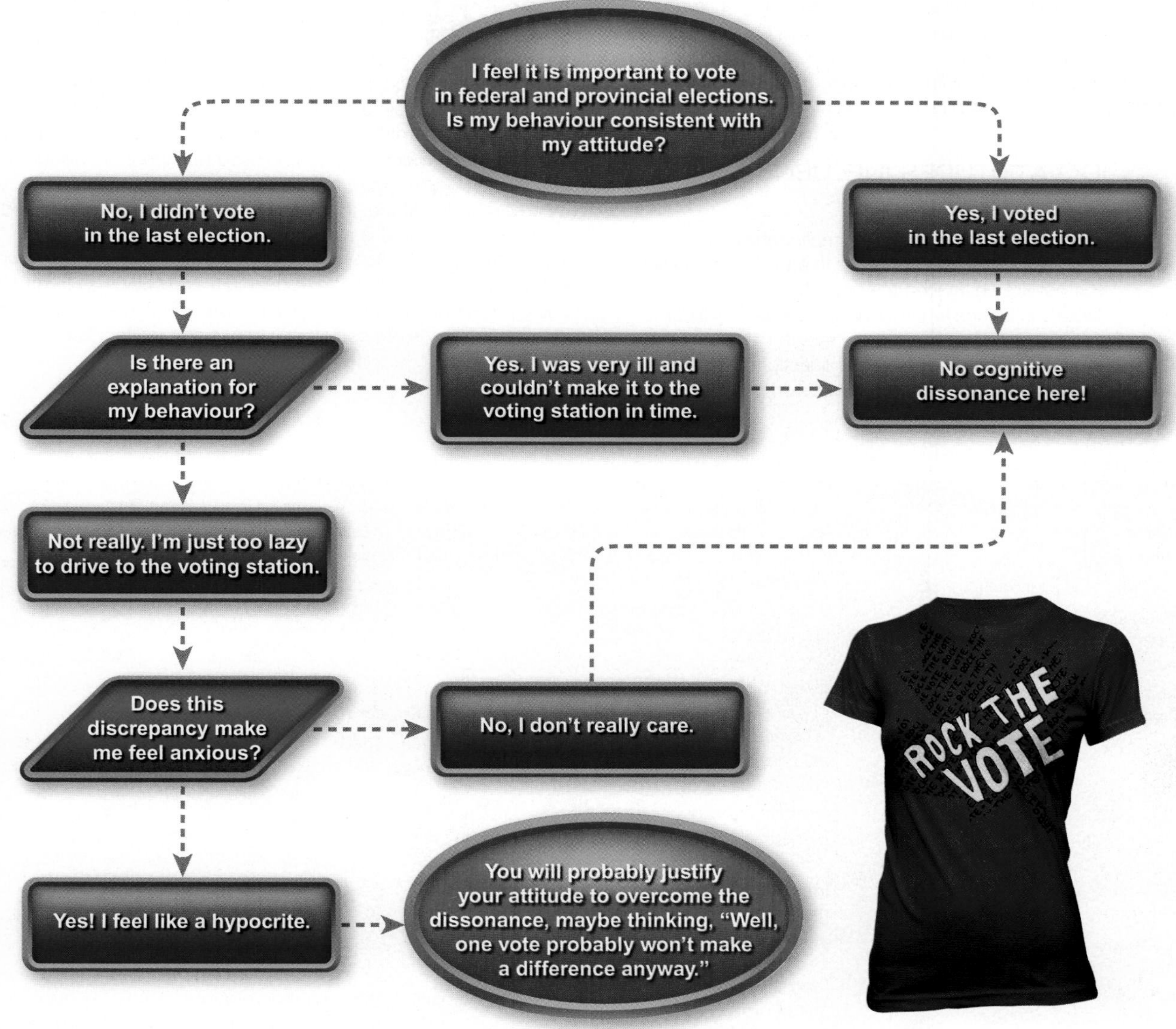


**Rock the Vote.** **Cognitive dissonance operates by arousing anxiety** due to an inconsistency between behaviour and attitude that we are motivated to eliminate.

CHAPTER

# 06 Review

## Summary

### HOW DO ATTITUDES DEVELOP? p. 98

• One way that attitudes çan arise is due to conditioning—either classical or operant. Classical conditioning creates an association between two mutually occurring events, while operant conditioning increases or decreases the frequency of behaviour with reinforcements and punishments.

• Attitudes can also arise due to observational learning, wherein we internalize the attitudes of others. In this way, attitudes can be passed on from one person to another.

• Attitudes can be held explicitly (those that are consciously known) or implicitly (associations of which people may not be aware). The methods necessary to assess these different types of attitudes vary considerably. Explicit attitudes can be assessed with simple self-report measures, while implicit attitudes require a subtle method such as the IAT.

### DO ATTITUDES INFLUENCE BEHAVIOUR? p. 103

• Attitudes do not inherently imply behaviour. Oftentimes people will believe in a cause or principle but not act on it when the opportunity arises. Many factors influence whether or not attitudes will come to impact behaviour. The core factors are the strength of the attitude, the specificity of the attitude to the behaviour in question, the accessibility of the attitude, and the result of rational decision making.

• The stronger an attitude is, the more likely it is to translate into behaviour. Likewise, the more specific the attitude is to the circumscribed behaviour, the more it will be relevant for that behaviour. The easier an attitude is to bring to mind, whether because of repeated exposure to it or recent exposure to it (both of which increase accessibility), the more it will influence behaviour. Finally, if rational thought leads to the decision that behaviour should be done based upon a held attitude, and it is decided that the behaviour can be done, it is more likely that the behaviour will arise.

### WHEN DOES BEHAVIOUR INFLUENCE ATTITUDES? p. 106

• One way in which attitude change occurs is via cognitive dissonance. If people find that they are behaving in a way that is inconsistent with their attitudes, they will shift their attitudes to better match the behaviour. This can be used to impact behaviour as well, by making people aware that they are behaving inconsistently with a cared-about attitude. In addition, the tendency to be affected by cognitive dissonance is affected by culture.

• Our attitudes can also shift based on observations of our own behaviour, our motivation to appear in a particular way to others, or by being more open to others' opinions after affirming core parts of our identity. When we are secure in who we are, we feel freer to consider others' ideas.

## Key Terms

**accessibility** the degree to which a concept is active in our consciousness *106*

**ambivalence** simultaneously experiencing strong contradictory emotions or motivations *98*

**attitudes** having an evaluative component toward a stimulus that is made up of affective, behavioural, and cognitive information *98*

**chronic accessibility** accessibility arising from frequent and recent exposure to a construct that has permanence—i.e., it is accessible all the time *106*

**classical conditioning** a type of learning by which a neutral stimulus gets paired with a stimulus (UCS) that elicits a response (UCR). Through repeated pairings, the neutral stimulus (CS) by itself elicits the response (CR) of the second stimulus *100*

**cognitive dissonance** the anxiety that arises from acting in a way discordant with one's attitudes. This anxiety is resolved by adjusting one's attitudes to be in line with the behaviour. *108*

**conditioned response (CR)** a learned response to the conditioned stimulus that was previously a neutral stimulus *100*

**conditioned stimulus (CS)** a stimulus that, only by repeated association with a particular unconditioned stimulus, comes to evoke the response associated with the unconditioned stimulus *100*

**explicit attitudes** attitudes of which one is aware and that one can control *98*

**Implicit Association Test (IAT)** a test that measures how easily we associate categories with positive or negative attitudes, including measures in categories ranging from racial and religious attitudes to attitudes about presidents. See implicit.harvard.edu/implicit/demo/. *102*

**implicit attitudes** attitudes that are automatically formed and activated without our even being aware of it *98*

**impression management** the process by which people either consciously or unconsciously attempt to monitor how they appear to others by regulating the information conveyed about themselves in a social interaction, and thus attitude change is more likely when counter-attitudinal behaviour occurs in public *110*

**mere exposure effect** the phenomenon whereby objects become better liked with exposure—we like things more as they become more familiar to us *100*

**name–letter effect** the tendency to show a preference for letters in our own name and prefer stimuli that contain those letters *101*

**observational learning** acquiring an attitude or behaviour due to the observation of others exhibiting that attitude or behaviour *101*

**operant conditioning** a type of learning in which the frequency of a behaviour is determined by reinforcement and punishment *101*

**post-decision dissonance** cognitive dissonance that results from having to reject one appealing choice in favour of another *109*

**self-affirmation theory** the theory that we are more open to attitudinal change when we have recently been given an opportunity to affirm our core values and identity *110*

**theory of planned behaviour** the theory that attitudes, social norms, and the perceived control of an individual lead to behaviour *105*

**unconditioned response (UCR)** a response that occurs automatically in reaction to some stimulus, without learning taking place *100*

**unconditioned stimulus (UCS)** a stimulus that elicits a response automatically, without learning taking place *100*

# Test Your Understanding

## MULTIPLE CHOICE

1. Which of these methods is best at measuring implicit attitudes?
   - a. observation
   - b. self-report
   - c. introspection
   - d. the IAT

2. Which of these events are we most likely to remember?
   - a. the A we got in social psychology
   - b. the F we got in social psychology
   - c. the sound of a clock ticking
   - d. the hue of the color magenta

3. You are afraid of thunder. I decide that every time there is a thunderstorm, I will make you hold a rabbit. Now you also fear rabbits. The rabbit is the
   - a. unconditioned stimulus.
   - b. unconditioned response.
   - c. conditioned stimulus.
   - d. conditioned response.

4. You made me a delicious dinner. Since I want more dinners made for me, I bring you wine and smile a lot when you cook for me. What am I engaging in?
   - a. positive reinforcement
   - b. negative reinforcement
   - c. positive punishment
   - d. negative punishment

5. Cognitive dissonance causes people to strive to diminish which personality trait?
   - a. guilt
   - b. hypocrisy
   - c. fear
   - d. prejudice

6. Why do implicit attitudes influence behaviour?
   - a. because associations in memory are activated outside of awareness
   - b. because we endorse implicit attitudes
   - c. because we mimic these attitudes in others
   - d. Implicit attitudes do not influence behaviour.

7. Hotel owners did not keep the Chinese couple from staying at their hotels in the research by LaPiere (1934). Which is least likely to be the reason?
   - a. the couple exhibited kindness
   - b. the couple spoke proper English
   - c. the generality of the stereotype versus the specificity of the couple
   - d. the owners really didn't mean it when they said they wouldn't admit a Chinese couple

8. Which influences the impact of attitudes on behaviour the least?
   - a. strength of the attitude
   - b. specificity of the attitude
   - c. superordinance of the attitude
   - d. accessibility of the attitude

9. When you act in a way that is different from how you believe you should, you
   - a. change your behaviour.
   - b. change your attitude.
   - c. a or b, depending on whether or not the behaviour can be changed and the strength of the attitude.
   - d. neither a nor b.

10. What is the best way to get others to listen to your opinions, based on attitude research?
    - a. talk louder
    - b. allow them to do something that affirms their own beliefs
    - c. try to provide proof for your opinions
    - d. show them that most people share your opinion

**ANSWERS:** 1. d; 2. b; 3. c; 4. a; 5. b; 6. a; 7. d; 8. c; 9. c; 10. b

## ESSAY RESPONSE

1. If some attitudes are acquired through conditioning, consider how we might overcome or undo attitudes that have negative impacts on our lives, such as prejudice.
2. Discuss how observational learning can overcome phobias.
3. When might attitudes influence behaviour versus not?
4. Think about how cognitive dissonance operates in the workplace. What from this chapter explains why paying employees more for better work is effective? How might employers increase workplace enjoyment, given that paying employees for work may reduce enjoyment of the tasks themselves?
5. Consider how impression management can impact your attitudes. What does it mean for the self and social relations to say that we change attitudes more when we behave counter-attitudinally in public?

## APPLY IT!

Think about your attitude toward school. Regardless of how positive or negative it is, what factors contributed to your acquisition of this attitude? Might conditioning or observational learning have played a role? Might cognitive dissonance be responsible for any decrements in your attitude toward school, perhaps after attending a few parties instead of studying? Or might impression management have kept any positive aspects of your attitude intact?

**Remember to check www.thethinkspot.ca for additional information, downloadable flashcards, and other helpful resources.**

## Health

When your parents or grandparents visited the doctor, they were probably asked about their medical histories, diets, and any genetic disorders. Today, medical doctors are increasingly incorporating a holistic view of health based on *the biopsychosocial model*—a concept that views health as the product of a combination of factors, including biological characteristics (e.g., genetic predispositions), behavioural issues (e.g., stress and relationships), and social conditions (e.g., family support or cultural influences). As such, a visit to a doctor today might include questions about one's lifestyle and any recent stressful events. The biopsychosocial model is the underlying concept behind the emerging discipline of health psychology.

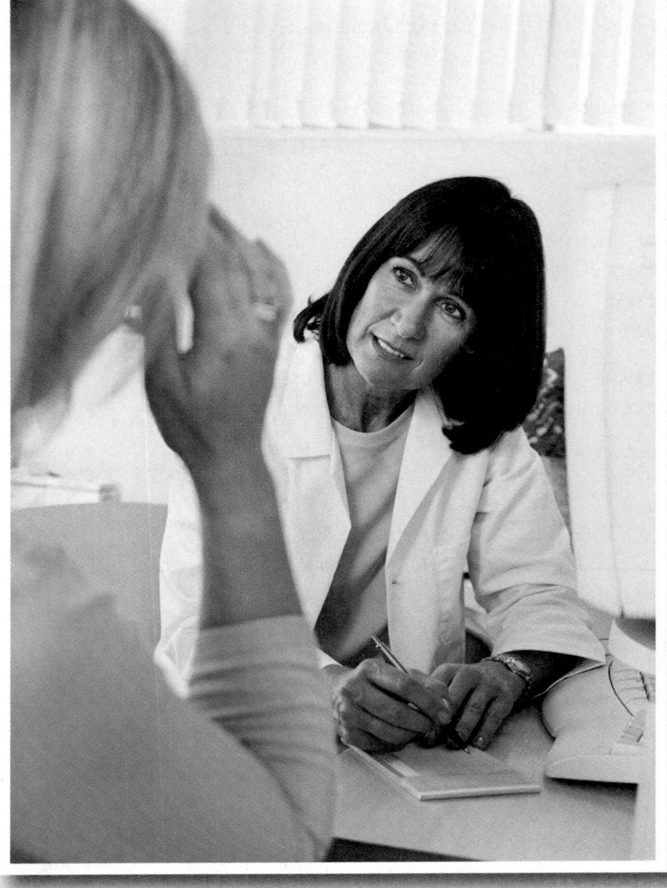

**When diagnosing a patient, health psychologists take psychosocial factors, such as stress, into consideration.**

In a fast-paced world, we increasingly encounter *stress*—an unpleasant physical response to events that make us feel threatened or upset our balance in some way. According to a 2009 survey by the Synovate research firm, financial matters (51 percent) and work (41 percent) are the top two major causes of stress in Canada (Sung, 2009). These are closely followed by family-related concerns (37 percent) and health-related concerns (32 percent). Further, this survey indicated that, in Canada, women are reporting higher levels of stress overall than men. Stress triggers can be divided into three main categories: *crises or catastrophes* (e.g., a natural disaster, motor vehicle accident, or terrorist attack), *major life events* (e.g., the death of a spouse, a divorce, or a job loss), and *daily stressors* (e.g., car problems, work issues, waiting in lines, or environmental factors such as noise, heat, and cold). Why do some people seem to bounce back from major catastrophes, while others fall apart over minor, daily stresses? Social psychology can help us understand these differences, aiding in the treatment of physical symptoms that manifest as a result of stress. It can also be applied to the health industry in an effort to prevent health problems, as in the following example.

> **"Why do some people seem to bounce back from major catastrophes, while others fall apart over minor, daily stresses?"**

Social psychologists often investigate the effectiveness of various methods of prevention with regard to health and well-being. For instance, most people would agree that reducing the rate of teen pregnancy and sexually transmitted diseases are desirable goals. But what is the best way to go about it? Analyses of school prevention programs have demonstrated that programs focusing only on abstinence are less effective than those that not only promote abstinence but also teach about contraception, sexually transmitted diseases, and relationships (e.g., Kohler, Manhart, & Lafferty, 2008; Trenholm et al., 2007). In addition to researching the effectiveness of various methods of prevention, social psychologists are also involved with changing people's attitudes toward serious health problems, and minimization of risk-taking behaviour. A key area of research is the prevention of alcoholism and unhealthy choices made while intoxicated. While approximately 11 percent of the Canadian population abuses alcohol (Veldhuizen, Urbanoski, & Cairney, 2007), there is particular concern over the 9.4 percent of youth aged 15 to 24 that report heavy frequent drinking (Health Canada, 2010). Addiction researchers have advocated for increased consideration of the social context of problematic drinking behaviours. Alcohol is associated not only with direct negative effects on health, but with *indirect effects* associated with poor decision making. Social psychologists have studied these effects as they relate to the theory of alcohol myopia: "a state of shortsightedness in which superficially understood, immediate aspects of experience have a disproportionate influence on behaviour and emotion, a state in which we can see the tree, albeit more dimly, but miss the forest altogether" (Steele & Josephs, 1990, p. 923). This idea helps to explain why alcohol use can be pleasurable, addictive, and destructive, all at the same time.

> Intoxicated people may focus on the perceived benefits of having intercourse rather than on the negative consequences of not using condoms.

In particular, the influence of alcohol myopia on attitudes and risk-taking behaviours has been the focus of several Canadian social psychologists at Queen's University and the University of Waterloo. One such area has been how alcohol influences our intentions concerning drinking and driving. Due to the impaired cognitive capacity caused by alcohol consumption, researchers found that intoxicated participants displayed less negative attitudes about drinking and driving when questioned about driving a short distance relative to drunk driving in general (e.g., MacDonald, Zanna, & Fong, 1995). Another area of investigation concerns risky sexual behaviour and condom use. Participants in multiple studies have reported more favourable attitudes and greater intentions to have unprotected sex when they are intoxicated than when they are sober (e.g., MacDonald, Zanna, & Fong, 1996; MacDonald, MacDonald, Zanna, & Fong, 2000). Consistent with alcohol myopia, these studies demonstrate that individuals tend to focus on the salient cues in their immediate environment rather than focus on the long-term consequences of their risky behaviours. For example, "intoxicated people may focus on the perceived benefits of having intercourse rather than on the negative consequences of not using condoms" (MacDonald et al., 1996, p. 763). As a result of these findings, this research group has tried to devise ways to reduce risky behaviours in such contexts. In a series of several clever studies in the laboratory and in bars in Alberta, the researchers manipulated the presence of impelling cues (e.g., likelihood of engaging in sexual intercourse) or inhibiting cues (e.g., likelihood of engaging in sexual intercourse without a condom), where the inhibiting conditions emphasized the unprotected nature of risky sexual behaviour (MacDonald, Fong, Zanna, & Martineau, 2000). When surveyed using questionnaires in Studies 1 and 2, intoxicated young men reported less intention to engage in unprotected sex when inhibiting cues were used, relative to high intentions in the presence of impelling cues. In Study 3, the researchers manipulated awareness cues by using hand stamps when patrons entered bars. Three cue manipulations were used: control (smiley face stamp), mild inhibiting (SAFE SEX stamp), and strong inhibiting (AIDS KILLS stamp). Again, their results suggested that strong inhibiting cues (i.e., a message that AIDS kills) was associated with decreased intentions to engage in unprotected sexual intercourse relative to the control or mild inhibiting groups. In an additional laboratory follow-up study, similar results were revealed. Overall, they concluded that "when inhibiting cues were salient, intoxicated participants were significantly less likely than their sober and placebo counterparts to report intentions to engage in unprotected sexual intercourse" (MacDonald et al., 2000, p. 617). The results of these studies can be applied to modification of the social messages or cues being presented to intoxicated individuals, such that powerful inhibiting cues and reminders (e.g., hand stamps, keychains) may decrease risky decisions such as having unprotected sex or drinking and driving. Developing techniques to encourage prevention of risky behaviours is just one example of the many useful ways social psychology can be put to practical use in the health industry.

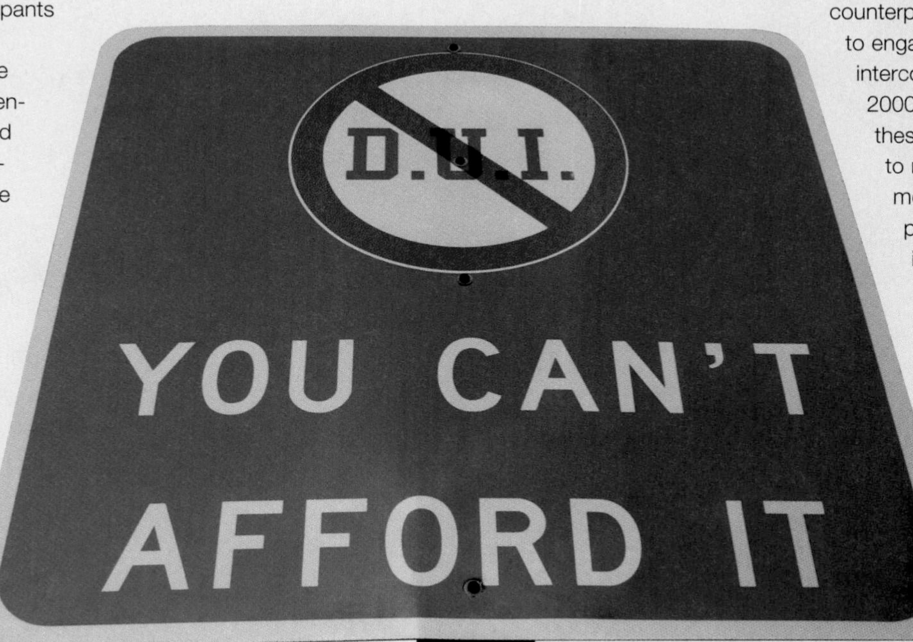


**Social psychological research has demonstrated that using potent reminders of the effects of risky behaviour when people are intoxicated may help them make healthier decisions.**

# THE POWER OF PERSUASION

<<< *Why are flowers the Mother's Day gift of choice?*

**WHAT** ARE PERSUASIVE MESSAGES?
**WHAT** PRINCIPLES CAN WE USE TO INFLUENCE OTHERS' BEHAVIOUR?
**WHAT** DOES RESEARCH TELL US ABOUT RESISTING PERSUASION TACTICS?
**WHEN** SHOULDN'T WE RESIST PERSUASION?

# How did

you celebrate last Mother's Day? Did you buy flowers, cards, and trinkets for your mother, grandmother, or any other special women in your life? Did you treat one of these women to one of the many well-advertised Mother's Day brunches at a local restaurant?

Overall, U.S. citizens spent nearly $16.3 billion on Mother's Day gifts in 2011, according to the National Retail Foundation (National Research Foundation, 2011). Similarly, Canadians spend an average of about $150 each on Mother's Day (Kimura, 2007). According to Nicholas D. Kristof, a columnist for the *New York Times*, this money could pay for the primary education of more than 60 million girls around the world currently not attending school—effectively ending female illiteracy (Kristof, 2010). In fact, the *Vancouver Sun* published a news report in 2011 detailing the historical roots of Mother's Day and how its founder, Anna Jarvis, denounced the commercialization of the holiday in 1923. She believed that "a single white carnation and a letter expressing love and appreciation were the appropriate ways to pay homage to mothers" ("The Story Behind Mother's Day," 2011). Billions of dollars go toward chocolate, roses, and greeting cards, and to what end? Do these material items contribute to the well-being of the world's mothers and future mothers? Was this the original intent of a day to honour mothers?

In addition to noting the impact this money could have on illiteracy, Kristof (2010) points out that there are other worthy causes that are more deserving of this money than a card that may well find its way into the recycling bin. He suggests that the money spent on one Mother's Day could instead go toward medical procedures that could improve the lives of mothers globally as well as save them from maternal complications. Wouldn't this be a better way to honour the mothers of the world?

When put so simply, it seems obvious what the answer *should* be. So why do we find ourselves pouring money into Hallmark and Carlton cards instead of global efforts to reduce maternal mortality? The answer is related to *persuasion*. Card stores, gift shops, and florists remind us "Don't forget Mother's Day!"—and they let us know just how to go about making sure we do not do so.



CHAPTER 07

**PERSUASION** the way people communicate in order to influence other people's attitudes and behaviours

**CENTRAL ROUTE** a type of processing that occurs when an individual has the ability and motivation to thoroughly listen to and evaluate a persuasive message

**PERIPHERAL ROUTE** a type of processing that occurs when an individual lacks the ability and motivation to thoroughly listen to and evaluate a persuasive message and is, therefore, influenced by external cues such as attractiveness of the speaker

# What Are Persuasive Messages?

What are you wearing? Why did you purchase these items? Did you do it because you really like the way your shoes and shirt look and fit? Or did you see a similar style in a magazine and decide it was a good look? Now scroll through your iPod or MP3 player. Why did you download these songs? Did you find them on your own? Or did a friend recommend that you listen to them? Maybe you heard a song played on a television show or commercial and just had to buy it. For example, independent musician Amy Seeley gained in popularity following the release of her song "Surprisingly So" on a widely played Canon camera commercial in 2010. Most of us would like to believe that we are independent thinkers, but persuasive forces are all around us. They are in our homes, governments, schools, and the media.

The study of **persuasion**, or the way people communicate in order to influence other people's attitudes and behaviours, became a central focus of social psychology after World War II and prompted an interest in the power of persuasive propaganda. Interest in persuasion has continued to grow since then, particularly in the past few years, as national and international events (e.g., economic crises, elections, the behaviour of soldiers overseas) have prompted individuals to question why we behave the way we do and what factors influence our actions.

For example, consider the downturn of the economy that has been evidenced in both Canada and the United States. Given our economic situation and all the hiring freezes that large and small industries have faced, why do we continue to spend money on impractical items? Persuasive forces can provoke irrational spending. What do you think of Kristof's (2010) ideas about Mother's Day spending? Has he persuaded you to swap the standard dozen roses and card for a donation to a worldwide educational fund or to a foundation that supports malnourished mothers? Probably not, given the amount of time you have spent convinced of the worth of flowers and cards as well as your mother's probable expectations of what constitutes a proper gift. However, if you (and she) haven't yet been persuaded by Kristof's message, it does not mean that you will never be convinced. As you will learn in this chapter, it's not always what is said, but how it's said, when it's said, and who says it that carries the power of persuasion.

## ROUTES TO PERSUASION

We all want to have what are the "right" attitudes and opinions, but the potential number of issues on which we can have opinions is infinite. It is nearly impossible to carefully scrutinize every message or evaluate all of the evidence when trying to arrive at a well-thought-out opinion, so in our search for what is "right," we must compromise by paying more attention to some information than we do to other information. Early research by Hovland and colleagues (1949, 1953) found that a message will be accepted based on three factors: the *communicator* of the message, the *content* of the message, and the *audience* receiving the message. This research was only the start. But before beginning to understand when people accept persuasive messages, it is important to understand what cognitive faculties enable or disable persuasion. Dual-process models of persuasion propose that it occurs through one of two routes: central or peripheral (e.g., Eagly & Chaiken, 1993, 1998; Petty & Cacioppo, 1981).

The **central route** is a type of processing that occurs when an individual has the ability and motivation to thoroughly listen to and evaluate a persuasive message. When booking a hotel for an upcoming vacation, a person using the central route might research the best rates, read several Hotels.ca reviews, and evaluate the amenities available at each option. This is the more analytical approach. Petty and colleagues (2004) argue that attitudes that are developed as a result of using the central route to persuasion "will be more persistent over time, will remain more resistant to persuasion, and will exert a greater impact on cognition and behaviour" (p. 75) in comparison to attitudes that are affected by using the peripheral route. For example, if you carefully consider the benefits of donating your Mother's Day gift money to a women's charity, weighing them against the cons, and decide to donate, you are more likely to continue to donate for years to come.

The **peripheral route** is the opposite of the central route. It is a type of processing that occurs when an individual lacks the ability and motivation to thoroughly listen to and evaluate a persuasive message and is therefore influenced only by external cues. Using the previous example, a person using this route might book a hotel based on the flashy photos on the hotel's website, a fun-sounding name, or other external factors (i.e., a friend went there and said it was good). This approach involves using more superficial information to make decisions. For example, if you see a beautiful bouquet of flowers and a sign that says, "Give your mom the gift of flowers," you might be more likely to buy these for your mother than to donate to a charity in her name.

<<< **Using sexy images to sell** products is a popular method of persuasion **because it doesn't just sell consumers a product;** it sells them a desired lifestyle.

Do you choose the clothes you wear, **or do clothing companies choose for you?**

As stated, opinions adopted due to central-route processing are more resistant to change. The reason for this is that when people have the available cognitive resources with which to consider an issue, they rely on the message as well as their own reflections. The more deeply an individual thinks about an issue, the more that attitude will resist change since the issue was considered more carefully. Keep in mind, however, that the link between attitudes and actual behaviour can be influenced by other factors, as we saw in Chapter 6. If we must make a snap judgment, even messages adopted via the peripheral route can bring about a change in behaviour. For example, if you had to choose a professor but did not have time to thoroughly research each one, how would you select among them? You might decide on a professor simply because one of your friends said he was "fun" (peripheral information) rather than looking up teaching reviews and reading comments on RateMyProfessor.ca (central information). Of course, as we saw in Chapter 4, first impressions may not always be accurate, so relying on peripheral-route processing is not always best.

As a result of these routes to processing, several counterintuitive effects can emerge. If we are presented with a poor argument in an attractive manner, such as an effort to make us buy overpriced clothing endorsed by celebrities, we may be persuaded if we process by the peripheral route. For example, while recently on a trip to New York City for a conference, one of the authors observed that her Canadian students "freaked out" over going to the store DASH that sells the Kardashian clothing line. In addition, a non-credible source may persuade us if the argument is strong and we process it via the central route. For example, a random classmate in your political science class might make a compelling argument for a political position that, after much deliberation, you decide is correct.

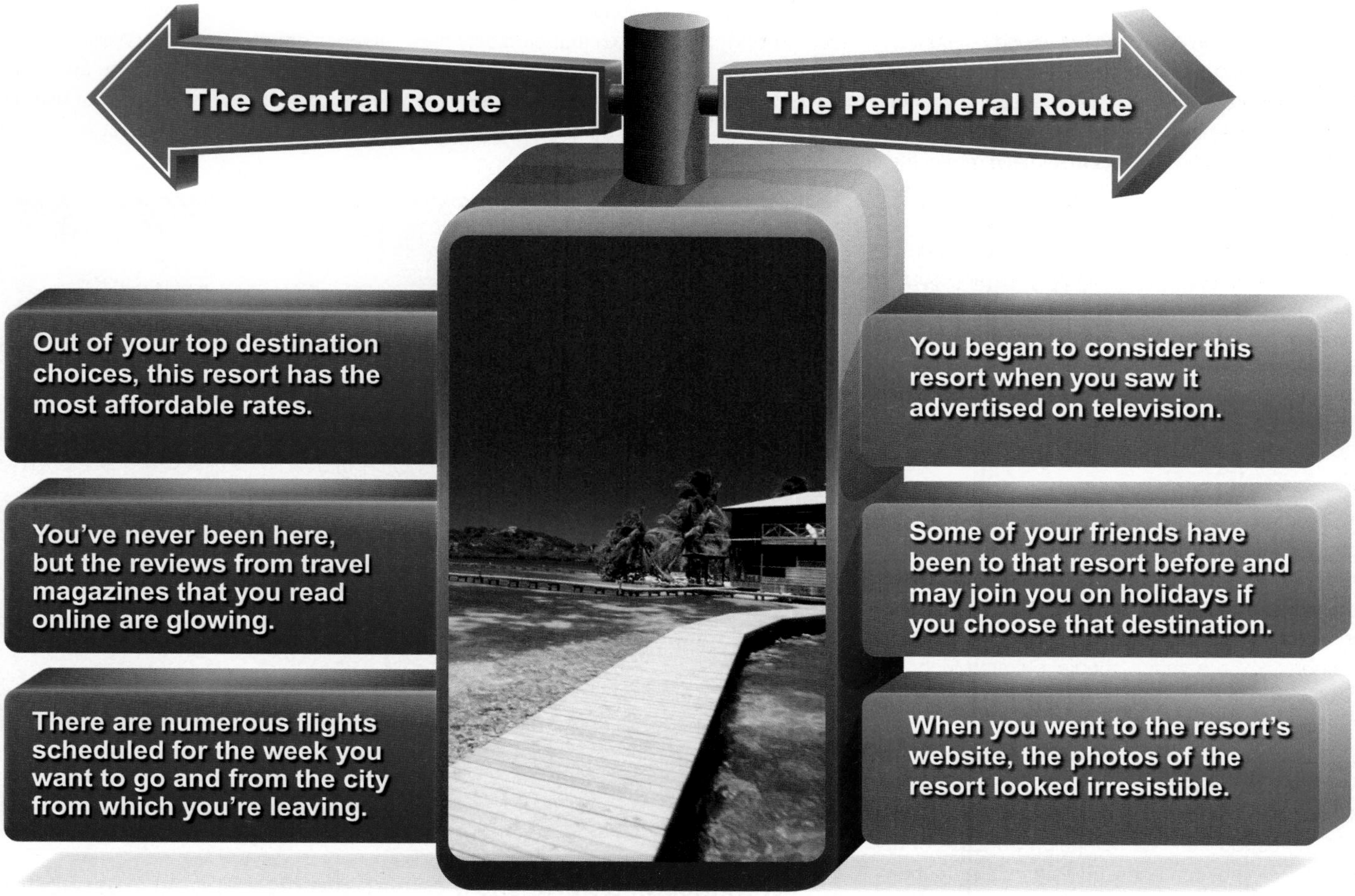

| The Central Route | The Peripheral Route |
| --- | --- |
| Out of your top destination choices, this resort has the most affordable rates. | You began to consider this resort when you saw it advertised on television. |
| You've never been here, but the reviews from travel magazines that you read online are glowing. | Some of your friends have been to that resort before and may join you on holidays if you choose that destination. |
| There are numerous flights scheduled for the week you want to go and from the city from which you're leaving. | When you went to the resort's website, the photos of the resort looked irresistible. |

**Which Way to a Tropical Resort Vacation?** When choosing a resort destination for a summer or winter holiday, **what types of information would influence you more?**

**ELABORATION LIKELIHOOD MODEL (ELM)** a model of persuasion that proposes two different routes, central and peripheral, that an individual may take when processing a message. The route is impacted by cognitive capacity and individual differences of the perceiver.

**SOURCE** the person or persons who deliver the message

**SLEEPER EFFECT** the effect whereby the persuasive impact of a non-credible source increases over time

## What Influences Which Route We Take?

So when do we use one route versus the other? This can be explained by the **Elaboration Likelihood Model (ELM)**, which provides a general framework for organizing and understanding the basic processes underlying the effectiveness of persuasive communication by emphasizing how people react to persuasive communication (Petty & Cacioppo, 1981, 1986). According to the model, people react to persuasive communication by reflecting on different aspects of a persuasive message as a function of their involvement in the message content and their ability to process the message.

In particular, when the message is important to us and we have the cognitive resources available to consider the arguments, we are more likely to use *systematic processing* (central route). On the other hand, if cognitive resources are limited or the message is not important to us, we are more likely to use *heuristic processing* or mental shortcuts (peripheral route) (Petty & Wegener, 1999). For example, imagine you receive a letter from your college or university regarding changes to your student health plan. If you have medical needs or use the plan to cover your medical expenses, you may take the time to review the changes in detail. Conversely, if you rarely use the health plan or don't really have many medical needs, you may not really care about the changes and only give the letter cursory attention. In fact, you may indicate your approval of these changes only because of a picture of an attractive student supporting the changes that appears in the notice. So then, what factors influence whether we process information via the central or peripheral route?

### THE SOURCE

When it comes to persuasive messages, whom the message comes from can be just as important as what is said. The person or organization who delivers the message is called the **source**. The source may be an actor or actress in a commercial, a celebrity spokesperson, or a major media outlet. Much like the packaging on a product, the *attractiveness of the source* can enhance the power of a persuasive message. This factor is the reason why young, attractive models are used in print ads and television commercials. Canadian brand Jacob did not hire Coco Rocha for its "Photoshop free" ad campaign because of her knowledge of the company or Photoshop technology; the company hired her because her physical attractiveness has the power to persuade consumers and sends a message that you can be beautiful without being "touched up" (Heaton, 2011). Research supports this idea; in a study that asked participants to collect signatures for a petition, researchers found that the success rate was 41 percent for attractive participants and only 32 percent for unattractive participants (Eagly & Chaiken, 1993). We will further explore the impact of attractiveness on social perception in Chapter 12, including if attractiveness can, at times, be a liability.

The limitations of attractiveness are revealed when an individual has a reason to value the *credibility of the source*. For example, you would likely take advice from soccer player David Beckham on which soccer ball is best for your intramural team, but you might not take his advice on how to rewire a light switch. If you read that a celebrity couple was breaking up, you'd be more likely to believe the rumour if it were written in the *New York Times* than if it were posted on a random celebrity gossip message board. Similarly, you would be more likely to follow skin care advice from a board-certified dermatologist than a cosmetic company representative at a department store. The credibility of a source is an important variable in persuasion. In most cases, the source's credibility is an advantage to message persuasiveness, and credibility can be increased by factors such as whether or not the source is perceived as having authority (see Pornpitakpan, 2004, for review). That said, a decrease in credibility can have a tremendous impact. For example, when political scandals are uncovered, the trustworthiness of particular candidates or political parties is diminished (e.g., Corman, Hess, & Justus, 2006). Similarly, the testimony of an eyewitness or a victim may be disbelieved if the person is not perceived as a credible source (e.g., Peace, Brower, & Rocchio, 2011). However, credibility's impact can wane. Research has shown that credibility has a **sleeper effect** (Hovland & Weiss, 1951). In other words, if you learn after receiving a message that the source is of low credibility, at the time you will discount the message, but over time you will tend to increasingly support it. The sleeper effect is less likely

**Even though a news show or website may appear trustworthy, always consider whether it is a credible source of unbiased information.**

to occur if people are informed of the source beforehand than if they receive the message and then find out the source. For example, Justin Long is known for being an actor, not a computer expert. But the more we see his Mac versus PC television commercials, the easier it becomes for us to accept his word on the subject of which computer to purchase. Counterintuitively, a low-credibility source can suppress initial attitude change but increase it over time.

Not all sources need to be as attractive as model Coco Rocha or as seemingly credible as CBC newscaster Peter Mansbridge to be persuasive; simply being similar to the message recipient can be effective. Research has shown that *sources that are similar to the recipient* are more persuasive than those that are different. Consider this: would you be more persuaded to see a movie that was suggested by your grandfather or your best friend? You and your friend likely have a similar idea of what is funny, scary, or compelling, so you would probably take your friend's suggestion over your grandfather's. Similarity can apply to a person's background, values, associations, appearance, or any of a number of factors. For example, student participants who were asked to read a persuasive essay on an environmental issue written by either a fellow schoolmate or a student from another university, were more likely to consider the arguments of classmates than those of strangers (Mackie, Worth, & Asuncion, 1990). Similarly, gender affinity also can influence persuasiveness. A recent analysis of Canadian voting patterns suggests that female voters are more likely to be convinced by and vote for women candidates, and vice versa for male voters (Goodyear-Grant & Croskill, 2011).

Message recipients can come to perceive similarities through various routes. The source might directly express attitudes that are similar to those of the recipient, or a third party might imply the presence of a similarity. It might even be the case that the person simply shares *incidental similarities* with us, such as having the same birthday (e.g., Burger, Messian, Patel, del Prado, & Anderson, 2004). That said, consumer research at the University of British Columbia has found that pointing out incidental similarities is only effective for persuasion if the relationship is expected to continue (i.e., through future interactions) and if the initial evaluation of the salesperson is not negative (Jiang, Dahl, Chattopadhyay, & Hoegg, 2009). Similarity is used to sell a variety of everyday items such as laundry detergent, toothpaste, and cereal. Advertisers establish a target audience (e.g., mothers of young children, seniors, middle-class men) and choose a spokesperson or an actor who appears to be a member of that target audience to promote their products or message (e.g., Bhatnagar & Wan, 2008). For example, the Proactiv skin care system and Cover Girl cosmetics primarily sell to young girls and women who have acne or regularly use makeup, so the companies have hired youthful stars such as Avril Lavigne, Jessica Simpson, and Taylor Swift to persuade young women to purchase their products.

Another factor influencing source effectiveness is the *likeability of the source*. Attractiveness and similarity are two factors that may increase liking, but no matter the form of liking, it has an impact. For example, persuasive messages from our own groups' members, who are generally more liked than members of other groups, are more effective (Mackie & Queller, 2000). In addition, those who are more attractive are more well liked, increasing communicator persuasiveness (e.g., Chaiken, 1979; Dion & Stein, 1978). Finally, your initial social evaluations of the communicator matter. If you are buying a car and the salesperson initially strikes you as being aggressive, underhanded, and insincere, you are unlikely to be persuaded by his or her pitch to sell you a car (e.g., Jiang et al., 2009).

It is important to note that most of these factors are *heuristics:* shortcuts that are used to form opinions. They involve use of the peripheral route to persuasion, rather than one that involves systematic processing.

**VALENCE** the degree of attraction or aversion that a person feels toward a specific object, event, or idea

**FEAR-BASED APPEAL** an attempt to provoke fear in the audience in order to persuade them not to do something

## THE MESSAGE

The actual message is obviously a critical factor in the effectiveness of persuasion. Whether it is verbal or visual, the message has the ultimate duty to get the job done. The message has two main characteristics: message content and message construction. *Message content* refers to the tactics that may be used to communicate a concept to an audience—the actual words or images used in the message. *Message construction* refers to how the message is put together (how information should be placed in a message, how long the message should be, and how often the message should be repeated).

### Message Content

When developing the message content, a source must consider the valence of the message. In psychology, **valence** refers to the degree of attraction or aversion that a person feels toward a specific object, event, or idea. This means that a source must decide if it wants its message to be positive or negative; does it want to attract or repel the audience? Negative messages are typically delivered with **fear-based appeals**.

^^^ Which one of these people is likely to **convince you that the iPad will revolutionize the way you study?**

Fear-based appeals attempt to provoke fear in the audience by depicting a personally relevant threat in order to persuade people to modify their behaviours. The effectiveness of fear-based appeals varies and can be affected by individual differences and whether the final message is one of fear or of how to take action to overcome the feared situation. Fear-based appeals seem to be most effective when they attempt to prevent a negative outcome, such as an anti-smoking commercial focusing on avoiding cancer rather than attempting to promote a positive outcome such as being healthy overall (Lee & Aaker, 2004).

That said, the amount of fear induced can negatively impact persuasion if it is enough to be overwhelming. In one study, researchers gave participants one of three messages about the dangers of not practicing proper oral hygiene habits. Each message varied in the level of intended fear. The study found that the negative message that stimulated mild fear resulted in the most improvement in oral hygiene habits, while the message that stimulated the most fear resulted in the least improvement (Janis & Feshbach, 1953). It may be that people were so afraid that they only wanted to turn away from the message, feeling hopeless rather than empowered enough to act. Fear-based approaches are often used to guide audiences away from behaviours that pose health risks. For example, the classic "This is your brain. This is your brain on drugs" campaign aimed to prevent teens from using drugs by inflicting the fear that their brains would fry like an egg if they did. These messages, however, are not always effective. In particular, they may be unsuccessful because they put the audience on the defensive and prompt members of the audience to argue against the message or dismiss it completely because they believe "that won't happen to me" (e.g., Liberman & Chaiken, 2009).

Recent research shows that how vulnerable a person is can affect his or her likelihood of being persuaded by a fear-based appeal. For example, if you have engaged in unprotected sex, advertising about HPV (human papillomavirus) featuring accounts from young women who engaged in "normal" sexual behaviours but contracted the virus may be effective in increasing your likelihood of getting vaccinated or engaging in protected sex in the future (e.g., Dal Cin, MacDonald, Fong, Zanna, & Elton, 2006; de Wit, Das, & Vet, 2008; Hynie, MacDonald, & Marques, 2006). Also, if a fear-based appeal shows how to *avoid* the fear-inducing event, and a feasible solution is provided, then a fear-based message may be successful—for example, getting vaccinated for tetanus or the H1N1 virus (e.g., Leventhal, Singer, & Jones, 1965).



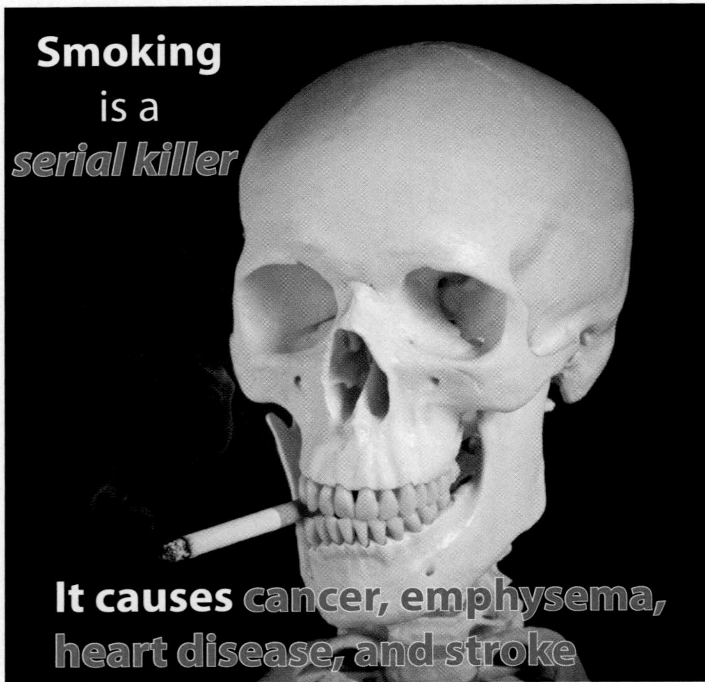


**Some public service announcements (PSAs) use fear-based approaches** in an attempt to persuade the public to avoid certain unhealthy behaviours.

Messages with a positive valence can also bring about a change in attitude. Studies suggest that health messages would actually be more effective if the content had a positive valence (e.g., Broemer, 2004). For example, an ad that shows a group of friends smiling and laughing while getting a ride home in a taxi would be more effective at convincing audiences not to drink and drive than showing a mangled car and an autopsy report on a drunk driver. But as we discussed earlier, sources must always take their audiences into account. Studies have shown that while people from individualist cultures are more likely to respond well to positive information, collectivistic individuals are more likely to focus on the negative (Noguchi, 2006). So a fear-based approach may be more effective in Japan or other non-Western cultures than in Canada or the United States.

### Message Construction

It's not always what is said but how it is said that is important, so when delivering a persuasive message, positive or negative, construction can be just as important as content. Something as simple as the *length of a message* can influence its effectiveness. The length of the message might serve as a peripheral cue that leads to an unfounded assumption, such as thinking that a longer message must have more support for its position (e.g., Petty & Cacioppo, 1984; Wood, 1985). When audiences make this assumption, longer messages will be more persuasive than shorter ones. Imagine you are reading a newspaper article on the benefits of eating raw versus cooked vegetables. If the article is a section feature rather than a short vignette, you may develop a more favourable opinion about the subject even if the quality of the information is identical to what would have been presented in the vignette. However, if you process the information via the central route, the length will not matter, only the strength of the argument itself. Further, the wording complexity and comprehensibility of the message will influence persuasion, as complex and convoluted arguments lead to greater peripheral processing (e.g., Hafer, Reynolds, & Obertynski, 1996).

The *strength of the message* indeed contributes to its persuasiveness; for example, those who provide compelling reasons for a request are more likely to get others to comply with the request (e.g., Langer, Blank, & Chanowitz, 1978). Furthermore, while it may seem that to be persuasive, you should focus on your side of the issue and present only the points that support your case, presenting both sides of the argument and refuting the points of the opposing opinion is the most effective method of persuasion (Crowley & Hoyer, 1994). This form of persuasion relies in part on the central route of processing, since it requires a well thought-out argument and rebuttal of others' arguments. It may be that presenting multiple sides of an issue and refuting counter-attitudinal arguments increases the strength of one's own argument (see Eisend, 2006).

The way in which people adopt opinions also shifts based on the *personal importance of the issue* at hand. When people care about an issue, they will expend the effort to deeply and carefully process the arguments in support of and against a given perspective—in other words, they will use the central route. In this case, the argument's strength determines the effectiveness of the persuasive message. However, for individuals not involved in or concerned with an issue, the characteristics of the source of the message will predominate in persuasion. In this case, the person will use the peripheral route (Petty, Cacioppo, & Goldman, 1981). Given that issues about which we care deeply are those whose messages we process centrally and systematically, these same issues, once we form an opinion on them, are resistant to further persuasion (e.g., Blankenship & Wegener, 2008; Zuwerink & Devine, 1996). That said, researchers at the University of Western Ontario have argued that when a message is highly relevant to us, we may expend *less* mental energy in processing the message and rely more on heuristics. However, this high relevance-heuristic processing effect depends upon your approach to ambiguous situations or arguments (e.g., Sorrentino, Bobocel, Gitta, Olson, & Hewitt, 1988). Individuals who are uncertainty-oriented tend to seek out more information in decision-making tasks (central route), whereas those who are certainty-oriented stick to what they know and what is familiar to them. As a result, certainty-oriented individuals engage in more heuristic processing when the message has high personal relevance due to familiarity and knowledge (Sorrentino et al., 1988).

Creating circumstances in which such "outcome-relevant involvement" is either high or low can generate motivation. **Outcome-relevant involvement** is the degree to which the economic or social outcome promoted in the message is important to the receiver (Slater, 1997). For example, a message about debt consolidation would have high outcome-relevant involvement to a person who is drowning in credit card debt and student loans. When outcome relevance is high, people are likely to engage in central-route processing. When outcome relevance is low, people are likely to engage in peripheral-route processing (e.g., Maio & Olson, 1995).

**OUTCOME-RELEVANT INVOLVEMENT** the degree to which the economic or social outcome promoted in a message is important to the receiver

Investment in the issue at hand is just one kind of motivation, and *motivation to understand the message* being delivered can increase the likelihood of central-route processing (Chaiken, 1980). Motivation is increased not only by the importance of the issue but also its proximity to us, both in time and in space, and so central route processing is increased by proximity as well. Further, if the message is tailored to the audience, it will be more persuasive (e.g., Noar, Harrington, & Aldrich, 1987). The central route is more time-consuming and difficult, so a person with less motivation is more likely to engage in peripheral processing, which is easier and requires less analysis (e.g., Gass & Seiter, 2003; Petty & Cacioppo, 1984).

## THE AUDIENCE

The intended audience of a persuasive message has a tremendous effect on how the message is crafted, as different audiences are influenced in different ways. Audiences are often identified by demographic factors such as age, gender, and education. Each of these demographics reacts to persuasive messages in its own unique way, but these are by far not the only characteristics of the audience that influence persuasion.

### Demographic Factors

Research has shown that *age* may be a factor in the effectiveness of persuasive efforts. Children, teens, and young adults are the most easily influenced by persuasive messages, making them appealing targets for advertisers. With regard to children, it is argued that they do not possess the cognitive strategies necessary for central-route processing and rely on heuristics or attractiveness of the desired object (e.g., Nairn & Fine, 2008). Why do you think sugary (and relatively unhealthy) cereals include children's toys and games and use cartoon figures for advertising? These are attempts to appeal to the target audience. With respect to teens and young adults, students aged 18 to 22 have more flexible attitudes than those aged 23 and older and a stronger tendency to submit to authority. As a result, this age group is more easily influenced by persuasive messages (Krosnick & Alwin, 1989). That said, both younger and older adults are more susceptible to attitude change than are middle-aged adults (e.g., Visser & Krosnick, 1998). In particular, older adults (aged 55–85) are more likely to be persuaded by emotionally meaningful messages related to love and caring than are younger adults (Fung & Carstensen, 2003). This holds true for people across several different ethnicities. Once again, the content and type of persuasive message matters.

Similarly, while both men and women are equally persuadable when they are not familiar with a topic, the type of persuasion strategy may be chosen according to apparent *gender differences* (e.g., Bisanz & Rule, 1989). This discrepancy is due to social roles (Eagly, 1978). In our culture, men tend to assert their independence from others, while women tend to concentrate on promoting cooperation with others. Since men and women react to persuasive messages differently, the type of persuasion strategy used on each gender is different. Women are often more influenced by face-to-face persuasion—which occurs in point-of-sale situations such as purchasing a car—than by impersonal strategies such as direct mail or email advertising. On the other hand, men often have the same reaction to both personal and impersonal messages (Guadagno & Cialdini, 2002). That said, recent research also suggests that both men and women can be equally persuaded by a virtual human or non-human character (e.g., cat), and that cross-gender interactions in persuasiveness are important to consider (Zanbaka, Goolkasian, & Hodges, 2006). Specifically, women are more persuaded by messages delivered by men, and men are more persuaded by messages delivered by women. This may be why beer advertisements (often targeted toward men) tend to feature attractive women, and cleaning advertisements (often targeted toward women) may feature male characters (e.g., Mr. Clean).

While sources might use different techniques to persuade their audiences based on gender, there is no formula for persuading any

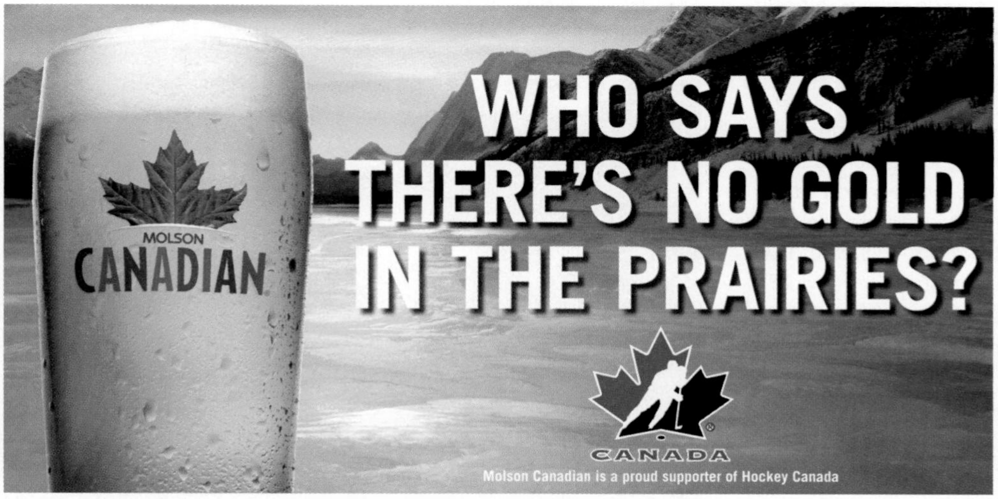

**Short messages** lend themselves to billboards and advertisements, **and comedy helps attract people's attention.**

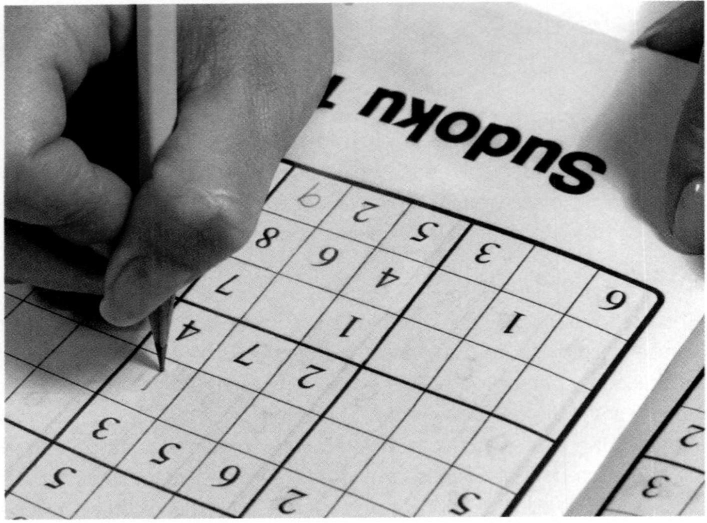


People with a high need for cognition may enjoy thought-provoking activities, such as solving Sudoku puzzles.

one demographic. The expression "There's a sucker born every minute" emphasizes the assumption that some people are more easily influenced by persuasive messages than others.

### Personality Factors



Susceptibility to persuasion, however, is a little more complex than simply having gullible genes. Several personality variables play a part in the persuasion process. One of these personality factors is a need for cognition. *Need for cognition* refers to an individual's tendency to engage in and enjoy effortful cognitive activity. Individuals who have a high need for cognition enjoy thinking abstractly, while those who have a low need for cognition do not seek out and may, in fact, try to avoid situations in which deep thought is needed (Cacioppo & Petty, 1982). Those with a high need for cognition prefer deliberate analysis, having an inherent desire to understand phenomena and a liking of critical thinking and, therefore, are likely to default to the central route rather than the peripheral. Individuals with a low need for cognition are more strongly influenced by peripheral cues such as attractiveness or celebrity endorsement of a product or behaviour in commercials and movies (e.g., Gibson & Maurer, 2000; Perlini & Hansen, 2001).

Research suggests that need for cognition also influences a person's *need for elaboration*. This means that individuals with a high need for cognition are more likely to ask questions and request more details about an issue than individuals with a low need for cognition (e.g., Cacioppo, Petty et al., 1996). These high-need individuals are likely to be persuaded by messages that can withstand scrutiny; therefore, the quality of the message is an important aspect of persuading this audience. Individuals who have a low need for cognition are more likely to be persuaded by secondary signals such as the attractiveness or popularity of the source (Cacioppo & Petty, 1982).

Susceptibility to persuasion is also influenced by a person's ability to self-monitor her actions. In Chapter 4, we learned that *self-monitoring* is the tendency to focus on situational or internal cues when deciding how to present the self in a particular situation (Snyder, 1979). In general, most people are concerned with self-presentation (the way they present themselves to others), but that does not mean they are concerned with self-monitoring (the extent to which they adjust their behaviours in response to different situations). Individuals who are high self-monitors promptly change their behaviours in response to the demands of a particular situation. Individuals who are low self-monitors have little concern for changing their behaviours and tend to uphold the same attitudes and opinions regardless of the demands of the situation. For example, a person who is a high self-monitor may frequently use profanity when around good friends, but may clean up his language when around his parents. However, if he is a low self-monitor, he is likely to engage in the same behaviour regardless of the context. He would continue to use profanity regardless of whether he was around his friends or his parents.

> "Individuals who are high self-monitors promptly change their behaviours in response to the demands of a particular situation."

People who are high self-monitors, then, are more susceptible to shifts in attitude or behaviour if such shifts would make them more agreeable to others. When selecting a romantic partner, high and low self-monitors have very different preferences. In one study, high self-monitors were more likely to choose attractive women with negative personalities, whereas low self-monitors were more likely to choose unattractive women with positive personalities (Snyder, Berscheid, & Glick, 1985). Similarly, a person with high self-monitoring might be persuaded to purchase an attractive, but impractical, sports car if that is valued by her social group, or to vote for a popular, but inexperienced, political candidate.

Even if a person is motivated to process a message due to personal relevance, self-monitoring, or a high need for cognition, if he lacks the ability to focus on the message, then he is still likely to engage in peripheral processing. The *inability to focus on a message* can be due to a lack of time or the presence of distractions. For instance, television advertisements are often less than a minute long, leaving you to rely on the peripheral aspects of the message—the models, the music, the visual effects—to process the information. In addition, if you are distracted, it is difficult or impossible to concentrate on the message and process information on a central level. Distractions thusly force a person to rely on peripheral cues to process messages (Petty, Wells, & Brock, 1976).

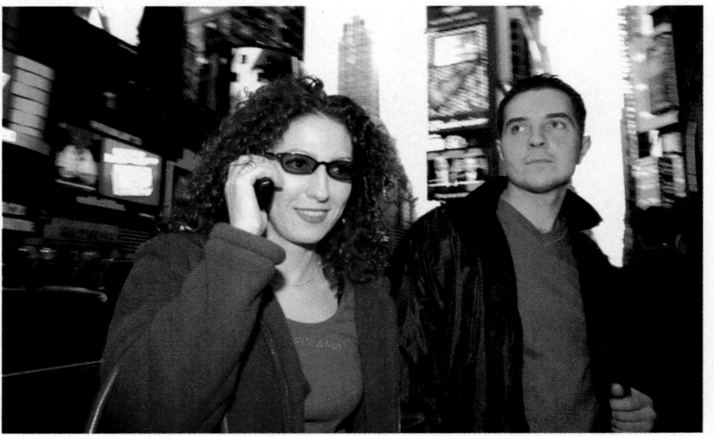

A distracted individual might have a limited ability to focus on the surrounding messages.

When processing a message while distracted, people tend to immediately accept the information they receive and then revisit the information later.

While it might seem reasonable that sources would want people to focus on their messages, distractions can be beneficial. A persuasive message can be enhanced by distracting the receiver long enough to prevent him or her from developing counterarguments. A political candidate might use vivid images and quick, catchy buzz words to distract the public's attention so that viewers do not examine the candidate's message, experience, or records too closely. If you have ever purposely waited until your parent was watching TV, reading a book, or was otherwise occupied to ask for a favour, then you may have experienced the benefits of distraction firsthand.

As you might expect, the *mood of an audience* can influence its susceptibility to persuasion. Have you ever wanted to ask a person for a favour but then held off because you wanted to wait until he or she was in a better mood before you made your plea? You do this because you know that people who are in good moods are more easily persuaded than those who are not. This is true because people who are in good moods typically wish to stay in those good moods, so they are less likely to disrupt their euphoria in order to process information carefully. This leads them to rely on peripheral cues rather than central cues when evaluating a message (e.g., Ruder & Bless, 2003; Sinclair & Mark, 1995). Sources will attempt to put their audience in a good mood by delivering positive emotional messages through words or images. For example, a laundry detergent company might use images of a sunny sky, crystal clear water, and sandy beaches to get a consumer in the mood to say "yes" to a product that has nothing to do with a tropical paradise (e.g., Soldat & Sinclair, 2001). That said, people in a positive mood may be more influenced by negative information presented in a message (e.g., Raghunathan & Trope, 2002). For example, if smokers are in a good mood and exposed to the negative health effects of smoking, they may experience more attitude change about smoking.

> "A political candidate might use vivid images and quick, catchy buzz words to distract the public's attention **so that viewers do not examine the candidate's message, experience, or records too closely.**"

Physical mood cues can affect a person's willingness to accept persuasive arguments as well. In one study, researchers asked participants to either nod their heads in agreement or shake their heads in disagreement while listening to a persuasive message (Briñol & Petty, 2003). Their findings indicated that the head movements had a significant effect on the participants' thoughts about the message. Nodding enhanced participants' confidence in their thoughts about the message, while shaking undermined it.

### Cultural Factors

Not all audiences have the same physical cues of happiness or agreement, which is why sources need to be knowledgeable about their audiences, especially if communication is occurring across cultures. For example, in Western cultures, the thumbs-up gesture indicates a positive emotion, as if to say, "Hey, all right," but in some Middle Eastern countries, it is considered an obscene gesture and can be the equivalent of giving the middle finger. So giving a movie "two thumbs up" in a country such as Iraq would not be a good way to persuade a person to rush to the theatre. Language also can be an issue. When Chevrolet introduced the Nova to Spanish-speaking countries, it created more laughter than sales because in Spanish "*no va*" translates to "it doesn't go."

These cultural differences may be easy to identify, and a source might alter its behaviour accordingly, but differences on intimate issues such as how people identify with themselves can be a bit more of a challenge. When cosmetic companies use slogans like "Maybe she's born with it. Maybe it's Maybelline," they are relying on a desire for a type of personal self-enhancement that may only apply to some Western cultures (Morling & Lamoreaux, 2008). The need to alter one's appearance in order to appear more attractive may seem universal in North America and western Europe, but this kind of sense of self is different from that of much of the rest of the world, particularly in Eastern cultures (e.g., Heine & Lehman, 1997).

In addition, Westerners have a tendency to think of individuals as having their own attitudes and beliefs. Some cultures have a broader sense of self and individuals within them think of themselves as members of a group with collective attitudes and beliefs. Persuasion in these types of cultures can be difficult because a source must aim to change the attitude of an entire group, not just the individual. This is not to say that individuals from these cultures would never form attitudes or participate in behaviours that go against the group, but the motivation to do so is much lower. These concepts are directly related to the ideas of individualism and collectivism discussed in Chapter 4.

In Canada and the United States, audiences have motivation to stray from the collective culture because we value individuality. That is why, for instance, companies such as Dell allow customers to customize their own laptop covers. Dell offers customers their choice of hundreds of different colour combinations and designs and even lets buyers engrave their company names, logos, or contact information on the laptops through laser etching. This type of customized laptop might be coveted in Western societies, but in a collectivist culture like that of Korea, this uniqueness might make a person feel uncomfortable. In Korea, things that are normal, regular, and traditional are the most desirable (e.g., Kim & Markus, 1999). When delivering persuasive messages to this audience, sources such as advertisers tend to promote concepts that represent cultural values.

<<< **A woman who is a high self-monitor might buy an expensive purse** if she is going to be in a crowd that values popular accessories.

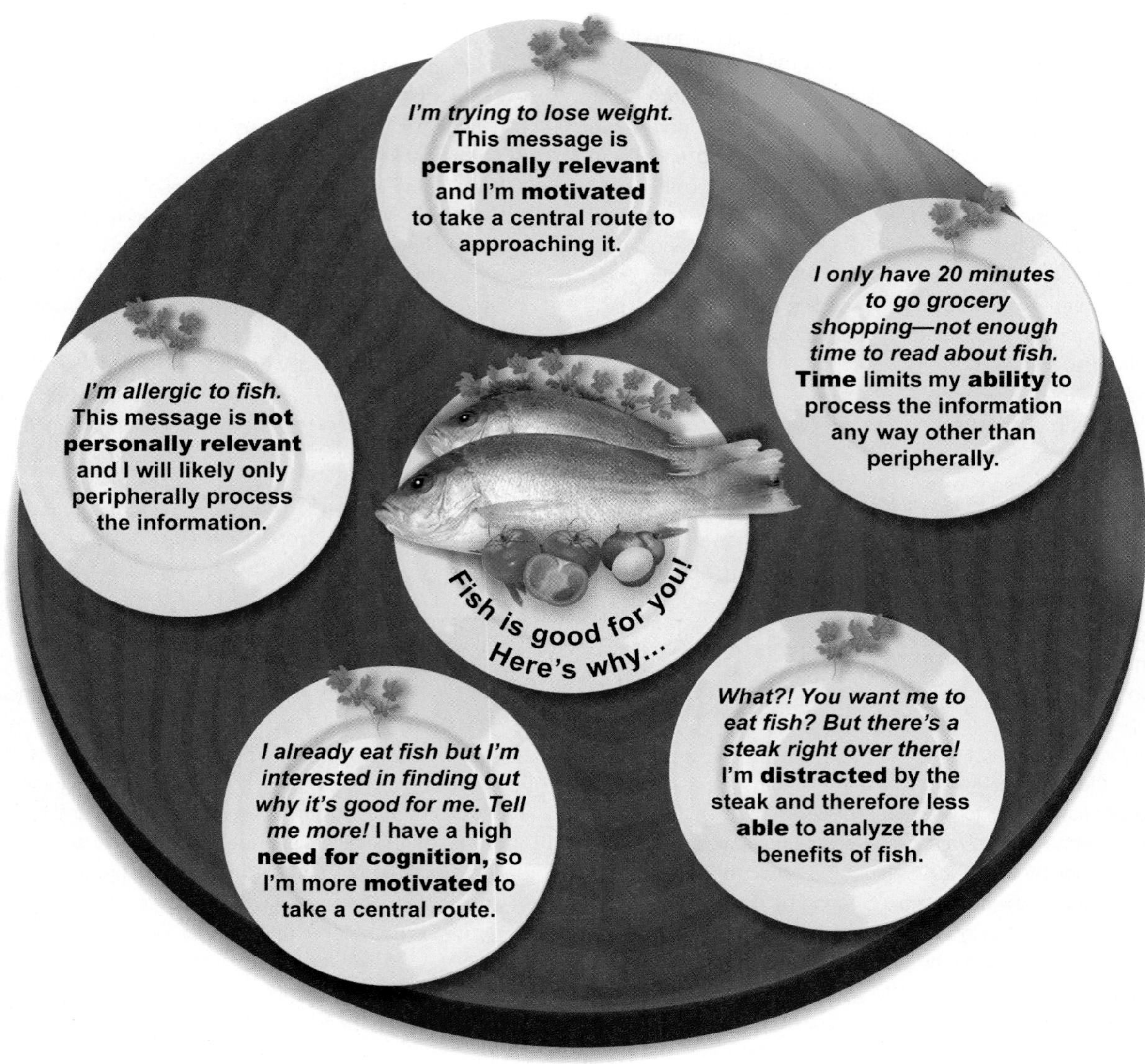




**How Will You Process This Message?** How likely are you to respond to an advertisement that promotes the benefits of eating fish?

> "When Chevrolet introduced the Nova to Spanish-speaking countries, it created more laughter than sales because in Spanish "no va" translates to "it doesn't go."

## What Principles Can We Use to Influence Others' Behaviour?

In his book *Influence* (1984), psychologist Robert Cialdini identified six persuasion techniques, or "weapons," that are useful in specific situations. "The Six Weapons of Influence" are reciprocation, commitment and consistency, social proof, liking, authority, and scarcity. In this chapter we will introduce you to these principles of persuasion; however, specific techniques used to get people to comply with your requests based on Cialdini's ideas will be discussed in Chapter 8.

### RECIPROCATION

The use of reciprocity capitalizes on our desire not to appear as moochers or freeloaders. Most of us do not want to feel indebted to another person or organization, so we often try to repay favours or acts of kindness. It's a classic case of the old give and take: If your friend helps you move a couch, you may return the favour by dog-sitting for a night. In some cases, this persuasion tactic can create an unequal exchange.

You've most likely used reciprocation as a persuasion tactic many times in your life. Have you ever helped out a classmate with a question or problem with the expectation that if *you* ever had a question or problem, that person would help you as a way to return the favour? You may even have saved "favour banks" with several people, passively keeping track of things you have done for others, records you can recall when you need a favour done. Charities such as the March of Dimes and the War Amps

>>> **Wal-Mart uses greeters to improve the mood of customers as they walk in the door.**

use the reciprocation technique when they send prospective donors personalized address labels and key tags as "free" gifts and then ask for donations. They hope to persuade people to make a donation by making them feel indebted to the organization because they accepted the gift, even though it was not solicited. Reciprocity has been found to occur even when the individual believes that the person who provided the original favour will not know that the favour was returned (e.g., Burger, Sanchez, Imberi, & Grande, 2009), suggesting that this norm does not operate out of a selfish desire for recognition of our acts but rather a desire to restore balance.

## COMMITMENT AND CONSISTENCY

In Chapter 6, we learned that people like to make sure that their attitudes are in line with their behaviours; if they are not, people experience an unpleasant tension called *dissonance*. Our attitudes include things we believe about ourselves—for instance, if we are reminded that we believe ourselves to be generous people, we will be more likely to donate to charities requesting money. Likewise, if we value being a good son or daughter, a florist is more likely to be persuasive at selling us flowers if it emphasizes in advertisements that good sons and daughters buy flowers, showing images of tearful, grateful mothers hugging their children. Similarly, when a person makes a commitment to something, particularly a verbal one, he typically feels internal and external pressures to meet that commitment. The person doesn't want to seem unreliable or weak willed. As such, he will be sure to act in a way that is consistent with that commitment. For example, if you wanted to find volunteers for a community outreach program, you might post fliers around campus or send out a mass e-mail to friends, asking people to show up for the program. While simply presenting the information to people may generate some volunteers, you would most likely have more success if you approached or called your friends and classmates personally and asked them to make a verbal commitment to volunteer.

Commitment and consistency is an effective persuasion weapon. Research studies have demonstrated that individuals who commit to one act are more likely to commit to a second act, even if it is inconvenient (e.g., Freedman & Fraser, 1966). Such techniques as initial agreement to a small request (foot-in-the-door technique) or terms of purchase (lowballing technique) will lead people to follow through with additional requests or changes to the terms of an agreement due to behavioural consistency (Cialdini, 2007). For the most part, once we have made a commitment to an act or position, we will act in accordance with it—even if it requires more of a burden. We will explore these ideas and specific techniques further in Chapter 8.

## SOCIAL PROOF

Social proof, the notion that others' actions suggest to us what is correct, has the power to change what we believe is true in our world. Imagine that you are driving a car and trying to make a left-turn exit out of a crowded mall parking lot. After several minutes of waiting, you finally reach the intersection, but there is a sign that says "No Left Turns." You notice that two cars in front of you turn left. What do you do? Many people would make the turn because the other cars did. This principle is often referred to as the *bandwagon effect*. For example, during Olympic Games or sports playoffs, if your favourite athlete or team is out of the running, you are likely to cheer for the team or person that sportscasters predict is the favourite to win or is a member of your country of origin. In the Stanley Cup 2011 playoffs in Vancouver, many fans jumped on the Canucks bandwagon to support the only remaining Canadian team in the series. That said, many Canadians took an alternative position and cheered for the Boston Bruins as that team had a greater number of Canadian players overall. Even in politics, our need for social validation can be evidenced; when individuals who are initially going to vote for a particular political candidate are told that another candidate is ahead in the polls, they may change their voting behaviour (e.g., Morwitz & Pluzinski, 1996). This premise also holds a lot of sway in helping behaviour, which will be explored in Chapter 13.

## LIKING

The notion of being persuaded more readily by people we like is a simple concept—we enjoy saying "yes" to requests from people we like and do not enjoy saying "yes" to people we don't like. So the more a person likes you, the more likely it is that you will be able to persuade him or her. For example, imagine you need to purchase a new laptop, so you go to a local electronics store to check out a few different models. The salesperson who helps you is very friendly and even compliments you on

^^^ Customization has become a **mainstay of Western culture, such as the ability to customize our laptop covers.**

**FOREWARNING** the process of being informed ahead of time that a favoured attitude will be challenged

your knowledge of computers. You were thinking about purchasing the laptop from an online retailer who offers a free case with each purchase, but you decide to buy the laptop from the store because the salesperson was so nice and helpful, and also because she complimented you.

Salespeople know likeability plays a huge role in their pursuits to persuade you to purchase items. Corporations know this as well, which is why companies such as Best Buy and Future Shop spend 5 percent of their payroll on training sales staff to, among other things, make a positive impression on customers (e.g., Kump, 2010). In fact, anyone who works in the human service industry recognizes that techniques such as flattery and ingratiation (see Chapter 8) induce liking, which can lead to effective persuasion (e.g., Drachman, DeCarufel, & Insko, 1978; Levine, 2003). The next time you want to ask a favour of a friend or attempt to get an extension on an assignment due date from your professor, try using this principle!

## AUTHORITY

In most societies, people are taught to respect authority, both implied and real, especially individual authority figures such as police officers, firefighters, and members of the military. If a police officer asked you to show a form of identification, you probably would not hesitate to take out your driver's licence. But authority figures are not just uniformed public servants; they can come in many different forms. A parent, teacher, pastor, doctor, hotel manager, grocery store supervisor, or any person with a badge or nametag can be seen as an authority figure. Let's say you are eating lunch at a table in a park. A person in plain clothes walks up to you and tells you that you have to move because the table is reserved for a private party. You might be hesitant to move because she does not seem to have any authority over the space. But if she pulls out a badge and states that she is a grounds supervisor for the parks department, wouldn't you be more likely to move? Your motivation in such a case may be less a belief that what the supervisor is doing is correct, and more of a fear of being penalized for inaction, but nonetheless you would act. Research has shown that even in the absence of an obvious punishment for inaction, people will obey authority figures—even to the point of administering lethal shocks to another person—and this will be discussed further in Chapter 8 (see Cialdini, 2007).

## SCARCITY

People want what they can't have. Diamonds are more valuable than quartz, not because they are necessarily more beautiful, but because they are more scarce. Emphasizing scarcity is a popular way of selling products (e.g., Worchel, Lee, & Adewole, 1975). Things such as limited-edition shoes or watches make consumers feel as if they have something special that has a value above the purchase price. For example, when the Nintendo Wii game systems were first introduced in Canada, they were extremely hard to come by, which enhanced the demand for this product. Additional examples can be seen with Apple products such as iPhones and iPads. That said, scarcity applies to more than just consumer products. Limited-time offers can occur in personal relationships. In order to get a person to go out on a date with you, you may project yourself as something special and highlight your unique qualities that cannot be found in anyone else (e.g., Gibbs, Ellison, & Heino, 2006; Whitty, 2008). In other words, you're not a dime a dozen, and you may not be "on the market" for long. Similarly, individuals have played "hard to get" or indicated that their time is scarce in order to increase their desirability to potential dating partners (e.g., Cialdini, 2008)

Asking a person to RSVP to an event is a **way of using commitment and consistency as a persuasive technique.**

> "In order to get a person to go out on a date with you, you may project yourself **as something special and highlight your unique qualities that cannot be found in anyone else.**"

# What Does Research Tell Us About Resisting Persuasion Tactics?

So now that you know all of the tactics that different sources use to persuade people, you must be wondering if it is inevitable that we will fall prey to these messages. But we are not defenceless against the power of persuasive messages (Wegener, Petty, Smoak, & Fabrigar, 2004). Our ability to resist persuasion is influenced by three factors: forewarning, reactance, and inoculation.

## FOREWARNING

If a friend yells "heads up" before tossing you an object, you are more likely to catch that object than if he just hurled it at you with no warning. This concept also applies to the processing of persuasive messages. When people are given **forewarning** about a persuasive message, they are being informed ahead of time that an attitude will be challenged. Forewarning allows a person to build up a defence or prepare to resist a persuasive message. For example, if you know ahead of time that a credit card company likes to try to convince customers to sign up optional features such as added insurance or rate protection programs, then you will be better prepared to say "no, thanks" when the bank representative offers you a deal on the unnecessary upgrades. In a study to examine the effects of forewarning, researchers measured the persuasiveness of a lecture given to teenagers arguing that teenagers should not be allowed to drive. The sample of teenagers was divided into two groups. One group was informed of the topic 10 minutes before the lecture started. The other group was not forewarned of the topic. The group that was forewarned was less convinced by the argument. This is because the delay between a warning and the delivery of a message gives people more time to generate arguments against the message (e.g., Petty & Cacioppo, 1977; Quinn & Wood, 2008).

**REACTANCE** the instinctive reaction of individuals to preserve their freedom when they feel it is threatened

## REACTANCE

Sometimes we build up such a resistance to a persuasive message that it can have a boomerang effect, making us believe exactly the opposite of what the source intends. This occurs frequently in relationships between parents and their children. Have your parents ever expressed disapproval of the person you were dating? How did you respond? Chances are, you ignored your parents' objections, or even liked the person all the more because of the disapproval. This boomerang effect is known as **reactance**. The reactance theory states that when individuals feel that their freedom is threatened, they instinctively want to preserve their freedom by acting in opposition to the freedom-threatening source (Brehm, 1966).

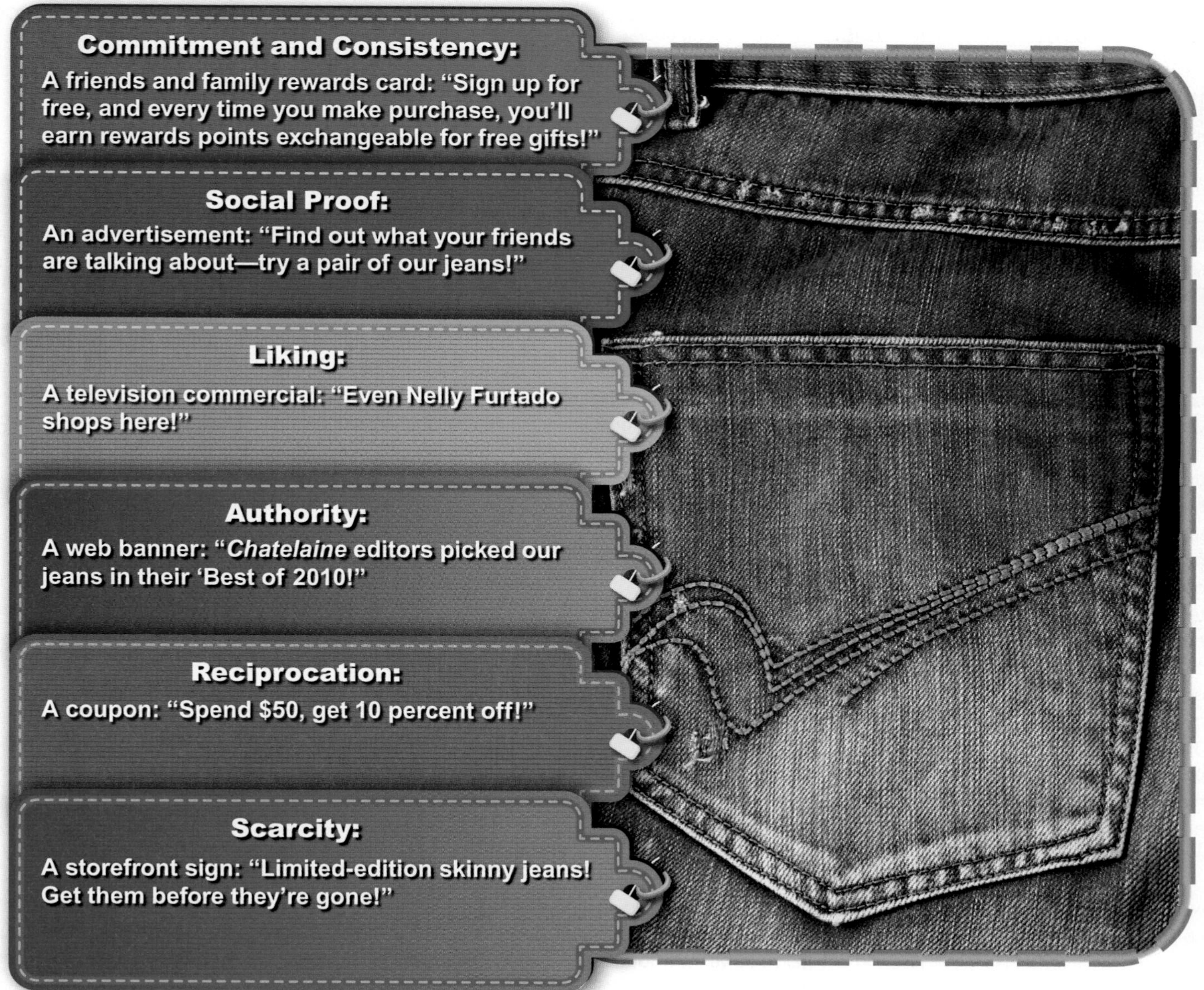

Commitment and Consistency:
A friends and family rewards card: "Sign up for free, and every time you make purchase, you'll earn rewards points exchangeable for free gifts!"
Social Proof:
An advertisement: "Find out what your friends are talking about—try a pair of our jeans!"
Liking:
A television commercial: "Even Nelly Furtado shops here!"
Authority:
A web banner: "*Chatelaine* editors picked our jeans in their 'Best of 2010!"
Reciprocation:
A coupon: "Spend $50, get 10 percent off!"
Scarcity:
A storefront sign: "Limited-edition skinny jeans! Get them before they're gone!"


**How Does the New Store at the Mall Get You in Its Pocket?** A single message can be delivered using each of **"The Six Weapons of Influence."**

**INOCULATION** the process of building up resistance to unwanted persuasion

Reactance explains why anti-drug campaigns sometimes backfire. Researchers have concluded that anti-drug ads might increase rather than decrease drug usage among college and university students. After presenting government-funded anti-drug ads to a sample group of 53 students, researchers found that three out of four students said that they had a *more* favourable impression of drugs after viewing the ads than they had previously. The researchers explained that students saw the ads as exaggerated and nonfactual, which created distrust of the source and its message (Meagher, 2004). So instead of convincing students that drugs are bad, the ads led students to believe that drugs aren't *that* bad. Reactance also explains why warning labels on violent movies or television shows increase viewership by inappropriate audiences. In a study that examined the effects of rating systems on young children, researchers found that ratings that indicated violent, sexual, and other graphic content had a deterrent effect on children younger than age eight but had an enticement effect on children older than 11, especially if they were male (Bushman & Cantor, 2003).

## INOCULATION

Just as we use vaccines to inoculate ourselves and build up resistance to diseases, we sometimes want to inoculate ourselves and build up resistance to persuasive messages. To protect a person against persuasion, McGuire and his colleagues (1961) developed a technique appropriately called **inoculation**, and proposed that individuals should be exposed to weak attacks on a favoured position (McGuire & Papageorgis, 1961). The attacks must be weak so that they do not alter the person's opinion on the subject. By defending against the weak attack, a person will be better prepared to face future, possibly stronger, attacks (McGuire, 1964). In the original work, to inoculate participants from arguments against brushing their teeth, participants were provided with some arguments against regular tooth-brushing that were then refuted, rendering them weak. These refutations resulted in more support for regular tooth-brushing after exposure to stronger anti-brushing messages (McGuire & Papageorgis, 1961). In their studies, the researchers were able to demonstrate that inoculation approaches were more powerful than telling a person that they currently have the correct opinion and should ignore any persuasive tactics (McGuire, 1964). This technique has many practical applications and is used in a variety of professional settings in which individuals regularly face attempts at persuasion. For example, defence attorneys might use inoculation in their opening statements. They may tell the jury, "The Crown Prosecutor will try to convince you that one 130-pound man is capable of carrying a 300-pound steel safe 200 yards on his own, in the middle of the day, undetected." The prosecution may have several strong arguments, but the defence wants to point out the weakest parts so that jurors build up a resistance to the prosecution's argument before stronger evidence is exposed in cross-examination.

However, these techniques to resist persuasion do not work equally well for all. The American Psychological Association developed a task force on advertising and children; it found that young children are not capable of employing these resistance techniques and lack the cognitive ability to critically think about advertising (e.g., Nairn & Fine, 2008). For instance, cereal manufacturers often include the disclaimer that cereal is *part of* a balanced breakfast. However, research argues that children do not understand this claim and, therefore, will equate the cereal with being a good breakfast in and of itself (Palmer & McDowell, 1981). As a result, in some countries (such as in the European Union), advertisements to children are restricted.

What would persuade you to try to **become more conscious about recycling?**

# When Shouldn't We Resist Persuasion?

Persuasion is not always something to be resisted; in some cases, it is to our benefit to carefully consider new opinions and maybe even shift our own to align with them. For example, in a study in which researchers first validated people's complaints about recycling (e.g., that it was inconvenient) but then delivered a persuasive message about recycling, researchers found success in getting people to partake in this beneficial behaviour (e.g., Werner, Stoll, Birch, & White, 2002). By "succumbing" to persuasion, people can adopt behaviours that benefit them and their environments.

In addition, there are behaviours that are not only beneficial to adopt but may be a matter of life and death. One of those behaviours is getting tested for HIV, the herpes virus, or other sexually transmitted diseases (STDs). In fact, many young adults fail to consider the consequences of unprotected sexual activity and tend to adopt "it won't happen to me" thinking in regard to STDs (e.g., Hynie et al., 2006). Further, people neglect getting vaccinated against such diseases for the same reasons. One factor that can influence this behaviour is framing the goal to get tested. Goals can be viewed using a *gain frame* (thinking about what you will gain by approaching them) or a *loss frame* (thinking about what you will lose by avoiding them) (for a review, see O'Keefe & Jensen, 2007). In the case of HIV testing, when people were certain they would test negative, gain-framing (reminding subjects of the peace of mind they would attain once tested) produced more persuasion. However, when people were uncertain, there was a slight increase in the rate of getting tested under loss-framing (reminding subjects of the potential problems they would face if they didn't get tested) (Apanovitch, McCarthy, & Salovey, 2003). Similarly, risky behaviours benefit from loss framing, while low-risk behaviours become more likely with gain framing. In one study, this translated to greater condom-related health behaviour, such as carrying condoms, when there was a gain frame but greater condom-related relational behaviour, such as talking to one's partner about using them, when there was a loss frame (Kiene et al., 2005). Goal framing can also have an impact on such behaviours as smoking cessation (Tasso et al., 2005) and frequency of breast self-examination (Meyerowitz & Chaiken, 1987).

Persuasion can be powerful, for better or worse. Whether it leads you to quit smoking, improve your health, or buy your mother flowers for Mother's Day, it affects your attitudes and behaviour all the time. In Chapter 8, we will explore other social influence tactics—including shifts in attitude and behaviour as a result of demands made by a perceived authority figure or another individual. We will examine in-depth the effects on one's own attitudes and behaviours that may emerge as a result of desires and compulsions to conform to group norms. As you read Chapter 8, keep in mind all we have learned so far, and how these persuasion techniques might apply to conformity in group situations as well.

## ACTION LEARNING

### Getting Fit and Persuasive

As you have learned from this chapter, persuasion is an art and a science (see Cialdini, 2008). Creating an effective persuasive message requires creativity as well as a keen understanding of the target audience.

Imagine that your student council is starting a campus-wide campaign to increase student use of the school's new fitness centre, the key to a new push toward health and well-being. The president of the student council has asked you to act as the psychology expert to design the message behind the campaign.

How would you create the persuasive message? Would you try to get students to follow the central or peripheral route? Consider the source, the message, and your audience prior to designing the campaign. Should you design two different advertisements? What measures would you take in minimizing resistance to your message? To design an effective campaign, you must take into consideration the factors that affect persuasion.

What you will learn from this action learning project:

1. How to bring about a change on campus
2. How to create a persuasive message
3. How to deliver a message through multiple routes

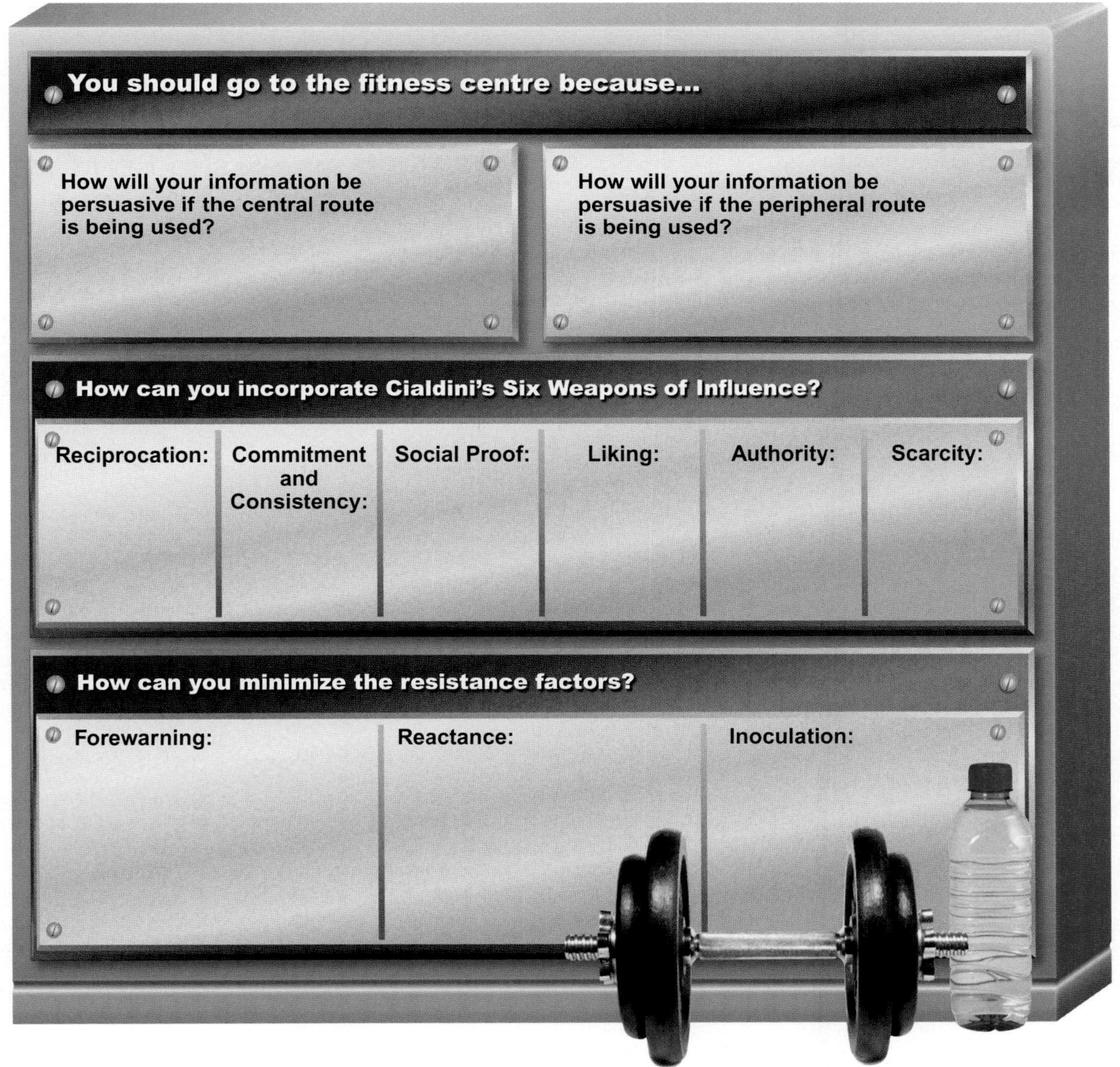

You should go to the fitness centre because...
How will your information be persuasive if the central route is being used?
How will your information be persuasive if the peripheral route is being used?
How can you incorporate Cialdini's Six Weapons of Influence?
Reciprocation:
Commitment and Consistency:
Social Proof:
Liking:
Authority:
Scarcity:
How can you minimize the resistance factors?
Forewarning:
Reactance:
Inoculation:


How will you **get your classmates in shape?**

# CHAPTER 07 Review

## Summary

### WHAT ARE PERSUASIVE MESSAGES? p. 118

• Persuasion is the strategy of communicating with other people in order to get them to behave in a certain way or change particular attitudes. A number of factors determine how the message recipient will process this information, and the recipient will do so via either the central route or the peripheral route.

• Not all persuasive messages are successful. If they were, recipients would have a harder time making decisions. The person trying to persuade the recipient must consider three factors: the source, or the entity delivering the message; the audience, or the demographics of who is to receive the message; and the message itself, and what tactics might be most suitable to delivering it.

### WHAT PRINCIPLES CAN WE USE TO INFLUENCE OTHERS' BEHAVIOUR? p. 126

• Psychologist Robert Cialdini has identified "Six Weapons of Influence" that people can use when developing persuasive messages. These are reciprocation, commitment and consistency, social proof, liking, authority, and scarcity. No one way is better than the other; the effectiveness of each depends on the context of the situation.

### WHAT DOES RESEARCH TELL US ABOUT RESISTING PERSUASION TACTICS? p. 128

• People are not always susceptible to even the best persuasive messages. This is due to three strategies for resisting persuasion: forewarning, reactance, and inoculation.

• When people are informed ahead of time—or forewarned—that they will be the recipient of a persuasive message, they are afforded the opportunity to think critically about the message they are to receive and to build up a defence against it. Sometimes, a persuasive message can have the boomerang effect, making us believe the exact opposite of what is intended. This is termed reactance. And finally, to inoculate yourself against persuasion, you can expose yourself to weaker attacks relating to the message and responses to them supporting your opinion. In doing so, you will be better prepared for possible stronger attacks in the future.

### WHEN SHOULDN'T WE RESIST PERSUASION? p. 130

• Sometimes it is not beneficial to resist persuasion. For example, sometimes persuasion can convince us to engage in actions that benefit to ourselves, such as getting tested for HIV, doing breast self-examinations, or getting vaccinated for tetanus or the H1N1 virus.



## Key Terms

**central route** a type of processing that occurs when an individual has the ability and motivation to thoroughly listen to and evaluate a persuasive message *118*

**Elaboration Likelihood Model (ELM)** a model of persuasion that proposes two different routes, central and peripheral, that an individual may take when processing a message. The route is impacted by cognitive capacity and individual differences of the perceiver *120*

**fear-based appeal** an attempt to provoke fear in the audience in order to persuade them not to do something *121*

**forewarning** the process of being informed ahead of time that a favoured attitude will be challenged *128*

**inoculation** the process of building up resistance to unwanted persuasion *130*

**outcome-relevant involvement** the degree to which the economic or social outcome promoted in a message is important to the receiver *123*

**peripheral route** a type of processing that occurs when an individual lacks the ability and motivation to thoroughly listen to and evaluate a persuasive message and is, therefore influenced by external cues such as attractiveness of the speaker *118*

**persuasion** the way people communicate in order to influence other people's attitudes and behaviours *118*

**reactance** the instinctive reaction of individuals to preserve their freedom when they feel it is threatened *129*

**sleeper effect** the effect whereby the persuasive impact of a non-credible source increases over time *120*

**source** the person or persons who deliver the message *120*

**valence** the degree of attraction or aversion that a person feels toward a specific object, event, or idea *121*

# Test Your Understanding

## MULTIPLE CHOICE

1. Which is an example of a message that would be persuasive if an individual were taking the central route?
   - **a.** a print ad that says "Your girlfriend will love these shoes"
   - **b.** a commercial that features an attractive model
   - **c.** a speech that uses colourful vocabulary
   - **d.** a food label that highlights nutritional benefits

2. If you do not have the motivation to listen to a central message, you are less likely to rely on cues such as
   - **a.** the length of the message.
   - **b.** the message source.
   - **c.** the facts in the message.
   - **d.** the sound of the message.

3. Which of the following audiences is most likely to have high outcome-relevant involvement with a message about the closing of a community senior centre?
   - **a.** the director of a community youth centre
   - **b.** a real estate developer
   - **c.** a person who attends the senior centre
   - **d.** a newspaper journalist

4. Which of Cialdini's weapons is being used if a source uses a police officer to deliver its message?
   - **a.** social proof
   - **b.** liking
   - **c.** reciprocation
   - **d.** authority

5. Which of the following factors is not a major influence on the source of a message?
   - **a.** attractiveness
   - **b.** scarcity
   - **c.** credibility
   - **d.** similarity

6. Which of the following activities is a person with a low need for cognition likely to enjoy?
   - **a.** doing crossword puzzles
   - **b.** examining food labels
   - **c.** reading owner's manuals
   - **d.** skimming the newspaper

**ANSWERS:** 1.d; 2. c; 3. c; 4. d; 5. b; 6. d; 7. b; 8. a; 9. b; 10. a

7. The tendency to focus on situational or internal cues when deciding how to present the self in a particular situation is called
   - **a.** self-realization.
   - **b.** self-monitoring.
   - **c.** self-sufficiency.
   - **d.** self-control.

8. When a person is in a good mood, she is likely to rely on
   - **a.** peripheral cues.
   - **b.** central cues.
   - **c.** motivation focus.
   - **d.** central focus.

9. Which of the following might initiate reactance?
   - **a.** a person being told the subject of a speech
   - **b.** a person being told that they can't do something
   - **c.** a person being told a weak message
   - **d.** a person being told multiple messages

10. What are the benefits of inoculation?
    - **a.** It gives a person time to build up a resistance to a message.
    - **b.** It lets a person know the source ahead of time.
    - **c.** It prevents a person from hearing strong arguments for a message.
    - **d.** It allows counter-arguments to be repeated.

## ESSAY RESPONSE

1. Think about the last time you made a decision. Did you come to this decision through the central route or the peripheral route? Explain why.
2. In what way can distraction enhance the persuasiveness of a message?
3. Imagine that you want to persuade a potential employer that you would be a great employee. Which one of Cialdini's "Six Weapons of Influence" would you use in your persuasive message?
4. How does self-monitoring prevent individuals from being persuaded?
5. What do you think causes some individuals to be persuaded by dangerous ideologies? What can be done to prevent this from happening?

## APPLY IT!

Find an advertisement for something you recently purchased. How much influence did this advertisement have on you? Is it using the central or peripheral route to appeal to consumers? Which of Cialdini's six weapons do you see at work?

**Remember to check www.thethinkspot.ca for additional information, downloadable flashcards, and other helpful resources.**

# THINK READINGS

SOCIAL INFLUENCE

# Indecent Influence: The Positive Effects of Obscenity on Persuasion

BY CORY R. SCHERER AND BRAD J. SAGARIN
Northern Illinois University, DeKalb, IL, USA

This experiment examined the effects of judicious swearing on persuasion in a pro-attitudinal speech. Participants listened to one of three versions of a speech about lowering tuition that manipulated where the word "damn" appeared (beginning, end, or nowhere). The results showed that obscenity at the beginning or end of the speech significantly increased the persuasiveness of the speech and the perceived intensity of the speaker. Obscenity had no effect on speaker credibility.

In 1939, David Selznick, producer of *Gone With the Wind*, was fined $5,000 by the Hollywood Production Code Commission for the profane word that ended Rhett Butler's famous line, "Frankly my dear, I don't give a damn" (Vertres, 1997). Sixty-five years later, US Vice President Dick Cheney used a substantially stronger word when he told Vermont Democratic Senator Patrick Leahy to, in the words of *The Washington Times*, "perform an anatomical sexual impossibility" (Simms, 2004, p. 98). The statement garnered no fine, and Cheney offered no apology. Indeed, in an interview with Neil Cavuto of Fox News, Cheney expressed no regrets, explaining instead that he "felt better afterwards" (FOXNews.com, 2004, ¶101).

Clearly, society's stance against swearing has become more relaxed in recent years. The increasing acceptability of swearing raises the possibility that obscenity could have a positive effect on the perceptions of the speaker. In fact, Cheney's use of obscenity actually endeared him to some. As blogger Ravenwood explained, "The more I hear about Vice President Dick Cheney telling Senator Patrick Leahy to go fuck himself, the better I like Cheney" (Ravenwood's Universe, 2004, ¶1). Along these lines, a poster to the bulletin board on Promote Liberty.org argued that Cheney's comment "shows a remarkable degree of restraint on the part of the Vice President yet a willingness to stand up for his personal honor and convictions" (FMeekins, 2004, ¶4).

The present experiment was designed to examine the effects of obscenity on the perceptions of a speaker and the persuasiveness of a speech. However, as the reactions to Cheney's statement suggest, obscenity may have its most positive effect when targeted at a congenial audience. Given this, the present experiment examined the persuasive impact of a single swear word incorporated into a pro-attitudinal speech. The present experiment also examined the effects of obscenity on the perceived intensity and credibility of the speaker.

## Swearing and Persuasion

What are the effects of swearing on the influence process? Past research suggests two possibilities: (a) increasing the perceived intensity of the communicator and (b) decreasing credibility.

### *Intensity*

Hamilton, Hunter, and Burgoon (1990) defined intensity as a stylistic feature of language that is expressed through emotionality and specificity. Emotional intensity is the degree of affect in the source's language. Obscene language can be seen as a form of intense language (Bradac, Bowers, & Courtright, 1979).

A study examining motivation for why people swear had female and male college students complete a survey to determine their beliefs about the common motives for their use of obscenity and why others use obscenity (Fine & Johnson, 1984). The study examined 10 possible motives: to express anger, to emphasize feelings, out of habit, peer pressure, to relieve tensions and frustrations, because the word is taboo, to act cool, to get attention, because the word is acceptable, and lack of another word. Across gender, the motives of expressing anger and emphasizing feelings were found to be of greatest importance.[1]

Fine and Johnson's (1984) results demonstrate that the emphasis of feelings is an important motive for swearing. Furthermore, people recognize that other people swear, in part, to emphasize feeling. In this regard, Mulac (1976) found that a speaker can demonstrate strong emphasis about a topic by using obscene language, but the obscene language detracts from other aspects of how the speaker is perceived. Nonetheless, in regards to persuasion, Fine and Johnson's results suggest that if an

When you read Chapter 11 about aggression, revisit this idea. How can language be used as a tool for aggression? Do you swear?

Would obscene language in a speech be a characteristic of a message using the central route to persuasion or the peripheral route to persuasion?

SOCIAL INFLUENCE Vol. 1, Issue 2, Pages 138–146 Copyright 2006 Psychology Press Ltd.

[1]Although people swear to express anger, they also swear to express other emotions such as happiness. At the 2003 Grammy awards, for example, Bono of the rock group U2 used an obscenity to express how happy he was with the fact that his band had just won an award.

audience hears a speaker swear when giving a speech on a particular topic, then the audience might infer that the speaker is emphasizing feelings. Acknowledgement of such a point might motivate the audience to take particular note of the argument and, quite possibly, to be especially influenced by the communication.

In fact, research supports the idea that speakers can increase persuasion by increasing the intensity of their language. According to a causal model by Bradac, Bowers, and Courtright (1980) based on reinforcement expectancy theory, language intensity influences attitude change through two steps: language intensity affects source evaluation and source evaluation affects attitude change. If swear words act as strong or intense language, then obscenity may increase persuasion in the same way as other forms of intense language. However, unlike some other forms of intense language, swearing may negatively impact source evaluation by reducing credibility.

### Credibility

In *Cursing in America*, Jay (1992) claims that cursing at an inappropriate time will reduce a speaker's credibility, persuasiveness, and perceived professionalism. Therefore, Jay cautions that swearing for persuasive reasons should be used only when the speaker has nothing to lose.

Past research on obscenity and persuasion supports Jay's (1992) concern. For example, Bostrom, Baseheart, and Rossiter (1973) examined reactions to people who swear. This experiment looked at the persuasive effects of three types of profane language: religious (e.g., damn), excretory (e.g., shit), and sexual (e.g., fuck) obscenity. The participants listened to a tape-recorded interview about a topic and evaluated the topic before and after listening to the tape. Overall, Bostrom et al. (1973) did not find support for the prediction that obscenity would increase persuasion. Another study conducted by Hamilton (1989) found that obscenity increased audience disgust with the message and negative perceptions of the source.

However, the lack of persuasion effects in these studies may have stemmed from the choice of topics, which were counter-attitudinal for most participants. For counter-attitudinal topics, listeners may use swearing as an excuse to reject the message. On the other hand, swearing may increase persuasion for pro-attitudinal topics. Nevertheless, given Jay's (1992) caution, the present experiment examined the possible detrimental effects of obscenity on the credibility of the speaker.

## The Current Experiment

The current experiment examined the effects of swearing on the persuasive impact of a speech and the intensity and credibility of the speaker. Because of the dearth of evidence for the persuasive power of obscenity, the present experiment used swearing in a manner optimized for its effectiveness: one relatively mild swear word ("damn") was placed at the beginning or end of a pro-attitudinal speech.

### Method

*Participants.* A total of 88 introductory psychology students from a large Midwestern university participated in partial fulfillment of a course requirement.

*Design and procedure.* The participants were randomly assigned to one of three conditions (no swear word, swear word at the beginning of the speech, swear word at the end). After giving informed consent, participants were seated in front of a computer and instructed to follow the instructions on the computer.

The computer played a 5-minute videotaped speech about the topic of lowering tuition at a different university, a pro-attitudinal topic of low relevance to the participants. When the participants finished watching the speech, they completed scales that measured their attitudes on the topic and their perceptions of the speaker. After the participants finished, they were probed for suspicion and debriefed.

*Materials.* There were three speeches of similar length. The speeches discussed the topic of lowering tuition at a different university. The speeches had a mixture of strong and weak arguments. Strong arguments included how students have to take into account how much school will cost when deciding where to go and how the school will be saving the students money. Weak arguments included how the school could use lowering tuition as a selling point and how the community will be more attractive to businesses because the students would have more money to spend in the town. Judicious swearing was operationalized as a single instance of the relatively inoffensive word "damn." The swear word appeared either at the beginning (". . . that lowering of tuition is not only a great idea, but damn it, also the most reasonable one for all parties involved.") or end ("Damn it, I think lowering tuition is a great idea.") of the speech. The control speech was the same speech without the swear word.[2]

The speeches were delivered in a video format on a computer screen using Medialab experimental software (Jarvis, 2002). The male speaker could be seen from mid-chest up in front of a neutral background. The speaker attempted to maintain the same tone for every speech.

There were two surveys that assessed the participants' attitudes about the speaker and the speech. The first survey was a nine-item scale that asked questions about the participants' attitudes toward the speaker. The questions of most interest were the three

Why is this important to the validity of the experiment? What would happen to the results if all of the arguments were either strong or weak?

Can you think of intense language that would be an alternative to swearing? How might the impact of swearing change depending on the source, the message, or the audience?

The researchers are utilizing replication, which you first learned about in Chapter 2, to build on previous findings about obscenity and persuasion. What are some other ways to replicate this idea?

[2]The experiment contained an additional condition with swearing in the middle of the speech. Unfortunately, this condition inadvertently confounded the placement of the swear word with its use (". . . then the alumni may feel that the damn school already has taken enough money from them."). This condition did not differ from the control condition on persuasion, speaker intensity, or speaker credibility, but given the confound, it is unclear whether the lack of an effect was due to the placement of the swear word or its use.

questions about the intensity of the speaker (how passionately, strongly, and enthusiastically did the speaker feel) and three questions about the credibility of the speaker (how credible, trustworthy, and knowledgeable the audience found the speaker). There were an additional three questions about how similar the speaker was to the participant (was the speaker like them, similar to them, and akin to them) that were used for further study. The second survey was a four-item scale that asked about the participants' attitudes about lowering tuition (how much did they like the idea of lowering tuition, how much did they think it was a good idea at the school that was implementing the plan, would they implement such a plan at their school, and did the speech make them feel more positive or negative towards the idea). All questions used similar seven-point response options with all points labelled (e.g., not at all credible, not credible, somewhat not credible, neutral, somewhat credible, credible, very credible).

*Think about the primacy and recency effects you learned about in Chapter 5. What can you conclude about these effects from the results of this experiment?*

*Do you think the results of this experiment would be the same had the use of obscenity been abundant?*

## Results

The purpose of the present experiment was to examine the effects of swearing on the perceptions of the speaker and the persuasiveness of the speech. These were tested using a series of univariate ANOVAs comparing the three conditions on each dependent variable (speaker intensity, speaker credibility, and attitude about topic; see Table 1). Each dependent variable displayed good internal consistency (intensity: $\alpha = .87$, credibility: $\alpha = .83$, and attitude about topic: $\alpha = .82$). Speaker intensity was correlated with speaker credibility ($r = .28$, $p = .009$) and with attitude about the topic ($r = .35$, p = .001). Speaker credibility did not correlate with attitude about the topic ($r = .12$, $p = .267$).

Swearing had a significant effect on participants' attitudes about lowering tuition, $F(2, 85) = 3.751$, $p = .027$. Follow-up contrasts showed that the speeches with the swear word at the beginning or end were significantly more persuasive than the control speech (see Table 1). The speeches with the swear word in the beginning and end did not significantly differ from each other. Swearing also had a significant effect on participants' perceptions of the intensity of the speaker, $F(2, 85) = 3.473$, $p = .035$. Follow-up contrasts revealed the same pattern as for attitudes about lowering tuition: swearing at the beginning or end of the speech led to significantly higher perceptions of speaker intensity than no swearing. Swearing did not significantly impact perceptions of speaker credibility, $F(2, 85) = 0.052$, $p = .945$.[3]

*Mediational analysis.* To test whether the effects of swearing on persuasion were fully or partially mediated by increased intensity, three regression analyses were conducted (Baron & Kenny, 1986). In each of these regressions, the three conditions were represented by two contrast vectors. Contrast vector 1 (CV1) compared the beginning and end conditions against the control condition. Contrast vector 2 (CV2) compared the beginning condition against the end condition. CV1 represented the comparison of interest. CV2 was included to fully represent the three conditions in the regression equations.

In the first regression, intensity was regressed on the contrast vectors. Consistent with the ANOVA results above, CV1 was a significant predictor of intensity, $B = -.395$, $SE_B = .152$, $\beta = -.270$, $t = -2.599$, $p = .011$. In the second regression, attitude toward lowering tuition was regressed on the contrast vectors. Also consistent with the ANOVA results, CV1 was a significant predictor of attitude toward lowering tuition, $B = -.938$, $SE_B = .352$, $\beta = -.276$, $t = -2.661$, $p = .009$. In the third regression, attitude toward lowering tuition was regressed on the contrast vectors and intensity. CV1 remained a significant predictor, $B = -.067$, $SE_B = .031$, $\beta = -.228$, $t = -2.131$, $p = .036$, although the beta was reduced somewhat, suggesting partial mediation. Speaker intensity approached significance, $B = .075$, $SE_B = .046$, $\beta = .174$, $t = 1.628$, $p = .107$. It should be noted, however, that although the experimental manipulation allows a causal interpretation of the effect of swearing on intensity and persuasion, the relationship between intensity and persuasion is correlational, and the data are consistent with other possible causal relationships.

## Discussion

The purpose of this experiment was to examine the effects of judicious swearing on persuasion in a pro-attitudinal speech. Results demonstrated that swearing at the beginning and at the end of the speech led to more positive attitudes about the topic and greater perceptions of speaker intensity. These results provide the first demonstration of the persuasive power of obscenity, and they suggest that judiciously used obscenity can increase persuasion, at least within the context of a pro-attitudinal speech.

Mediational analyses suggested that speaker intensity partially mediated the effects of swearing on persuasion, although the effect of intensity on persuasion in the final regression equation was not statistically significant. This may be due to a lack of statistical power. Additional research should be conducted to further test the mediational effect. These findings are congruent with the idea that language intensity can lead to higher levels of attitude change and they suggest that swear words can be used in a similar way to other forms of intense language.

In the present experiment, swearing had no impact on speaker credibility. In

[3]When looking at the expertise and trustworthiness components of credibility separately, the results were similarly nonsignificant—expertise: $F(2, 85) = 0.184$, $p = .832$, trustworthiness: $F(2, 85) = 0.224$, $p = .800$.

**Table 1** Effects of One Swear Word on Persuasiveness of a Speech and Perceptions of the Speaker

| | *No obscenity (control)* | *Obscenity at the beginning* | *Obscenity at the end* |
|---|---|---|---|
| Attitude about lowering tuition | 4.14 $SD = 0.40$ | $4.42^a$ $SD = 0.45$ | $4.34^a$ $SD = 0.41$ |
| Speaker intensity | 4.40 $SD = 1.03$ | $4.89^a$ $SD = 0.81$ | $5.02^a$ $SD = 0.98$ |
| Speaker credibility | $4.91^a$ $SD = 0.73$ | $4.91^a$ $SD = 0.75$ | $4.98^a$ $SD = 0.76$ |

Scales range from 1–7 with higher s indicating more persuasion, greater intensity, and greater credibility. Means within a row that share a superscript are not significantly different.

regards to credibility, it is possible that swearing may be affecting credibility both positively and negatively, leading to an overall null effect. Obscenity could impact credibility positively because the use of obscenity could make a credible speaker appear more human. Consistent with this, Aune and Kikuchi (1993) found that language intensity increased source credibility in a pro-attitudinal message. However, obscenity could also impact credibility negatively because the use of obscenity could be seen as inappropriate for a credible speaker. Future work is needed to tease apart the relationship between swearing and the different aspects of credibility: expertise and trustworthiness. It is also possible that credibility would have greater importance in a counter-attitudinal speech in which the audience might be motivated to reject the speech by derogating the qualities of the speaker.

*Limitations and future directions.* As described above, the present experiment was designed to examine the persuasive power of obscenity in an optimal setting: a pro-attitudinal speech containing a single, relatively mild swear word. Future studies could examine whether obscenity's persuasive effect is limited to this domain. Are there situations in which obscenity can increase persuasion even in a counter-attitudinal speech? Would obscenity be more or less useful if the message arguments are all strong or weak? What would be the effects of using stronger (and potentially more offensive) swear words? Would an increase in the number of swear words increase their persuasive impact? It might be the case that the effects of swearing on persuasion are curvilinear; additional swear words may increase a message's persuasive impact only to the extent that they are perceived as appropriate. Once the swearing becomes excessive, however, it may backfire.

Manuscript received 11 April 2005

Manuscript accepted 11 April 2006

**Which of Cialdini's six weapons of influenced discussed in Chapter 7 does this idea apply to?**

## References

Aune, R. K., & Kikuchi, T. (1993). Effects of language intensity similarity on perceptions of credibility, relational attributions, and persuasion. *Journal of Language and Social Psychology, 12,* 224–238.

Baron, R. M., & Kenny, D. A. (1986). The moderator–mediator variable distinction in social psychological research: Conceptual, strategic, and statistical considerations. *Journal of Personality and Social Psychology, 51,* 1173–1182.

Bostrom, B. N., Baseheart, J. R., & Rossiter, C. M. (1973). The effects of three types of profane language in persuasive messages. *The Journal of Communication, 23,* 461–475.

Bradac, J., Bowers, J., & Courtright, J. (1980). Lexical variations in intensity, immediacy and diversity: An axiomatic theory and causal model. In R. N. St. Clair & H. Giles (Eds.), *The social and psychological contexts of language* (pp. 294–317). Newbury Park, CA: Sage.

Bradac, J., Bowers, J. A., & Courtright, J. (1979). Three language variables in communication research: Intensity, immediacy and diversity. *Human Communication Research, 5,* 257–269.

Fine, M. G., & Johnson, F. L. (1984). Female and male motives for using obscenity. *Journal of Language and Social Psychology, 3,* 59–74.

FMeekins (2004, July 3). Hillary high horse. Message posted to http://www.promoteliberty.org/phpbb2/viewtopic.php?t = 65

FOXNews.com (2004). *Transcript: Interview with Dick Cheney,* Retrieved September 20, 2004, from http://www.foxnews.com/printer_friendly_story/0,3566,123792,00.html

Hamilton, M., Hunter, J., & Burgoon, M. (1990). An empirical investigation of an axiomatic model of the effect of language intensity on attitude change. *Journal of Language and Social Psychology, 9,* 235–255.

Hamilton, M. A. (1989). Reactions to obscene language. *Communication Research Reports,* 6, 67–69.

Jarvis, B. (2002). MediaLab2001 (Version 2002.1.4) [Computer software]. New York: Empirisoft Corporation.

Jay, T. (1992). *Cursing in America.* Philadelphia: John Benjamins Publishing Company.

Mulac, A. (1976). Effects of obscene language upon three dimensions of listener attitude. *Communication Monographs, 43,* 300–307.

Ravenwood's Universe (2004). *Cheney said what needed to be said,* Retrieved September 20, 2004, from http://www.ravnwood.com/archives/003261.shtml

Simms, P. (2004, July 26). New details surface. *The New Yorker,* Retrieved September 20, 2004, from http://www.newyorker.com/shouts/content/?040726sh_shouts

Vertes, A. D. (1997). *Selznick's vision: Gone with the Wind and Hollywood filmmaking.* Austin, TX: University of Texas Press.

# SOCIAL INFLUENCE: SHOULD WE RESIST?

<<< *What do our names for these drinks tell us about social influence?*

**HOW** DO UNINTENTIONAL SOCIAL INFLUENCES CHANGE OUR BEHAVIOUR?
**WHAT** IS CONFORMITY, AND HOW DOES IT INFLUENCE BEHAVIOUR?
**HOW** DO OTHERS INTENTIONALLY INFLUENCE OUR BEHAVIOUR?
**HOW** DO AUTHORITY FIGURES GET US TO OBEY THEM?

It's your summer vacation, and you've decided to join your friend Malcolm for a visit to his hometown in Glasgow, Scotland, where you have never visited before. You're at the movie theatre one night, ordering snacks before you head in to see the movie. You have your candy and your popcorn, and you are just about to order a beverage. You open your mouth, ask for what you want to drink, and the woman behind the concessions counter looks at you like you have two heads.

Confused, you turn to Malcolm, who immediately starts to laugh. Why? What's so funny about asking for something to drink? To you, what you've ordered makes perfect sense, but Malcolm and the woman behind the counter have grown up calling those carbonated beverages something else entirely. In fact, these beverages have many different names, depending on where you are in the world—"pop" in Canada, "soda" or "bubbler" or "co-coler" in various places in the United States, "scoosh" or "ginger" in Scotland, "cooldrink" in South Africa, "lolly water" in Australia, or "fizzy drink" in certain places in the United Kingdom. Wherever you go, they're calling it something else (von Schneidemesser, 1996)!

In addition, these naming differences are not restricted to pop only. For example, sandals worn in the summer are called "thongs" in Western Canada and "flip-flops" in Eastern Canada. These differences are, perhaps surprisingly, the topic of much debate and research. People can get quite heated about which is the "right" name—in fact, bring the question up in the cafeteria at school and see what happens. If you have friends from different parts of the world, chances are you'll find yourself in the middle of an argument! The fact that people in different regions conform by using certain names for beverages is an illustration of social influence, a concept that will be discussed in great detail in this chapter. We are going to introduce you to the ways in which our behaviour can be influenced through both unintentional (i.e., social norms, conformity) and intentional (i.e., compliance and obedience) processes. As you read, think about how you might behave the next time you go to the movies with Malcolm—would you continue to order using the word you're accustomed to using, or would you bend to the expectations of the people around you in this unfamiliar city?



CHAPTER 08

**CHAMELEON EFFECT** the non-conscious mimicry of the postures, mannerisms, facial expressions, and other behaviours of one's interaction partner, such that one's behaviour passively and unintentionally changes to match that of others in one's current social environment

**SOCIAL ROLE** expectations for the ways in which an individual should behave in a given situation

# How Do Unintentional Social Influences Change Our Behaviour?

You are at a party with friends. It's a great place to observe the ways in which people interact, so you decide to sit back and watch what's going on around you. In the corner, you see your friend Mark talking to Jane, who you know he likes. You notice she has a habit of rubbing her arm as she speaks with Mark. As you watch them, you notice that Mark has started rubbing his arm when he talks, too. Now, if you weren't studying social psychology, you probably would not have been observing their behaviours closely enough to pick up on this. It leaves you wondering, though. Is Mark intentionally mimicking Jane's behaviour, and for what benefit?

It's highly unlikely that Mark is *intentionally* rubbing his arm. In fact, it is highly unlikely that he is even fully conscious of the fact that he is doing so—or that Jane is rubbing hers. Instead, Mark is probably exhibiting what is known as the **chameleon effect**. Coined by Chartrand and Bargh (1999, p. 893), this term refers to "the non-conscious mimicry of the postures, mannerisms, facial expressions, and other behaviours of one's interaction partner, such that one's behaviour passively and unintentionally changes to match that of others in one's current social environment."

This effect was first demonstrated in a study where students had a 10-minute interaction with a confederate under the guise of discussing photographs for use in another experiment (Chartrand & Bargh, 1999). The students each interacted with two different confederates in two separate sessions. During the interactions, the confederates varied their mannerisms, smiling, shaking their feet, or rubbing their faces; the second confederate would exhibit mannerisms that the first had not. The researchers observed that students smiled more times per minute when partnered with a smiling confederate rather than a neutral one, and shook their feet or rubbed their faces more often when that behaviour was exhibited by the confederate. If you are thinking the students might have been mimicking the confederates on purpose, Chartrand and Bargh (1999) thought of that, too. At the end of each session, they asked the students if anything had stood out about the other participant. Not one student pointed out the target mannerisms, demonstrating that the chameleon effect is not conscious.

The term *chameleon effect* describes the tendency to non-consciously mimic the behaviours of someone with whom one is interacting.

So what is the mechanism behind this chameleon effect, which calls to mind the lizard's ability to match its surroundings? Chartrand and Bargh (1999) point to a perception-behaviour link through which perceiving an action displayed by another person makes someone more likely to perform that same action. The chameleon effect may serve an important social function; being "in sync" with someone else's behaviours and mannerisms allows for easier interactions between people. In a second experiment by Chartrand and Bargh (1999), confederates matched the behaviours of some study participants but not others. The participants who had been mimicked responded more favourably to the confederate than those who had not been. It may be that we mimic others when we want to be liked or are feeling a bit out of place. It certainly explains why Mark was rubbing his arm, doesn't it? Similarly, think of why it is that when you see someone else yawning, you usually end up yawning too. Research has demonstrated that seeing a yawning face stimulates "mirror neurons" in the brain, which our responsible for mimicking witnessed actions (e.g., Provine, 2005; Rizolatti & Craighero, 2004).

The chameleon effect is just one way in which we describe the social influence exerted upon us in our daily lives. Social influence occurs when our attitudes, cognitions, or behaviours are affected by another person or group. As mentioned above, social influences can be intentional ways others try to change our behaviour, such as in persuasion (which you learned about in Chapter 7), compliance, and obedience. We'll discuss the last two later in the chapter. On the other hand, social influence can occur unintentionally or without our awareness, such as with the roles and norms that guide our behaviour and how we conform to others around us. In fact, social roles and social norms are key concepts in the development of social influences.

## SOCIAL ROLES

Monique is a 21-year-old woman. She is a student, majoring in psychology, who also works part-time at Canadian Tire and volunteers once a week at the local animal shelter. She is the sister of seven-year-old twin boys, lives with her parents, and spends most Saturdays with her girlfriends at the beach. While all of this adds up to make one individual person, do you think Monique's behaviours and mannerisms remain exactly the same as she moves through all of these spheres of her life? Of course not. At the beach, you'll find Monique wearing a bathing suit and laughing loudly as she goofs around with her friends. When she babysits her brothers, she can't show the same behaviours—she must be a responsible older sister. At work, she wears her Canadian Tire uniform, which is clothing you would never see her wearing in class, and the way she interacts with customers is very different from the way she does with her friends at the beach. Though she is still Monique in all of these settings, she must play different roles throughout her life, and these roles dictate which behaviour is called for. Through the course of your day, your **social role,** or the expectations for the ways in which you should behave in a given situation, may

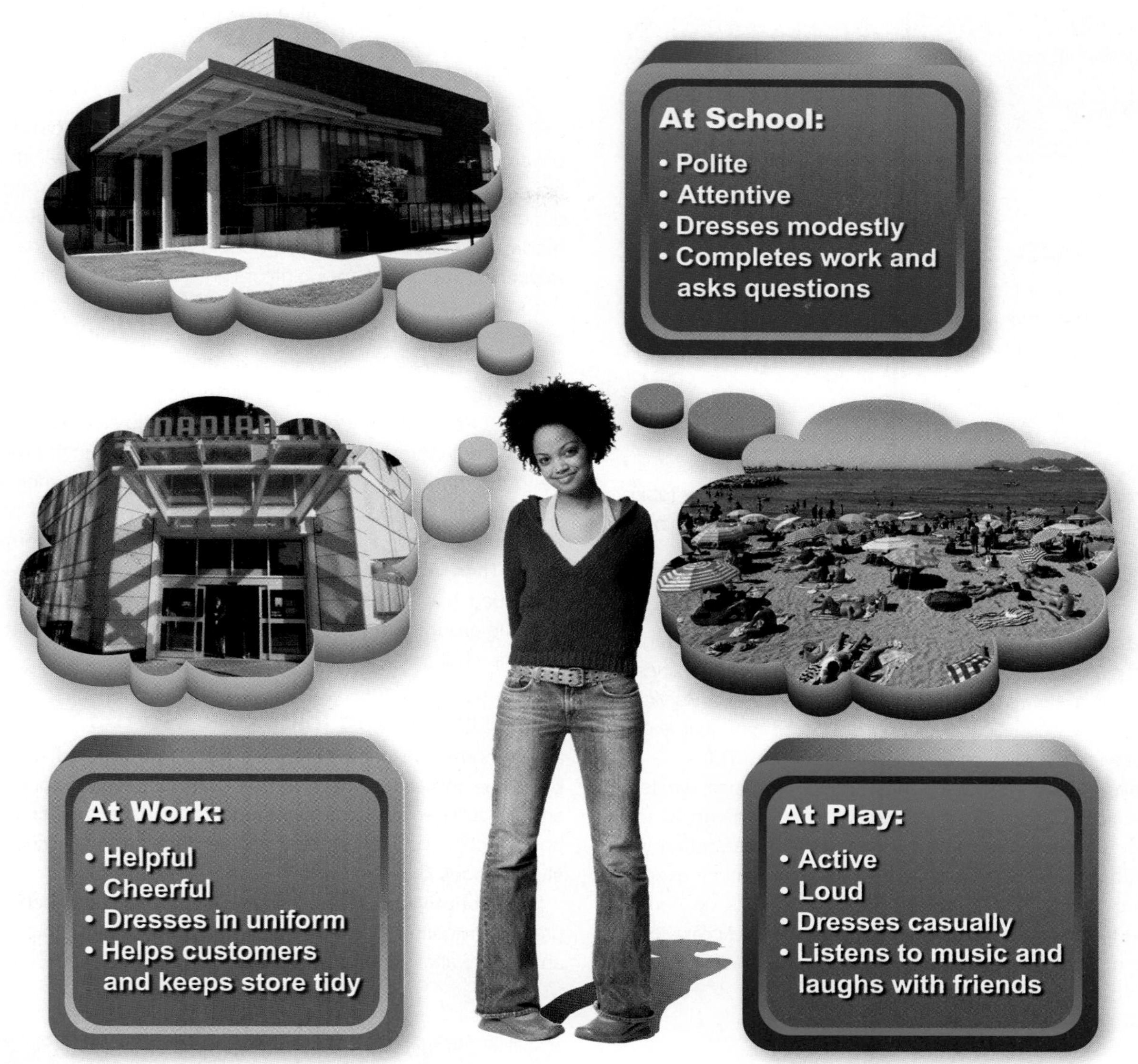


**Monique's Social Roles.** **As we move through the day,** we change our behaviours to meet the expectations of various social roles.



change many times. Think about all of the different circles in which you move as a student, a member of your family, an employee, and so on. How do you behave differently in your social roles?

The social influence exerted by the expectations of social roles is pretty well ingrained. We expect people within certain roles to act a certain way. How would you react if you saw one of your professors dancing at a local club? It might throw you off, because you expect him to behave within the confines of his social role of "professor." Remember, though, that he, like you, has many other social roles—you just normally do not see him in those roles. This explains the odd feeling that sometimes comes with seeing someone "out of context."

Fulfilling the expectations of social roles can have serious consequences, as evidenced in a classic study known as the Stanford Prison Experiment (e.g., Haney & Zimbardo, 1998; Zimbardo, 1971). College students volunteered to spend time in a simulated prison in Stanford's psychology department. Half of the students took on the role of guards, while the other half became prisoners. The "guards" were given billy clubs and permission to enforce rules. Very quickly, the students settled into their roles—and the expectations that came along with those roles. The guards devised humiliating punishments for the prisoners, some of whom rebelled and some of whom became apathetic to the situation. The students fell so fully into their roles that the researcher had to call off the two-week experiment after only six days (see www.prisonexp.org for a detailed overview of this research). How do you think the lessons of this study can be applied to social roles outside of the laboratory? Zimbardo (2007) has argued that our social contexts often dictate behaviour, and can make ordinary people perform extraordinary actions (whether they are positive or negative).

**SOCIAL NORMS** patterns of behaviour that are accepted as normal, and to which an individual is expected to conform in a particular group or culture.

**DESCRIPTIVE NORMS** how people typically behave in a given group or situation

## SOCIAL NORMS

Imagine you are visiting your friend Olivie in Paris. When she introduces you to her family, each member greets you warmly, giving you a quick kiss on each cheek. You find this is repeated when you meet some of Olivie's friends for lunch. You are not used to making such close contact with unfamiliar people, but you know this kind of greeting is common in France, so you relax and accept the warm gesture. You expect lunch to be rather quick, maybe an hour if you get caught up in conversation, but three hours pass without anyone making a move to leave the table. You're feeling a little antsy, since you are not used to lingering so long, but it seems normal to everyone else, so you just go along with it.

Hand-in-hand with social roles go **social norms**. These are the patterns of behaviour that are accepted as normal, and to which an individual is expected to conform in a particular group or culture. You might think of them as rules indicating how you are expected to behave. These rules can be *explicit* (a sign saying "No Shirt, No Shoes, No Service" posted on the door of a convenience store) or *implicit* (you just *know* you're not supposed to stand close to someone using an ATM).

In many ways, social norms are internalized. Because we feel uncomfortable about violating social norms, we often conform to the group norm so we don't stick out and we do not even realize that we are doing so! In fact, in new situations such as those you might experience when visiting Olivie in Paris, people are likely to pick up norms quickly by looking to those around them to model expected behaviour. Of course, this is not limited to vacations in foreign cities—think about the last time you started at a new job or school. How did you learn what was expected of you? We want to be accepted, so we accept the influence of social norms. But how do these norms develop in the first place?

In the first half of the 20th century, one of the founders of social psychology, Muzafer Sherif (1937), set out to answer this question. He wanted to know how norms develop and how strong their influence can be. In his approach to answering these questions, Sherif made use of a setup in which people are placed in a dark room and exposed to a stationary point of light. In this situation, most people perceive that the light is moving because there are no points of reference for location or distance in a completely dark room. This perception of movement is called the *autokinetic phenomenon*. You may be asking yourself at this point "What does this have to do with social norms?" Sherif knew that people perceive the stationary light as moving different distances. By placing several people in the room at once, he found that those people influenced one another when asked what the light was doing. There was no discussion or debate between participants, but after several trials they would start to conform to a group norm. Then, when people were exposed to the light individually, they continued to describe the movement in ways that were consistent with the group norm. Sherif (1937) had demonstrated that norms can change what people actually believe.

### Descriptive and Injunctive Norms

Social norms describe behaviour that is considered to be "normal," but does this single definition fit every situation? Consider drinking among college and university students. Is there a difference between how much a "normal" student *should* drink and how much a "normal" student *does* drink?

**Descriptive norms** describe how people typically behave in a given group or situation. These are generally pretty easy to follow. There isn't anything to analyze, as they are based on raw behaviour. You might think

Social norms dictate many areas of our lives—**even the ways in which we greet one another—and** can vary greatly from one situation or culture to another.

of descriptive norms as birds in a flock or fish in a school, following the behaviour of those around them. In the example of drinking behaviour, students tend to drink alcohol relative to how much they perceive others around them are drinking (Lee et al., 2007). **Injunctive norms**, on the other hand, involve perceptions of which behaviours are acceptable or unacceptable. Injunctive norms are behaviours of which people typically *approve* or *disapprove* of in a given group or situation. For example, students may find it acceptable to drink heavily around their friends on the weekend, but this may not be acceptable at home or at the campus pub during the week. Subscribing to these norms is based on understanding the moral rules of a society. Both kinds of norms motivate human action. Every day, you see examples of people doing what is socially approved and of people simply doing what is popular!

A perfect example of this is littering, for which the *injunctive* norm has become that one should not litter. Cialdini and his colleagues (1994) set up an experiment in which they hoped to manipulate norms that would lead people to litter. They gave people an opportunity to litter after finding flyers on their car windshields. The environment varied—it was either clean or fully littered—and the researchers added another variable by having a confederate either model littering or throwing the flyer in a trashcan. By introducing these variables, they were manipulating the perceived *descriptive* norm. They found that people were more likely to litter when they watched a confederate model littering, particularly in areas that were already fully littered. Cialdini and his fellow researchers (2004) also found that people were least likely to litter when they watched a confederate litter in a clean environment. They speculated that this was because the confederate's action drew attention to the anti-littering descriptive norm represented by the clean environment (Cialdini, 2004).

**INJUNCTIVE NORMS** behaviours of which people typically *approve* or *disapprove* of in a given group or situation

**PLURALISTIC IGNORANCE** a type of norm misperception that occurs when each individual in a group privately rejects the norms of the group, but believes that others accept them

PEDIATRIC ONCOLOGY WAITING ROOM
A CHILD'S WISH IS WAITING.
YOU CAN HELP MAKE IT COME TRUE.
Every 40 minutes, the Make-A-Wish Foundation® grants the wish of a child with a life-threatening medical condition — being a veterinarian for a day, meeting a favourite entertainer or going anywhere their imagination takes them. You can help make wishes happen. Visit www.makeawish.ca today.
MAKE-A-WISH. Canada
© 2010 Make-A-Wish Foundation. All marks are the property of the Make-A-Wish Foundation


**Public service announcements tend to be more effective when** they display injunctive norms of what we should be doing**—such as giving sick children hope by helping their dreams come true.**

Descriptive norms are often called upon in public service announcements (PSAs). For example, an anti-domestic violence PSA by the Homefront organization depicts a man in a restaurant beating up a waitress after she spills coffee on him, and no one intervening in the assault. However, Cialdini (1994) would have argued that while this PSA may be powerful, it demonstrates a descriptive norm of people not interfering in violence. In fact, he advocated that public service announcements would be more effective if they identified what people *should* be doing (injunctive norms) rather than what people *are* doing (descriptive norms). Some recent PSAs appear to have listened to Cialdini's advice. A recent series of television advertisements reflects people in a variety of situations modelling helpful behaviour (i.e., giving up their seat on the subway for a pregnant woman) and corresponding praise for such kindness (see peopleforgood.ca). In addition, certain organizations, such as the *Make a Wish Foundation*, regularly utilize these principles in their campaigns.

## Pluralistic Ignorance

As was stated before, people tend to accept social norms out of the desire to be accepted. What happens, though, when our drive to be accepted is so strong that we go along with social norms despite privately rejecting them? What happens when each individual in a group engages in this outward acceptance and private rejection, believing that everyone else accepts the norm?

You've probably seen this phenomenon demonstrated in one or more of your classes along the way. Let's say you are in a difficult math class, and you're just not getting it. Your professor asks if anyone has any questions. "Yes! About a hundred!" you think, but before raising your hand, you look around the room. All of your classmates are staring straight ahead, and no other hands are raised. You don't want to look stupid—after all, it seems like everyone else is getting it—so you keep your hand down. Only a week later, when the professor ditches a lesson plan in favour of reviewing the material based on the class's dismal performance on a quiz, do you figure out that everyone else felt just like you did. Of course, most of the time, we do not ever get any hints that pluralistic ignorance has been at work.

**Pluralistic ignorance** is a type of norm misperception that occurs when each individual in a group privately rejects the norms of the group, but believes that others accept them. It also often plays out in the development (or non-development!) of romantic relationships. Out of fear of rejection, you might not pursue someone in whom you are interested, fearing the person is not into you. Of course, the other person is feeling

**SYMBOLIC SOCIAL INFLUENCE** a type of influence that occurs when we change our behaviour according to the mental representation of others and our relationships with them

**CONFORMITY** a type of social influence in which an individual changes his or her behaviours to stay in line with social norms

exactly the same way and doesn't call you, which only serves as evidence for your suspicion that he is not interested. Your failure to call serves as the same evidence for him, and you both end up missing out on a potential relationship.

### Symbolic Social Influence

So what happens when people seem to influence our behaviour even from afar? Imagine you have moved away from home to attend college or university, and you have just discovered that your roommate has been stealing money from your room. What would you do? It is likely that you are going to think of what your parents or best friend would do if they were in the same situation. Other people influence our thoughts and actions even when they are not directly trying to change our behaviour! This is called **symbolic social influence**—that is, influence resulting from our evaluation of how important others in our life would interpret our behaviour even though they are not even present (e.g., Bargh & Williams, 2006; Forgas & Williams, 2001). For example, Fitzsimons and Bargh (2003) found that the psychological presence of others activates goals and values that are represented by our relationship with those individuals. In their study, participants were more likely to help a stranger after thinking of a friend compared to a co-worker.

We carry with us mental representations of people who matter to us (i.e., parents, friends, partners) and often ask ourselves what they would do in the same situation (e.g., Gillath et al., 2006). For example, if you are debating getting a tattoo and you know your parents would not approve, you may choose not to get the tattoo after all. While symbolic social influence can make us think twice about doing things we want to do but maybe shouldn't, it can also prevent us from acting in ways that may harm us. Consider Casey, a first-year university student who has had a few too many alcoholic drinks with his friends and is debating driving home even though he should not. His father always told him "better safe than sorry," and with that in mind, he chooses to take a taxi home. Even though his father was not physically present when Casey made this choice, Casey's decision was influenced by his mental representation of his dad. In fact, this occurs more often than we realize, for when our "conscience" kicks in and influences our actions, these reminders tend to reflect the values and morals of important people in our lives.

So far, we have learned about descriptive and injunctive norms, pluralistic ignorance, and symbolic influence—but what keeps us following these rules of unintentional social influence?

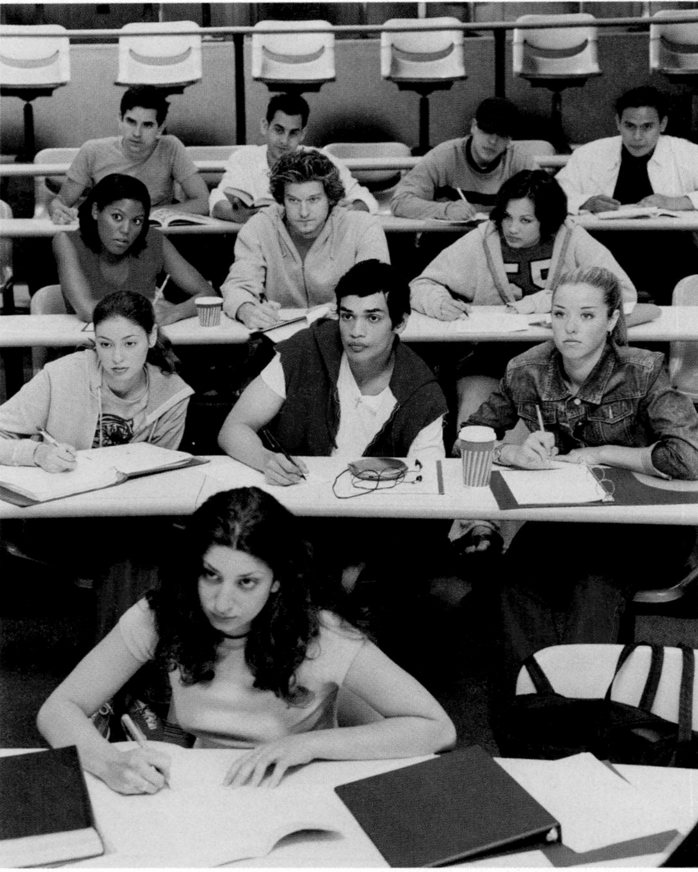

^^^ They might all be confused, **but pluralistic ignorance leads them to stay silent** for fear of looking stupid in front of their classmates.



## What Is Conformity, and How Does It Influence Behaviour?

Let's say you are in line at the grocery store, and you're in a real hurry. Ahead of you are three people, each with 15–20 items in their baskets. The second person in line has reached into her purse only to pull out, of all things, a cheque book. You feel like you're going to be in line forever. So why don't you just step in front of the woman with the cheque book and get on with your day? It sounds crazy to even suggest it, doesn't it? People just don't do things like that. But why? **Conformity** is the driving force that keeps you following social norms like patiently waiting your turn in the grocery store. It's a type of social influence in which we change our behaviours to stay in line with those norms.

This concept was first explored in a classic study by Solomon Asch in the early 1950s. Asch wanted to explore the forces of social influence, particularly those that come into play when our own judgments or actions don't match up with those reached or demonstrated by others. He asked study participants to respond to a series of problems in which they were asked to select which of three comparison lines was the same length as a standard line. Each participant was joined by several other participants who were, unbeknownst to the original participant, really confederates, meaning they were part of the research team. For many of the problems, the assistants stated incorrect answers out loud, before the participant gave an answer. All of the confederates gave the same incorrect answer.

Keep in mind, these judgments were quite simple, so it must have seemed odd to the participants that these other people were agreeing on an answer that was clearly incorrect. What was the participant to do? Should he be the "odd man out" and give the correct answer, or go along with the group, despite knowing that the answer they gave was most likely wrong? Asch (1951, 1955) found that most people chose the latter. Although he reported that many subjects experienced observable conflict with publicly conforming, 37 percent of all answers conformed to what the confederates answered. Some people even reported "I am

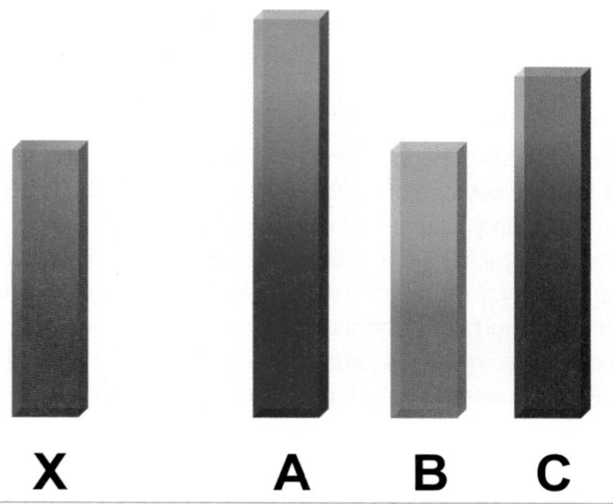
X
A
B
C

∧∧∧ **For Asch's study, participants were asked to** identify which of the three comparison lines on the right matched the length of the standard line on the left.

**PUBLIC CONFORMITY** a type of conformity that occurs when we feel pressured to conform to group norms. When publicly conforming, people pretend to agree with the group, but privately think the group is wrong

**PRIVATE CONFORMITY** a type of conformity that occurs when people truly believe the group is right; occurs even in the absence of group members

**INFORMATIONAL SOCIAL INFLUENCE** a type of influence that occurs when one turns to members of one's group to obtain accurate information

**NORMATIVE SOCIAL INFLUENCE** a type of influence that occurs when one goes along with a group because one wants to be accepted

wrong; they are right" when questioned. It is important to note that although 75 percent of subjects conformed at least once across the 12 trials, participants could also sometimes resist conformity. Of the subjects, 95 percent did provide at least one correct answer going against the group at least once.

Many of the participants in Asch's experiment were probably exhibiting **public conformity,** which occurs when we feel pressured to conform to group norms. When publicly conforming, people pretend to agree with the group, but privately think the group is wrong. **Private conformity,** on the other hand, occurs when people truly believe the group is right. This type of conformity occurs even in the absence of group members.

There are actually two different kinds of influence that lead to conformity. When you turn to members of your group to obtain accurate information, you are demonstrating **informational social influence.** There are various situations in which this might occur, such as when a situation is ambiguous and you're not sure what to do, or when immediate action is necessary during a crisis. In such cases, we depend upon others for what to do, or to ease our fears. Informational social influence most often leads to *private conformity* to the group's views. For example, imagine you were out with your friends and you witnessed a crime. One of your friends, who generally has a good memory, describes the perpetrator as wearing a "blue" coat and a beard, but you don't distinctly remember either of these details. You are likely to assume your friend has the correct information and these details may even become incorporated into your own memory (e.g., Clark & Wells, 2008). On the other hand, **normative social influence** occurs when you go along with a group because you want to be accepted. This kind of influence and the resulting public conformity were demonstrated in Asch's line experiment. Despite their feelings that the group was wrong, participants were still highly likely to give the group's answers as their own. Sometimes, we would rather be wrong than risk social disapproval. If you have ever wanted to be a part of a group, whether a peer group, sorority, special club, sports team, or other type of social group, you likely experienced this type of social influence as you were trying to "fit in."

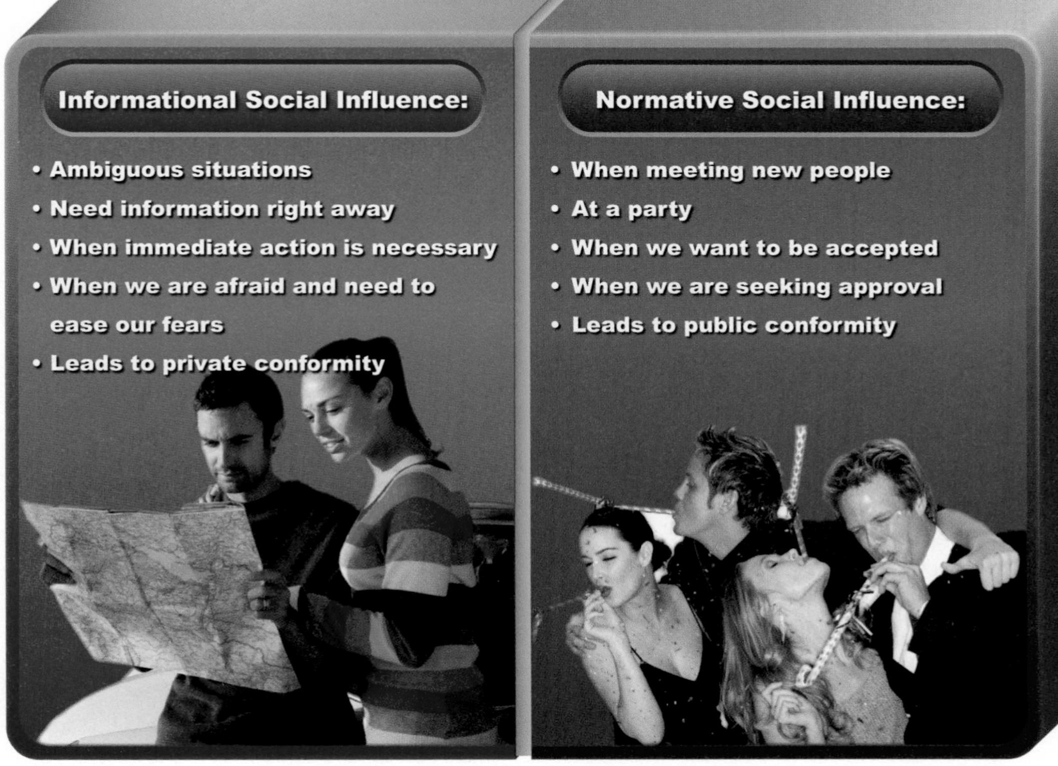
Informational Social Influence:
• Ambiguous situations
• Need information right away
• When immediate action is necessary
• When we are afraid and need to ease our fears
• Leads to private conformity
Normative Social Influence:
• When meeting new people
• At a party
• When we want to be accepted
• When we are seeking approval
• Leads to public conformity

<<< **Social Influence: Informational or Normative?** **Seeking information or striving to be accepted?**

**SOCIAL IMPACT THEORY** a theory which suggests that social influence depends on the strength, immediacy, and number of source persons relative to the target person(s)

## FACTORS AFFECTING CONFORMITY

By now, you have likely thought of various examples from your own life where you have conformed to what others were doing either for informational or normative purposes. You may even have asked yourself why you conformed. Recent research has shown how conformity manifests in the brain! It seems that our brains are wired to put out an alert when we make the 'mistake' of being too different from others (Klucharev, Hytonen, Rijpkema, Smidts, & Fernandez, 2009). In conjunction with our brains, certain features of our social environments also make us more or less likely to conform.

### Characteristics of the Group

You've just settled in to study for tomorrow's huge exam. Your grade in the class is on the edge, and if you do well tomorrow morning, you might just make an A. You've promised yourself you won't be distracted, that you'll keep your mind focused on the goal. Suddenly, your roommate bursts through the door, exclaiming, "25 cent wing night! Come on, we'll go for like an hour, and then you'll still have plenty of time to study." It's easy to turn him down, with a promise to go next week and an explanation that your grade is riding on this exam. He leaves you alone, and you open your text, a little disappointed that you can't join him, but proud of yourself for sticking to your guns.



Let's rewind. Now, instead of your roommate bursting through the door, it's your roommate *and* four of your friends. Suddenly it's a lot harder to say "no," isn't it? As the size of a group increases, so does the impact of conformity. Asch's experiment demonstrated this. When participants faced their tasks with only one confederate present, almost every participant went with his or her original answer without being swayed by the confederate. When two confederates were present, 14 percent of the participants conformed to the influence of the group, giving the wrong answer on at least one trial. Adding another confederate led to 32 percent of all answers conforming to the group norm (Asch, 1951, 1955). However, there is a limit to the number of individuals that can continue to increase the level of conformity. In Asch's work, adding three individuals led to an increase in conformity, but after that, the addition of another person did not significantly affect levels of conformity (Asch, 1956; Gerard, Wilhelmy, & Conolley, 1968). Thinking about the example from the beginning of this chapter, the next time you go to the movies in another country, you might be more likely to conform to the local name for that drink if you're surrounded by people in line than if it were just you and the server behind the counter.

This effect can be explained by **social impact theory** (Latane, 1981), which suggests that social influence depends on the strength, immediacy, and number of source persons relative to the target person(s). The strength of a source comes from status, ability, or relationship to a target person. You're more likely to be influenced by someone you see as competent or of higher status than yours. Immediacy has to do with how close a source person is to a target person. You're more likely to use the local name for that carbonated beverage at the concessions counter than the one you use back home, miles and miles away. Finally, as the number of source people increases, so does their influence. Again, think about that line of people behind you. If there were just one person behind you, you wouldn't be nearly as likely to conform to giving that local name.

### Demographic Variables

The degrees to which people conform, and in what situations, are not one-size-fits-all. Likelihood of conformity is dependent upon factors such as age, gender, and culture. You probably already know from your own experience that conformity to norms set by one's parents decreases with age, as conformity to norms set by one's peers increases. One classic study of students in the third, sixth, ninth, 11th, and 12th grades confirmed this (Berndt, 1979). Students responded to hypothetical situations in which peers encouraged them to behave in antisocial, prosocial, or neutral ways. For all types of behaviour, peer conformity peaked in sixth or ninth grade. In a second study by the same researcher, children in those same grades responded to situations testing conformity to peers or parents. As you might have already guessed from your own experience, conformity to parents decreased steadily with age and was negatively correlated with conformity to peers.

Let's say you are talking with a group of friends about plans for Friday night. Three of the people in the group want to go to a party a friend is having, but one isn't interested. She would much rather go into the city to hear a classmate's band play. Ten minutes of arguing later, the dissenter has started to cave, saying, "OK, maybe the party would be more fun, but I'm not sure." After another five minutes, she's in complete agreement that everyone will go to the party. Do you think this conformity would have been more or less likely if the dissenter had been a man? It seems like an odd question, but gender plays a role in how likely a person is to conform.

Traditionally, women tend to be more concerned with interpersonal relationships than men are. As such, are women more readily influenced to conform? Not necessarily. However, some research has demonstrated that when women are in group pressure situations (i.e., under surveillance by group members), they are more likely to conform than their male counterparts (e.g., Eagly & Chrvala, 1986). So it would seem that gender is a factor in conformity in group pressure situations, but what about in private situations? If there is no one around to observe any change that may take place, women don't conform any more or less than men do. Why, if a woman would not conform privately, would she be so much more likely to bend to group pressure? Some researchers believe it is due in part to the expectations of women in many societies. Women are often expected to foster interpersonal relationships and encourage harmony within a group. Often, this is accomplished through giving in to the group (e.g., Wood & Stagner, 1994).

"Why, if a woman would not conform privately, would she be so much more likely to bend to group pressure?"

These gender differences do, however, depend on familiarity with material, which determines how comfortable people are with a given task. In one study, male and female participants were asked to answer questions on stereotypically feminine, masculine, or gender neutral topics. They were also given the percentage of people who agreed or disagreed with each question. Female participants conformed to the majority more on the masculine items, while men conformed more with the feminine items (Sistrunk & McDavid, 1971). Faced with unfamiliar material, people are more likely to go with the group. In another study, men resisted influence to conform to incorrect answers about stereotypically masculine topics, while women held their ground on stereotypically feminine topics, showing that comfort with a topic leads to less conformity (Cacioppo & Petty, 1980). So unless you are familiar with topics such as turbine engines (stereotypically male) or skin moisturizer (stereotypically female), you are probably likely to go along with whatever answer is provided by the respective gender if questioned on these topics.

Cultural differences also play a major role in an individual's likelihood to conform. In a meta-analysis of conformity studies using a task similar to that in Asch's classic work, researchers found that countries with collectivist cultures tend to show higher levels of conformity than those with more individualistic cultures (Bond & Smith, 1996). Why? In collectivist countries, conformity is often seen as the "glue" that holds society together, whereas in individualistic cultures, conformity is usually seen as something to be avoided (e.g., Kim & Markus, 1999; Smith, Bond, & Kağitçibaşi, 2006). Of course, these are not hard and fast rules. Women and individuals from collectivist cultures may be more likely to conform in general, but it depends on the situation and task. Some scholars also argue that display rules—rules governing what behaviours are appropriate in certain situations—may constrain the expression of individualism even in collectivistic cultures. In a comparison of Japanese and Canadian students, researchers at the University of Toronto found that Japanese students still possessed the desire to be unique, but that they did not experience satisfaction from "standing out" unlike their Canadian counterparts (Tafarodi, Marshall, & Katsura, 2004).

## HOW DO WE RESIST CONFORMING?

In July 2010, the prime minister of Iceland, Johanna Sigurdardottir, made history—for the second time. In 2009, she became the world's first openly gay head of state, and in 2010, she and her partner of seven years took advantage of the full marriage equality in Iceland and were married. Though Iceland is one of the few nations around the world that allows marriage equality for gay and lesbian citizens, there is still some bias present (Melloy, 2010). Imagine the pressure to conform that people in positions of power must feel. All eyes are on them, and the public will judge. Sigurdardottir may very well have decided to conform to the prescribed image for a head of state, but instead she chose to live her life according to what is right for her and for her family. The drive toward conformity is a strong one, but it is one that can, and sometimes should, be resisted.

### The Presence of a Dissenter

Let's say you don't agree with a policy at your school. Would you make your voice heard? It can be pretty scary to resist conformity on your own, can't it? This is where the power of having an ally comes in. If someone else present dissents from the majority opinion, you may find it easier to dissent yourself. In Asch's line study, he found that the introduction of a confederate who agreed with the study participant reduced conformity by about 80 percent (Asch, 1951). In another set of experiments, Allen and Levine (1969) demonstrated that people conformed to the group less often when a confederate didn't go along with the majority. In addition, they found that even a seemingly incompetent ally decreased conformity (Allen & Levine, 1971). Simply having another person who is willing to stand up to the majority can have a powerful effect.

### Motivation

The issue of conformity is a complicated one, particularly in an individualistic society such as Canada, in which individual freedoms are highly valued, yet people for the most part are expected to conform to social norms. To some people, the very word calls to mind weak-minded individuals who blindly go along with society. Of course, it's not that simple or that dreadful. Indeed, we all conform to some degree, and conformity can be positive. Can you imagine what would happen if we all refused to conform to the social norms associated with waiting in line at the grocery store or obeying traffic signals?

Resistance to conformity is driven by a high need for individuality, particularly in situations in which people feel they're just one of the crowd. This motivates behaviours that are aimed at re-establishing a sense of being different. Individuals who demonstrate a high need for uniqueness are less swayed by the pressure to conform and agree less with the majority (Imhoff, 2009). In addition, recent research has demonstrated that nonconformity may serve evolutionary purposes, and manifest differently in men and women when trying to attract potential mates (Griskevicius, Goldstein, Mortensen, Cialdini, & Kenrick, 2006). Specifically, men may engage in more nonconformity to display themselves as different and desirable, whereas women tend to conform more to mate preferences established by men.

Despite the image of the "nonconformist" in popular culture as a sullen teen who rejects anything "normal," resistance to conformity can have a profound impact. In many cases throughout history, we have nonconformists to thank for social progress, particularly since the punishment for resisting conformity can sometimes be great. Without the willingness of key individuals to resist conformity, would women have been allowed to vote in Canada? Would the civil rights and anti-slavery movements in the United States have gotten off the ground? Would Sigurdardottir be able to live her life openly? Often, the

^^^ Icelandic prime minister Johanna Sigurdardottir broke conformity when **she became the first openly gay head of state, and she did so again when she married her long-time partner in July 2010.**

**MINORITY INFLUENCE** a process in which a small number of people within a group guide a change in the group's attitude or behaviour

**COMPLIANCE** a form of social influence involving direct requests from one person to another

motivation to resist conformity comes from a deep belief that large-scale societal change is necessary.

### Minority Influence

Most of the time, the social influence of conformity is carried out by a majority. Sometimes, though, we find cases of **minority influence**, a process in which a small number of people within a group guide a change in the group's attitude or behaviour. How does this work? When the minority is very firm in their beliefs, unwilling to give in to pressure from the majority, others start to believe that those in the minority may actually be right.

Research has shown that, while people publicly shy away from aligning themselves with a deviant point of view, minority influence can be profound, leading to the private conformity that comes with an actual change in viewpoint (e.g., Wood, Lundgren, Ouelette, Busceme, & Blackstone, 1994). This can, in fact, lead to an improvement in thinking, as an exposure to a strong opposing viewpoint forces cognitive effort and leads to more original thinking (Erb, Bohner, Schmilzle, & Rank, 1998). In Chapter 7, we discussed how people can be persuaded when they use systematic processing and the message is important, and these processes help minority opinions be heard!

> "Conformity can help us take care of ourselves and those around us."

Of course, conformity can be a positive force. As we discussed earlier, conformity to the injunctive norm of not littering and to another, more recently developed injunctive norm—recycling—has led to greater stewardship of the environment. Conformity can help us take care of ourselves and those around us. Think about the norms at your school. The expectation to conform to campus values such as the rejection of cheating and plagiarism serves to protect students. It might be rejected by "nonconformists," but these individuals often are not thinking about how the full picture of conformity can benefit society.

As we have seen, various social processes influence our behaviour, and we are unaware of them for the most part. However, sometimes we are all too aware of someone trying to change how we act or what we believe. The latter half of this chapter deals with these intentional social influences.

## How Do Others Intentionally Influence Our Behaviour?

Your sister has just come home from the mall. As soon as she gets in the door, she throws a shopping bag from Gap into your lap. "I can't believe I just bought that," she groans. You pull a dress from the bag. It's not ugly, really, but it is definitely not *her*. You ask her why she bought it. She answers, "I tried it on and didn't really like it, but the saleswoman said it looked really good. Before I knew it, I was at the register with that dress in my hand. I'm returning it tomorrow!" How often have you agreed to do something simply because somebody asked you to do it? Doing favours for friends, letting people cut ahead of you in line at the store, buying something you don't really want because a salesperson nudges you toward purchasing it—these are all examples of **compliance**. Compliance is a form of social influence involving direct requests from one person to another.

### HOW DO WE GET PEOPLE TO COMPLY WITH REQUESTS?

The effect of simply requesting a certain behaviour of an individual has been studied in various situations, including a study involving a copy machine at a library. Three different requests for cutting in line were used (Langer, Blank, & Chanowitz, 1978). For the first, participants were asked, "Excuse me. I have five pages. May I use the Xerox machine?" In the second version, the words "because I'm in a rush" were added to the request. In the third, participants were asked, "Excuse me. I have five pages. May I use the Xerox machine because I have to make some copies?" Both the second and third versions include the word *because*, which would signal a *reason* for having to cut in line. Look again at the third, though, and you'll find that there isn't any real reason given. This didn't seem to matter, though. While more study participants complied when the request was justified (94 percent complied with the second request, compared to the 60 percent who did with the first request), the *appearance* of a reason was all that was needed. Given the third request, in which no justification was actually given, 93 percent of participants still complied. Remember the concept of automatic processing from Chapter 3? Sure sounds like it's at work here, doesn't it? Words aren't even always necessary

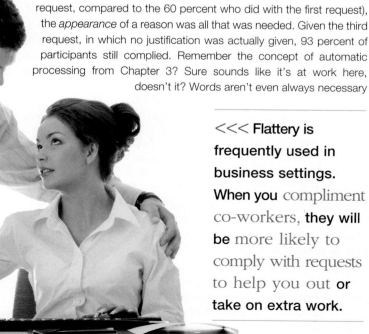

<<< **Flattery is frequently used in business settings. When you** compliment co-workers, **they will be** more likely to comply with requests to help you out **or take on extra work.**

for compliance (e.g., Briñol & Petty, 2003), but we do rely on several principles to get others to comply with our requests.

In the mid-1990s, Cialdini determined that the best way to study compliance was to study individuals who depended upon their abilities to persuade others. He called these individuals *compliance professionals*—individuals such as salespeople, people who work in advertising, fund-raisers, politicians—anyone whose livelihood is directly tied to his or her powers of persuasion. To study these individuals and their methods of prompting compliance, Cialdini went undercover, working in fund-raising, sales, and other fields that depend upon compliance. He found that while people may use many different methods of gaining compliance, all of these methods are based on six principles. They are *friendship* or *liking*, *commitment or consistency*, *scarcity*, *reciprocity*, *social validation*, and *authority* (Cialdini, 1994). We first discussed these as "Weapons of Influence" in Chapter 7, and now we will explore each of these in more detail and the compliance tactics associated with each.

## Friendship or Liking

Let's say your friend has asked you to save him a seat at the movies. No problem, right? Now let's say the same request has been made by a stranger or by someone you don't like. Suddenly, the likelihood of your compliance is pretty low, right? It seems fairly obvious—we are more likely to comply with requests from people we like than with those from people we don't like or don't know.

Persuasive techniques that take advantage of this principle are called **ingratiation techniques**—techniques in which we get others to like us so they are more likely to comply with a request. Flattery is a great example of this—remember your sister and the dress she didn't like but bought anyway? Even just a *sense* of familiarity can affect degrees of compliance. Researchers have found that participants were more likely to agree to a request for a donation to charity from a stranger who had the same first name or birthday than when there were no such similarities between the participant and the stranger (e.g., Burger, Messian, Patel, del Prado, & Anderson, 2004). As small as the connection might be, it still enhanced the drive to comply.

## Commitment or Consistency

You're heading into class when a classmate approaches, asking you to sign a petition to stop animal testing in the campus labs. If you already agree with his or her position, you're far more likely to sign than if you disagree. This is an illustration of the commitment or consistency principle of compliance. Once you're already committed to a position, you are more willing to comply with requests that reflect that position.

One persuasive technique that depends upon this principle is the **foot-in-the-door technique**, which begins with a small request. Once that request is granted, the requester makes a larger target request. You've seen this in play if you've ever been to a large "warehouse" store like Costco or Superstore. It's so easy to take that free sample, isn't it? The requester knows that once that sample is in your hands, it will be easier to persuade you to comply with the target request: buying the full-sized product. Research suggests that this technique does indeed lead to increased compliance (Freedman & Fraser, 1966).

Another technique based on the commitment or consistency principle is the **lowball technique**. In this technique, once an individual agrees with an offer, the requester adds on additional costs, making the offer less attractive. Why, after an offer has been made less attractive, doesn't the target of the offer just walk away? This is where the idea of commitment comes in. Once the initial commitment has been made, it's harder to say "no," even when the offer has changed. For example, your friend asks you

**INGRATIATION TECHNIQUES** techniques in which we get others to like us so they are more likely to comply with a request

**FOOT-IN-THE-DOOR TECHNIQUE** a compliance technique that begins with a small request that, when granted, leads to a larger request

**LOWBALL TECHNIQUE** a compliance technique in which a target accepts a "low-cost" offer, only then to be told that there are additional hidden costs

**DOOR-IN-THE-FACE TECHNIQUE** a compliance technique in which the requester makes an initial offer that is much larger than the target offer, in the hope that the final offer will have the appearance of the requester doing a favour for the target person

"Why, after an offer has been made less attractive, **doesn't the target of the offer just walk away?**"

to drive him or her to the airport so he or she can fly home to visit his or her parents. Only after you've already agreed does he or she mention that his or her flight is at 7 a.m. and that you'll need to pick him or her up at 5 a.m. Had your friend mentioned the time before you complied with the request, you might not have agreed to the arrangement. As unattractive as the prospect of getting up at 4 a.m. to drive to the airport may be, you probably won't back out now because you have already made the commitment.

## Scarcity

If something is hard to get or if supplies are running out, you're more likely to comply with a request. Items that seem to be in short supply suddenly seem more desirable, and we don't want to feel left out. Think about what happens around the holiday season at the end of each year. There's usually some hot new toy or gadget that's the "must have" gift of the year, whether it be the new iPhone or iPad, a Wii or Xbox, or Tickle-Me-Elmo. How many news stories have you heard about parents getting into fist-fights over these toys? One classic study confirmed the effectiveness of perceived scarcity when participants were asked to rate the attractiveness of, and the price they would pay, for cookies (Worchel, Lee, & Adewole, 1975). The researchers found that ratings were significantly higher when there were only two cookies in the jar as opposed to when there were 10 cookies available. It's the principle of scarcity at work!

## Reciprocity

When you do a favour for someone, you expect he or she will be willing to do one for you next time you ask, right? The principle of reciprocity works because you are usually more willing to comply with a request from someone who has previously complied with a request from you.

The principle of reciprocity is central to a method known as the **door-in-the-face technique**. Here, the requester makes an initial offer that is much larger than the target offer, in the hope that the final offer will have the appearance of the requester doing a favour for the target person. This technique comes into play in a classic study carried out by Cialdini and his colleagues where they asked college students if they would be willing to commit to unpaid positions as counsellors for juvenile delinquents for two hours a day for the next two years (Cialdini, Vincent,

**THAT'S-NOT-ALL TECHNIQUE** a compliance technique in which an initial request is followed by adding something that makes the offer more attractive

**OBEDIENCE** a form of social influence in which an individual orders another person to do something

Lewis, Catalan, Wheeler, & Darby, 1975). Not one person agreed. However, when the request was modified to ask the students to serve as chaperones on a two-hour trip to the zoo with the juvenile delinquents, half of the students agreed. When the zoo request was made without the initial proposition of a counselling position, only 17 percent of the students complied. In the end, it appeared that the researchers were making an offer of reciprocity—that they were willing to help the students out by making the offer more manageable (Cialdini et al., 1975).

Another technique that depends upon the principle of reciprocity is the **that's-not-all technique**. Using this technique, an initial request is followed by adding something that makes the offer more attractive. Infomercials are notorious for using this technique—in fact, the very words "That's not all!" are often used in those television advertisements. If you have ever watched infomercials on late-night television, you have been exposed to this technique and may have even bought products you didn't really need! This technique works in part because it seems like a negotiation, even though it's used when the target of the request hasn't yet had a chance to respond to the offer. For example, Burger (1986) conducted a study selling cupcakes with an added bonus of two "free" cookies or just selling cupcakes alone. Although the price was the same for both deals (75 cents), people purchased the "that's not all!" cupcakes 73 percent of the time relative to 40 percent for the cupcakes alone. As a salesperson adds additional products or incentives, the customer feels an obligation to purchase the product because it seems that the salesperson is making concessions—again, tapping into that principle of reciprocity.



## Social Validation

The principle of social validation depends upon our willingness to comply with a request that is in line with what we believe is the norm for people like ourselves. We want to fit in (again, the power of social norms at work!), so we go along with requests that seem to match up with what others are doing. In fact, the principle of social validation was the one Cialdini (2001) most often encountered during his studies of compliance. He argues that when we see other people performing a recommended action, we are more likely to do so ourselves, especially if they are similar to us (Cialdini, 2008). Think about all of the ads you have seen or heard in which a company claims its product is the best-selling or most popular on the market—it's the principle of social validation at work. Unfortunately, social validation may take the form of peer pressure to perform negative behaviours. However, recently some scholars have tried to design positive peer pressure techniques to encourage appropriate behaviour based on social validation—such as comparing exercise regimes and *healthy* eating choices through cellphones for female teens rather than using diet pills and potentially developing eating disorders (Toscos, Faber, An, & Gandhi, 2006).

## Authority

After an appointment with a doctor, you're most likely going to follow her advice or pick up the medication she prescribed. When you see a police car flashing its lights behind you, you're most likely going to pull over. We are generally more likely to comply with requests from people who appear to have authority (Cialdini, 2008). Even when the authority figure is not directly in our presence, we are still likely to obey. For example, when you see photo radar signs, are you more likely to obey the speed limit? This influence often comes from the perception that authority figures are experts. In the next section, you will read about just how far this compliance can go, and the dangers that are associated with an excessive drive toward complying with authority figures.

**Two for the price of one?** The that's-not-all technique relies on the principle of reciprocity, **throwing in something extra to make you feel like you're getting something free.**

# How Do Authority Figures Get Us to Obey Them?

In Chapter 2, you were introduced to Stanley Milgram's infamous studies on **obedience**, a form of social influence in which an authority figure is able to simply order someone to do something. His experiments, in which he led study participants to believe they were administering electric shocks to an unseen person whenever that person gave an incorrect answer to a question, rocked the world of social psychology and brought ethical concerns to the forefront of discussions of (and subsequent changes to) acceptable research methods because participants believed they were administering potentially lethal shocks to another individual (Milgram, 1963). Despite Milgram's assertion that he debriefed all participants and a survey showing that 84 percent of participants were either "glad" or "very glad" to have participated in the experiment, ethical concerns prevent research like his from being conducted today.

The principle of authority that plays a part in driving compliance is the central factor in obedience, and Milgram's research depended upon perception of authority. When one experiment was conducted in a lab at Yale University, and run by a research scientist, the study resulted in 70 percent of participants continuing to administer shocks to the generator's limit. When Milgram ran his studies out of a ramshackle lab with no associations with Yale, the rate of obedience with

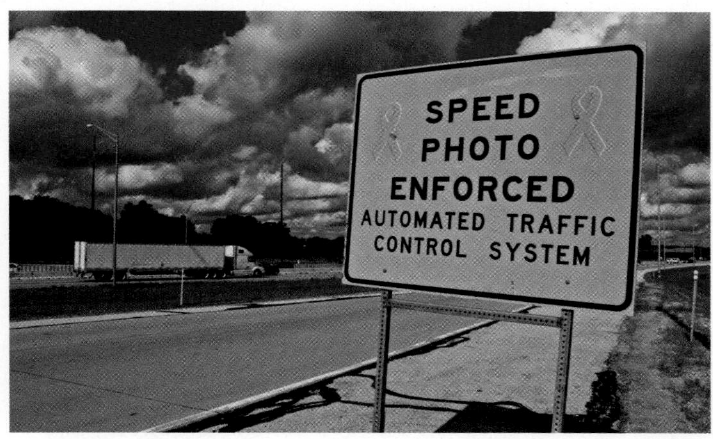


^^^ **If you saw this photo radar sign, would you slow down, knowing that** the police have the authority to give you a ticket **or suspend your license for speeding?**

administering the shocks dropped to 48 percent. Further, when the experimenter was not perceived to be a scientist, but instead another participant, compliance dropped to 20 percent (Milgram, 1963, 1965).

We'd probably like to think that an experiment like Milgram's wouldn't get the same results today. But nearly 50 years later, despite ethical constraints, researchers have recently been able to replicate Milgram's experiment.

Professor and social psychologist Jerry Burger (2009) observed that many people assume that the lessons of the Holocaust and an awareness of the dangers of blind obedience would lead people to resist the pressure of the authority figure. As such, these individuals believed that if Milgram's experiment were repeated, the results would be drastically different. Unfortunately, this was not the case. To comply with ethics guidelines, Burger (2009) put several safeguards in place. He lowered the top range of the generator to 150 volts, the level in Milgram's study at which nearly every participant paused and expressed reluctance to continue (see Packer, 2008). In addition, participants in Burger's study were told at least three times they could withdraw and still receive the $50 payment. They were also given a lower sample shock (to show the generator was real) than that given in Milgram's study. His study may not have directly mimicked Milgram's, but it is nonetheless useful. What he found may be a bit disheartening though. Despite our supposed awareness of the dangers of blind obedience, and the historical examples of the horrors that can result, Burger's experiment resulted in only slightly lower levels of obedience than those found in Milgram's original work (Burger, 2009). So have we really changed all that much if we are willing to blindly follow the orders of an authority figure just because they told what to do?

## ACTION LEARNING

### Using Compliance Techniques

Is there a particular cause about which you care deeply, one for which you feel you could do something major, if only you had some assistance from your peers or the community? Now that you have learned about a variety of compliance techniques based on Cialdini's (1994) six principles, why not apply them and finally drum up some of that support you've been hoping for?

Turn on the television, and you'll see compliance principles and techniques used in an effort to get you to do your part as a consumer. Research has demonstrated that compliance techniques are useful in more noble pursuits as well. For example, people have been asked to contribute money ($1.00) to a museum children's program using three different compliance techniques: foot-in-the-door, door-in-the-face, and the lowball procedure (e.g., Brownstein & Katzev, 1985). In general, the researchers found that the lowball procedure was the most effective of the three techniques, and that the foot-in-the-door technique was the least effective. Why do you think the compliance techniques varied in their effectiveness in this scenario? Which of the various compliance techniques do you think might be most effective in asking for support for your selected cause?

For this project, select a cause for which you wish to garner support from your community. In order to test compliance techniques, remember that there should be some request you will make of your potential supporters. For example, maybe you are concerned with homelessness and feeding the poor so you might seek donations for a local shelter. Perhaps you would like better support for local animal shelters through money or volunteer hours. What about support for programs for disadvantaged children and youths, such as Big Brothers and Big Sisters or the Boys and Girls Club of Canada? Here are some ideas for determining what your possible cause could be:

1. An organization for which you would like to raise money through an event such as a bake sale or through directly asking for donations (e.g., your psychology club, a local children's school, or a homeless shelter).
2. An elected position, such as on your school's student government, to bring about change
3. A research fund or drive to which you would like to contribute money
4. Another cause that is important to you

Select three compliance techniques and/or principles (e.g., foot-in-the-door, door-in-the-face, and scarcity) and write out in your own words how they work. Apply the three techniques to your chosen cause by developing three different requests that can be used to ask for support. Next, contact the director of your chosen cause and get approval and the proper information concerning volunteer fundraising for an organization. Then approach people in your community and ask for support using one of the requests you developed, using the three requests on different people. Evaluate which of the techniques is most successful—do they all work equally well, or is one more successful than the others? Are there any additional factors that may have affected rates of compliance?

What you will learn from this action project:

1. Explain how three compliance techniques work.
2. Use compliance techniques to request support for a selected cause, and help contribute to that cause.
3. Evaluate which compliance technique is most successful for use in supporting a selected cause.

## Using Compliance Techniques for a Good Cause

| What Cause Is Important to You? | |
|---|---|
| Technique 1: | Results: |
| Technique 2: | Results: |
| Technique 3: | Results: |
| Which compliance technique is most successful for your cause? | |



## OBEDIENCE OUTSIDE THE LAB

Would you eat a big jar of worms right now? How about let yourself be locked in a glass box full of snakes and cockroaches? Of course not, right? The very idea of doing either of these things seems just plain crazy. Now, what if you could win a trip to Toronto or New York or Las Vegas or a new car by doing one of these things? *What if you were on television*? Reality shows like *Fear Factor*, which feature stunts like the ones above (and those would be considered tame by the show's standards!), depend upon contestants' willingness to do things they would not normally do. The contestants do these things for prizes, yes, but many believe the real motivation comes from being on television. Of course, we don't only see the potential dangers of obedience carried out in reality television. There are plenty of real-world examples that serve as warnings against blind obedience.

Think about the prisoner abuses carried out by American soldiers who were "just following orders" at Abu Ghraib in Baghdad. Similarly, several Canadian soldiers were charged with the murder of Somalian teenager Shidane Arone in 1993 after beating, sodomizing, burning, threatening, kicking, and abusing the youth and taking "trophy" pictures of the incident. When the trials began for soldiers involved in both of these incidents, the question on everyone's mind was: What makes "good" people do bad things? Based on his research and the famous Stanford Prison Experiment (discussed earlier), Zimbardo (2007) argued that social modelling and group conformity, paired with stress and a lack of accountability, played roles in the obedience that led soldiers to act in appalling ways (Dittman, 2004). On a smaller scale, but no less horrifying, is the story of a nightmarish interrogation that took place at a McDonald's in Mt. Washington, Kentucky. Following instructions given by a "police officer" on the phone, the store manager subjected a terrified employee to an "examination" and sexual abuse carried out by the manager's fiancée. The man on the phone was, of course, not a police officer. Rather, this was the latest in a long line of hoax calls carried out by a voyeuristic prison guard (ABC News, 2005). The perceived authority of the caller coupled with the presentation of an unfamiliar situation led the store manager to blindly trust and obey the voice on the phone.

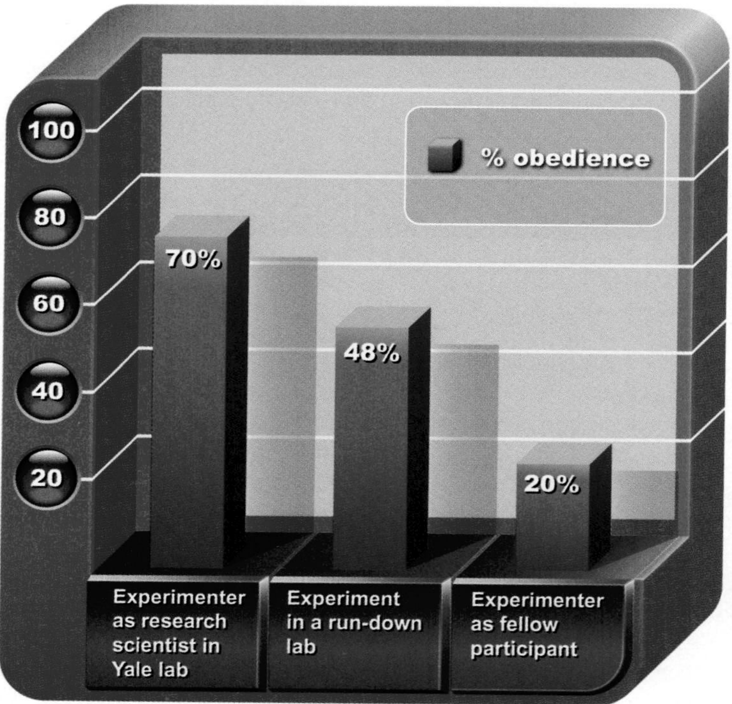


*Source:* From the book "Obedience to Authority" by Stanley Milgram, Harper & Row, 1974.

**Degrees of Disobedience.** Whether or not we obey depends upon the perceived level of authority, **as demonstrated in Milgram's controversial study on obedience.**

### Bringing Milgram to Prime Time

The motivation of the promise of TV time was illustrated, to disturbing effect, on French television in March 2010. Eighty contestants on a game show signed contracts in which they agreed to inflict electric shocks on other contestants. They were told that there would be no prizes, as it was a new show and this was a test episode, but were offered a small fee for their participation. The setup was much like that in Milgram's experiment. Contestants were instructed to administer an electric shock, up to 460 volts, to another contestant whenever he answered a question incorrectly. The overwhelming majority obeyed, despite his screams of protest. When the final shock of 460 volts was administered, the man fell silent—presumably he had passed out or even died. Only 16 of the 80 contestants stopped before that last shock. What could drive people to follow orders until they potentially killed a man?

> "When the final shock of 460 volts was administered, the man fell silent—**presumably he had passed out or even died.**"

As it turned out, this was no game show. The contestant being shocked was an actor, who screamed and writhed as the "shocks" were administered. It was all for a documentary called *Game of Death*, which cast a critical eye on the trend of reality television, in which contestants are asked to carry out harmful or humiliating tasks. Many of the "contestants" in the show later said they wanted to stop, but that they were convinced by the presenter to keep going. One admitted with regret that she kept going despite the fact that her grandparents were Jewish Holocaust victims.

Has television become the ultimate authority? *Game of Death* producer Christophe Nick argued that on television, under the guise of a game, you can get people to do anything. Even if your partner screams, you are still in a game. In a game, he said in an interview about the documentary, the rules are skewed. A psychologist involved with the show said the results serve as a lesson that rules must be explained to children, rather than simply imposed upon them, and that people must be taught to disobey when a situation calls for it (Chazan, 2010).

### Cults and Obedience

Obedience also can have drastic consequences when leaders of cult-like organizations order their members to perform heinous or self-destructive acts. In the late 1970s, members of the Peoples Temple cult, led by Jim Jones, were ordered to commit mass suicide in what became known as "Jonestown" in Guyana. Large vats of Kool-Aid were laced with cyanide, and though a few people escaped, the vast majority of his group obeyed. Some helped their children drink the Kool-Aid before drinking it themselves, their final act of obedience to their leader. Similarly, followers of the Order of the Solar Temple in Quebec, Switzerland, and France were either murdered or committed mass suicide by a variety of methods in the mid-1990s. Orders to harm others are by no means uncommon within these organizations (i.e., the murders committed by members of the Manson Family under the instruction of Charles Manson). That said, being ordered to perform criminal actions does not relieve individuals of criminal responsibility, but can lead people to act in ways they would not otherwise (see Zimbardo, 2007).

## STRATEGIES FOR RESISTING OBEDIENCE

Despite the power exerted by authority figures, there are ways in which obedience can be resisted (Burger, 2009; Milgram, 1963). This can be done by changing authority or changing proximity (also see Packer, 2008).

### Changing Authority

One way in which obedience can be resisted is by taking away the perceived authority level from the authority figure. Remember that Milgram (1963) did not get nearly as many people to comply when the person urging them to push the button was perceived to be another participant, rather than a researcher. We often believe authority figures are willing to take responsibility for actions they have ordered. If it is perceived that the person does not have a high enough level of authority, people are less willing to follow her orders.

### Changing Proximity

It's a classic suspense-movie scenario. You can stop one of three events, and you must make a choice between them. One will result in the death of your best friend, the second will result in the deaths of 20 people in your town, and the third will result in the deaths of 200 people in a foreign country. If your instinct is to save your friend, you are not alone. Proximity is a powerful factor. Because you are more proximal to your best friend, you are naturally more inclined to want to save him. In Milgram's study, he found that obedience levels were significantly reduced the closer the participant was to the person being shocked, with the lowest levels occurring when participants were required to touch their partners. Proximity of the authority figure was also a factor, with lower levels of obedience when the experimenter gave instructions over the phone or via a tape recorder, rather than in person (Milgram, 1963).

Often, as Milgram discovered, we behave in ways that cognitively, we don't necessarily want to. Social roles and norms play a large part in defining how we think we should behave and how we do behave. This sometimes results in obeying and conforming, but it also helps us persuade others to conform in ways we wish them to. These social influence techniques can be used to both harm and help. So next time you change your attitudes or behaviours, consider the influence that others have on your decision.

**Jim Jones and the members of the Peoples Temple** serve as a haunting example of just how far obedience can go.

CHAPTER
# 08 Review

## Summary

### HOW DO UNINTENTIONAL SOCIAL INFLUENCES CHANGE OUR BEHAVIOUR? p. 140

- Social influence occurs when our attitudes or behaviours are affected by another person or group. This influence is rooted in social roles and social norms.
- We expect people within certain social roles to act according to our expectations for those roles. Social norms might vary from culture to culture and group to group, and provide guidance for how we are expected to behave in a particular place or group. Descriptive norms describe how people typically behave, while injunctive norms define what is acceptable behaviour.

### WHAT IS CONFORMITY, AND HOW DOES IT INFLUENCE BEHAVIOUR? p. 144

- Through changing our behaviours to stay in line with social roles and social norms, we engage in conformity. Conformity can be public, which occurs when one feels pressure to follow a group, or private, which occurs when one comes to truly believe that the group is right.
- There are many reasons for conforming, including when we need to decide what to do in an ambiguous situation, or when we want to be accepted by the group. Conformity is affected by group size as well as demographic variables.

### HOW DO OTHERS INTENTIONALLY INFLUENCE OUR BEHAVIOUR? p. 148

- Compliance is based on six basic principles, upon which different compliance techniques are built. These techniques are used to influence someone through a direct request. Often, all that is needed for compliance is the appearance of a reason.

### HOW DO AUTHORITY FIGURES GET US TO OBEY THEM? p. 150

- The findings of Stanley Milgram's infamous 1963 study still hold true today—people seem to be willing to follow the orders of an authority figure, even if it means hurting someone else. The effect has been made even greater with the invention of various reality television shows.
- While there are certainly positive aspects to authority and obedience, there are many dangers associated with the kind of blind obedience seen in Milgram's study. Levels of obedience can be changed by changing the authority level of the person giving orders or by changing proximity.

## Key Terms

**chameleon effect** the non-conscious mimicry of the postures, mannerisms, facial expressions, and other behaviours of one's interaction partner, such that one's behaviour passively and unintentionally changes to match that of others in one's current social environment *140*

**compliance** a form of social influence involving direct requests from one person to another *148*

**conformity** a type of social influence in which an individual changes his or her behaviours to stay in line with social norms *144*

**descriptive norms** how people typically behave in a given group or situation *142*

**door-in-the-face technique** a compliance technique in which the requester makes an initial offer that is much larger than the target offer, in the hope that the final offer will have the appearance of the requester doing a favour for the target person *149*

**foot-in-the-door technique** a compliance technique that begins with a small request that, when granted, leads to a larger request *149*

**informational social influence** a type of influence that occurs when one turns to members of one's group to obtain accurate information *145*

**ingratiation techniques** techniques in which we get others to like us so they are more likely to comply with a request *149*

**injunctive norms** behaviours of which people typically *approve* or *disapprove* in a given group or situation *143*

**lowball technique** a compliance technique in which a target accepts a "low-cost" offer, only then to be told that there are additional hidden costs *149*

**minority influence** a process in which a small number of people within a group guide a change in the group's attitude or behaviour *148*

**normative social influence** a type of influence that occurs when one goes along with a group because one wants to be accepted *145*

**obedience** a form of social influence in which an individual orders another person to do something *150*

**pluralistic ignorance** a type of norm misperception that occurs when each individual in a group privately rejects the norms of the group, but believes that others accept them *143*

**private conformity** a type of conformity that occurs when people truly believe the group is right; occurs even in the absence of group members *145*

**public conformity** a type of conformity that occurs when we feel pressured to conform to group norms. When publicly conforming, people pretend to agree with the group, but privately think the group is wrong *145*

**social impact theory** a theory which suggests that social influence depends on the strength, immediacy, and number of source persons relative to the target person(s) *146*

**social norms** patterns of behaviour that are accepted as normal, and to which an individual is expected to conform, in a particular group or culture *142*

**social role** expectations for the ways in which an individual should behave in a given situation *140*

**symbolic social influence** a type of influence that occurs when we change our behaviour according to the mental representation of others and our relationships with them *144*

**that's-not-all technique** a compliance technique in which an initial request is followed by adding something that makes the offer more attractive *150*

# Test Your Understanding

## MULTIPLE CHOICE

**1.** People most likely engage in the chameleon effect to

- **a.** allow for easier interaction through shared mannerisms.
- **b.** make fun of someone.
- **c.** subtly influence another person's behaviour.
- **d.** exert power over one another.

**2.** Muzafer Sherif studied social norms using

- **a.** the chameleon effect.
- **b.** the autokinetic phenomenon.
- **c.** brain imaging.
- **d.** surveys.

**3.** _____ norms involve perceptions of what we should do in a typical setting.

- **a.** Social
- **b.** Injunctive
- **c.** Descriptive
- **d.** Confederate

**4.** Which is an example of pluralistic ignorance?

- **a.** Ten people at a party drink five beers each, believing that the rest of the group finds this normal and acceptable. Privately, all of them believe it to be excessive, but don't want to look stupid.
- **b.** In Asch's line trials, the participants gave the wrong answers because those were the answers given by a group of confederates.
- **c.** A student raises his hand in class to ask about a lecture because he thinks everyone else might have been confused by it.
- **d.** All of these are incorrect.

**5.** _____ is a type of social influence in which we change our behaviours to stay in line with norms.

- **a.** Compliance
- **b.** Obedience
- **c.** Conformity
- **d.** Norm adjustment

**6.** Some studies have shown that women are more likely than men to

- **a.** conform to group opinions.
- **b.** resist conformity.
- **c.** conform to group opinions only in private situations.
- **d.** conform to group opinions only in public situations.

**7.** _____ is a form of social influence involving direct requests.

- **a.** Conformity
- **b.** Compliance
- **c.** Pluralistic ignorance
- **d.** A social role

**ANSWERS:** 1. a; 2. b; 3. b; 4. a; 5. c; 6. d; 7. b; 8. d; 9. b; 10. a

**8.** Which of the following is an example of the door-in-the-face technique?

- **a.** getting a free sample at the food court in the mall and then being asked if you want to buy a sandwich
- **b.** being offered a coupon for milk in exchange for buying cookies, only to be told after you've agreed to buy the cookies that they are out of milk
- **c.** being told that there are only five left of the shirt you are on the fence about ordering
- **d.** being asked to make a $100 donation and then to make a $25 donation when the first request is refused

**9.** Which of the following is an example of the lowball technique?

- **a.** getting a free sample at the food court in the mall, then being asked if you want to buy a sandwich
- **b.** agreeing to a flight and hotel vacation package through a travel agent, and when the agent adds on extra service fees, you still purchase it
- **c.** being told that there are only five left of the shirt you are on the fence about ordering
- **d.** being asked to make a $100 donation and then to make a $25 donation when the first request is refused

**10.** Burger's 2009 study found that

- **a.** Milgram's 1963 findings have not changed much over time.
- **b.** people are less likely to obey authority figures than they were in the 1960s.
- **c.** compliance techniques are based on six principles.
- **d.** people are willing to do just about anything on television.

## ESSAY RESPONSE

1. Provide examples of three social roles that you fill. How does your behaviour change between these roles? Why?
2. You have been asked to plan a public service campaign for a social issue. Explain how you would use what you have learned about descriptive and injunctive norms to shape the campaign.
3. Choose a situation such as a trip to the grocery store or driving to work. Name one descriptive norm for people in that situation, and one injunctive norm. What is the difference?
4. Describe examples of when informational social influence and normative social influence might occur. What is the difference between the two?
5. How might you design an ethically acceptable experiment to test the boundaries of obedience? Why would this experiment be effective?

## APPLY IT!

Think of a social norm you can safely (and legally!) break. Do so. What happens? Observe the reactions of your breaking that norm.

**Remember to check www.thethinkspot.ca for additional information, downloadable flashcards, and other helpful resources.**

# THE POWER OF THE GROUP

*<<< When you are involved in group work, are you a leader or a follower?*

**WHAT** DEFINES A GROUP?
**HOW** DOES A GROUP INFLUENCE INDIVIDUAL BEHAVIOUR?
**HOW** DOES A GROUP MAKE DECISIONS?
**WHAT** ARE THE CAUSES OF GROUP CONFLICT?
**HOW** ARE CONFLICTS AMONG GROUPS RESOLVED?

On January 28, 1986, the world was shocked when the *Challenger* space shuttle exploded only seconds after launching. While the explosion itself was an incredible tragedy that included the death of seven individuals, what is perhaps more upsetting is that it could have possibly been prevented. Reports indicate that engineers and other workers found problems with equipment on the shuttle, but no one went through the process of properly addressing these issues. Though individuals had identified problems, the groups of people working on the shuttle launch refused to acknowledge the problems or to delay the launch until the problems were resolved. This sad example of what we call "groupthink" indicates how groups can alter an individual's behaviour. Though some found errors, the collective response was simply to drive forward and complete the ultimately fatal launch (Esser, 1998). The *Challenger* launch is an example of how a group can negatively impact a person's behaviour. But fortunately, group interaction doesn't always have to have a negative result.

People join groups for all kinds of reasons. Some people happen to end up in a group together simply because they are in the same place at the same time, although these people are not united. Some individuals look actively for groups to join because they want to make new friends, while others want to work collaboratively to accomplish a common goal. Some people may live alone and crave the social interaction that groups provide, while others like the diversion from the stress of everyday life.

Most people become part of at least one group in one way or another, and every group serves a different purpose. A group can consist of two or three people, such as a study group, or it can be larger and include hundreds or thousands of members, like a political party. Sometimes our membership in a group is temporary—such as participation in an intramural sports team—while other times it may be lifelong, such as membership within a religious group. The accepted behaviours of a group become norms for us as individuals and determine how we act when surrounded by other members. Whether we are functioning as part of a family or as members of a social committee, the influence of the group leads us down paths we would not normally walk alone.

This chapter will help you to understand what defines a group, how groups influence individual behaviour, and the factors that determine how decisions are made within groups. We will also take a look at conflicts, their causes, and methods for solving them.



# CHAPTER 09

**GROUP** two or more people who are seen as a unit and interact with one another

**COHESION** the degree to which a group is connected

## What Defines a Group?

A **group** is defined as two or more people who are seen as a unit and interact with one another (Shaw, 1981). Some groups—such as sports teams or work groups—have members who know each other personally and work together in order to achieve a common goal. The members of these groups recognize themselves as being part of a group. Other groups contain people who do not know each other and are grouped together only by similar interests or characteristics. Your sex, culture, and race place you within groups, but you don't necessarily know every other person in those groups. For example, you probably connect more strongly with other people who speak your language than with those who do not, whether or not you have personal interactions or relationships with them. Another example of unintentional groups involves fans of a particular sports team. For example, when it was announced that the Winnipeg Jets would be re-established in Manitoba for the 2011 NHL season, fans of the original team were thrilled by the news and could be considered a group of "Jets fans" even though they are spread across Canada (Wiebe, 2011). You may be grouped in with these people simply because you share some type of commonality.

We all join groups; sometimes our memberships are short-lived, like when you're part of a group waiting in line at a Subway restaurant. Other times, we belong to groups for life, like our families or religious groups. Regardless of how long you are in a group or how insignificant it might seem, each group you are part of serves a different purpose and might influence your behaviour differently.



### COHESION

Groups have different degrees of **cohesion,** or the extent to which they are connected. They may be comprised of a random selection of people who have little in common with one another, except that they find themselves in the same place at the same time. For example, if you are waiting in line for a drink from Booster Juice, there is no reason to assume you share any of the same characteristics or goals as the people in front of you or behind you. But you *are* all there for a reason—you want a tasty, delicious beverage! This is the only factor making you cohesive as a group.

^^^ Religious groups have a high level of cohesion because their members share a belief that the group has great importance. **What else creates cohesion in a religious group?**

On the other hand, groups can be made up of people who are united in terms of a shared intimacy, history, or background, as in the case of religious groups or families. People in these groups tend to have high levels of communication with each other, as well as common goals and a shared belief that the group is of great importance. They also have a high level of cohesion, exhibit improved performance, and are usually more subject to stereotypes because their behaviours are consistent over time (Evans & Dion, 1991). Furthermore, they are often stereotyped because their particular characteristics make them more distinguishable from other groups (Yzerbyt, Corneille, & Estrada, 2001). Most established groups possess common motives and goals, as well as defined roles and statuses. This, in turn, results in the formation of a social rank or hierarchy of dominance among group members (Bettencourt, Charlton, Dorr, & Hume, 2001). Groups are also characterized by their accepted

>>> Groups come in all shapes and sizes. **Most have common goals that determine the actions of each individual.** How many groups do you belong to?

norms and values, as well as a clear system of rewards and penalties when those norms are upheld or violated (Sherif & Sherif, 1956).

Group cohesiveness also can vary within the same social grouping. For example, one of the authors of this text (KP) joined a slo-pitch softball team several years back and takes her commitment to being a member of team sports very seriously. As a result, she rarely misses games and actively participates in team activities. That said, there are other people on the team who show up for games infrequently and do not become part of the cohesive unit that forms the core of the team. So you could say that some people have low cohesiveness with the group, whereas others have high cohesiveness.

Another component of groups involves shared goals and outcomes. To accomplish this, people serve different roles in order to fulfill various goals in a group. In some cases, roles are assigned or voted upon, like that of a psychology student club president, whereas in other cases, people acquire roles due to their personal characteristics. Think about the group of friends with whom you spend the most time. Often one friend is better at making decisions for the group, while another helps keep peace when conflict arises. Think about the Stanford Prison Experiment (Zimbardo, 1969), discussed in Chapter 2. The students chosen to be prisoners quickly fell into their roles and demonstrated varied behaviour ranging from rebellion to emotional distress. The guards in the prison adopted different approaches to their newfound power in relation to one another: some were harsher with prisoners, while others attempted to compensate or help prisoners through lenience. Though the students were initially all just volunteers, they quickly embraced their designated roles and were influenced by the behaviour of the group to which they were assigned.

## How Does a Group Influence Individual Behaviour?

Regardless of the social network to which we may belong, the group often influences our individual behaviour. We are not always simply *in* a group; we become *part* of it. For example, when New Democratic Party (NDP) leader Jack Layton passed away in August 2011 ("Jack Layton Remembered," 2011), the social network Facebook provided a demonstration of group behaviour. Many people changed their status to reflect their sympathies and united in a common sentiment across Canada (Kennedy & Boswell, 2011). Furthermore, some individuals who were not supporters of the NDP expressed that they felt guilty for not changing their status because it made them seem callous. Indeed, the authors of this textbook know of a few people who made the decision to update their Facebook pages because they felt group pressure to do so. Our own actions are often a result of the presence (whether physical or mental) of other people. This includes experiences within our families or workplaces and extends to our relationships with friends.

In fact, recent research indicates that your friends can affect your health just as much as your family can. In a long-term study of 12,067 people, researchers found that a person's social network can influence alcohol intake (Rosenquist, Murabito, Fowler, & Christakis, 2010). Think about it. If your friends spend Friday and Saturday nights drinking, you probably do too. Specifically, the study showed that an individual who spends a lot of time with a heavy drinker is 50 percent more likely to drink to excess as well. It further showed that 36 percent of participants in situations where only a friend of a friend was a heavy drinker also displayed excessive drinking. When attempting to treat a person for alcoholism, his or her social networks should be taken into account as a possible hindrance to the attainment of sobriety (Rosenquist et al., 2010). This is just one example of the many impacts a group such

**Experienced athletes typically feel more driven to succeed** when they are being watched.

as one's social network can have on one's life. Being around others can influence a person to act in certain ways, whether negatively or positively. Have you ever shown up for a class for which your professor was 10 or 15 minutes late? There were probably students who thought it was a good idea to leave before waiting a sufficient amount of time for the teacher to arrive. The original idea to leave may have been the suggestion of just a couple of people. However, after some of the other students who had planned to wait discussed the idea with their classmates, the suggestion to leave became more appealing and acceptable to them. The group influence moved these individuals to make a decision that they might not have made alone.

Groups can and do move us to action. If you've ever been at a sporting event or a rock concert, you are probably aware of your inclination to ramp up your behaviour as the crowd grows. Conversely, groups also influence us to choose *not* to act on occasion. Have you ever not voiced your opinion because you thought the rest of the group would not agree with you? Worrying what other people might think is a part of human nature that has both benefits and drawbacks, which you will see shortly. Three examples in which the presence of others affects individual behaviour include *social facilitation*, *social loafing*, and *deindividuation*.

"Groups can and do move us to action. If you've ever been at a sporting event or a rock concert, you are probably aware of your inclination to ramp up your behaviour as the crowd grows."

### SOCIAL FACILITATION

You probably possess a talent or a set of skills that others may not. If you are a gifted and confident singer, you are likely to show even more proficiency in front of an audience. To many skilled performers, the feeling of being "on stage" propels them to perform with even more accuracy and passion than if they were alone. This trend toward stronger performance

**SOCIAL FACILITATION** the enhancement of a well-learned performance when other people are present

**EVALUATION APPREHENSION** the idea that one's performance will be hindered or heightened due to approval or disapproval from others

**DISTRACTION CONFLICT THEORY** the idea that a person performing a task in front of others experiences a conflict of attention between the audience and the task at hand, thus increasing the motivation to succeed when completing simple tasks

in the presence of others is called **social facilitation.** We discussed this concept in Chapter 1, including seminal research by Norman Triplett (1898), who demonstrated that the performance of cyclists was heightened and racing times were faster when they competed against other cyclists than when they raced against a timer. Zajonc (1965) later developed this idea into the *theory of social facilitation*. However, while having others present can facilitate performance, some studies have shown that the presence of others can at times hinder performance—a process known as social inhibition (Zajonc, 1965). Think of a time when you had to make an oral presentation to your class. If public speaking does not come naturally to you, or if it frightens you, then you may not have performed as well as you wanted. Hindered performance in the company of others tends to occur with activities that individuals find somewhat difficult. Zajonc (1965) noted that when we have an audience, we become stimulated to succeed at the task at hand. This results in physiological arousal, which leads us to perform our *dominant response* (i.e., what is most common for us in that situation). If the task is a familiar one, our dominant response will most likely result in improved performance. However, if the task is less familiar, decreased performance can often occur because our dominant tendency isn't as established as it is in a more familiar task. Depending on our dominant response to a given task, the presence of an audience may have a positive or negative impact on our success (Lambert et al., 2003). However we end up responding, we can see that being in front of an audience strongly influences us.

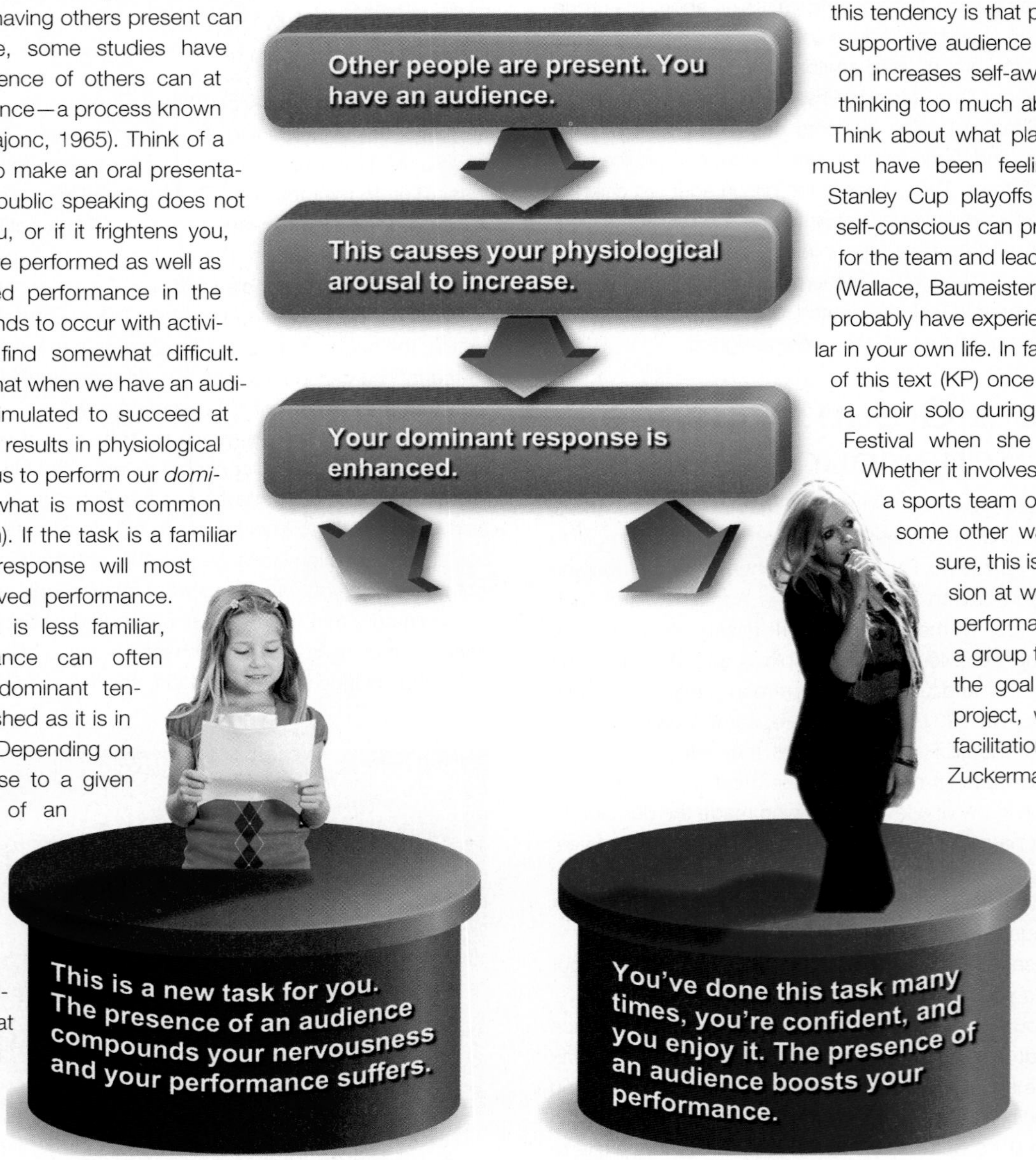

### What Leads to Arousal?

We evidently experience increased arousal when we are in the presence of an audience. Why is this? Research indicates there are three factors that may lead to increased arousal: *mere presence* (discussed above), *evaluation apprehension,* and *distraction.*

**Evaluation apprehension** is the idea that one's performance will be hindered or heightened due to approval or disapproval from others. When we feel that we will be judged by the people watching us, we become self-conscious and thus apprehensive about our abilities, and these feelings can negatively affect our performance. A classic example of evaluation apprehension can be seen in sports teams or athletes "choking" during the most important game or event of the season. In many different sports, studies have shown that some teams have greater tendencies to lose critical games—such as championship playoffs—on their home turfs (Baumeister & Steinhilber, 1984). A rationale for this tendency is that performing in front of a supportive audience when the pressure is on increases self-awareness and leads to thinking too much about what is at stake. Think about what players for the Canucks must have been feeling during the 2011 Stanley Cup playoffs in Vancouver. Being self-conscious can produce harmful results for the team and lead to devastating losses (Wallace, Baumeister, & Vohs, 2005). You probably have experienced something similar in your own life. In fact, one of the authors of this text (KP) once flubbed the words to a choir solo during the Kiwanis Musical Festival when she was in junior high. Whether it involves messing up a play on a sports team or making a mistake in some other way when under pressure, this is evaluation apprehension at work. Even focusing on performance while completing a group task, instead of having the goal of learning from the project, will lead to the social facilitation effect (Gagné & Zuckerman, 1999).

Social facilitation also may be explained by the **distraction conflict theory,** which is the idea that a person performing a task in front of others experiences a conflict of attention between the

Other people are present. You have an audience.
This causes your physiological arousal to increase.
Your dominant response is enhanced.
This is a new task for you. The presence of an audience compounds your nervousness and your performance suffers.
You've done this task many times, you're confident, and you enjoy it. The presence of an audience boosts your performance.

**Social Facilitation: When the Going Gets Tough.** The presence of an audience can propel us to excel at the task at hand if it is something we are comfortable doing. **But research has shown that the less capable we are at a task, the more poorly we will perform in front of an audience.**

audience and the task at hand (Baron, 1986). When the individual is tackling simple tasks, this can increase his or her motivation to succeed because of the awareness that he or she is being watched. But if the task is difficult, studies show that the time it takes to complete it increases with the presence of an audience, making it harder for us to focus (e.g., Baron, Moore, & Sanders, 1978; Groff, Baron, & Moore, 1983). As a result, we are more likely to revert to our dominant responses, whether that means taking on tasks we are skilled at or engaging in mental short-cuts such as stereotypes (e.g., Lambert et al., 2003). For instance, do you ever find yourself struggling to parallel park with a passenger in the car more so than you do when you're driving alone?

> Do you ever find yourself struggling to parallel park with a passenger in the car **more so than you do when you're driving alone?**

## SOCIAL LOAFING

Around the same time that Triplett (1898) was conducting his work with cyclists, Ringelmann's research on the influence of groups revealed that the presence of others actually *decreased* performance in certain group tasks where individual contributions were not identified (Ringelmann, 1913; see Chapter 1). This occurrence, known as **social loafing**, is the tendency among individuals performing a group task to exert less effort than if they were performing the task alone. For example, Latane, Williams, and Harkins (1979) conducted a study in which they asked individuals to clap and shout as part of a group or by themselves. They found that when performing alone, participants clapped and shouted much louder than when they were a member of a group.

The reasoning for this phenomenon is that people feel *less* pressure to perform to the best of their abilities when they know others will pick up the slack. People working in a group feel less responsible to give it their all because the burden is not solely theirs. As a result, they are less concerned about the opinions of others and do not experience social facilitation or inhibition. Social loafing also occurs because group members feel their contribution is not that important (as in the clapping and shouting example above) (Latane et al., 1979). Further, when groups lack cohesiveness (e.g., when assigned instead of self-chosen), our tendency to engage in social loafing may be increased (Karau & Williams, 1997).

This phenomenon is experienced by adults and children alike and may be evidenced in children as young as five (Smith, Kerr, Markus, & Stasson, 2001). In addition, recent research suggests that even people in online communities and online

**A study led by Ingham and colleagues (1974) showed that when blindfolded students were led to believe that others were pulling behind them in a game of tug of war,** they exerted less effort than when they knew they were pulling alone.

**SOCIAL LOAFING** occurs when individuals make less of an effort when attempting to achieve a particular goal as a group than they would if they were attempting to achieve the goal on their own

groups engage in social loafing when they don't believe their individual knowledge contributions or inputs are being monitored (Shiue, Chiu, & Chang, 2010). That said, it should be noted that there are differences that affect the level of social loafing among individuals—for instance, the need for cognition. If you need to understand and acquire the skills or knowledge stemming from a group project, you are less inclined to loaf because the contributions you make are more valuable to you and your future goals (Smith et al., 2001).

Interestingly, the prevalence of social loafing is influenced by cultural factors. While we all may have a tendency to "loaf off" at various times, members of collectivistic cultures are *less* likely to engage in this behaviour than are members of individualist cultures. Within individualistic cultures, prevalence of social loafing is further influenced by gender. In general, men tend to be more individualistic than women, causing men to be more prone to social loafing (Karau & Williams, 1993). That said, people in collectivistic cultures, such as those found in East Asia, are generally more interconnected, so they tend to understand the necessity of each person contributing to the group effort. These cultures are more aware of the impact of social loafing on the group. Because of this awareness, social loafing is less prevalent in such cultures (e.g., Karau & Williams, 1993; Wagner, 1995). Take a moment to think about how social loafing might manifest in a multicultural society such as ours in Canada. Reflect on group work you have had to do either at school or a place of employment that involved individuals of different cultural backgrounds. Did you notice a difference in people's tendency to engage in social loafing? If not, do you think "Canadian" individualistic norms may have influenced this behaviour?

In your academic career, you have probably been involved in numerous group assignments. Depending on your experiences and your own work habits, you may already have formed an opinion on the positives or negatives of group work. Do you prefer to work alone or with a group? If you do not like working in groups, what are some of your reasons? You are probably well aware of the inclination of some students to perform less work within a group, leaving the bulk of the productivity to fall upon the more motivated students. Usually, if individual performance is not assessed, or if all students are given the same grade, social loafing may occur (e.g., Aggarwal & O'Brien, 2009; Comer, 1995; North, Linley, & Hargreaves, 2000).

### What Reduces Social Loafing?

It may seem unavoidable that certain people will exert less commitment to a group project; however, social loafing is *less* likely to occur when one of three things happens. The first is when group members believe that their *individual work will be acknowledged by the assessor.* When a member knows that his or her personal contributions will be validated, he or she tends to exert more effort because there is more at stake for him or her personally. Williams, Nida, Baca, and Latane (1989) demonstrated this idea through their research. Specifically, they found that relay swimmers achieved faster results when their individual times were recognized than when their times were lumped in with the group's.

Another factor that reduces social loafing is an *increase in each group member's level of commitment* (Karau & Williams, 1993). This is more likely to happen when it is established that each person's contributions are necessary for a successful outcome. The belief that one's personal work will have a positive bearing on the entire group's performance causes an individual to work harder and more steadily toward the common goal. Related to this is the level of group cohesion. For example, Karau and Williams (1997) found that groups of strangers tended to be associated with more social loafing, whereas groups of friends experienced greater social compensation. Therefore, *increasing group cohesiveness* will likely increase commitment to the group and subsequent effort towards a desirable outcome, which is a method that coaches use to attempt to improve performance (e.g., Høigaard, Säfvenbom, & Tønnessen, 2006).

A third factor in the reduction of social loafing is *task importance*. When there is more at stake for team members personally, they are more motivated to put forth greater effort in their personal contributions. For example, people in an office collaborating on a group project that has the potential to yield them promotions will view the task as having greater importance. With the possible outcome of a pay raise, individuals are more motivated to work harder, despite other members' less fervent efforts. In one study, researchers found that students who were assigned to evaluate a plan that would require all final exams to be comprehensive

## ACTION LEARNING

### Practise Reducing Social Loafing

How many times have you found yourself frustrated because you felt that you were taking on more than your fair share of a group project? How many times have you found yourself on the other side of the line, kicking back and letting others take on more responsibility for the work? What influenced your choices in these cases?

Next time you are assigned to work on a group project with other students, apply this action learning project. Consider the potential impact social loafing may have on your group. Explain to your classmates what social loafing is. Chances are they already know people slack off in groups, but what they don't know is that it's something social psychologists study. Let the other students know that there are some solutions to social loafing—making each group member's contributions identifiable, increasing the level of individual commitment, and increasing the importance of the task.

Brainstorm with your group members how you can apply these three solutions to social loafing to your project in order to ensure that your work as a group is productive and meaningful. Once the project is complete, write up a summary of the techniques you used and evaluate their effectiveness. Share your results with the rest of your classmates.

What you will learn from this action project:

1. Use social psychological principles to increase the productivity and success of a working group.
2. Educate others about resolving the problems associated with group work to enhance each individual's experience.
3. Practise strategies to help you become an effective leader in future group projects.

**Eliminating the Loafing.** How will you eliminate social loafing **on your next group project?**

were more inclined to loaf when this proposal did not affect their own courses but rather those of future students or students at other institutions (Brickner, Harkins, & Ostrom, 1986). Increasing the personal importance of the task to the students caused the students to be more motivated to put forth effort and not loaf.

## DEINDIVIDUATION

Can a group lead us to lose our senses of self and engage in behaviours that we normally wouldn't perform if we were by ourselves? This occurrence, known as **deindividuation**, happens when a person lets go of self-consciousness and control and does what the group is doing—usually with negative goals or outcomes. Deindividuation occurs when individuals feel anonymous within a group and because of that anonymity, also feel empowered to act upon a situation.

Mobs, especially sports mobs, are an excellent example of deindividuation. We have seen multiple examples of this in relation to Canadian NHL hockey, most recently when Vancouver Canucks fans rioted following their team's loss against the Boston Bruins in the final game of the 2011 Stanley Cup playoffs. Unfortunately, this behaviour is nothing new. Riots by fans (and players) occurred following team losses (and wins!) in the NHL playoffs in 1986 (in Montreal), 1993 (in Montreal), 1994 (in Vancouver), 2006 (in Edmonton), and 2008 (in Montreal) ("Hockey Riots," 2011). In all of these cases, numerous people were arrested, significant damages were incurred by businesses and the cities involved (e.g., $2.5 million in 1993 in Montreal), and many innocent bystanders and participants were injured. What would cause people to act like this?

Zimbardo (1969) identified three antecedent conditions associated with deindividuation: *arousal*, *anonymity*, and *reduced feelings of responsibility*. Following the 2011 loss by the Canucks, fans were frustrated and angry, both of which are emotions associated with physiological arousal. In addition, the large number of fans in the crowd and on the streets gave individuals the feeling of anonymity. Because people were experiencing arousal, and a sense of anonymity, they felt less individual responsibility for their actions. This explains why groups of people in certain cults or in mobs experience a loss of self-restraint and subsequently commit acts that they normally would not if they were alone.

The theory of deindividuation has been tested in several experiments. For example, Zimbardo (1970) set up a paradigm in which two groups of women engaged in a task that required them to decide how much electric shock would be administered to the "participants" of a study. (Note: no actual shocks were administered.) One group of women wore hoods that obscured all of their faces except their eyes, while the other group of women remained uncovered. The researchers found that, when given a choice, the hooded students would have administered twice as much electric shock to the subjects as the women who were not hidden behind the hoods (Zimbardo, 1970). Similarly, a study conducted by Diener, Fraser, and Kelem (1976) found that children who wore costumes (facilitating anonymity) and were a part of a group chose to steal candy and money more often than those who were identified by name or those who were presented with the choice to steal by themselves. The highest instance of stealing candy and money was in the groups of children in costumes who were not asked to identify themselves. Clearly, what provoked the transgression in the study was the combination of both anonymity and group behaviour.

Children in costumes that created a sense of anonymity chose to steal candy more often when they were in a group **than when they were alone or had been identified by name.**

**DEINDIVIDUATION** the tendency for an individual within a group to let go of self-awareness and restraint and do what the group is doing

"The researchers found that, when given a choice, **the hooded students would have administered twice as much electric shock to the subjects as the women who were not hidden behind the hoods.**"

This understanding of human behaviour can explain why people in certain cult-type organizations become moved to commit acts of violence—the deindividuation propels them toward more active participation in the group experience. As we see in these two studies, the women and the children who experienced the most deindividuation were most likely to choose the more violent or less acceptable choice. For these members, if everyone around them was doing something, and if they couldn't be identified, it felt acceptable to go along with the group mentality. Police agencies across Canada and the United States have reported trends that link deindividuation with increased potential for bias (Hodgson, 2001).

In one of the most famous examples of group members experiencing deindividuation, the Heaven's Gate cult committed group suicide in March 1997. The leader of the cult, Marshall Applewhite, convinced the group that suicide was the only way to take their souls to the next spiritual level. Though their ages ranged from mid-20s to early 70s, all of the members of the cult participated in the suicide. Their identification with the group and the resulting behaviour illustrates classic deindividuation. Another common example of this is manifested in the way soldiers are processed into boot camp and training. The soldiers are stripped of everything that differentiates them from each other, including their hair. They are required to dress

**SOCIAL DECISION SCHEMES** rules that guide how the initial distribution of views of each group member influences the final group decision

**RISKY SHIFT** the tendency for people in groups to take greater risks than if the actions were to be taken by individual members alone

in uniforms and behave according to standards set by the Canadian Forces. This causes a loss of self, and ultimately a stronger identification with the group orchestrating that loss.

As we learned in Chapter 4, the way a person identifies himself or herself is linked to his or her behaviour. Think back to our discussion of self-awareness—how might that connect to the concept of deindividuation? As Mullen, Migdall, and Rozell (2003) discovered in their study on self-awareness, when individuals feel anonymous they experience a decreased self-awareness and decreased social identity. The researchers asked participants to fill out a survey on identity in four different scenarios: in front of a mirror, wearing a hood, after filling out a family tree, and in a controlled environment with no additional variables. The results demonstrated that participants who wore the hood felt less self-aware and less able to identify themselves socially. The hood created a loss of identity, and so deindividuation occurred. That said, recent research has proposed the SIDE model of deindividuation—*social identity deindividuation* (Postmes, Spears, & Lea, 1999). This model argues that deindividuation occurs not because there is a loss of identity, but because there is a shift from identification with oneself to identification with the group. Once the person has made this shift, this leads them to conform to the group's norms. Whether a person loses his self-awareness and conforms to the group or actually adopts the group's identity, deindividuation results in a person acting like other members of a group instead of the way he would alone.



Recent developments in social media and the use of the internet for communication, dating, business, and networking has led scholars to examine this method of communication in relation to deindividuation (Kabay, 2001). Postmes et al. (1999) argued that computer-mediated communication is particularly susceptible to social identity deindividuation and possible negative group influence, such as stereotyping and discrimination. In addition, researchers at the University of Guelph found that the sense of anonymity the internet provides can accentuate the influence of gender and racial stereotypes on our communication and behaviour (Christofides, Islam, & Desmarais, 2009). Many forms of social media rely on establishing a username, allowing individuals to be who they want to be. Furthermore, in online gaming communities, research has demonstrated that individuals create entire online personas (avatars) and may act more impulsively and conform to stereotypes about their avatars more often than if they were not under the veil of anonymity (e.g., Yee, Ducheneaut, Yao, & Nelson, 2011). As a result, people may be more open to engaging in cyber-bullying and other aggressive behaviours (Wade & Beran, 2011).

Membership in some groups is structured around conformity and deindividuation, **such as being a soldier in the Canadian Forces.**

# How Does a Group Make Decisions?

Think about a group to which you belong. Have any recent decisions been made that affected the entire group? Maybe at your restaurant job, management made the decision to pool tips to be divided among the staff instead of letting each person keep the tips he or she earned individually. Or maybe your class voted to change a due date for an assignment so that it was better suited to people's schedules. If a decision was made recently, did you agree with it? Do you think it was fairly made? The sections that follow present four factors that affect group decision making: *social decision schemes*, *group polarization*, *groupthink*, and different *leadership styles*.

## SOCIAL DECISION SCHEMES

When examining how groups make decisions, researchers have noticed that we are often able to predict a group decision on the basis of the group's pre-existing views and features of the group itself (Kerr, MacCoun, & Kramer, 1996). For example, a meta-analysis of jury research has revealed that the initial verdict favoured by the majority of people on a jury is likely to reflect the final verdict outcome 90 percent of the time (e.g., Devine, Clayton, Dunford, Seying, & Pryce, 2000; Sandys & Dillehay, 1995). In particular, these predictions may be based on the types of rules that we tend to utilize when making decisions in groups. These rules, called **social decision schemes,** guide how the initial distribution of views of each group member influences the final group decision (Davis, 1973). Four primary social decision schemes are employed in various situations. The *majority-wins rule* applies when a group opts for whatever position is initially supported by most group members. The *truth-wins rule* occurs when the correct solution or decision will ultimately be accepted by group members as they recognize its accuracy. The *first-shift rule* applies when groups tend to adopt a decision that is consistent with the first shift in opinion show by any member. And finally, *unanimity* requires that all persons agree on the outcome, which is often imposed by the criminal justice system (Devine et al., 2000).

In addition to these schemes, many group decisions also may be more "risky" than those made by individuals. **Risky shift** describes the tendency for people in groups to take greater risks than individual members would (Stoner, 1961). The belief is that the shared risk makes each person's individual risk seem less hazardous. This may be why, in part, groups appear to have a preference for risk and may succumb to groupthink (Whyte, 1998). Risky shift is somewhat related to social loafing, in that it involves less accountability on the part of an individual. Wallach, Kogan, and Bem (1962) found that in a group setting, people are more willing to take greater risks because responsibility is spread out among members, and the support of others lessens anxiety over a risky choice. Another reason for risky shift is that highly confident risk takers in the group tend to persuade less confident group members to take greater chances (Collins & Guetzkow, 1964). Further, group members' social standings are often determined by the extent to which they will take risks, causing people to take more chances in order to maintain a high status within the group (Brown, 1965). Bateson (1966) offered an additional suggestion that this shift occurs when members increasingly focus on a risky action until they become so used to the notion that the perceived risk lessens.

## GROUP POLARIZATION

While initially it seemed that people tended to make riskier decisions in group contexts, other research has discovered that the group setting can actually lead to more conservative decisions. This occurrence can be a result of a phenomenon known as *group polarization*. **Group polarization** is the tendency for an attitude or a belief to become magnified for individual group members after discussing an issue with the group as a whole (Moscovici & Zavalloni, 1969; for a review, see Isenberg, 1986). The dominant attitude among group members becomes stronger when people discuss their feelings—whether favourable or oppositional—about a certain topic (e.g., Brauer, Judd, & Jacquelin, 2001; Sunstein, 2002). Let's say you had a problem with a recent rash of burglaries in your neighbourhood, and you talked to neighbours who shared your thoughts and feelings about the events. As a group, you would become more inclined to feel threatened and want to take measures to protect yourselves. Because of the group's supporting beliefs, all members might experience a heightened conviction in their opinion. A common tendency is for group members to feed on the emotions of others and become even more passionate—in this case incensed—about an issue.

There are essentially two causes of group polarization. The first is *social comparison*, which occurs when individuals are conscious of how others perceive them, and adjust accordingly in order to retain a favourable position within a group (Isenberg, 1986). In this instance, individuals are constantly evaluating the norms of the group as they perceive them, and then repositioning themselves to suit that group dynamic. The other cause is *persuasion,* or persuasive arguments, as we discussed in Chapter 7. In both cases, the result of the influence is group polarization.

**GROUP POLARIZATION** the tendency for an attitude or belief to become magnified within a group after members discuss an issue among themselves

Given that social comparison and persuasion play a role in this phenomenon, it should not surprise you to learn that group polarization frequently occurs in juries during deliberation. In one study, jurors watched a re-enactment of a murder trial, and the results of the deliberation demonstrated group polarization. Before meeting to deliberate, most jurors leaned toward a guilty verdict, but after deliberation, they felt that not only should the verdict be guilty, but that the punishment should be more extreme than they had indicated prior to discussion with other jurors (e.g., Hastie, Penrod, & Pennington, 2002). One exception to group polarization occurs in juries when the initial verdict is not guilty and also when the evidence is not incriminating (e.g., Devine et al., 2000; MacCoun & Kerr, 1988). This usually results in significantly more lenient sentences after deliberation. If even a minority of the jury leans toward acquittal, if there is a not-guilty verdict or less incriminating evidence, the jurors will move toward a more lenient sentence (instead of always tending toward harsher sentences even if there is a dissenting voice of leniency in the group).

You also can get a glimpse at group polarization any day by surfing the internet. The web is an abundant source of group forums, message boards, and chat and game rooms that allow millions of users to share their thoughts and feelings, participate in hobbies, and empathize or commiserate with one other. For example, websites devoted to self-help groups, such as Alcoholics Anonymous or those for military wives, offer virtual meeting places for people with similar interests and concerns to encourage one another and give and receive support in their struggles. Sunstein (2001) discusses the phenomenon of people choosing to interact with only those people who share their prejudices and ideas. This choice to filter out opposing viewpoints can certainly be harmful to open dialogue and exposure to new ideas. One study found that extremist websites feed off of connectivity to other extremist sites, and often the links between these sites escalate the hate and prejudice already present on a site (Gertsenfeld, Grant, & Chang, 2003).

Thankfully, most websites aren't used to espouse racism or spread hateful messages, as we know. The social networking site Facebook is teeming with groups and fan pages, which users can "like" in an effort to back any given cause, and many virtual groups provide millions of people the opportunity to find solace or comfort in the company of people who believe what they believe. Think about the sites you visit on the internet. Do any of these offer group membership, whether formally or informally? What are some of the groups you belong to within those social networks? What are the shared beliefs? Do you see an inclination within yourself to feel more passionately about your views after communicating with the people in the groups to which you belong?

Taking $1,000 with you to Las Vegas and gambling with it.
Contributing $1,000 to a pool of cash to gamble with along with your friends on a group trip to Las Vegas.

<<< **When the Group Takes a Gamble: Which Seems Riskier?** It's easier for an individual to make a riskier move in a group **because the responsibility of a poor result is then diffused.**

**GROUPTHINK** a manner of thinking that happens when the desire for harmony in a decision-making group overrides a realistic evaluation of other solutions

**GROUP NORMS** rules or expectations regarding desirable behaviours that group members strive to follow

## GROUPTHINK

**Groupthink** is a manner of thinking that happens when group members, faced with an important decision, become so focused on the decision being passed smoothly that they overlook other, possibly more fruitful, options (Janis, 1982). The mentality of the group can actually produce negative results because their desire for harmony supersedes a practical evaluation of other solutions. Being caught up in the group's goals can skew decision making and produce unanticipated consequences, as we learned from the chapter opener regarding the *Challenger* space shuttle disaster.

Groupthink usually occurs when two factors are present: a *strong unity among group members*, and *emergent group norms*. **Group norms** are rules or expectations regarding desirable behaviours that group members strive to follow. Group norms determine the behaviour of members in an attempt to maintain harmony within the group. Individuals not wanting to cause problems or be judged by the group are swayed by the motivation to preserve and act accordingly with group norms.

Janis (1982) coined the term *groupthink* after examining the Bay of Pigs invasion of 1961. The Bay of Pigs invasion is historically considered a complete and perfect failure. U.S. president John F. Kennedy and his advisors, who attended some of the country's best universities, approved an invasion of Cuba using Cuban exiles as invaders (so as not to appear involved themselves). One of the biggest mistakes of the United States was counting on situations that never came to fruition, nor seemed likely to happen in the first place, such as assuming exiles would use guerrilla warfare in nearby mountains, which in fact turned out to be too difficult. Fidel Castro's soldiers easily captured the exiles, and the mission was subsequently linked to the U.S. government. What seemed like a sound plan quickly turned disastrous and left Kennedy's advisors wondering what went wrong. Janis determined that Kennedy's cabinet was so overconfident and enthusiastic in their mission that they did not entertain any possible problems with the plan. The group stifled any dissenters in order to preserve the self-assurance in which the newly elected administration revelled.



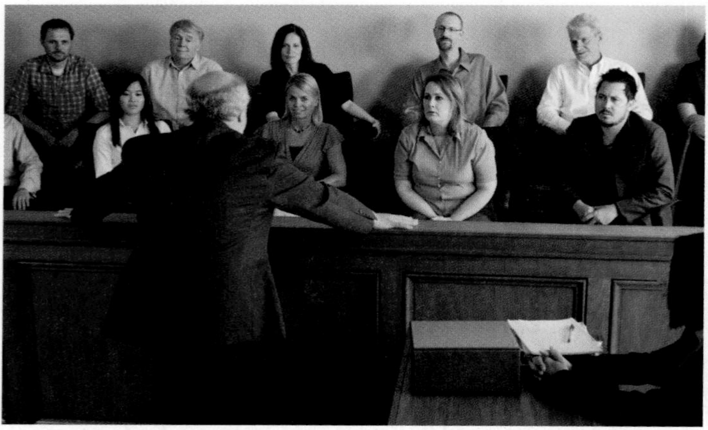

**If you were a juror in a criminal trial and had to determine the verdict of a trial with 11 other people,** what processes do you think would influence your group decision?

**Engineers opposed the launch of the *Challenger* in 1985 because of potential dangers caused by freezing temperatures.** Group pressures to launch, however, took precedence over the engineers' warnings and resulted in the destruction of the shuttle and the lives of all seven on board.

While this decision-making disaster initiated an investigation of group decision-making processes, other scholars have attempted to determine what features of groups can lead to biased outcomes. Researchers at the University of Western Ontario found that the orientation of groups (i.e., whether they are certainty oriented or uncertainty oriented) influences decision outcomes, which also are dependent on whether the leadership style is open or closed (Hodson & Sorrentino, 1997). In particular, certainty-oriented groups under conditions of open leadership made the least biased decisions when determining a legal case outcome, and tended to discuss more facts and engage in debate for longer durations than other group types. Identification with the group also affects individuals' susceptibility to groupthink. For example, Packer (2009) examined group relations with regard to problems on a university campus. He found that participants who only weakly identified with their group (i.e., university students) would only express their concerns about a collective problem (e.g., binge drinking or campus security) if they felt that other people in the group would agree with them. Conversely, those who strongly identified with the group expressed their concerns independent of whether they felt the rest of the group would agree or disagree. Packer (2009) concluded that group members who are more vigilant are more likely to prevent group harm, whereas group members who hold back maintain a "spiral of silence," with potentially disastrous consequences. In an analysis of classic decision-making blunders, Whyte (1998) also found that lack of vigilance and a preference for risk is associated with a sense of collective group efficacy, which leads to higher group cohesion and greater biased outcomes.

That said, Janis (1982) also believed that groupthink is preventable and can be avoided by following a few simple practices: being *open to criticism*; *working with diverse people*, including members outside of the group; and *training members in group decision making*. One study found that groups whose norms include being open to constructive criticism tend to make better decisions (e.g., Postmes, Spears, & Cihangir, 2001). Willingness to listen to outside opinions helps prevent the groupthink mentality. For example, open communication and seeking advice from members not directly involved in the group decision can be effective at generating dissent and avoiding bias (Maharaj, 2008). Another method of preventing groupthink is to ensure a diverse group of people is involved in decision making. A study that included racially diverse people with various backgrounds discovered that the groups with more diversity resulted in more varied opinions and essentially less groupthink (Antonio et al., 2004). Another key to eradicating groupthink is to educate the group making the decisions about the dangers of bias and of groupthink itself (Stewart & Stasser, 1995). Finally, researchers have found that information sharing and discussion of opposing views in decision-making sessions can lead to better decisions (e.g., Larson, Foster-Fishman, & Keys, 1994; Packer, 2009).

## LEADERSHIP STYLES

Another factor that affects the process of group decision making is the type of leader the group has. While good leaders possess similar traits, they are separated into two categories: **transformational** and **transactional**. Transactional leaders are those who reward good behaviour but ultimately only take action when something goes wrong. Transformational leaders work on building relationships and group goals throughout their time in leadership. Both types are effective, but transformational leaders tend to produce better performance among the group because they nurture trust among members and build identification with, and excitement for, lofty group goals. Transformational leaders welcome new approaches for problem solving and create internal motivation among group members (Charbonneau, Barling, & Kelloway, 2001).

Charismatic, transformational leaders often believe that when people are inspired by a passionate and visionary leader, they will follow more easily due to genuine admiration. Furthermore, they believe that the best way to motivate followers is to envelop them in enthusiasm and energy for the tasks at hand. Transformational leaders strive to transform not only the group as a whole but also the members within the network, believing that members will transform themselves through their contributions to the group. These leaders view their followers as products of the transformation; however, when the group and its members are happy with the way things are and do not want to be transformed, transformational leaders are likely to become frustrated. Some names of transformational leaders you might recognize are Jack Layton (NDP leader), Steve Jobs (CEO of Apple, Inc.), and Pierre Trudeau (prime minister of Canada). Each of these people were considered transformational leaders during their lives. Another lesser-known example is Chief of the Defence Staff General Rick Hillier, who led the Canadian Forces by having a clear vision of the future of the military, being proactive rather than reactive, and inspiring others to actively engage in becoming transformational leaders themselves (Mitchell, 2010). Further, research has suggested that transformational leadership in military settings can be applied at many different rank levels, positively influence performance outcomes, and promote development of better leaders in subordinate positions (Bradley & Charbonneau, 2004).

One of the disadvantages of transformational leadership is that followers can mistake their leader's passion and confidence for what is actually taking place. Just because a leader is excited and determined to succeed does not necessarily mean that the group will prevail. While passionate leaders have indeed accomplished great things, a successful outcome is not always the case. For example, a charismatic leader may lead a protest march concerning some political or human rights issue, but he or she may be ultimately disregarded by those in positions of power (i.e., government). Transformational leaders also can become burdens to their followers by way of their relentless energy for accomplishing a goal. While a leader's energy is a necessary ingredient in getting people motivated, it can often backfire and cause people to give up—especially if they do not see progress being made. A final drawback to the style of transformational leaders is their inclination to not see the details but rather focus on the end product. If no one takes care of the details for them, these leaders often end up failing.

**TRANSFORMATIONAL LEADER** a leader who believes in inspiring his followers with energy and devotion, thereby transforming the group and its members

**TRANSACTIONAL LEADER** a leader who believes in a ladder of authority and considers people on lower rungs to be subordinates and therefore required to follow the instructions set forth by their manager; this type of leader rewards good work and works efficiently to solve problems

Transactional leaders, while also successful, tend to see less fruitful results than transformational leaders. Although there has been much debate about its limitations, transactional leadership continues to be a popular approach with many directors. These leaders believe in a clear ladder of authority and consider people on lower rungs to be subordinates and therefore required to follow the instructions set forth by their manager. In fact, transactional leadership has been described as a management approach to leading a company or group of people (Bradley & Charbonneau, 2004). Transactional leaders reward good work and work efficiently to solve problems (Burns, 1978). They assume that individuals work harder when they are aware of potential rewards for producing results, as well as penalties for not working effectively. While the consequences of poor work are not always explicit, transactional leaders ensure that those under their direction understand that there will be punishments for not keeping pace.

Have you ever been a leader in a group? Perhaps you were a summer camp counsellor or the head of a youth group in your hometown. Or maybe you plan to become a leader in your career, such as a teacher or principal or police sergeant. Based on the descriptions of the two types of leadership styles, what kind of leader do you want to be, or what kind of leader have you been in the past?

Certain traits have been associated with great leaders, and both men and women can be effective leaders. However, many people do

Do you consider Prime Minister Stephen Harper **a transformational or transactional leader?**

**CONFLICT** the perceived incompatibility of actions, goals, or ideas
**REALISTIC GROUP CONFLICT** the theory that conflict stems from competition for limited resources such as money, land, power or other resources

not consider women to be as effective leaders as men, an assessment that often places an undue burden on women, who can and do make skilled, successful leaders. For example, one study found that women in leadership roles received more negative criticism when they made specific comments and offered arguments on a given topic than men in the same scenario who said the same things as the women (Butler & Geis, 1990). What's more, people tend to negatively judge and devalue the authority of female leaders who express anger, whereas men are viewed as more powerful and better leaders when they become angry (Brescoll & Uhlmann, 2008). People also tend to look down upon women who take on more traditionally "male" leadership styles, such as autocratic or directive styles, or when they occupy historically male-dominated positions (Eagly, Makhijani, & Klonsky, 1992). Further, women may experience stereotype threat when in leadership roles, leading to a decrease in their effectiveness as a leader (Davies, Spencer, & Steele, 2005). That said, a meta-analysis of leadership styles across men and women revealed that women tend to take a more transformational approach to leadership relative to the transactional "management" methods employed by many men (Eagly, Johannesen-Schmidt, & van Engen, 2003). The role of women in politics also is changing in North America, as there is a greater acknowledgement that women can be effective leaders—for example, Supreme Court of Canada Chief Justice Beverley McLachlin and U.S. Secretary of State Hillary Clinton. In fact, Canadians tend to promote female political leadership more than our American counterparts. For example, in 2011, a record-setting 76 women were elected as members of Parliament to serve in the Canadian House of Commons (total of 308 seats; approximately 25 percent), in comparison to 72 women who serve as members of the U.S. Congress (total of 435 seats; approximately 16.5 percent) ("Record Number," 2011).

Whether male or female, strong leaders often possess the same traits. They are consistently intelligent, dominant, and extroverted, and they can initiate, plan, and delegate responsibilities. They also tend to be decisive, use shrewd judgment, and be strong communicators (Zaccaro, 2007). Think of one of your favourite teachers. He or she likely possesses most of these traits. Men and women both have the ability to lead, and each can do so transactionally or transformationally.

**Regardless of their professional performances, female** politicians and judges, such as Supreme Court of Canada Chief Justice Beverley McLachlin, endure a certain type of scrutiny **that their male counterparts do not.**



## What Are the Causes of Group Conflict?

Leadership isn't the only element that contributes to the success or failure of a group. We experience conflicts every day, whether within ourselves, or with other people, times, or events. Not a day goes by in which we are not faced with some sort of problem that requires a solution. If you were to reflect upon this day, in particular, you could probably come up with a handful of conflicts you have already resolved or plan to resolve. **Conflict** can be defined as the perceived incompatibility of actions, goals or ideas. Conflicts are usually most intense when they involve groups of people. In this section, we will look at the usual causes of conflicts, as well as common attempts to solve them.

With one look at a news channel, you are bombarded with stories of conflicts between groups. Anti-abortion protestors regularly quarrel with pro-choice abortion clinic employees and patients; Liberals frequently clash with Conservatives; celebrities who want more privacy consistently fight with paparazzi; and oppressed groups in war-torn countries riot against dictators and military control. Conflict is an inevitable part of life. There are numerous reasons why people enter into conflicts. The causes are similar on all scales—from the smallest dispute, such as a quarrel with a spouse or loved one, to a racial clash among citizens of the same country, to an international conflict among warring nations. No matter how big or small the conflicts, the reasons we enter into them are very similar. The most prevalent factors that lead to conflict are *realistic group competition*, *attribution bias*, *communication errors*, and *biased perceptions*.

### REALISTIC GROUP CONFLICT

When groups of people compete for resources, they enter into **realistic group conflict** (e.g., Coser, 1956; Sherif, 1966). Think back to our discussion in Chapter 1 of the Robbers Cave Experiment conducted by Sherif (1961), involving two groups of boys at summer camp (the Eagles versus the Rattlers). These two groups functioned independently of each other until, after a time, they were brought together. The two groups had already formed bonds, and once they were confronted with each other, their identification as separate groups in competition with one another increased. This type of conflict stems from the threat of not having access to limited resources, such as money, land, or power. Even if the people in these groups come from the same backgrounds and lead similar lives, much like the boys at the camp, a desperate need for resources can quickly catapult them into competition and conflict. For example, Southern Nigeria is plagued by fighting over its oil resources. Instead of being used to eliminate poverty and stave off pollution, the resources are a cause of conflict as different groups attempt to acquire more oil and exert power over one another (Harsch, 2007). Another instance is that of Sierra Leone's "blood diamonds," the small diamonds that are smuggled and sold to finance violent battles over control of the diamond fields (Harsch, 2007).

### ATTRIBUTIONAL BIASES

When we judge others' personalities based on incomplete evidence, such as an isolated act or behaviour, the fundamental attribution error is likely to occur (first discussed in Chapter 5). If you have ever witnessed a stranger yelling at her children in a supermarket, you probably assumed that the woman was a bad mother who had no patience for her children.

Your judgment was based on what you saw in an isolated timeframe. What you probably did not take into account was that the woman may have been having a bad day and that her children may have been behaving in a way she had already warned them about several times. She could have been a very loving mother who doted on her children. Under similar circumstances as the mother at the grocery store, we, or people we know well, might have acted in the same way. When we form these opinions without knowing the relevant context, we are demonstrating attributional bias. So how can attribution bias contribute to creating conflict? When we erroneously judge the cause of people's behaviour, we may act based on our assumptions. For example, imagine you approached the mother at the grocery store and told her she was being abusive to her children and that you were going to phone Child Protective Services. What do you think her reaction would have been? It is likely that an argument of some sort would have ensued.

Another manifestation of this type of bias is termed **hostile attribution bias** (Dodge, Price, Bachorowski, & Newman, 1990). This type of bias occurs when people assume that the intentions of another person are hostile and intended to inflict harm or stress on their own lives. Baron and Richardson (1994) determined that hostile attribution bias causes people to assume an antagonistic intent on the part of others, even when there is none. This generally shows up when the wronged party feels disrespected or threatened in some manner and may, as a result, react to the behaviour in an aggressive way (Halligan, Cooper, Healy, & Murray, 2008). Researchers at Queen's University have developed a questionnaire to assess the extent to which people engage in these hostile interpretations (Simourd & Mamuza, 2000). Recent research suggests that the hostile attribution bias can occur in both direct and cyber-aggression situations (Pornari & Wood, 2010). In addition, certain personality features, such as psychopathy and depressive attributional styles, are related to increased hostile attributions and generating conflict among others (Vitale, Newman, Serin, & Bolt, 2005).

In everyday life, this bias could occur anywhere, such as at a nightclub. If you walked up to the bar to order a drink and there was a group of people looking in your direction and laughing, you might assume they were laughing at you. You would also probably feel that they were being hostile toward you and that they were mean people. This, in turn, would cause you to feel hostility toward them for laughing (and maybe even become violent or antagonistic with the group). What you would not have realized is that they were laughing at a funny commercial on the TV behind you.

Blaming other people when we do not achieve our own goals is also a feature of attribution bias. As humans, when we feel that our goals have been obstructed, we generally try to pinpoint the reasons for the negative outcome. Assuming that another party has interfered with our goals can lead to an intense conflict, even if other people actually had no involvement in the situation. Being biased in attributing blame for an unrealized goal plays an important role in conflict and can often cause disputes that did not need to take place.

In conflict over the scarce mineral resource of diamonds, **factions in Sierra Leone often come to bloody battles for control of the lucrative diamond fields.**

**HOSTILE ATTRIBUTION BIAS** bias that occurs when people assume that the intentions of another person are hostile

**BIASED PERCEPTION** the belief that we are justified in our own thoughts and actions but that others are biased in their beliefs and behaviours

In order to avoid these biases and the reactions they cause within us, it is wise to have a general awareness of these tendencies. By noticing our incomplete understanding of other people's intentions, we can begin to release the negative bias when a situation arises and avoid making incorrect attributions.

## COMMUNICATION ERRORS

Another reason for conflict stems from communication errors. The way we communicate with each other often leads to conflict, since all of us have different ways of expressing ourselves. We each bring to the table different behaviours, perspectives, and backgrounds that are not always compatible with those of the people with whom we interact. If you grew up in a family in which members communicated by yelling, you might enter into a conflict later on with someone who grew up in a family where yelling did not occur. If you attended schools where teachers constantly praised your efforts—whether or not you produced excellent results—you might enter into conflict with a college professor who criticizes your work, even though you have put forth great effort.

Have you ever known a person who was very blunt in the way he criticized you? Instead of phrasing his criticism in a helpful or polite way, it seemed as if he came right out and judged you in a manner that hurt your feelings or made you angry. Studies have revealed that this type of disapproval can result in vengeful feelings on the part of the wronged person and can lead to a series of conflicts that do not necessarily involve people with opposing views (e.g., Baron, 1990; Cropanzano, 1993).

## BIASED PERCEPTION

A third cause of conflict stems from a **biased perception** of the intentions of others. This occurs when we think we are justified in our own thoughts and actions but believe that others are biased in *their* beliefs and behaviours. Perceiving other people in this manner often amplifies differences in opinions and unduly stresses conflicts of interest among groups or individuals. Studies have shown that a biased perception occurs most often for groups or individuals in powerful or controlling positions, where they tend to believe that their stance is more rational or neutral than it actually is (Keltner & Robinson, 1997). A biased perception among powerful groups often leads to an inaccurate opinion of other groups with opposing viewpoints.

One method researchers use to examine the effects of social conflict is called the "Prisoner's Dilemma" (Rapoport, 1960). Let's say Alex and Jack are caught vandalizing a dorm room as part of a prank against other students. Campus security knows Alex and Jack committed the prank together, but the security guard only has adequate evidence for a lesser punishment. The guard decides to offer an incentive to each one as he

**BARGAINING** a means of resolving conflict that involves each side of the dispute making offers, counteroffers, and concessions

interrogates them separately. He tells each student that if one of them confesses and the other doesn't, the confessor will get immunity, while the student who does not confess will get kicked out of his dormitory—a punishment to the fullest extent. If both Alex and Jack confess, they will each be punished by having to clean the men's bathrooms for a semester. But if neither confesses, each will receive only a mark on his record—a mere slap on the wrist. If you were Alex and had no way of talking to Jack, what would you do? The choice you make will almost surely cause a conflict based on how you and Jack perceive each other's actions.

Another manifestation of biased perception is in *hostile media phenomenon*. This occurs when a person views supposedly unbiased media coverage as biased against whatever perspective they hold. In a study on hostile media phenomenon, researchers discovered that participants assumed the media held a bias against whatever position they held, no matter which side of the argument they were on (Vallone, Ross, & Lepper, 1985). More recently, researchers at Carleton University found that unbiased media coverage concerning particular ethnic groups and conflicts evoked strong group identity and ingroup biases and the perception by members of these ethnicities that the media was not objective. (Matheson & Dursun, 2001). This can influence attitudes concerning voting, allegiance to certain groups, racial identity, and aesthetic "ideals" portrayed by the media (e.g., Fujioka, Ryan, Agle, Legaspi, & Toohey, 2009; Wei, Chia, & Lo, 2011). Here we see bias perception occurring between individuals and the media.

| | Criminal 1: Confess | Criminal 1: Doesn't confess |
|---|---|---|
| **Criminal 2: Confess** | A: 3 years, B: 3 years | A: 0 year, B: 15 years |
| **Criminal 2: Doesn't confess** | A: 15 years, B: 0 year | A: 1 year, B: 1 year |

Just like Alex and Jack (above), our biased perceptions of others' behaviour, **and how we believe they are likely to act,** can influence our decisions.

# How Are Conflicts Among Groups Resolved?

It has been said that every problem has a solution—or that there *are* no problems, only solutions. Resolving conflict is such a necessary action that entire law firms are dedicated to solving disagreements between groups. People who possess strong negotiating skills can make healthy livings from the conflicts of others. Negotiation occurs everywhere, every day, in businesses and non-profit organizations, as well as in government, during legal proceedings, and among nations. It also happens in personal situations such as marriage, divorce, and parenting. The two most common forms of resolving group conflict are bargaining and a process known as GRIT. These techniques can be used in personal relationships and also in international relations.

## BARGAINING

When you first got your driver's licence, you probably tried to convince your hesitant parents to let you borrow the car on a Friday night. Maybe they did not want you to take it out and they told you their reasons for their reluctance. You probably countered with your own reasons as to why it would be a good idea. Ultimately, if they allowed you to borrow the car for the night, you probably had to make some concessions, such as agreeing to be home by a certain hour or allowing only one other person to ride with you. In order to persuade your parents to come to a decision that would make everyone happy, you went through the process of bargaining.

**Bargaining**, also known as *negotiation*, is the most common means for resolving a conflict. It occurs when two disputing parties come together, either in person or through representatives, to discuss ideas for resolving their disagreements. Bargaining typically involves each party making offers, counteroffers, and concessions in order to reach a resolution. People involved in bargaining try to establish trust with the opposition and find similarities between the two groups. They also strive to understand the conflicting position and share ideas that will convince the other side to agree upon a resolution (Mnookin, 2010). Conflict is resolved when the opposing sides are able to devise and agree upon a compromise. Sometimes, however, neither side will accept the terms of the proposed agreement, leading to the conflict growing while the parties remain deadlocked.

Bargaining occurs in a few ways. The people involved in the process use specific tactics in order to convince the opposing side to concede to their desires by diminishing their goals so that they will instead settle for something less desirable. Negotiators do this, first by offering an extreme proposal that favours the side that wants it. Then, they try to convince the opponent to make more concessions than they normally would. Third, they express that their party will cease negotiations if they do not get what they want and will instead find someone else who either will offer better results or agree to their terms as is (Thompson, 1998).

Negotiators view the bargaining process as having two potential outcomes: one in which there is a winner and a loser, and one in which everyone wins. The latter result is generally more preferable since it provides gains for the individuals on both sides of the conflict. In order to achieve this "win–win" outcome from the bargaining process, each side must exhibit not only the willingness to listen to what the other side wants, but also possess a genuine concern for what is important to the opponent. That said, the focus of

> **Negotiation occurs everywhere, every day, in businesses and non-profit organizations, as well as in government, during legal proceedings, and among nations.**

**GRIT** "graduated and reciprocated initiatives in tension reduction," a step-by-step formula for de-escalating a conflict that involves unilateral concessions and quick reciprocation by the opposition

the negotiation process may be influenced by culture. For example, one study comparing negotiation situations in Canada (individualistic) and China (collectivistic) found that Canadian negotiators were more focused on economic gains than were Chinese negotiators, whose goal was to maintain good bargaining relationships (Ma et al., 2002).

In fact, formalized systems of bargaining are a part of many institutions within Canada that have employee unions to represent the interests of all workers at a company. When unions act on behalf of their members, they engage in collective bargaining to negotiate terms of their employment (e.g., wages, benefits). However, collective bargaining by unions is not always effective and may lead to dissatisfaction of employees—both on group and individual levels. For example, the Canadian Union of Postal Workers (CUPW) attempted to bargain regarding issues of health and safety, and was continually denied recognition of these problems by Canada Post. As a result, Canada Post workers went on strike in June 2011, until they were ordered back to work through the enactment of new legislation by the federal minister of labour. This resulted in a form of imposed settlement, with neither side happy with the resolution of this conflict ("Canada Post Union," 2011). In fact, the CUPW has challenged the fairness of this legislation, and at the time of this writing has been granted a new hearing in court in January 2012 concerning the legislation and a biased choice of arbitrators in the dispute (Canadian Union of Postal Workers, 2011).

Think of a time when you bargained personally with someone else like a parent or your significant other, resulting in either a win–win or a win–lose deal. What concessions did either you or the other person make? What techniques did you each use to get what you wanted? What factors went into making the ultimate decision? If you won the conflict, how did you feel for yourself and for the other person? If you lost, what impression did you take away from the other person?

## GRIT

Defusing a conflict can seem almost impossible when both parties are set on having their own way. Even if a person or group on one side of the dispute wants to take actions that might end or change the conflict, doing so imposes great risks for the entire group. Individuals within a group who take measures to find a way to agree with the opposition might be viewed as traitors by their own groups. People on opposite sides of the disagreement are likely to be angry or mistrustful of each other and might reject any peacemaking attempts. They might misunderstand measures to resolve the conflict and view the negotiators as devious or deceitful. A way to try to avoid these pitfalls is to use what is known as "graduated and reciprocated initiatives in tension reduction," or **GRIT**, which is a step-by-step formula for de-escalating a conflict (Osgood, 1962). The term GRIT was later used to stand for "gradual reduction in tension" because that is precisely what it helps people do—work gradually through a problem with the use of compromise to reduce tension between opposing groups.

Using the GRIT method, one party involved in the dispute begins to weaken the conflict by making a small concession to the opposing side and then asking them to concede something as well. If the adversary accepts the concession and makes an equal compromise, then the first party makes a second concession, setting in place a chain of peacemaking measures (Conflict Research Consortium, 1998). These concessions include taking responsibility for previous errors, or simply expressing the willingness to begin compromising (Kriesberg, 2003). The goal of GRIT is to establish trust and cooperation between disputing groups, leading to quick reciprocation in the form of concessions made by either side. The idea behind it is that it increases one party's credibility and persuades the other party to act in a similar manner of concession-making.

When disputing parties use the GRIT method, conflicts become more manageable and thus more easily resolved. The GRIT formula results in a higher probability of both parties feeling satisfied with the ultimate agreement, as well as the transformation of their opinions of the opposing side. In a study of this method, researchers found that 90 percent of the conflicts that used GRIT were resolved with a mutually beneficial agreement, whereas only 65 percent of the disputes treated with a non-GRIT approach resulted in mutually beneficial outcomes (Lindskold & Han, 1988).

An understanding of the influence groups can have on our personal behaviour, as well as the reasons we enter into conflicts and the means for resolving them, can assist you in the way you relate to other people. Specifically, being aware of social facilitation, social loafing, and evaluation apprehension can help you understand why you behave in certain ways in front of others. Now that you're aware of deindividuation, group polarization, and groupthink, you'll be conscious of how a group dynamic changes your opinion or causes you to make choices you might not otherwise make. With an understanding of leadership styles, factors that cause conflict, and ways to defuse conflict, you can operate in groups of varied dynamics and help solve problems. And a greater awareness of human behaviour in groups can allow you to move beyond asking why people act the way they do and begin asking how you can take measures to improve group interactions and resolve conflicts effectively.

**What differences do you think we might have seen in resolving the mail strike** if Canada Post and the Canadian Union of Postal Workers had used the GRIT method?

# CHAPTER 09 Review

## Summary

### WHAT DEFINES A GROUP? p. 158

• A group is defined as two or more people who appear to be united to some extent. Most groups are formed intentionally and have members who know each other personally and work together in order to achieve a common goal. Some groups, however, are formed solely as a result of common characteristics, such as race or gender.

• Most groups possess common motives and goals, as well as established roles and clear statuses, meaning that there is a social rank or hierarchy of dominance among group members. Groups are also characterized by their accepted norms and values, as well as a clear system of rewards and penalties when those norms are adhered to or violated.

### HOW DOES A GROUP INFLUENCE INDIVIDUAL BEHAVIOUR? p. 159

• Social facilitation affects individual behaviour in that the presence of other people can drive a person to perform better than when alone. The effects of social loafing on individual behaviour can be seen when a group task causes some members to put forth less effort when they know others will carry the weight of the project.

• Deindividuation affects an individual when a person lets go of self-consciousness and control and does what the group is doing, usually with negative goals or outcomes. This occurs when a person is moved by the group experience and does things that, without the group for support, she would not normally do.

### HOW DOES A GROUP MAKE DECISIONS? p. 164

• Many groups are moved to make decisions after group polarization has occurred. Group polarization is the tendency for an attitude or belief to become magnified for group members after discussing an issue with the group. The dominant attitude among group members becomes stronger when people discuss their feelings—whether favourable or oppositional—about a certain topic.

• Groups often make decisions when influenced by groupthink. This manner of thinking happens when group members, faced with an important choice, become so focused on making a smooth, quick decision that they overlook other, possibly more fruitful, options. The mentality of the group can actually produce negative results because their desire for harmony supersedes a practical evaluation of other solutions. Being caught up in the group's goals can skew decision making and produce unanticipated consequences.

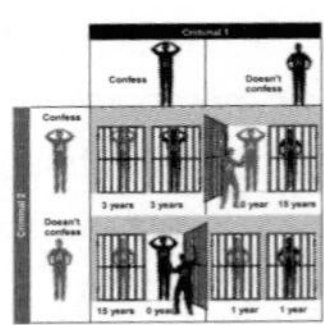

### WHAT ARE THE CAUSES OF GROUP CONFLICT? p. 168

• Conflict often exists within groups through incompatible goals or ideas. Groups may experience conflict due to competition for resources (realistic group conflict), attributional biases, communication errors, and biased perceptions of the intentions of others.

### HOW ARE CONFLICTS AMONG GROUPS RESOLVED? p. 170

• Groups typically use the process of bargaining in order to resolve conflict. This involves the two disputing parties coming together to discuss ideas for resolving their disagreements. Bargaining typically includes each party making offers, counteroffers, and concessions in order to reach a resolution.

• GRIT is a method that allows parties to work gradually through a problem with the use of compromises. One party begins to weaken the conflict by making a small concession to the opposing side and by asking them to concede something as well. If the adversary accepts the concession and makes an equal compromise, then the first party makes a second concession, setting in place a chain of peacemaking measures.

## Key Terms

**bargaining** a means of resolving conflict that involves each side of the dispute making offers, counteroffers, and concessions *170*

**biased perception** the belief that we are justified in our own thoughts and actions but that others are biased in their beliefs and behaviours *169*

**cohesion** the degree to which a group is connected *158*

**conflict** the perceived incompatibility of actions, goals, or ideas *168*

**deindividuation** the tendency for an individual within a group to let go of self-awareness and restraint and do what the group is doing *163*

**distraction conflict theory** the idea that a person performing a task in front of others experiences a conflict of attention between the audience and the task at hand, thus increasing the motivation to succeed when completing simple tasks *160*

**evaluation apprehension** the idea that one's performance will be hindered or heightened due to approval or disapproval from others *160*

**GRIT** "graduated and reciprocated initiatives in tension reduction," a step-by-step formula for de-escalating a conflict that involves unilateral concessions and quick reciprocation by the opposition *171*

**group** two or more people who are seen as a unit and interact with one another *158*

**group norms** rules or expectations regarding desirable behaviours that group members strive to follow *166*

**group polarization** the tendency for an attitude or belief to become magnified within a group after members discuss an issue among themselves *165*

**groupthink** a manner of thinking that happens when the desire for harmony in a decision-making group overrides a realistic evaluation of other solutions *166*

**hostile attribution bias** bias that occurs when people assume that the intentions of another person are hostile *169*

**realistic group conflict** the theory that conflict stems from competition for limited resources such as money, land, power or other resources *168*

**risky shift** the tendency for people in groups to take greater risks than if the actions were to be taken by individual members alone *164*

**social decision schemes** rules that guide how the initial distribution of views of each group member influences the final group decision 164

**social facilitation** the enhancement of a well-learned performance when other people are present 160

**social loafing** occurs when individuals make less of an effort when attempting to achieve a particular goal as a group than they would if they were attempting to achieve the goal on their own 161

**transactional leader** a leader who believes in a ladder of authority and considers people on lower rungs to be subordinates and therefore required to follow the instructions set forth by their manager; this type of leader rewards good work and works efficiently to solve problems 167

**transformational leader** a leader who believes in inspiring his followers with energy and devotion, thereby transforming the group and its members 167

# Test Your Understanding

## MULTIPLE CHOICE

**1.** Which of the following is not a trait of a typical group?
- **a.** similar beliefs
- **b.** anger over perceived injustices
- **c.** cohesion
- **d.** the presence of leaders and followers

**2.** Which psychological researcher is credited with being the first to study the theory of social facilitation?
- **a.** Baron
- **b.** Ringelmann
- **c.** Zajonc
- **d.** Triplett

**3.** Which of the following is not a reason that social loafing occurs?
- **a.** the feeling of less accountability
- **b.** less pressure to perform when others will pick up the slack
- **c.** the fear of performing when there is an audience
- **d.** the feeling that an individual's contribution is not important

**4.** Which term describes the tendency for a person in a group to lose self-awareness and go along with the group?
- **a.** deindividuation
- **b.** social loafing
- **c.** bargaining
- **d.** social facilitation

**5.** Which term best describes the tendency for group members to develop a more extreme position when in a group setting?
- **a.** groupthink
- **b.** deindividuation
- **c.** group polarization
- **d.** social loafing

**6.** Which of the following is not true of transformational leaders?
- **a.** They nurture trust among group members.
- **b.** They are passionate and energetic.
- **c.** They create intrinsic motivation within their followers.
- **d.** They believe in punishment for poor work.

**7.** What is an example of attribution bias?
- **a.** You see a stranger kick a soda machine and assume that he is an angry person.
- **b.** You believe you are justified in your own thoughts and actions but think that other people are biased in their beliefs and behaviours.
- **c.** Your professor harshly criticizes your work and you develop a dislike for her.
- **d.** You give a fantastic oral presentation because you enjoy public speaking.

**ANSWERS:** 1. b; 2. d; 3. c; 4. a; 5. c; 6. d; 7. a; 8. c; 9. d; 10. c

**8.** Which is not involved in the bargaining process?
- **a.** One side makes an initial offer.
- **b.** The other side makes a counter offer.
- **c.** One side makes a concession with no expectation that the opposition will also make a concession.
- **d.** Both sides try to find similarities with each other.

**9.** How can the bargaining process be influenced by culture?
- **a.** Collectivistic cultures focus on individual and economic gains.
- **b.** Individualistic cultures focus on maintaining good bargaining relationships and keeping the bargaining process fair to all groups involved.
- **c.** Collectivistic cultures rarely engage in bargaining as it does not serve the best interests of the group and minimizes group goals.
- **d.** Individualistic cultures focus on individual and economic gains.

**10.** Which is a step-by-step method for resolving a conflict?
- **a.** hostile attribution bias
- **b.** realistic group conflict
- **c.** GRIT
- **d.** none of the above

## ESSAY RESPONSE

**1.** Explain how deindividuation involves aspects of both social facilitation and social loafing.

**2.** How can a group member strive to decrease social loafing among other members?

**3.** Describe how and where group polarization occurs on the internet. Find an example and explain how group polarization came about and what the implications could be.

**4.** Discuss the differences between a transactional and a transformational leader. What are the drawbacks of each, and which style do you think is better?

**5.** Give an example of an imaginary conflict that could use GRIT as a solution. Devise potential elements of the conflict, as well as potential concessions made by both sides, and then determine the ultimate outcome.

## APPLY IT!

Write a journal entry about a time when you exhibited attribution bias. What happened to cause you to make a judgment? Do you think you were fair in your criticism? Now that you understand what fundamental attribution error is, how could that knowledge have affected your understanding of the other person? How will you use this understanding in future, similar scenarios?

**Remember to check www.thethinkspot.ca for additional information, downloadable flashcards, and other helpful resources.**

## Law

As you learned in Chapter 9, groups can wield quite a bit of influence over individuals. One field in which this is prominently illustrated is law. In criminal or civil trials in which juries are involved, once the jury has been presented with all the available evidence in a case, several factors may influence the decision-making process.

Social psychologists have conducted research in two key areas. One area of investigation is how *extra-legal factors* (i.e., factors not directly related to the case or evidence) influence jury decision making. For example, scholars have investigated how the races of the defendant and the juror may interact. Research shows that when race is not a prevalent factor during a trial, jurors tend to favour defendants of their own race or ethnic background (Sommers & Ellsworth, 2000). In a real-life example, when former football star O.J. Simpson was on trial for the murder of his ex-wife Nicole Brown and her friend Ronald Goldman, jury consultants for the defence team predicted that race would play an important part in the trial and that black women would prove to be Simpson's strongest defenders. A consultant for the prosecution came up with similar findings. However, prosecutor Marcia Clark rejected the advice, believing that black women would turn on Simpson when they heard about his history of domestic violence. The results of the 1995 trial supported the consultants' findings—Simpson was acquitted after just four hours of jury deliberation (Toobin, 1996). That said, a meta-analysis by researchers in Canada and the United States has revealed that racial biases in jurors are not inevitable, and that these are often evidenced more when racial minority groups serve as mock jurors or judges (Mitchell, Haw, Pfeifer, & Meissner, 2005). In particular, in jury simulation studies, there tends to be greater leniency when the race of the defendant and the participant match if the evidence against the accused is weak. That said, if the evidence is strong, minority groups tend to cast the accused as "the black sheep" of their race and judge them more harshly (e.g., Taylor & Hosch, 2004).

**Social psychologists work with experts to examine multiple areas of a trial, including evaluating the credibility of testimony, jury decision making, and what factors (e.g., race or gender) influence case outcomes.**

Gender also plays a role in legal decision making, both on the part of the defendant and experts. In their study on gender stereotypes associated with expert testimony, York University researcher Schuller and her colleagues (2005) found that the gender of an expert interacts with the complexity of the expert's testimony. Specifically, male experts who present complex testimony have more of an influence on case outcomes, whereas female experts who present non-complex testimony are more influential. In addition, research has found that the presence of an expert who testifies about poorly understood phenomena, such as Battered Woman Syndrome, leads to more lenient verdicts (e.g., Schuller & Hastings, 1996; Schuller & Jenkins, 2007; Schuller & Vidmar, 1992). Further, when the gender of the expert matches the gender orientation of the case (e.g., price fixing in a tire/automotive business versus a cosmetics company), the expert's testimony has more influence over case outcomes (i.e., damages awarded; McKimmie, Newton, Terry, & Schuller, 2004).

Attractiveness also influences our judgments of guilt or innocence. Research suggests that the attractiveness of a defendant may play a part in decisions made within the legal system, including the likelihood of a guilty verdict and the length of sentence given (Downs & Lyons, 1991; Lieberman, 2002). Studies have consistently found that individuals considered physically unattractive are rated as more likely to commit criminal behaviour (MacLin & Herrera, 2006). Why might this be the case? Researchers suggest that a less attractive defendant may look more like the "type of person" to commit a crime, that people perceive crimes committed by more attractive defendants to be less serious, and that society holds a general belief that attractive people are unlikely to participate in criminal actions (Nauert, 2010). Faces that look stereotypically criminal are identified more often in police lineups and tend to be remembered better by witnesses and victims.

"Faces that look stereotypically criminal are identified more often in police lineups and tend to be remembered better by witnesses and victims."

This criminal face bias tends to involve a greater perception that features such as scars, pock marks, tattoos, small or "beady" eyes, and long or shaggy hair are associated with criminality (Flowe & Humphries, 2011). As you can imagine, these features also tend to be associated with unattractiveness.

"Does the concept of "innocent until proven guilty" automatically make juries inclined to favour the defendant?"

In addition, emotionality or expressed emotion is relevant to credibility judgments. For example, researchers have reported that rape victims who present as emotional (i.e., sobbing, trembling) are more likely to be believed by police, juries, and judges than those who present as unemotional (i.e., restrained, controlled) (e.g., Ask & Landström, 2010; Wessel, Drevland, Eilertsen, & Magnussen, 2006). In fact, MacLin, Downs, MacLin, and Caspers (2009) found that defendants who displayed remorse in their facial expressions were given more lenient verdicts by mock jurors than were those who had angry facial expressions. Further, recent research by Peace, Brower, and Rocchio (2011) has found that the bizarreness of a victim's or witness's testimony affects ratings of credibility: more bizarre claims are less likely to be believed by mock judges, and tend to result in a disbelief of witness testimony. These findings are critical as defendants may attempt to feign emotional expressions or fake details of their claims to lend credibility to a "story."

The second major area of investigation for social psychologists is *group decision-making processes* (see Devine, Clayton, Dunford, Seying, & Pryce, 2000). Most juries are not in agreement when they first enter the jury room. However, nearly all manage to reach a consensus following deliberations, indicating that some form of group influence has occurred. In the classic film *Twelve Angry Men*, Henry Fonda stars as a juror who is firmly convinced that the defendant is not guilty, ultimately transforming an 11–1 jury in favour of conviction into a 12–0 jury in favour of acquittal. Research suggests that this situation would be extremely unlikely in a real trial; majority opinion usually prevails. One study found that nine out of 10 juries reach the verdict favoured by the majority on the first ballot (Kalven & Zeisel, 1966). However, minority influence occasionally sways a jury's verdict, particularly if those in the minority are confident, persistent, and consistent in their opinions (Gordijn, De Vries, & de Dreu, 2002).

The influence of a group may also result in group polarization, as jury discussions can magnify jurors' initial viewpoints, making them more extreme. Does the concept of "innocent until proven guilty" automatically make juries inclined to favour the defendant? Research suggests that most jurors become more lenient during deliberations, particularly if the evidence is not highly incriminating (e.g., Hastie, Penrod, & Pennington, 1983; MacCoun & Kerr, 1988). In addition, juries that are initially leaning toward acquittal will rarely return a conviction (Stasser, Kerr, & Bray, 1981). This tendency to favour the accused is known as the *leniency bias*, a phenomenon that likely occurs because jurors in favour of acquittal need only produce a reasonable doubt in their fellow jurors, whereas those in favour of conviction must eliminate any doubt at all.

An awareness of the types of biases that occur in and out of the courtroom can help to reduce prejudicial behaviours in the legal system. Social psychological research is used to educate juries and law enforcement officials about the possibility of bias and plays an important role in bias reduction.

**Are juries biased in favour of more attractive defendants? Research shows that attractive people receive lighter sentences than their average-looking peers. An example is Karla Homolka, Canada's notorious sex killer and former partner of serial rapist/killer Paul Bernardo.**

# STEREOTYPES, PREJUDICE, AND DISCRIMINATION: CAUSES AND CONSEQUENCES

<<< Even though you may not realize it, you likely hold beliefs about characteristics of individuals of certain ethnicities.

**WHAT** ARE STEREOTYPES, PREJUDICE, AND DISCRIMINATION?
**HOW** DO WE MEASURE STEREOTYPES, PREJUDICE, AND DISCRIMINATION?
**WHAT** ARE THE SOURCES OF STEREOTYPING AND PREJUDICE?
**WHAT** ARE THE CONSEQUENCES OF STEREOTYPING?
**HOW** CAN WE COMBAT STEREOTYPING AND PREJUDICE?

# You may

believe that due to our multicultural society, Canadians are more tolerant and have displayed less prejudice and discrimination throughout our history—especially if you are a member of a majority group. But are you correct? Consider the following examples.

Our history is replete with examples of discrimination against blacks, Jews, Asians, women, and the list goes on. For example, thousands of Japanese Canadians in British Columbia were removed from their homes and forced into confinement in work camps during World War II. Following the Pearl Harbor attack in 1941, it was believed that individuals of Japanese descent might be involved in sabotage or espionage. After the war had ended, Japanese Canadians were given the "choice" of leaving British Columbia or being repatriated to Japan. Many chose to move to the greater Toronto area and work within the food services or agricultural industry growing produce or labouring for local farmers. No formal apology was issued by the Canadian government until 1988 (Roberts-Moore, 2002). More recently, a Jewish businessman was denied his purchase of a cottage on Lake Huron because of a protest by the property association. In addition, a Trinidadian man was accepted by the Canadian military and later deported due to his Asian ancestry (Walker, 1997).

Yet another example involves hundreds of thousands of Aboriginal children who were removed from their homes and placed in the Canadian Indian residential school system in order to assimilate them into the "Canadian"—i.e., white European-based—culture. Within this system, they were physically and sexually abused, and punished for engaging in any behaviour that was considered part of their Aboriginal ethnicity. In fact, the mandates of the system have been considered a form of cultural genocide as authorities attempted to "kill the Indian in the child." Schools were set up all across Canada, with the last residential school in Saskatchewan closing in 1996. In September 2007, a $1.9 billion compensation program was implemented in an attempt to rectify past abuses, and a formal apology was issued in June 2008 by Prime Minister Stephen Harper ("A Timeline," 2008)

While you may think we have learned not to be prejudiced in modern times, research has demonstrated that we all have biases against certain groups. Have you ever moved to the opposite side of the street when individuals of a different ethnicity approached on a sidewalk? Have you ever locked your car doors in neighbourhoods associated with certain groups of people? Have you ever treated customers differently based on physical, age-related, or racial characteristics? In this chapter, we will discuss how it is that we may become prejudiced against others and what we can do to eliminate (or minimize) these biases.



# CHAPTER 10

**PREJUDICE** a negative learned attitude toward particular groups of people

**DISCRIMINATION** a behaviour directed toward a group of people based solely on their membership in that group

**STEREOTYPE** a belief about the characteristics of a group of people ok to have two entries for this term?

## What Are Stereotypes, Prejudice, and Discrimination?

In the past decade, there has been a widespread resurgence of prejudice and discrimination against individuals of the Muslim faith or countries associated with war and terrorism. Following the terrorist attacks on the World Trade Center towers in New York City on September 11, 2001, any person who defined himself or herself as Muslim was considered a terrorist by hyper-patriotic white Americans, and some were overtly discriminated against and harmed. The Canadian Council of Muslim Women reported that approximately 30 percent of Muslim women experienced unfair treatment or discrimination in the 10 years following 9/11, including graffiti on one woman's property reading "Kill Muslim Dogs" in Hamilton, Ontario (Patel, 2011). That said, negative feelings toward Muslims in Canada existed well before this time and have led to discrimination charges being made against various governmental organizations.

> Prejudice and discrimination have to do with attitudes and behaviours. **Prejudice is the affective or attitudinal component of the equation, and discrimination is where our behaviour comes in.**

In 1999, Muslim Iranian-Canadian Ali Tahmourpour pursued his dream of being a member of the Royal Canadian Mounted Police (RCMP) and began his training at the Depot Academy in Regina, Saskatchewan. After four months of training, he was told that he "didn't measure up" and was booted out of training. This began an eight-year legal fight against the RCMP and an official investigation into charges of harassment and discrimination that were perpetrated by several instructors. For example, Tahmourpour was ridiculed for writing in Persian script and wearing a religious pendant, and was constantly told he was "a loser," "a coward," "[f—ing] useless," and "incompetent." In April 2008, the Canadian Human Rights Tribunal ordered the RCMP to pay approximately $1 million to Tahmourpour to compensate for the abuses he experienced and to cover his lost wages and legal bills. The ruling also dictated that the RCMP must reinstate him in their police training program. In addition, mandatory diversity and cultural awareness programs were to be instituted by the RCMP for all cadets and instructors to prevent further discrimination ("RCMP Faces," 2008). While these outcomes don't erase the abuses faced by Tahmourpour and many others, they are a step in the right direction.

Both of these examples demonstrate the differences between stereotypes, prejudice, and discrimination. **Prejudice** refers to negative *feelings or attitudes* about particular groups of people. For example, if an individual states "I hate Muslims" or "Aboriginals are disgusting," he is demonstrating an explicit prejudiced attitude and negative feelings about certain people simply based on their membership in a particular group. Unfortunately, prejudice often leads to **discrimination**, which refers to *behaviours* that are directed against people solely because they are members of a particular group. The insults and abuses experienced by Muslim men and women, as in Tahmourpour's case described above, are examples of discrimination, as was the treatment of Aboriginal children at the residential schools across Canada. Prejudice and discrimination have to do with attitudes and behaviours. Prejudice is the affective or attitudinal component of the equation, and discrimination is where our behaviour comes in. They have their roots in a cognitive component that starts with automatic processing—that "shortcut" thinking that leads us to make sweeping generalizations called stereotypes (Steele, Choi, & Ambady, 2004). A **stereotype** refers to a *belief* about the characteristics of a particular group of people, such as some people's belief, in the years following the 9/11 attacks, that all Muslims were involved in terrorist organizations (e.g., Khan, 2002; Patel, 2011).

Most of us would probably strongly reject the idea that we hold prejudices or that we actively discriminate against people on the basis of their race, gender, or sexual orientation. However, we are all guilty of forming stereotypes—whether we admit it to ourselves or not. Stereotypes can contain negative or positive information; think about the stereotype that all Asians are smart, or the one that says all Africans are good at sports. That said, it is important to remember that even if a stereotype seems to say something good about someone, it is still an overgeneralization that can lead to prejudice.

Have you ever been cut off in traffic by an elderly driver and instantly thought to yourself that people over the age of 75 shouldn't be allowed on the road? Or have you seen a group of young men wearing hooded sweatshirts and nervously crossed to the other side of the street? Do you buy into the assessment that all Italians are good lovers or that "white men can't jump"? Our brains save us time and energy by classifying people and objects into categories, and stereotyping provides us with useful basic information about the world around us. However, this tendency can often lead us to draw false conclusions about people, resulting in prejudice and discrimination. Your response to encountering that group of young men wearing hoodies is an example of a stereotype that has led to discrimination—the choice to cross the street because you don't want to go anywhere near them. Once a stereotype has been formed, it is difficult to dispel, because it is often activated automatically and we have a tendency to reject new information that does not support our stereotype and accept only information that encourages our preconceived viewpoint (i.e., the confirmation bias we discussed in Chapter 2; see Nickerson, 1998). Alternatively, we may subtype a stereotyped target who doesn't end up fitting the stereotype, deciding that she isn't really part of that group, or is somehow an exception to the rule (e.g., Kunda & Oleson, 1997; Weber & Crocker, 1983).

Although stereotypes are difficult to dispel, they are not static. Stereotypes change as a group's role changes over time, and are determined by social norms regarding what behaviour is acceptable or unacceptable. For example, within the Canadian criminal justice system, a man could not be charged with sexual assault against his wife until after 1983. Before that time, a woman was considered to be a man's property, and violence that happened within the home was deemed a "private" matter that was separate from the "public" matters that police attended to (Tang, 1998). In addition, stereotypes of groups also change as group status changes (e.g., Ross & Nisbett, 1991). In fact, changes in Canadian rape legislation during the 1980s reflected both the growing influence of women's rights movements and advocacy groups in challenging unfair social categorizations, and a changing view that these organizations should not just be perceived as feminist trouble makers (Tang, 1998).

## IS PREJUDICE ON THE DECLINE?

Although there is little doubt that attitudes have changed overall, prejudice still exists in various forms. Recent research shows that 20 percent of gay, lesbian, and bisexual persons have experienced a crime based on their sexual orientation (Herek, 2009). Religious groups are also an ongoing target—eight years after 9/11, 58 percent of Americans felt that there remained "a lot of discrimination against" Muslims (Pew, 2009). Recently, Americans and Canadians alike have demonstrated strong opposition to the Islamic community's desire to build a mosque near the Ground Zero memorial site in New York City, with some individuals being very vocal about their disagreement (Jia, Karpen, & Hirt, 2011).

The examples above indicate that prejudice has not been dispelled but has merely transitioned into a more subtle form—with people unwilling to admit, either to themselves or others, how they truly feel. This argument, that prejudice and discrimination is not gone but is simply more subtly expressed, is supported by behavioural bias identified in various social experiments. In one case, researchers sent 5,000 resumes out in response to 1,300 employment advertisements. Applicants who were randomly assigned typically "white" names, such as Emily or Greg, received one call-back for every 10 resumes sent. Applicants who were randomly assigned typically "black" names, such as Lakisha or Jamal, received one call-back for every 15 resumes sent—a far lower success rate than their white-sounding counterparts (Bertrand & Mullainathan, 2004).

Many white people, some argue, have learned to say the right thing but have not truly internalized the ideals that would classify them as non-racist (Jackman & Jackman, 1983). Psychologists Dovidio and Gaertner (2000) coined the term **aversive racism** to describe the attitudes of people who openly endorse egalitarian views but discriminate in subtle ways they are able to rationalize. They investigated changes in aversive racism over a 10-year period and found that self-reported prejudice was lower in 1998 to 1999 than it was in 1988 to 1989 but that white participants showed discrimination against black job candidates when differences between the strengths of each candidate was ambiguous (Dovidio & Gaertner, 2000). That said, recent research on social media indicates that individuals may express more racist attitudes in online forums even though they may personally disapprove of prejudice. For example, Tynes and Markoe (2010) stated that students showed mild approval of depictions of racial biases (i.e., a "gangsta" party) on social networking sites but privately found such displays offensive. Interestingly, in research with minority groups in Canada, black and Muslim groups acknowledged that people *explicitly* held negative attitudes toward their groups, but believed that people *implicitly* liked their group more than they overtly expressed (Peach, Yoshida, Spencer, Zanna, & Steele, 2011).

**AVERSIVE RACISM** the attitudes of people who openly endorse egalitarian views but discriminate in ways they're able to rationalize

Despite these demonstrations of more covert prejudice, *overt discrimination* still occurs, as demonstrated by the continued existence of hate groups. For example, groups such as the Northern Alliance, Tri-City Skinheads, Western Canada For Us, Final Solution Skins, Canadian Heritage Alliance, the Aryan Resistance Movement, and the Canadian Association for Free Expression all endorse views of white supremacy and Neo-Nazi sentiments against blacks, Jews, and more recently, anyone of Middle Eastern descent (Westcoast Coalition for Human Dignity, 2003). For example, in 1998, a group of skinheads in Surrey, B.C., was charged with the murder of Sikh temple caretaker Nirmal Singh Gill ("Crown Seeks Life," 1999). While not all of these groups engage in violence, several have been associated with assaults, gay-bashing, racially motivated crimes, and murder.

Hate crimes in Canada are an ongoing concern. On April 28, 2009, a 15-year-old Asian male was charged with assault following a high-school fight in which he was defending himself from racial taunts and attacks by non-Asian students. Following the charges, hundreds of students from the school rallied to defend the boy and protest how the York Regional Police had treated him (Clarkson, 2009). Unfortunately, cases where minority groups are targeted as perpetrators and/or victims are not isolated.

In a *Juristat* article on Canadian hate crimes in 2009, Dauvergne and Brennan (2011) report that although hate crimes account for approximately 1 percent of all crimes known to police, there has been a recent increase in hate crimes (violent and non-violent) from previous years. That said, in a General Social Survey in 2009, Canadians indicated that only one-third of hate crimes are actually reported to the police, so this rate may be a drastic underestimation of discrimination in Canada. Of the hate crimes reported, motivations most commonly involved race (54 percent), religion (29 percent), or sexual orientation (13 percent). These motivations also are associated with regional

<<< **From the late 1800s until the 1990s, hundreds of thousands of** Aboriginal children were stripped of their culture at residential schools across Canada **because of the belief that Indian children were undisciplined savages.**

RACISM an institutional practice that discriminates against individuals on the basis of their race

SEXISM an institutional practice that discriminates against individuals on the basis of their gender

differences: racially motivated crimes were highest in Hamilton and Calgary, religious-based crimes were highest in Winnipeg and Montreal, and crimes based on sexual orientation highest in Vancouver. Further, these statistics indicate that the greatest amount of violence occurred in hate crimes motivated by homophobia (Dauvergne & Brennan, 2011).

## TYPES OF PREJUDICE AND DISCRIMINATION

You might think of prejudice and discrimination as being personal issues, but in fact some types of prejudice are institutionalized. **Racism** and **sexism** are examples of institutional practices that result in discrimination against individuals on the basis of their race or gender.

### Racism

Imagine being denied a table in a restaurant or the ability to attend a certain school purely on the basis of the colour of your skin. Under the Common Schools Act in Canada, racial segregation was a reality until the 1980s, denying blacks equal access to schools, creating separate "black only" schools, and denying admittance into "white" schools. The last segregated school in Canada, located in Nova Scotia, was closed in 1983. Although racial segregation was banned and integration was mandated, the debate about segregation has taken an interesting turn in recent years. For example, the State of Connecticut threatened to pull funding from the primarily black-enrolled Capital Preparatory Magnet School unless the principal increased the number of white students in the school to approximately 25 percent of the student body. Some individuals have questioned this resistance to desegregation, arguing that it may cause black children to develop racial prejudices against white students ("Are Magnet Schools," 2011). In Toronto, the District School Board announced its plans to embed the city's first Africentric High School inside Oakwood Collegiate in order to boost rates of achievement and graduation among minority populations (Wong, 2011). This announcement has fallen under heavy anti-segregation criticism. Interestingly, though, black Canadians were deeply upset by barriers to the proposed segregation, as some feel it is a way to boost cultural enrichment and decrease school drop-out rates (Brown & Popplewell, 2008). However, others have argued that current segregated learning systems, such as Toronto's First Nations School, should serve as an example of what happens when vulnerable minority populations are further separated from the larger learning community (Wong, 2011).



Even as early as the 1940s, researchers were investigating the potential negative effects of segregation in schools. In the famous *Brown v. Board of Education of Topeka, Kansas* case, heard by the U.S. Supreme Court in 1947, lawyers referred to research by Clark and Clark (1947) that provided evidence for the destructive effects of racial segregation. The Clarks produced drawings and dolls of black and white children and asked a number of black preschool and elementary school children to indicate their preferences. They also asked the children to colour line drawings using the crayon that was closest to their own skin colour. Results showed that black children often preferred the white doll and drawing and often coloured the line drawing a shade lighter than their skin tones. Some of the children's responses indicated that they perceived white as "good" and "pretty," and thought of black as "bad" and "ugly," leading the researchers to conclude that even at the tender age of six or seven, black children had already accepted their inferior status in society (Clark & Clark, 1947). Further, research at McGill University has demonstrated how segregation can promote ingroup favouritism (i.e., preference for members of one's own group) and outgroup prejudice even in children as young as five years (Aboud, 2003). By illustrating how the "separate but equal" system reinforced negative stereotypes and a sense of inferiority among black children, the "doll test" assisted in ending racial segregation across North America.

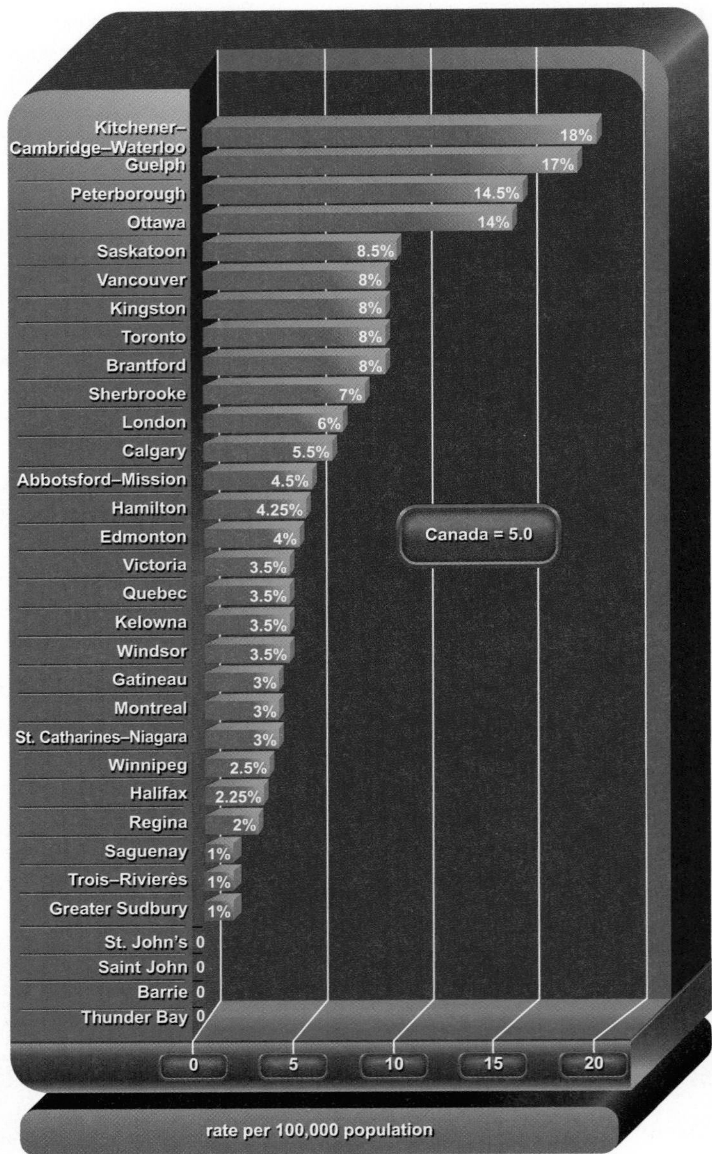


**Hate Crime in Canada. While reported hate crimes only account for approximately 1 percent of all crime,** there are many variations across metropolitan areas in Canada. **How does your city measure up?**

Although the last segregated school was closed in Nova Scotia in 1983, there has been a recent push by educational boards in Ontario to establish segregated schools for "at-risk" minority populations such as First Nations, black, and Middle Eastern.

While discrimination based on racial segregation has been minimized in recent years, **racial prejudice**—the tendency to hold a hostile attitude toward an individual because of his or her racial background—remains a cause for concern. In Canada, scholars have argued that despite our multicultural society, there is still a predominant "white racial identity" that equates being white with normalness (Crawford, 1998). Crawford argued that this identity is maintained through the construction of stereotypes associated other races with negative attributes (e.g., Natives as lazy alcoholics), and the view that other races are "newcomers" or "foreigners" who are only Canadian due to the stamp of an immigration official (Shadd, 1989). This is further reflected in research that has shown that we have a tendency to be able to recognize faces of familiar others, including those in our own racial groups, more readily than those of different racial groups (see Meissner & Brigham, 2001, for a review of this concept). The tendency has even been demonstrated in infants as young as three months old (e.g., Bar-Haim, Ziv, Lamy, & Hodes, 2006; Kelly, Quinn, Slater, Lee, Ge, & Pascalis, 2007). In fact, different areas of the brain become more active when recognizing someone of the same race versus someone of a different race (e.g., Golby, Gabrieli, Chiao, & Eberhardt, 2001; Ronquillo et al., 2007). That said, the cross-race effect likely results from familiarity with one's own race and may be reversed if we become intimately familiar with another race. In a study of Korean children who were adopted by white families when they were between the ages of three and nine, researchers found that the children were better able to recognize white faces than Asian ones. Conversely, Korean children who grow up in Korea are better able to recognize Asian faces than white ones (Sangrigoli, Pallier, Argenti, Ventureyra, & de Schonen, 2005).

Like stereotypes, prejudices toward groups also change over time, depending on the concerns and ideologies of a given group, as well as current events. In recent years, prejudice against immigrants has risen, with Germans harbouring more prejudices toward Turks, British toward West Indians and Pakistanis, Americans toward Latin Americans, and Canadians against anyone of Middle Eastern descent (e.g., Esses, Dovidio, & Hodson, 2002; Pettigrew & Tropp, 2006). In recent years, groups of American citizens, part of the Minutemen movement, have taken it upon themselves to patrol the Mexico–United States border, looking for people crossing into the United States illegally. Hundreds of volunteers, taken in by the rhetoric of the movement, have participated in these patrols—sometimes with deadly results, as in the case of the shooting of a 10-year-old girl and her father (McKinley, 2009). Further, a recent report issued by the Royal Canadian Mounted Police indicated that youths and young adults are being encouraged to engage in racially-motivated violence through online forms of social media, including games such as "Bye, Bye Mosque" and "Ethnic Cleansing" ("Shocking Online," 2011). This trend is disturbing and reflects that stereotypes, prejudice, and discrimination based on race are still very much alive and (un)well in today's society (e.g., Blatz, Schumann, & Ross, 2009).

**RACIAL PREJUDICE** the tendency to hold a hostile attitude toward an individual because of his or her racial background

**GENDER PREJUDICE** the tendency to hold a hostile attitude toward an individual because of his or her gender

**GENDER STEREOTYPES** people's ideas about how men and women behave based on socially and culturally defined beliefs

## Sexism

In a 2009 case in British Columbia, Ronald Morrison was rejected for a health care position he had applied for in a senior's home, even though he had superior qualifications for the job, including education as a residential care aide. He sought damages and was awarded $12,000 from the B.C. Human Rights Tribunal ("B.C. Health-Care Worker," 2009). In another recent case, more than 400 female nurses who work for the Canada Pension Plan were awarded compensation for years of sex discrimination in wages, as males performing the same job were receiving twice the pay ("Nurses Get," 2011). And female lawyer Jaime Laskis, a graduate of the prestigious Dalhousie Law School, is currently suing a New York law firm where she was employed and experienced sexual discrimination. Her male co-workers are alleged to have said that "women who take maternity leave will be taken off the partner track," that Laskis "needed to be more than just a pretty face," and that law schools are "full of pretty women pretending to get a legal education" (*Laskis v. Osler, Hoskin & Harcourt LLP,* 2011).

Unfortunately, cases such as this are not that uncommon. Both men and women may be subject to gender discrimination or **gender prejudice** in the workplace, in which they are treated unequally due to attitudes based on their sex. Such prejudice arises from **gender stereotypes**—people's ideas about how men and women behave based on socially and culturally defined beliefs. Often, gender stereotypes are used to rationalize a group's role, in that women are perceived as more nurturing and men more assertive and business minded—which translates into a perception of which professions are "appropriate" for each gender. Gender stereotypes differ from other stereotypes because they are prescriptive rather than merely descriptive—in other words, they indicate what many people in a particular culture believe that men and women *should* be. These stereotypes are reinforced by common phrases such as "Big boys don't cry" and "Girls don't play with trucks." Studies show that gender stereotypes are formed very early in life and are dramatically influenced

**AMBIVALENT SEXISM** the contradictory attitudes of hostile sexism and benevolent sexism

by gender-specific cues in an infants' environment (e.g., Serbin, Poulin-Dubois, & Eichstedt, 2002). For example, Université du Québec à Montréal researchers found that the colours parents choose to dress their children in and the toys provided for them to play with reinforce traditional gender roles (Pomerleau, Bolduc, Malcuit, & Cossette, 1990).

As gender roles have evolved in society, gender stereotypes have also improved in some measure (e.g., Eagly, 1987; Nelson & Robinson, 2006). However, recent data shows that sexism within cultures is still evident and is directly associated with gender inequality across 57 different societies (Brandt, 2011). Further, even though women may work in male-oriented fields and men in female-oriented professions, behaviours within these cross-over jobs still vary. For example, in a study of male nurses in Nova Scotia, Evans (2002) found that they were "cautious caregivers" and faced concerns such as the sexualization of their physical touch or being labelled as homosexual. Further, women in positions of leadership (e.g., politics, the military) are often perceived as less effective than their male counterparts, which may result in such women identifying more with the masculine stereotype in their behaviours (e.g., Boyce & Herd, 2003; Eagly & Karau, 2002; Norris & Wylie, 1995). In general, sexism can lead to acts of violence and hate against individuals based on their gender. Globally, up to six out of ten women experience sexual or physical violence in their lifetimes due to sex discrimination (United Nations, 2010).

Interestingly, psychologists have found that gender attitudes are often contradictory. This phenomenon has been called **ambivalent sexism** (Glick & Fiske, 2001). On the one hand, men experience *hostile sexism,* in which they feel resentful about women's abilities and make derogatory remarks about the female sex. On the other hand, men also experience *benevolent sexism*, feeling paternalistic toward women and wanting to demonstrate chivalrous behaviour. While the latter is a more acceptable form of sexism, and influences the perceived attractiveness of women who embody these ideals (i.e., needing a man to take care of them; Lau, Kay, & Spencer, 2008), it still contributes to negative female stereotypes. In a study of 19 nations across six continents, Glick and others (2000) found evidence of ambivalent sexism all over the world, noting that it is most prevalent in people from countries with the greatest degree of economic and political inequality between the sexes.

Another type of institutionalized prejudice is *heterosexism*. Despite recent legislation permitting same-sex marriages in Canada, negative attitudes toward these marriages still exist, as well as biases against hiring homosexual persons in a variety of settings (e.g., Buchner & Huen, 1998; Smith, 2005). Poteat and his colleagues have argued that homophobic attitudes are a product of socialization, often involving peer groups in adolescence, and may lead to feelings of superiority and differential treatment on the part of heterosexual persons (Poteat, 2007; Poteat et al., 2007). These feelings then lead to internalized ideals of what should and should not constitute sexual relationships (Szymanski, Kashubeck-West, & Meyer, 2008).

<<< Studies suggest that children learn traditional gender roles **at a young age.**

## Prejudice Is Not Just About Race or Sex

Prejudice, and subsequent discrimination, also can occur on the basis of superficial distinctions between individuals. Think back to the opening of Chapter 1 of this text, where we described the Robbers Cave Experiment and how young boys at summer "camp" became prejudiced against each other in a very short period of time even though they were all the same age, gender, and race. As tensions grew between the two groups, prejudiced attitudes were expressed. The Eagles had written off their fellow campers, the Rattlers, as a rough bunch who swore too much, while the Rattlers made equally negative snap judgments about the Eagles. These attitudes were quickly expressed and discriminatory acts began when the Rattlers won a crucial tug-of-war competition. The Eagles responded by stealing their rival's flag and burning it. Goaded into action, the Rattlers raided the Eagles' camp, stealing the group leader's jeans and painting them orange. They carried the jeans as a flag the next day, emblazoned with the taunt "The Last of the Eagles." Incensed, the Eagles launched a retaliatory raid on the Rattlers' camp, flinging dirt around the cabin and overturning camp beds (Sherif, Harvey, White, Hood, & Sherif, 1954). The rivalry between the Eagles and the Rattlers might sound like the content of a recent episode of *Survivor* or a similar reality show, but this level of antagonism is expressed in everyday life on the basis of superficial distinctions between individuals, such as what sports team they belong to. This may result from intergroup rivalry and defining your own group as "us" and the other group as "them." As soon as these group divisions are in place, both children and adults begin to identify more with their own group and may consider the other group "different" or "outcasts" and demean them in some way. How many times have you made fun of members of another sports team even though, in reality, the members of the other team are just like you?

Another potent example of how superficial groupings can lead to discrimination was conducted not long after the Robbers Cave Experiment. In 1968, Jane Elliott, a teacher from the United States, demonstrated the arbitrary nature of prejudice by initiating a polarizing activity with her third-grade students. Elliott's activity was prompted by the assassination of prominent black civil rights activist Martin Luther King, Jr. Unsure of how to explain to her young students what King stood for and why he was killed, Elliott decided to teach her students, all of whom were white, what it is like to be discriminated against. Elliott divided her students into two groups, those with blue eyes and those with brown eyes. The blue-eyed group, or Blues, were designated the superior group, and the brown-eyed group, or Browns, were designated the inferior group. As the inferior group, the Browns were told that they were less intelligent and less important than their fellow students, and Elliott constantly belittled them. Eventually, the Blues joined in on the discriminatory behaviour, making judgments against and showing hatred toward those in the inferior group. The next day, Elliott reversed the experiment, making the Browns the superior group, and the brown-eyed students expressed the same prejudiced behaviour toward the Blues (Tozer, Violas, & Senese, 1993). While Elliott's activity was simply a demonstration rather than an experiment in discrimination (and used methods that are ethically questionable—something that social psychologists have also had to deal with), it does expose the irrational nature of discrimination.

How much of a role do prejudice and bigotry play in your life? Have you ever been the victim of prejudice or bigotry, or have you ever been the perpetrator of this behaviour? If you are a member of a minority group, you may have sometimes felt unjustly judged by other members of society. If you are a member of a majority group, you may have acted superior to a member of a minority group. As a society, we are programmed to assume that the divide that instigates prejudice between minority and majority groups is based on race, gender, or other socially significant factors (e.g., white versus Aboriginal, men versus women, homosexual versus heterosexual, able-bodied versus disabled). Our social norms support this idea, but social psychologists argue that discrimination also can be based on factors that are purely arbitrary and meaningless, such as height, hair colour, or even shoe size. These kinds of seemingly insignificant factors can instigate discrimination just as easily as skin colour or gender. Elliott's classroom activity highlights just how random and powerful prejudice can be. The Blues were quick to embody their initial superiority, while the Browns readily accepted their inferiority. You can watch footage of Elliot's demonstration in the documentary *A Class Divided* on the PBS website: www.pbs.org/gbh/pages/frontline/shows/divided/.

**In tests that use virtual reality simulation,** participants are more likely to mistakenly shoot at an image of a black person than at an image of a white person.

## How Do We Measure Stereotypes, Prejudice, and Discrimination?

What does it mean to be prejudiced? Is prejudice a conscious decision that we make or an automatic response? A study by Devine (1989) indicates that stereotypes may bias our perceptions and responses, even if we don't personally agree with them. The mere fact that we are aware of a particular stereotype through images in the media or through stories told by family members or friends is enough to automatically activate the stereotype when we encounter members of the group involved.

So if stereotyping is a function of automatic processing, does that mean that stereotyping is inevitable? Can stereotyping be prevented? The answer is complex—stereotyping is not something that can be flipped on and off like a switch. Yes, stereotypes are triggered automatically, as evidenced in Devine's study. However, there are factors that make activation more or less likely to happen. Some stereotypes come to mind more quickly and easily for some people than for others. This depends upon one's environment. Activation of a stereotype for someone who is Aboriginal is going to happen more easily for someone living near a Native reserve than for someone living in a primarily white community. Additionally, while stereotypes can be activated even in people who don't express much prejudice, triggers are usually much stronger in people who already feel prejudice toward a certain group.

> "If stereotyping is a function of automatic processing, **does that mean that stereotyping is inevitable?**"

So how do we measure stereotypes if they are automatically activated and we may not even be aware of them? Researchers often use what are called *covert measures* in order to assess these types of implicit attitudes. One of the most commonly used measures is the Implicit Association Test (IAT), which measures the amount of time it takes participants to associate faces with positive or negative words (i.e., pairing a white face with the word *good* or an Aboriginal face with the word *bad*). Studies using the IAT have found that most people hold implicit negative stereotypes about people of a difference race from themselves (e.g., Greenwald et al., 1998, 2000). Further, these implicit attitudes can have negative consequences for the interpretation of others' faces, behaviour, or ambiguous scenarios. For example, Hugenberg and Bodenhausen (2003) have associated stronger implicit prejudices on the IAT with increased perceptions of anger in ambiguous racial faces.

Based on these ideas, Correll and colleagues (2002), as well as Greenwald et al. (2003), have developed virtual reality simulations used

**OLD-FASHIONED (OR OVERT) RACISM** overt, oppressive acts and feelings toward a group of people based on their race

**MODERN (OR COVERT) RACISM** negative feelings toward a group of people based on their race, manifested in more subtle forms of racism

**OLD-FASHIONED SEXISM** overt sexism, characterized by the endorsement of traditional gender roles, differential treatment of men and women, and stereotypes about lesser female competence

**MODERN SEXISM** internalized negative feelings toward a group of people based on their gender, characterized by a denial of continued discrimination, antagonism toward women's demands, and lack of support for policies designed to help women in work and education

to assess implicit racial attitudes. In these simulations, student participants are invited to "shoot" or "not shoot" images of men who suddenly appeared onscreen holding either a gun or a harmless object such as a flashlight or a bottle. Given less than one second to respond to each figure, the students (who were predominantly white or Asian) wrongly shot at black targets 35 percent of the time, compared with a 26 percent error rate for white targets. Similar studies concluded that when primed with black faces, people were more likely to mistake a harmless object for a gun than when confronted with white faces (e.g., Judd et al., 2004; Payne, 2001). Studies such as these may help to explain why unarmed black men such as Steven Eugene Washington, who was shot by police in Los Angeles in March 2010, lose their lives simply for reaching into a pocket or touching a waistband while being confronted by law enforcement officials.

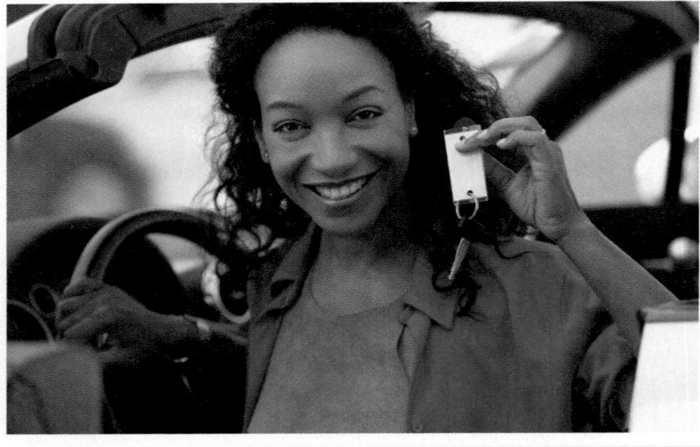

**Will the dealer charge this woman more because of her race and gender?** According to researchers, black women pay up to 8 percent more for a new vehicle than white males.



Neurological research also is being used as a covert measure to assess for negative implicit biases. These studies indicate that people have a natural tendency to classify others as part of a racial "ingroup" or "outgroup." By tracking event-related brain potentials (ERPs), which reflect brain electrical activity in response to discrete stimuli, researchers are able to examine the range of processes that occur when people perceive racial ingroup and outgroup members. Studies have shown that stereotype-based processing is evident within 100 milliseconds of encountering a stigmatized group member (Ito, Thompson, & Cacioppo, 2004).

What about prejudiced attitudes that we are aware of? Researchers have noted a difference between **old-fashioned racism**—overt oppressive acts and feelings—and **modern racism**—more internalized feelings that other racial groups are "taking over" and a general attitude that discrimination no longer exists and that policies such as affirmative action are therefore unnecessary (e.g., Gawronski, Peters, Brochu, & Strack, 2008; McConahay, 1986). Similarly, studies also have found a similar distinction between **old-fashioned sexism** and modern beliefs about women, noting that although overt sexism is less common in today's society, **modern sexism**—characterized by the denial of continued discrimination, antagonism toward women's demands, and a lack of support for policies designed to help women in work and education—is alive and well (Swim et al., 1995). *Self-report scales* have been designed to assess each of these attitudes, and include questions on the topics of racism or sexism in a Likert format. This enables participants to choose *strongly agree, agree, neutral, disagree*, or *strongly disagree* in response to statements such as "Over the past few years, Aboriginals have received more economically than they deserve." In general, studies have found that reported levels of modern racism or modern sexism are higher relative to the old-fashioned forms (Gawronski et al., 2008).

But do these attitudes translate into real-world behaviours? Some studies would suggest they do. When a research team visited car dealers and used a uniform strategy to try to negotiate the lowest price on a new car, they discovered that the dealers altered their "best price" according to the buyer's race and gender (Ayres, 1991). Other studies have noted discrepancies between the treatment of different racial groups at police checkstops. While drivers of any race are equally likely to be pulled over, certain racial groups are searched and threatened more often ("Black, Latino Drivers," 2007).

# What Are the Sources of Stereotyping and Prejudice?

Imagine you are talking to your friends about what they are going to dress up as for Halloween, and you get an assortment of costume responses such as "a cowboy," "a rapper," "an Indian," "a male fashion designer," and "a terrorist." Why is it that, as you read them, these terms likely conjured up images of certain attributes associated with particular racial or social groups? Where do these perceptions come from? Stereotypes and prejudice originate from several different sources: how we were brought up, the way that our brains classify individuals as part of an ingroup or an outgroup, and motivating factors such as group competition and individual emotional status.

## SOCIAL LEARNING

Imagine growing up in a household in which the use of derogatory terms such as *fag* and *dyke* was actively encouraged. Your attitude toward the homosexual community would likely be very different than if you grew up in a same-sex household or a household in which the use of such terms resulted in being deprived of television for a week. Just as children will copy aggressive behaviours by role models (Bandura, 1973), they often form their attitudes about people in different groups by watching and listening to their parents. For example, if a child hears a parent express a negative opinion about someone who holds different religious beliefs, or sees a parent avoid interacting with people who hold these beliefs, the child is more likely to form negative beliefs about people in this group (Towles-Schwen & Fazio, 2001). Similarly, children who are raised by obese mothers tend to exhibit more positive attitudes toward individuals who are obese, whereas children who are raised by slender mothers show an implicit preference for slimmer individuals (Rudman, Phelan, & Heppen, 2007).

Parents are not the only people who are capable of influencing our attitudes and behaviours—peers, too, serve as yardsticks by which we measure our social responses. When a friend or classmate expresses a prejudiced attitude, laughs at a joke that invokes a stereotype, or takes part in a discriminatory act, he contributes to the formation and perpetuation of stereotypes (Crandall, Eshleman, & O'Brien, 2002). For example, studies have shown that when white students hear other whites express racist views, they are less likely to take an anti-racist stance in the presence of those peers (e.g., Blanchard, Crandall, Brigham, & Vaughn, 1994). Further, Poteat and his colleagues have found that homophobic attitudes are heavily influenced by peer group identification during adolescence, but still vary within groups, particularly with respect to gay men (Poteat, 2007; Poteat, Espelage, & Green, 2007).

Another source related to social learning is the concept of the **authoritarian personality**, a personality type that favours obedience to authority and intolerance of people lower in status (Adorno et al., 1950). In an attempt to get at the psychological roots that allowed Nazi Germany to lead the killing of millions of people, they found that individuals who showed hostility toward Jews also showed hostility to other minorities. These people also shared the traits of submission to authority and intolerance for weakness. Generally, such people face harsh discipline as children, and they project their fears and hostility onto others. However, positive interracial contact between highly authoritarian individuals can help to reduce prejudice (Dhont & Van Hiel, 2009).

## COGNITIVE SOURCES

Many of us like to think that we are immune from stereotyping, but numerous everyday experiences tell us otherwise. Imagine you are driving to visit a friend and another car cuts in front of you at an intersection. You glare out of your window at the other driver and notice that he or she is of the opposite gender. What do you say? Most people have a tendency to use a flurry of expletives, followed by a comment about what bad drivers men or women are. Why is this type of interaction such a common phenomenon? In part, it happens because our brains classify people and objects into categories according to their race, gender, or other common attributes (e.g., Bar-Haim et al., 2006; Sherman et al., 2009). Recall the Robbers Cave Experiment discussed earlier in the chapter and how the members of the Eagles camp discriminated against members of the Rattlers camp solely because they belonged to a different campsite. Due to this social grouping, each group developed prejudiced attitudes and later discriminatory behaviour (i.e., stealing or intentionally damaging the other groups property) (Sherif et al., 1961).

This process of **social categorization** helps us to form impressions quickly and enables us to use previous experiences to shape new interactions. For example, if you have had problems communicating with an older person because she is hard of hearing, you might develop a tendency to speak more slowly and loudly around people over a certain age when you first meet them. University of Waterloo's Kunda and Spencer (2003) state that social categorizations involve both *stereotype activation* (i.e., accessibility and automatic activation of the stereotype) and *stereotype application* (i.e., using a stereotype to make group judgments). In particular, these scholars have argued that these two processes are divergent and that one can activate stereotypes without applying them. For example, they discuss one of their studies in which white participants expected to discuss a neutral topic (health policy) or a sensitive topic (immigration policy) with an Asian Canadian (Hoshino-Browne & Kunda, 2000). In this study, they found that when motivated to avoid appearing prejudiced, participants expressed less negativity toward immigration than if they were having a conversation with someone of the same ethnicity as themselves. As such, Kunda and Spencer (2003) believe that the application of stereotypes can be inhibited by motivations to avoid prejudice and by comprehension goals that lead individuals to correct their own stereotypical judgments. For example, if you see an elderly woman, you may experience an automatic activation of a stereotypical belief that she is frail or hard of hearing, but you may not act on this because you say to yourself, "That is not fair of me to think that, not all older people are fragile!".

**AUTHORITARIAN PERSONALITY** a personality type that favours obedience to authority and intolerance of people lower in status

**SOCIAL CATEGORIZATION** the process of dividing people into categories according to their race, gender, and other common attributes

Studies have shown that the stereotype activation—or the practice of placing people into categories—begins at a very early age. Young babies are able to differentiate between people in various racial groups, showing a preference for faces that belong to their own race (e.g., Bar-Haim et al., 2006). In addition, researchers at Concordia University have reported that infants as young as 18 months of age already demonstrate gender stereotypes when looking at toys that are stereotypically male (i.e., toy trucks) or female (i.e., dolls) and learn appropriate gender schemas quite rapidly (e.g., Eichstedt, Serbin, Poulin-Dubois, & Sen, 2002; Serbin et al., 2001). Further, these authors found that females tend to develop these stereotyped preferences earlier than males. Other studies have reported that by the age of four, children are demonstrating clear ingroup biases, which may lead to outgroup prejudice (e.g., Aboud, 2003; Cameron, Alvarez, Ruble, & Fuligni, 2001).

Categorizing individuals into ingroups and outgroups might save our brains time and energy, but it is not without consequences. Researchers have found that people tend to learn features about majority groups earlier than features about minority groups. When we learn about minority groups, we focus on features that *differentiate* them from the majority, magnifying perceived differences between groups (Sherman et al., 2009). Because we have a tendency to exaggerate the differences between our own ingroups and other outgroups, minimizing perceived similarities and maximizing perceived differences, stereotypes are formed and reinforced. This cognitive habit is explained by two phenomena—the *outgroup homogeneity effect* and *ingroup favouritism*.

### Outgroup Homogeneity

Think back to a sports match you have played in the past. You may be a valuable member of a team: the top goal scorer, the fastest runner, or the strongest defender. Other members of your team probably have

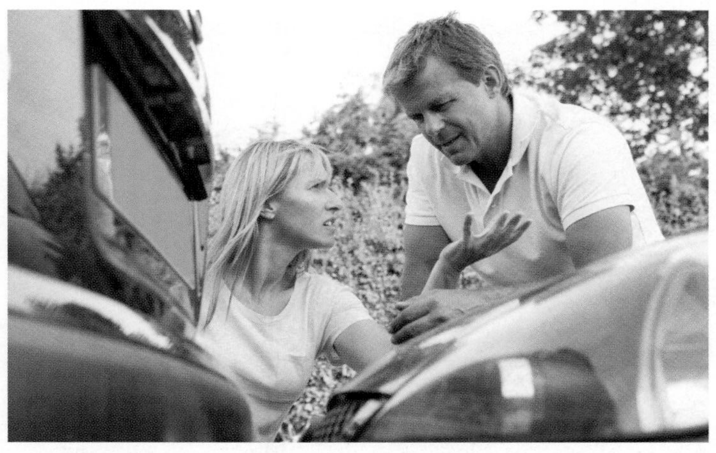

>>> **We all like to think that we don't stereotype,** but negative interactions between drivers of the opposite sex frequently prove otherwise.

**OUTGROUP HOMOGENEITY EFFECT** the tendency to see outgroup members as similar to one another but ingroup members as diverse individuals

**INGROUP FAVOURITISM** the natural tendency to favour an ingroup versus an outgroup

**SOCIAL DOMINANCE ORIENTATION** seeing one's own group as naturally superior to other groups

**ULTIMATE ATTRIBUTION ERROR** the tendency to explain the behaviour of groups in terms of internal dispositional factors, without taking the situational constraints into consideration

their own unique capabilities on the field, and you may socialize with them after training, familiarizing yourself with their likes and dislikes, their family backgrounds, and their goals and aspirations. Now picture one of the teams against which you have played. Do you see the players as similar individuals with unique qualities or as a single entity that must be defeated? In all likelihood, you take the latter view, perceiving the rival team as a homogenous group with few individual characteristics.

The **outgroup homogeneity effect** refers to our tendency to see outgroup members as similar to one another, but ingroup members as diverse individuals. This effect is evident in numerous situations around the world. You have probably heard liberals refer to conservatives as a group of "gun-toting religious nuts" and listened to conservatives dismiss liberals as "bleeding-heart socialists." Teenagers are often categorized as rude, thoughtless, and uncivilized, while the elderly are frequently thought of as stubborn, helpless, or old-fashioned. To ingroup members, people within an outgroup may even seem to look alike. For example, people are less accurate when it comes to distinguishing and recognizing faces of racial outgroups, especially if they are unfamiliar with these other groups (e.g., Chiroro, Tredoux, Radaelli, & Meissner, 2008; Tanaka, Kiefer, & Bukach, 2004). The difficulty with cross-race identification has proven to be tragic in some instances, such as the North Carolina case in which Jennifer Thompson falsely identified Ronald Cotton as the man who raped her in 1984. Cotton spent 11 years in prison before being exonerated by DNA evidence (Roth, 2010). This case represents only one of many misidentifications (e.g., Dwyer, 2007). In fact, approximately 40 percent of wrongful convictions have involved cross-race misidentifications (Roth, 2010).



Why do we tend to perceive outgroups as homogeneous? One reason is a lack of familiarity. If we have little personal contact with a particular group of people, we are unlikely to notice subtle differences between them and more inclined to lump them all together as a group. We may perceive our own ingroup to be homogeneous when we first join but change our opinion over time as we become more familiar with individual group members (Ryan & Bogart, 1997). For example, during the Robbers Cave Experiment, none of the boys in either camp initially knew one another, yet by the end of the first week, each group had established a coherent identity with leaders, social norms, and hierarchies. A lack of familiarity with the other group—the outgroup—resulted in stereotyping and name-calling, with each group making sweeping generalizations about the other (Sherif et al., 1961).

## Ingroup Favouritism

As soon as groups are formed, people have a natural tendency to favour an ingroup over an outgroup. This **ingroup favouritism** is so strong that we even categorize ingroup words such as we or us more favourably than outgroup words such as *they or them* (Otten & Wentura, 1999). Ingroup favouritism often results in discriminatory behaviour. Although studies within the Canadian legal system have found attractiveness of the defendant to be more predictive of lenient verdicts (Bagby, Parker, Rector, & Kalemba, 1994), studies based in the United States have noted that jurors often give shorter sentences to those accused of a crime when the accused is within their same ethnic group (e.g., Sommers & Ellsworth, 2000). Why might this occur?

One reason for ingroup favouritism is self-interest; we are more likely to favour those in our ingroup because they are more likely to favour us in return (Vivian & Berkowitz, 1992). During the Robbers Cave Experiment, the Eagles were more likely to support members of their own camp, who could provide them with food, prizes, and help with chores, than members of the Rattlers' camp who were of no practical use to them. As illustrated by the strong group bonds within the two camps, ingroup favouritism is more likely when people identify heavily with their group and when group norms are a prominent part of group mentality (Gagnon & Bourhis, 1996). Further, people sometimes see their own groups as naturally superior to other groups. This is referred to as having a **social dominance orientation** (e.g., Pratto et al., 1994; Sidanius & Pratto, 1999). Those who hold this orientation believe social groups should be ordered according to worth, and that superior groups should have more wealth and power. People with such an orientation usually hold negative stereotypes and prejudices against other groups, often out of a fear that the "superior" group's status is being somehow threatened (Esses & Hodson, 2006). That said, if individuals with high social dominance orientation have experienced positive intergroup contact, some research has found this to reduce prejudiced attitudes (e.g., Dhont & Van Hiel, 2009; Hodson, 2008).

### Attributional Biases

In Chapter 5, we discussed attribution errors that we make for others' behaviours. The fundamental attribution error is the tendency to focus on dispositional (personal) explanations for an individual's behaviour, without taking the situation into consideration. Likewise, attribution errors may be applied to an entire group. When we begin to favour an ingroup over an outgroup, we risk committing an **ultimate attribution error**—the tendency to explain the behaviour of groups in terms of internal dispositional factors,

<<< Children are more likely to recognize faces from within their own racial group, **or the racial group with which they are most familiar.**

without taking the situational constraints into consideration (Pettigrew, 1979). Thus, negative outgroup behaviour is attributed to dispositional attributes of the entire group. For example, you read a newspaper report about an Aboriginal man stabbing someone and conclude that it happened because all Native men are violent or dangerous. In contrast, positive outgroup behaviour is attributed to an exceptional case or an example of good fortune. For example, you read a newspaper report about a woman taking over a company and conclude that she must be related to the owner. Several studies support this view. For example, researchers found that white students were more likely to think a shove was violent (due to dispositional factors) when it came from a black person than when it came from a white person (Duncan, 1976). Gender prejudice is also evident with regard to ultimate attribution errors. Upon reviewing 58 separate experiments, researchers found that male successes in traditionally masculine tasks were more likely to be considered a result of ability than were female successes. Meanwhile, male failures were more likely attributed to poor luck or low effort than were female failures (e.g., Conway & Vartanian, 2000; Swim & Sanna, 1996).

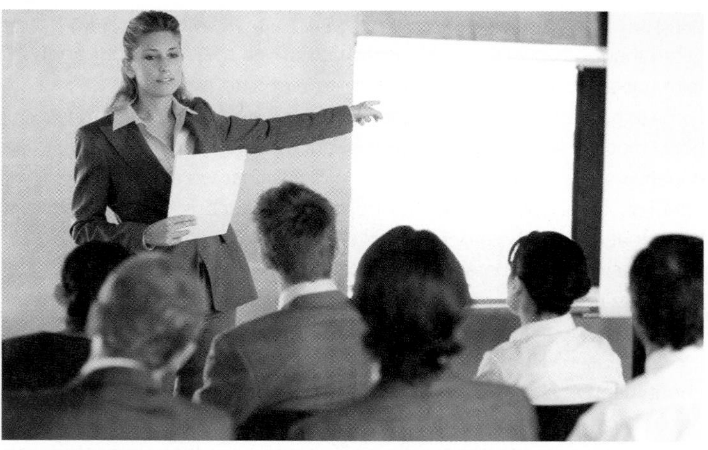

**Was this woman simply in the right place at the right time, or did her capable personality and hard work propel her to the top?** Studies show that female successes are more likely to be attributed to luck than to ability.

Another attributional bias is the **just-world hypothesis**, in which people believe that victims of misfortune deserve what happens to them (Hafer & Bègue, 2005). According to the hypothesis, we have a strong desire or need to believe that the world is a predictable, dependable place, where people get what they deserve. To live happy, fulfilling lives, we have to assume that our actions will have predictable consequences. As a result, when we encounter evidence that suggests the world is not a reliable, fair place to live, we attempt to restore the balance by convincing ourselves that no injustice has occurred. For example, a recent survey of 1,000 Londoners found that one in 10 respondents believed that most rape claims are "probably false," and more than half of the female respondents thought that there were situations in which the rape victim was to blame for the attack. Almost 20 percent of people agreed that a rape victim was partly to blame for being attacked if she went to the attacker's home (Bindel, 2010). By deciding that a woman has done something "wrong" by having a drink with a defendant or wearing provocative clothing, female jurors at a rape trial are able to reassure themselves that rape won't happen to them as long as they don't do anything similar. We invoke the just-world hypothesis every time we tell ourselves that a homeless person is simply lazy and needs to get a job, that an AIDS patient must be promiscuous or a drug addict, or that a person imprisoned for a crime he or she didn't commit must have done something wrong to arouse suspicion in the first place.

**JUST-WORLD HYPOTHESIS** the tendency for people to believe that the world is fair and just; therefore, victims of misfortune deserve what happens to them

**REALISTIC GROUP CONFLICT THEORY** the idea that when different groups are in competition for resources, they tend to close ranks, favouring ingroup members and discriminating against outgroup members

**RELATIVE DEPRIVATION** discontent caused by the belief that we might fare badly in comparison with people in other groups

## MOTIVATIONAL FACTORS

Imagine you are going camping for the weekend with friends or family. When you get to the campsite, you find that there is a limited supply of hot water in the showers and very little firewood with which to start a campfire. Another group arrives late in the afternoon and pitches their tent next to yours. Are you more likely to welcome the new arrivals or suddenly become possessive over the firewood and the hot water? According to the **realistic group conflict theory**, when different groups are in competition for resources, they tend to close ranks and favour ingroup members while discriminating against outgroup members (Esses, Jackson, & Armstrong, 1998). Animosity between different racial groups and different genders is therefore a result of individuals' self-interest in terms of competition for land, wealth, or even jobs when the economy is in decline. During the Robbers Cave Experiment, the Rattlers and the Eagles became possessive over their campground and their baseball diamond as soon as an element of competition was introduced to the summer camp experience. In fact, there are a variety of sources of threat that lead to negative prejudiced attitudes against outgroups (Riek, Mania, & Gaertner, 2006).

In the current economic climate, you may have noticed an increase in grumblings about the number of immigrants coming to Canada and the United States and "taking our jobs," as well as a stronger push for tighter border controls. For example, Esses and her colleagues from the University of Western Ontario examined attitudes toward immigration following the 9/11 terrorist attacks. They reported that in the aftermath of these events, there would be increased prejudices associated with "foreigners" and a heightened sense of threat that would exacerbate negative views on immigration. Further, economic hardships as a result of terrorism and the political climate would lead to further competition for scarce resources (i.e., jobs), and also serve to increase negativity surrounding immigration policies (Esses, Dovidio, & Hodson, 2002). Further, when equally skilled and hardworking immigrants are able to compete effectively in the job market, greater threat is perceived, resulting in more prejudiced attitudes (e.g., Zárate, Garcia, Garza, & Hitlan, 2004). Threat also may lead us to revert to our own gender-stereotyped behaviours and preferences (i.e., men should be strong and in charge and women should be vulnerable and needing the support of a man) in order to maintain the status quo (Lau et al., 2008).

Discontent caused by the belief that we might fare badly in comparison with people in other groups is known as **relative deprivation**. For example, if you are told that you, as a Canadian, are unlikely to get accepted to your university of choice because the school is prioritizing applications from foreign students, you are more likely to hold prejudiced attitudes toward foreign students and support policies that limit the number of non-Canadian students at your university. This similar sense of deprivation can be seen in the sentiments of white Canadians who have lamented over difficulties getting jobs in city police departments or the Royal Canadian Mounted Police because these organizations are favouring applications from minorities and women. A blog post on September 24, 2010, titled "RCMP: You're White and Male? You Need Not Apply!" clearly reflects this sense of relative deprivation.

Relative deprivation describes the feeling of being threatened by another group; by the same token, we want to be part of a successful group. According to *social identity theory*, part of our self-esteem is derived from the groups to which we belong—when we affiliate with successful groups, our feelings of self-worth increase (Tajfel & Turner, 1986). Sporting events often arouse positive feelings of self-worth; you may have cheered when Sydney Crosby scored the game-winning goal for the Canadian Men's Hockey Team in the 2010 Olympic Gold Medal game against the United States, or witnessed the recent demonstration of national pride in Spain following the final of the 2010 soccer World Cup. Sometimes, it doesn't take much to identify as part of a group. This is shown through the *minimal ingroup paradigm*. Even members of randomly determined groups in which members are unfamiliar with each other feel connected and will show preference for one another (Tajfel & Billig, 1974).

The flipside of social identity theory is that although belonging to a particular group may help to build feelings of self-worth and self-esteem, it often occurs at the expense of outgroups. Derogating outgroup members leads to increases in self-esteem, especially when our ingroup is important to us (e.g., Branscombe & Wann, 1991; Hodson, Dovidio, & Esses, 2003). For example, one study found that threatening individuals' self-esteem by giving them false task-failure feedback automatically caused an increase in their tendency to stereotype others. When white students received negative feedback from an experimenter, they became more likely to make word completions related to black stereotypes than participants who received positive or no feedback. For example, they would be more likely to complete the stem –ITOR as *JANitor* rather than *MONitor*. It seems that, unfortunately, negative evaluations of those who belong to stereotyped groups can serve to restore our damaged self-esteem (Spencer, Fein, Wolfe, Fong, & Dunn, 1998; Fein & Spencer, 1997). Logically, one might conclude that people with high self-esteem need not participate in ingroup favouritism; however, it appears that the opposite is true. Research suggests that people with high self-esteem favour their own groups to a greater extent than those who have low self-esteem (Aberson, Healy, & Romero, 2000).

What factors affect our tendency to put down other groups and strongly favour our own? The practices of ingroup favouritism and outgroup derogation are more likely to occur under three specific conditions. *First, being part of a small minority ingroup inspires greater group loyalty* than being part of a majority group because members feel unique (Brewer & Pickett, 1999). Have you ever heard of a White Studies Club? How about the Heterosexual Historical Society? Chances are these groups do not exist because people in majority groups are unable to distinguish themselves from the masses through their skin colour or sexuality. However, you have probably noticed an Asian students union; a lesbian, gay, bisexual, and transgender community centre; or a muslim community association in your local area. Second, a person's status within a group can also influence how likely she is to put down members of outgroups. *Those with marginal status are more likely to derogate others,* particularly in front of ingroup members. A study by Noel, Wann, and Branscombe (1995) found that peripheral members of fraternities and sororities were more likely to put down outgroups in public than in private, presumably because they wanted to demonstrate their group-oriented behaviour to core fraternity or sorority members in order to gain acceptance. Finally, *when ingroups as a whole feel threatened with inferiority, they are more likely to take pleasure in another group's failure*—a concept known as intergroup schadenfreude. For example, during a study of Dutch soccer fans, researchers found that participants took greater pleasure in the defeat of Germany (their neighbour and rival) in the 1998 soccer World Cup quarterfinals when they were reminded that their own team also had lost games; thus their status as a superior ingroup was threatened (Leach, Spears, Branscombe, & Doosje, 2003).

## Moods and Emotions

Most of us would be horrified to think that being in a good mood might bring out subconscious prejudices within us; however, research suggests that both positive and negative emotions may affect our ability to think clearly, resulting in a tendency to resort to preconceived stereotypes (e.g., Fordham & Ketteridge, 1998). For example, when we are in a good mood, we are less likely to think things through carefully. Whereas negative emotions such as sadness indicate that we need to pay close attention to people around us, positive emotions such as happiness imply that systematic processing is unnecessary (Schwarz, 1990).

This is just like persuasion. Recall what you learned in Chapter 7—when we're happy, we don't want to think too much. Researchers tested this theory by inducing mood states in a group of participants (Bodenhausen, Kramer, & Süsser, 1994). Some were asked to write about happy past experiences (inducing a positive mood condition), while others were asked to write about neutral experiences (inducing a neutral mood condition). The participants were then presented with a description of a student allegedly involved in misconduct (such as assaulting someone or cheating on a test). When asked to rate the student's guilt, participants in happy moods were more likely than those in neutral moods to rate "Juan Garcia" guilty compared with the identical "John Garner." Another study found that students who had been put in positive moods by being given favourable feedback about a previous task were more likely to shoot Muslim targets in a computer game than students in neutral moods (Unkelbach, Forgas, & Denson, 2007).

Negative moods can also affect our tendencies to resort to stereotypes. Emotions that

<<< **According to the realistic group conflict theory,** competition between groups increases when resources are scarce, **which can lead to negative feelings.**

^^^ Members of small minority groups tend to feel greater loyalty than individuals in majority groups **because members of the minority group feel unique.**

arouse us (i.e., anger or fear) reduce the amount of cognitive resources available to us and limit our ability to think clearly and logically, thus increasing the likelihood of stereotyping. A study by Wilder (1993) showed that people who are anxious are less likely to differentiate among members of a group and will assimilate a deviant member into the group as a whole rather than acknowledging the individual as a contradiction of the stereotype. Similarly, Brock University researchers Hodson and Costello (2007) found that sensitivity to disgust leads to more negative attitudes toward outgroups, and in particular those concerning immigrants, foreigners, and anyone classified as socially deviant. Other emotional states may also affect our judgment—as noted earlier, when we are feeling low about ourselves, we are more likely to derogate others.

## What Are the Consequences of Stereotyping?

Are there any real dangers to stereotyping? Most psychologists would argue "yes," as the practice of pigeonholing others into specific categories influences our perception of other people and affects our behaviours, as well as the behaviours of the stereotyped groups. To illustrate the first point, researchers Darley and Gross (1983) asked subjects to rate the academic ability of a young girl named Hannah, who was shown on video taking an achievement test. The subjects were led to believe that Hannah came from either a high or a low socioeconomic background. Those who believed that Hannah came from a higher socioeconomic background rated her as having significantly higher motivation and cognitive skills than those who believed she came from a lower socioeconomic background. Even though the material shown on the video was ambiguous (Hannah answered some questions correctly and some incorrectly), the subjects cited specific elements of her behaviour during the test as "evidence" of her ability level.

**STEREOTYPE THREAT** fear or anxiety held by people in minority groups that they might conform to a negative cultural stereotype

Our tendency to search for information that supports our initial viewpoint is known as confirmation bias. For example, in the "Little Hannah" study described previously, participants already believed that children from higher socioeconomic groups were more capable than children from lower socioeconomic groups and looked for information in the video to support their beliefs. We are guilty of using confirmation bias every time we get stuck behind a particularly slow mother and child at a supermarket checkout and conclude that all mothers with young children will delay us in a line. In reality, the situation may have occurred only a handful of times, but our natural instinct is to remember stereotype-consistent information and forget or ignore stereotype-inconsistent facts, such as the times when we encounter a highly efficient family at a checkout, a polite teenager, or a capable elderly driver (e.g., Ensslen & Peace, 2010; Lyons & Kashima, 2003).

Stereotyping not only influences our perception of other people; it can ultimately lead us to interact with people in ways that influence their behaviour. When this occurs, it is known as a *self-fulfilling prophecy*—a belief that causes itself to be true. For example, Rosenthal and Jacobson's (1968) "bloomers" study discussed in previous chapters demonstrated how teachers treated children who had been identified as "gifted" differently than those who had not. As a result, when the students who had been singled out were retested at the end of the school year, the researchers discovered that their IQ scores had risen by 10 to 20 points. Although in this instance, the self-fulfilling prophecy brought about a positive impact, in many cases, it can limit people as a result of others' negative expectations. For example, research demonstrated that nonverbal cues from interviewers elicited poor performance of job applicants (Word, Zanna, & Cooper, 1979). Studies also have shown that men in high-power positions give subordinate women fewer assignments than their male counterparts and generally have lower expectations of them in the workplace (e.g., Vescio, Gervais, Snyder, & Hoover, 2005). As a result, women in subordinate positions feel less confident and their performances suffer, fulfilling their bosses' expectations that they are not as competent as their male peers. For example, in a study by researchers at Queen's University, the interactions of nurses and physicians were examined in relation to gender (Zelek & Phillips, 2003). The authors reported that sex-role stereotypes influenced behaviour, including the fact that nurses felt they had to work harder and tended to defer to male physicians more often than if the physician was female. Every time we talk down to someone of a different race, treat an elderly person as frail and incompetent, or patronize someone with a physical disability, we are helping to create a self-fulfilling prophecy.

### STEREOTYPE THREAT

A further consequence of stereotyping is **stereotype threat**, or being at risk of confirming the negative stereotype about a group one belongs to.

<<< Could your happy mood inadvertently **cause you to rely on stereotypes?**

**Stereotyping and Prejudice**

**Social Learning**
- punishment or reward for behaviour
- observation of others' behaviour

**Cognitive Bias**
- outgroup homogeneity
- ingroup favouritism

**Motivational Factors**
- realistic group conflict theory
- social identity theory
- mood and emotion



**Sources of Stereotyping and Prejudice.** Stereotyping and prejudice **originate from several different sources.**

For example, although he might not believe it, a person from a low socioeconomic group may be aware that societal expectations with regard to his career prospects are extremely low; people would not generally expect someone who grew up in "the hood" to become the CEO of a high-ranking company. As a result, that person may feel additional pressure when he attends a job interview, negatively impacting his performance during the interview. A study by Steele and Aronson (1995) gave black and white college students at Stanford University a difficult test using items from a standardized verbal exam. One group of students was told that their performance on the exam would prove to be a good indicator of their underlying intellectual abilities, while a second group was told that the test was simply a problem-solving exercise and was not diagnostic of ability. The results showed that black students performed equally well as white students when the test was non-diagnostic but much worse when they believed the test was indicative of their intelligence levels. Steele and Aronson (1995) concluded that the black students, while just as intelligent as their white counterparts, performed worse when their racial identity was made salient.

Similar results have been found with other stereotyped groups. When researchers showed male and female undergraduates (all of whom were good at math) a set of six television commercials before asking them to complete a difficult math test, the female undergraduates' performance on the test differed according to the content of the commercials they had seen. Those who were shown commercials containing female stereotypes (i.e., an advertisement depicting a woman so excited about an acne product that she bounced on her bed) scored lower than their male peers on the test, whereas those who were shown counter-stereotypical commercials (i.e., an advertisement showing a woman exhibiting detailed knowledge of auto engineering) scored equally high (Davies, Spencer, Quinn, & Gerhardstein, 2002). In fact, gender stereotypes about performance on stereotypically "gendered" abilities such

We have a tendency to remember information that supports preconceived stereotypes, **but are they always correct?**

as math and science for men and arts and sociology for women have been the focus of much research on stereotype threat (e.g., Spencer, Steele, & Quinn, 1999; Steele, Reisz, Williams, & Kawakami, 2007). While this effect is consistent across conditions where stereotypes are activated, research also has demonstrated that stereotype threat can be reversed if participants are told information that contradicts the stereotype (Steele, Spencer, & Aronson, 2002).

# How Can We Combat Stereotyping and Prejudice?

Is anyone immune to stereotyping? Recent research indicates that one particular group of people might be able to avoid forming racial stereotypes. A study of 20 children with the neurological disorder Williams Syndrome (WS) found that the youngsters did not engage in racial bias about other ethnic groups (Santos, Meyer-Lindenberg, & Deruelle, 2010). Twenty children with the disorder and 20 children who did not have WS were asked to associate pictures of light-skinned and dark-skinned people with characters in stories. Children without WS tended to associate positive characteristics with pictures of light-skinned children and negative characteristics with pictures of dark-skinned children, whereas children with the disorder showed no signs of racial bias. Since the youngsters with WS retained the same patterns of gender stereotyping shown in other children, the researchers speculated that racial bias stems from a different brain process. People with WS show abnormal activity in the amygdala—the part of the brain involved in responding to social threats and triggering unconscious negative emotional reactions to people of a different race. Racial stereotypes, therefore, are likely linked to social fear. Although the results of the Williams syndrome study may provide us with valuable information about the causes of stereotypes and prejudice (and possible solutions to help combat them), the research is preliminary and will need to be replicated in larger samples and among different age groups before reliable conclusions can be drawn (see Chapter 2 for more information about research methods).

The brain's preference for automatic processing that leads to snap judgments about outgroups and favouritism toward ingroups is strong,

Anxiety caused by the belief that we might inadvertently conform to a negative cultural stereotype may affect our performance at school and in the workplace.

**CONTACT HYPOTHESIS** the belief that increased communication and contact between different racial groups reduces levels of prejudice and discrimination

and it can lead to biases that we aren't fully aware are there. Several techniques, however, can help combat the stereotypes that lead to discrimination and prejudice against others, such as increased equal contact with people in minority groups, increased interdependence between groups, better education, and improved personal motivation. Apologies in the aftermath of prejudice and discrimination also play an important role. Most of the techniques rely on harnessing the more effortful controlled processing that forces us to look objectively at the world around us rather than making an easy, quick assessment.

## CONTACT HYPOTHESIS

As the Clarks demonstrated with the "doll test" in the 1940s (referred to earlier in this chapter), racial segregation reinforces discrimination and causes children who are considered members of an outgroup to develop a sense of inferiority and self-hatred. Conversely, the **contact hypothesis** argues that increased communication and equal contact between different racial groups reduces levels of prejudice and discrimination. For example, in a study of two public housing projects in New York City that were desegregated in the late 1940s, researchers found that randomly selected white housewives held their black neighbours in higher esteem and were considerably more in favour of interracial housing (75 percent to 25 percent) than housewives who lived in segregated developments (Deutsch & Collins, 1951). However, other studies showed little decrease in prejudice following desegregation, with some even noting an increase (see Wong, 2011). In a review of existing data on the contact hypothesis, Pettigrew and his colleagues have concluded that contact situations that fostered the development of friendship are the most likely to reduce prejudice (Pettigrew, 1998; Pettigrew & Tropp, 2000). For example, York University researchers found that approach behaviours (i.e., asking another person for assistance, engaging in conversation) fostered a reduction in implicit racial biases (Kawakami, Phills, Steele, & Dovidio, 2007). Approach behaviours are likely interpreted as positive in connotation and friendly, relative to merely "exposure." Friendship interpretations are important because they generate positive orientations, such as empathy, and reduce negative emotions, such as anxiety (Pettigrew, 1998). Contact, in and of itself, is not sufficient to reduce prejudice, and in some cases can actually increase prejudice. For example, prisoners who are exposed to multi-racial situations where contact is forced, negative, and within confined locations may experience an increase in prejudiced attitudes (e.g., Casciani, 2003; Dhont & Van Hiel, 2009). That said, Hodson (2008) reported that when individuals who have a social dominance orientation are exposed to other racial groups in conditions favourable for positive interactions—even within prisons—ingroup biases decrease.

## GROUP INTERDEPENDENCE

In 1954, Gordon Allport theorized that increased contact between minority groups was not sufficient to reduce prejudice, but decreased prejudice may occur in four conditions: when both groups have equal status within a situation, when they have institutional support (e.g., the support of laws, authorities, or customs), when there is intergroup cooperation, and when both groups have common goals (Allport, 1954). The Robbers Cave Experiment provides a useful example of the last two conditions; when the camp's water supply was shut down and both the Eagles and the Rattlers had to work together in order to fix an outlet faucet, the two

**JIGSAW CLASSROOM TECHNIQUE** a teaching method that focuses on small-group activities and fosters a cooperative rather than competitive environment

teams celebrated their joint success without name calling or bickering about which group should get a drink first. These instances of cooperation demonstrate what are called superordinate goals—goals that require cooperation from all members of a group in order to succeed (Gaertner et al., 2000). This method of intergroup cooperation is used within today's classrooms to reduce racial conflict and promote better learning. The **jigsaw classroom technique**, developed by Aronson and colleagues (1978), uses a cooperative jigsaw structure, in which each student's role is essential for the successful completion of a project. For example, imagine you are testing children on past prime ministers of Canada (e.g., Trudeau, Mulroney, Chrétien), and each member of the group is given a piece of information on each former PM. In order for the group (and its individual members) to succeed, they need to share information with each other. This encourages both contact and cooperation, and has been found to improve intergroup relations (Gaertner et al., 2000).

> "Contact situations that fostered the development of friendship are the most likely to reduce prejudice **because friendship tends to generate positive orientations, such as empathy, and reduce negative emotions, such as anxiety.**"

## EDUCATION

Stereotyping can be reduced through training and education. Recall our discussion earlier in this chapter about how schoolteacher Jane Elliott decided to give her class a lesson about discrimination based on eye colour. After telling students that people with blue eyes were clever, quick, and likely to succeed, whereas people with brown eyes were untrustworthy, lazy, and stupid, she divided the class into blue-eyed and brown-eyed children and laid out a set of rules in which the superior group had extra privileges. Elliott discovered that the children's attitudes quickly changed: blue-eyed students became arrogant and behaved aggressively toward brown-eyed children on the playground, while brown-eyed children became timid and subdued. When Elliott told the class a few days later that she had made a mistake and swapped the colour superiorities around, the same situation happened in reverse (Tozer, Violas, & Senese, 1993).

Research shows that participating in demonstrations of discrimination such as the one described here is an effective technique for reducing prejudice. However, it is important for people to actually participate in an exercise. Merely watching a lecture or a video does not seem to change prejudiced attitudes (Byrnes & Kiger, 1990). In fact, Aboud and Doyle (1996) found that children who display high-prejudiced attitudes demonstrate *decreases* in negative racial attitudes following discussions with a low-prejudiced friend who emphasizes cross-racial similarities. Other types of education include training in statistical reasoning to learn about how we often mistakenly pair two things together. On a computer simulation task, police officers are initially more likely to shoot unarmed black suspects than unarmed white suspects, but following repeated computer training that shows a lack of connection between a suspect's race and the likelihood that he or she is carrying a weapon, officers are able to eliminate racial bias (Plant, Peruche, & Butz, 2005). Another study demonstrated that diversity training can reduce implicit racial prejudice. Researchers found evidence that participants' cognitive processes actually changed as stereotyping was reduced (Rudman, Ashmore, & Gary, 2001). A variety of programs are now available that teach both children and adults about group categorizations, diversity, similarity, and culturally relevant factors that aid in reducing intergroup bias (Stephan & Vogt, 2004).

## MOTIVATION

Can we become less prejudiced simply by choosing to do so? Although stereotyping is (to an extent) an automatic response, being motivated to reduce our reliance on stereotypes is a key factor in eliminating prejudice. For example, a study was conducted in which participants were asked to decide whether an object presented along with a black face or a white face was related to sports. The researchers found that, although participants tended to misidentify neutral objects as sports-related when depicted with black faces, this bias could be eliminated with training. The researchers also noted that participants who were highly motivated to respond without prejudice were especially effective at eliminating the bias (Peruche & Plant, 2006).

Sometimes, when people are made aware of their stereotypical attitudes, they will make a conscious effort to change their beliefs and behaviours. Monteith's (1993) research suggests that low-prejudiced individuals who are made aware of their prejudiced responses feel a strong sense of guilt and self-dissatisfaction and subsequently make an effort to inhibit responses to racist or homosexual jokes. Even high-prejudiced individuals who are confronted about their prejudiced comments are less likely to espouse their views in the future. However, their motivation usually stems from a desire to avoid being perceived by others as prejudiced, rather than a desire to eliminate prejudice itself (Plant & Devine, 1998). In general, though, an awareness of the language we use and the comments we make can reduce the use of stereotypes, especially if we have a personal desire to do so. Further, researchers at the University of Western Ontario have found that activating non-prejudiced goals and egalitarianism-related views can create cognitive inconsistencies that may prompt behaviour change. As such, when people are made aware of their prejudiced attitudes, cognitive dissonance can be used to change either the attitude or the behaviour (Gawronski, Peters, Brochu, & Strack, 2008).

## THE ROLE OF APOLOGY

While the above techniques can be useful in preventing or reducing prejudice *before* it occurs, apologies have often been required in the aftermath of discriminatory behaviour. For example, formal governmental apologies have been issued following cases of historical injustice and racism, such as the Indian residential school system and Japanese work camps in Canada (discussed in the chapter opener). Although apologies have been issued for such wrongs, do they make a difference in intergroup relations? In a review of apology literature, Blatz and Philpot (2010) identify that apologies to wronged groups can lead to forgiveness, but only under certain circumstances. Philpot and Hornsey (2008) found that for incidents that were recent and unintended (e.g., friendly fire incidents between U.S. and Canadian soldiers in Afghanistan), apologies can be effective in reducing prejudice and animosity. However, when apologies were offered for historical and intentional abuses, they did little to promote forgiveness. Intentionality is just one of the moderators of the effectiveness of apologies.

Apologies also are influenced by the extent to which the wrongdoers express remorse, the time lapsed since the harm, the level of empathy expressed, the sincerity of the apology, and the offending party's acknowledgment of responsibility for their actions. As you can imagine, insincere apologies that lack remorse are viewed as more of an insult and may seem to perpetuate covert racism. Fontaine (1998) discussed an article published in the *Alberta Report* following the federal government's official apology for the abuse and mistreatment of Aboriginal children sent to residential schools, titled "The Holocaust That Never Happened," which displayed an image of smiling Aboriginal children at school. These types of behaviours lead to an increased divide and a sense that apologies are intended as public tokens of "feeling sorry" while modern covert racism still exists. That said, apologies can increase positive thoughts toward other groups and lead to improved intergroup relations (Blatz, Schumann, & Ross, 2009). Genuine apologies and attempts to amend for past wrongs can reduce feelings of victimization (see Wohl, Hornsey, & Bennett, 2011). For example, Canada is in the process of building the Canadian Museum for Human Rights in Winnipeg, to acknowledge past wrongs, promote education, and prevent future injustices.

While stereotypes, prejudice, and discrimination occur, we hope that use of these techniques, along with education regarding negative attitudes and behaviour, can help to reduce intergroup conflict.

## ACTION LEARNING

### The Jigsaw Classroom

Following the desegregation of schools in both Canada and the United States, Aronson and his colleagues noted that the fear and distrust felt by various racial groups toward each other was being fuelled by a competitive element within the classroom. They shifted the emphasis from competition to cooperation by developing a learning technique in which classes were divided into small groups that were diversified in terms of race, ethnicity, and gender. Each student within the group was responsible for one specific part of a project and, just as in a jigsaw puzzle, each student's part was essential for the successful completion of the project. Once the students had completed their research, they had to report back to the rest of their group, encouraging each member to listen to one another in order to learn the necessary material. The researchers noted that this new method encouraged children who were typically unwilling to speak up in class to participate, increasing their self-confidence. It also encouraged children who would usually ridicule others to help them out for the sake of the group, fostering better group relations. Aronson's jigsaw technique has since been used in many other settings, including businesses, in order to facilitate social learning, increase self-confidence, and reduce stereotyping and prejudice.

Select a group that you would like to work with—maybe a campus club, members of your dormitory, or children in a local school. Choose a skill or an idea that would be worthwhile to learn and divide participants into small groups. Assign individuals within each group a task, making sure that the number of tasks is equivalent to the actual number of individuals. Once the tasks are complete, have the groups reunite to share their new knowledge with one another, and then have the entire group come back together to share what they have learned. How did this technique work out? Did you find that individuals and groups cooperated well together? What are the advantages of using this method?

What you will learn from this action project:

1. Learn how to implement a technique to foster cooperation among individuals.
2. Learn how to reduce competitive instincts within a large-group setting.
3. Get firsthand experience with a social psychologically tested concept to reduce stereotyping.

If you would like to learn more about the jigsaw classroom, visit www.jigsaw.org.

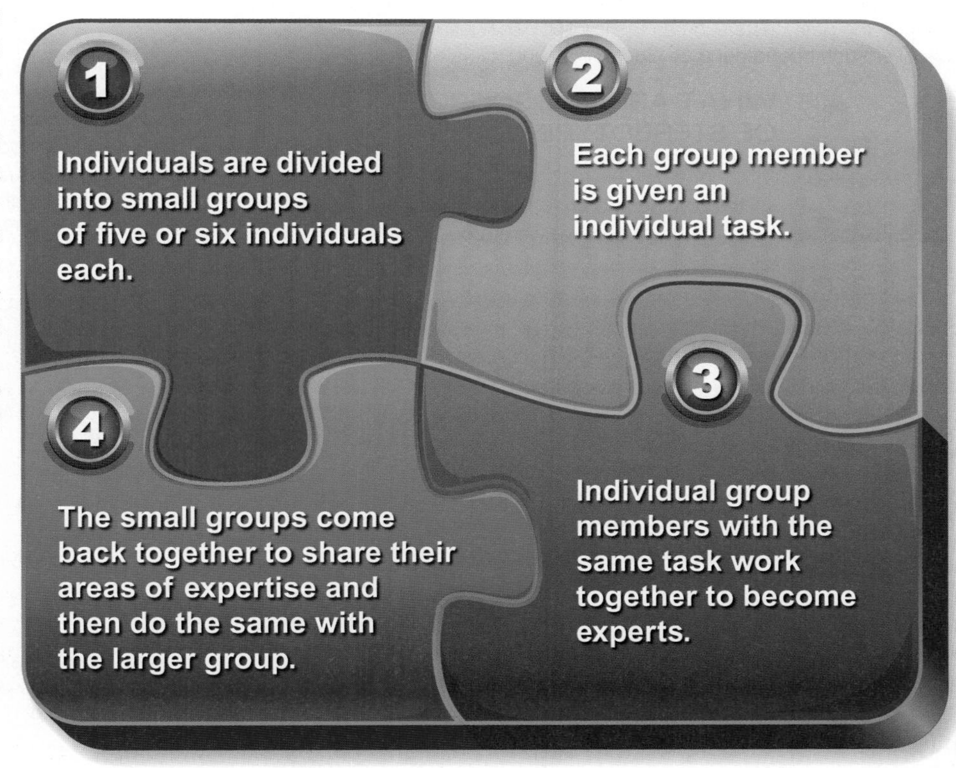

1
Individuals are divided into small groups of five or six individuals each.
2
Each group member is given an individual task.
3
Individual group members with the same task work together to become experts.
4
The small groups come back together to share their areas of expertise and then do the same with the larger group.


>>> **The Jigsaw Classroom. The jigsaw classroom technique** fosters cooperation and reduces stereotyping and prejudice.

CHAPTER
# 10 Review

## Summary

### WHAT ARE STEREOTYPES, PREJUDICE, AND DISCRIMINATION? p. 178

- Prejudice is a negative learned attitude toward particular groups of people. Prejudice often leads to discrimination, or negative behaviour directed toward members of a particular group. Common types of prejudice are racial prejudice and gender prejudice.
- Stereotypes may bias our perceptions and responses even if we do not personally agree with them. Neurological studies indicate that people have a natural tendency to classify others as part of a racial "ingroup" or "outgroup." This often translates into real-world behaviours, such as racial profiling.
- Overt discrimination still occurs, as seen in the existence of hate groups and hate crimes. However, it is less common in modern society. Covert prejudice and aversive racism are still prevalent in our society, and often involve various forms of racism and sexism.

### HOW DO WE MEASURE STEREOTYPES, PREJUDICE, AND DISCRIMINATION? p. 183

- The discussion of stereotypes goes back to the difference between automatic and controlled processing, as stereotyping is a function of the quicker automatic processing. Researchers have found different measures of stereotyping and racism in the distinction between old-fashioned and modern racism.
- Covert measures of prejudice work to uncover bias that is unconscious, and often unintended. While some people say prejudice is a thing of the past, tests such as the Implicit Association Test help to uncover such phenomena as hidden bias and aversive racism.

### WHAT ARE THE SOURCES OF STEREOTYPING AND PREJUDICE? p. 184

- Stereotyping and prejudice originate from several different sources: how we were brought up, the way that our brains classify individuals as part of an ingroup or an outgroup, and motivating factors such as group competition and individual emotional status.
- Groups are motivated to compete for resources, such as jobs, land, or wealth. When resources are scarce, groups tend to close ranks, favouring ingroup members and discriminating against outgroup members.

### WHAT ARE THE CONSEQUENCES OF STEREOTYPING? p. 189

- Stereotyping influences our perception of people and their behaviour. Our natural instinct is to remember stereotype-consistent information but to ignore information that contradicts the stereotype. When we interact with people based on a preconceived stereotype, we influence their behaviour, creating a self-fulfilling prophecy.
- A further consequence of stereotyping is stereotype threat, or the fear held by people in minority groups that they might conform to a negative cultural stereotype. Anxiety caused by stereotype threat affects people's performances at school and in the workplace.

### HOW CAN WE COMBAT STEREOTYPING AND PREJUDICE? p. 191

- We can attempt to combat stereotypes and prejudice using four different techniques: increased contact with people in minority groups, increased interdependence between groups, better education, and improved personal motivation. Apologies for historical injustices can help to ease group tensions, but only if they are perceived as genuine and perpetrators take responsibility for their actions.
- The jigsaw classroom is one example of increasing interdependence between groups. Students work in a cooperative rather than competitive environment, gaining self-confidence and learning how to work with people from different racial and ethnic groups.

## Key Terms

**ambivalent sexism** the contradictory attitudes of hostile sexism and benevolent sexism *182*

**authoritarian personality** a personality type that favours obedience to authority and intolerance of people lower in status *185*

**aversive racism** the attitudes of people who openly endorse egalitarian views but discriminate in ways they're able to rationalize *179*

**contact hypothesis** the belief that increased communication and contact between different racial groups reduces levels of prejudice and discrimination *191*

**discrimination** a behaviour directed toward a group of people based solely on their membership in that group *178*

**gender prejudice** the tendency to hold a hostile attitude toward an individual because of his or her gender *181*

**gender stereotypes** people's ideas about how men and women behave based on socially and culturally defined beliefs *181*

**ingroup favouritism** the natural tendency to favour an ingroup versus an outgroup *186*

**jigsaw classroom technique** a teaching method that focuses on small-group activities and fosters a cooperative rather than competitive environment *192*

**just-world hypothesis** the tendency for people to believe that the world is fair and just; therefore, victims of misfortune deserve what happens to them *187*

**modern (or covert) racism** negative feelings toward a group of people based on their race, manifested in more subtle forms of racism *184*

**modern sexism** internalized negative feelings toward a group of people based on their gender, characterized by a denial of continued discrimination, antagonism toward women's demands, and lack of support for policies designed to help women in work and education *184*

**old-fashioned (or overt) racism** overt, oppressive acts and feelings toward a group of people based on their race *184*

**old-fashioned sexism** overt sexism, characterized by the endorsement of traditional gender roles, differential treatment of men and women, and stereotypes about lesser female competence *184*

**outgroup homogeneity effect** the tendency to see outgroup members as similar to one another but ingroup members as diverse individuals *186*

**prejudice** a negative learned attitude toward particular groups of people *178*

**racial prejudice** the tendency to hold a hostile attitude toward an individual because of his or her racial background *181*

**racism** an institutional practice that discriminates against individuals on the basis of their race *180*

**realistic group conflict theory** the idea that when different groups are in competition for resources, they tend to close ranks, favouring ingroup members and discriminating against outgroup members *187*

**relative deprivation** discontent caused by the belief that we might fare badly in comparison with people in other groups *187*

**sexism** an institutional practice that discriminates against individuals on the basis of their gender *180*

**social categorization** the process of dividing people into categories according to their race, gender, and other common attributes *185*

**social dominance orientation** seeing one's own group as naturally superior to other groups *186*

**stereotype** a belief about the characteristics of a group of people ok to have two entries for this term? *178*

**stereotype threat** fear or anxiety held by people in minority groups that they might conform to a negative cultural stereotype *189*

**ultimate attribution error** the tendency to explain the behaviour of groups in terms of internal dispositional factors, without taking the situational constraints into consideration *186*

# Test Your Understanding

## MULTIPLE CHOICE

1. Which of the following is an example of modern racism?
   - **a.** dismissing the idea that racism exists in today's culture
   - **b.** supporting the segregation of white people and black people
   - **c.** refusing to hire a person of an ethnic minority because of the colour of his or her skin
   - **d.** banning people of a particular race from a restaurant or other business

2. Ambivalent sexism is most likely to occur
   - **a.** in developed countries.
   - **b.** in developing countries.
   - **c.** in countries where men and women have equal rights and equal opportunities.
   - **d.** in countries where there is a high degree of economic and political inequality between the sexes.

3. Which of these statements about stereotyping is NOT true?
   - **a.** We form stereotypes very early on in life.
   - **b.** Stereotyping is avoidable if children are taught early in life.
   - **c.** Awareness of a stereotype in the media is enough to activate it in real life.
   - **d.** Stereotyping is an automatic process that helps us classify people and objects.

4. What does the Implicit Association Test (IAT) primarily measure?
   - **a.** gender bias
   - **b.** racial bias
   - **c.** political bias
   - **d.** age bias

5. Stereotyping and prejudice can originate from all of the following except
   - **a.** social learning.
   - **b.** cognitive bias.
   - **c.** geographical origin.
   - **d.** motivational factors.

6. The inability to accurately distinguish people of other races results from
   - **a.** ingroup favouritism.
   - **b.** ultimate attribution error.
   - **c.** the just-world hypothesis.
   - **d.** the outgroup homogeneity effect.

7. Terry's classmates have been hiking all morning and decide to stop for lunch at the same time as another group. When Terry's teacher enters the shop, she notices that there are not enough sandwiches for both groups. Because there are only enough sandwiches for one group, Terry's group starts to make comments about the competitiveness of the second group. At the same time, the other group starts calling Terry's group names because they are buying up all the sandwiches. This demonstrates
   - **a.** the realistic group conflict theory.
   - **b.** intergroup schadenfreude.
   - **c.** social identity theory.
   - **d.** the contact hypothesis.

8. If we are in a good mood, we are
   - **a.** less likely to stereotype others.
   - **b.** more likely to stereotype others.
   - **c.** unable to stereotype others.
   - **d.** equally likely to stereotype others.

9. Which of these techniques does not help to combat stereotyping and prejudice?
   - **a.** increased contact with people in minority groups
   - **b.** increased interdependence between groups
   - **c.** increased personal motivation
   - **d.** increased competition between groups

10. Hannah walks past a homeless man on the street and tells herself that he is probably a drug addict who is entirely responsible for his own situation. Hannah is using
    - **a.** the just-world hypothesis.
    - **b.** confirmation bias.
    - **c.** the contact hypothesis.
    - **d.** a stereotype threat.

**ANSWERS**: 1. a; 2. d; 3. b; 4. b; 5. c; 6. d; 7. a; 8. b; 9. d; 10. a

## ESSAY RESPONSE

1. What are the differences between old-fashioned prejudice (for example, old-fashioned racism and old-fashioned sexism) and modern prejudice? Provide an example of each.
2. Describe the main principles of the jigsaw classroom technique and explain how it utilizes one of the four methods used to combat prejudice.
3. Explain how social categorization contributes to the formation and reinforcement of stereotypes.
4. Describe the advantages and disadvantages of belonging to an ingroup. Include examples of the outgroup homogeneity effect and ingroup favouritism in your answer.
5. Explain how our perceptions of other people may result in a self-fulfilling prophecy. Include an example of a self-fulfilling prophecy in your answer.

## APPLY IT!

Find a newspaper or magazine article that discusses the consequences of gender prejudice around the world (e.g., sex-selective abortion in India or China). What are the long-term implications of such prejudice? What measures are being taken to prevent it?

**Remember to check www.thethinkspot.ca for additional information, downloadable flashcards, and other helpful resources.**

# THINK READINGS

Based on your reading of the research presented in Chapter 10, what are other potential variables that could impact this relationship?

Were you raised in an environment where people openly discussed race? What role do you think cognitive dissonance (see Chapter 6) played in the discomfort these parents felt?

NEWSWEEK

## See Baby Discriminate

By PO BRONSON AND ASHLEY MERRYMAN

Published: September 5, 2009

Kids as young as 6 months judge others based on skin color. What's a parent to do?

At the Children's Research Lab at the University of Texas, a database is kept on thousands of families in the Austin area who have volunteered to be available for scholarly research. In 2006 Birgitte Vittrup recruited from the database about a hundred families, all of whom were Caucasian with a child 5 to 7 years old.

The goal of Vittrup's study was to learn if typical children's videos with multicultural storylines have any beneficial effect on children's racial attitudes. Her first step was to give the children a Racial Attitude Measure, which asked such questions as:

How many White people are nice?
(Almost all) (A lot) (Some)
(Not many) (None)
How many Black people are nice?
(Almost all) (A lot) (Some)
(Not many) (None)

During the test, the descriptive adjective "nice" was replaced with more than 20 other adjectives, like "dishonest," "pretty," "curious," and "snobby."

Vittrup sent a third of the families home with multiculturally themed videos for a week, such as an episode of *Sesame Street* in which characters visit an African-American family's home, and an episode of *Little Bill,* where the entire neighborhood comes together to clean the local park.

In truth, Vittrup didn't expect that children's racial attitudes would change very much just from watching these videos. Prior research had shown that multicultural curricula in schools have far less impact than we intend them to—largely because the implicit message "We're all friends" is too vague for young children to understand that it refers to skin color.

Yet Vittrup figured explicit conversations with parents could change that. So a second group of families got the videos, and Vittrup told these parents to use them as the jumping-off point for a discussion about interracial friendship. She provided a checklist of points to make, echoing the shows' themes.

"I really believed it was going to work," Vittrup recalls.

The last third were also given the checklist of topics, but no videos. These parents were to discuss racial equality on their own, every night for five nights.

At this point, something interesting happened. Five families in the last group abruptly quit the study. Two directly told Vittrup, "We don't want to have these conversations with our child. We don't want to point out skin color."

Vittrup was taken aback—these families volunteered knowing full well it was a study of children's racial attitudes. Yet once they were aware that the study required talking openly about race, they started dropping out.

It was no surprise that in a liberal city like Austin, every parent was a welcoming multiculturalist, embracing diversity. But according to Vittrup's entry surveys, hardly any of these white parents had ever talked to their children directly about race. They might have asserted vague principles—like "Everybody's equal" or "God made all of us" or "Under the skin, we're all the same"—but they'd almost never called attention to racial differences.

They wanted their children to grow up colorblind. But Vittrup's first test of the kids revealed they weren't colorblind at all. Asked how many white people are mean, these children commonly answered, "Almost none." Asked how many blacks are mean, many answered, "Some," or "A lot." Even kids who attended diverse schools answered the questions this way.

More disturbing, Vittrup also asked all the kids a very



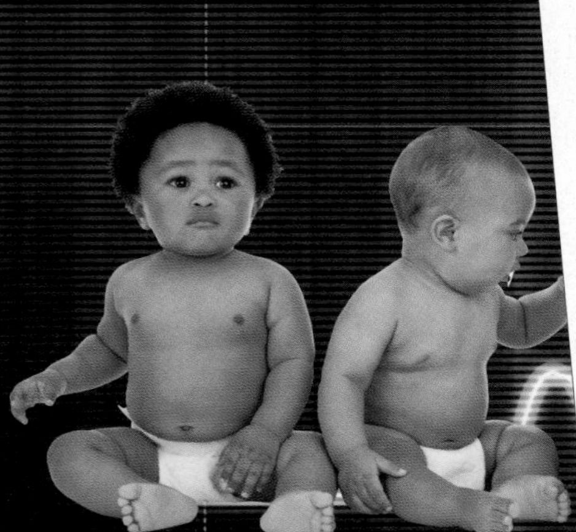

blunt question: "Do your parents like black people?" Fourteen percent said outright, "No, my parents don't like black people"; 38 percent of the kids answered, "I don't know." In this supposed race-free vacuum being created by parents, kids were left to improvise their own conclusions—many of which would be abhorrent to their parents.

Vittrup hoped the families she'd instructed to talk about race would follow through. After watching the videos, the families returned to the Children's Research Lab for retesting. To Vittrup's complete surprise, the three groups of children were statistically the same—none, as a group, had budged very much in their racial attitudes. At first glance, the study was a failure.

Combing through the parents' study diaries, Vittrup realized why. Diary after diary revealed that the parents barely mentioned the checklist items. Many just couldn't talk about race, and they quickly reverted to the vague "Everybody's equal" phrasing.

Of all those Vittrup told to talk openly about interracial friendship, only six families managed to actually do so. And, for all six, their children dramatically improved their racial attitudes in a single week. Talking about race was clearly key. Reflecting later about the study, Vittrup said, "A lot of parents came to me afterwards and admitted they just didn't know what to say to their kids, and they didn't want the wrong thing coming out of the mouth of their kids."

We all want our children to be unintimidated by differences and have the social skills necessary for a diverse world. The question is, do we make it worse, or do we make it better, by calling attention to race?

The election of President Barack Obama marked the beginning of a new era in race relations in the United States—but it didn't resolve the question as to what we should tell children about race. Many parents have explicitly pointed out Obama's brown skin to their young children, to reinforce the message that anyone can rise to become a leader, and anyone—regardless of skin color—can be a friend, be loved, and be admired.

Others think it's better to say nothing at all about the president's race or ethnicity—because saying something about it unavoidably teaches a child a racial construct. They worry that even a positive statement ("It's wonderful that a black person can be president") still encourages a child to see divisions within society. For the early formative years, at least, they believe we should let children know a time when skin color does not matter.

What parents say depends heavily on their own race: a 2007 study in the *Journal of Marriage and Family* found that out of 17,000 families with kindergartners, nonwhite parents are about three times more likely to discuss race than white parents; 75 percent of the latter never, or almost never, talk about race.

In our new book, *NurtureShock*, we argue that many modern strategies for nurturing children are backfiring—because key twists in the science have been overlooked. Small corrections in our thinking today could alter the character of society long term, one future citizen at a time. The way white families introduce the concept of race to their children is a prime example.

For decades, it was assumed that children see race only when society points it out to them. However, child-development researchers have increasingly begun to question that presumption. They argue that children see racial differences as much as they see the difference between pink and blue—but we tell kids that "pink" means for girls and "blue" is for boys. "White" and "black" are mysteries we leave them to figure out on their own.

It takes remarkably little for children to develop in-group preferences. Vittrup's mentor at the University of Texas, Rebecca Bigler, ran an experiment in three preschool classrooms, where 4- and 5-year-olds were lined up and given T shirts. Half the kids were randomly given blue T shirts, half red. The children wore the shirts for three weeks. During that time, the teachers never mentioned their colors and never grouped the kids by shirt color.

The kids didn't segregate in their behavior. They played with each other freely at recess. But when asked which color team was better to belong to, or which team might win a race, they chose their own color. They believed they were smarter than the other color. "The Reds never showed hatred for Blues," Bigler observed. "It was more like, 'Blues are fine, but not as good as us.'" When Reds were asked how many Reds were nice, they'd answer, "All of us." Asked how many Blues were nice, they'd answer, "Some." Some of the Blues were mean, and some were dumb—but not the Reds.

Bigler's experiment seems to show how children will use whatever you give them to create divisions—seeming to confirm that race becomes an issue only if we make it an issue. So why does Bigler think it's important to talk to children about race as early as the age of 3?

Her reasoning is that kids are developmentally

**If these children did not learn to stereotype and hold negative opinions about other races, then this suggests that racism isn't fully the result of social learning. If it's not, then why do you think these children came to such conclusions?**

**What is your opinion? What is the most ideal way to handle this topic with children? After learning about stereotype threat in Chapter 10, how do you think discussing U.S. President Barack Obama's race would affect both black and white children?**

**How does this experiment compare to Jane Elliott's blue eyes/brown eyes demonstration?**

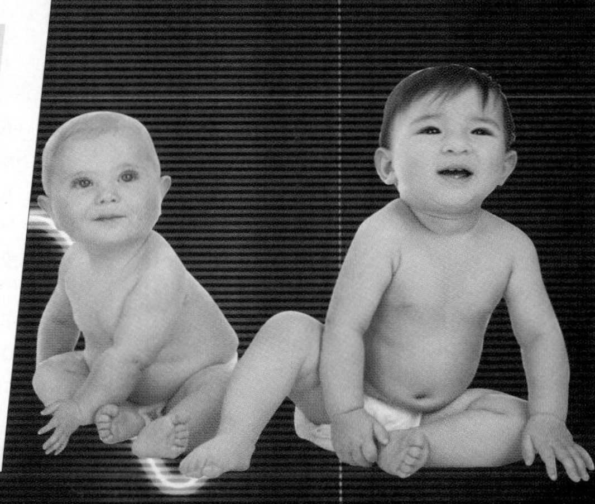

*What does this tell us about the nature-or-nurture debate first discussed in Chapter 1? Do you think the results of this experiment give us any definitive evidence for one side or the other?*

*Think about how the Diverse Environment Theory is similar to the contact hypothesis you learned about in Chapter 10.*



prone to in-group favoritism; they're going to form these preferences on their own. Children naturally try to categorize everything, and the attribute they rely on is that which is the most clearly visible.

We might imagine we're creating color-blind environments for children, but differences in skin color or hair or weight are like differences in gender—they're plainly visible. Even if no teacher or parent mentions race, kids will use skin color on their own, the same way they use T-shirt colors. Bigler contends that children extend their shared appearances much further—believing that those who look similar to them enjoy the same things they do. Anything a child doesn't like thus belongs to those who look the least similar to him. The spontaneous tendency to assume your group shares characteristics—such as niceness, or smarts—is called essentialism.

Within the past decade or so, developmental psychologists have begun a handful of longitudinal studies to determine exactly when children develop bias. Phyllis Katz, then a professor at the University of Colorado, led one such study—following 100 black children and 100 white children for their first six years. She tested these children and their parents nine times during those six years, with the first test at 6 months old.

How do researchers test a 6-month-old? They show babies photographs of faces. Katz found that babies will stare significantly longer at photographs of faces that are a different race from their parents, indicating they find the face out of the ordinary. Race itself has no ethnic meaning per se—but children's brains are noticing skin-color differences and trying to understand their meaning.

When the kids turned 3, Katz showed them photographs of other children and asked them to choose whom they'd like to have as friends. Of the white children, 86 percent picked children of their own race. When the kids were 5 and 6, Katz gave these children a small deck of cards, with drawings of people on them. Katz told the children to sort the cards into two piles any way they wanted. Only 16 percent of the kids used gender to split the piles. But 68 percent of the kids used race to split the cards, without any prompting. In reporting her findings, Katz concluded: "I think it is fair to say that at no point in the study did the children exhibit the Rousseau type of color-blindness that many adults expect."

The point Katz emphasizes is that this period of our children's lives, when we imagine it's most important to not talk about race, is the very developmental period when children's minds are forming their first conclusions about race.

Several studies point to the possibility of developmental windows—stages when children's attitudes might be most amenable to change. In one experiment, children were put in cross-race study groups, and then were observed on the playground to see if the interracial classroom time led to interracial play at recess. The researchers found mixed study groups worked wonders with the first-grade children, but it made no difference with third graders. It's possible that by third grade, when parents usually recognize it's safe to start talking a little about race, the developmental window has already closed.

The other deeply held assumption modern parents have is what Ashley and I have come to call the Diverse Environment Theory. If you raise a child with a fair amount of exposure to people of other races and cultures, the environment becomes the message. Because both of us attended integrated schools in the 1970s—Ashley in San Diego and, in my case, Seattle—we had always accepted this theory's tenets: diversity breeds tolerance, and talking about race was, in and of itself, a diffuse kind of racism.

But my wife and I saw this differently in the years after our son, Luke, was born. When he was 4 months old, Luke began attending a preschool located in San Francisco's Fillmore/Western Addition neighborhood. One of the many benefits of the school was its great racial diversity. For years our son never once mentioned the color of anyone's skin. We never once mentioned skin color, either. We thought it was working perfectly.

Then came Martin Luther King Jr. Day at school, two months before his fifth birthday. Luke walked out of preschool that Friday before the weekend and started pointing at everyone, proudly announcing, "That guy comes from Africa. And she comes from Africa, too!" It was embarrassing how loudly he did this. "People with brown skin are from Africa," he'd repeat. He had not been taught the names for races—he had not heard the term "black" and he called us "people with pinkish-whitish skin." He named every kid in his schoolroom with brown skin, which was about half his class.

My son's eagerness was revealing. It was obvious this was something he'd been wondering about for a while. He was relieved to have been finally given the key. Skin color was a sign of ancestral roots.

Over the next year, we started to overhear one of his white friends talking about the color of their skin. They still didn't know what to call their skin, so they used the phrase "skin like ours." And this notion of ours versus theirs started to take on a meaning of its own. As these kids searched for their identities, skin color had become salient.

Soon, I overheard this particular white boy telling my son, "Parents don't like us to talk about our skin, so don't let them hear you."

As a parent, I dealt with these moments explicitly, telling my son it was wrong to choose anyone as his friend, or his "favorite," on the basis of skin color. We pointed out how certain friends wouldn't be in our lives if we picked friends for their color. Over time he not only accepted but embraced this lesson. Now he talks openly about equality and the wrongfulness of discrimination.

Not knowing then what I do now, I had a hard time understanding my son's initial impulses. Katz's work helped me to realize that Luke was never actually colorblind. He didn't talk about race in his first five years because our silence had unwittingly communicated that race was something he could not ask about.

The Diverse Environment Theory is the core principle behind school desegregation today. Like most people, I assumed that after 30 years of desegregation, it would have a long track record of scientific research proving that the Diverse Environment Theory works. Then Ashley and I began talking to the scholars who've compiled that very research.

In the summer of 2007, led by the Civil Rights Project, a dozen scholars wrote an amicus brief to the U.S. Supreme Court supporting school desegregation in Louisville, Ky., and Seattle. By the time the brief reached the court, 553 scientists had signed on in support. However, as much as the scientists all supported active desegregation, the brief is surprisingly circumspect in its advocacy: the benefits of desegregation are qualified with words like "may lead" and "can improve." "Mere school integration is not a panacea," the brief warns.

UT's Bigler was one of the scholars heavily involved in the process of its creation. Bigler is an adamant proponent of desegregation in schools on moral grounds. "It's an enormous step backward to increase social segregation," she says. However, she also admitted that "in the end, I was disappointed with the amount of evidence social psychology could muster [to support it]. Going to integrated schools gives you just as many chances to learn stereotypes as to unlearn them."

The unfortunate twist of diverse schools is that they don't necessarily lead to more cross-race relationships. Often it's the opposite. Duke University's James Moody—an expert on how adolescents form and maintain social networks—analyzed data on more than 90,000 teenagers at 112 different schools from every region of the country. The students had been asked to name their five best male friends and their five best female friends. Moody matched the ethnicity of the student with the race of each named friend, then compared the number of each student's cross-racial friendships with the school's overall diversity.

Moody found that the more diverse the school, the more the kids self-segregate by race and ethnicity within the school, and thus the likelihood that any two kids of different races have a friendship goes down.

Moody included statistical controls for activities, sports, academic tracking, and other school-structural conditions that tend to desegregate (or segregate) students within the school. The rule still holds true: more diversity translates into more division among students. Those increased opportunities to interact are also, effectively, increased opportunities to reject each other. And that is what's happening.

As a result, junior-high and high-school children in diverse schools experience two completely contrasting social cues on a daily basis. The first cue is inspiring—that many students have a friend of another race. The second cue is tragic—that far more kids just like to hang with their own. It's this second dynamic that becomes more and more visible as overall school diversity goes up. As a child circulates through school, she sees more groups that her race disqualifies her from, more lunchroom tables she can't sit at, and more implicit lines that are taboo to cross. This is unmissable even if she, personally, has friends of other races. "Even in multiracial schools, once young people leave the classroom, very little interracial discussion takes place because a desire to associate with one's own ethnic group often discourages interaction between groups," wrote Brendesha Tynes of the University of Illinois at Urbana-Champaign.

All told, the odds of a white high-schooler in America having a best friend

*Think about your own school and the schools you've attended in the past. Have you witnessed the same phenomenon? Why do you think this is the case? What implications might it suggest?*

*What do you think is the reason for children's need for ingroups and outgroups? What are the potential consequences?*

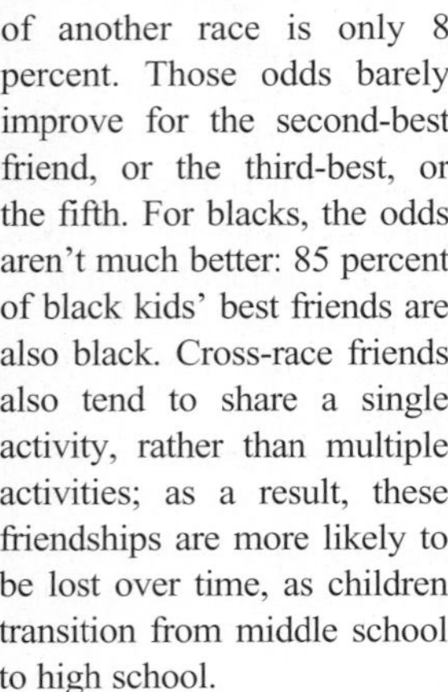

of another race is only 8 percent. Those odds barely improve for the second-best friend, or the third-best, or the fifth. For blacks, the odds aren't much better: 85 percent of black kids' best friends are also black. Cross-race friends also tend to share a single activity, rather than multiple activities; as a result, these friendships are more likely to be lost over time, as children transition from middle school to high school.

I can't help but wonder—would the track record of desegregation be so mixed if parents reinforced it, rather than remaining silent? It is tempting to believe that because their generation is so diverse, today's children grow up knowing how to get along with people of every race. But numerous studies suggest that this is more of a fantasy than a fact.

Is it really so difficult to talk with children about race when they're very young? What jumped out at Phyllis Katz, in her study of 200 black and white children, was that parents are very comfortable talking to their children about gender, and they work very hard to counterprogram against boy-girl stereotypes. That ought to be our model for talking about race. The same way we remind our daughters, "Mommies can be doctors just like daddies," we ought to be telling all children that doctors can be any skin color. It's not complicated what to say. It's only a matter of how often we reinforce it.

*In Chapter 10, you learned about old-fashioned and modern racism and sexism. How might the two different types of racism and sexism play a role in Katz's observation?*

Shushing children when they make an improper remark is an instinctive reflex, but often the wrong move. Prone to categorization, children's brains can't help but attempt to generalize rules from the examples they see. It's embarrassing when a child blurts out, "Only brown people can have breakfast at school," or "You can't play basketball; you're white, so you have to play baseball." But shushing them only sends the message that this topic is unspeakable, which makes race more loaded, and more intimidating.

To be effective, researchers have found, conversations about race have to be explicit, in unmistakable terms that children understand. A friend of mine repeatedly told her 5-year-old son, "Remember, everybody's equal." She thought she was getting the message across. Finally, after seven months of this, her boy asked, "Mommy, what's 'equal' mean?"

Bigler ran a study in which children read brief biographies of famous African-Americans. For instance, in a biography of Jackie Robinson, they read that he was the first African-American in the major leagues. But only half read about how he'd previously been relegated to the Negro Leagues, and how he suffered taunts from white fans. Those facts—in five brief sentences were omitted in the version given to the other children.

After the two-week history class, the children were surveyed on their racial attitudes. White children who got the full story about historical discrimination had significantly better attitudes toward blacks than those who got the neutered version. Explicitness works. "It also made them feel some guilt," Bigler adds. "It knocked down their glorified view of white people." They couldn't justify in-group superiority.

Minority parents are more likely to help their children develop a racial identity from a young age. April Harris-Britt, a clinical psychologist and professor at the University of North Carolina at Chapel Hill, found that all minority parents at some point tell their children that discrimination is out there, but they shouldn't let it stop them. Is this good for them? Harris-Britt found that some preparation for bias was beneficial, and it was necessary—94 percent of African-American eighth graders reported to Harris-Britt that they'd felt discriminated against in the prior three months.

But if children heard these preparation-for-bias warnings often (rather than just occasionally), they were significantly less likely to connect their successes to effort, and much more likely to blame their failures on their teachers—whom they saw as biased against them.

Harris-Britt warns that frequent predictions of future discrimination ironically become as destructive as experiences of actual discrimination: "If you overfocus on those types of events, you give the children the message that the world is going to be hostile—you're just not valued and that's just the way the world is."

Preparation for bias is not, however, the only way minorities talk to their children about race. The other broad category of conversation, in Harris-Britt's analysis, is ethnic pride. From a very young age, minority children are coached to be proud of their ethnic history. She found that this was exceedingly good for children's self-confidence; in one study, black children who'd heard messages of ethnic pride were more engaged in school and more likely to attribute their success to their effort and ability.

That leads to the question that everyone wonders but rarely dares to ask. If "black pride" is good for African-American children, where does that leave white children? It's horrifying to imagine kids being "proud to be white." Yet many scholars argue that's exactly what children's brains are already computing. Just as minority children are aware that they belong to an ethnic group with less status and wealth, most white children naturally decipher that they belong to the race that has more power, wealth, and control in society; this provides security, if not confidence. So a pride message would not just be abhorrent—it'd be redundant.

Over the course of our research, we heard many stories of how people—from parents to teachers—were struggling to talk about race with their children. For some, the conversations came up after a child had made an embarrassing comment in public. A number had the issue thrust on them, because of an interracial marriage or an international adoption. Still others were just introducing children into a diverse environment, wondering when and if the timing was right.

But the story that most affected us came from a small town in rural Ohio. Two first-grade teachers, Joy Bowman and Angela Johnson, had agreed to let a professor from Ohio State University, Jeane Copenhaver-Johnson, observe their classrooms for the year. Of the 33 children, about two thirds were white, while the others were black or of mixed-race descent.

It being December, the teachers had decided to read to their classes '*Twas the Night B'fore Christmas*, Melodye Rosales's retelling of the Clement C. Moore classic. As the teachers began reading, the kids were excited by the book's depiction of a family waiting for Santa to come. A few children, however, quietly fidgeted. They seemed puzzled that this storybook was different: in this one, it was a black family all snug in their beds.

Then there was the famed clatter on the roof. The children leaned in to get their first view of Santa and the sleigh as Johnson turned the page—

And they saw that Santa was black.

"He's black!" gasped a white little girl.

A white boy exclaimed, "I thought he was white!"

Immediately, the children began to chatter about the stunning development. At the ripe old ages of 6 and 7, the children had no doubt that there was a Real Santa. Of that they were absolutely sure. But suddenly there was this huge question mark. Could Santa be black? And if so, what did that mean?

While some of the black children were delighted with the idea that Santa could be black, others were unsure. A couple of the white children rejected this idea out of hand: a black Santa couldn't be real.

But even the little girl the most adamant that the Real Santa must be white came around to accept the possibility that a black Santa could fill in for White Santa if he was hurt. And she still gleefully yelled along with the Black Santa's final "Merry Christmas to All! Y'all Sleep Tight."

Other children offered the idea that perhaps Santa was "mixed with black and white"—something in the middle, like an Indian. One boy went with a two-Santa hypothesis: White Santa and Black Santa must be friends who take turns visiting children. When a teacher made the apparently huge mistake of saying that she'd never seen Santa, the children all quickly corrected her: everyone had seen Santa at the mall. Not that that clarified the situation any.

The debate raged for a week, in anticipation of a school party. The kids all knew Real Santa was the guest of honor.

Then Santa arrived at the party—and he was black. Just like in the picture book.

Some white children said that this black Santa was too thin: that meant that the Real Santa was the fat white one at Kmart. But one of the white girls retorted that she had met the man and was convinced. Santa was brown.

Most of the black children were exultant, since this proved that Santa was black. But one of them, Brent, still doubted—even though he really wanted a black Santa to be true. So he bravely confronted Santa.

"There ain't no black Santas!" Brent insisted.

"Lookit here." Santa pulled up a pant leg.

A thrilled Brent was sold. "This is a black Santa!" he yelled. "He's got black skin and his black boots are like the white Santa's boots."

A black-Santa storybook wasn't enough to crush every stereotype. When Johnson later asked the kids to draw Santa, even the black kids who were excited about a black Santa still depicted him with skin as snowy white as his beard.

But the shock of the Santa storybook was the catalyst for the first graders to have a yearlong dialogue about race issues. The teachers began regularly incorporating books that dealt directly with issues of racism into their reading.

And when the children were reading a book on Martin Luther King Jr. and the civil-rights movement, both a black and a white child noticed that white people were nowhere to be found in the story. Troubled, they decided to find out just where in history both peoples were.

***In what ways is this an illustration of the process of downward social comparison you learned about in Chapter 4? What might the impacts be on children of majority and minority races?***

***Both white and black students had trouble accepting this idea. You first learned about schemas in Chapter 3, and this is an example of the cognitive effort it takes when people's deeply ingrained schemas are challenged.***

# AGGRESSION

*<<< Girls are often the surprising culprits behind bullying and cyberbullying.*

**WHAT** IS THE NATURE OF AGGRESSION?
**WHAT** ARE THE THEORIES OF AGGRESSION?
**WHAT** INFLUENCES AGGRESSION?
**HOW** CAN WE REDUCE AGGRESSION?

In the fall of 1997, 14-year-old Reena Virk was bullied and brutally murdered in Saanich, British Columbia. This tragic event received an enormous amount of media attention and is a poignant example of youth violence and female bullying. Reena was a teenager from a traditional Native family; her parents were Jehovah's Witnesses and were ostracized even within their own culture. She was desperate to fit in and was continually taunted and rejected by her peers at school. On November 14, 1997, Reena was invited to a "party" underneath a local bridge where teenagers used to hang out to drink alcohol and smoke marijuana. Upon her arrival, Virk was swarmed by a group of seven girls and one boy. Reena was repeatedly punched, kicked, and hit, had cigarettes stubbed out on her head, and some group members attempted to set her hair on fire. Reena managed to walk away after the first attack but was followed by Kelly Ellard and Warren Glowatski and attacked a second time. This time, Reena was not so lucky. They proceeded to beat her again and held her head under water until she drowned. While many of the girls received fines or minor jail terms for their involvement in the crime, Glowatski was sentenced to life in prison and released on full parole in June 2010. Kelly Ellard, the other major player in the homicide, has undergone three trials and been convicted of murder twice. In June 2009, the Supreme Court of Canada overturned her final appeal and she is currently serving a life sentence (with no eligibility for parole for seven years) for second-degree murder ("The Murder of Reena Virk," 2009).

Social and educational psychologists recognize the kind of situation described here as a new kind of bullying. Unlike the male social-delinquent stereotype of the past, these new bullies are generally good looking, athletic, accomplished students, who also may be female and are comfortable around authority figures. This case and a rash of other bullying-related deaths have influenced a number of anti-bullying laws (Hampson, 2010). In addition, researchers at the University of Western Ontario have begun to closely examine female bullying and correlates of aggression (Leschied, Cummings, Van Brunschot, Cunningham, & Saunders, 2000).

The way teens bully has changed as well. The internet has taken bullying out of the schoolyard and into cyberspace, and mobile devices facilitate harassment 24 hours a day. Cyberbullying includes the use of texts, IMs, social media, websites, or emails to threaten, intimidate, or humiliate a person; often resulting from other sources of frustration, anger, retaliation, or boredom. Four in ten teens have experienced cyberbullying, and girls are twice as likely to be the victims *and* perpetrators of this kind of harassment (University of Gothenburg, 2010).

# CHAPTER 11

**AGGRESSION** behaviour, either verbal or physical, that is used to intentionally harm another individual

**HOSTILE (AFFECTIVE) AGGRESSION** behaviour that occurs when the primary goal of an action is to make the victim suffer

**INSTRUMENTAL AGGRESSION** behaviour that occurs when the primary goal of an action is not to make the victim suffer but to attain a non-injurious goal

## What Is the Nature of Aggression?

Consider the following situations. (1) A woman walking home from a night out with friends is knocked out with a mallet and sexually assaulted. (2) A man is sitting at a red light. When the light turns green, the person in the car behind him lays on the horn and yells at the man to move. (3) A teenager is texting while driving and rear-ends another vehicle, killing a family of four. (4) A pet owner hits his dog with a rolled-up newspaper after the dog disobeys him.

Which of these instances is considered aggression? Your answer will depend on your definition of the term. Many people assume that aggression involves inflicting harm on another person, but what if the harm was unintentional, such as in the case of the teenager? And what if no physical harm occurs, as in the case of the man at the red light? And what if the target is not a person, as in the case of the pet owner? Aggression takes many forms and can have multiple effects, so it can be tricky to specifically define. **Aggression** can be generally defined as a behaviour, either verbal or physical, that is used to *intentionally harm* another individual.

Engaging in acts of aggression seems to be the way many people attempt to release frustration or address conflicts. If you flip on the news or open a newspaper, you will read about acts of sexual assault, murder, and assault with a weapon. These are the types of behaviours you may primarily associate with aggression. What you may not realize is that there are probably acts of aggression in your everyday life that fly under the radar, such as a verbal argument with a co-worker, a harsh email from a friend, or a case of the silent treatment from a significant other. These behaviours may not seem overtly aggressive, but when you examine the purpose of the acts—to harm another—then the aggression behind them is revealed. Social psychologists are interested in the causes of aggressive behaviour and have sought to achieve a better understanding of its nature through research. They anticipate that the better we understand human nature, the better equipped we are to prevent aggressive acts. Let's examine what social psychologists already know about aggression.

Aggression comes in two forms: hostile and instrumental. **Hostile (or affective) aggression** occurs when anger leads to aggression and the primary goal of an action or behaviour is to make the victim suffer. Individuals who participate in emotional aggression, then, are simply seeking to harm or injure the target of their attack. The attack on Reena Virk is an example of emotional aggression. The group of six girls, including Kelly Ellard as the ringleader, and one male, Warren Glowatski,

> "Aggression takes many forms and can have multiple effects, so it can be tricky to specifically define."

kicked, punched, burned, and beat Reena. Following her attempted escape, they held her head underwater and drowned her ("The Murder of Reena Virk," 2009). The purpose of the attack was clearly to cause harm to the attackers' "target." This form of violence differs from *reactive (or hot-blooded) aggression*, which occurs in response to some type of provocation (e.g., a wife comes home and finds her husband in bed with another woman and kills them both; Woodworth & Porter, 2002).

In contrast, **instrumental aggression** occurs when the primary goal of the action is not to make the victim suffer, but to attain a non-injurious goal (e.g., money, control or power, sex). An individual who participates in instrumental aggression will harm or injure another as a way of obtaining various rewards such as control of a situation or improved self-esteem. For example, CFL linebackers breaking through an offensive line and knocking the quarterback of the opposing team down would be classified as instrumental aggression. The motivation behind the action is not to physically harm the quarterback; it's to establish dominance for the aggressor's own team and to keep the opponent away from the end zone in an ultimate effort to win the game.

Instrumental aggression is often used as a method of coercion to help a person "get his or her way." Acts of intimidation, such as threatening injury or demanding control, demonstrate behaviour intended to improve the aggressor's situation

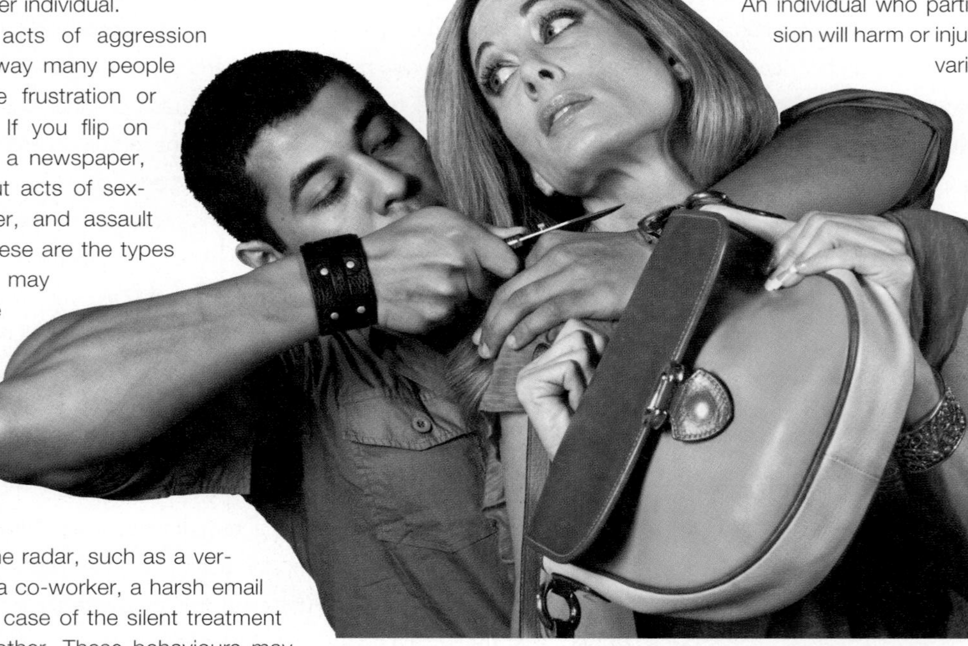

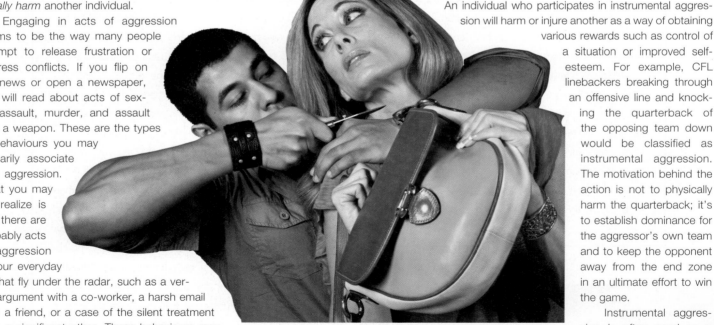

**Crimes such as mugging, theft, and assault with a weapon can be forms of** instrumental aggression when the primary goal is obtain money, not to harm another.

and harm another in the process. An angry diner who yells at a waitress and demands to be compensated for unsatisfactory service is exhibiting instrumental aggression. At times, the primary goal of this type of aggression is hard to detect, such as when the goal involves a person's sense of self. When people participate in instrumental aggression to improve their self-esteem, they attempt to build themselves up by bringing others down. For example, bullies often tease others as a way to make themselves feel better.

## GENDER DIFFERENCES

When we think of an act of hostile aggression, we often think of the aggressor as male. This is because of the informal assumption that males are more aggressive than females. This notion is supported by the overwhelming number of reports of male aggression in the news and other forms of media, as well as by research. When asked whether they had ever participated in any aggressive actions, males reported a higher incidence of aggressive behaviour than did females (Harris, 1994). Furthermore, males are more likely than females to be targets of aggression (e.g., Buss, 2004; Daly & Wilson, 1989).

While these studies support what many of us already believe, further research on gender differences in aggression reveal that the issue is a bit more complex (e.g., Bettencourt & Miller, 1996; Lightdale & Prentice, 1994). Meta-analysis and reviews of literature suggest that gender differences are not that large, and the disparity in aggression between genders is dependent on how aggression is defined (e.g., Bettencourt & Miller, 1996; Card, Stucky, Sawalani, & Little, 2008). Studies have found that males ultimately tend to be more physically aggressive, while females are more relationally aggressive (e.g., Anderson & Huesmann, 2003; Crick & Grotpeter, 1995). In other words, female aggression is more likely to manifest itself through hurting relationships by engaging in gossip, excluding a person from a group or activity, or telling lies (e.g., Crick & Rose, 2000; Huesmann et al., 2003; Tapper & Boulton, 2004, 2005).

Provocation, or the lack thereof, considerably affects this disparity. When men are provoked in any way, they are significantly more likely to act aggressively than are females. However, when provocation is not involved, the disparity seems to disappear (Bettencourt & Miller, 1996). Similarly, gender differences in aggression are heightened in situations in which aggression is required or expected, typically by some sort of social role. The term "man up," used in situations where a man is expected to take an aggressive approach to something, exemplifies this type of social expectation (Baron & Richardson, 1994). However, recent Canadian developmental research suggests that boys engage in physical aggression more than girls, even from a young age (i.e., 17 months), and these differences do not appear to be moderated by socialization (e.g., Baillargeon et al., 2007).

**DIRECT AGGRESSION** an action or a behaviour that is clearly derived from the aggressor and is aimed directly at the target

**INDIRECT AGGRESSION** an action or a behaviour that is not clearly derived from the aggressor, and where it is not obvious to the target that he or she has been the victim of aggression

The type of aggression also affects the disparity. Research has shown that males are more likely than females to participate in direct aggression (e.g., Archer, 2004; Card et al., 2008). **Direct (or overt) aggression** is an action or a behaviour that is clearly derived from the aggressor and is aimed directly at the target—for example, punching, pushing, yelling, and using insulting language. On the other hand, females are more likely than males to participate in indirect aggression. **Indirect (or covert) aggression** is an action or a behaviour that is not clearly derived from the aggressor, where it is not obvious to the target that he or she has been the victim of aggression. Examples of this include spreading rumours and gossiping, creating social isolation, or framing others for something they did not do. So while a man is more likely to get into a brutal brawl with someone, a woman is more likely to spread a nasty rumour (e.g., Eagly & Wood, 1991). Further, individuals who gossip tend to externalize blame to others more often (e.g., Watson, 2011) and

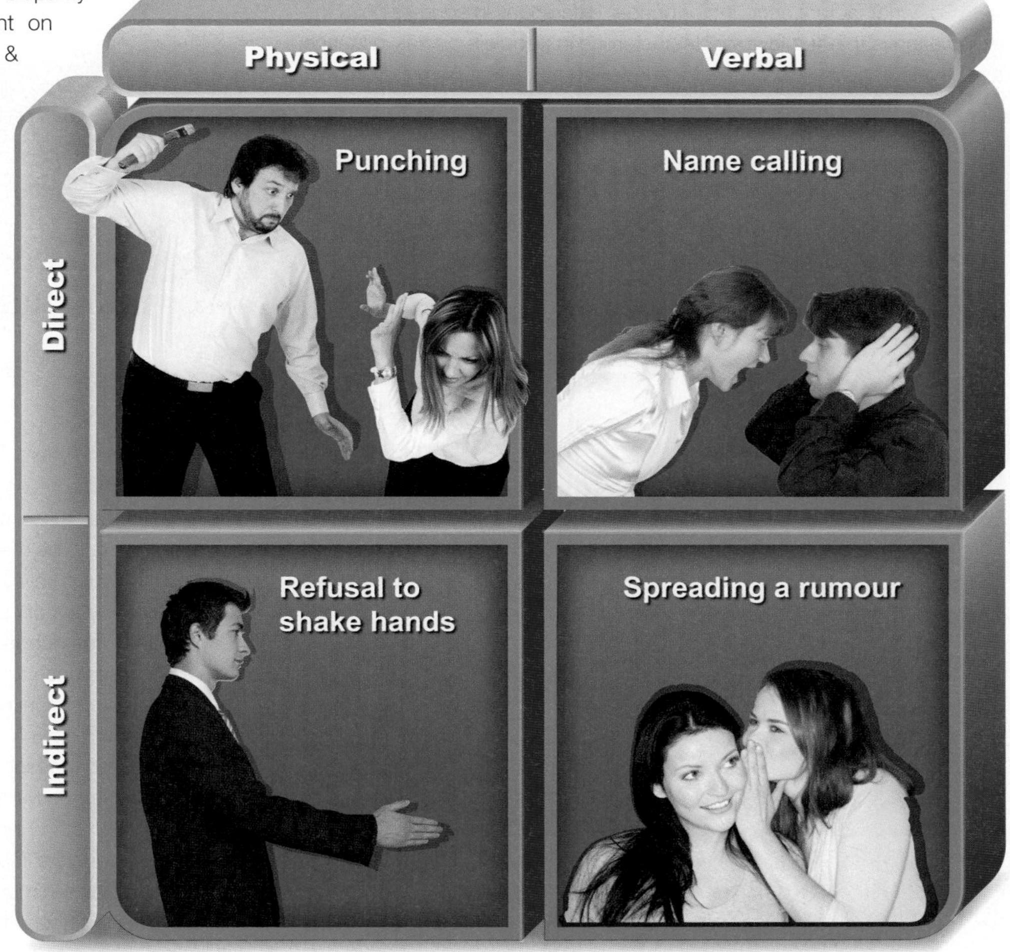

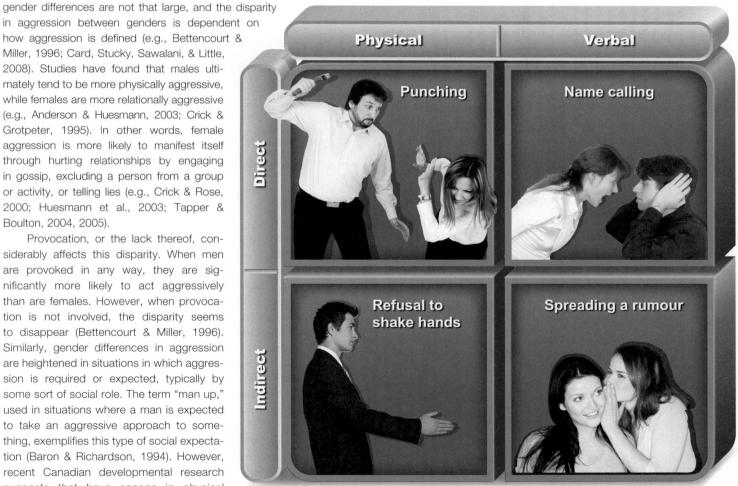

**Types of Aggression.** **Aggression can be a combination of** direct, indirect, verbal, and physical behaviour.

**EXPRESSIVE VIEW OF AGGRESSION** a view of aggression as a way to express anger and reduce stress

**INSTRUMENTAL VIEW OF AGGRESSION** a view of aggression as a way to gain social or material rewards

**CULTURE OF HONOUR** a culture in which strong norms suggest that aggression is an appropriate response to an insult or threat to one's honour

may react to direct aggression in a more hostile manner. This helps to explain recent findings that gender differences in indirect aggression are negligible (Card et al., 2008).

Research suggests that men and women also differ when it comes to their respective attitudes toward aggression. Men tend to report less guilt or anxiety about their aggressive behaviour than women, while women report more concern about the possibility that their aggressive behaviour could cause a threat to their personal safety, as in the case of retaliation. Research also suggests that men and women are apt to have contrasting views of what aggression represents and what the purpose of aggressive acts is. Women tend to hold an **expressive view of aggression**, in which aggression is used as a way to express anger and reduce stress. Men, on the other hand, tend to hold an **instrumental view of aggression**, in which the aggression is used to gain personal, social, or material rewards (e.g., Campbell, Muncer, & Gorman, 1993).

So, what factors account for gender differences in aggression? One explanation is that the levels of testosterone in people's bodies influence their levels of aggression (e.g., Mazur & Booth, 1998; Olweus, Mattson, Schally, & Low, 1988). Men naturally have more testosterone, so they tend to be more aggressive. Correlational studies show that there is a relationship between the amount of testosterone and the level of aggression in young boys (e.g., Chance, Brown, Dabbs, & Casey, 2000), delinquent adults (e.g., Banks & Dabbs, 1996), and in women in general (e.g., Dabbs & Hargrove, 1997).

However, it is important to note that additional research suggests that it is not the level of testosterone alone that accounts for increased aggression. Research comparing individuals of different income levels finds that men with high income levels have low rates of delinquency, regardless of their levels of testosterone, yet the rate of delinquency for low-income men varies with level of testosterone (e.g., Dabbs & Morris, 1990). Several groups of Canadian researchers have looked at socialization and gender roles and found that males and females are taught differently about the costs and benefits of aggression (e.g., Vaillancourt & Hymel, 2004), although underlying differences in the type of aggression displayed may still exist (e.g., Baillargeon et al., 2007). There isn't just one reason for the gender differences in aggression; hormone levels, gender roles, and methods of socialization all contribute to the way men and women exhibit aggression.

In 2008, teenagers Amina and Sarah Yaser Said were shot to death by their father **because they supposedly dishonoured their family by dating non-Muslim boys.**

## CULTURAL DIFFERENCES

While we often think of aggression as triggered by the actions of another person, it can also be triggered by cultural factors. A culture's system of values, beliefs, and norms may suggest that aggression is appropriate or even necessary in certain circumstances. Countries with individualistic cultures, such as Canada and the United States, have different ways of thinking and behaving than those with collectivist cultures, such as China and India. These differences, along with general beliefs and values, contribute to the varied ways aggression manifests itself in different cultures.

> "A culture's system of values, beliefs, and norms may suggest that aggression is appropriate or even necessary in certain circumstances."

In cultures where the law is weak and citizens need to protect themselves, the act—or even the threat—of violence is considered to be essential. Under these conditions, any threat to a person or his or her possessions must be met with retaliation or he or she could be viewed as an easy target and have his or her survival put at risk. Social psychologists refer to these types of cultures as **cultures of honour** (Nisbett & Cohen, 1996). In cultures of honour, strong norms suggest that aggression is an appropriate response to an insult or threat to one's honour.

The Southern United States was one of the first focuses of social psychologists' research on cultures of honour. One study by Nisbett and Cohen (1996) found higher instances of violence in that region. In another study, Southerners were more likely than Northerners to respond with aggression and show physical signs of distress when their honour was challenged by insults (Cohen et al., 1996). You may have also witnessed this type of culture in movies. In an old western, a cattle driver might challenge a crooked sheriff to a duel because the sheriff insulted the man's livelihood. Or in a Japanese period piece, you may see a young warrior set out on a mission to seek revenge on a man who dishonoured the young warrior's family. While these situations often seem larger than life onscreen, they remain present in the real world.

Cultures of honour often exist in conditions where law enforcement is weak or lacking, wealth is portable and can be stolen, and financial security is absent (Cohen & Nisbett, 1997). It may seem like this type of culture died with the Wild West, but there are several present-day examples of cultures of honour around the world (Sev'er & Yurdakul, 2001). Individuals in cultures of honour sometimes perpetrate *honour killings*, which have become a searing human rights issue. Honour killings occur when one family member kills another because the victim has somehow "shamed" the family. Typically, this is perpetrated by a father, brother, or husband on a daughter, sister, or wife. Honour killings are based on the belief that women are considered the property of the family and their bodies are repositories of the family's honour (Amnesty International, 2010). If a woman or girl is accused, or even suspected, of participating in behaviour that could damage the reputation of her family, she is likely to endure brutal retaliation from fellow family members. This retaliation can result in serious bodily injury and even death.

In 1997, Marzouk Abdel Rahim, a tile maker from Cairo, brutally murdered his 25-year-old daughter and then dismembered her body because he felt that her relationship with a male friend dishonoured their family. Abdel Rahim displayed no regrets for his action, and in a statement to the press declared that, "honour is more precious than my own flesh and blood." He served only two months in jail for his crime (Jehl, 1999). Similarly, 26-year-old Turkish immigrant Fadime Sahindal was murdered by her father in Sweden in order to restore honour to his family name. Sahindal opposed an arranged marriage that was set up for her, and secretly dated another man. When her father found out, he uttered death threats and stalked Fadime for a period of four years before finally murdering her (Mojab & Hassanpour, 2003).

Honour killings are most prevalent in Arab nations, where traditions are tightly adhered to. Leaders of these nations are often close-lipped about the subject, but some governments, such as Jordan's under King Abdullah, have lifted the lid on public discussion of honour killings. They have worked in conjunction with modernizers and traditionalists to respond to this issue with appropriate sensitivity. Arabs contend that attention to their society's role in the phenomenon of honour killings is a result of the Western world's tendency to see them as backward. They argue that in individualistic cultures such as Canada or the United States, when a man kills his wife based on the suspicion that she is cheating, it is viewed as a crime of passion. Or when a gang member kills a member of a rival gang because the rival disrespected, or "dissed," one of his boys, it is seen as an unfortunate consequence of urban living. But when crimes with similar motivations happen in the Arab world, they are considered barbarous and incomprehensible (Jehl, 1999). Still, despite these arguments, the fact remains that Western nations punish murderers regardless of their motivation, while many Arab governments traditionally choose to look the other way or merely issue slaps on the wrist when it comes to honour killings.

# What Are the Theories of Aggression?

Through formal and informal observation, we know that human beings frequently engage in aggressive behaviour, but we don't know exactly *why*. The nature of aggression, the forces from which it originates, and the factors that impact its occurrence are contentious topics among social psychologists (e.g., Baron & Richardson, 1994; Geen & Donnerstein, 1998). Theoretical perspectives on aggression typically fall into several general categories: instinct, biology, frustration, and social learning.

**INSTINCT THEORY** a theory in which aggression is an innate and inevitable force

## INSTINCT AND EVOLUTION

Psychologists who follow the **instinct theory** believe that aggression is an innate and inevitable force. Sigmund Freud and Konrad Lorenz were two of the leading proponents of this theory. Freud believed that aggression stems from a self-destructive impulse—a behaviour Freud referred to as the "death drive." He believed that humans must act out that impulse in order to release negative energy and return to a state of calm. Lorenz agreed that aggression is unlearned and universal, but viewed the behaviour from an evolutionary perspective. He believed that through evolution, humans developed a fighting instinct similar to that found in animals (Lorenz, 1963/2002). Over the course of many years, our ancestors found that aggressive behaviour benefited them as a method of gaining resources, eliminating competition, threatening

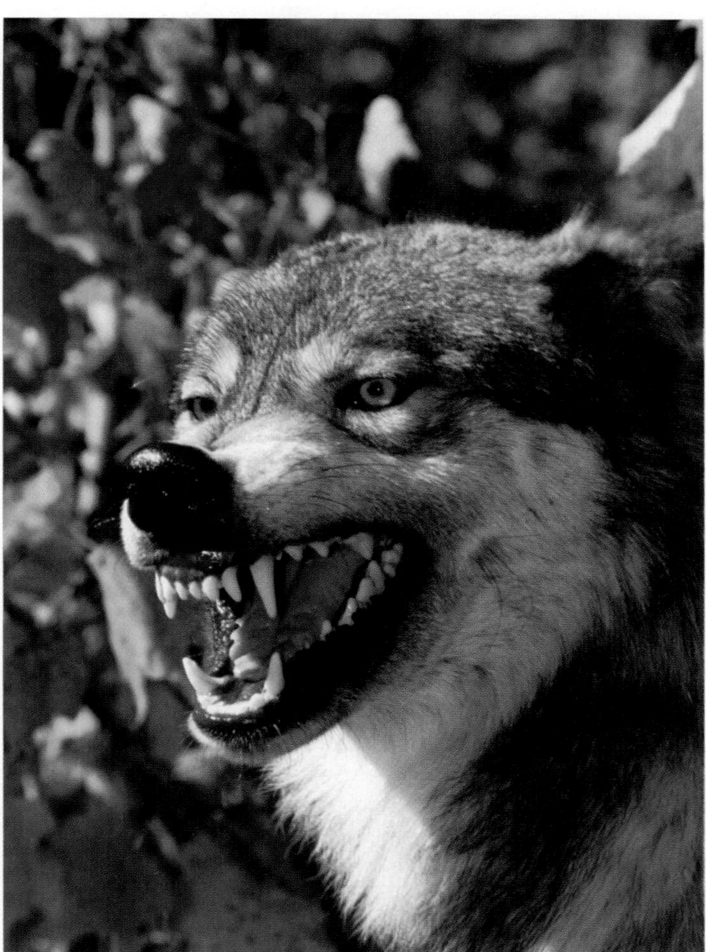

Instinct theory suggests that humans, **like animals in the wild, have an innate desire to protect their personal safety, their family's safety,** and their possessions through aggressive behaviour.

rivals, and defending against assailants. According to instinct theory, the natural need for aggression gets stronger over time until the pressure is released through aggressive acts, akin to a hydraulic engine, producing catharsis (Macmillan, 1997).

Instinct theory is not without flaws. For one thing, it does not take into account the differences in aggressive behaviour among various societies. If all humans share the same desire to act aggressively, how can we explain why some societies are historically peaceful while others are violent, or why every human does not overtly express her aggressive desires (Hornstein, 1976)? Instinct theory must concede that the way humans express their aggression is a learned behaviour, regardless of whether that expression is physical, verbal, direct, or indirect. For example, you and your friend might both have the innate desire to act aggressively, but you may have learned to express that aggression by verbally venting to others while your friend may have learned to release aggression through physical force. Another problem with instinct theory is that the logic behind it is circular. When a person asks why people aggress, the answer is that it is due to instinct. When discussion about how we know aggression is instinctual arises, instinct theory falls back on the simple fact that people do aggress.

Another related theory that looks at our origins for explanations of aggression is evolutionary theory. This theory examines the evolutionary drive to survive and posits that our aggression evolved out of necessity in order for us to simply exist (Lorenz, 1963/2002). One study claims that the need to obtain limited resources necessary for survival resulted in adaptive aggressive behaviour (Tooby & Cosmides, 1988). Further, males and females evolved different aggressive mechanisms based on needs associated with competition and nurturing (Eliot, 2009). It is important to remember that simply because the need arose and aggression became a part of the evolutionary process, this doesn't necessarily mean all humans are aggressive.



## BIOLOGICAL FACTORS

Another way of explaining the individual differences in aggressive behaviour is by considering biological factors. Our individual biological makeup is believed to be a fundamental factor that influences our behaviour. Like blue eyes or detached earlobes, a tendency toward extreme aggression can be genetic. Researchers in the Netherlands discovered a genetic mutation in a Dutch family that appears to cause periodic outbursts of aggression in its maternally linked male possessors (Morell, 1993). Similarly, researchers in Toronto have found that the presence of certain enzymes (i.e., monoamine oxidase A) may regulate key hormones associated with childhood aggression, such as serotonin, norepinephrine, and dopamine, and variants in these enzymes were present in a sample of male children diagnosed with childhood-onset aggression (Beitchman, Mik, Ehtesham, Douglas, & Kennedy, 2004). However, over-generalizing the results of genetic and hormonal research could be dangerous, as people could push for prenatal screening for the "aggressive gene" or genes that control the regulation of certain hormones. This information is, however, another step closer to answering the central questions about the origins of aggression.

When trying to identify aggressive behaviour, research can look directly at the brain. Scientists have used the single photon emission computerized tomography (SPECT) system to identify regions of the brain that relate to aggression. SPECT generates a color picture of the blood flow and activity in the brain (Hirono, 2000). Unusual increases and decreases in activity that are vital to causing aggression are typically found in the left temporal lobe. Aggressive men tend to have too much or too little activity in that area, limiting their ability to control their actions. Identifying the areas of abnormality allows doctors to prescribe customized drug treatment for individuals to help balance the activity in their brains.

### Biochemical Influences

Conflicting studies have shown that heredity alone cannot determine whether or not a person is going to behave aggressively. An individual's blood chemistry also influences the propensity to aggressive behaviour. If you've ever watched an episode of MTV's *The Jersey Shore* and observed cast members getting into drunken bar brawls, then you know that alcohol can unleash aggression when individuals are provoked. Laboratory experiments and legal statistics back up that observation (Graham, West, & Wells, 2000). Alcohol has a tendency to enhance aggressive behaviour by reducing people's self-awareness and their ability to self-monitor while focusing their attention on provocative sources (Bartholow & Heinz, 2006). In one study, people who had consumed alcohol were more likely to give a higher number of electric shocks to an opponent than those who hadn't had alcohol, even if they were not doing so in response to provocation (Bailey & Taylor, 1991). While aggressive behaviour does not occur in every person who throws back a drink, it does have a strong correlation with heavy drinking, especially in the case of those who already expect that their disposition will become more aggressive when alcohol is involved (e.g., Barnwell, Borders, & Earleywine, 2006). In fact, research has found that five factors seem most prominently related to alcohol-related aggression in bars: "risk-taking effects of alcohol, cognitive impairment from alcohol, hyperemotional effects of alcohol, 'macho' subculture, and permissive environment" (Graham et al., 2000, p. 847).

"If you've ever watched an episode of MTV's *The Jersey Shore* and observed cast members getting into drunken bar brawls, then you know that **alcohol can unleash aggression when individuals are provoked.**"

Human hormones, and particularly testosterone, can also be a key biological factor that influences aggressive behaviour. Research investigating testosterone levels, crime, and prison misbehaviour of 692 prison inmates found that male inmates who had committed personal crimes that were violent or sexual in nature had higher testosterone levels than inmates who committed property crimes of larceny, drug possession, and burglary. They also found that those inmates with higher levels of testosterone violated more prison rules, especially rules that involved confrontation (Dabbs, Carr, Frady, & Riad, 1995). While testosterone, like aggression, is typically associated with men, it impacts women as well. In one study, women who were given doses of testosterone so that their levels of the hormone became equal to those of men became less aware of aggression-deterring threat signals like facial expressions of anger, fear, and disgust, making them more susceptible to aggression themselves (van Honk & Schutter, 2007). Similarly, high doses of anabolic steroids (which increase testosterone) influence serotonin receptor activity in animals (e.g., Ricci, Rasakham, Grimes, & Melloni, 2006) and may be associated with a "shorter fuse" and greater interpretation of aggression-eliciting cues in humans. Injecting a person with testosterone, male or female, will not automatically make him or her aggressive, but in general, higher levels of this hormone are associated with aggressive behaviour when a person is provoked, just as lower levels are associated with less aggressive behaviour. Further, other sex hormones such as androgens may be important in the expression of aggression (e.g., Soma, Scotti, Newman, Charlier, & Demas, 2008).

Researchers can also look directly at brain activity. Low levels of the neurotransmitter serotonin can cause compromised impulse control in the frontal lobes, as serotonin plays a considerable role in the regulation of emotions and social functioning, domains that are closely related to aggression (e.g., Beitchman et al., 2004). Research has shown that in humans as well as primates, low serotonin is often found in violence-prone children and adults. As with genetics, however, it is not accurate to simply state that biochemical makeup can create an individual who is predisposed to aggressive behaviour. For example, the behaviour of aggression-prone individuals such as psychopaths results from a combination of brain abnormalities, biological factors, and the interpretation of situational cues (e.g., Blair, 2001, 2007; Glenn & Raine, 2009). There has been no evidence to support the idea of a "violent brain" that works independently from a person's surroundings and circumstances, so we must understand that there are environmental as well as natural factors that influence aggressive behaviour.

## FRUSTRATION AGGRESSION

As a student, you probably understand frustration all too well. You spend hours studying for a test, but end up with a less than impressive grade. You need to get to class, but you cannot find your keys or bus pass anywhere and you need them to get to school. These types of situations will typically lead to **frustration**, which is a feeling of being upset or annoyed by the inability to reach a goal or perform an activity.

The **frustration aggression theory** (Dollard et al., 1939) suggests that frustration precedes aggression. This theory states that frustration triggers the inclination for aggression because our motivation for aggression increases when our current behaviour is interrupted or we are prevented from reaching a goal. What do you do when you can't find lost keys or other misplaced important items? Do you forcefully toss around nearby objects or mumble obscenities to yourself? A classic study of the frustration aggression theory occurred in 1941, when researchers showed a group of children a room full of attractive toys but did not allow all of the children to play with the toys right away. Researchers found that the children who had to delay their play, and thus became frustrated, engaged in more aggressive behaviour in their play once they were allowed access to the toys (Barker, Dembo, & Lewin, 1941). Other sources of frustration, such as relative deprivation, also have been proposed to lead to aggression. We experience relative deprivation when we compare ourselves to others and feel deprived of something, leading to feelings of frustration (e.g., Bernstein & Crosby, 1980; Crosby, 1976; Merton & Kitt, 1950). For example, if your older brother or sister continually gets special treatment from your parents and you do not, this will lead to frustration, resentment, and aggressive actions against your sibling. Later research, however, failed to find more than mild support of this theory, so it cannot be concluded that frustration alone leads to aggression or that aggression is always preceded by frustration (e.g., Burstein & Worchel, 1962).

**FRUSTRATION** a feeling of being upset or annoyed by the inability to reach a goal or perform an activity

**FRUSTRATION AGGRESSION THEORY** a theory which states that frustration precedes aggression because our motivation for aggression increases when our current behaviour is interrupted or we are prevented from reaching a goal

**COGNITIVE-NEOASSOCIATION THEORY** a theory which suggests that when a person experiences something with a negative result, such as pain or discomfort, aggressive behaviour can often occur in the wake of that experience

In 1989, Leonard Berkowitz revised the frustration aggression theory; he found that frustration produced anger, and anger could then lead to aggression, but did not necessarily always do so. This revision, known as the **cognitive-neoassociation theory**, posits that when a person experiences something with a negative result, such as pain or discomfort, aggressive behaviour can often occur in the wake of that experience (Berkowitz, 1998). Anger or negative feelings are believed to "ready" a person to act aggressively when we are blocked from obtaining an expected goal. However, aggressive reactions also may depend on the presence of aggression-eliciting stimuli. In particular, when a person is simply in the presence of an object related to aggression (i.e., a gun versus a badminton racket), that person is more likely to display aggression (Berkowitz & LePage, 1967). Thus, aggression-related cues tend to facilitate or increase the likelihood that an individual may act aggressively, especially if he or she has been negatively primed (or aroused) previous to exposure (Berkowitz, 1998).

<<< **Authorities investigated the role of** "roid rage"—caused by an increase in testosterone due to anabolic steroids—**in professional wrestler Chris Benoit's killing of his wife and child and his subsequent suicide.**

**SOCIAL LEARNING THEORY** a theory which suggests that human aggression is largely learned by observing the aggressive behaviour of other people and is reinforced by consequences such as punishment or reward in the individual's environment

**MODELLING** a process in which one person engages in behaviour that is mimicked by another person

**REINFORCEMENT** an action or a process that strengthens a behaviour

## SOCIAL LEARNING

**Social learning theory** suggests that human aggression is largely learned by observing the aggressive behaviour of other people and is reinforced by consequences such as punishments or rewards in the individual's environment. Alberta-born psychologist Albert Bandura developed social learning theory, also referred to as social cognitive theory, during the 1960s.

### Modelling

Bandura conducted several studies involving observational learning, or modelling. **Modelling** is a process by which a person mimics another's behaviour. Bandura believed that children could learn to engage in aggressive behaviour by observing that behaviour, both in real life and in the media (Bandura, Ross, & Ross, 1963). Bandura's famous Bobo doll study exhibited the power of modelling on aggression in children. In the study, a sample of preschool-aged children watched a video that showed an adult forcefully tossing, kicking, and punching an inflatable toy, which researchers referred to as a Bobo doll (a five-foot-tall doll with a weighted bottom that would pop back up when it was knocked down). The adults in the video displayed very specific physical and verbal signs of aggression, including striking the doll with a mallet, sitting on the doll, punching it in the nose, tossing it in the air, and repeating phrases such as, "sock him," "kick him," "hit him down," "throw him in the air," and "pow." The children were then placed in a mildly frustrating situation in which they were given some of their favourite toys only to have them taken away a few minutes later.

The children were eventually introduced to the Bobo doll along with other toys such as stuffed animals, baby dolls, and crayons. Without the children's knowledge, researchers observed the children for 20 minutes. The observers noted that the children who watched the video of the adults striking the Bobo doll were far more likely to strike their own dolls than a control group who did not watch the video (Bandura, Ross, & Ross, 1961), showing that the children learned to display aggression. The Bobo doll study, along with follow-up studies that involved exposure to pre-recorded aggression (Bandura, 1973), was one of the first lines of research to suggest a link between violence on TV and violence in real life. We will discuss this link in more detail later on in this chapter.

### Reinforcement

The second component of social learning theory is reinforcement. **Reinforcement** is an action or process that strengthens a behaviour, and is a part of operant conditioning, which we discussed in Chapter 6. Reinforcement can be positive (adding in something that is pleasant or desirable) or negative (the removal of an unpleasant or aversive stimulus).

While one would think that aggressive behaviour is typically met with punishment (e.g., a teenager getting suspended from school for fighting), it is frequently met with positive reinforcement that might not be considered. For example, if a man knocks a woman down and steals her purse, the man's aggressive behaviour is rewarded with the valuable contents of the woman's purse. In another Bobo doll study, children watched one of three videos of an individual either being punished, rewarded, or receiving no consequences for aggressing against the Bobo doll (Bandura, 1965). The children who had seen the individual rewarded for beating up the Bobo doll showed the same behaviour toward doll. An unexpected finding, however, was that children who watched the video that resulted in no consequences also engaged in aggressive behaviour toward the doll, perhaps because it appeared that they could engage in violence without being punished. Therefore, children who learn to associate aggressive behaviour with positive reinforcement will be more likely to participate in aggressive behaviour in the future than children who learn to associate the behaviour with punishment (e.g., Bandura, Ross, & Ross, 1961).

Reinforcement can come from the behaviour of parents and peers, as well as from media sources such as television, movies, and video games. For example, Carnagey and Anderson (2005) conducted a

>>> **Frustration aggression theory suggests that** waiting in a long line might trigger aggressive behaviour.

> Reinforcement can come from the behaviour of parents and peers, as well as from media sources such as television, movies, and video games.

**GENERAL AGGRESSION MODEL (GAM)** a theory that builds on the social learning theory and provides a more integrative framework for specific theories of aggression by including situational and personal variables

study in which participants were asked to play one of three versions of a car-racing video game: a version in which all violence was punished (i.e., points were deducted), a version in which all violence was rewarded (i.e., points were added), and a nonviolent version in which aggressive behaviour had no impact on the player's score. Results of their research showed that rewarding violent game actions increased hostile emotions, aggressive thinking, and aggressive behaviour in participants. Punishing violent behaviour increased hostile emotions; however, it did not increase aggressive behaviour or aggressive thinking. The results suggest that positive reinforcement of violent actions can increase aggressive behaviour, cognitions, and affect (Carnagey & Anderson, 2005).

## GENERAL AGGRESSION MODEL

The **General Aggression Model (GAM)** builds on the social learning theory and provides a more integrative framework for specific theories of aggression by including different types of input variables (Anderson, Bushman, & Groom, 1997). According to GAM, two major types of input variables can trigger events that may eventually lead to blatant aggression—factors that relate to current situations, or *proximal factors*, and factors that influence aggression over a longer period of time, or *distal factors* (Anderson & Carnagey, 2004). Proximal factors include elements of the present situation (i.e., provocation, mood, pain/discomfort, social stress, and aggressive primes) as well as personal factors (i.e., self-esteem, beliefs and attitudes about aggression, personality traits). For example, individuals who score high on trait aggressiveness and irritability tend to engage in more aggressive behaviours, whether provoked or unprovoked (Bettencourt, Talley, Benjamin, & Valentine, 2006). Distal factors include environmental modifiers (i.e., family and cultural norms, media violence), as well as biological factors (i.e., hormones and genetics) that can increase or reduce risk of aggression (e.g., Anderson & Huesmann, 2003; Carnagey & Anderson, 2005).

**Social learning theory suggests that** observing others act aggressively serves as a model of behaviour **that we mimic, as in Bandura's classic Bobo doll research (see Bandura, 1965).**

**AVERSIVE EXPERIENCE** an undesirable experience that may include pain, discomfort, overcrowding, or attack

Input variables must influence several different processes at a variety of levels before they can increase or decrease aggressive behaviour. GAM suggests three routes of influence: affective state, cognitive state, and arousal state (Anderson & Carnagey, 2004). The affective state filters information and can initiate aggressive feelings and their outward signs, such as an angry glare or "the evil eye." The cognitive state processes information and can initiate aggressive thoughts or can stir up beliefs and attitudes about aggression. The arousal state determines what stimulates a person and can increase personal excitement. Depending on an individual's understanding of a present situation and the environmental factors involved, he or she employs either thoughtful action (e.g., restraining his or her anger) or impulsive action (e.g., releasing his or her anger through aggressive acts). This chain of events ultimately determines whether, and in what form, aggression occurs (Bushman & Anderson, 2002).

# What Influences Aggression?

Now that you understand the various theories of aggression, let's examine specific factors and conditions that may influence aggression. Based on surveys, correlational and experimental studies, social psychologists have found that aversive experiences, cues in the environment, and the effects of the media can create a powerful cocktail for personal aggression.

## AVERSIVE EXPERIENCES

Imagine you are at a summer music festival. It's one of the hottest days of the year, and it seems like everyone in a 50-kilometre radius is in attendance. The crowd is so dense that you hardly notice the broken bottle under your feet, and you end up slicing your foot on it as you make your way toward the main stage. The cut is pretty deep and painful, so you know that you need to find a first aid tent to get help. Moving back through the crowd is nearly impossible. Your foot is beginning to throb, and the sun is beating down on you. How are you feeling right now? Are you cursing under your breath about the people who carelessly discarded their bottles on the ground? Are you tempted to shove all the people in front of you in order to make your way out of the crowd? Even a typically passive person could be tempted to act aggressively during such an aversive experience.

An **aversive experience** is an undesirable experience that may include pain, discomfort, overcrowding, or attack. For example, research on crowd behaviour has found that overcrowding, in a variety of contexts, increases the rate of both verbal and physical aggression (e.g., Graham, Bernards, Osgood, & Wells, 2006; Ng, Kumar, Ranclaud, &

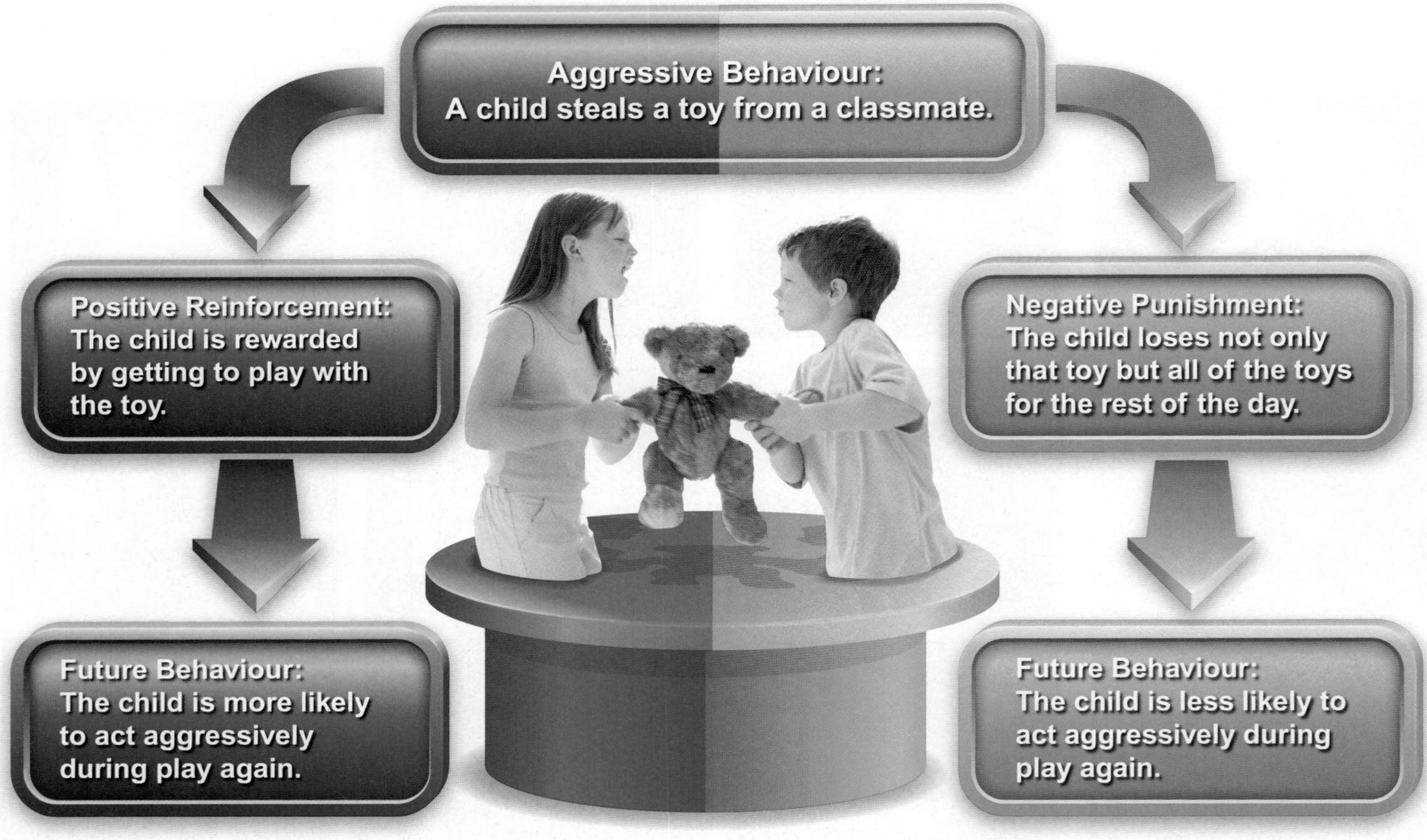


**The Reinforcement Chain Reaction.** When aggressive behaviour is met with positive reinforcement, it is more likely to lead to future aggressive behaviour than when it is met with negative punishment.

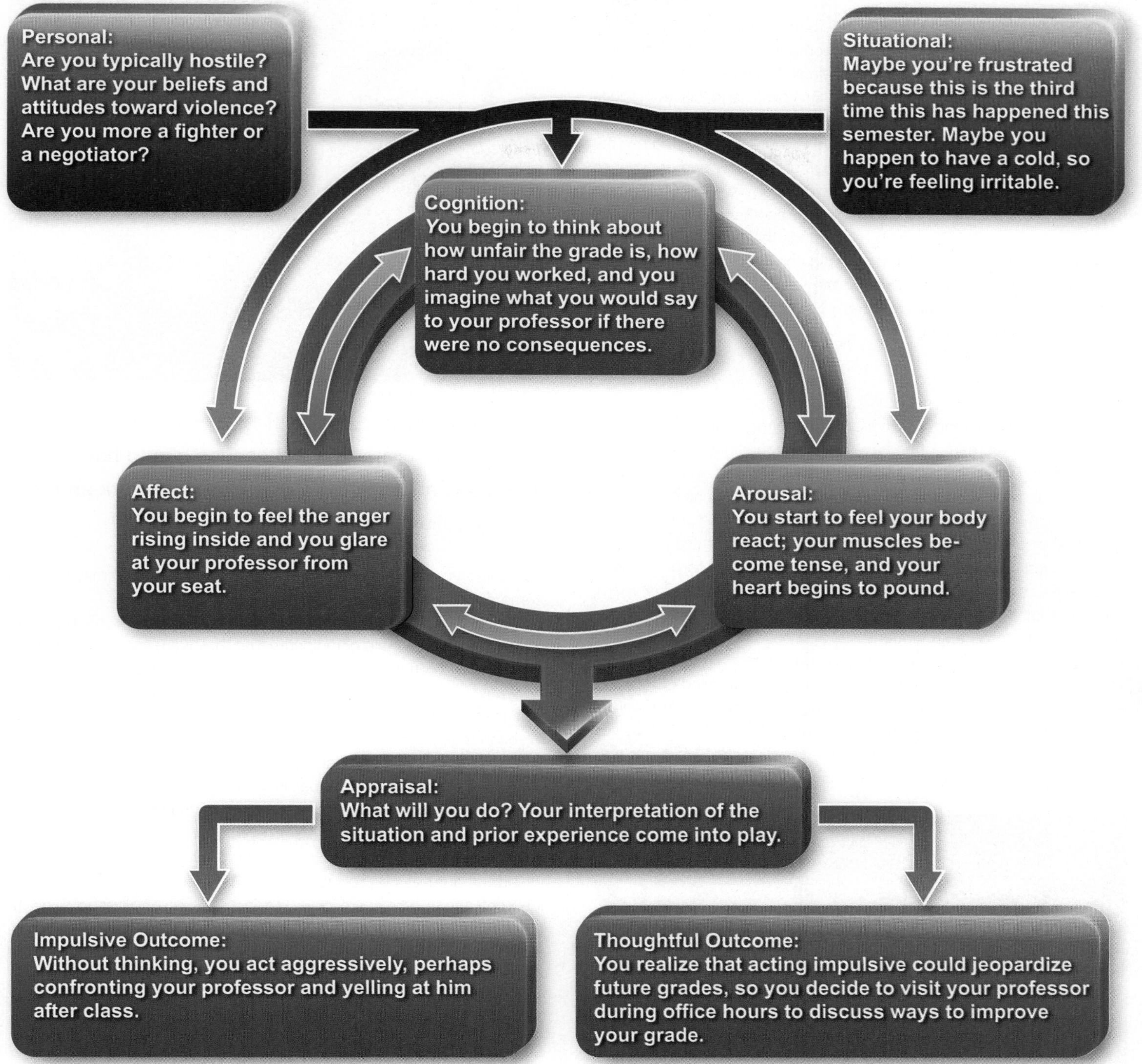

Personal:
Are you typically hostile? What are your beliefs and attitudes toward violence? Are you more a fighter or a negotiator?
Situational:
Maybe you're frustrated because this is the third time this has happened this semester. Maybe you happen to have a cold, so you're feeling irritable.
Cognition:
You begin to think about how unfair the grade is, how hard you worked, and you imagine what you would say to your professor if there were no consequences.
Affect:
You begin to feel the anger rising inside and you glare at your professor from your seat.
Arousal:
You start to feel your body react; your muscles become tense, and your heart begins to pound.
Appraisal:
What will you do? Your interpretation of the situation and prior experience come into play.
Impulsive Outcome:
Without thinking, you act aggressively, perhaps confronting your professor and yelling at him after class.
Thoughtful Outcome:
You realize that acting impulsive could jeopardize future grades, so you decide to visit your professor during office hours to discuss ways to improve your grade.


*Source*: Based on Bushman, B. J., & Anderson, C. A. (2002). Violent video games and hostile expectations: A test of the General Aggression Model. *Personality and Social Psychology Bulletin*, *28*, 1679–1689.

**The General Aggression Model.** The General Aggression Model (GAM) looks at the person in the given situation. It proposes that aggression is affected by several factors, including both proximal and distal factors that influence our cognitions, affect, and arousal when interpreting others' behaviour and deciding on our own reactions.

Robinson, 2001; Regoeczi, 2003). Studies have shown a link between increased aggression and higher temperatures due to the increase in physical arousal and discomfort that accompanies higher temperatures (Anderson, Deuser, & DeNeve, 1995). Pain also can be a powerful force that increases aggression in humans. Berkowitz and his colleagues conducted a study in which students submerged one hand in either tepid water or bitterly cold water. The students whose hands were in the bitterly cold water described more feelings of irritability and annoyance than those whose hands were in the tepid water. This group was also more willing to inflict an unpleasant noise on another study participant. These results prompted Berkowitz to conclude that aversive experience, rather than frustration, is the primary instigator of aggressive behaviour. It may be the culprit for bringing out the worst in us, as those made miserable often make others miserable (Berkowitz 1983, 1989, 1998). Misery loves company, right?

The arousal a football player receives from vigorous exercise **may cause him to have increased anger when a play does not work and the referee yells at him.**

## AROUSAL

It is easy to comprehend how certain experiences can spark aggressive behaviour, as many of us have been in conditions that make our blood boil (e.g., being stuck in a stuffy plane stranded on the runway). What about experiences that make our hearts pound? Types of arousal such as those associated with exercise or sexual excitement can have an effect on our aggression. Imagine that you've just had a vigorous workout at the gym; you took a lung-busting cardio class or lifted some serious weights. When you get back to the locker room, you find that the showers are out of order, so you can't clean up before you go to an appointment that you have scheduled. What do you do? Do you forcefully throw down your towel? Do you go to the front desk and give the gym manager a piece of your mind? Since this is merely a hypothetical situation and you have not actually received the physiological arousal from a workout, you may not think that you would have a very strong reaction to this situation. But what you may not realize is that the arousal you receive from a workout may work up some aggressive feelings.

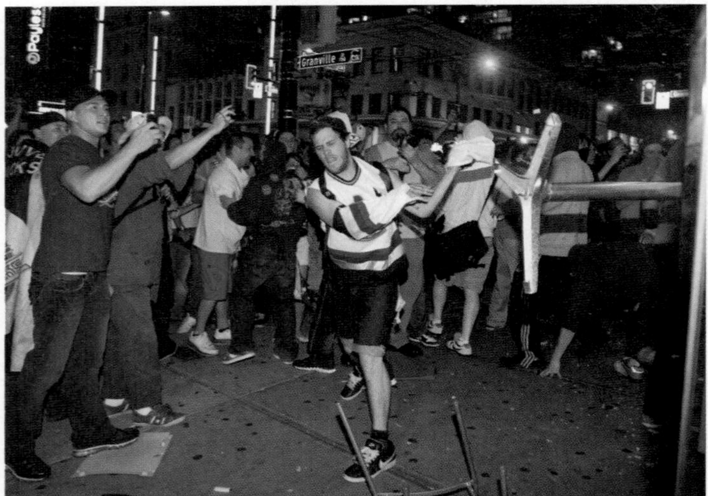

**During the Stanley Cup 2011 riot in Vancouver,** the loss by the Canucks and overcrowding on the streets were aversive experiences **that may have influenced aggressive responses.**

In a classic study of arousal and aggression, Schachter and Singer (1962) told male participants that they were involved in a study on vitamin injections and visual skill. Each participant was asked if he would be willing to receive an injection of "Suproxin," a name that was invented by the experimenters. The students who agreed to the injection received either adrenaline or saline, the latter of which served as a placebo. The individuals who were injected with the adrenaline were divided into three groups: informed (those who were told that the "Suproxin" produced side effects such as hand shaking and heart pounding, and who were therefore prepared for the effects of the adrenaline), misinformed (those who were told to expect effects that would not actually be produced by the drug, such as numb feet), and ignorant (those who were given no instructions of what to expect). Participants were then placed in a waiting room in which a confederate would either create a euphoria situation by entertaining the participant or an anger situation by annoying the participant. In both the euphoria situation and the anger situation, the informed group showed the least emotion. Researchers concluded that this occurred because participants had an explanation for why they felt aroused (the injection). They believed that it wasn't the confederate's behaviour that was making their body react—it was the drug. On the other hand, the misinformed and ignorant groups showed both increased happiness and increased anger in the simulated situations because they could not explain why their feelings were aroused.

These findings support the researchers' concept of a two-factor theory of emotional states that explains how appraisal shapes emotion. The theory says that physiological arousal in different emotions is completely the same; we simply label the arousal according to the information that we have available (Schachter & Singer, 1962). Under this principle, the anger you might feel in response to the situation at the gym could be reduced if you understood that physiological arousal had revved up your emotions. Other research notes that any arousal, even sexual arousal, can increase aggression (e.g., Cantor, Zillmann, & Einseidel, 1978; Seto, Maric, & Barbaree, 2001). It is important to note that arousal can be misinterpreted, and that cognitions about physiological arousal also can serve to decrease aggression (e.g., Tyson, 1998).

That said, we should remember that arousal is not a necessary component of emotions (Reisenzein, 1983) and that evidence for the two-factor theory is mixed (e.g., Marshall & Zimbardo, 1979; Maslach, 1979). However, another theory that builds on the two-factor idea is the excitation-transfer theory (Zillmann, 1983, 1996): a person may experience arousal in one situation, and that may not fully dissipate before another situation occurs. The excitement from the first situation can transfer to another event, and the same kind of arousal (e.g., anger, aggression) also will transfer to that second scenario. For example, if a man is reprimanded at work and becomes upset, he may return home and display anger toward his family, even though his anger is actually meant for the workplace.

## CUES IN THE ENVIRONMENT

What do you think of when you see a gun? Safety, danger, or violence? According to Berkowitz and other psychologists, the sight of a weapon such as a gun is an environmental cue that can prime aggressive thoughts (e.g., Anderson, Benjamin, & Bartholow, 1998; Berkowitz, 1993). In a study conducted by Berkowitz and LePage (1967), participants were given electric shocks by a study administrator. Later, the participants were given the opportunity to shock the administrator. During the study, some participants were sitting at a table with the shock machine and two badminton rackets; others were at a table with both the machine and a 12-gauge shotgun and a 38-calibre revolver. All objects were supposedly left behind from a previous experiment. The results showed that participants who sat at the table with the guns gave more electric shocks to the administrator than those participants who sat at the table with the racket (Berkowitz & LePage, 1967). Berkowitz conducted a similar follow-up study with children. He found that children

You're waiting in line at a hot dog stand on the beach on a sweltering day. The line is long, and all you want is some water. As you wait, the experience becomes more and more aversive. What would trigger an aggressive action?
Arousal: As the sun beats down on you, your heart rate increases, your skin feels like it's burning, and you begin to sweat.
Angry feelings: You think about how thirsty you feel, and you start to get angry at how long the line is taking. Why would serving hot dogs take this much time?
Aggressive thoughts: It occurs to you that you could just cut in line; after all, these people want hot dogs and you just want water. Or maybe you envision yourself telling the kids behind the stand to hurry it up.
You can't take it anymore! Will you take aggressive action?

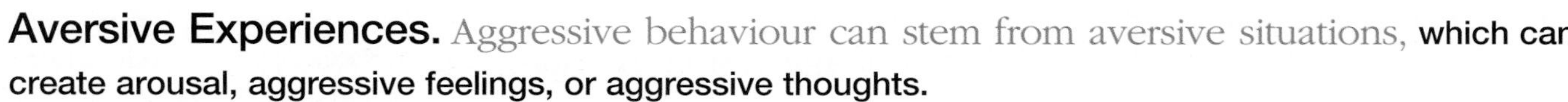
**Aversive Experiences.** Aggressive behaviour can stem from aversive situations, which can create arousal, aggressive feelings, or aggressive thoughts.

who had recently played with toy guns were more willing to knock down another child's tower of blocks (Berkowitz, 1968).

These studies suggest that environmental cues such as guns can create hostile thoughts and subsequently instigate aggressive actions. Berkowitz associates the rate of handgun crime with handgun ownership. Though controversial, Berkowitz's claim is supported by statistics showing that gun owners are 2.7 times more likely to be murdered, almost always by a family member or close friend who would have been most likely to have had visual exposure to the gun (Kellerman, 1993). That said, while Edmonton was recently labelled the murder capital of Canada in 2011, this city does not have the highest rates of gun registration per capita in the province or country (Staples, 2011). Research has found that the weapon-priming effect may be dependent on the perception of the weapon, and whether the gun is viewed as a tool of violence, rather than a hunting tool. Bartholow et al. (2005) demonstrated this when hunters saw a hunting rifle and did not experience an increase of aggressive thoughts, while non-hunters did experience an increase. According to the General Aggression Model, such differences in interpretation of cues can make the difference between an aggressive or passive response (Anderson & Carnagey, 2004).

## MEDIA VIOLENCE

Famed film director Oliver Stone is quoted as saying, "Film is a powerful medium. Film is a drug. Film is a potential hallucinogen. It goes into your eye. It goes into your brain. It stimulates, and it's a dangerous thing. It can be a very subversive thing" (British Broadcasting Corporation, 1995). While Stone's comments may be slightly tongue-in-cheek, many people believe that violence in the media is a very real threat to our society. They feel that exposure to aggressive behaviour via television, movies, music, or books can cause children and even adults to act aggressively. This belief has been supported by research (e.g., Bushman & Anderson, 2001; Bushman & Huesmann, 2001) and many health organizations, but as you have learned so far in this chapter, aggression is not as simple as "monkey see, monkey do." It is generally agreed upon that media has some influence on behaviour, but how and to what extent? There are correlational studies on this subject, from which we can only infer a relationship, and then there are experimental studies, which allow us to isolate possible causal variables (review research methodology in Chapter 2). Let's examine this issue, but keep in mind that the results of the research should not be interpreted to mean that all people who watch television or play video games will commit acts of violence.

### Models Aggression

On April 20, 1999, two male students walked into Columbine High School in Littleton, Colorado, wearing black trench coats and toting semi-automatic handguns, shotguns, and explosives. Within an hour, the boys killed 12 fellow students, one teacher, and themselves. One week later, on April 27, 1999, a 14-year-old boy brought a rifle to W. R. Myers High School in Taber, Alberta, and opened fire, killing one student and injuring another ("Tragedy in Taber," 2004). To witnesses, these events were like scenes right out of a movie. Were they? Many different factors were blamed for these tragedies—poor parental supervision, bullying by peers, signs of depression, and the availability of guns.

But it was exposure to violence in the media that drew the most attention in both of these cases. In the Columbine shootings, the attack was nearly identical to a fantasy scene from the 1995 film *The Basketball Diaries*, in which the protagonist (played by Leonardo DiCaprio) walks down the halls of his school in a trench coat and randomly shoots classmates with a shotgun. Similarly, psychologist Dr. John Satterberg said the Taber shooting resulted from the teen's obsession with violent movies and video games ("Tragedy in Taber," 2004). Many people believe that children and adults exposed to violent behaviour through the media will likely model that behaviour in real life, as in Bandura's Bobo doll study, discussed earlier (e.g., Freedman, 2002; Kirsh, 2012). While these events were eerily similar to violent media (right down to the trench coat attire), we shouldn't assume that these acts were perpetrated solely because of the influence of media. There were many factors at play here, including the reality that each of these boys were social outcasts, and had been bullied.

Television in particular is often pinpointed as the largest provider of violent messages, as it is the most accessible medium to the average Canadian. For example, a study in 1982 found that aggression in both Canadian and American television programs was portrayed regularly (9 physically aggressive acts and 7.8 verbally aggressive acts per program hour) and rarely were alternatives to aggression sought. In fact, aggression was often portrayed as comical and consequences to aggressive behaviour were generally absent (Williams, Zabrack, & Joy, 1982). Imagine how much aggression is displayed in current television programming, in our culture of apparent acceptance of violence as entertainment. That said, while it might be common for some children to imitate the kicks they see in a kung fu cartoon or some adults to try to replicate a grappling move they see during a televised mixed martial arts fight, this does not mean that everyone is likely to model violent behaviour displayed through the media. If that were the case, millions of people would tote samurai swords and administer violent vengeance on anyone who crossed them, à la Uma Thurman in Quentin Tarantino's graphically violent *Kill Bill* movies.

There are certain things we can look at to get a glimpse into the likelihood of aggression in children. Dodge's social information processing theory is a five-step model that outlines a child's response to a problematic situation (e.g., Crick & Dodge, 1994; Dodge, 1986). The five steps—encoding social cues, interpreting social cues, searching for a response, evaluating a response, and enacting—can be applied to how children process information coming from the media. A child moves through the model successfully, or possibly is hindered by bias and deficient ability to process the situation. The child who fails to navigate the problem is more likely to exhibit aggressive behaviour. Research has proposed that cognition mediates aggression in children, and may ultimately help mitigate aggression in children if they can learn to respond to problems in different ways (Kirch, 2012).

Does this collection of guns ignite feelings of aggression in you?

### Primes Aggression

The media does not have to be a how-to guide in order to influence aggression; it can simply *prime* thoughts and feelings of aggression, which may eventually lead to aggressive behaviour. Violent video games are often accused of priming aggressive thoughts and feelings in children and teens (Anderson, Gentile, & Buckley, 2007). In a study investigating the effect that violent video games have on aggression, researchers randomly assigned two video games to members of a group of 43 participants. Some played *Mortal Kombat* (a violent video game), and others played *Tiger Woods PGA Tour* (a nonviolent video game). After the participants played their assigned game, they performed a retaliation reaction time task with a study administrator. The participant set the punishment levels (punishment was in the form of noise) for the administrator during the task. Researchers found that the participants who played the violent video game used higher levels of noise when they were in the punisher role. It was concluded that the violent video game primed the aggressive feelings of participants, causing them to act out their aggression on the study administrator (Bartholow & Anderson, 2002).

Music, and particularly music with explicit lyrics, is also a media source that can prime aggressive behaviour. In the way that "Let's Get It Started" by the Black Eyed Peas might get you pumped to perform your best in a game, songs with violent lyrics might get you primed for aggression. In a 2006 study, participants were asked to listen to either a song with misogynistic lyrics such as Bloodhound Gang's "A Lapdance Is So Much Better When the Stripper's Crying," and Dr. Dre's "Bitches Ain't Shit," or a song with more neutral lyrics such as Miley Cyrus's "The Climb" (Fischer & Greitemeyer, 2006). Participants were told that they were participating in a music survey. After participants listened to their assigned song, they were asked to prepare a sample of hot sauce for another participant, either male or female, who was secretly one of the study administrators. The participants heard the confederate state that they did not enjoy spicy foods and were told that they could dish out as large of a sample as they wished with the knowledge that the "participant" would be required to drink the entire sample. The results of the survey showed that participants who heard the misogynistic lyrics gave more hot sauce to female administrators than to male administrators. The group who listened to the neutral lyrics did not show this discrepancy. The results of this study suggest that misogynistic lyrics can prime aggressive feelings against women and cause individuals to model the behaviour described in the lyrics.

> ". . .whether violence is expressed on television, in music, or in a violent video game, a person's arousal, affect, and cognitions about the media are likely to moderate whether he or she will engage in violence."

### Repeated Exposure to Violence

As we discovered from social learning theory, aggressive responses are stimulated in individuals either by their personal experiences or by their observation of others. Actors on television or in the movies serve as models for viewers, and with more than half of major actors shown on network television continuously involved in violent interactions, it is likely that television actors are frequent models of aggressive behaviour. As we learned from Bandura, viewers are likely to imitate aggressive models if the behaviour is rewarded or goes unpunished. Repeated exposure to rewarded or unpunished violence may lead viewers to believe that if others can constantly behave aggressively without being punished, then that behaviour is acceptable for them as well. In a recent analysis, more than 5,000 hours of programming on network and cable broadcasts showed violence being rewarded 15 percent of the time and unpunished 73 percent of the time (Federman, 1997). For example, popular programs such as FX's *The Shield* and Showtime's *Dexter* frequently exhibit violent behaviour being rewarded.

**DESENSITIZATION** a process through which physiological reactions to violence are reduced as a result of repeated exposure

This repeated exposure to violent media, particularly violence that is rewarded, can desensitize a viewer to the violence. When **desensitization** occurs, a viewer's physiological reactions to violence are reduced as a result of repeated exposure. According to an American Psychological Association task force report on television and society, by the time the average child completes elementary school, he or she will have viewed more than 8,000 murders and more than 100,000 other assorted acts of violence on television (also see Williams et al., 1982). The emergence of online streaming of television shows on computers and personal mobile devices allows even more frequent and extreme acts to be displayed inside and outside the home.

That said, whether violence is expressed on television, in music, or in a violent video game, a person's arousal, affect, and cognitions about the media are likely to moderate whether he or she will engage in violence. As per the General Aggression Model, both proximal (current situational variables and personal factors) as well as distal (environment and biology) can serve to increase or decrease risk of aggression (see Anderson et al., 2007). For example, if a young teen spends a few hours playing violent video games but is not normally aggressive or short-tempered and has many prosocial values, he will not inevitably engage in violence as a result of his video games. This also applies to whether the teen plays six hours of violent games per day or does so only occasionally. Predicting the outcomes of these various factors is much more complex that simply stating that violent media exposure causes aggression.

## SOCIAL MEDIA

While television, music, and video games play a significant role in desensitization, social media have increasingly been a vehicle for predators to perpetrate aggression. Earlier in this chapter, we discussed how the use of social media, such as Facebook and chat programs, may result in cyberbullying (e.g., Mishna et al., 2009). These communication channels have also been used to locate or lure in potential victims of violence. For example, convicted Edmonton killer Mark Andrew Twitchell used dating sites to lure unsuspecting men into his "kill room." He posed as a single woman and asked men to meet him in his garage, which he was using as a set for a horror movie he was filming. One potential victim escaped, but Johnny Altinger was not so lucky. On October 10, 2008, he arrived at Twitchell's garage and was never seen alive again. Several days later, Twitchell hacked into Altinger's email account and sent a message (pretending to be Johnny) indicating that he had met a woman and was going on a tropical vacation for weeks. His remains were not discovered until June 2010, when Twitchell provided police with a Google Maps printout of where Altinger's body was. Twitchell was convicted of first-degree murder in April 2011 ("The Mark Twitchell Case," 2011). While this case is extreme, it illustrates just one of many ways in which social media and dating sites have been used to perpetrate aggression. For example, online messages have been used to organize meeting places for hazing rituals or flash mobs. Online stalking and harassment also has increased worldwide, as more sophisticated technology is developed to recognize and track people from photos or personal information (Schrammel, Köffel, & Tscheligi, 2009). Further, videos posted on YouTube or other websites have been used as a recruitment tool for gangs. Only recently, following the riots across England in August 2011, has new legislation been proposed by England's Labour MP Heidi Alexander to give police and internet providers permission to remove online videos that could incite violence (Halliday, 2011). As you can see, aggression is not solely produced in reaction to violent video games or programs on television.

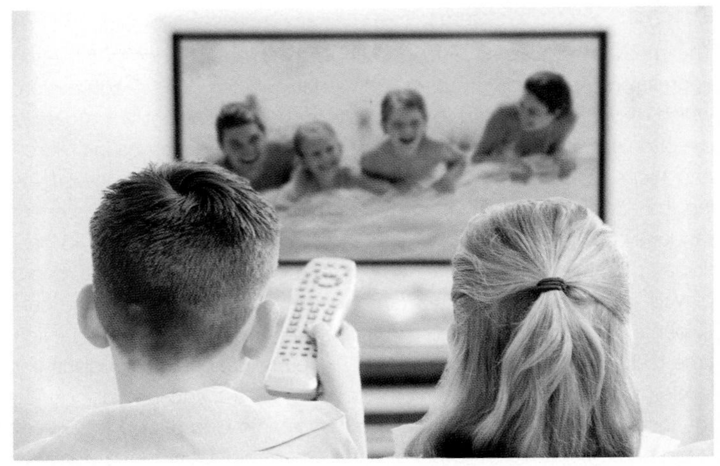

**Research has reported that approximately 81 percent of parents have seen their** children imitate either positive (e.g., helping) or aggressive (e.g., punching or hitting) behaviours they see modelled on TV.

# How Can We Reduce Aggression?

Let's think about what we have learned so far in this chapter. Observations, genetics, biochemical makeup, culture, aversive experiences, arousal, environmental cues, and the media can all potentially lead us to act aggressively. With all of these factors encouraging us to act aggressively, why isn't everyone in the world in constant opposition? Well, aggression is not inevitable. In fact, recent studies show that the rate of violent crimes are actually decreasing overall in Canada and the United States (e.g., Anderson & Huesmann, 2003; "Violent Crime," 2009). Aggression can be reduced and even prevented in many cases through several strategies. The source of the aggression might affect which prevention strategy is most effective in any given situation.



## PUNISHMENT

As we learned from Bandura's social learning theory, children are likely to model aggressive behaviour if they see that behaviour rewarded. Similarly, they are less likely to model aggressive behaviour if that behaviour is punished. For example, when the children in the Bobo doll study were shown a video that displayed an adult kicking the doll and then getting yelled at for doing so, the children were less likely to model the aggressive form of play.

Unfortunately, punishment alone is not completely effective because several types of aggression stem from impulsive reactions. A man punches another man who makes a quick and threatening move toward him. A woman yells out a threatening curse word when the person in the car next to her cuts her off. When people act impulsively, they do not have time to think about the consequences of their actions. Let's use capital punishment as an example. This punishment is used as a deterrent for heinous crimes such as murder; however, murders are typically committed on impulse and without premeditation (reactive aggression; see Woodworth & Porter, 2002). The vast majority of evidence has demonstrated that capital punishment is no more effective than imprisonment as a deterrent for murder (e.g., Donohue & Wolfers, 2006; Hjalmarsson, 2009). This evidence has led to a widespread abolishment of the death penalty in Canada and in many states in the United States. Despite fears of an increased homicide rate, when Canada abolished the death penalty in 1976, rates actually decreased (Vidmar & Dittenhoffer, 1981). This was explained via the *brutalization hypothesis*, which posits that lethal punishment brutalizes the population into believing that violence is an acceptable form of punishment (Cochran & Chamlin, 2000). Even for non-physical aggression, individuals may not think about the possible consequences or punishment for their behaviour. The assailants in Reena Virk's case, discussed in the opening of the chapter, most likely did not consider that spreading rumours and bullying could cause a person's death and subsequently send them to jail.

One of the major flaws in the use of punishment as a method to reduce aggression is that it does not show the individual an example of acceptable behaviour. It does not draw a distinction between how a situation is handled with aggression and how it can be appropriately handled without aggression. In fact, studies evaluating the use of physical punishment by parents on their child's subsequent behaviours have reported an increase in aggressive actions (e.g., Durrant, Rose-Krasnor, & Broberg, 2003). Use of aggression to punish aggression sends the message "aggression is okay." However, beliefs concerning the appropriate use of physical punishment have shifted, and a recent survey in Quebec suggests that parents report seeking alternative forms of discipline (Clément & Chamberland, 2007).

## MODELLING NON-AGGRESSION

Just as the modelling concept can lower inhibitions and encourage imitation when aggressive behaviour is observed, it can also increase self-control and encourage obedience when non-aggressive behaviour is observed (e.g., Ostrov, Gentile, & Crick, 2006). A television program that shows a protagonist who typically does the "right thing" (e.g., solves conflicts with peaceful discussion, displays self-control) can serve as a non-aggressive model. Incorporating these types of models in children's lives through positive television programming or organizations such as Big Brother, Big Sister can help children learn how to control their aggression and become less violent adults. Further, parents who use proactive strategies for resolving conflict also serve as positive role models for their children.

## TRAINING

One of the best methods for reducing aggression is to prevent it before it happens. Training individuals to engage in non-aggressive conflict resolution strategies can help to accomplish this. Wilson and Lipsey (2006) collected data from 249 studies of school violence prevention programs and found that these types of programs were effective in reducing violence, particularly in the case of programs that engaged students with behavioural problems. In these programs, students were taught problem-solving skills, conflict resolution techniques, and emotion-control strategies. After completion of a given program, the percentage of students who participated in violent or disruptive behaviour was reduced from 20 percent to 13 percent (Wilson & Lipsey, 2006). The kids who were charged in the Reena Virk murder case are prime examples of those who should participate in programs that work to prevent violence in schools—perhaps if people are given non-violent tools to deal with peers with whom they have conflicts, fewer stories like Reena's will end so tragically.

<<< **How often do you wish that you could immediately take back something you have said in a verbal argument?** Many of our aggressive acts are triggered by impulse, so we do not take the time to consider the consequences.

# ACTION LEARNING

## Action Learning Project: Reducing Aggression

The tragedies at Columbine and Taber that were previously mentioned unfortunately have not been the only occurrences of this type. Among other recent school violence incidents, the murderous rampage at Virginia Polytechnic Institute in 2007, perpetrated by Seung-Hui Cho, resulted in 32 deaths before he killed himself. What can be done to protect students from violence from elementary school all the way through college or university? What have you learned in this chapter that applies?

Consider teaching others to reduce and even prevent violence by introducing the General Aggression Model. Design a violence prevention workshop for children based on the GAM. Use the chart below to organize your ideas, and draw out the model in terms that a young child could understand. Be sure to simplify the terms and concepts. Explain how this type of education could decrease some of the bullying that children and teenagers experience at school. Contact your campus child development centre or a local elementary school to see if you can share your project with them. Ask your instructor if you can present your project in class to show how social psychology can be applied.

What you will learn from this action learning project:

1. How social psychology theories can help reduce or even prevent aggression
2. How to educate others about reducing aggression
3. How children react to non-aggressive modeling

**How Will You React? Explaining the General Aggression Model to Children**

| | | | |
|---|---|---|---|
| ***Inputs*** | Personal: | | Situation: |
| ***Routes*** | Affect: | Cognition: | Arousal: |
| ***Outcomes*** | Thoughtful Action: | | Impulsive Action: |

# CHAPTER 11 Review

## Summary

### WHAT IS THE NATURE OF AGGRESSION? p. 204

• Social psychologists are interested in what causes aggressive behaviour and have sought for several years to achieve a better understanding of its nature through research. They anticipate that the better we understand human nature, the better equipped we are to prevent aggressive acts.

• Aggression comes in two forms: hostile (affective) and instrumental. Hostile aggression occurs when the primary goal of an action or behaviour is to make the victim suffer. Individuals who participate in hostile aggression, then, are simply seeking to harm or injure the target of their attack. Instrumental aggression occurs when the primary goal of the action is not to make the victim suffer but to attain a non-injurious goal. An individual who participates in instrumental aggression will harm or injure another as a way of obtaining various rewards such as control of a situation or improved self-esteem.

• While we often think of aggression as being triggered by the actions of another person, it can also be triggered by cultural factors. A culture's system of values, beliefs, and norms may suggest that aggression is appropriate, or even necessary, in certain circumstances. In cultures where the law is weak and citizens need to protect themselves, the act or even the threat of violence is considered to be essential.

### WHAT ARE THE THEORIES OF AGGRESSION? p. 207

• Freud believed that aggression stems from a self-destructive impulse and that humans must act out that impulse in order to release negative energy and return to a state of calm—a behaviour Freud refers to as a "death drive." Lorenz believed that through evolution, humans developed a fighting instinct similar to that found in animals.

• Social learning theory suggests that human aggression is largely learned by observing the aggressive behaviour of other people and is affected by consequences such as punishment or reward in the individual's environment. Psychologist Albert Bandura developed social learning theory, also referred to as social cognitive theory, during the 1960s.

• The General Aggression Model (GAM) builds on the social learning theory and provides a more integrative framework for specific theories of aggression by including input variables. According to the GAM, two major types of input variables can trigger events that may eventually lead to blatant aggression—factors that relate to current situations, or situational factors, and factors that relate to the individuals involved, or personal factors.

### WHAT INFLUENCES AGGRESSION? p. 212

• There are several factors that influence aggression, including aversive experiences, arousal, and cues in the environment. Aversive experiences can come in the form of pain, discomfort, or personal attacks. Arousal from sources such as exercise and sex can be transformed into aggression. Environmental cues such as guns or other weapons increase the likelihood of aggression.

• Viewing violence either in person or on television can increase aggressive behaviour, particularly when individuals are provoked. It can also desensitize viewers to violence, making them less aware of the harmful results of their actions.

### HOW CAN WE REDUCE AGGRESSION? p. 218

• Aggression is not inevitable. It can be reduced and even prevented in many cases through several strategies. The source of the aggression might impact which prevention strategy is most effective in a given situation.

• Children are likely to imitate aggressive behaviour if they see that behaviour rewarded. Similarly, they are less likely to imitate aggressive behaviour if that behaviour is punished.

• Just as the modelling concept can lower inhibitions and encourage imitation when aggressive behaviour is observed, it can also increase self-control and encourage obedience when non-aggressive behaviour is observed.

## Key Terms

**aggression** behaviour, either verbal or physical, that is used to intentionally harm another individual *204*

**aversive experience** an undesirable experience that may include pain, discomfort, overcrowding, or attack *212*

**cognitive-neoassociation theory** a theory which suggests that when a person experiences something with a negative result, such as pain or discomfort, aggressive behaviour can often occur in the wake of that experience *209*

**culture of honour** a culture in which strong norms suggest that aggression is an appropriate response to an insult or threat to one's honour *206*

**desensitization** a process through which physiological reactions to violence are reduced as a result of repeated exposure *217*

**direct aggression** an action or a behaviour that is clearly derived from the aggressor and is aimed directly at the target *205*

**expressive view of aggression** a view of aggression as a way to express anger and reduce stress *206*

**frustration** a feeling of being upset or annoyed by the inability to reach a goal or perform an activity *209*

**frustration aggression theory** a theory which states that frustration precedes aggression because our motivation for aggression increases when our current behaviour is interrupted or we are prevented from reaching a goal *209*

**General Aggression Model (GAM)** a theory that builds on the social learning theory and provides a more integrative framework for specific theories of aggression by including situational and personal variables *211*

**hostile (affective) aggression** behaviour that occurs when the primary goal of an action is to make the victim suffer *204*

**indirect aggression** an action or a behaviour that is not clearly derived from the aggressor, and where it is not obvious to the target that he or she has been the victim of aggression *205*

**instinct theory** a theory in which aggression is an innate and inevitable force *207*

**instrumental aggression** behaviour that occurs when the primary goal of an action is not to make the victim suffer but to attain a non-injurious goal *204*

**instrumental view of aggression** a view of aggression as a way to gain social or material rewards *206*

**modelling** a process in which one person engages in behaviour that is mimicked by another person *210*

**reinforcement** an action or process that strengthens a behaviour *210*

**social learning theory** a theory which suggests that human aggression is largely learned by observing the aggressive behaviour of other people and is reinforced by consequences such as punishment or reward in the individual's environment *210*

# Test Your Understanding

## MULTIPLE CHOICE

1. Which of the following situations is an example of hostile (affective) aggression?
   - **a.** A baseball player rushes the pitcher's mound after being hit by a ball.
   - **b.** A basketball player elbows an opponent in the eye after a rebound.
   - **c.** A football player knocks down a receiver after he catches the ball.
   - **d.** A soccer player steps on the foot of an official while going for the ball.
2. What group would most likely be the target of aggression?
   - **a.** men
   - **b.** teens
   - **c.** the elderly
   - **d.** women
3. Which of the following is an example of indirect aggression?
   - **a.** a verbal insult to a person's face
   - **b.** a punch in the stomach
   - **c.** a rumour that is told in secret
   - **d.** a noticeable snub at a party
4. What is the flaw in the instinct theory?
   - **a.** It only applies to animals and does not apply to human behaviour.
   - **b.** It does not take into account the differences in behaviour between individuals.
   - **c.** It does not include verbal aggression.
   - **d.** It does not take history into consideration.
5. Which of the following is not a biological force of aggression?
   - **a.** genetics
   - **b.** biochemical makeup
   - **c.** hormones
   - **d.** observations
6. Reinforcements influence aggression by
   - **a.** creating additional frustration.
   - **b.** rewarding behaviour.
   - **c.** regulating stimuli.
   - **d.** increasing environmental cues.
7. According to GAM, what are elements of a given situation that can increase aggression?
   - **a.** biological variables
   - **b.** situational factors
   - **c.** personal factors
   - **d.** instinct variables
8. Which of the following is not an element of an aversive experience?
   - **a.** discomfort
   - **b.** knowledge
   - **c.** attack
   - **d.** pain
9. Through what method of influence does television induce violence?
   - **a.** modelling
   - **b.** authoritarianism
   - **c.** frustration
   - **d.** reiteration
10. Which of the following is a method to reduce aggression?
    - **a.** increased arousal
    - **b.** genetic engineering
    - **c.** non-aggressive modelling
    - **d.** appraisal

**ANSWERS:** 1. a; 2. d; 3. c; 4. b; 5. d; 6. b; 7. b; 8. b; 9. a; 10. c

## ESSAY RESPONSE

1. Is the fighting a soldier engages in during wartime considered emotional or instrumental aggression? Why? Can it be both?
2. Give an example of a culture of honour in Canada and explain the forces that impact that culture.
3. How do biological factors work with environmental factors to impact aggression?
4. What reinforcements and punishments (positive and negative) might be involved in a physical fight between two men over a woman they both have interest in?
5. How strongly does television influence your behaviour? Have you ever modelled the behaviour of an actor?

## APPLY IT!

Conduct your own study on the effects of violent song lyrics. Ask your friends to bounce a ball against a wall as they listen to a song that includes lyrics about violence and then a song that includes neutral lyrics. Notice the change, if any, in the force your participant uses while listening to each song.

**Remember to check www.thethinkspot.ca for additional information, downloadable flashcards, and other helpful resources.**

How does this relate to what you just learned about sex differences in aggression? Could aggression in men be more biologically based, relative to women, who may be more influenced by social and environmental factors?

In Chapter 9 we discussed the Prisoner's Dilemma game. If you could detect a "cheater" or a liar based on how his or her face looks, what type of advantage do you think that would give you in group decisions? How does this correspond to what you learned about deception detection in Chapter 5?

When you read Chapter 2 about operational definitions, think about how this applies to defining a vague concept like aggression. Do button presses reflecting an intention to 'steal points' really reflect aggression?

ink about what you learned out attribution in Chapter 5. hen you first meet other ople, how do you use their cial cues to judge their person- ty and disposition?

PSYCHOLOGICAL SCIENCE

*Research Report*

# Facial Structure Is a Reliable Cue of Aggressive Behavior

JUSTIN M. CARRÉ,[1] CHERYL M. McCORMICK,[1,2] and CATHERINE J. MONDLOCH[1,2]

[1]*Department of Psychology and* [2]*Centre for Neuroscience, Brock University*

**ABSTRACT**—*Facial width-to-height ratio is a sexually dimorphic metric that is independent of body size and may have been shaped by sexual selection. We recently showed that this metric is correlated with behavioral aggression in men. In Study 1, observers estimated the propensity for aggression of men photographed displaying neutral facial expressions and for whom a behavioral measure of aggression was obtained. The estimates were correlated strongly with the facial width-to-height ratio of the stimulus faces and with the actual aggression of the men. These results were replicated in Study 2, in which the exposure to each stimulus face was shortened to 39 ms. Participants' estimates of aggression for each stimulus face were highly correlated between Study 2 (39-ms exposure) and Study 1 (2,000-ms exposure). These findings suggest that the facial width-to-height ratio may be a cue used to predict propensity for aggression in others.*

The human face is a basis for judgments about gender, ethnicity, attractiveness, emotion, and personality traits (Zebrowitz, 2006). In fact, personality attributions based on the characteristics of the face show high rates of consensus across observers (Penton-Voak, Pound, Little, & Perrett, 2006; Todorov, Mandisodza, Goren, & Hall, 2005), are made very quickly (Bar, Neta, & Linz, 2006; Willis & Todorov, 2006), and, for certain traits, are somewhat accurate (Penton-Voak et al., 2006). People are relatively good at identifying "cheaters" in a Prisoner's Dilemma game based on facial photographs (Verplaetse, Vanneste, & Braeckman, 2007), and women's judgments of men's interest in infants based on their faces predicted their actual interest in infants (Roney, Hanson, Durante, & Maestripieri, 2006). There is some evidence that "baby facedness," characterized by round faces and big eyes, is associated with social, intellectual, and physical weakness (Zebrowitz, Fellous, Mignault, & Andreoletti, 2003). Also, people are accurate in estimating the physical strength and fighting ability of others based on facial information (Sell et al., 2009), although the facial metrics used to make such judgments are not well understood.

Recently, Weston, Friday, and Lio (2007) identified a sexually dimorphic characteristic of the face that was independent of body size from a morphometric analysis of an ontogenetic series of human skulls. They found that the growth trajectories of males and females diverged at puberty for bizygomatic width and not for upper facial height (from the upper lip to the mid-brow), leading to a width-to-height facial dimorphism (greater ratio in men than in women). They proposed that the sexual dimorphism in facial width-to-height may reflect a sexual selection pressure that is independent of selection for body size.

We recently reported that individual differences in the facial width-to-height ratio (WHR) accounted for a significant proportion of variance in aggressive behavior in men, but not women, tested in the laboratory (Carré & McCormick, 2008). Aggression was measured in the lab using a modified version of the point-subtraction aggression paradigm, in which players have continuous access to three buttons: Pressing one button earns points, pressing another protects the player from having points stolen, and pressing the third button steals points from a fictitious opponent to no benefit to the player. Aggression is defined as the number of button presses on that third button. Facial WHR was correlated with actual aggression in men ($r = .38$), but not women. A similar finding was obtained in elite male hockey players when aggression was defined as the number of penalty minutes per game. The goal of the current study was to determine whether observers' estimates of propensity for aggression are correlated with individual differences in the facial WHR, a finding that would suggest that this facial metric could be used to predict another's propensity for aggressive behavior.

Here, we asked observers to estimate the propensity for aggression of men photographed displaying neutral facial expressions and for whom a behavioral measure of aggression previously had been obtained (Carré & McCormick,

Address correspondence to Cheryl M. McCormick, Department of Psychology and Centre for Neuroscience, Brock University, 500 Glenridge Ave., St. Catharines, Ontario, Canada L2S 3A1, e-mail: cmccormick@brocku.ca.

2008). In the first study, participants viewed the stimulus faces for 2,000 ms; in the second study, participants viewed the stimulus faces for 39 ms.

## METHOD

### Participants

Two samples of undergraduate students (Study 1: 16 women, 15 men; mean age = 19.94 years, *SD* = 2.05 years; Study 2: 16 women, 0 men; mean age = 19.38 years, *SD* = 1.41 years) received course credit for participation. The procedures were approved by Brock University's Research Ethics Board.

### Stimuli

Photographs were obtained from a sample of 37 men for which aggressive behavior and facial WHR was quantified previously (see Carré & McCormick, 2008). These men were volunteers from an introductory psychology participant pool who received a $5 honorarium and course credit for their participation. Aggressive behavior was measured using a modified version of the point subtraction aggression paradigm, a well-validated laboratory task (e.g., Cherek, Schnapp, Moeller, & Dougherty, 1996). The facial WHR of the men was measured using NIH ImageJ software and involved the landmarks originally used by Weston et al. (2007). Specifically, the distance between the left and right zygion (bizygomatic width) was divided by the distance between the upper lip and mid-brow (upper facial height) to yield the facial WHR (see Fig. 1). For the studies described here, the sample of stimulus faces was reduced to include only Caucasian men without facial hair (to avoid judgments based on stereotypes) and displaying neutral expressions (*n* = 24, mean age = 19.08 years, *SD* = 1.41 years). Faces were converted to 8-bit gray scale, standardized using a hairline-chin distance of 400 pixels, and placed within a black background.

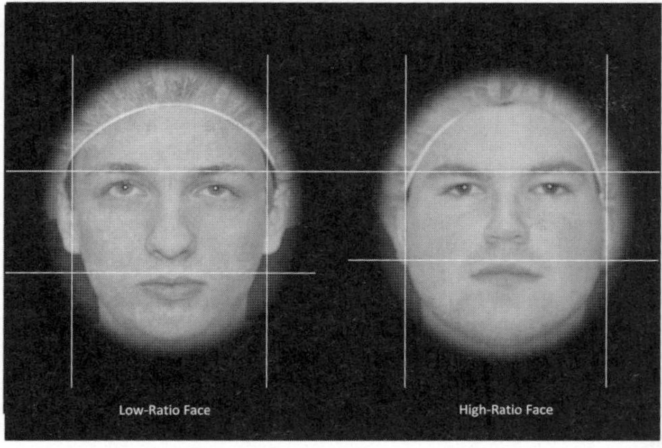


**Fig. 1.** Examples of stimuli used in Studies 1 and 2. The faces differ in width-to-height ratio (i.e., high and low ratios). The lines drawn on the faces were not shown to observers, and are included here to illustrate the landmarks used to measure the width-to-height ratio.

### Procedure

In the first study, stimulus faces were presented on a black background using E-Prime software on a 14-in. LCD monitor. Images were approximately 17 cm wide by 20 cm high (or 15.2 × 12.9 visual degrees when viewed from 75 cm). Faces were presented in random order for 1,000 ms to familiarize the participants with the range of faces. Participants were told how the aggressive behavior of the men had been assessed. Next, each face was presented for 2,000 ms (fully randomized), after which the question "How aggressive would this person be if provoked?" appeared on a black background along with a 7-point Likert scale (1 = *not at all aggressive*, 7 = *very aggressive*). Participants were given unlimited time to make their response on a numerical keypad, which then caused the next stimulus face to appear. After completing the estimates of aggression, participants rated each face for dominance, masculinity, trustworthiness, and attractiveness using 7-point Likert scales (order of these four ratings was fully counterbalanced). In sum, each face was presented a total of six times, once for familiarization and once for each of the five traits, and the entire set of faces was rated on one attribute at a time. Estimates of aggression were highly correlated with ratings of dominance ($r$ = .92), masculinity ($r$ = .86), trustworthiness ($r$ = –.90), and attractiveness ($r$ = –.57). Only estimates of aggression and of dominance were correlated significantly with the facial WHR ($r$ = .59 and $r$ = .54, respectively). However, given the specific evaluative context (i.e., participants were told of the objective measure of aggression; Oosterhoff & Todorov, 2008) and the high degree of association of the five ratings, statistical analyses used estimates of aggression only.

In the second study, presentation of a stimulus face was preceded by a central fixation cross that appeared for 500 ms. A face was then presented for 39 ms (order of faces was fully randomized and without any prior familiarization to the faces), after which the question "How aggressive would this person be if provoked?" appeared on a black background along with a 7-point Likert scale (1 = *not at*

*As a dependent variable (see Chapter 2), do you think this measure of aggression would be different if the researchers asked about aggression that was not provoked? Think about what you have learned about the causes of aggressive behaviour.*

*Based on what you learned about stereotypes in Chapter 10, how do you think race would influence these judgments? How might different facial expressions (i.e., anger) interact with race to produce different interpretations?*

*all aggressive,* 7 = *very aggressive*). As in Study 1, participants were told how the aggressive behavior of the men had been assessed before the presentation of stimulus faces.

### Statistics

Cronbach's alpha was calculated to examine the consistency of the ratings of estimated aggression across individual participants. For each participant within each study, we calculated the correlation between the estimate of aggression for the 24 faces and both the facial WHR and actual aggression of the stimulus faces. One-sample $t$ tests were computed to test the primary hypothesis that these correlations would be significantly different from the null hypothesis (i.e., no association). For each stimulus face, we calculated the mean estimated aggression across participants and correlated that with both the facial WHR and the actual aggression of the stimulus face. The correlation between estimates of aggression in Study 1 and Study 2 was also calculated for each face. Significance level was set at $p < .05$, two-tailed, for all analyses.

*Do you think the results of this experiment would be different if culture and anger expressions had been considered and a different measure of "actual aggression" had been used?*

## RESULTS

### Study 1

The estimates of aggression were highly consistent across individual observers (Cronbach's $\alpha$ = .95). Single-sample $t$ tests comparing individual correlations to a null value of zero showed that estimated aggression was positively associated with the facial WHR of the stimulus faces: male observers, $t(14) = 16.94$, $p < .001$, $p_{rep} > .99$; female observers, $t(15) = 9.23$, $p < .001$, $p_{rep} > .99$; combined, $t(30) = 16.41$, $p < .001$, $p_{rep} > .99$ (Fig. 2). These $t$ tests also indicated that estimated aggression was positively associated with actual aggression of the stimulus faces: male observers, $t(14) = 6.95$, $p < .001$, $p_{rep} > .99$; female observers, $t(15) = 8.81$, $p < .001$, $p_{rep} > .99$; combined, $t(30) = 11.21$, $p < .001$, $p_{rep} > .99$ (Fig. 2). The mean estimated aggression for each face across participants was associated with both the facial WHR ($r = .59$, $p < .002$, $p_{rep} = .98$) and actual aggression ($r = .42$, $p = .04$, $p_{rep} = .89$) of the stimulus faces (Fig. 2).

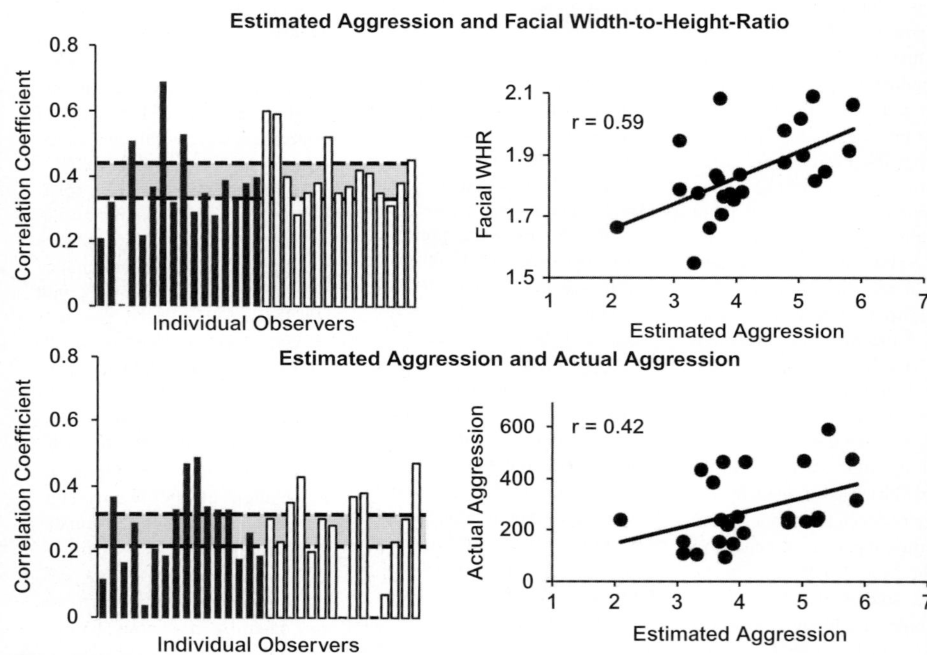


**Fig. 2.** Results from Study 1: relationships between observers' estimates of the pictured individuals' aggression and (a) width-to-height ratio (WHR) of the facial stimuli and (b) the pictured individuals' actual aggression. The bar graphs show the relationships for each individual observer (stimuli viewed for 2,000 ms each). Black bars indicate female observers ($n$ = 16); white bars indicate male observers ($n$ = 15). Shaded areas represent the 95% confidence intervals (CIs). The mean $r$ value for the relationship between estimated aggression and WHR was .38 (95% CI = .33–.43), and the mean $r$ value for the relationship between estimated aggression and actual aggression was .27 (95% CI = .21–.31). The graphs on the right show facial WHR and actual aggression as a function of estimated aggression, across participants.

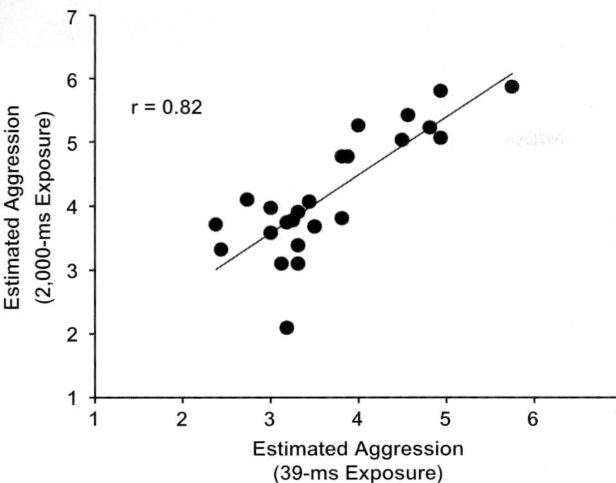


**Fig. 3.** Relationship between observers' estimates of the pictured individuals' aggression in Study 1 (2,000-ms exposure) and in Study 2 (39-ms exposure). The plotted points represent individual stimulus faces; each point shows the average estimate of aggression for a stimulus across participants in Study 1 and across participants in Study 2.

### *Study 2*

The estimates of aggression were highly consistent across individual observers (Cronbach's $\alpha$ = .89). Also, estimates of aggression among these participants were highly correlated with estimates of aggression from participants in Study 1, who were given 2,000-ms exposure to the stimulus faces, $r = .82$, $p < .001$, $p_{rep} > .99$ (Fig. 3). Single-sample $t$ tests comparing individual correlations to a null value of zero showed that estimated aggression was positively associated with both the facial WHR, $t(15) = 10.24$, $p < .001$, $p_{rep} > .99$, and actual aggression of the stimulus faces, $t(15) = 4.49$, $p < .001$, $p_{rep} > .99$. The mean estimated aggression for each face across participants was associated with the facial WHR but not with actual aggression, $r = .70$, $p < .001$, $p_{rep} > .99$, and $r = .31$, $p = .14$, $p_{rep} = .79$ (Fig. 4).

## DISCUSSION

The results indicate that observers can make accurate judgments of propensity for aggression from faces displaying neutral expressions, even when exposure to the faces is limited to 39 ms. In both Study 1 and Study 2, individual participants reliably judged men with larger facial WHRs as more aggressive; across participants, faces with larger WHRs were rated as more aggressive than faces with smaller WHRs. The strong correlation between estimated aggression and facial WHR suggests that this facial metric may be one of the facial cues used to make accurate estimates of aggression.

It is not surprising that participants' estimates of aggression were correlated more strongly with facial WHR than with actual aggression. Whereas facial WHR is a stable facial characteristic that provides a static estimate of the propensity for aggression, any actual behavioral aggression will vary over time (e.g., as a function of state or situation). Indeed, it is impressive that the correlation between estimates of aggression and actual aggression of the stimulus faces was as high in the current study ($r = .42$ and $r = .31$) as was the correlation between facial WHR and actual aggression in our original study ($r = .38$; Carré & McCormick, 2008). Furthermore, facial WHR is only one of many cues to propensity for aggression.

Future research should investigate whether the facial WHR meets the criteria for an "honest signal" of aggressive potential, similar to honest signals guiding interindividual behavior in other species (Setchell, Smith, Wickings, & Knapp, 2008; Tibbetts & Dale, 2004). Honest signals are used in other species as a means to gauge one's relative status within the hierarchy (Setchell et al., 2008; Tibbetts & Dale, 2004) and may serve to modulate adaptive behavior (Senar & Camerino, 1998; Tibbetts & Lindsay, 2008). The ability to gauge aggressive behavior from neutral faces may reflect an overgeneralization of emotional expressions (Montepare & Dobish, 2003). In other words, neutral faces may be evaluated according to their similarity to certain emotional expressions, such as anger and happiness, which may in turn be used by perceivers to guide adaptive social behavior (e.g., approach/avoidance; Oosterhof & Todorov, 2008). Notably, angry facial expressions consist of lowering the brow and raising the upper lip, a facial movement that inevitably increases the facial WHR and, by implication, increases the saliency of the "signal" advertising propensity for aggression. Thus, it is also possible that the relationship between facial WHR and aggression reflects social conditioning whereby a person's aggressive behavior has been shaped by others' expectations of their aggressive behavior. Furthermore, it may be some other cue in the face correlated with the facial WHR that is influencing estimates of aggression. For example, using computer-generated faces, Todorov, Baron, and Oosterhof (2008)

*Why do you think these results are different from Study 1, even though the only change was a shorter stimulus display? Do you think that when we make snap judgments, we may interpret people as being more aggressive based on their facial structure, relative to when we have more time to carefully examine someone's face? Are we necessarily accurate all the time?*

*In what other situations do you think interpretation of facial expressions of emotion may be critical to decision making and social behaviour? Think about the Applying Social Psychology sections throughout this text.*

*How does this statement relate to research on emotional expressions that are recognized cross-culturally (discussed in Chapter 5)? Are we taught to express certain emotions certain ways, or is there a biological basis for some emotional expressions, such as anger and fear?*

*Think about the different theories of aggression presented in Chapter 11. How could you interpret these results within the framework of instinct theory and evolutionary theory?*

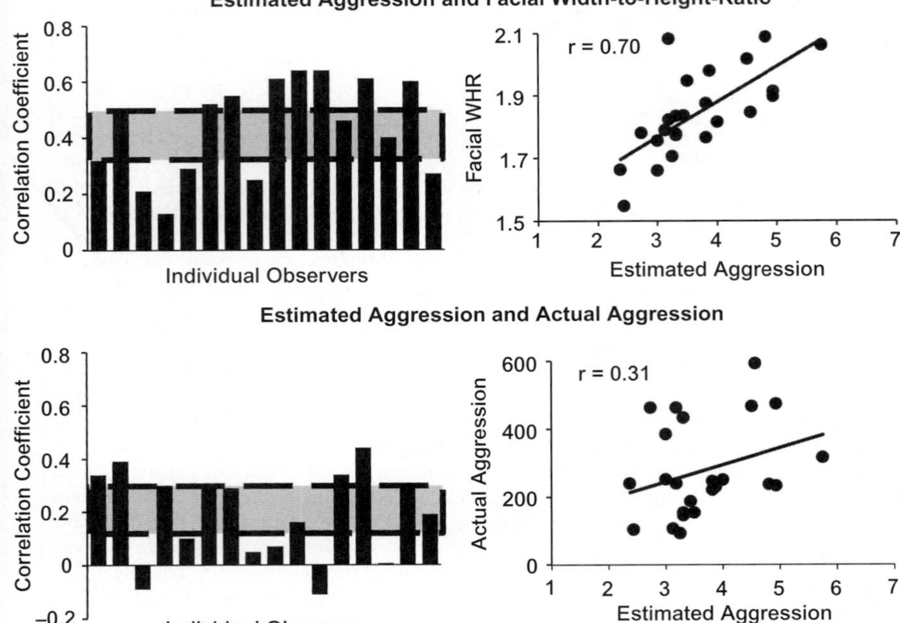


**Fig. 4.** Results for Study 2: relationships between observers' estimates of the pictured individuals' aggression and (a) facial width-to-height ratio (WHR) and (b) the pictured individuals' actual aggression. The bar graphs show the relationship for each individual observer ($n$ = 16; stimuli viewed for 39 ms). Shaded areas represent the 95% confidence intervals (CIs). The mean $r$ value for the relationship between estimated aggression and WHR was .44 (95% CI = .35 – .53), and the mean $r$ value for the relationship between estimated aggression and actual aggression was .19 (95% CI = .10 – .28). The graphs on the right show facial WHR and actual aggression as a function of estimated aggression, across participants.

found that variation in the brow ridge, cheekbones, chin, and nose sellion (i.e., where the nose and brow meet) were related to observer ratings of trustworthiness, a social attribute that is negatively correlated with aggression. Thus, it will be important to test whether the facial WHR predicts aggression independently of these other cues. Nevertheless, the present results raise the possibility that subtle differences in facial structure influence trait judgments, which may, in turn, guide social behavior.

***Acknowledgments***—We thank Mark Vida and Alexandra Hatry for technical assistance. C.M.M. and C.J.M. hold Natural Sciences and Engineering Research Council (NSERC) Discovery Grants. J.M.C. holds an NSERC Canada Graduate Scholarship.

## References

Bar, M., Neta, M., & Linz, H. (2006). Very first impressions. *Emotion, 6*, 268–278.

Carré, J.M., & McCormick, C.M. (2008). In your face: Facial metrics predict aggressive behaviour in the laboratory and in varsity and professional hockey players. *Proceedings of the Royal Society B: Biological Sciences, 275*, 2651–2656.

Cherek, D., Schnapp, W., Moeller, F., & Dougherty, D. (1996). Laboratory measures of aggressive responding in male parolees with violent and non-violent histories. *Aggressive Behavior, 22*, 27–36.

Montepare, J.M., & Dobish, H. (2003). The contribution of emotion perceptions and their overgeneralizations to trait impressions. *Journal of Nonverbal Behavior, 27*, 237–254.

Oosterhof, N.N., & Todorov, A. (2008). The functional basis of face evaluation. *Proceedings of the National Academy of Sciences, USA, 105*, 11087–11092.

Penton-Voak, I.S., Pound, N., Little, A.C., & Perrett, D.I. (2006). Personality judgments from natural and composite facial images: More evidence for a "kernel of truth" in social perception. *Social Cognition, 24*, 490–524.

Roney, J.R., Hanson, K.N., Durante, K.M., & Maestripieri, D. (2006).

Reading men's faces: Women's mate attractiveness judgments track men's testosterone and interest in infants. *Proceedings of the Royal Society B: Biological Sciences, 273*, 2169–2175.

Sell, A., Cosmides, L., Tooby, J., Sznycer, D., von Rueden, C., & Gurven, M. (2009). Human adaptations for the visual assessment of strength and fighting ability from the body and face. *Proceedings of the Royal Society B: Biological Sciences, 276*, 575–584.

Senar, J.C., & Camerino, M. (1998). Status signalling and the ability to recognize dominants: An experiment with siskins (*Carduelis spinus*). *Proceedings of the Royal Society B: Biological Sciences, 265*, 1515–1520.

Setchell, J.M., Smith, T., Wickings, E.J., & Knapp, L.A. (2008). Social correlates of testosterone and ornamentation in male mandrills. *Hormones & Behavior, 54*, 365–372.

Tibbetts, E.A., & Dale, J. (2004). A socially enforced signal of quality in paper wasps. *Nature, 432*, 218–222.

Tibbetts, E.A., & Lindsay, R. (2008). Visual signals of status and rival assessment in *Polistes dominulus* paper wasps. *Biology Letters, 4*, 237–239.

Todorov, A., Baron, S.G., & Oosterhof, N.N. (2008). Evaluating face trustworthiness: A model based approach. *Social Cognitive and Affective Neuroscience, 3*, 119–127.

Todorov, A., Mandisodza, A.N., Goren, A., & Hall, C.C. (2005). Inferences of competence from faces predict election outcome. *Science, 308*, 1623–1626.

Verplaetse, J., Vanneste, S., & Braeckman, J. (2007). You can judge a book by its cover: The sequel. A kernel of truth in predicting cheating detection. *Evolution and Human Behavior, 28*, 260–271.

Weston, E.M., Friday, A.E., & Lio, P. (2007). Biometric evidence that sexual selection has shaped the hominin face. *PLoS ONE, 2*, 1–8.

Willis, J., & Todorov, A. (2006). First impressions: Making up your mind after 100-ms exposure to a face. *Psychological Science, 17*, 592–598.

Zebrowitz, L.A. (2006). Finally, faces find favour. *Social Cognition, 24*, 657–701.

Zebrowitz, L.A., Fellous, J.M., Mignault, A., & Andreoletti, C. (2003). Trait impressions as overgeneralized responses to adaptively significant facial qualities: Evidence from connectionist modeling. *Personality and Social Psychology Review, 7*, 194–215.


(RECEIVED 1/19/09; REVISION ACCEPTED 3/19/09)

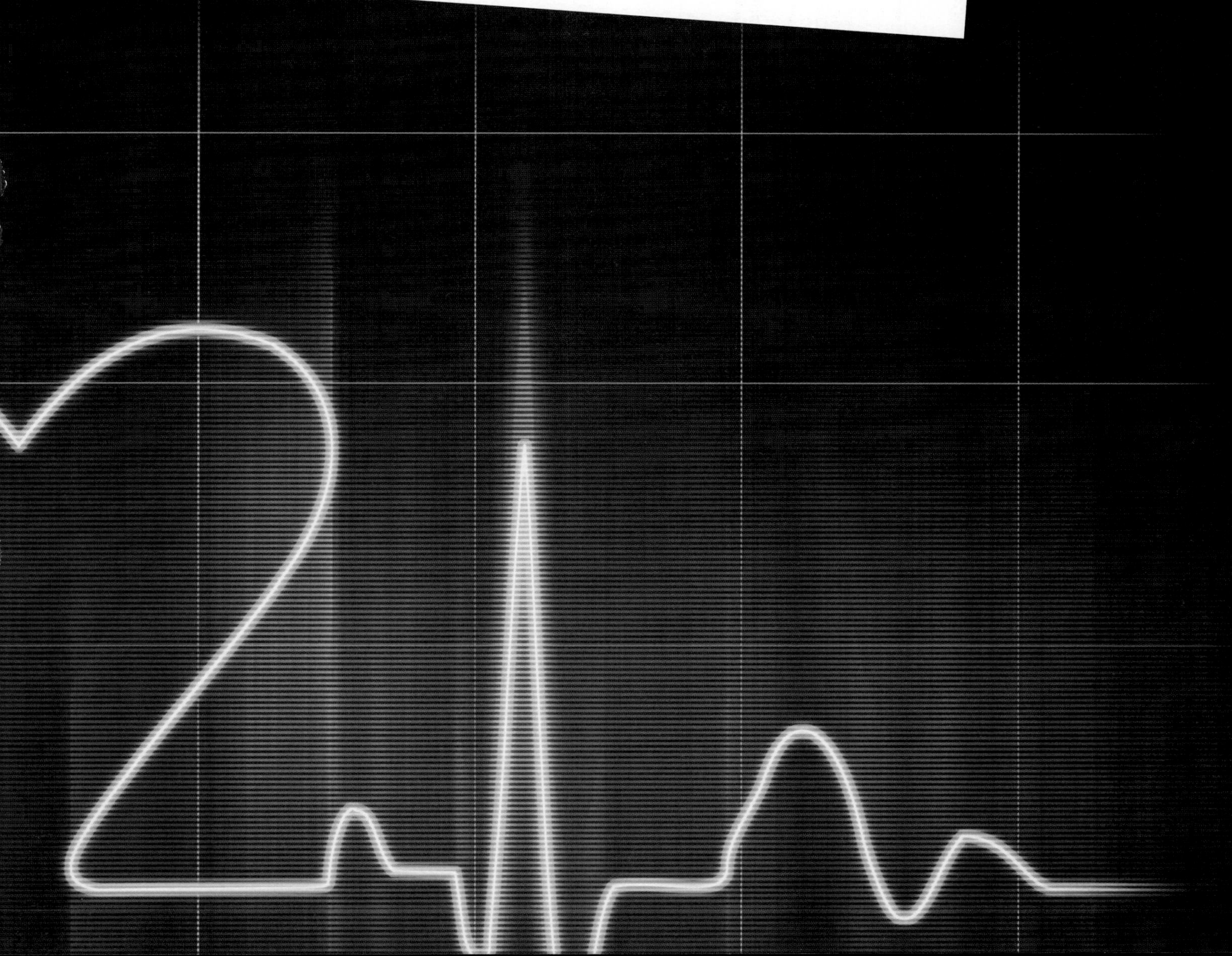

# ATTRACTION AND CLOSE RELATIONSHIPS

<<< *How do our best friends become our best friends?*

**HOW** DO EARLY PARENT–CHILD INTERACTIONS IMPACT FUTURE RELATIONSHIPS?
**WHAT** LEADS TO ATTRACTION?
**WHAT** FACTORS INFLUENCE AND DEFINE ROMANTIC LOVE?
**HOW** ARE RELATIONSHIPS MAINTAINED?
**WHAT** ROLE DOES CONFLICT PLAY IN RELATIONSHIPS?

# CHAPTER 12

Kristine knows what she'll hear before she even picks up the phone.

"Hello Cyril, it's Minerva calling. How are you doing, *dawwwling*?"

They developed these personas to provide an extra excuse to call one another. It's been the routine for nearly 15 years now, ever since Kristine moved away to Halifax to further her education, leaving her best friend Tanya back in Calgary. Every week, without fail, Tanya's phone rings. The two women sit in their living rooms in Alberta and Nova Scotia and talk about everything that's happened over the week.

As she waits for this week's call and the familiar question, Kristine reflects on the more than 15 years that have been marked by this friendship. *I don't know what I would do without her*, she thinks, recalling Tanya's soothing voice on the other end of the line when Kristine's mother was diagnosed with cancer and the joyful tears they shed together when something great would happen to either one of them. They know everything about each other and have been each other's support through it all: challenging and debating with each other, discussing relationships, deciding where to go to graduate school, and supporting each other through moves, children, illnesses, and successes. Deep in thought about her relationship with Tanya, Kristine is startled when the phone rings. She smiles, settles into the cushions of the sofa, and picks up the phone, eager to hear her best friend's voice on the other end.

"Hello Cyril, it's Minerva calling . . . "

Reading about Kristine and Tanya, were you reminded of a close relationship you have? How does this relationship impact your life? What drew you to this person in the first place? In this chapter, you will explore how attraction leads to relationships (both close friendships and romantic relationships), and how those relationships are developed and defined.

**NEED FOR AFFILIATION** the desire to establish and maintain rewarding interpersonal relationships

It might seem like an obvious conclusion, but studies have demonstrated that friendships foster a sense of positive well-being across a person's lifetime (Holder & Coleman, 2009). Friends boost our self-esteem, sense of subjective well-being, and happiness, and they help us to learn social roles and norms that allow us to succeed within a group (e.g., Baumeister & Leary, 1995; Hartup & Stevens, 1997; Rubin & Thompson, 2002).

It's not just our social lives that benefit from friendship. Numerous longitudinal studies have shown that both men and women with close friends actually have better health outcomes than people without such friendships. People with solid networks of friends are happier (e.g., Argyle, 1987; Holder & Coleman, 2009) and generally live longer than those who are not as social (e.g., Giles, Glonek, Luszcz, & Andrews, 2005). In fact, recent studies have found that low levels of social interaction can be as detrimental to health as behaviours such as smoking, a lack of exercise, alcoholism, and obesity (e.g., Holt-Lunstad, Smith, & Layton, 2010). Further, negative social interactions, such as social exclusion or rejection, activate the same parts of the brain that respond to physical pain (Eisenberger, Lieberman, & Williams, 2003).

> **As a parent interacts with an infant, he or she lays the groundwork for how the infant will experience interpersonal relationships over her lifetime.**

So it would seem that friendship is good for us. What, though, draws us to other people in the first place? Our urge to surround ourselves with other people is driven by the **need for affiliation**, or the desire to establish and maintain rewarding interpersonal relationships (e.g., Baumeister & Leary, 1995; MacDonald & Leary, 2005; McAdams, 1989). Of course, this motive is different for everyone—you might describe yourself as a "people person," while someone else might consider herself a "loner"—but the general tendency is toward achieving a balance. In one study, researchers asked college students to carry pagers for four days. When the pagers went off, as triggered by the researchers, students recorded whether they were alone or with others at that moment, as well as whether they *wanted* to be alone or with others at that time. The response a student gave usually predicted the situation he or she would be in the next time the pager went off. For example, a student who said she wanted to be alone when paged at 1 p.m. would then be found alone when paged at 2 p.m. This study demonstrated how people achieve a balance in their social interactions, according to their need to be with others to seek solitude at various parts of the day (O'Connor & Rosenblood, 1996). Further, University of Waterloo researcher La Guardia and her colleagues have found that supporting our friends' need for autonomy and varying need for affiliation leads to greater relationship quality and better psychological health (e.g., Deci, LaGuardia, Moller, Scheiner, & Ryan, 2006).

That said, some researchers have questioned whether social interactions have changed in recent years. With increased use of the internet, and the advent of social networking and communication sites such as messenger programs, chat rooms, MySpace, Facebook, and Twitter (not to mention online gaming communities such as the World of Warcraft and Lord of the Rings), how are social relationships influenced? Does the development of new social technology lead to increased or decreased feelings of well-being? One study by Kraut et al. (1998) found that increased use of the internet for social relations leads to a decline in interpersonal and family interactions, and social activities, as well as an increase in depression and feelings of loneliness. However, other studies have demonstrated that for individuals who report low self-esteem and low life satisfaction, use of Facebook helps to improve their sense of well-being and social interactions offline as well as online (Ellison, Steinfield, & Lampe, 2007). Thus, while in-person friendships generally fulfill our need for affiliation the best, some individuals may benefit from online social interactions when these are lacking otherwise—in particular if these are used to bridge online relations to offline friendships (e.g., Ellison et al., 2007). Offline friendships also are often maintained and may be strengthened by online communications—and some evidence suggests that most individuals frequently use social media to stay in touch with friends made elsewhere (Kraut et al., 2003).

The affiliation motive describes our desire to have rewarding interpersonal relationships. What, though, leads to a rewarding relationship, and how do we define what it means to be rewarding? The specifics are different for everyone, but at the basic level, there are certain characteristics that define attraction, close relationships, and the attachment styles we use in forming bonds with others throughout our lives.

## How Do Early Parent–Child Interactions Impact Future Relationships?

The first personal contact most people make is with a parent. From the moment we take our first breaths, we are ready to interact with other people. It's well known that infants are highly sensitive to facial expressions as well as sounds and movements made by people. Think about the times you have seen a baby interact with an adult—the adult probably engaged in baby talk and shot big grins and other exaggerated facial expressions at the baby. As he did, the baby might have cooed or giggled. The baby is being entertained, but there is deeper work going on here. As a parent interacts with an infant, he or she lays the groundwork for how the infant will experience interpersonal relationships over her lifetime.

Our brains are wired to encourage this interaction. When faced with nonthreatening signals from a stranger, the hormone *oxytocin*, which facilitates social recognition, is released. This leads to a feeling of trustworthiness (Zak, Kurzban, & Matzner, 2005). This is important in facilitating relationships as we come into contact with new people, and the same principle is at work between parents and children. Oxytocin has been linked to a clearly defined set of maternal bonding behaviours such as affectionate touch and vocalizations, as well as frequent checking of the infant, leading some researchers to consider it a "bonding hormone" (e.g., Feldman, Weller, Zagoory-Sharon, & Levine, 2007). Oxytocin also is linked to feeling calm and connected, which encourages the behaviours that will educate the infant about positive social interactions.

Though many people assume the strongest bond between a parent and child is that involving the mother, a similar biological encouragement for cuddling has been found in fathers. In fact, it seems that men are as "hardwired" to bond with their children as women are (Gordon,

Zagoory-Sharon, Leckman, & Feldman, 2010). In support of this, Feldman et al. (2007) found that oxytocin levels also increased in fathers after their child is born, and that these levels continued to increase the more men cuddled their babies, leading to a sense of calm satisfaction for both father and infant. Of course, it's all for a reason. The loop has to start with positive interaction with the baby (Shellenbarger, 2009).

Developmentally, these first human interactions are critical to our attitudes about ourselves, others, and trust. Long before a child acquires any language skills, he has already started developing a style of interacting with others. This is called an **attachment style** (Bowlby, 1969, 1973), or the degree of security experienced in interpersonal relationships (Ainsworth et al., 1978).

**ATTACHMENT STYLE** the degree of security experienced in interpersonal relationships

**INTERPERSONAL TRUST** the belief that people are generally trustworthy and dependable and the attitude that underlies the development of attachment styles

**SECURE ATTACHMENT STYLE** the most successful of the attachment styles, characterized by high self-esteem and high interpersonal trust

## ATTACHMENT STYLES

You might be surprised to learn that much of what we know about attachment begins with taking baby rhesus monkeys away from their mothers. Psychologist Harry Harlow (1958) gave baby monkeys a choice of surrogate "mothers" after being separated from their birth mother—one made of terrycloth and another made of wire. He found that the monkeys clung to their cloth mother for security and comfort, and chose the wire mother only when it provided food. He also found that the monkeys, after being separated from their cloth mothers for a few days and then reunited, clung to the surrogates in lieu of exploring their surroundings. Through these studies, he illustrated the importance of physical connection and that feeding was not, as previously thought, the most important factor in bonding.

Based on these findings, John Bowlby (1969, 1973) conducted research with humans that led to the conclusion that infants develop two basic attitudes during early interactions with adults: *self-esteem and interpersonal trust*. Self-esteem is developed through the emotional reactions of the infant's caregiver. A caregiver who smiles at and cuddles the infant helps to build a sense that the infant is valued and loved, while a caregiver who behaves coldly toward the infant is laying the groundwork for the child to feel unloved and unvalued. In conjunction with self-esteem, the infant develops a perception that the caregiver is trustworthy and reliable (or the opposite). **Interpersonal trust**, which involves the belief that people are generally trustworthy and dependable, is the attitude that underlies the development of attachment styles. In order to assess these, Mary Ainsworth and her colleagues (1978) developed the Strange Situation paradigm, in which a mother and baby would be introduced to an unfamiliar woman. The baby would briefly be left with the woman and then would be left alone. It was found that the children were less confident in exploring and playing when their mothers were not present. Ainsworth and Bowlby conducted such important work that it didn't just add to the scientific literature, it also influenced public policy involving children (e.g., see Bretherton, 1992, for a review of their work and its impact).

> "Self-esteem is developed through the emotional reactions of an infant's caregiver."

Basically, attachment styles can be boiled down to a formula describing the levels of self-esteem and interpersonal trust. A person can be high in both, low in both, or high in one and low in the other. These attachment styles, developed so early in life, have a great impact on our adult lives. Bowlby (1988) argued that there is a link between the type of attachment style an infant has and the type of relationships that he will have later in life, and others have echoed this argument (e.g., Feeney & Noller, 1990; Shaver & Hazan, 1993). In fact, levels of physical affection, distress, marital status, and marital success may be predicted from knowing both partners' attachment styles (e.g., Banse, 2004; Fraley, 2002). This is the case for both opposite-sex and same-sex relationships (e.g., Ridge & Feeney, 1998; Robinson, 1999). There is some disagreement when it comes to the number of styles, but following the above formula gives us four basic attachment styles.

### Secure Attachment Style

If a person is high in both self-esteem and interpersonal trust, she has a **secure attachment style**. Seven in 10 infants, and about as many adults, exhibit this type of attachment style (e.g., Baldwin et al., 1996; Jones & Cunningham; 1996; Mickelson, Kessler, & Shaver, 1997). This is the most successful of the attachment styles. People

<<< **Our very first interactions** have profound impacts on our later interpersonal relationships.

**FEARFUL-AVOIDANT ATTACHMENT STYLE** the most insecure of the attachment styles, characterized by low self-esteem and low interpersonal trust

**PREOCCUPIED ATTACHMENT STYLE** a conflicted, insecure attachment style characterized by low self-esteem and high interpersonal trust

with this style tend to form lasting and satisfying relationships over the courses of their lives.

### Fearful-Avoidant Attachment Style

At the other end of the spectrum, someone who is low in both self-esteem and interpersonal trust is described as having a **fearful-avoidant attachment style**. People with this style are usually unable to form close relationships, or their relationships are not fulfilling. Several studies have demonstrated that people with this attachment style tend to focus on how they are similar to or different from their friends, which strongly impacts the natures of the relationships (Gabriel et al., 2005). Further, research has linked this attachment style to engaging in verbally and physically abusive behaviours against intimate partners (e.g., Dutton, Saunders, Starzomski, & Bartholomew, 1994).

### Preoccupied Attachment Style

People who are low in self-esteem but high in interpersonal trust exhibit the **preoccupied attachment style**. This style is also referred to as

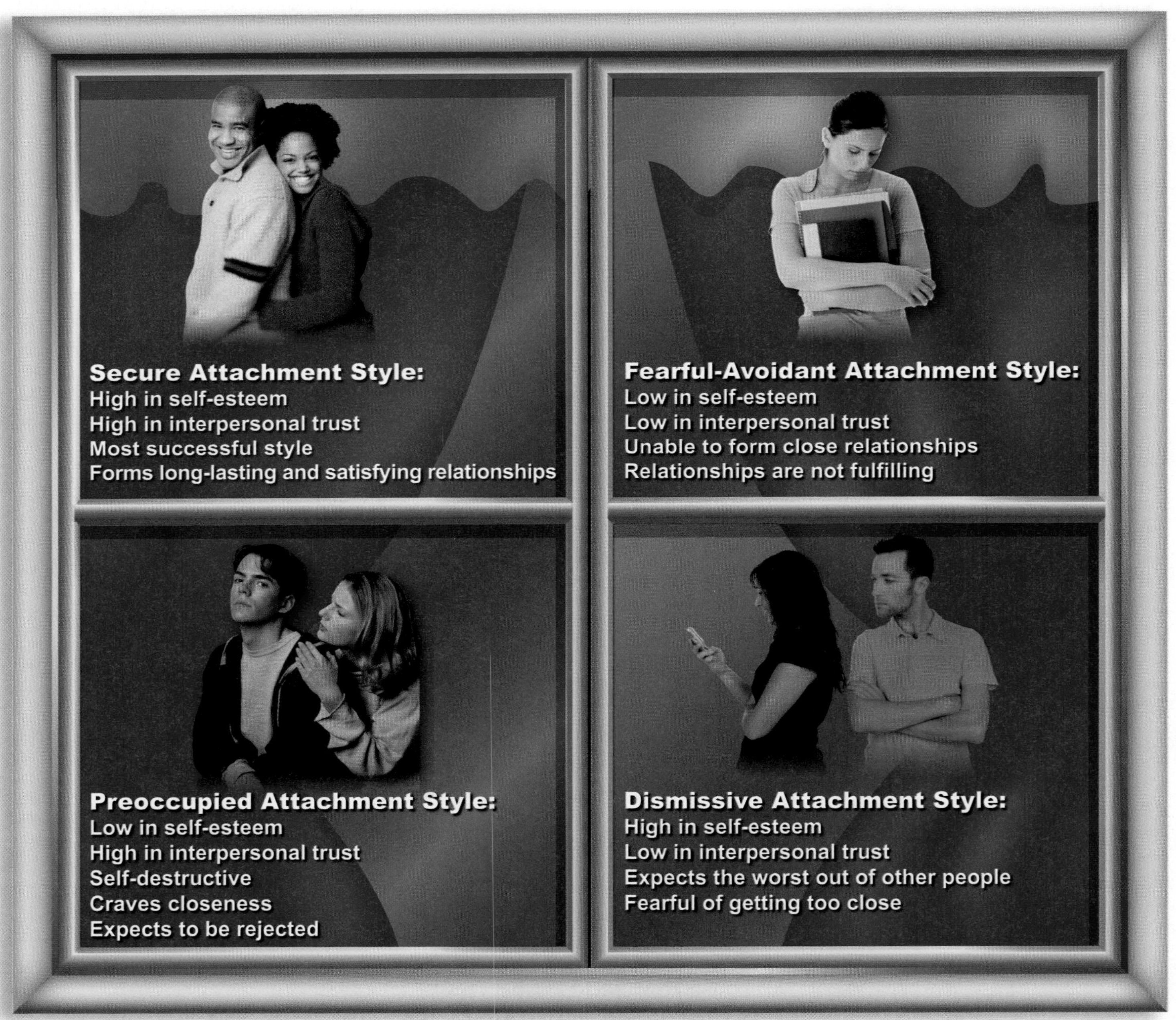

Secure Attachment Style:
High in self-esteem
High in interpersonal trust
Most successful style
Forms long-lasting and satisfying relationships
Fearful-Avoidant Attachment Style:
Low in self-esteem
Low in interpersonal trust
Unable to form close relationships
Relationships are not fulfilling
Preoccupied Attachment Style:
Low in self-esteem
High in interpersonal trust
Self-destructive
Craves closeness
Expects to be rejected
Dismissive Attachment Style:
High in self-esteem
Low in interpersonal trust
Expects the worst out of other people
Fearful of getting too close


**Attachment Styles.** The relationship between self-esteem and interpersonal trust **defines your attachment style.**

"anxious-ambivalent." They find it easy to form relationships, as they crave closeness and the approval of others. The preoccupied attachment style can be seen as a bit self-destructive, as for all of their craving for closeness, people with this style expect to be rejected because they believe they are not worthy of attention or love. Anxious lovers tend to report more emotional ups and downs with their relationships than those with secure or avoidant styles (Davis, Shaver, & Vernon, 2004). It's also been demonstrated that individuals with this style perceive their partners as less supportive within their relationship than do those who do not have this attachment style (e.g., Campbell, Simpson, Boldry, & Kashy, 2005; Collins & Feeney, 2004).

### Dismissive Attachment Style

A combination of high self-esteem and low interpersonal trust results in the **dismissive attachment style**. The high self-esteem leads people to believe they are worthy of good relationships, but the low level of interpersonal trust means they expect the worst of others and therefore are fearful of getting close to people. This attachment style has been linked to the development of a variety of negative behaviours, such as violent and sexual offenses? (e.g., Ward, Hudson, & Marshall, 1996) and some eating disorders (e.g., anorexia; Ward, Ramsay, & Treasure, 2000).

### Can Attachment Styles Change?

Once an attachment style has been established, it is not necessarily set in stone. Many social psychologists believe it remains constant (e.g., Klohnen & Bera, 1998). However, there is certainly evidence that our relationship experiences, both good and bad, can lead to changes in attachment style (e.g., Baldwin & Fehr, 1995; Brennan & Bosson, 1998; Keelan, Dion, & Dion, 1994; Scharfe & Bartholomew, 1994). For example, people who have relationship experiences that leave them feeling vulnerable (e.g., a traumatic breakup, abuse) have been found to changes attachment styles (e.g., Davila & Cobb, 2003; Muller, Sicoli, & Lemieux, 2000). Of course, this can go both ways; a particularly positive relationship experience can lead to an increase in secure attachment style (Ruvolo, Fabin, & Ruvolo, 2001). Further, some research suggests that there is within-person variability in attachment styles across the various people we interact with, including our parents, partners, and best friends

**DISMISSIVE ATTACHMENT STYLE** a conflicted, insecure attachment style characterized by high self-esteem and low interpersonal trust

(La Guardia, Ryan, Couchman, & Deci, 2000). Though our attachment styles took form when we were infants, they continue to shape the way we interact with our friends and romantic partners for the rest of our lives. They also play a role in what attracts us to others and how we define our experiences of love.

## What Leads to Attraction?

"All the girls get prettier at closing time, oh, they all begin to look like movie stars . . . If I could rate them on a scale from one to 10, I'm looking for a nine but eight could work right in. Few more drinks and I might slip to five or even four" (Baker-Knight, 1975).

Attraction is a funny thing, isn't it? As tongue-in-cheek as the song "Don't the Girls All Get Prettier at Closing Time" might be, it voices an astute observation of the game of finding love. You might even be surprised to learn that this song's thesis was actually used as a hypothesis for a study on attraction conducted by Pennebaker and his colleagues (1979). Those "beer goggles" that people joke about have some truth to them—both men and women are perceived as more attractive by members of the opposite sex (the study didn't consider potential same-sex pairings) as a night out at a bar progresses. It might not have anything to do with the beer, either. It could be that, as the clock ticks away, people who want to meet a potential partner readjust the way they see the "options" around them.

What is it, though, that creates a sense of attraction, anyway? Of course, we're not just talking about attraction to potential romantic partners, but potential friends as well. In many ways, attraction boils down to just being around someone.

### PROXIMITY, MERE EXPOSURE, AND INTERACTION

It's the first day of new student orientation. Brian is in the dining hall, surrounded by a sea of unfamiliar faces. He gets his lunch and sits down at his assigned table with the rest of his orientation group, feeling so overwhelmed, he barely even glances at the student next to him. The next day, he finds himself sitting next to the same person again, and they introduce themselves. Brian and Keith chat a little about how orientation is going and about what classes they are going to be taking. A few days

<<< As the night goes on and the prospect of going home alone looms, **do people become more attractive to one another?**

**PROXIMITY** physical closeness; the smaller the physical distance, the more likely the two people will experience repeat contact, which could lead to the development of mutual attraction

**MERE EXPOSURE** the hypothesis that the mere repeated exposure of an individual to a stimulus is enough for an increase in favourable response to that stimulus

later, in his first day of English Literature, Brian notices that Keith is in the same class. They decide to sit next to one another—after all, it's nice to see a familiar face, isn't it? By the end of the school year, Brian and Keith are close friends and decide to become roommates for the next school year.

Obviously, attraction has to start with contact. You can't get to know someone and decide if you are a good match for friendship or a romantic relationship without first meeting. This is why attraction starts with your physical surroundings. The people with whom you come into contact are determined by where you work, what classes you take, what dorm you live in, and so on. The repeated contact that results from these arrangements is based on **proximity**, the physical closeness between two individuals (Festinger, Schachter, & Back, 1950). The smaller the physical distance, the more likely the two people will experience repeat contact, and the development of mutual attraction. Numerous studies have shown that proximity is one of the best predictors of friendship (e.g., Festinger, Schachter, & Back, 1950; McPherson, Smith-Lovin, & Cook, 2001). For example, Back, Schmukle, and Egloff (2008) found that when students were randomly assigned seats for a semester, the students sitting together felt friendlier toward one another in comparison to other students sitting farther away from one another.

In Brian and Keith's example, you can see why proximity is so important. Related to this is the concept of *functional distance*, which describes how often individuals come into contact with one another. Functional distance contributes to relationship development (Newcomb, 1961). People who live or work close to one another are more likely to become acquainted and form friendships. People are also generally more likely to form relationships with—or at least favour—individuals they anticipate meeting, due to an effect called "anticipation of interaction." Studies have found that when female college or university students were given information about two women and were told they were going to interact with one of them, they consistently preferred the woman they were told they were going to meet (e.g., Bond & Dutton, 1973; Darley & Berscheid, 1967; Miller & Marks, 1982).

The effect created by proximity is called **mere exposure**, which hypothesizes that the mere repeated exposure of an individual to a stimulus is enough for an increase in favourable response to that stimulus (Zajonc, 1968). The effect of mere exposure was demonstrated in a study conducted in a university course. Moreland and Beach (1992) had one assistant attend class 15 times over the course of a semester, a second attend 10 times, a third attend five times, and a fourth that did not attend a single class. None of the assistants actually interacted with the students. At the end of the semester, when the students were shown photos of the four assistants and asked how much they liked each one, it was found that the number of times an assistant had been present in class was directly related to how much she was liked (Moreland & Beach, 1992). The mere exposure effect even works with photographs. For example, when participants view photographs of faces (repeated and unrepeated) and then assign likability and similarity ratings, they tend to assign higher ratings and exhibit more a greater physiological response to faces they have seen before (e.g., Harmon-Jones & Allen, 2001; Moreland & Zajonc, 1982). In other words, the more you see a person, the more likely you are to like that person. This might not work, though, when an initial response is negative—in fact, repeated exposure in that case can lead to even stronger dislike!

Of course, the reason that proximity and mere exposure are so important to attraction is that they lead to interaction. It is only through interaction that people learn enough information about each other to find out if they are a good match. Sometimes, though, interaction comes without proximity. In fact, use of the internet as a form of social interaction may decrease the extent to which spatial proximity is required for relationships to exist (Merkle & Richardson, 2000). Interactions through social networking sites such as Facebook don't benefit from geographic proximity, but they can still have positive effects. During studies in which people met online prior to meeting in person, they tended to report more favourable impressions of one another in comparison with

<<< Attraction starts with proximity and mere exposure. **The simple fact that two students are in the same class makes it more likely that they will become friends.**

pairs who first met in person (e.g., McKenna, Green, & Gleason, 2002). In addition, attraction was related to perceived similarity prior to meeting and how well people are "matched" (e.g., Byrne, Ervin, & Lamberth, 1970). This is related to the anticipation effect described above—our sense of familiarity with individuals we interact with through online venues is greater, leading to higher degrees of liking (e.g., Mantovani, 2001). Further, similar attraction cues are relevant for both online and in-person initiation of relationships, including proximity as well as physical attractiveness (e.g., Billedo, 2009). New proximity-based smartphone applications take advantage of this by allowing people to digitally start a date with individuals who are in close geographic proximity. Proximity, mere exposure, and interaction make up just one piece of the puzzle, though. Another factor that plays a major role in pulling people together is the perception of physical attractiveness.

## THE IMPACT OF PHYSICAL ATTRACTIVENESS

You're waiting at a bus stop when an individual approaches you with a clipboard, asking if you'd like to sign a petition against a U.S.-based corporation (e.g., Wal-Mart) being built in your small Canadian community that is filled with many independent and small business owners. This person flashes you a smile with amazing white teeth. You notice the person has really nice eyes and a great body. Does this matter? Could the fact that this person is highly attractive have anything at all to do with whether or not you add your name to the petition? You might like to think the answer is no, that you'll choose whether or not to sign the petition based on how you feel about the issue.

As much as we might not want to admit it, a person's level of attractiveness does impact interactions with others. Research using this petition scenario found that the more attractive the experimenter was, the more signatures he was able to get (Chaiken, 1979). The findings suggest that attractive individuals wield more persuasive power than their unattractive counterparts. Additional research has revealed advantages such as the tendency for physically attractive men and women to earn more money than their peers (e.g., Hamermesh & Biddle, 1994). Further, income studies in Canada have suggested that attractiveness is more predictive of salary differences for men than for women (i.e., more attractive men gained significant economic returns relative to unattractive men; Roszell, Kennedy, & Grabb, 1989). This discrepancy has been called a "plainness penalty" and is associated with salaries that are 5 to 10 percent lower than those of attractive individuals (Hamermesh & Biddle, 1994; Watkins & Johnston, 2000).

So if attraction is related to salary discrepancies, does it also contribute to differences in the perception of skills and productivity? The answer is a resounding yes! The empirical literature is replete with examples of attractive individuals being associated with more positive skills, traits, and personal worth (e.g., Perlini, Bertolissi, & Lind, 1999; Perlini & Hansen, 2001; Tews, Stafford, & Zhu, 2009; Watkins & Johnston, 2000) and perceived as lacking in negative attributes such as criminality (e.g., Saladin, Saper, & Breen, 1988). Even your ratings of your professors may be influenced by attractiveness. For example, Hamermesh and Parker (2005) found that professors who were considered better-looking received higher ratings for their instructional skills from students. Similarly, ratings of likeability and skill on websites such as RateMyProfessor.com also may be influenced by attractiveness. Consider the faculty at your college or university and see if the ratings differ.

Wait a minute, though. What about all of those sayings like "beauty is in the eye of the beholder"? If physical attractiveness is a subjective measure, how can it be studied in this way? It could be that physical attractiveness is actually an objective characteristic that can be measured and studied. People tend to assume that what is considered attractive differs greatly between people and cultures, but it turns out that's not necessarily true. Studies that have examined the question of physical attractiveness as an objective characteristic have found that the concept of attraction really doesn't differ across cultures (e.g., Cunningham, Roberts, Wu, Barbee, & Druen, 1995). In fact, many studies have reported a high degree of similarity in standards of attractiveness across cultures (e.g., Dion, Pak, & Dion, 1990; McArthur & Berry, 1987). Yet another study showed that even as children, people of different cultural backgrounds found the same features, such as big eyes and prominent cheekbones, attractive in photographs of people of different races, genders, and ages (Langlois, Ritter, Roggman, & Vaughn, 1991). This indicates a generalized definition of what is considered attractive. It also demonstrates that preferences for attractiveness are not, as previously thought, gradually learned through socialization but may be somehow "hardwired." For example, researchers have found that even infants look longer at and seem to prefer attractive female faces (e.g., Quinn, Kelly, Lee, Pascalis, & Slater, 2008).

"What about all of those sayings like **"beauty is in the eye of the beholder"?**"

Interestingly, though, social psychologists have demonstrated that people show a preference for faces in which the features aren't very different from an "average" face. Langlois and Roggman (1990) presented college students with actual yearbook photos and computerized photos that "averaged" the features from four to 32 of the consistently preferred yearbook photos. Their results indicated that participants showed a preference for the created faces over the actual ones. In fact, the more faces that had been averaged (i.e., across 32 relative to four photos), the more the students liked them. The researchers speculated that this preference may be due to the perceived familiarity of those computerized faces—because they incorporate so many faces, they are less distinctive and therefore seem more familiar (Langlois & Roggman, 1990). Further, familiar or "averaged" faces provide cues to trustworthiness and attractiveness (e.g., DeBruine, 2005; Halberstadt & Rhodes, 2000). This effect of preference for "averaged" images has been found to extend to nonhuman species and even inanimate objects (Halberstadt & Rhodes, 2003). That said, some faces do appear to be particularly attractive, and are still rated higher than averaged faces (e.g., DeBruine, Jones, Unger, Little, & Feinberg, 2007).

Facial studies on averaging also show a preference for facial images that are symmetrical, in which the left and right side are mirror images of one another (see Rhodes, 2006, for a review). Yet another study further demonstrated our preference for symmetry; participants were more attracted to dancers whose features were physically symmetrical (Brown et al., 2005). Although much of the research uses self-reporting of perceptions of attractiveness, other research has used physiological measures such as facial EMGs that are not as susceptible to biased responses and have found similar results (Winkielman, Halberstadt, Fazendeiro, & Catty, 2006). An additional consideration in attractiveness research should be the context in which stimuli are presented, as these can influence ratings of attractiveness and desire for affiliation (e.g., Honey & Coulombe, 2009).

### Why Is Attraction Important?

It's pretty clear from the research we've discussed that being attractive is a desirable trait and can impact interpersonal relationships. Physical appearance is the most visible trait in social interactions, and for better or worse, it has a high degree of impact on those interactions. Attractiveness influences not only whom we choose to interact with but also the personality traits that attractive and unattractive individuals are believed to possess. Folk psychology has long contained theories that a given person's outward appearance is enough to forecast personality. For example, Dion, Berscheid, and Walter (1972) reported that participants rated physically attractive individuals as higher in desirable personality traits and expected them to lead better lives (e.g., be better husbands or wives). Other studies have shown that attractive people are perceived as being more successful, happier, more sociable, and better job applicants than unattractive individuals (e.g., Cash, Gillen, & Burns, 1977; Eagly, Ashmore, Makhijani, & Longo, 1991; Hatfield & Sprecher, 1986; Watkins & Johnson, 2000). Collectively, these experiments have uncovered the existence of a "what is beautiful is good" stereotype, characterized by an assumption that physically attractive people are somehow "better" in other aspects of life, and that their lives are happier (see Dion et al., 1972). These studies also serve as further evidence of a somewhat universal standard of attractiveness. If standards varied widely, then this stereotype would not hold much weight in our daily interactions as well as in our friendships and in interpersonal attraction.

## ACTION LEARNING

### "What Is Beautiful Is Good"

In a study on the "what is beautiful is good" stereotype, researchers found a physical attractiveness stereotype, characterized by an assumption that attractive people have better personalities and lives (Dion, Berscheid, & Walster, 1972). The researchers also concluded that physical attractiveness can have a profound impact on social interactions and influence. They point out that the advantage physically attractive people have in dating may be even greater than previously assumed because of the belief that beautiful people attract wealth and happiness.

They concede that they don't know how the stereotype determines patterns of social interaction but that it would be strange if people didn't behave in line with the stereotype and that social interaction shaped by the stereotype has been reported anecdotally. As an example of this, they point to previous research showing that even social workers used to dealing with many kinds of people often find it difficult to think of a pretty woman as having committed a crime. Beautiful women, it seems, are not often convicted (Dion, Berscheid, & Walster, 1972). Do you agree with these conclusions, or do you believe something else could explain the way the "what is beautiful is good" stereotype is at play?

Think about the influence of attraction on your interactions with others. Has an individual's level of attractiveness influenced whether or not you pursued a relationship with that person? To show the impact that level of attractiveness has on our perceptions of others, replicate research testing the "what is beautiful is good" stereotype. Consider showing people two different images of a male or female target person (make sure that the target individuals share the same basic demographics). Ask 10 other people to rate the level of attractiveness of each of the target individuals. Then ask a series of other questions to determine if attractiveness impacts the impression that was formed. For example, you may want to ask how much money people think the target individuals make on a scale of 1 (very low amount) to 7 (very high amount), or how likely they would be to interact with each target person on the same scale.

You may want to revisit Chapter 2, on research methods, to help plan this research. Develop a hypothesis. When you have completed your research, consider alternative explanations for your findings. Did your demonstration go as planned or were there issues that may have affected your results? Share your results with your classmates and discuss how the "what is beautiful is good" stereotype may have influenced your perceptions of others.

What you will learn from this action project:

1. Develop a hypothesis concerning how level of attractiveness affects interactions.
2. Prepare a social psychological study to test a question.
3. Analyze the results of a social psychological study.

<<< **Examples of the photos you might use for your target individuals.** Be sure your selected individuals match across all traits other than their levels of attractiveness.

> Physical appearance is the most visible trait in social interactions, and for better or worse, it has a high degree of impact on those interactions.

**MATCHING HYPOTHESIS** the hypothesis that people are more likely to form longstanding relationships with others whose social attributes match with theirs and with those who are similar in physical attractiveness

**PROPORTION OF SIMILARITY** an equation that divides the number of topics on which two people express similar views by the total number of topics on which they have communicated, resulting in a prediction of attraction

**REPULSION HYPOTHESIS** states that similarity doesn't actually have any effect on attraction

**RECIPROCITY** the exchange of what we receive for what we get, which can include liking those who like us back

### SIMILARITY

Opposites attract. It's a fact of life, right? Repeated over and over in popular culture (i.e., songs, romantic comedies and other movies), it's become one of those hard and fast truths about dating—you just have to be different for it to work. Just how many television sitcoms have you seen that start out with the couple absolutely hating one another and then falling madly in love? Studies of relationships, however, have largely contradicted this popular belief.

Overall, we tend to like people who are similar to us in terms of demographics, attitudes/values, or experiences. This can be explained by the **matching hypothesis** (Goffman, 1952), which specified that people are more likely to form long-standing relationships with others whose social attributes match theirs. This is true of romantic relationships as well as friendships (Cash & Derlega, 1978). Research has shown that pairs based on complementary interests and behaviours are more attracted to one another and have better, longer-lasting relationships (e.g., Aube & Koestner, 1995; Byrne et al., 1970). Others have shown that partners with similar levels of physical attractiveness express more liking for each other (e.g., Walster, Walster, Berscheid, & Dion, 1971). Of course, couples don't *always* match in levels of attractiveness. However, research has documented that matching attitudes, senses of humour, and attachment styles can result in initial attraction even when physical attractiveness varies between partners (e.g., Buss & Barnes, 1986; Byrne, 1961; Klohnen & Luo, 2003; Murstein & Christy, 1976; Feingold, 1988).

In fact, this tendency toward pairing with people with whom we share similar traits can actually be expressed as a proportion! That's right—there is a formula that can predict attraction between two individuals. The **proportion of similarity** divides the number of topics on which two people express similar views by the total number of topics on which they have communicated (Byrne & Nelson, 1965). The proportion that results can then be put into a formula that predicts attraction—the higher the proportion of similarity, the more the pair will like one another. On the contrary, the **repulsion hypothesis** states that similarity doesn't actually have any effect on attraction (Rosenbaum, 1986). Instead, people are repulsed by dissimilarity. While Rosenbaum's ideas were shown to be wrong (e.g., Smeaton, Byrne, & Murnen, 1989), there is still value to the research. Although it may not lead to repulsion, dissimilarity does have a slightly stronger effect on attraction than does similarity, especially when individuals differ in terms of core group memberships such as ethnicity, sexual orientation, and values (e.g., Pilkington & Lydon, 1997; Tan & Singh, 1995).

### RECIPROCITY

Similarity is just one factor that helps to predict attraction; another is **reciprocity**, which is the exchange of what we receive for what we get, which can include liking those who like us back (e.g., Aron, Dutton, Aron, & Iverson, 1989; Kenny, 1994). Many people begin friendships or romantic relationships based on this belief—we are attracted to those who like us. The belief that someone likes you can lead you to reveal more about yourself to the person over time (Collins & Miller, 1994). This helps to build trust in a relationship, which in turn strengthens it. We like people who share personal information with us (e.g., Archer & Burleson, 1980; Vittengl & Holt, 2000). That said, this may depend somewhat on culture in terms of how reciprocity is defined. For example, González, Moreno, and Schneider (2004) found that Canadian youths related friendship to the reciprocity of self-disclosure, whereas Cuban teens placed more emphasis on reciprocal helping. Independent of how it is defined, reciprocal actions are important for the formation and maintenance of close relationships.

## What Factors Influence and Define Romantic Love?

Paul and Maria have been hanging out with the same group of friends since they all started school together last year. They've always liked one another, but lately things have just been *different*. When they're out with their friends, they find themselves sitting right next to each other more and more often. To top it off, Maria will sometimes catch Paul looking at her and then turning away, and she could swear she sees him blushing!

Obviously, these two are attracted to one another, but what factors will turn this attraction into a romantic relationship? For the most part, romantic love can be influenced by the same factors that affect other relationships. Paul and Maria are affected by proximity and mere exposure since they're in the same group of friends, and they enjoy the same activities—there you see similarity and the matching hypothesis at play.

### THE ROLE OF GENDER

As Paul and Maria move toward a romantic relationship, they are probably seeking different things from the relationship. Much of this has to do with their individual personalities, of course, but some can also be attributed to their genders. For men and women in heterosexual relationships, different aspects of potential mates carry more weight than others. Evolutionary psychologists suggest that whether or not we are interested in becoming parents, our genetic histories and our ancestors' drives to pass on their genes play a major role in our selections of romantic partners.

Our preferred mate choices, these psychologists argue, are based on reproductive potential, which is manifested in different ways in males and females (e.g., Geary, Vigil, & Byrd-Craven, 2004). For example,

**PASSIONATE LOVE** a state of intense longing for union with another

**EXCITATION TRANSFER** the process by which arousal from one stimulus can be transferred to the second stimulus, a person

evolutionary psychologists suggest that men have developed a more powerful desire for a variety of sex partners, with the explanation that more partners means more opportunities to successfully reproduce (Buss, 2002). There may be a reason for the emphasis men seem to place on physical attractiveness in potential female partners, according to evolutionary determinants. Beauty may be associated with fertility, and early men may have had more reproductive success with female mates selected according to physical attractiveness, which is indicative of youth and good health—both considered important in the process of reproduction and childbirth. There may also be evolutionary reasons for men's preferences for "beautiful" long hair and symmetrical faces (e.g., Hughes, Harrison, & Gallup, 2002; Jacobi & Cash, 1994). While a man may not be looking to start a family with every woman he dates, he still may be predisposed to seek out women who are considered beautiful (Buss, 2002).

Women, of course, are also drawn to potential mates that are physically attractive, as discussed earlier in this chapter. Evolutionary psychologists suggest that women don't care as much about physical attractiveness in men because men's reproductive years aren't as limited as women's are; therefore, youth is not as much of a factor in mate selection. Instead, they argue that women are more highly attracted to men who have access to resources, because those resources translate to an ability to protect and care for a family (e.g., Buss, 2002; Kenrick, Neuberg, Zierk, & Krones, 1994).

Now, before you throw this book across the room, grumbling that you can't just make broad generalizations about what men and women are looking for in their romantic partners, you should know that not everyone agrees with this perspective. Research indicates that *both* women and men prefer wealthy and healthy mates (Miller, Putcha-Bhagavatula, & Pederson, 2002). Further, Canadian researchers have noted that cultural and contextual influences may now be more powerful than evolutionary ones (e.g., Dion & Dion, 1993; Honey & Coulombe, 2009), and that reproductive potential as an explanation for romantic relationships is not universally accepted. In fact, gender differences are not as great when individuals are asked about long-term relationship goals (Kenrick, Sadalla, Groth, & Trost, 1990). Both genders are more selective when it comes to picking a long-term mate (Stewart, Stinnett, & Rosenfeld, 2000). Another criticism of the evolutionary perspective is its lack of explanation for male homosexuality. However, new research by scholars at the University of Lethbridge suggests that male same-sex attraction can be explained by the kin selection hypothesis (e.g., Vasey & VanderLaan, 2010). According to this hypothesis, homosexual men may perpetuate family genes by acting as "helpers in the nest," helping with the care of nieces and nephews (also see Forrester, VanderLaan, Parker, & Vasey, 2011).



## PASSIONATE LOVE

As Paul and Maria fall in love with one another, their relationship is new and exciting. They find that their feelings are intense, at some times even overwhelming. They spend all of their free time together and one's heart seems to skip a beat when the other approaches. Paul and Maria are in the throes of **passionate love**, defined by Hatfield (1988) as a state of intense longing for union with another. This can be assessed using Hatfield and Sprecher's (1986) Passionate Love Scale, in which ratings are provided for feelings for another person on a range from "extremely passionate" to "extremely cool." This measure has been used in family therapy with adolescents, who aren't quite sure how to deal with the intensity of passionate love, experiencing these feelings for the first time. In fact, researchers contend that the first appearances of passionate love coincide with puberty (Hatfield & Sprecher, 1986; Hatfield, 1988).

^^^ Once mutual attraction has been established, **how does it turn into a romantic relationship?**

Hatfield (1988) theorizes passionate love, identified by such behaviours as a couple gazing into one another's eyes and feeling like they're on an emotional "roller-coaster," as the steering of a state of arousal into an emotional state. She maintains that heightened arousal is the same no matter what emotion is involved. Think about it. If your heart is pounding and your body is trembling, you might be experiencing fear, anger, or joy, but the physical response is the same. By this theory, any source of arousal should intensify feelings of passion—as long as a possible target of that passion is present. Could a fearful situation, then, lead to feelings of love?

### Can Fear Lead to Passionate Love?

It's a classic action movie scene. A beautiful woman is in danger. Maybe she's been kidnapped, or has been locked in a cage with a hungry tiger, or is being dangled off the edge of a skyscraper by a crazed villain. Whatever the circumstances may be, the hero swoops in and saves the day. Then what happens? They fall madly in love, of course!

It's easy to roll our eyes at these romantic pairings between heroes and their damsels in distress, but they could actually reflect a basic truth about passionate love. There's some pretty substantial evidence showing that sexual attraction occurs with increased frequency when people are in strong emotional states. The **excitation transfer** process suggests that arousal from one stimulus, a scary movie or a roller-coaster, can be transferred to the second stimulus, a person (Zillmann, 1971). The evidence includes studies such as the classic Capilano Suspension Bridge experiment by Dutton and Aron (1974) in Vancouver, B.C., in which male passersby were contacted by an attractive female interviewer

> It's easy to roll our eyes at these romantic pairings between heroes and their damsels in distress, **but they could actually reflect a basic truth about passionate love.**

**COMPANIONATE LOVE** the affection we feel for people with whom our lives are deeply intertwined

**TRIANGULAR THEORY OF LOVE** Robert Sternberg's theory that love is made of three components: intimacy, passion, and commitment

either on a fear-arousing suspension bridge or a non-fear-arousing bridge. Participants who were approached on that bridge misattributed their arousal (marked by racing heart rate and heavier breathing) to the woman interviewing them rather than to the bridge. These men were more likely to call the woman after the experience than those who met her on the non-fear-arousing bridge. The differences were not present for subjects who were contacted by a male interviewer (Dutton & Aron, 1974). In a study of real-life romantic partners, researchers found that participants engaged in more affiliative behaviours following an arousing movie relative to non-arousing movie (Cohen, Waugh, & Place, 1989). More recently, Meston and Frohlich (2003) replicated these effects with individuals who were either waiting in line for a roller-coaster ride (low arousal) or had just gotten off a roller-coaster ride (high arousal). Participants' ratings of attractiveness and dating desirability for target photographs were higher when shown following the roller-coaster ride, but only if they were on the ride with a non-romantic partner (Meston & Frohlich, 2003). Therefore, the passionate love reflected in those action movies may contain a few realistic elements!

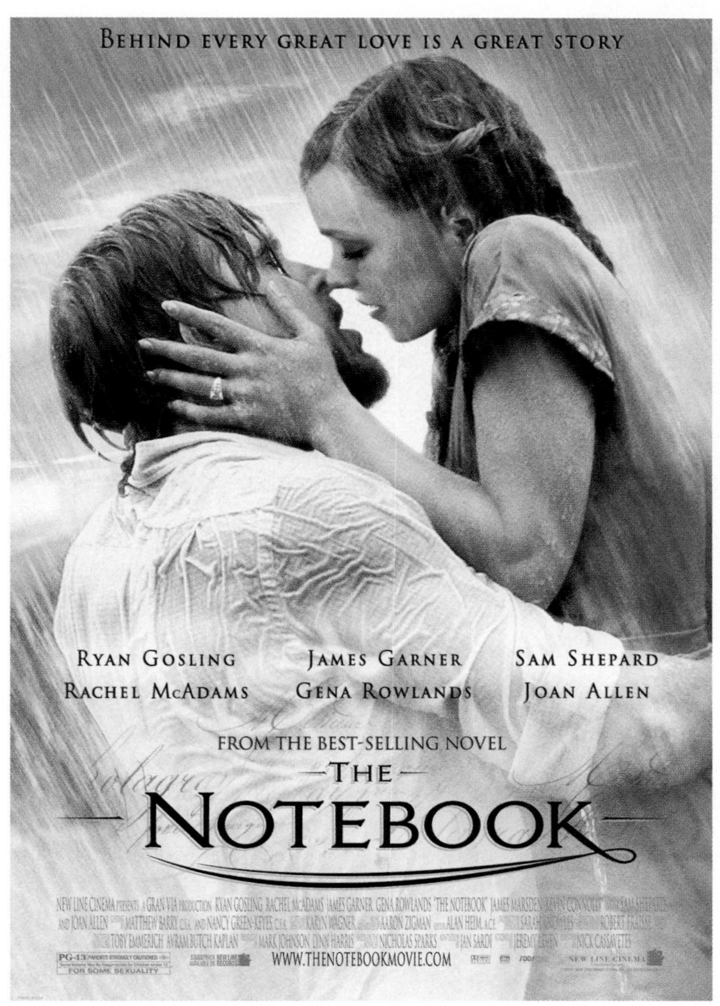

BEHIND EVERY GREAT LOVE IS A GREAT STORY
RYAN GOSLING
JAMES GARNER
SAM SHEPARD
RACHEL McADAMS
GENA ROWLANDS
JOAN ALLEN
FROM THE BEST-SELLING NOVEL
THE NOTEBOOK
WWW.THENOTEBOOKMOVIE.COM


When two people are in the throes of passionate love, **they feel as if they cannot live without each other.**

## COMPANIONATE LOVE

Maybe their relationship progresses to the point that Paul and Maria get married. After years together, their state of passionate love shifts into a different kind of love. While passionate love is intense and exciting, **companionate love** is more stable and calm. It's the affection we feel for people with whom our lives are deeply intertwined. Companionate love is characterized by shared attitudes, values, and life experiences, as well as deep feelings of trust in the other person (Hatfield, 1988). Passionate love is thrilling, but eventually all thrills must come to an end. That doesn't mean the relationship ends or the love stops, though. It just changes into the more sustainable and comfortable companionate love.

Sometimes, though, this cooling of passionate love goes through a transitional period. As the excitement and novelty fade, people can become disillusioned, particularly if they believe romance is essential for the continuation of a marriage. Some social psychologists believe rising divorce rates can be attributed in part to the rising importance of intense positive emotional experiences, like the "high" of passionate love (see Reis & Aron, 2008). It's hard to keep that kind of emotional state up, but that doesn't stop some people from clinging to the dream (Simpson, Campbell, & Berscheid, 1986). More recent research suggests that being in a long-term relationship doesn't necessarily mean one has to give up on passionate love and make a complete shift to companionate love. And sometimes our conceptualization of what love is changes with a changing relationship (e.g., Fehr, 2006). Romantic love can exist in long-term marriages and is in fact a sign of well-being and high self-esteem in long-married couples (e.g., Acevedo & Aron, 2009).

## THE TRIANGULAR THEORY OF LOVE

As the relationship between Paul and Maria develops and changes, we call it love, but what does that mean? What components add up to create love? Robert Sternberg (1986, 1997) found a way to explain it through his **triangular theory of love**. He suggests that there are three components that make up love: *intimacy* (feelings of closeness and connectedness), *passion* (physical attraction and sexual consummation), and *commitment* (both in the decision that one loves another and to maintain the love). The amount of love felt by an individual depends on the strength of these components, and the kind of love depends on the strength of each component in relation to the others.

We've discussed passionate and companionate love, but Sternberg's triangular model actually results in *eight* different types of love, as people can experience love as all three components, two of the components,

**Passionate Love:**

- Characterized by intense longing for one's partner
- Thrilling
- Roller-coaster of emotions
- First experienced in adolescence
- Can be triggered by scary or intense experiences
- Often present at the beginning of a romantic relationship

**Companionate Love:**

- Calm and stable
- Characterized by shared values and life experiences
- Marked by a deep sense of trust
- Most often present in couples that have been together for a long time



**Passionate and Companionate Love.** Over time, the thrill of new love usually fades, and a calmer kind of love takes its place.

just one of them, or even none of them (Sternberg, 1986). Where might companionate love and passionate love (which Sternberg describes as romantic love) fall on the model? Think about what characterizes those types of love, and which of the three components would be strongest.

## ROMANTIC LOVE ACROSS CULTURES

If Paul and Maria had grown up in a country such as China or India, would they place as much importance on the connections they are forming with each other now? Would they even see each other as potential partners, or envision marrying one another?

Definitions of romantic love vary across cultures. University of Toronto researchers have explored differences in romantic love along the lines of individualist and collectivist cultures, and found that viewpoints can be quite different (Dion & Dion, 1993, 1996). Romantic love seems to be a more important basis for marriage in individualist cultures such as Canada and the United States than it is in collectivist cultures such as India, China, and Japan. Likewise, individualist cultures place more value on psychological intimacy between romantic partners. The research also discussed the impact of individualism on romantic love, particularly the aspects of individualism that make developing psychological intimacy problematic (Dion & Dion, 1993). Other research has determined that there are some similarities in the way different cultures conceptualize love. For example, Hong Kong Chinese and British respondents in one study both showed at least a moderate belief in the role of predestiny and fate in relationship development (e.g., Goodwin & Findlay, 1997). The Chinese respondents, however, scored significantly higher on endorsement of those beliefs than their British counterparts did.

Not all romantic relationships are based on initial passionate love. For example, studies on arranged marriages in India find that even

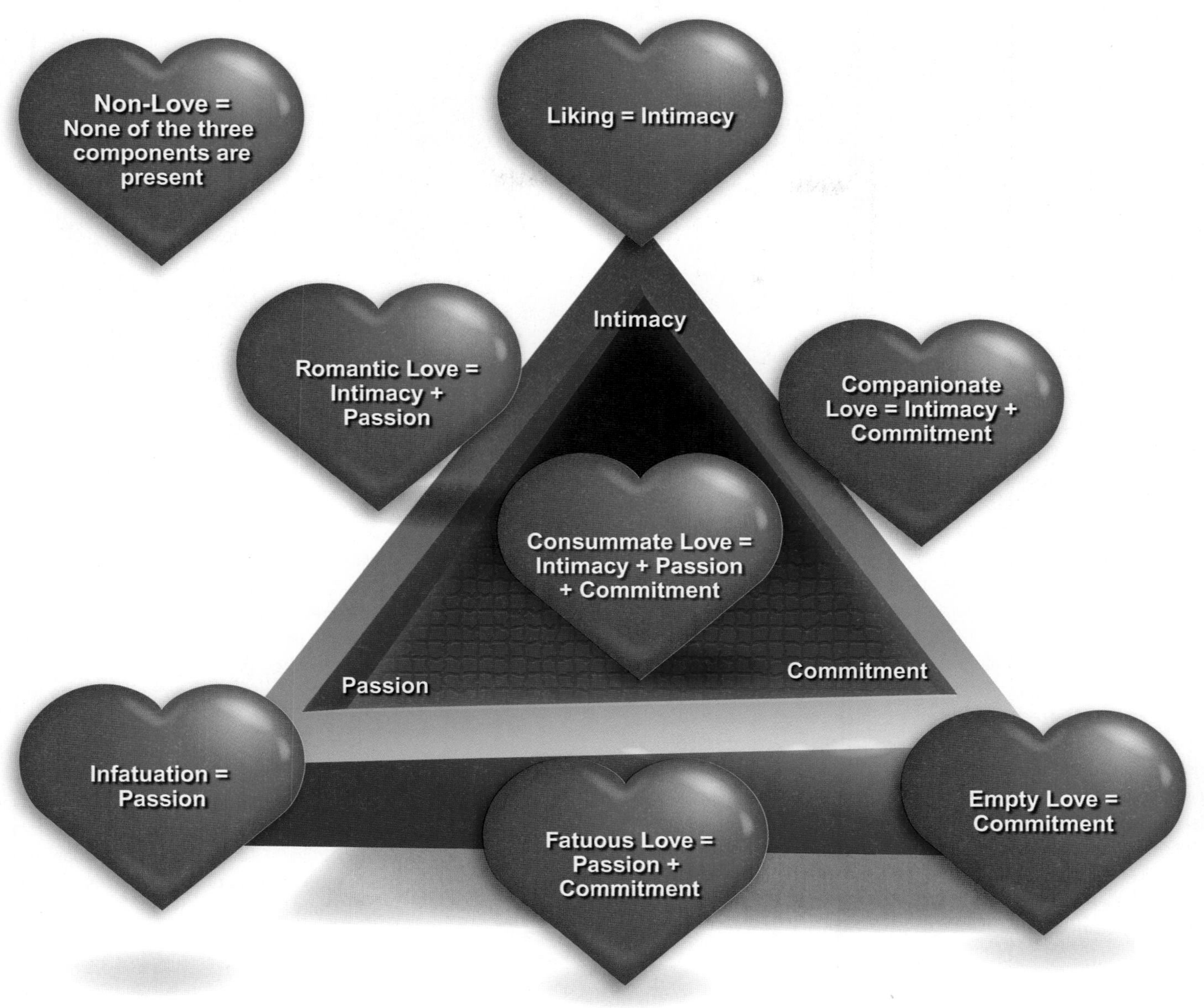


<<< **Sternberg's Triangular Theory of Love.** Through different arrangements of three basic components of love (intimacy, commitment, and passion), **eight distinct types of love can be experienced.**



though these unions are not by choice, there is no difference in the long-term satisfaction within the relationships in comparison to marriages of choice (e.g., Gupta & Singh, 1982; Myers, Madathil, & Tingil, 2005). There are also cultural considerations in the question of marital satisfaction. In Canada, many people cannot imagine being paired off for an arranged marriage, but some research shows that people in arranged marriages actually experience more satisfaction than those who choose their partners (Xiaohe & Whyte, 1990). However, as mentioned above, other research shows little difference between arranged and non-arranged marriages (e.g., Myers et al., 2005). Further, differential emphasis on the importance of love and marriage may differ within one's own country. For example, Quebec has experienced more declines in marriage rates in comparison to the rest of Canada, in part due to differing norms, cultural heritage, and greater emphasis on sexual freedoms (Pollard & Wu, 1998).

## IS MARRIAGE THE END GOAL OF ROMANTIC LOVE?

In imagining Paul and Maria moving through the stages of a relationship, we've assumed that they get married, but not all romantic relationships end in marriage. Some people see marriage as the "goal" of a romantic relationship, but should it be? Research to determine whether marriage has a positive effect is complicated. Some research shows that marriage benefits individuals' economic well-being, the well-being of their children, and their overall health (e.g., Lerman, 2002; Schoenborn, 2004). Other studies show that it's not marriage alone that predicts better health and well-being—that people must be *satisfied* with their marriages to reap these benefits. These studies suggest that single individuals generally have better health than their unhappily married counterparts (e.g., Holt-Lunstad, Birmingham, & Jones, 2008).

**SOCIAL EXCHANGE THEORY** an economic model of human behaviour in which people make decisions based on maximizing benefits and minimizing costs in relationships

**EQUITY THEORY** a theory that relationships are most satisfying when the ratio between benefits and contributions is similar for both partners

**INVESTMENT** resources that have been devoted to a relationship that cannot be retrieved

**EXCHANGE RELATIONSHIP** a relationship in which partners expect strict reciprocity

**COMMUNAL RELATIONSHIP** a relationship in which partners expect mutual responsiveness to one another's needs

^^^ What keeps couples together? **The answer may lie in several theories of relationship maintenance.**

It must be noted, too, that most of the research on marriage and long-term relationships has been on opposite-sex couples. Part of the reason for this has been the legal bans on same-sex marriages within many countries. However, we can assume that same-sex couples would also experience the same benefits and challenges of marriage. In fact, a recent study suggests that the ban on gay marriage has had a negative impact on the mental health of gay, lesbian, and bisexual individuals (Mustanski, 2010). The study found an increase in mood disorders, generalized anxiety disorder, and alcohol use disorders among gay, lesbian, and bisexual individuals living in places with gay marriage bans. In addition to illustrating the ill effects of keeping people from the benefits of marriage, this study clearly demonstrated the negative effect of institutionalized discrimination. Other recent research looking at same-sex couples who are in civil unions or long-term relationships adds support to the idea that same-sex couples experience the same benefits from long-term relationships as do opposite-sex couples (e.g., Balsam, Beauchaine, Rothblum, & Solomon, 2008; Gottman, Levenson, Swanson, Swanson, Tyson, & Yoshimoto, 2003). A longitudinal study by Kurdek (2004) showed that same-sex couples were just as happy as, if not happier than, opposite-sex couples (see Peplau & Fingerhut, 2007, for a review of research on same-sex couples).



# How Are Relationships Maintained?

So far, we've discussed how friendships and romantic relationships start, but how do people keep them going? There have been several theories proposed to predict how long and how well a relationship is maintained.

## SOCIAL EXCHANGE THEORY

The first of these theories is the **social exchange theory** (Thibaut & Kelley, 1952, 1959), an economic theory of behaviour that argues that people base behaviours on maximizing benefits and minimizing costs in relationships. Following this theory, relationships that offer more benefits and fewer costs (including the work it takes to maintain the relationship) will naturally last longer and be more fulfilling than those that carry more costs and fewer benefits. The frequency and rate of increase of rewards also matter—couples who experience greater increases in rewards over the course of a relationship tend to stay together longer (e.g., Assh & Byers, 1990; Berg & McQuinn, 1986). The same effect has been found in heterosexual couples as well as homosexual couples (Kurdek, 1991).

Of course, timing is everything. The social exchange theory doesn't usually apply to the early stages of a relationship. People don't tend to worry about costs of relationship in the first throes of passion or during the honeymoon (Hays, 1985). In addition to timing, another important consideration is how well rewards actually address each partner's needs—social exchange isn't just about quantity, but *quality* (Lawrence et al., 2008). A partner can buy you gifts daily, but if they do not really reflect you or the things you like, then they do not enhance fulfillment in a relationship.

## EQUITY THEORY

Have you ever been in a relationship in which you felt you worked much harder than the other person, and that he or she got more out of it without having to lift a finger? Chances are, it didn't last too long. This can be explained through the **equity theory** (Walster, Walster, & Traupmann, 1978), which states that relationships are most satisfying when the ratio between benefits and contributions is similar for both partners (for a review of this theory, see Sprecher & Schwartz, 1994; Van Yperen & Buunk, 1994). That said, this theory isn't without its critics, who argue that the evidence is sometimes contradictory to the theory. However, Van Yperen and Buunk (1990) propose that there are individual differences in importance of equity. For example, if couples place high importance on exchange, then the perception of equity is important to the satisfaction level of the relationship in comparison to couples who do not. For example, some couples who live according to traditional sex roles may not have equity per se, but this may be less important for *both* partners in the relationship, and as a result it may not diminish satisfaction.

## THE INVESTMENT MODEL

Once you've devoted certain things to a relationship—time, self-disclosure, energy—there is no way to get them back. These resources that cannot be retrieved are **investments** (Rusbult, 1983, 1991). The investments you make in a relationship are directly linked to the commitment you feel to that relationship. If you've put a lot into it, it's harder to break it off. Think about someone you've dated for two weeks versus someone you've dated for two years—you're generally more willing to work through problems if you have more invested in a relationship. Research findings tend to support this model across time (Rusbult, 1983).

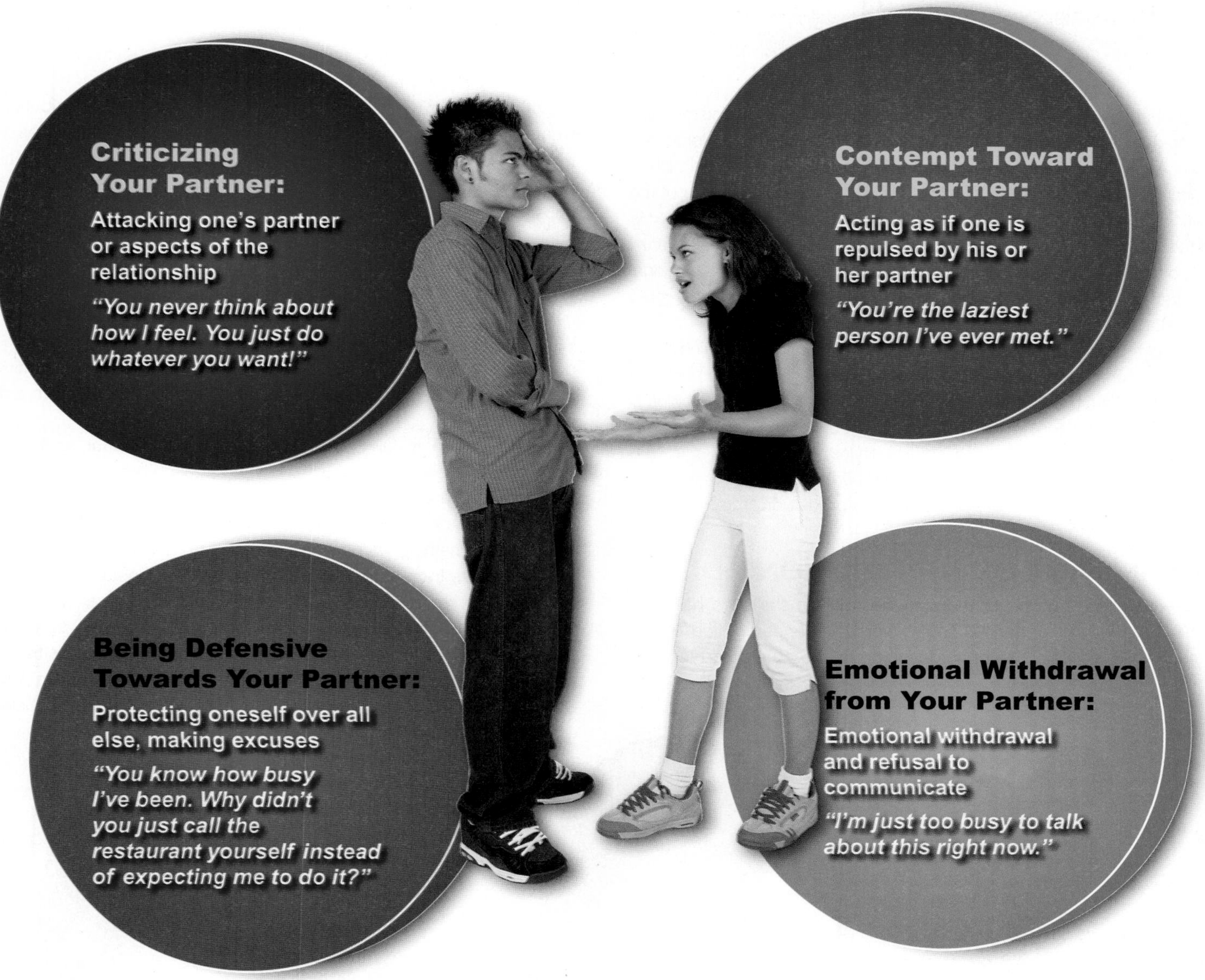


**Four Types of Conflict.** The presence of these forms of conflict can bring about the end of a relationship.

## EXCHANGE AND COMMUNAL RELATIONSHIPS

Yet another way of looking at the maintenance and satisfaction of relationships is through examining the differences between exchange and communal relationships (Clark, 1984). **Exchange relationships** are those in which partners expect strict reciprocity, while **communal relationships** are those in which partners expect mutual responsiveness to one another's needs. Exchange relationships are usually limited to strangers and casual acquaintances, or between business partners. Strong communal relationships, on the other hand, exist between close friends, romantic partners, and family members. In these relationships, people seek to take care of one another without expecting anything in return (for a review of these types of relationships, see Clark & Pataki, 1995).

# What Role Does Conflict Play in Relationships?

"I just don't even want to look at you right now!" she yells and, before you know it, the door has been slammed in your face. What started out as a perfectly normal evening has now somehow ended in a massive fight, and you're not even sure how you got there. Fighting with a friend or lover is never fun, but it certainly isn't unusual. Relationships have the potential to improve your mood and overall health, but they aren't without their challenges. All close relationships will involve some conflict—it simply can't be avoided.

While conflict can be part of a healthy relationship, there are certain conflict styles that can be quite destructive. In fact, leading marriage

**NEGATIVE ATTRIBUTIONAL STYLE** a style that occurs when a person explains his or her partner's behaviours in negative ways

researcher John Gottman (1994) identified four styles (criticism, contempt, defensiveness, stonewalling) and called them the "Four Horsemen of the Apocalypse" because they can usher in the end of a relationship. *Criticism* is characterized by attacking aspects of one's partner or of the relationship. *Contempt* is marked by one acting as if he is repulsed by his partner. One exhibits *defensiveness* when she will protect the self over all else, often through making excuses, and *stonewalling* involves emotional withdrawal and refusal to communicate. They all sound like they could kill a relationship, don't they?

And they can; research has shown that relationships in which these behaviours are shown lead to lower satisfaction over time in women, and in highly anxious persons in general (e.g., Campbell, Simpson, Boldry, & Kashy, 2005; Huston & Vangelisti, 1991). Further, there are gender differences in the use of these conflict styles; for example, men are more likely to use stonewalling. Gottman (1994) also argues that stonewalling and contempt are especially likely to predict divorce.

## THE IMPACT OF ATTRIBUTIONS

Sarah is walking out of her morning class when she sees her boyfriend, Will, waiting for her. Without a word, he hands her two tickets to see Great Big Sea, one of her favourite bands. She'd had to work when tickets for the show went on sale, and had been disappointed that she was going to miss out on seeing them. Looking at the tickets, and then at Will's smiling face, she thinks, "Best boyfriend ever! He is so sweet!"

In Chapter 5, you learned about Kelley's theory of attributions, where we attribute behaviours to internal or external causes as we try to make sense of what is going on around us. Usually, we make beneficial attributions for things that happen to ourselves and our loved ones. You might make an excuse for your partner's negative behaviour, attributing it to an external factor. For example, "My partner is not working right now because the job market is bad." Positive behaviour, like Will buying Sarah those Great Big Sea tickets, is attributed to an internal factor—that Will is a thoughtful boyfriend and cares about Sarah. What if, though, Sarah didn't attribute Will's positive behaviour to a positive factor? What if she instead attributed it to something negative? Let's say, upon seeing the tickets, Sarah's first thought was "What did he do this time?"

Here, Sarah is falling into a **negative attributional style**. This occurs when a person explains his or her partner's behaviours in negative ways. We're all familiar with the classic scenario, often used in comedy, in which a man brings his wife flowers, only to have her assume he's done something wrong—he's cheating on her or has screwed up at work. These traps lead to lower marital satisfaction, usually because they increase conflict within a relationship and may lead to aggressive behaviours (e.g., Assh & Byers, 1990; Scott & Straus, 2007). In a study of attribution, researchers asked married couples to rate their trust in their partners and then to discuss a common relationship problem (Miller & Rempel, 2004). After the discussion, participants rated the beliefs they'd had about their partners during the discussion. Two years later, the participants were once again to rate their beliefs about their partners. People who had made negative

Is seeing your partner talk to an **attractive person** enough to get you feeling jealous? **There could be an evolutionary reason for this.**

attributions in the first part of the study reported less trust in their partners during the two-year follow-up. Likewise, people who reported lower trust in the first part of the study made negative attributions for their partners' behaviour in the second part of the study (Miller & Rempel, 2004).

## THE GREEN-EYED MONSTER

How do you feel when you see your partner chatting up an attractive person at a party? It's normal to feel a little pang of jealousy over any potential threat to your relationship. Men and women both experience jealousy, but do they experience it in the same ways, and in reaction to the same experiences?

Once again, evolutionary psychologists have a possible answer. Participants in one study were asked to imagine their partners flirting with someone at a party (Dijkstra & Buunk, 1998). Male participants were more jealous when they imagined their partners flirting with someone powerful and successful, while female participants were more likely to report feelings of jealousy when imagining their partners flirting with really physically attractive people (Dijkstra & Buunk, 1998). Evolutionary psychology suggests that men should fear sexual infidelity because it could result in the use of their resources to raise another man's child. A woman, on the other hand, would be more threatened by emotional infidelity because it threatens resources that support her children.

The potential for jealousy over different behaviours also seems to be divided along gender lines (e.g., Levy & Kelly, 2010). When men and women were asked if they would be more upset if their partner had sexual intercourse with or formed a deep emotional attachment to another person, 60 percent of the men said they would be more upset by sexual infidelity. Of the women who were surveyed, 83 percent said they would be more upset by the emotional infidelity (Buss, Larsen, Westen, & Semmelroth, 1992). That said, others argue that sex differences in jealousy that have been revealed by research are inconsistent and lack empirical validity (e.g., Edlund & Sagarin, 2009).

## ARE THERE BENEFITS IN THE DISSOLUTION OF A RELATIONSHIP?

Sometimes people just drift apart. Nothing bad has happened; it's just that the relationship has run its course. This is common with friendships, but the same is not generally true with romantic relationships or marriages. The dissolution of a marriage can be particularly difficult, as all of the energy a couple has put into building a life together can suddenly seem like a waste of time. Our automatic response tends to be to see breakups as a bad thing. One's trust in others takes a hit, belongings are divided, friends choose sides—it can be hard to see much good coming out of the dissolution of a relationship. Why, then, do so many people say, "It's for the best"?

There's no doubt that the end of a relationship causes feelings of sadness, but there is some positive effect. Think of it this way: Everything you learned about yourself in the formation, duration, and dissolution of a relationship only makes you better prepared for the next one. Evidence of personal growth can be divided into several groupings: person positives, relational positives, and environment positives (Tashiro & Frazier, 2003). *Person-positive* personal growth is marked by the development of attitudes such as greater confidence in what experiences you can handle. *Relational positives* involve lessons about yourself in relation to others, such as learning relationship skills or knowing not to let yourself fall so hard so quickly. Finally, *environment positives* focus on the world around you. You might see a break-up as a way to refocus on the importance of your friends or schoolwork. So although the dissolution of a relationship may be painful, it may be "for the best" when you gain these benefits from it in order to have better relationships in the future!



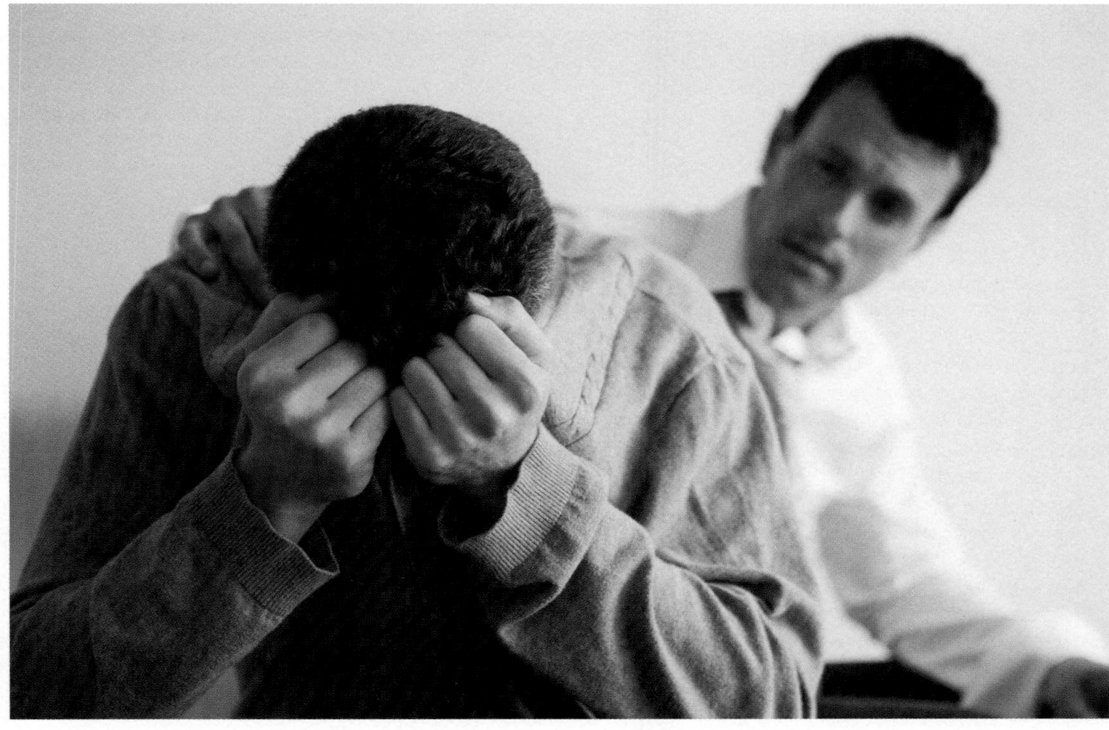

>>> **"Hey, man, it's all for the best."** Is there truth in these commonly used words of comfort?

CHAPTER

# 12 Review

## Summary

### HOW DO EARLY PARENT–CHILD INTERACTIONS IMPACT FUTURE RELATIONSHIPS? p. 230

- Our brains are wired to encourage interaction between parents and children. The release of the hormone oxytocin leads to feelings of trust and calm.
- Early interactions with parents and caregivers lead to the development of attachment styles. These styles describe the relationship between self-esteem and interpersonal trust. They affect the way we define and interact within relationships.

### WHAT LEADS TO ATTRACTION? p. 233

- Attraction starts with proximity, which leads to repeated contact between people. This repeated contact, described as mere exposure, increases the likelihood of attraction.
- Physical attraction impacts interaction; we are more likely to react positively to someone who is physically attractive. We are also attracted to people with whom we share similar traits or beliefs.

### WHAT FACTORS INFLUENCE AND DEFINE ROMANTIC LOVE? p. 237

- Romantic relationships are defined in terms of passionate and companionate love. Passionate love is frequently seen at the beginning of a relationship, when two people feel intense longing toward one another. It usually cools into the more stable and calm companionate love.
- Robert Sternberg's triangular theory of love describes the relationship between three possible components of love. His model results in eight different types of love.

### HOW ARE RELATIONSHIPS MAINTAINED? p. 242

- Social exchange theory argues that relationship satisfaction comes from weighing the benefits of a relationship against the costs. Similar to this is equity theory, in which relationship maintenance can be predicted based on similarity between partner's ratios of benefits to contributions in a relationship.
- The more you've invested in a relationship, the more you're willing to work at maintaining it.

### WHAT ROLE DOES CONFLICT PLAY IN RELATIONSHIPS? p. 243

- Conflict is a normal part of any relationship; however, there are four conflict styles, identified by Gottman, that usually result in the end of a relationship. The negative attributional style can also cause serious problems within a relationship.
- The dissolution of a relationship is often considered a bad thing, but it can result in personal growth. This growth is measured in three types of positive outcomes.



## Key Terms

**attachment style** the degree of security experienced in interpersonal relationships *231*

**communal relationship** a relationship in which partners expect mutual responsiveness to one another's needs *242*

**companionate love** the affection we feel for people with whom our lives are deeply intertwined *239*

**dismissive attachment style** a conflicted, insecure attachment style characterized by high self-esteem and low interpersonal trust *233*

**equity theory** a theory that relationships are most satisfying when the ratio between benefits and contributions is similar for both partners *242*

**exchange relationship** a relationship in which partners expect strict reciprocity *242*

**excitation transfer** the process by which arousal from one stimulus can be transferred to the second stimulus, a person *238*

**fearful-avoidant attachment style** the most insecure of the attachment styles, characterized by low self-esteem and low interpersonal trust *232*

**interpersonal trust** the belief that people are generally trustworthy and dependable and the attitude that underlies the development of attachment styles *231*

**investment** resources that have been devoted to a relationship that cannot be retrieved *242*

**matching hypothesis** the hypothesis that people are more likely to form longstanding relationships with others whose social attributes match with theirs and with those who are similar in physical attractiveness *237*

**mere exposure** the hypothesis that the mere repeated exposure of an individual to a stimulus is enough for an increase in favourable response to that stimulus *234*

**need for affiliation** the desire to establish and maintain rewarding interpersonal relationships *230*

**negative attributional style** a style that occurs when a person explains his or her partner's behaviours in negative ways *244*

**passionate love** a state of intense longing for union with another *238*

**preoccupied attachment style** a conflicted, insecure attachment style characterized by low self-esteem and high interpersonal trust *232*

**proportion of similarity** an equation that divides the number of topics on which two people express similar views by the total number of topics on which they have communicated, resulting in a prediction of attraction *237*

**proximity** physical closeness; the smaller the physical distance, the more likely the two people will experience repeat contact, which could lead to the development of mutual attraction *234*

**reciprocity** the exchange of what we receive for what we get, which can include liking those who like us back *237*

**repulsion hypothesis** states that similarity doesn't actually have any effect on attraction *237*

**secure attachment style** the most successful of the attachment styles, characterized by high self-esteem and high interpersonal trust *231*

**social exchange theory** an economic model of human behaviour in which people make decisions based on maximizing benefits and minimizing costs in relationships *242*

**triangular theory of love** Robert Sternberg's theory that love is made of three components: intimacy, passion, and commitment *239*

# Test Your Understanding

## MULTIPLE CHOICE

1. The hypothesis that repeated contact with a stimulus is enough for an increase in favourable response to that stimulus is called
   - **a.** mere exposure.
   - **b.** proximity.
   - **c.** interaction.
   - **d.** attachment.
2. Studies of the concept of physical attractiveness across cultures have found that
   - **a.** people from collectivist countries tend to favour smaller features.
   - **b.** collectivist cultures place very little emphasis on physical attractiveness.
   - **c.** there is very little difference in what is considered physically attractive by people from different cultures.
   - **d.** people from individualist cultures tend to favour large eyes and prominent cheekbones.
3. According to evolutionary psychologists,
   - **a.** men seek out physically attractive mates, while women seek out mates with access to resources.
   - **b.** there is really no difference in what men and women want in a potential romantic partner.
   - **c.** women seek out younger mates, while age isn't a factor for men.
   - **d.** women seek out mates who are physically attractive, but men value youth above all in a partner.
4. Interaction between parents and their infants is encouraged by the release of
   - **a.** melatonin.
   - **b.** oxytocin.
   - **c.** adrenaline.
   - **d.** estrogen.
5. Which attachment style results from low self-esteem paired with high interpersonal trust?
   - **a.** secure attachment style
   - **b.** fearful-avoidant attachment style
   - **c.** preoccupied attachment style
   - **d.** dismissive attachment style
6. Which attachment style results from high self-esteem paired with low interpersonal trust?
   - **a.** secure attachment style
   - **b.** fearful-avoidant attachment style
   - **c.** preoccupied attachment style
   - **d.** dismissive attachment style
7. The type of love often seen in long-term relationships and characterized by stability and calm is called
   - **a.** passionate love.
   - **b.** comfortable love.
   - **c.** companionate love.
   - **d.** real love.
8. Sternberg's triangular theory of love describes the relationship between
   - **a.** intimacy, loneliness, and passion.
   - **b.** intimacy, passion, and commitment.
   - **c.** commitment, loneliness, and attractiveness.
   - **d.** commitment, passion, and loyalty.
9. One of the "Four Horsemen," *stonewalling* involves
   - **a.** emotional withdrawal.
   - **b.** acting as if you are repulsed by your partner.
   - **c.** ignoring everything your partner says.
   - **d.** complaining about your partner.
10. When one explains his or her partner's behaviour in a negative way, he or she is showing evidence of
    - **a.** criticism.
    - **b.** denial.
    - **c.** contempt.
    - **d.** negative attributional style.

**ANSWERS:** 1. a; 2. c; 3. a; 4. b; 5. c; 6. d; 7. c; 8. b; 9. a; 10. d

## ESSAY RESPONSE

1. Explain the process that leads to attraction, using an example.
2. Is physical attractiveness a subjective trait, or can it be measured objectively? Explain your reasoning.
3. Define each of the four attachment styles, and give an example of a representative relationship for each.
4. Compare and contrast passionate and companionate love. How does one lead to the other?
5. How does the negative attributional style lead to distrust and negative feelings in a relationship?

## APPLY IT!

Choose five of the eight possible types of love from Sternberg's triangular theory of love. Find examples from television, movies, or books that exemplify each of the types you selected. How do these examples reflect these types of love?

**Remember to check www.thethinkspot.ca for additional information, downloadable flashcards, and other helpful resources.**

# THINK READINGS

Why do you think vulnerability can play such a large part in the success of a relationship? Think about what you learned in Chapters 4 and 5. How might self-disclosure play a role in romance?

Epstein attributes this effect in large part to an increase in people opening up to one another. But what role do you think proximity, mere exposure, and interaction—factors you learned about in Chapter 12—played in his experiment?

SCIENTIFIC AMERICAN MIND

## How Science Can Help You Fall in Love

By ROBERT EPSTEIN

Published: January/February 2010

***Nothing is more fulfilling than being in a successful love relationship. Yet we leave our love lives entirely to chance. Maybe we don't have to anymore***

The best way to get students interested in scientific studies is to give them hands-on experiences that get them excited about the subject matter. In chemistry courses, teachers accomplish that with test tubes and mysterious liquids. In a course I taught recently at the University of California, San Diego, on relationship science, I piqued my students' interest with exercises on, well, *love*.

To begin, I invited eight students who did not know each other to come to the front of the auditorium, where I paired them up randomly. I then asked each individual to rate, on a scale of 1 to 10, how much he or she liked, loved, or felt close to his or her partner. Then I asked the couples to look deeply into each other's eyes in an exercise I call Soul Gazing.

There was some giggling at first and then some very intense gazing. After two minutes, I again asked for the numbers. The result? A modest 7 percent increase in loving (meaning 1 point added for one person in one couple), an 11 percent increase in liking, and a whopping 45 percent increase in closeness. There were gasps and cheers in the audience. When I asked everyone in the class to pair up for two minutes of gazing, 89 percent of the students said the exercise increased feelings of intimacy.

And that was just the beginning....

### Eye Contact

About 50 percent of first marriages fail in the U.S., as do two thirds of second marriages and three quarters of third marriages. So much for practice! We fail in large part because we enter into relationships with poor skills for maintaining them and highly unrealistic expectations. We also tend to pick unsuitable partners, mistakenly believing that we are in love simply because we feel physical attraction.

That combination of factors sets us up for failure: eventually—often within a mere 18 months—the fog of passion dissipates, and we begin to see our partner with new clarity. All too often we react by saying, "Who are *you?*" or "You've *changed.*" We might try hard for years after that to keep things going, especially if children are in the picture. But if we start out with the wrong person and lack basic tools for resolving conflicts and communicating, the chances that we will succeed are slim to none.

Over the years, having looked carefully at the fast-growing scientific literature on relationship science and having conducted some new research of my own, I have come to believe that there is a definite fix for our poor performance in romantic relationships. The fix is to extract a practical technology from the research and then to teach people how to use it.

At least 80 scientific studies help to reveal how people learn to love each other. A 1989 study by psychologist James D. Laird of Clark University and his colleagues inspired my Soul Gazing exercise. The researchers showed that mutual eye gazing (but not gazing at hands) produced rapid increases in feelings of both liking and loving in total strangers. Mutual gazing is like staring, but with an important difference: for many mammalian species, staring is both intended and received as a threat. Try it on a New York subway if you have any doubts about its efficacy. In mutual gazing, however, people are giving each other permission to stare; that is, they are being vulnerable to each other, and that is the key element in emotional bonding. The vulnerability created when people are in

### Fast Facts

#### Lessons on Love

1 » About half of first marriages fail in the U.S., as do two thirds of second marriages and three quarters of third marriages. We fail in large part because we enter into relationships with poor skills for maintaining them and highly unrealistic expectations.

2 » The fix for our poor performance in romantic relationships: extract a practical technology from scientific research on how people learn to love each other—and then teach individuals how to use it.

3 » A study of arranged marriages in which love has grown over time hints that commitment, communication, accommodation and vulnerability are key components of a successful relationship. Other research indicates that sharing adventures, secrets, personal space and jokes can also build intimacy and love with your partner.

SCIENTIFIC AMERICAN MIND, Vol. 20, Pages 26–33 Copyright 2010 Scientific American

war zones can create powerful emotional bonds in seconds, and even hostages sometimes develop strong attachments to their captors, a phenomenon called the Stockholm syndrome.

Signs of vulnerability in an animal or another person bring out tendencies in many people to provide care and protection—to be drawn to that being and to like or even love him or her. And as research in social psychology has shown for decades, when a person is feeling vulnerable and thus agitated or otherwise aroused, he or she often looks around for clues about how to interpret and label those feelings. The body is saying, "I'm aroused, but I'm not sure why," and the environment is suggesting an answer, namely, that you're in love.

## A Technology of Affection

Soul Gazing is one of dozens of exercises I have distilled from scientific studies that make people feel vulnerable and increase intimacy. Love Aura, Let Me Inside and Secret Swap are other examples of fun, bond-building activities that any couple can learn and practice [*see box on preceding page*].

Students could earn extra credit in my course by trying out such techniques with friends, romantic interests or even total strangers. More than 90 percent of the students in the course reported using these methods successfully to improve their relationships, and more than 50 of the 213 students submitted detailed reports about their experiences. Nearly all the reports documented increases in liking, loving, closeness or attraction of between 3 and 30 percent over about a month. In a few cases, ratings tripled. (Students did not need to enhance their relationships to receive extra credit; all they had to do was document their use of the techniques.)

The few exceptions I saw made sense. One heterosexual male saw no positive effects when he tried the exercises with another male; moreover, the experience made him "uncomfortable." When he tried them with a female, however, his intimacy ratings increased by 25 percent—and *hers* increased by 144 percent!

A student named Olivia attempted the exercises with her brother, mother, a good friend and a relative stranger. Soul Gazing failed with her brother because he could not stop giggling. When she and her mom tried the Secret Swap—an activity that creates vulnerability when people disclose secrets to each other—intimacy ratings increased by 31 percent. Exercises she tried with her friend boosted ratings between 10 and 19 percent, but most impressive was the outcome of gazing with someone she barely knew: a 70 percent increase in intimacy.

One student did the assignment with her husband of five years. The couple, Asa and Gill, tried out eight different exercises, and even though their "before" scores were usually very high (9s and 10s), every exercise they tried increased their scores by at least 3 percent. Overall, Asa wrote, "I noticed a drastic change in our bond for one another. My husband seems more affectionate now than he was, for which I am really grateful." She also reported a bonus: a substantial drop in the frequency with which she

## Love-Building

### *Exercises*

Here are some fun exercises, all inspired by scientific studies, that you can use to deliberately create emotional intimacy with a partner— even someone you barely know:

**1 »** **Two as One.** Embracing each other gently, begin to sense your partner's breathing and gradually try to synchronize your breathing with his or hers. After a few minutes, you might feel that the two of you have merged.

**2 »** **Soul Gazing.** Standing or sitting about two feet away from each other, look deeply into each other's eyes, trying to look into the very core of your beings. Do this for about two minutes and then talk about what you saw.

**3 »** **Monkey Love.** Standing or sitting fairly near each other, start moving your hands, arms and legs any way you like—but in a fashion that perfectly imitates your partner. This is fun but also challenging. You will both feel as if you are moving voluntarily, but your actions are also linked to those of your partner.

**4 »** **Falling in Love.** This is a trust exercise, one of many that increase mutual feelings of vulnerability. From a standing position, simply let yourself fall backward into the arms of your partner. Then trade places. Repeat several times and then talk about your feelings. Strangers who do this exercise sometimes feel connected to each other for years.

**5 »** **Secret Swap.** Write down a deep secret and have your partner do the same. Then trade papers and talk about what you read. You can continue this process until you have run out of secrets. Better yet, save some of your secrets for another day.

**6 »** **Mind-Reading Game.** Write down a thought that you want to convey to your partner. Then spend a few minutes wordlessly trying to broadcast that thought to him or her, as he or she tries to guess what it is. If he or she cannot guess, reveal what you were thinking. Then switch roles.

**7 »** **Let Me Inside.** Stand about four feet away from each other and focus on each other. Every 10 seconds or so move a bit closer until, after several shifts, you are well inside each other's personal space (the boundary is about 18 inches). Get as close as you can without touching. (My students tell me this exercise often ends with kissing.)

**8 »** **Love Aura.** Place the palm of your hand as close as possible to your partner's palm without actually touching. Do this for several minutes, during which you will feel not only heat but also, sometimes, eerie kinds of sparks.

*—R.E.*

**ROBERT EPSTEIN** is a contributing editor for *Scientific American Mind* and former editor in chief of *Psychology Today*. He holds a Ph.D. in psychology from Harvard University and is a longtime researcher and professor. He is currently working on a book called *Making Love: How People Learn to Love and How You Can Too (www.MakingLoveBook.com).*

***What do you think of Epstein's exercises? How do you think you would feel if you tried them with a significant other, a family member, or a stranger?***

## Extra Credit for Love

Jocelyn, aged 21, and Brian, aged 25, are students at the University of California, San Diego, where they tried some of the love-generating techniques they learned in the author's class on relationship science. These graphs show changes in feelings of liking (blue), closeness (pink) and loving (red) over six weeks. Each week the students tried one exercise. At the outset, they liked each other fairly well but experienced little closeness or love. In the first week, the gazing technique had a big effect on closeness, especially for Brian. By the sixth week, Jocelyn's love for Brian had risen from a 1 to a 6 on a 10-point scale, and Brian's love for Jocelyn had climbed from a 2 to a 7. Brian and Jocelyn might have made progress without the exercises, but both felt the activities had helped.

*These ideas are examples of Chapter 12's discussion of similarity and of the chameleon effect. Think about the people you have dated or been attracted to in the past. Do these concepts apply to your experiences?*

*Schemas about what love is and should be differ across cultures, as Epstein describes in this article. In Chapter 3, you learned about the role optimism can play in our lives. How do you think the Western idea of destiny's role in love can make us happy or unhappy?*

and her spouse called attention to their past mistakes. This change probably came about because the couple was now, as a result of my course, broadly interested in enhancing their relationship.

### Taking Control

The students in my course were doing something new—taking *control* over their love lives. We grow up on fairy tales and movies in which magical forces help people find their soul mates, with whom they effortlessly live happily ever after. The fairy tales leave us powerless, putting our love lives into the hands of the Fates.

But here is a surprise: most of the world has never heard of those fairy tales. Instead more than half of marriages on our globe are brokered by parents or professional matchmakers, whose main concerns are long-term suitability and family harmony. In India an estimated 95 percent of the marriages are arranged, and although divorce is legal, India has one of the lowest divorce rates in the world. (This is starting to change, of course, as Western ways encroach on traditional society.)

Young couples in India generally have a choice about whether to proceed, and the combination of choice and sound guidance probably accounts for the fact that studies of arranged marriages in India indicate that they measure up well—in, for example, longevity, satisfaction and love—against Western marriages. Indeed, the love experienced by Indian couples in arranged marriages appears to be even more robust than the love people experience in "love marriages." In a 1982 study psychologists Usha Gupta and Pushpa Singh of the University of Rajasthan in Jaipur, India, used the Rubin Love Scale, which gauges intense, romantic, Western-style love, to determine that love in love marriages in India does exactly what it does in love marriages here: it starts high and declines fairly rapidly. But love in the arranged marriages they examined started out low and gradually *increased*, surpassing the love in the love marriage about five years out. Ten years into the marriage the love was nearly twice as strong.

How do they do it? How do people in some arranged marriages build love deliberately over time—and can we do it, too?

Over the past few years I have been interviewing people in arranged marriages in which love has grown over time. One of these couples is Kaiser and Shelly Haque of Minneapolis,

## Studies in Intimacy

Dozens of scientific studies illuminate how people fall in love—and hint at techniques for building strong relationships. Here are 10 kinds of investigations that are helping to inspire a new technology of love.

**1 » Arousal.** Studies by researchers such as psychologist Arthur Aron of Stony Brook University show that people tend to bond emotionally when aroused, say, through exercise, adventures or exposure to dangerous situations. Roller coaster, anyone? See the Falling in Love exercise on page 29.

**2 » Proximity and familiarity.** Studies by Stanford University social psychologists Leon Festinger and Robert Zajonc and others conclude that simply being around someone tends to produce positive feelings. When two people consciously and deliberately allow each other to invade their personal space, feelings of intimacy can grow quickly. See the Let Me Inside exercise on page 29.

**3 » Similarity.** Opposites sometimes attract, but research by behavioral economist Dan Ariely of Duke University and the Massachusetts Institute of Technology and others shows that people usually tend to pair off with those who are similar to themselves—in intelligence, background and level of attractiveness. Some research even suggests that merely imitating someone can increase closeness. See the Monkey Love exercise on page 29.

**4 » Humor.** Marriage counselors and researchers Jeanette and Robert Lauer showed in 1986 that in long-term, happy relationships, partners make each other laugh a lot. Other research reveals that women often seek male partners who can make them laugh—possibly because when we are laughing, we feel vulnerable. Know any good jokes?

**5 » Novelty.** Psychologist Greg Strong of Florida State University, Aron and others have shown that people tend to grow closer when they are doing something new. Novelty heightens the senses and also makes people feel vulnerable.

**6 » Inhibitions.** Countless millions of relationships have probably started with a glass of wine. Inhibitions block feelings of vulnerability, so lowering inhibitions can indeed help people bond. Getting drunk, however, is blinding and debilitating. Instead of alcohol, try the Two as One exercise on page 29.

*(continue)*

who have been happily married for 11 years and have two bright, welladjusted children. Once he had a secure life in the U.S., Kaiser, an immigrant from Bangladesh, returned to his native country to let his family know he was ready for matrimony. The family did the rest. After just one meeting with Shelly—where, Kaiser said, there was "like at first sight"—the arrangements were made. "We've grown to love each other and to get to know each other over time," Kaiser says. "The sparks are getting bigger, and I think we can do even better in the future."

Kaiser and Shelly are not atypical. A study that Mansi Thakar, a student at the University of Southern California, and I presented at the November 2009 meeting of the National Council on Family Relations included 30 individuals from nine countries of origin and five different religions. Their love had grown, on average, from 3.9 to 8.5 on a 10-point scale in marriages lasting an average of 19.4 years.

These individuals identified 11 factors that contributed to the growth of their love, 10 of which dovetailed beautifully with the scientific research I reviewed in my course. The most important factor was commitment, followed by good communication skills. The couples also identified sharing secrets with a spouse, as well as accommodation—that is, the voluntary altering of a partner's behavior to meet the other person's needs. Seeing a spouse in a vulnerable state (caused by injury or illness) was also singled out. There are many possible lessons here for Westerners, among them: do things deliberately that make you vulnerable to each other. Try experiencing danger, or thrilling simulations of it, as a couple.

The results conflicted with those of American studies in only one respect: several of the subjects said their love grew when they had children with their spouse. Studies in the U.S. routinely find parenting to be a threat to feelings of spousal love, but perhaps that tendency results from the strong feelings and unrealistic expectations that launch our relationships. The stress of raising children tends to disrupt those expectations and ultimately our positive feelings for each other.

## Creating Love

A careful look at arranged marriage, combined with the knowledge accumulating in relationship science, has the potential to give us real control over our love lives—without practicing arranged marriage. Americans want it all—the freedom to choose a partner and the deep, lasting love of fantasies and fairy tales. We can achieve that kind of love by learning about and practicing techniques that build love over time. And when our love is fading, we can use such techniques to rebuild that love. The alternative— leaving it to chance—makes little sense.

**"A careful look at arranged marriage, combined with the knowledge accumulating in relationship science, has the potential to give us real control over our love lives."**

*How might a person's gender affect the way one person in a couple reacts to the other in a vulnerable state? What did you learn in Chapter 12 about the way men and women differ in expressing their affection for each other?*

## Further Reading

- **An Exploratory Study of Love and Liking and Type of Marriages.** Usha Gupta and Pushpa Singh in *Indian Journal of Applied Psychology,* Vol. 19, pages 92–97; 1982.
- **Love Games.** Mark Robert Waldman. Tarcher/Putnam, 2000.
- **Steps toward the Ripening of Relationship Science.** Harry T. Reis in *Personal Relationships,* Vol. 14, pages 1–23; 2007.
- **Handbook of Relationship Initiation.** Susan Sprecher, Amy Wenzel and John Harvey. Psychology Press, 2008.
- The author's ongoing survey of arranged marriages (including how to participate) is at **http://ArrangedMarriageSurvey.com**
- Test your relationship skills at **http://MyLoveSkills.com**

**7 »** **Kindness, accommodation and forgiveness.** A variety of studies confirm that we tend to bond to people who are kind, sensitive and thoughtful. Feelings of love can emerge especially quickly when someone deliberately changes his or her behavior—say, by giving up smoking or drinking—to accommodate our needs. Forgiveness often causes mutual bonding, because when one forgives, one shows vulnerability.

**8 »** **Touch and sexuality.** The simplest touch can produce warm, positive feelings, and a backrub can work wonders. Even getting very near someone without actually touching can have an effect. Studies by social psychologist Susan Sprecher of Illinois State University, among others, also show that sexuality can make people feel closer emotionally, especially for women. There is danger here, however: confusing sexual attraction with feelings of love. You cannot love someone without knowing him or her, and attraction blinds people to important characteristics of their partner.

**9 »** **Self-disclosure.** Research by Aron, Sprecher and others indicates that people tend to bond when they share secrets with each other. Once again, the key here is allowing oneself to be vulnerable. See the Secret Swap exercise on page 29.

**10 »** **Commitment.** We are not that good at honoring our relationship commitments in the U.S., but studies by researchers such as psychologist Ximena Arriaga of Purdue University suggest that commitment is an essential element in building love. People whose commitments are shaky interpret their partners' behavior more negatively, for one thing, and that can be deadly over time. Covenant marriage—currently a legal option only in Arizona, Arkansas and Louisiana— is a new kind of marriage (emerging from the evangelical Christian movement) involving a very strong commitment: couples agree to premarital counseling and limited grounds for divorce. Conventional marriage in America can be abandoned easily, even without specific legal cause (the so-called no-fault divorce).

—R.E.

What do you think the answer is? Are any couples in your family the result of an arranged marriage? How would you feel if you knew that your parents would choose your future spouse?

# PROSOCIAL BEHAVIOUR: WHY WE HELP AND WHY WE DON'T

<<< **_Would you volunteer your time to help collect donations for a charity?_**

**WHY** DO WE HELP?
**WHEN** DO WE HELP?
**WHAT** ARE OTHER INFLUENCES ON HELPING?
**HOW** CAN WE INCREASE PROSOCIAL BEHAVIOUR?

# In October

2011, a two-year-old Chinese toddler named Yueyue got separated from her mother and wandered onto a street within a busy marketplace in Foshan, China. The toddler was hit several times by passing vehicles and lay bleeding in the road while more than 18 bystanders failed to help, including a mother with her child (Osnos, 2011). Why would all these people fail to help this poor little girl? One reason is that, unlike Canada, China does not have Good Samaritan laws to protect the legal rights of people who get involved and help in emergency situations (i.e., they are at risk of getting sued; Krueger, 2011). Another factor, developed from years of social psychological research, is what is known as the *bystander effect*—where the presence of others leads to less helping by any one individual.

Psychological research has investigated the factors that contribute to and impede helping behaviour. Moreover, there has been extensive debate about what helping *is*. In other words, is helping always a selfish act, or can it be done purely selflessly? If you engage in volunteer work or help out a friend by lending her money, is it true that you get no gratification from this? For example, many people put together Christmas hampers or donations for underprivileged children. While this may involve some cost to the giver, there is also the reward that giving makes *us* feel good. "The Money Song," from the Broadway musical *Avenue Q*, contains the line "When you help others, you can't help helping yourself" (Lopez & Marx, 2003). If that's true, can helping others ever be a truly selfless act? In order to answer this question, it is important to understand the reasons, both emotional and intellectual, for people's inclination to help.

In this chapter, we will examine the many factors that contribute to why people help others. We will also explore the different kinds of helping—selfish and selfless—in order to determine what differentiates them and to what extent it matters. We will investigate the five-step model that determines when people will help and when they will not, and what the obstacles are to providing and receiving help. Finally, we will explore how we might increase helping behaviour, both in our own lives and in the lives of others.

CHAPTER 13

**PROSOCIAL BEHAVIOUR** behaviour designed to help another person

**EGOISTIC** having a selfish motivation for helping

**ALTRUISTIC** having a selfless motivation for helping

**NEGATIVE STATE RELIEF MODEL** a model which posits that the reason people help others is to improve their own negative mood

**EMPATHY** having compassion for others and a feeling of seeing the world through the eyes of another individual

# Why Do We Help?

Helping behaviour, in the psychological literature, has been shown to take many forms. Broadly speaking, **prosocial behaviour** is behaviour intended to benefit others; it is a positive form of social action (Bierhoff, 2002). This form of behaviour can be either **egoistic**, meaning that it is done for selfish reasons, or **altruistic**, meaning that it is done for purely selfless reasons. Recently, some scholars also have further divided egoistic prosocial behaviour into two forms: one that is *proactive* (i.e., associated with some type of gain and non-emotional) and another that is *reactive* (i.e., based on the level of positive emotional arousal we get from an individual) (Boxer, Tisak, & Goldstein, 2004).

Why might someone decide to help or not to help, and what motivations might underlie that decision? Can you think of a time in Canadian history when many individuals engaged in prosocial behaviour?

In the wake of the fires that resulted in the evacuation of more than 10,000 residents in Slave Lake, Alberta, in May 2011, the rates of donations of necessary items like clothing and toiletries, as well as financial donations, skyrocketed (McLean, 2011). Facebook and Twitter sites were quickly established for donations, and the response was immediate. One organizer of donation efforts was astonished when the membership on the Facebook donation page jumped from fewer than 100 to more than 500 people within a matter of hours. Emergency shelters were established in both small towns and larger centres such as Grande Prairie and Edmonton, and donation efforts reached such a fevered pitch they were termed the "spirit no one can extinguish" ("A Spirit," 2011). In fact, so many donations of material goods were received that there was a shortage of people available to transport them to the displaced residents, and some donations of children's toys, books, games, and clothing ended up in a Calgary landfill ("Slave Lake Donations," 2011).

Why were so many people eager to donate during a crisis but reluctant to donate during ordinary times? One possible explanation is that when our sense of safety is threatened by uncontrollable natural or human-made disasters, such as wildfires or nuclear disasters, we respond by reaffirming our commitment to important values that make us feel safe or useful (e.g., Skitka, Saunders, Morgan, & Wisneski, 2009). In the case of the outpouring of help during and immediately after the Slave Lake fires, another possibility is that the personal relevance of the attacks made helping others somewhat soothe the trauma. In an editorial for the *Edmonton Sun* (2011), the author stated, "As quickly as thousands of people here rushed to help victims of the Japanese nuclear accident, we know they'll do the same to help good people in their own backyard as they struggle to get back on their feet." Indeed, recent neurobiological research has shown that making charitable donations activates the same brain regions—the regions of the *mesolimbic reward* system—that are activated upon the receipt of monetary rewards (Moll et al., 2006). This suggests that giving to those in need makes a person feel just as good as if she had just received a reward. Another possibility is that, after the fires, people helped out of genuine empathy toward the displaced residents and their families. In truth, there are many possible reasons, all of which are likely to be true to some extent, for some people.

Next, we will consider some of the predominant theories of why people help when they do (see Penner, Dovidio, Piliavin, & Schroeder, 2005, for a review). Keep in mind, though, that it is rare that there is only one reason. In truth, it is far more likely that, at any given time, there are multiple motives behind the decision to help.

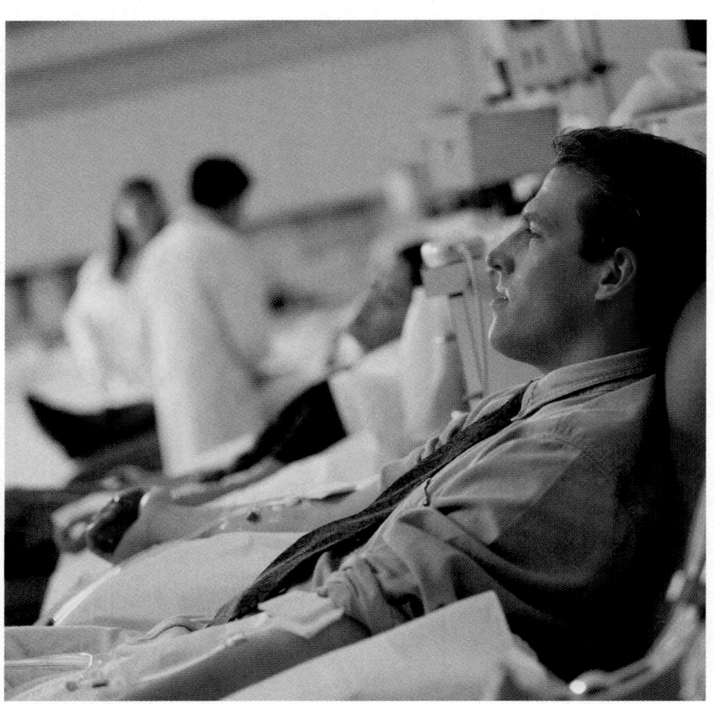

Why do we engage in actions, **such as donating blood,** that will benefit others?

## EGOISTIC MODELS

Several models postulate that selfish motivations are at the core of people's decisions to help others. Specifically, the *negative state relief model* and *cost-benefit analysis* are two models that describe how people consider the outcomes of their helpful behaviours.

### Negative State Relief Model

People will provide help to others to feel good about themselves. Prosocial behaviour has positive psychological effects on individuals; most notably, it increases their happiness (Piliavin, 2003). People will also provide help to alleviate their negative state while observing or thinking about another's suffering; this is known as the **negative state relief model** (Cialdini, Kenrick, & Baumann, 1982). Witnessing another's suffering can induce **empathy**—which includes both a *cognitive* and *emotional* component and includes the feeling of compassion for others and that of seeing the world through the eyes of another individual (e.g., Eisenberg & Miller, 1987; Eisenberg et al., 1989). If a friend complains about his tough class for the third day in a row, you feel compassion toward him, and you imagine how he feels to be overwhelmed by coursework. Seeing him in distress motivates you to help him in an effort to alleviate his suffering. So you offer to spend a couple of hours helping him organize his notes, hoping it will give him some relief. In fact, in an examination of fund-raising requests made through public service announcements, University of Alberta researcher Fisher and his colleagues (2008) found that when the appeals were focused on helping other people, a greater presence of negative emotional content led to a greater number of calls to offer assistance or pledges.

You might also help someone in order to help yourself, which also fits this model. Selfish motives such as gaining respect from your peers, making yourself feel better, or actually being rewarded can lead to helping (e.g., Batson, 1998; Simpson & Willer, 2008). Whatever the reason, the negative state relief model of motivation can actually lead to sustained helping. When researchers investigated volunteers' motives for helping people with AIDS and tracked how long those volunteers continued to work, they found that people who were there for more selfless reasons were actually *less likely* to keep volunteering. Somewhat unexpectedly, the people who were volunteering for more selfish reasons, such as wanting to make friends or develop their resumé, kept volunteering longer (Omoto & Snyder, 1995). These incentives usually lead to increases in prosocial behaviour, but from an egotistical standpoint (Simpson & Willer, 2008).

## Cost-Benefit Analysis

People are more inclined to help others when their own outcomes can be improved by helping. They will weigh the needs of the other person with their own needs to determine if helping will prove too costly to themselves. This decision-making process is termed a **cost-benefit analysis** (e.g., Dovidio, Piliavin, Gaertner, Schroeder, & Clark, 1991). It includes weighing any potential threats to the self, including personal harm, emotional harm, and any harm that may befall one's reputation due to association with a member of a stigmatized group (e.g., Batson, O'Quin, Fultz, Vanderplas, & Isen, 1983; Edelmann, Childs, Harvey, Kellock, & Strain-Clark, 1984; Snyder, Omoto, & Crain, 1999). People are not only motivated to help when it does not cause them harm; they will also help if it brings them rewards, such as money (e.g., Wilson & Kahn, 1975), improved mood (e.g., Gueguen & De Gail, 2003), improved skill (e.g., Perlow & Weeks, 2002), increased popularity and recognition from others (e.g., Fisher & Ackerman, 1998; Reddy, 1980), maintenance of a good reputation (e.g., Johnson, Erez, Kiker, & Motowidlo, 2002), personal gratification (e.g., Smith, Keating, & Stotland, 1989; Utne & Kidd, 1980), or even a simple "thank you" (e.g., McGovern, Ditzian, & Taylor, 1975).

**COST-BENEFIT ANALYSIS** the act of weighing the relative costs and benefits of helping to decide whether or not to provide help

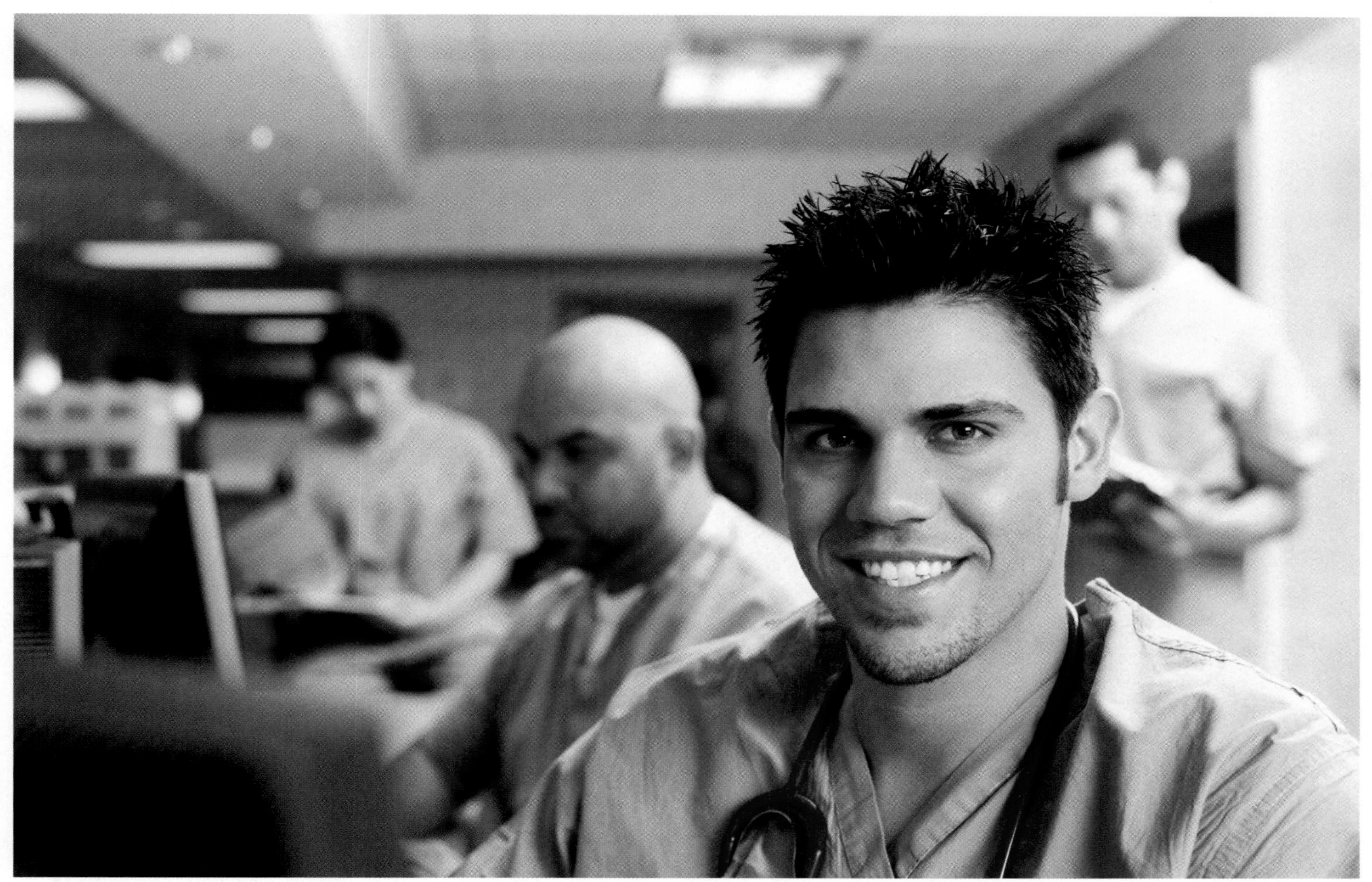

People sometimes help others for their own gain, such as when people do internships. **Doing the work for free benefits the employer and also provides benefits to the student, such as increased skill and experience, as well as a reference.**

**EMPATHY-ALTRUISM MODEL OF PROSOCIAL BEHAVIOUR** a model which suggests that true altruism is a product of empathy; this empathy can create nurturing feelings toward a target or a goal to increase the target's welfare

In addition to the motivation people have to improve their frame of mind, their existing mood impacts the perceived costs and benefits of helping. Those in *good moods* will be more likely to focus on the rewards of helping rather than the costs, and these rewards will come to mind more easily. Even finding a dime or getting a cookie can enhance one's mood and subsequently increase the desire to help others (e.g., Isen, Clark, & Schwartz, 1976; Isen, Shalker, Clark, & Karp, 1978). Moreover, people will also help others in an effort to try and maintain their own existing positive moods—to avoid it slipping because of the other person's dilemma (e.g., Wegener & Petty, 1994). In this way, mood further impacts people's tendency to provide help.

## ALTRUISTIC MODEL OF HELPING

In contrast to the above-mentioned models that propose that helping is driven by egoistic motivations, the **empathy-altruism model of prosocial behaviour** suggests that helping can occur for altruistic reasons as well (Batson, 1991). Specifically, the theory states that an individual will be more likely to help another person if that other person's welfare is at stake. This is particularly the case if the helper has nurturing feelings toward the other person. In fact, protecting another's well-being is often enough to encourage helping behaviour, even if no egoistic motivations to help exist (Batson & Oleson, 1991) and even when helping is costly to oneself (Toi & Batson, 1982). For example, the bystanders who rushed to the aid of victims trapped in a plane crash in British Columbia (discussed later in this chapter) were motivated by empathy and provided help in a situation that was dangerous (Lee, Carman, & Duggan, 2011). This suggests that people truly can help in selfless ways—that altruistic behaviour exists and is not an artifact of egoistic motivations.

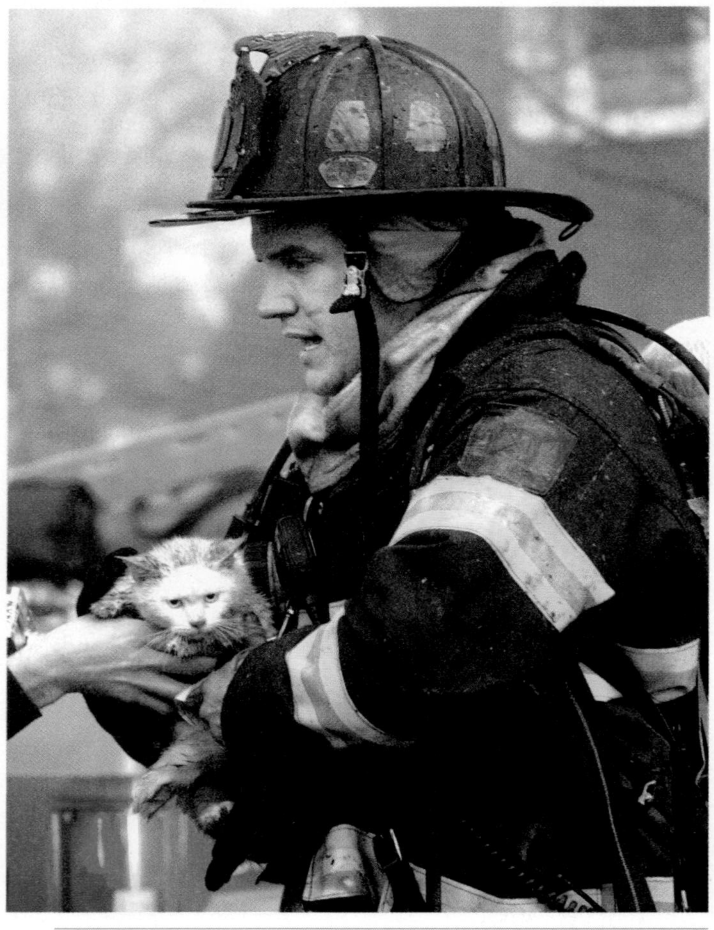

People will help those in need if they feel nurturing feelings toward them, **even in the absence of any selfish motivations.**

During the 1980s, researchers published several studies testing the empathy-altruism model (e.g., Batson, Duncan, Ackerman, Buckley, & Birch, 1981; Batson et al., 1988). They wanted to show that ego-based motives cannot explain the helping that takes place when people feel empathy. Participants were presented with a woman named "Elaine." To elicit empathy, participants were told that Elaine was very much like them in terms of values and interests. After watching Elaine react badly to a pair of electric shocks, participants were told they could take the remaining eight shocks for her. Half were told they could leave if they didn't take the shocks for Elaine, and the other half were told they must stay and watch Elaine take the rest. People who were given the choice to leave did so—except when they felt empathetic concern for Elaine. When empathy was introduced, it didn't matter if they were given an escape option—people stayed and helped.

"When empathy was introduced, it didn't matter **if they were given an escape option—people stayed and helped.**"

Although taking the perspective of another individual can impact helping, Batson's model is not without criticism. Critics say that conditions leading to empathy also lead to a greater sense of overlap between the self and the other. They argue that this means that the impulse to help isn't just a selfless response to the suffering other, but is also directed toward the self. When this overlap was considered in studies, the impact of empathy was eliminated (e.g., Cialdini, Brown, Lewis, Luce, & Neuberg, 1997; Schaller & Cialdini, 1988).

Batson and colleagues proposed that the reason prosocial behaviour increases with the presence of nurturing feelings and the desire to increase another's welfare is because these emotions involve empathy (e.g., Batson, 1991; Batson et al., 1981; Toi & Batson, 1982). The researchers found that heightened feelings of empathy do indeed predict altruism—helping when no selfish reasons are present. However, there is considerable debate as to whether an altruistic personality really exists. Even if we do not receive tangible awards for helping, there are other intangibles that certainly compensate us—such as feeling good about helping someone.

## NORMS

There are two social norms that may influence when people engage in prosocial behaviour: *reciprocity* and *social responsibility*. These norms can operate without our being aware of them and drive us to certain behaviours without our knowledge. For example, when social norms related to helping are activated or made salient to individuals (e.g., through reading a story about helping), people are more likely to help others in unrelated situations (Harvey & Enzle, 1981). Norms also can motivate us consciously, whether through a desire to conform to society's standards for their own sake or through an awareness of how certain behaviours might benefit us and/or others. For example, in team projects, it has been found that certain personality characteristics (such as agreeableness) are important for establishing helping norms within a group context (Raver, Ehrhart, & Chadwick, in press). Of course, there are regional differences in helping within Canada. When a friend of the authors moved from Halifax to Edmonton, she was shocked at how helpful others were to strangers. On the other hand, when one of the authors of this text (KP) lived in the Maritimes, she found people, in general, to be much more friendly and easy-going than those in Western Canada, which resulted in greater prosocial behaviours. Some of these differences are argued to depend on population density, where the denser the population is, the less likely people are to help strangers (Levine, Martinez, Brase, & Sorenson, 1994).

### Reciprocity Norm

One such norm is the **reciprocity norm**, which suggests that people usually help others who have helped them (e.g., Dovidio & Penner, 2007; Wilke & Lanzetta, 1970). Doing a favour for someone increases the likelihood of getting that favour returned (e.g., Regan, 1971). In fact, this inclination toward reciprocating is even present in children as young as 21 months old. In a study done by Dunfield and Kuhlmeier (2010), babies were introduced to two actresses. One offered each baby a toy, but due to the incline of the table, the toy rolled away and the child was unable to receive it. The other actress showed the baby the toy but did not offer it. In both cases, the child did not gain access to the toy. Then, the two actresses sat next to each other in front of the baby. The experimenter then placed a toy on the table in front of the baby so that it fell off, and both actresses reached for the toy but were unable to get it. The baby could reach the toy, however, and, upon picking it up, was more likely to hand the toy to the actress who had tried to give the baby the toy earlier. In this way, babies remembered an attempt at helpful behaviour and returned the favour, thus supporting the idea of the reciprocity norm (Dunfield & Kuhlmeier, 2010).

But what if the baby had been able to get the toy? Would the positive outcome overwhelm the effect of reciprocity? In this same study, some babies were exposed to one actress who, as in the first study, attempted to give the child the toy but could not. Instead of also being exposed to an actress who would not give the baby the toy, however, they were introduced to an actress who successfully gave the baby the toy. In this second stage, babies were no more likely to give the toy to the actress who succeeded than the one who did not. Even infants were able to recognize that the two actresses' intentions were the same—both positively oriented toward the infant—and they responded with reciprocation to both (Dunfield & Kuhlmeier, 2010). From this young age on, reciprocity norms are often established as the basis of "good" relationships in both family and peer contexts (Laursen & Hartup, 2002). These norms are then reinforced throughout our lives by having others do favours for us (Hoffman, McCabe, & Smith, 1998). Further, we are more likely to help others who are helpful in general or who have been observed helping a different person (Seinen & Schram, 2006). This suggests that prosocial behaviours are not solely determined by reciprocity.

**RECIPROCITY NORM** the idea that if others help us, we should help them, and that if we help them, they will help us

**SOCIAL RESPONSIBILITY NORM** the idea that we have social responsibility to help others; the extent to which this extends to outgroup members varies by culture

### Social Responsibility Norm

Another norm that impacts helping is the **social responsibility norm**. It states that a person will feel more compelled to help others if he feels a sense of responsibility to his society and its members (Berkowitz & Daniels, 1963). One prominent example of this is donations to charity and social activism—people giving time or money to causes in which they believe.

To investigate rates of charitable giving, Canadian researchers at *The Fraser Institute* have calculated the Generosity Index (based on tax-filed donations and the percentage of personal income donated) for provinces and territories across Canada, as well as in the United States ("Canadians Behind U.S.," 2010; LeRoy, Gabel, & Veldhius, 2003). They found that Manitoba, Ontario, Prince Edward Island, and Saskatchewan have the highest level of charitable giving, whereas Yukon, Nunavut, Northwest Territories, and Quebec have the lowest. In addition, although rates of charity donations have decreased, the depth of this generosity has increased—meaning that although fewer people are making donations, those who do donate are giving more (LeRoy et al., 2003). That said, using this measure, the levels charitable giving for all of Canada fall well below those of the United States ("Canadians Behind U.S.," 2010).

These data suggest that *cultural norms* also may influence helping behaviour (e.g., Betancourt, Hardin, & Manzi, 1992). For example, one study reported that East Indians are more likely than Americans to offer bone marrow for transplant to a wide variety of potential recipients—including strangers on the other side of the world (Baron & Miller, 2000). Similarly, within business contexts, members of collectivistic cultures are more likely to help whomever needs assistance, whereas individualistic cultures tend to help more according to the reciprocity norm—that is, they will help people whom they expect to need help from in the future (Perlow & Weeks, 2002).

People expect that those for whom they do a favour will do a favour back when requested, **and indeed that reciprocity tends to occur.**

**KIN SELECTION** the tendency of people to help their biological relatives over nonfamily members, even at great cost to themselves, thus favouring the reproductive success of one's relatives over his or her own survival

**RECIPROCAL ALTRUISM** the belief that helping others increases the likelihood that others will help us or our kin in return

Besides giving money to charitable organizations, individuals who hold fast to the norm of social responsibility often help in other ways, such as volunteering for fund-raisers, crisis lines, soup kitchens, or animal shelters. In addition, this norm corresponds with the "helping movements" that have been initiated worldwide (e.g., Pay It Forward Foundation; People for Good), discussed later in this chapter. For an account of an American family that embodies the definition of this norm, read *The Power of Half* by father–daughter team Kevin and Hannah Salwen (2010) and consider what you could do to embrace this norm.

What makes some people give so incredibly generously—such as donating thousands of dollars or goods to hunger relief efforts—while others give nothing? Even on a much smaller scale, what leads a person to help (e.g., offering an elderly person a seat on the subway or bus) when so many people do not? One reason these helping differences occur is that we are willing to give generously only when we feel that the victims are not responsible for their situation. If we cast blame on the victim, we will not help. Consider the perception of some individuals toward AIDS patients who become ill due to a transfusion, versus their perception of those who become ill due to unsafe sex or drug use (e.g., Chapple, Ziebland, & McPherson, 2004; Marlow, Waller, & Wardle, 2010). Even medically trained staff exhibit less helping toward patients whose injuries they perceive to be avoidable (Mackay & Barrowclough, 2005). However, as you learned in Chapter 5, people vary in the sorts of causes for which they will provide help, and this variation is partly based on their morals and ideologies. For example, liberals are more likely to help people with afflictions perceived to have controllable causes than are conservatives (Skitka, 1999).



## EVOLUTIONARY REASONS

Some theorists speculate that we help others because it promotes the evolution of our species and the continuation of our genetic line. It has been suggested that genes "selfishly" desire to be passed on to promote species survival and in doing so, create unselfish behaviour in the individual organism (Dawkins, 1976). This line of thought is not necessarily opposed to the cultural, emotional, and intellectual lines of reasoning discussed earlier, but it places the most emphasis on genetics as the source of our varied motivations to help. This theory basically argues that genes are only out for themselves.

The theory also includes the concept of **kin selection**, which refers to the tendency of people to help their close relatives, even at great cost to themselves. This favours the reproductive success of the person's relatives over her own survival. This is illustrated by a study on Samoan homosexual men by researchers at the University of Lethbridge. Vasey and VanderLann (2010) have noted a group of men, called *fa'afafine* in Samoa, that indirectly contribute to the survival prospects of their family's genes by offering help and support to their nieces and nephews (also see Vasey, Pocock, & VanderLaan, 2007). These same findings have been replicated in a population of androphilic males (i.e., those sexually attracted to adult males) in Canada, in which there were greater expressions of altruism toward kin in comparison to non-kin children (Forrester, VanderLaan, Parker, & Vasey, 2011).

> People's tendencies to help out in certain ways **can vary based on specific cultural norms.**

Additional studies support the theory of kin selection. Burnstein, Crandal, and Kitayama (1994) found that study participants were more likely to help individuals who were genetically related to them, especially in life-or-death situations. Other research has suggested that it is important to look at not only genetic closeness but also emotional closeness (e.g., Korchmaros & Kenny, 2001). When participants were asked to decide to which family member they would donate an organ, decisions were based partly on kinship and partly on emotional closeness (for a review of kin selection, see Stewart-Williams, 2007). With respect to the latter point, the concept of reciprocal altruism provides as explanation as to why we help unrelated others. **Reciprocal altruism** reflects the idea that helping others increases the likelihood that others will help us or our kin in return (see Penner et al., 2005). Therefore, even though the people we help may not be genetically related to us, such as our best friends, we know they will help us and our families throughout our lives.

That said, some scholars argue that engaging in "strong reciprocity" (i.e., voluntary cooperation and punishment of non-cooperators) and other helping norms cannot be explained solely by evolutionary theories such as kin selection or reciprocal altruism (Fehr, Fischbacher, & Gächter, 2002). They argue that evolutionary pressures do not explain why we often engage in unselfishly motivated or sometimes dangerous helping.

# When Do We Help?

Many theories, then, provide possible explanations for why we help when we do. Each of these explanations may hold true in its own relevant circumstances, but knowing *why* people help when they do is only part of the story. It is also important to understand *when* people will help, and one major theory proposed during the late 1960s and early 1970s by social psychologists Latane and Darley has made a tremendous contribution toward this understanding.

## THE DECISION MODEL OF BYSTANDER INTERVENTION

The examination of social influences on helping was initiated, to a large extent, by a shocking incident the occurred in 1964 in New York City. A young woman, named Kitty Genovese, was brutally murdered outside her home. While this, in and of itself, was unfortunately nothing new, what shocked the nation was that she had been stabbed repeatedly and cried out for help within earshot of 38 people, but the original news reports indicated that not one of these people did anything to help (Gansberg, 1964). The attacker left the scene and twice returned to it, continuing his assault, and Kitty kept crying for help, but still no one came. This version of the story has since been shown to be untrue. As it turns out, more than one person did call the police, but Kitty had crawled out of sight, and so it was unclear that she continued to need help. In addition, many people thought that it had been a lovers' quarrel rather than a stabbing. One man shouted at the attacker, causing him to flee. While the original version of the story was what prompted the wealth of research done on helping behaviour, the true version of the story also reveals many of the core reasons why people choose not to provide help.

Kitty Genovese's murder was not an isolated occurrence. In 1974, 25-year-old Sandra Zahler was beaten to death in an apartment of the building that overlooked the site of the Genovese attack. Neighbours again said they heard screams and "fierce struggles" but did nothing (McFadden, 1974). In 1995, a woman named Deletha Ward was severely beaten by a man before she jumped into a river to escape from the attack, resulting in her death. No one on the bridge where this extended and brutal attack occurred attempted to intervene ("Jury Convicts," 1996). Even in the past few years, there have been several horrifying stories of failure to help others in dire situations. In 2007, LaShanda Calloway was stabbed and lay dying in a convenience store in Kansas while witnesses watched, continued shopping, or in one case, stopped to take a picture of her with a cellphone. Not one of these people phoned emergency services. In 2008, Dewayne Taylor was attacked by an unknown assailant with a hammer on a Philadelphia subway. Surveillance video showed at least 10 people who witnessed the attack but did nothing to intervene ("Police Arrest Man," 2008). In 2009, a 15-year-old girl in Richmond, California, was savagely beaten and gang raped during a high school dance, while at least 10 people watched and did nothing ("Police: People Watched," 2009). Most recently, the case in China profiled at the beginning of this chapter demonstrates that bystanders often fail to act or help in emergency situations.

Is this effect a result of cultural norms? In light of recent events, scholars have argued a resounding no. While discussions surrounding Yueyue's case have focused on China's authoritarianism, societal collectivism (which discourages individual action), and lack of Good Samaritan laws (i.e., those that offer protection from legal ramifications to people that help in an emergency), this is not a uniquely collectivistic or individualistic phenomenon—as seen in the cases above. So, is Canada any different from China in this respect? Consider an example: 82-year-old Doreen Wallace fell in the lobby of the Greater Niagara General Hospital on October 8, 2011, and broke her hip. She lay face down, bleeding, and in pain, while multiple people walked by her, including medical professionals, but was told by nurses and a security guard that she needed to call an ambulance to take her to a hospital—even though she was already in the lobby of one (Stone & Boyle, 2011). Writers for *The Huffington Post* argue that our failure to offer help in such situations is symptomatic of societal moral bankruptcy (Kielburger & Kielburger, 2011). However, situational and personal factors influence our willingness to help others.

Darley and Latane (1968) were pioneers in the effort to understand when people will help and when they will not, using both laboratory experiments and field research. Throughout

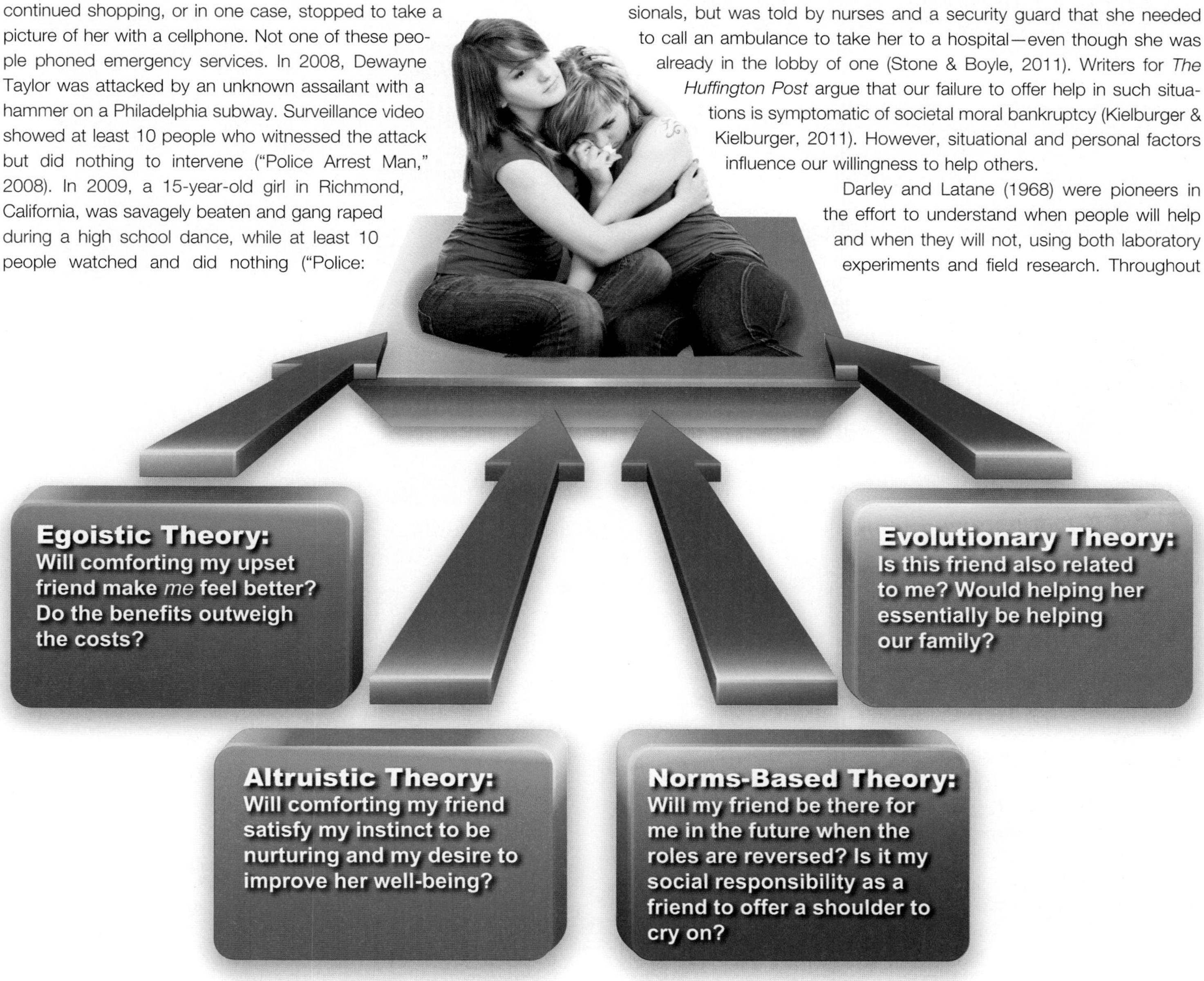

Egoistic Theory:
Will comforting my upset friend make *me* feel better? Do the benefits outweigh the costs?
Altruistic Theory:
Will comforting my friend satisfy my instinct to be nurturing and my desire to improve her well-being?
Norms-Based Theory:
Will my friend be there for me in the future when the roles are reversed? Is it my social responsibility as a friend to offer a shoulder to cry on?
Evolutionary Theory:
Is this friend also related to me? Would helping her essentially be helping our family?

<<< **Getting by with a Little Help from Your Friends.** Each theory that has been offered to explain helping behaviour provides different reasons for such behaviour—**and more than one can apply in a given situation.**

**_An emergency occurs:_ Someone is attacked outside.**

**_Notice the emergency:_ You hear the victim's screams.**

**Obstacles**

You don't notice because you're thinking about the argument you had with a friend, or you're busy watching your favourite TV show.

**_Interpret the situation as requiring help:_ You hear the victim cry for help.**

**Obstacles**

The situation is ambiguous; it could just be your neighbours arguing. Also, if your other neighbours aren't interfering, nothing is probably wrong to begin with.

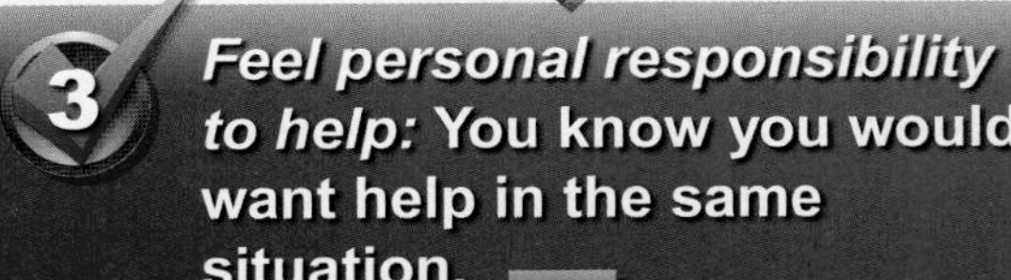

**_Feel personal responsibility to help:_ You know you would want help in the same situation.**

**Obstacles**

If you can hear them, your neighbours can, too, and surely someone else will take action, so there's no need for you to get involved.

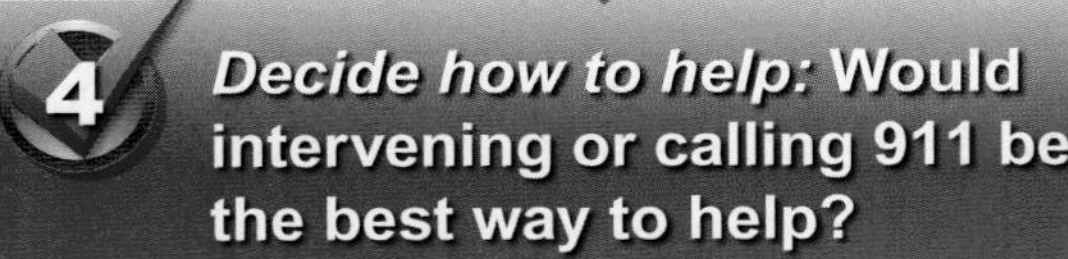

**_Decide how to help:_ Would intervening or calling 911 be the best way to help?**

**Obstacles**

You don't know how to help. You'll feel embarrassed if the police show up for no real reason, and you certainly don't want to risk becoming a second victim of an attack.

**_Provide the help:_ To ensure your personal safety as well, you decide to dial 911.**

**When Will You Help?** Darley and Latane (1968) argue that these steps must be followed to permit helping in an emergency to occur; however, there are many obstacles that stand in the way, as illustrated by the deaths of Kitty Genovese and two-year-old Yueyue in China.

their research, they discovered that as the number of people present during an emergency increases, each individual is less likely to help—a phenomenon known as the **bystander effect** (Latane & Darley, 1968). Have you ever witnessed another person trip and fall and injure themselves? Have you witnessed someone experiencing a seizure or a medical emergency? Have you ever witnessed a mugging or attack on another person? It is likely that in your lifetime, you have witnessed a variety of situations requiring help or intervention—but did you help? In order to try to explain situations in which people help or don't help, Darley and Latane (1968) developed the **decision model of bystander intervention**, a series of criteria that must be met before a bystander will provide help in an emergency.

**STEP 1:** *Noticing (or failing to notice) that there is a need for help.* The tendency to notice a need is influenced by factors such as being distracted, in a hurry, or focused internally on your thoughts. Concerns about oneself can therefore affect whether or not a need for help is even noticed. In other words, if you are preoccupied with thoughts about tomorrow's exam, you will be self-focused rather than other-focused, and therefore distracted from external cues for helping.

In one of their studies, Darley and Batson (1973) sent seminary students to an adjacent building for an appointment, and in the process, the students crossed paths with a confederate of the researchers who was sitting in a doorway, clearly in distress. Of the students who had been sent to the appointment with no sense of urgency, almost two-thirds stopped to help the man. Those who had been sent off in a hurry and told they were late were far less likely to help. In fact, only 10 percent of "late" participants stopped to help the man. Interestingly, the "appointment" the students were to attend was to give a presentation on the parable of the Good Samaritan (which advocates treating others as you would like them to treat you)—and still they didn't stop to offer help! This demonstrates that one's thoughts, as well as many aspects of one's environment, can act as distractions from an external situation.

**STEP 2:** *Correctly interpreting the situation as an emergency*. In the second step, the bystander must interpret the situation as requiring help. Ambiguous situations are thus responded to less readily. For example, have you ever seen a visually impaired person crossing the street? You may wonder, "Does that person need help? Will he be offended if I offer to help, or will he appreciate the gesture?" In situations like this, helping is less common.

Another factor that contributes to bystander inaction in a potential emergency is called **pluralistic ignorance** (Latane & Darley, 1968). This is when a person may privately think there may be an emergency, but seeing others do nothing leads her to infer that there is no need to provide help. In their study to test this concept, Latane and Darley (1968) placed participants in a room to answer a questionnaire. As they did, smoke began streaming into the room. When participants were alone, 75 percent reported the smoke. When participants were accompanied by two confederates who ignored the smoke, only 10 percent of them reported the smoke. Further, when they were accompanied by two other *participants*, neither of whom was told what was going on and both of whom saw the smoke, only 38 percent reported the smoke.

In Kitty Genovese's case, when the neighbours reported believing the attack to be a lovers' quarrel, their belief was likely validated, in part, by each neighbour seeing the other neighbours do nothing—at least nothing that they could see, such as someone running outside to stop the attacker. In this way, the inaction of others confirmed the belief that nothing was wrong. In addition, when Kitty's lungs were punctured after the initial attack, and she crawled away in an effort to escape, this may have confirmed bystanders' belief that the screaming was part of an interpersonal argument, and that the situation must have resolved itself. Therefore, if a situation is ambiguous and/or we don't visibly see others helping, this decreases our own likelihood of helping as we may not believe our help is needed.

**BYSTANDER EFFECT** a phenomenon in which as more people are present, each individual is less likely to help

**DECISION MODEL OF BYSTANDER INTERVENTION** the model derived by Bibb Latane and John Darley that explains the five steps required to provide help to someone in need and what can interfere with successful completion of each of these steps

**DIFFUSION OF RESPONSIBILITY** a decreased feeling of responsibility to help in a group; if an emergency arises in a group setting, it is less likely that any one person will help than if someone was witnessing the emergency alone, because being in a group decreases each person's feeling of personal responsibility to help

**PLURALISTIC IGNORANCE** a form of misperception where individuals within a group believe that other group members are behaving the way they are because they have additional knowledge about the context or situation

**STEP 3:** *Feeling personally responsible for helping*. Upon recognizing the need for help, people must then feel a personal responsibility to help. According to the bystander effect, the more people who witness an event, the less likely any individual is to help ("The Bystander Effect," 2011). But why does this happen? This effect can be explained by each person feeling less of a personal responsibility for providing help; this is called **diffusion of responsibility**. In fact, even thinking about other people can reduce the likelihood of helping (Garcia, Weaver, Moskowitz, & Darley, 2002). If a person feels responsible for helping, then he or she is more likely to do so. In Darley and Latane's (1968) study examining the bystander effect, participants were exposed to the sounds of another student having an epileptic seizure. These sounds made very clear what was happening and that help was needed. Participants who were alone were faster to report the emergency than those who believed they were in the company of others—they were not actually able to see these others, but believed they were nearby. The more people participants believed were present, the slower they were to respond.

Moreover, sometimes we do not take responsibility for helping because we are embarrassed about interfering with the outcome or feel regret for a past failure to help. What if we do something wrong? What if we have misinterpreted a situation? For example, in 1993, 38 people witnessed two 10-year-old boys dragging a two-year-old boy for 2.5 miles but did not interfere because the older boys said that they were the young boy's brothers. The two-year-old, James Bulger, was subsequently brutally murdered by those boys. It is fair to suppose that each person who saw the boy being dragged along and did nothing will regret it for the rest of his or her life. A lesson learned the hard way—if something seems amiss, and you hesitate to act out of embarrassment, it's often worth it to set those feelings aside and act anyway. You might just save a life.

**STEP 4:** *Deciding if you have the necessary skills required to help*. In the next step of the decision model of bystander intervention, people must decide how to assist the person in need. If an obvious solution presents itself, people are more likely to provide effective help. However, if they do not know *how* to help, they are less likely to help, may hesitate to act, or may be too embarrassed to even try to help. For instance, those trained in first aid or CPR are more likely to provide

^^^ When in the company of others, **we are less likely to help a person in need than when we are alone.**



help than those not trained (e.g., Cramer, McMaster, Bartell, & Dragna, 1988; Shotland & Heinold, 1985). This also relates to your confidence in your competence and skills. Imagine that it has been several years since you have taken a first aid course, and you have forgotten most of what you have learned. Would you feel comfortable performing CPR on a drowning victim? Would you know how to respond to someone having a seizure? Probably not. However, if you have been trained in first aid or are confident in your abilities, you will likely intervene. For example, not too long ago, one of the authors of this text (KP) was in a restaurant and witnessed a person who was waiting for a table fall to the ground and begin seizing. People formed a circle around the young woman, but no one knew what to do. Thankfully, KP had previously worked within residential care homes with several epileptic clients, knew how to respond appropriately, and provided help to the young woman. Thus, having any information regarding how to help, and being confident in your ability to use that information, would be beneficial in increasing the amount of help given.

**STEP 5**: *The actual provision of help*. The final step in the decision model involves engaging in helping behaviour. In doing this, bystanders must consider a variety of factors, including how to implement their chosen way of helping. One important thing to note is that helpers must consider their own safety as well. If direct intervention is possible, then it ought to be done. However, if the person providing help places her own life at risk, and thus may not be of much assistance to the victim either, it might be better to provide help in a more indirect way, such as by calling 911. That said, there are emergencies in which there is no time to call for help, and people act spontaneously, independent of personal risk. On October 27, 2011, Flight 204 from Vancouver to Kelowna crashed into Russ Baker Way in Richmond, British Columbia. Although the pilot was killed on impact, the other seven passengers and one co-pilot were trapped in the burning wreckage. Several bystander citizens were heralded as heroes for jumping from their cars, running to the burning plane, and pulling all of the passengers and crew to safety. One of these heroes, Jeremy Kerr, was quoted in the *Vancouver Sun* as saying that he didn't know why he helped out but that waiting was not an option (Lee et al., 2011). In many places, the value of helping others is held in such high regard that laws and rules have been created to protect people who act in good faith to help others. Good Samaritan laws in Canada focus on protecting people from being prosecuted or sued for injury or wrongful death as a result of helping another person. In Europe, the philosophy behind Good Samaritan laws is quite different—there, the failure to help someone in need when one is able to do so is actually criminalized.

## USING THE FIVE STEPS TO HELP

Even those who put themselves at risk to help others are not always assisted. In 2010, a homeless man in Queens, New York, named Hugo Tale-Yax rushed to the aid of a woman who was being attacked. During the intervention, he was stabbed. He bled to death on the sidewalk as no fewer than 20 people walked by and did nothing (Livingston, Doyle, & Mangan, 2010). People's failure to help others in serious situations is not

# ACTION LEARNING

## Decision Model of Bystander Intervention

College and university campuses can often be dangerous places for young women. A 2010 survey of well-respected schools in the United States revealed that three-quarters of the universities and the areas around them had sex offence rates that were 83 percent higher than the national average for sexual assault (Sullivan, 2010). What may surprise you is that Canada has been found to have higher rates of sexual assault on campuses (including acts ranging from unwanted touching to rape) than the United States ("Sexual Assault," 2010; Wong, 2010). But just as every student has a right to pursue an education at your school, every student also has the right to feel secure. You and your fellow students can work together as a community to promote a safe environment, but how would you respond if you saw someone being attacked? How would you respond if *you* were attacked?

Using what you have learned about Latane and Darley's five-step model of helping, design an educational campaign to help students become more knowledgeable about how to act in an emergency—both as the victim and as a potential witness. Imagine your school's website administrator has asked you to design a page to help students understand what to do in case of an emergency such as sexual assault. How would you describe and make the five-step model engaging for your classmates? Describe each step thoroughly, and don't forget to include a description of all of the obstacles that can arise when attempting to provide help. Make sure to do research on what's available on your campus. For instance, in discussing Step 4 (deciding how to help), be sure to include all resources available to students at your school. Consider resources such as campus crisis hotlines, SafeWalk, and ways to get in touch with campus security, as well as the closest locations for emergency phones and safe houses. Find out what your school has to offer. Also consider resources that do not currently exist but could be implemented at your school.

What you will learn from this action learning project:

1. Understand how to use social psychological research to increase prosocial behaviour, and consider how to make your campus environment a safer place.
2. Learn how to teach people to monitor their own behaviour in order to avoid falling prey to the obstacles to helping someone.
3. Become more likely to provide help in future situations. Experiments by Beaman and his colleagues (1978) demonstrated that when individuals learn about research on why people do and do not provide help, they are more likely to take responsibility in a situation that looks like someone needs help.

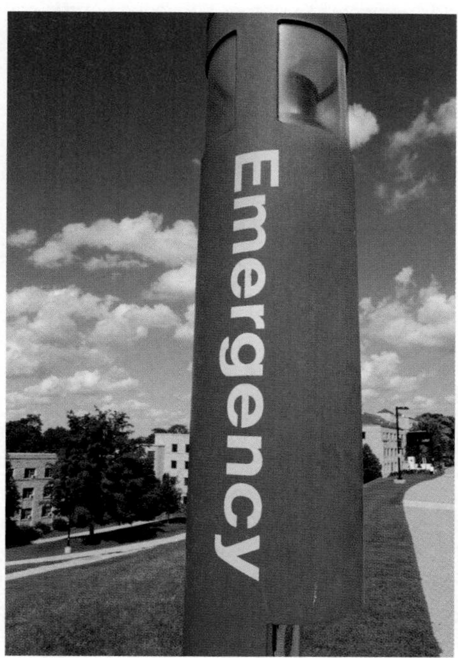


uncommon, and no number of heinous occurrences seems to prevent it from happening again and again. So what can we do to ensure that help is provided when it is needed?

Based on the research presented above, one approach is to try to reduce the ambiguity of the situation. Specifically, it is important to make it clear that there is indeed an emergency occurring, and that it is something in which others should intervene (Clark & Word, 1972). For instance, if you are being robbed, it might be wise to yell out quite specifically that you are being robbed and that someone should call 911. You might also benefit from stating that you do not know your attacker so that others do not think it is a lovers' quarrel, like in Kitty Genovese's situation (Shotland & Straw, 1976). In addition, to avoid diffusion of responsibility, if it is possible to select a bystander and request help specifically from him, do so, and make eye contact if you can (e.g., Moriarty, 1975; Shotland & Johnson, 1978; Shotland & Stebbins, 1980). By isolating one person and pleading with him for help, it becomes clear that he is the only person who can help, and is thus *responsible* for helping. Making such a clear request for assistance from an individual increases your odds of getting the help you need. People often believe that if they request help, others will not offer it, but this is not the case (Flynn & Lake, 2008). People can be quite responsive to direct requests for assistance in clear emergency situations.

# What Are Other Influences on Helping?

In addition to the decision model of bystander intervention, there are other factors that contribute to increased or decreased likelihood of someone choosing to help another person in need.

## MOOD

Earlier in the chapter, you saw how one model of helping suggests that we help others to alleviate negative emotions. Can a positive mood also impact helping? Some studies have found that being in a good mood can lead to an increase in helping behaviour by bystanders (e.g., Carlson, Charlin, & Miller, 1988; Isen, Clark, & Schwartz, 1976; North, Tarrant, & Hargreaves, 2004). In one study, participants were more likely to help others after experiencing positive events that presumably put them in a good mood, such as receiving cookies or finding a dime left in a payphone (Isen & Levin, 1972). According to industrial-organizational psychologists, good mood within the workplace increases organizational spontaneity—which, in this context, refers to helping co-workers, protecting the organization, making constructive suggestions, developing oneself, and spreading goodwill (George & Brief, 1992). In general, when you are in a good mood, you don't want to destroy that mood. Therefore, some researchers argue that we help others in an effort to maintain that good mood (e.g., Isen & Levin, 1972; Wegener & Petty, 1994). That said, if helping is going to cause distress or unpleasant emotions, we may not want to help for the same reason (e.g., Miller, 2009).

Another reason people are more helpful when they are in a good mood is that a good mood raises self-awareness. As you learned in Chapter 4, this heightened sense of self-awareness causes us to match our behaviour to our actual self. In fact, we are more likely to engage in helping behaviours when in front of a mirror, a situation in which, as research has shown, we become more self-aware (Batson et al., 1999). While positive moods may increase our self-awareness, they tend to decrease our other-awareness at the same time (Carlson et al., 1988). Have you ever been in a great mood and been so caught up in your own daydreams and happy thoughts that you have not noticed something around you, like someone calling your name? As a result of our increased self-awareness, we may be *less likely* to even notice or correctly interpret a situation as an emergency that requires our help (Steps 1 and 2 in the decision model discussed above).

"Can a positive mood **also impact helping?**"

## SIMILARITY

Similarity also plays a role in likelihood of being helped. People are more likely to help others who are perceived to be similar to them than those individuals who are not (Dovidio, 1984). This effect will even be present in people who share the same birthday (Burger, Messian, Patel, del Prado, & Anderson, 2004). This may be the case, in part, because similarity leads to attraction (Byrne, 1971). What is similar is familiar, and people prefer what is familiar (Zajonc & Rajecki, 1969). This similarity can consist of being part of the same group, even if the party in distress is a stranger. In one study, students were made to think about their favourite soccer team, thereby activating their identity as a fan of that team (i.e., their ingroup). Each participant was then made to walk to another building, purportedly to be shown a video. On the way, they encountered a student who was injured and either wearing a shirt of the participant's favourite team, a shirt of a competitor, or a shirt with no team name. The injured student received more help when wearing a shirt of the participant's favourite team than when wearing either of the other kinds of shirts (Levine, Prosser, Evans, & Reicher, 2005). Generally speaking, we are more likely to help ingroup rather than outgroup members.

When it comes to similarity and demographics, things get a little complicated. Reviews show that the impact of race on helping is particularly complex (e.g., Crosby, Bromley, & Saxe, 1980; Saucier, Miller, & Doucet, 2005). For example, 79-year-old Turkish Canadian Yusuf Hizel, who was robbed aboard a Toronto subway in April 2010, was not assisted by the nearly two dozen people who witnessed the event (O'Toole, 2010). Did his minority ethnicity or age play a role? Conversely, none of the same-race witnesses helped Kitty Genovese or Deletha Ward (discussed previously). So what is the influence of race on helping? Some research shows that we are more likely to help same-race victims (e.g., Benson et al., 1976; Gaertner, 1973; Sissons, 1981). However, much of this research is done only with black and white participants, and the results are therefore limited. Other studies involving face-to-face interactions find that individuals are more likely to help victims of different races (e.g., Dutton, 1971; Katz, Sohn, & Zalk, 1975). In addition, more recent research examining volunteerism and race has found that different racial groups are approximately equal in their attendance at volunteer training sessions (Morrow-Howell, Elliott, & Ozawa, 1990).

## ATTRACTION

Another factor is attraction, whether due to appearance, behaviour, or other qualities (e.g., Dovidio & Gaertner, 1983; Harrell, 1978; Kelley & Byrne, 1976; Kleinke, 1977; Wilson, 1978). For instance, Benson, Karabenick, and Lerner (1976) showed that even when helping is anonymous and there is only a very slim chance of ever meeting the person helped, the attractiveness of the person requiring assistance influences helping behaviour. Specifically, this study showed that people were more likely to help others whom they perceived as attractive (Benson et al., 1976). More recently, Danzis and Stone-Romero (2009) reported that the attractiveness-helping relationship may be moderated by the gender of the helper.

<<< Would **attractiveness** make you more likely to **help someone else?**

Specifically, males were equally likely to help attractive and unattractive females in a group business project, but females offered more help to unattractive females. Further, attractiveness can override our tendency to help only those we perceive as similar to ourselves, and can increase helping of outgroup members (Stürmer, Snyder, & Omoto, 2005).

## GENDER

There have been some differences found in how men and women help and the situations in which they will help. First and foremost, faculty at the Canadian University College have found that within friendships, women help more than men (e.g., George, Carroll, Kersnick, & Calderon, 1998). Men tend to be more likely to help in "heroic" ways, such as assisting with car trouble or rescuing a drowning child (e.g., Eagly & Crowley, 1986; Penner, Dertke, & Achenbach, 1973; Piliavin & Unger, 1985). On the other hand, women tend to help in more long-term, nurturing ways, such as providing emotional support or taking in an elderly parent (e.g., Aries & Johnson, 1983; McGuire, 1994). The source of these differences may not be genetic, but instead may be due to gender norms prescribing that men should be heroic and women should be nurturing (recall our discussion of gender stereotypes in Chapter 10), or perhaps men's and women's beliefs about their own capabilities (Eagly & Crowley, 1986). A woman may not believe she has the strength to pull a child out of the pounding waves, and a man may not believe that he would know how to tend to the needs of an elderly person.

In other studies, gender has been found to influence whom we offer help to and accept assistance from. Specifically, we are more likely to seek help from individuals of our own gender (Baron, 1997). However, although females are more likely to offer to help other females, males may be somewhat more likely to offer help to females (Eagly & Crowley, 1986). These gender effects also may be influenced by attributions of responsibility, as men tend to help less when they attribute responsibility to the person needing help (MacGeorge, 2003). Cross-cultural studies support the idea that social norms heavily influence gender differences in helping (Johnson et al., 1989). Interpretations of sexual orientation also influence helping behaviour. For instance, Gore, Tobiasen, and Kayson (1997) found that when a male or female caller made a telephone call to a participant and asked for help with reaching a girlfriend or boyfriend, 80 percent of heterosexuals received help, in comparison to 48 percent of homosexuals.

## MIMICRY

Another positive influence on helping is mimicry. People tend to mimic one another somewhat automatically and will even mimic strangers in their language and bodily gestures. This mimicry tends to increase prosocial behaviour (e.g., Chartrand & Bargh, 1999; van Baaren, Horgan, Chartrand, & Dijkmans, 2004). For example, van Baaren, Holland, Kawakami, and van Knippenberg (2004) conducted a series of studies in which participants were mimicked by a research confederate and then placed in a situation in which they would have the opportunity to help the original experimenter or a new experimenter that came in to assist with the project. The results showed that, across all studies, participants who were mimicked were more helpful and generous toward others than were participants who hadn't been mimicked (van Baaren et al., 2004). Further, we are more helpful not only toward the person who mimicked us, but also toward others even peripherally involved in a situation. Being mimicked seems to increase prosocial orientations, and can even lead to greater charitable donations made by participants (e.g., Stel, van Baaren, & Vonk, 2007).

> "If others act as we do, **we infer that they are similar to us.**"

One possible reason for the mimicry–helping relationship is that if others act as we do, we infer that they are similar to us. Another possibility is that this mimicry is an effort on our part to develop a common way of interacting—a shared perspective on the world and the way in which "things are done." Research has shown that establishing a shared reality with another person is a crucial way in which people bond and understand their worlds, and such a bond and shared understanding could promote helping behaviour between people (Hardin & Higgins, 1996). Mimicry also may lead to feelings of empathy. For example, Stel and Vonk (2010) reported that mimickers experienced more empathy in comparison to non-mimickers, increasing the likelihood of helping behaviours. In studying mimicry, neuroscience complements social psychological research. Researchers have identified mirror neurons—brain cells that respond both when an action is performed and

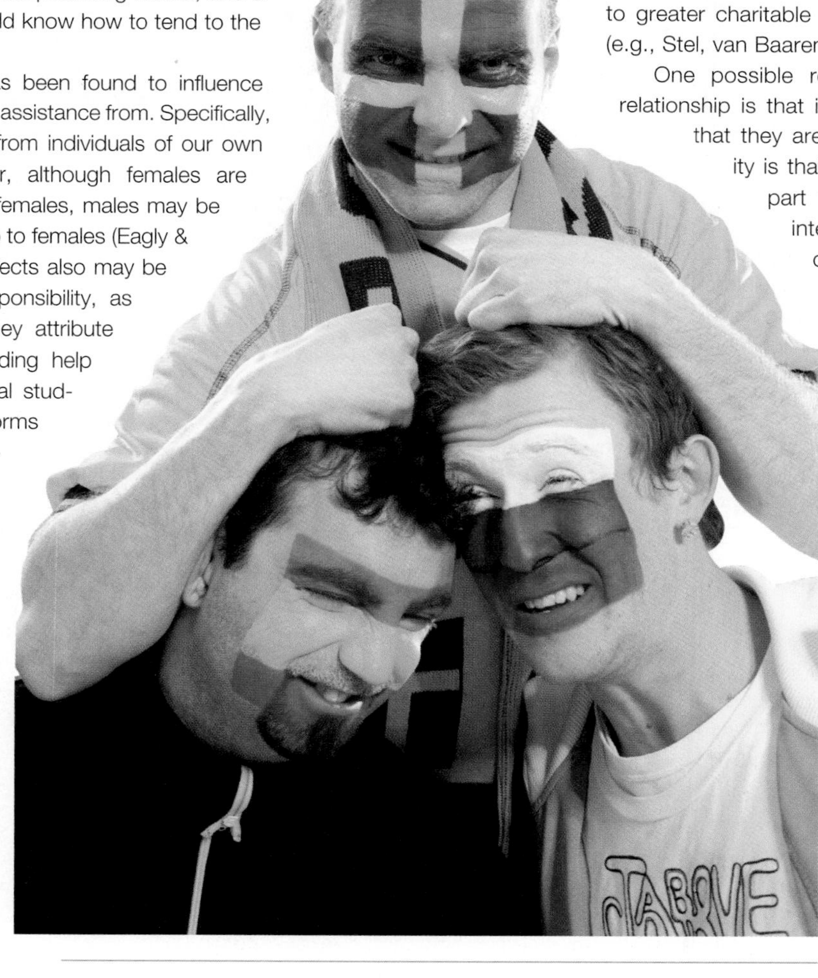

**We are less likely to help people** in whom we perceive a lack of similarity to ourselves.

**ALTRUISTIC PERSONALITY** a proposed personality composite consisting of five traits, each of which correlates positively with helping behaviour: empathy, internal locus of control, belief in a just world, a sense of social responsibility, and low egocentrism

when that same action is observed in another—in both monkeys and humans (Iacoboni et al., 1999). Some researchers think that mirror neurons are critical to understanding the function of mimicry (Ramachandran, 2006). Although this research is still in its infancy, the findings provide an interesting neurological look at empathy.

## ALTRUISTIC PERSONALITY

In addition to all of these situational factors, one dispositional one may exist—an **altruistic personality**. Individuals thought to have this personality possess five traits that research has shown seem to correlate with helping behaviour: empathy, an internal locus of control (leading those people to consider themselves responsible for and able to control the circumstances around them), belief in a just world, a sense of social responsibility, and low egocentrism (e.g., Bierhoff, 2002). In an examination of traits associated with people who helped victims of traffic accidents, Bierhoff, Klein, and Kramp (1991) found that each of these traits was prevalent to a high degree. As such, they may be used to predict people's tendencies to engage in helping behaviours. Recent evidence also suggests that genetic and dispositional influences (i.e., temperament) on helping behaviour become increasingly important as we age, whereas helping when we are younger is determined more by environmental and situational factors (e.g., Hastings, Rubin, & DeRose, 2005; Scourfield, John, Martin, & McGuffin, 2004).



## MODELLING

Another factor that increases the likelihood of help being given is the modelling of prosocial behaviour (Bryan & Test, 1967). As discussed in previous chapters, people learn how to behave in part by observing how others behave (Bandura, 1962, 1965). The same is true with regard to helping behaviour. If people observe others engaging in prosocial behaviour—whether in the moment of an emergency or during repeated occasions earlier in their lives—they are more likely to do so themselves. This is often where parenting styles and responses to childhood emotion come into play. Canadian research has shown that how a parent deals with childhood problems and how parents act can influence later displays of prosocial behaviour; tolerant and non-punitive parenting has been associated with increased prosocial actions (e.g., Roberts, 1999; Romano, Tremblay, Boulerice, & Swisher, 2005). Positive interactions between parents and children may be critical in fostering an environment in which prosocial values and norms can be modelled to young children, and consistently reinforced (Knafo & Plomin, 2006). Similarly, childhood involvement in positive families, recreational activities, and neighbourhood groups may increase prosocial actions (King et al., 2005). Even as adults, being exposed to prosocial role models increases our likelihood of helping. In a classic study of prosocial modelling, participants witnessed a driver in need being helped by

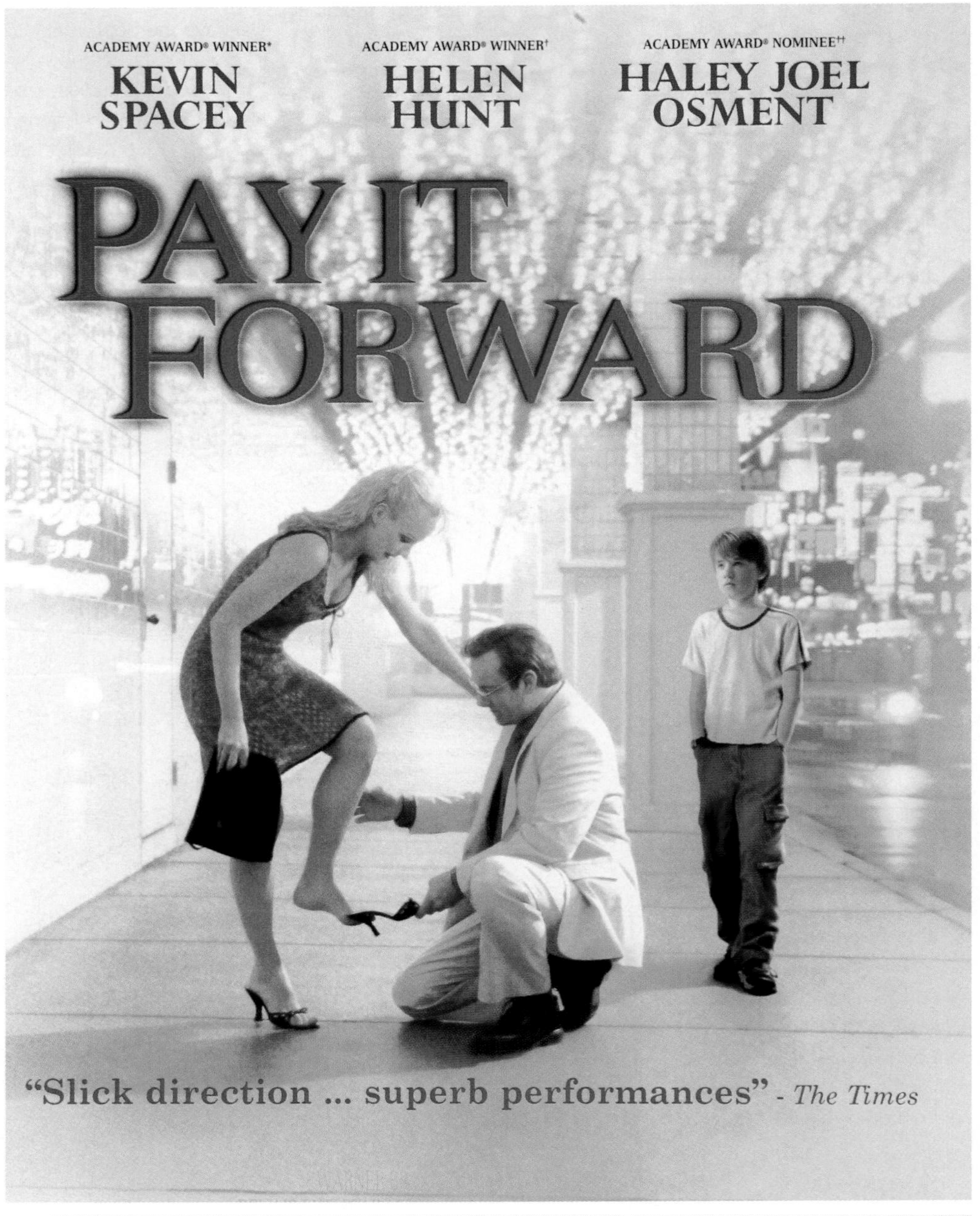

ACADEMY AWARD® WINNER*
KEVIN SPACEY
ACADEMY AWARD® WINNER†
HELEN HUNT
ACADEMY AWARD® NOMINEE††
HALEY JOEL OSMENT
PAY IT FORWARD
"Slick direction ... superb performances" - The Times


**Children, as well as adults,** are more likely to engage in helpful acts after witnessing others—even those in the media—do so.

^^^ **Modelling Prosocial Behaviour.** If we are exposed to role models who exhibit prosocial behaviour, **we are more likely to exhibit such behaviours ourselves.**



another person (Bryan & Test, 1967). Sometime later, they encountered another driver in need who was not being helped. Seeing the first driver being helped increased the likelihood of participants helping the second driver (though it's worth noting that these drivers were alone, so the bystander effect is not applicable here). In this way, people use others' actions as cues for what they should do themselves, and these actions may activate schemas associated with helping behaviours.

Role models need not be physically present—they can be media figures as well (Forge & Phemister, 1987). Whether exposed to positive role models on *The Littlest Hobo* or on *Corner Gas* (i.e., animal or human models), both children and adults alike are influenced by, and learn from, these models. Following the release of the popular movie *Pay It Forward* in 2000, the Pay It Forward Foundation was established, and the principle of doing a favour and requesting that the favour recipient pass the good deed on to someone else, rather than "returning the favour," has become a movement around the world. At present, over 35 countries have participated in an annual International Pay It Forward Day (April 26) to inspire acts of kindness (see payitforwardday.com). Did the actors in this movie realize what an impact the film would have? We often try to emulate the behaviour of those that are famous, such as what they wear or how they act—so why not copy their helping behaviour? Research suggests that this is exactly what we do when prosocial acts are displayed in the media (e.g., Sprafkin, Liebert, & Poulos, 1975). In a meta-analysis of models for children's behaviour found on television, children who watched prosocial content had more positive interactions with others,

> "Children who watched prosocial content had more positive interactions with others, **exhibited more altruistic behaviour, held fewer stereotypes, and were less aggressive.**"

exhibited more altruistic behaviour, held fewer stereotypes, and were less aggressive (Mares & Woodward, 2005). In addition, older children (around age six) benefited more than younger children (around age three), perhaps because they had the intellectual capacity to understand the meaning of the modelled behaviour. Conversely, children who are exposed to aggressive media content engage in less prosocial behaviour both within games and in terms of real-world helping (Anderson et al., 2010).

In modern society, helping behaviour also can be modelled via social media, such as Facebook or Twitter. For example, Facebook is often used as a method to collect donations for the Multiple Sclerosis Society and Juvenile Diabetes Foundation, and seeing people donate to friends' causes may increase a person's chance of helping. Further,

**JUST-WORLD HYPOTHESIS** the perception that people get what they deserve, based on the belief that the world is a fair and just place

posts and requests for people to become active in social causes (e.g., rescuing and finding homes for injured or stray animals) can help to promote this behaviour in others.

### HOW IT FEELS TO BE HELPED

One final factor that influences helping is the way it feels to be helped. At first, it might seem that those being helped should be grateful—and in some cases, such as emergencies, they are. However, they aren't always grateful. Let's say you just finished working on a paper for your English Literature course. You feel like you know a lot about the subject, and you are proud of your work. As it's coming out of the printer, your roommate happens to pick it up and immediately starts pointing out places in which it could be improved. How would that make you feel? Most likely, you would feel insulted. Research has shown that help that threatens one's self-esteem, or is associated with an air of superiority, is unwelcome (e.g., Nadler, Fisher, & Itzhak, 1983; Shrout, Herman, & Bolger, 2006). If we *feel* like we need help, we feel bad (Newsom, 1999). Help provided by enemies or someone with many resources has a negative effect on the person being helped (e.g., Nadler & Fisher, 1974; Nadler, Fisher, & Streufert, 1974; Penner et al., 2005). Overall, help is best received when the person being helped believes the helper is genuinely interested in helping and is not doing so to humiliate, patronize, or demean (Ames, Flynn, & Weber, 2004). In addition, when another person engages in a reciprocal helping interaction with us, we feel a sense of gratitude, which further enhances the likelihood that we will help in future situations (Tsang, 2006).



> "Research has shown that help that threatens **one's self-esteem, or is associated with an air of superiority, is unwelcome**"

## How Can We Increase Prosocial Behaviour?

Now that we know what leads to prosocial behaviour and what precludes it, how can we attempt to increase it in the general population? As we learned in Chapters 7 and 8, whether or not we get what we want often depends on the way we ask. As we saw earlier, modelling helping behaviour increases the likelihood of it occurring (e.g., Bryan & Test, 1967; Romano et al., 2005). As such, by modelling helping behaviour to other people, we can increase the chances that they will step up and help us when needed (e.g., Schnall, Roper, & Fessler, 2010). In fact, researchers working in conjunction with the Correctional Service of Canada have recognized that modelling prosocial behaviour must be incorporated into offender treatment and rehabilitation programs to promote prosocial rather than antisocial actions (Bonta & Andrews, 2007). Besides modelling, there are several other ways in which we can increase our likelihood of helping others.

### ATTRIBUTIONS

You're eating lunch with a friend when he casually asks if he can borrow your notes for the afternoon class you have together. "I just didn't bother taking any," he says, "and we have that exam on Friday." How would you react? Is it likely that you would comply with his request? Now, what if he'd said, "I try to take organized notes, but I feel like I'm looking at gibberish when I try to study. Would you please help me out?" Chances are, you'd be more likely to help him in the second scenario, right? A research study tested that very same scenario, except the request was made by phone. The caller received much more help when he claimed to have tried and failed than when he admitted to not even bothering with taking notes (Barnes, Ickes, & Kidd, 1979).

When we consider helping others, a certain degree of importance is placed on our feelings about the person's responsibility. Even when the situation is less cut and dry, the effect is more or less the same (e.g., Dooley, 1995). It seems we tend to be more willing to help others when we feel a situation is, to some degree, out of their control. If people are perceived as being responsible for their plight, we are less likely to help them (see Hafer & Bègue, 2005, for a review). This effect is related to what is known as the **just-world hypothesis**, which states that because we have a need to believe that the world is a fair and just place, we also believe that people get what they deserve (Lerner & Miller, 1978). For example, in November 2011, a man choked to death on the street while witnesses walked by; no one intervened and no one called 911. Why did no one help this man? Aside from the diffusion of responsibility by the presence of a number of people, the man was homeless, Aboriginal, and intoxicated. Does your interpretation of the situation change based on this information? Our sense of responsibility to help decreases when we believe those in need of help are not worthy of such actions. Unfortunately, our attributions of responsibility are often incorrect when we encounter minority groups, AIDS patients, rape victims, or homeless persons (Furnham, 2003). That said, our attributions can change if we perceive ourselves to be more similar to the person in need of assistance (Burger, 1981). Perhaps if we alter our social categorizations to include all people as humans, rather than as persons of certain races, genders, or statuses, we will be more likely to help (e.g., Dovidio et al., 1997; Levine, Prosser, Evans, & Reicher, 2005).

> "When we consider helping others, a certain degree of importance **is placed on our feelings about the person's responsibility.**"

### EDUCATION

People are receptive to learning about different behavioural choices and the psychological principles that attempt to explain them. This effect is what Gergen (1973) termed the **enlightenment effect**, and it suggests that learning about psychology can bring about changes in behaviour. Research has shown that learning about the bystander effect results in an increase in helping in group situations (Beaman et al., 1978). Thus, by reading this chapter and learning about what leads to helping behaviour and what blocks or discourages it, you are already modifying your own future behaviour. From now on, when you encounter an emergency situation, you will be aware of the bystander effect and may be more conscious of the fact that you are only failing to help because there are others around. And perhaps you will then help, and maybe even save a life.

This awareness not only extends to how you will react in an emergency situation, but also how you will go about your day-to-day life. You may not be able to make a grand gesture, like the individuals who donated hundreds of thousands of dollars to the earthquake and tsunami victims in Japan in March 2011, but you'll be surprised at the differences that small prosocial acts can make. In fact, a new Canadian movement called People for Good celebrates both everyday and grand-scale prosocial acts by asking people to donate generosity (i.e., be kind and generous to others) and to reinforce prosocial acts and share them with others. This group also has released a series of advertisements to educate others about their belief that if people helped more often, prosocial behaviour would not seem so strange or out of place. We challenge you to take what you have learned from this chapter, and the text as a whole, and apply it to your life!

**ENLIGHTENMENT EFFECT** the effect wherein learning about how humans fall prey to obstacles to helping can aid us in overcoming those obstacles in the future; it extends to benefits from learning about other human biases

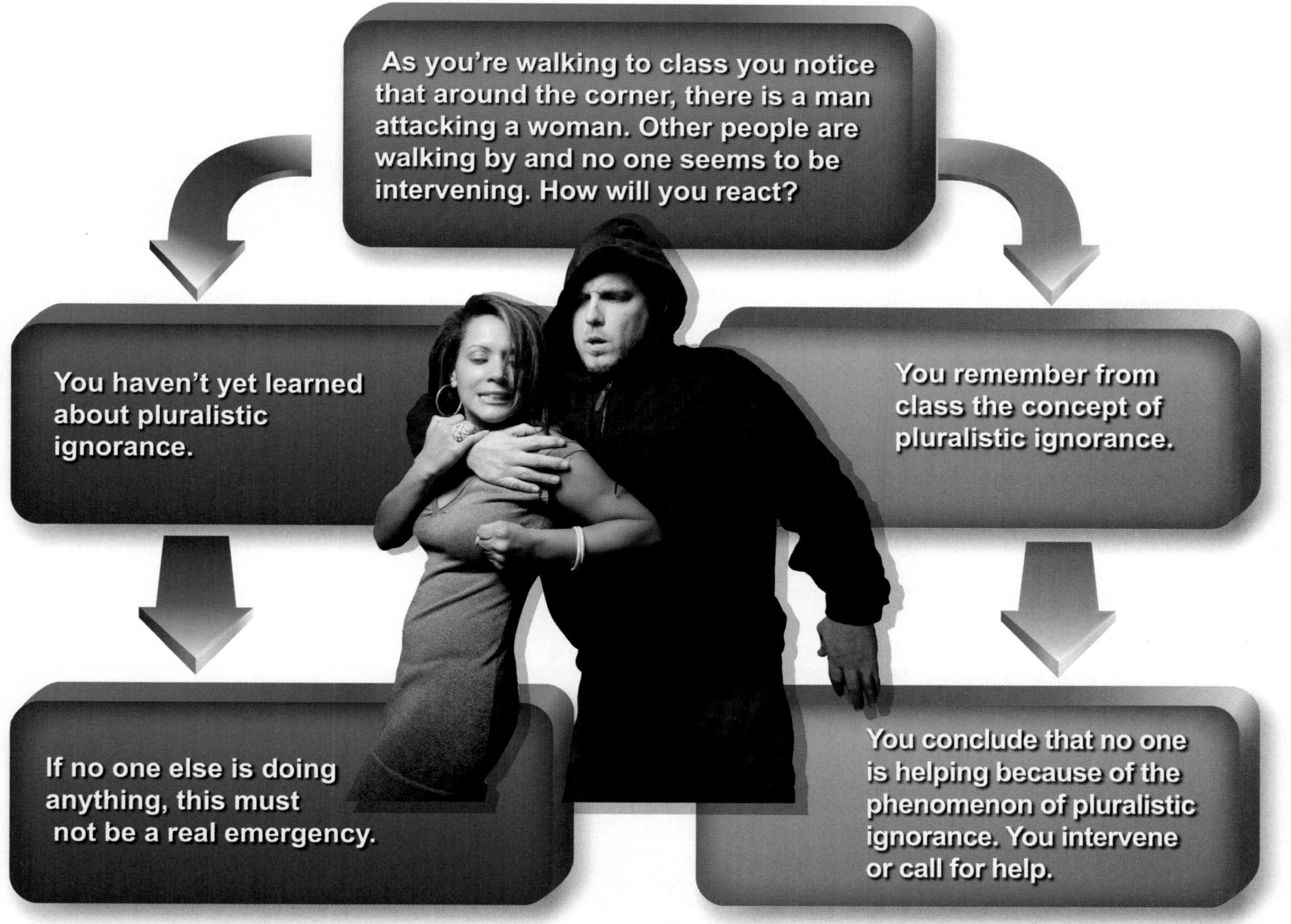


**Enlightened About Pluralistic Ignorance.** By learning about psychological theories that help you understand your own thought processes and behaviours, **you can avoid falling prey to the obstacles that may prevent you from helping others in need.**

# CHAPTER 13 Review

## Summary

### WHY DO WE HELP? p. 254

• People may provide each other with help, otherwise termed *prosocial behaviour*, for a variety of reasons. Some of these reasons may be egoistic (selfishly motivated) or altruistic (selflessly motivated).
• Egoistic models of prosocial behaviour include the influences of existing negative mood, the desire to improve one's mood, and the relative costs and benefits of helping. Being in a negative mood, having no desire to improve one's mood, and perceiving more costs than benefits tend to decrease helping.
• Altruistic models of prosocial behaviour include the influences of empathy, nurturing feelings toward the target, and a goal to promote the target's welfare on the likelihood of helping behaviour. Each of these factors tends to increase helping.
• Models that discuss the influence of norms suggest that the norm of reciprocity increases helping, because we expect that if we help others, they will help us (and they often do). They also suggest that social norms about when helping is appropriate impact our tendency to help.

### WHEN DO WE HELP? p. 258

• According to the decision model of bystander intervention, there are five steps that are required for helping to occur: noticing the emergency, interpreting the situation as an emergency, feeling a personal responsibility to help, deciding how to help, and providing the help.
• Being aware of the obstacles that arise in completing each step can enable you to overcome them. People do not notice emergencies because they are focused on their own concerns or are otherwise distracted—or the event is not clear or nearby. People do not interpret situations as emergencies when they are ambiguous, when the relationship between the parties involved is unclear, or when pluralistic ignorance occurs; if others do not seem to think there is an emergency, we decide there must not be one. People do not accept responsibility for helping in groups—all the more when other people are present (diffusion of responsibility). Finally, people will not be able to decide how to help if they do not have the appropriate knowledge set or are insecure in that knowledge.

### WHAT ARE OTHER INFLUENCES ON HELPING? p. 263

• Many other factors can influence helping behaviour. Some of these factors include the helper's mood, the similarity of the helper to the target person, the attractiveness of the target person (whether physical or in terms of personality), the gender, the behavioural mimicry of the helper, the helper having the five traits composing an "altruistic personality," and the modelling of helping behaviour.
• People do not always welcome help. Sometimes it is embarrassing to need help because people sometimes want to feel self-sufficient. People often do not like to be helped with matters that are tied to their self-esteem. In particular, they want to be able to accomplish things on their own in areas important to them. If the helper exudes superiority while helping, it will also make the help less welcome and less appreciated. Indeed, such assistance may hurt more than it helps.

### HOW CAN WE INCREASE PROSOCIAL BEHAVIOUR? p. 268

• People's tendency to help can be increased by others modelling prosocial behaviour to them. Models can be real-life people or people in the media. Older children tend to benefit more from this sort of modelling, and it is prosocial behaviour that must be modelled for helping to increase—not just positive behaviour in general.
• By being educated about psychological principles related to prosocial behaviour, you can apply them to your real-life situations and possibly catch yourself before you decide not to help someone who is truly in need.

## Key Terms

**altruistic** having a selfless motivation for helping *254*

**altruistic personality** a proposed personality composite consisting of five traits, each of which correlates positively with helping behaviour: empathy, internal locus of control, belief in a just world, a sense of social responsibility, and low egocentrism *266*

**bystander effect** a phenomenon in which as more people are present, each individual is less likely to help *261*

**cost-benefit analysis** the act of weighing the relative costs and benefits of helping to decide whether or not to provide help *255*

**decision model of bystander intervention** the model derived by Bibb Latane and John Darley that explains the five steps required to provide help to someone in need and what can interfere with successful completion of each of these steps *261*

**diffusion of responsibility** a decreased feeling of responsibility to help in a group; if an emergency arises in a group setting, it is less likely that any one person will help than if someone was witnessing the emergency alone, because being in a group decreases each person's feeling of personal responsibility to help *261*

**egoistic** having a selfish motivation for helping *254*

**empathy** having compassion for others and a feeling of seeing the world through the eyes of another individual *254*

**empathy-altruism model of prosocial behaviour** a model which suggests that true altruism is a product of empathy; this empathy can create nurturing feelings toward a target or a goal to increase the target's welfare *256*

**enlightenment effect** the effect wherein learning about how humans fall prey to obstacles to helping can aid us in overcoming those obstacles in the future; it extends to benefits from learning about other human biases *269*

**just-world hypothesis** the perception that people get what they deserve, based on the belief that the world is a fair and just place *268*

**kin selection** the tendency of people to help their biological relatives over nonfamily members, even at great cost to themselves, thus favouring the reproductive success of one's relatives over his or her own survival *258*

**negative state relief model** a model which posits that the reason people help others is to improve their own negative mood *254*

**pluralistic ignorance** a form of misperception where individuals within a group believe that other group members are behaving the way they are because they have additional knowledge about the context or situation *261*

**prosocial behaviour** behaviour designed to help another person *254*

**reciprocal altruism** the belief that helping others increases the likelihood that others will help us or our kin in return *258*

**reciprocity norm** the idea that if others help us, we should help them, and that if we help them, they will help us *257*

**social responsibility norm** the idea that we have social responsibility to help others; the extent to which this extends to outgroup members varies by culture *257*

# Test Your Understanding

## MULTIPLE CHOICE

**1.** Charitable donations activate the same brain region that is activated when

**a.** we smile.
**b.** we receive a monetary reward.
**c.** we eat something we like.
**d.** we are praised by a classmate.

**2.** Which of these does not factor into a cost-benefit analysis?

**a.** emotional harm to oneself
**b.** someone saying "thank you"
**c.** increased popularity from helping
**d.** emotional harm to the target

**3.** Why does positive mood influence helping?

**a.** Rewards are more accessible.
**b.** Penalties are more accessible.
**c.** You like the target better.
**d.** None of these

**4.** In the empathy-altruism model of prosocial behaviour, what promotes helping?

**a.** similarity
**b.** nurturing feelings
**c.** reciprocity norm
**d.** attraction

**5.** According to research, if you give someone a pop and then ask him to buy your raffle tickets, he will

**a.** buy more tickets.
**b.** want to buy more tickets but not do it.
**c.** offer to tell friends about the raffle.
**d.** offer you a pop.

**6.** According to the decision model of bystander intervention, why might we not notice a need for help?

**a.** distractions
**b.** being self-focused
**c.** distance from event
**d.** all of the above

**7.** If others do not act as though there is an emergency happening, you will interpret the event as a nonemergency. This is called

**a.** diffusion of responsibility.
**b.** egoism.
**c.** reciprocity effect.
**d.** pluralistic ignorance.

**8.** People who have decided to help must figure out how to do so. What is not something that would stop them at this stage?

**a.** feeling embarrassed
**b.** limited time to help
**c.** having no training in how to help
**d.** lack of confidence in how to help

**9.** Which of these is a trait not necessarily possessed by someone with an altruistic personality?

**a.** empathy
**b.** social responsibility
**c.** extroversion
**d.** belief in a just world

**10.** Sometimes we don't want to be helped. Which of these is not a reason why?

**a.** The person has fewer resources than we do.
**b.** Doing it on our own is important to our self-esteem.
**c.** The helper exudes superiority.
**d.** The person has more resources than we do.

**ANSWERS:** 1. b; 2. d; 3. a; 4. b; 5. a; 6. d; 7. d; 8. b; 9. c; 10. a

## ESSAY RESPONSE

**1.** Consider the negative state relief model. Can we ever say for sure that this is not the cause of a given helpful behaviour? What might we have to do to discount the possibility that the improvement of negative mood is the cause?

**2.** What does it take to help when doing so is costly to oneself? Consider the research in this chapter in your explanation.

**3.** The reciprocity norm was shown by infant research to be somewhat innate. What are the possible reasons for this? Consider evolutionary possibilities as well as perspectives regarding the individual's and culture's interests.

**4.** Consider why attraction might lead us to help someone whom we are likely never to meet. Discuss any egoistic, altruistic, normative, and alternative reasons that may exist.

**5.** Modelling has profound effects on long- and short-term behaviour. Discuss some ways in which parents can inadvertently influence their children and we can inadvertently influence our peers.

## APPLY IT!

Think about any time you've been out with your friends and seen a scuffle of some sort. Maybe you saw a couple fighting outside a restaurant. Maybe you saw two men shouting about something on the street. Maybe you saw a woman striking a child, or a man dragging an animal down the street. How could you have fairly assessed whether or not there was an emergency? How could you have responded in a way that would have provided needed help to a potential victim while still ensuring your own safety?

**Remember to check www.thethinkspot.ca for additional information, downloadable flashcards, and other helpful resources.**

# THINK READINGS



**Based on what you learned in Chapter 13, which influences on prosocial behaviour might this symbolic association be most closely linked to?**

**This result demonstrates the reciprocity norm discussed in Chapter 13. But how might an egoistic model of prosocial behaviour explain the outcome? How would an altruistic model of helping explain it?**

PSYCHOLOGICAL SCIENCE

## The Smell of Virtue: Clean Scents Promote Reciprocity and Charity

By KATIE LILJENQUIST, CHEN-BO ZHONG and ADAM D. GALINSKY

Published: February 4, 2010

"*The smell and taste of things remain poised a long time . . . and bear unfaltering, in the tiny and almost impalpable drop of their essence, the vast structure of recollection.*" (Proust, 1928, p. 65)

As Proust's words so eloquently express, a familiar smell can transport us to an exact time and place in our past. Indeed, psychologists have found that scents can dutifully retrieve images and feelings from the deepest recesses of the mind (Chu & Downes, 2000; Doop, Mohr, Folley, Brewer, & Park, 2006). Not only do smells activate memories, they can also influence judgment (Schnall, Haidt, Clore, & Jordan, 2008) and even regulate behaviour. For example, Holland, Hendriks, and Aarts (2005) found that exposure to citrus cleaning scents enhanced the mental accessibility of cleaning-related constructs and led participants to maintain a cleaner environment while eating.

Based on the symbolic association between physical and moral purity, we introduce a provocative possibility: clean smells might not only regulate physical cleanliness, but may also motivate virtuous behaviour. Indeed, moral transgressions can engender literal feelings of dirtiness (Zhong & Liljenquist, 2006). Just as many symbolic associations are reciprocally related (Lakoff, 1987), such as coldness and loneliness (Zhong & Leonardelli, 2008) or darkness and depravity (Frank & Gilovich, 1988), morality and cleanliness may also be reciprocally linked. In the current research, we investigate whether clean scents can transcend the domain of physical cleanliness and promote virtuous behaviour.

### Experiment 1: Promoting Reciprocity

Experiment 1 tested the impact of clean scents on reciprocating trust. We chose this behaviour because Aristotle advocated justice in exchange as a primary "moral virtue" (Aristotle, c330BC/1999) and because studies have indentified traits like fairness and generosity as central to moral identity (Aquino & Reed, 2002).

Twenty-eight participants (12 female) were individually assigned to either a *clean-scented* room or a *baseline* room. The only difference between the two rooms was a spray of citrus-scented Windex in the clean-scented room.

In both conditions, participants engaged in a one-shot anonymous trust game (Berg, Dickaut, & McCabe, 1995) involving two parties: a sender and receiver. In a typical trust game, the sender is given money that he can choose to keep or "invest" with an anonymous receiver. Any money sent is tripled, and the receiver then decides how to split the tripled money. For example, if the sender passes all of the money and the receiver reciprocates this trust by returning half of the tripled amount, both would be better off. However, sending money can be risky if the receiver chooses to exploit the sender and keep all the invested money (Camerer, 2003).

All the participants in the current experiment were told they had been randomly assigned to play the role of the *receiver* and that their ostensible counterpart had decided to send them the full amount ($4) which was now tripled to $12. They had to decide how much money to keep or return to the sender. Participants could exploit their counterpart by keeping all the money or they could honor the trust by returning some portion to the other party.

As predicted, participants in the clean-scented rooms returned significantly more money than those in the baseline condition, $t(26) = 2.64$, $p = .01$, $d = 1.03$ (see Table 1). The clean-scented room led participants to resist exploitation and reciprocate the trusting behaviour of the sender.

### Experiment 2: Promoting Charity

Experiment 2 was designed to replicate the conceptual pattern of Experiment 1 by exploring whether clean scents would motivate another aspect of moral virtue: charity (Aristotle, c330BC/1999; Machan, 1998). Ninety-nine

 

**Table 1** Reciprocation of trusting behaviour in Experiment 1. Volunteerism and donation rate in Experiment 2. Standard deviations are in parentheses.

| | Experiment 1 | Experiment 2 | |
|---|---|---|---|
| | Money Returned | Volunteering Interest | Willingness to Donate |
| **Clean Scent** | \$5.33 (2.01) | 4.21 (1.86) | 22% |
| **Baseline (No Scent)** | \$2.81 (2.81) | 3.29 (2.04) | 6% |

undergraduate students (50 female) were individually assigned to either a *clean-scented* room (sprayed with Windex) or a *baseline no-scent* room and asked to work on a packet of unrelated tasks. Included in the packet was a flier requesting volunteers for a charity, Habitat for Humanity. Participants indicated their interest level in volunteering for future Habitat efforts (1–7 scale), specified the activities they would like to assist with, and selected whether they wanted to donate funds to the cause (yes/no). To rule out mood as a driver of the effects of clean scents, participants completed a shortened version of the PANAS (Watson, Clark & Tellegen, 1988).

As predicted, participants in the clean-scented environment expressed greater interest in volunteering than control participants, $t(97) = 2.33$, $p = .02$, $d = .47$. Additionally, a greater proportion of participants in the clean-scented rooms indicated a willingness to donate money, $\chi^2(1, N = 99) = 4.78$, $p = .03$ (see Table 1). Room scent had no impact on positive nor negative affect ($p$'s > .20), and when controlling for affect, room scent continued to have a significant effect on volunteerism and donation rate ($p$'s < .05). Because our charity measures captured intentions, future research should measure behaviour directly.

## Discussion

Two experiments demonstrated that clean scents not only motivate clean behaviour, but also promote virtuous behaviour by increasing the tendency to reciprocate trust and to offer charitable help. Capitalizing on the fact that abstract concepts are often symbolically derived from the concrete environment (Emerson, 1836), our results suggest that olfactory cues can trigger virtuous behaviours that are related to cleanliness at only a symbolic level. The link from cleanliness to virtuous behaviour appears to be a nonconscious one: in neither experiment did participants recognize an influence of scent on their behaviour, and in Experiment 2, perceived cleanliness did not differ by condition nor correlate with the effects.

These findings carry important implications for environmental regulation of behaviour. Evidence abounds of how people lose their moral footing, how saints become sinners. However, there is much less understanding of what can lead sinners toward the path of virtue. By demonstrating that the association between morality and cleanliness is bidirectional, the current research identifies an unobtrusive way—a clean scent—to curb exploitation and promote altruism.

Beyond olfactory cues, there is the possibility that visual cleanliness can also influence morality (Liljenquist, Zhong, & Galinsky, 2008), which is consistent with the "broken windows" theory of crime that argues damage and disrepair in the environment promote lawless behaviour. The current findings suggest there is some truth to the claim that cleanliness is next to godliness; clean scents summon virtue, helping reciprocity prevail over greed, and charity over apathy.

## References


Aquino, K., & Reed, A. II. (2002). The self-importance of moral identity. *Journal of Personality and Social Psychology, 83*, 1423–1440.

Aristotle. (1999). *Aristotle: Nicomachean ethics*. (T. H. Irwin, Trans.). Indianapolis, IN: Hackett Publishing Company. (Original work published c330BC).

Berg, J., Dickaut, J., & McCabe, K. (1995). Trust, reciprocity and social history. *Games and Economic Behavior, 10*, 122–42.

Camerer, C. (2003). *Behavioral game theory: Experiments in strategic interaction*. Princeton, New Jersey: Princeton University Press.

Doop, M., Mohr, C., Folley, B., Brewer, W., & Park, S. (2006). Olfaction and memory. In W. Brewer, D. Castle, & C. Pantelis (Eds.), *Olfaction and the brain*. (pp. 65–82) Cambridge: Cambridge University Press.

Emerson, R. W. (1836). Nature. In A.R. Fersonson & J.F. Carr (Eds.), *The essays of Ralph Waldo Emerson* (pp. 315–332). Cambridge, MA: Belknap Press.

Frank, M. G., & Gilovich, T. (1988). The dark side of self-and social perception: Black uniforms and aggression in professional sports. *Journal of Personality and Social Psychology, 54(1)*, 74–85.

Holland, R.W., Hendriks, M., & Aarts, H. (2005). Smells like clean spirit: Nonconscious effects of scent on cognition and behavior. *Psychological Science, 16(9)*, 689–693.

Lakoff, G. (1987). *Women, fire, and dangerous things*. Chicago, IL: University of Chicago Press.

Liljenquist, K. A., Zhong, C., & Galinsky, A. D. (2008, August). Environmental cleanliness and the regulation of ethical behavior. In F. Gino (Chair), *Environmental and outcome-based influences on unethical behavior*. Paper presented at Academy of Management, Anaheim, CA.

Machan, T. R. (1998). *Generosity: Virtue in the civil society*. Washington D.C.: Cato Institute.

Proust, M. (1928), *Swann's way* (C. K. Scott-Moncrieff, Trans.). New York: The Modern Library.

Schnall, S., Haidt, J., Clore, G. L., & Jordan, A. H. (2008). Disgust as embodied moral judgment. *Personality and Social Psychology Bulletin, 34*, 1096–1109.

Watson, D., Clark, L. A., & Tellegen, A. (1988). Development and validation of brief measures of positive and negative affect: The PANAS scale. *Journal of Personality and Social Psychology, 54*, 1063–1070.

Wilson, J. Q., & Kelling, G. L. (1982). Broken windows: The police and neighborhood safety. *Atlantic Monthly, 249*, 29–38.

Zhong, C. B., & Leonardelli, G. J. (2008). Cold and lonely: Does social exclusion literally feel cold? *Psychological Science, 19(9)*, 838–842.

Zhong, C., & Liljenquist, K. A. (2006). Washing away your sins: Threatened morality and physical cleansing. *Science, 313*, 1451–1452.


If cleanliness was able to motivate people to return a favour, how did it motivate people to behave prosocially of their own accord? Why might the negative state relief model factor into this?

How might this finding factor into whether or not a person chooses to give money to a homeless person? How does it tie into the idea that attraction and similarity influence helping behaviour?

Now that you have a well-rounded idea of the different ways research methods are implemented in social psychology, how would you use replication to strengthen the finding of this experiment?

# GLOSSARY

**accessibility** the degree to which a concept is active in our consciousness (p. 106)

**actor-observer effect** the tendency people have to make dispositional inferences for others' behaviour but situational attributions for their own (p. 86)

**affective forecasting** the process of predicting the impact future events will have on our overall emotional states (p. 64)

**aggression** behaviour, either verbal or physical, that is used to intentionally harm another individual (p. 204)

**altruistic** having a selfless motivation for helping (p. 254)

**altruistic personality** a proposed personality composite consisting of five traits, each of which correlates positively with helping behaviour: empathy, internal locus of control, belief in a just world, a sense of social responsibility, and low egocentrism (p. 266)

**ambivalence** simultaneously experiencing strong contradictory emotions or motivations (p. 98)

**ambivalent sexism** the contradictory attitudes of hostile sexism and benevolent sexism (p. 182)



**amygdala** a small structure found in the medial temporal lobe of the brain's limbic system that is involved in automatic processing and emotion (p. 45)

**anchoring and adjustment heuristic** a heuristic in which we use a number as a starting point on which to anchor our judgment (p. 49)

**applied research methods (in social psychology)** "pure" research that is driven by curiosity or obtaining scientific knowledge about some phenomenon (p. 5)

**archival studies** research that entails culling information from existing records ranging from magazine articles to website analytics (p. 27)

**attachment style** the degree of security experienced in interpersonal relationships (p. 231)

**attitudes** having an evaluative component toward a stimulus that is made up of affective, behavioural, and cognitive information (p. 98)

**attribution** deciding who or what is responsible for the outcome of a situation; another way we cope with failure and respond to success in order to maintain self-esteem (p. 69)

**authoritarian personality** a personality type that favours obedience to authority and intolerance of people lower in status (p. 185)

**automatic processing** the processing of information "on the fly," using schemas as shortcuts (p. 44)

**availability heuristic** a rule used to estimate the likelihood of a given occurrence based on how easily one can recall an example of that occurrence (p. 46)

**aversive experience** an undesirable experience that may include pain, discomfort, overcrowding, or attack (p. 212)

**aversive racism** the attitudes of people who openly endorse egalitarian views but discriminate in ways they're able to rationalize (p. 179)

**bargaining** a means of resolving conflict that involves each side of the dispute making offers, counteroffers, and concessions (p. 170)

**base rate fallacy** an erroneous conclusion reached when the representativeness heuristic is used to draw a conclusion without considering the base rate (p. 48)

**basic research methods (in social psychology)** the application of basic research to solve practical problems in the real world (p. 5)

**belief in a just world** people have to believe the world is fair and adjust their other beliefs to maintain that stance by concluding that bad things happen to bad people and good things happen to good people (p. 85)

**belief perseverance** holding on to one's beliefs, even in the face of contradictory evidence (p. 90)

**biased perception** the belief that we are justified in our own thoughts and actions but that others are biased in their beliefs and behaviours (p. 169)

**bi-directional causality** a situation in which variable X could cause variable Y or vice versa (p. 30)

**BIRGing** "basking in reflected glory," a strategy by which we reinforce our positive self-concepts by identifying ourselves with successful others (p. 71)

**bystander effect** a phenomenon in which as more people are present, each individual is less likely to help (p. 261)

**case studies** in-depth analyses of an individual, group, or event (p. 27)

**central route** a type of processing that occurs when an individual has the ability and motivation to thoroughly listen to and evaluate a persuasive message (p. 118)

**chameleon effect** the non-conscious mimicry of the postures, mannerisms, facial expressions, and other behaviours of one's interaction partner, such that one's behaviour passively and unintentionally changes to match that of others in one's current social environment (p. 140)

**chronic accessibility** accessibility arising from frequent and recent exposure to a construct that has permanence—that is, it is accessible all of the time (p. 106)

**classical conditioning** a type of learning by which a neutral stimulus (UCS) gets paired with a stimulus that elicits a response (UCR). Through repeated pairings, the neutral stimulus (CS) by itself elicits the response (CR) of the second stimulus (p. 100)

**cognitive dissonance** the anxiety that arises from acting in a way discordant with one's attitudes. This anxiety is resolved by adjusting one's attitudes to be in line with the behaviour. (p. 108)

**cognitive-neoassociation theory** a theory which suggests that when a person experiences something with a negative result, such as pain or discomfort, aggressive behaviour can often occur in the wake of that experience (p. 209)

**cohesion** the degree to which a group is connected (p. 158)

**collectivism** a cultural focus on the self as interdependent and defined by the connectedness of people to one another—in particular, the people closest to them (p. 63)

**communal relationship** a relationship in which partners expect mutual responsiveness to one another's needs (p. 242)

**companionate love** the affection we feel for people with whom our lives are deeply intertwined (p. 239)

**compliance** a form of social influence involving direct requests from one person to another (p. 148)

**conditioned response (CR)** a learned response to the conditioned stimulus that was previously a neutral stimulus (p. 100)

**conditioned stimulus (CS)** a stimulus that, only by repeated association with a particular unconditioned stimulus, comes to evoke the response associated with the unconditioned stimulus (p. 100)

**confirmation bias** the tendency to notice information that confirms one's beliefs and to ignore information that disconfirms one's beliefs (p. 9)

**conflict** the perceived incompatibility of actions, goals, or ideas (p. 168)

**conformity** a type of social influence in which an individual changes his or her behaviours to stay in line with social norms (p. 144)

**confound** any difference other than the levels of the independent variable between the experimental group and the control group (p. 33)

**contact hypothesis** the belief that increased communication and contact between different racial groups reduces levels of prejudice and discrimination (p. 191)

**control group** the group that does not get the main treatment in an experiment, but is used as a baseline to compare results with the experimental group (p. 31)

**controlled processing** a type of mental processing that takes purposeful thought and effort as decisions or courses of action are weighed carefully (p. 44)

**CORFing** "cutting off reflective failure," a strategy by which we try to disassociate ourselves from others who have failed or behaved poorly (p. 71)

**correlational research** research in which researchers do not manipulate variables but observe whether there is a relationship between two variables (p. 29)

**correspondence bias** the tendency of people to make dispositional attributions for others' behaviours (p. 83)

**correspondent inference theory** the theory that people base their inferences regarding the source of others' behaviours on whether or not the behaviour was freely chosen, if the consequences are distinctive, and if the behaviour was socially desirable (p. 82)

**cost-benefit analysis** the act of weighing the relative costs and benefits of helping to decide whether or not to provide help (p. 255)

**counterfactual thinking** the tendency to imagine alternative outcomes for an event (p. 52)

**covariation theory** the theory that people base their inferences regarding the source of others' behaviours on whether or not there is a consensus regarding the way one ought to respond, the distinctiveness of the response, and the consistency of the person's response across situations (p. 82)

**culture of honour** a culture in which strong norms suggest that aggression is an appropriate response to an insult or threat to one's honour (p. 206)



**debriefing** a procedure that involves giving participants a full explanation of the hypothesis being tested, procedures used to deceive participants, and the reasons for the deception (p. 35)

**deception** providing participants with false or incomplete information (p. 34)

**decision model of bystander intervention** the model derived by Bibb Latane and John Darley that explains the five steps required to provide help to someone in need and what can interfere with successful completion of each of these steps (p. 261)

**deindividuation** the tendency for an individual within a group to let go of self-awareness and restraint and do what the group is doing (p. 163)

**dependent variable** the variable an experimenter does not control that is used to measure whether the change in the independent variable has an effect (p. 30)

**descriptive norms** how people typically behave in a given group or situation (p. 142)

**descriptive research** research used to obtain information regarding the current status of a population or phenomena to describe the who, what, when, where, and how questions with respect to variables or conditions in a situation (p. 26)

**desensitization** a process through which physiological reactions to violence are reduced as a result of repeated exposure (p. 217)

**differential construal** the act of judging circumstances differently (p. 9)

**diffusion of responsibility** a decreased feeling of responsibility to help in a group; if an emergency arises in a group setting, it is less likely that any one person will help than if someone was witnessing the emergency alone, because being in a group decreases each person's feeling of personal responsibility to help (p. 261)

**direct aggression** an action or a behaviour that is clearly derived from the aggressor and is aimed directly at the target (p. 205)

**discrimination** a behaviour directed toward a group of people based solely on their membership in that group (p. 178)

**dismissive attachment style** a conflicted, insecure attachment style characterized by high self-esteem and low interpersonal trust (p. 233)

**dispositional attribution** inferring that a person's traits, something internal, caused his or her behaviour (p. 82)

**distraction conflict theory** the idea that a person performing a task in front of others experiences a conflict of attention between the audience and the task at hand, thus increasing the motivation to succeed when completing simple tasks (p. 160)

**door-in-the-face technique** a persuasive compliance in which the requester makes an initial offer that is much larger than the target offer, in the hope that the final offer will have the appearance of the requester doing a favour for the target person (p. 149)

**double-blind study** a study in which neither the experimenter nor the participant knows which group is experimental and which is control (p. 34)

**downward social comparison** the process of comparing yourself to someone who is less capable or worse off than you are (p. 71)

**egoistic** having a selfish motivation for helping (p. 254)

**Elaboration Likelihood Model (ELM)** a model of persuasion that proposes that there are two different routes, central and peripheral, that an individual may take when processing a message. The route is impacted by cognitive capacity and individual differences of the perceiver (p. 120)

**empathy** having compassion for others and a feeling of seeing the world through the eyes of another individual (p. 254)

**empathy-altruism model of prosocial behaviour** a model which suggests that true altruism is a product of empathy; this empathy can create nurturing feelings toward a target or a goal to increase the target's welfare (p. 256)

**enlightenment effect** the effect wherein learning about how humans fall prey to obstacles to helping can aid us in overcoming those obstacles in the future; it extends to benefits from learning about other human biases as well (p. 269)

**equity theory** a theory that relationships are most satisfying when the ratio between benefits and contributions is similar for both partners (p. 242)

**evaluation apprehension** the idea that one's performance will be hindered or heightened due to approval or disapproval from others (p. 160)

**evolutionary perspective** a perspective that focuses on the physical and biological predispositions that result in human survival (p. 6)

**exchange relationship** a relationship in which partners expect strict reciprocity (p. 242)

**excitation transfer** the process by which arousal from one stimulus can be transferred to the second stimulus, a person (p. 238)

**experimental group** in an experiment, the group that gets the main treatment or manipulation (p. 31)

**experimental research** research that attempts to control all the factors (like a potential third variable) that may affect the results of an experiment (p. 30)

**experimenter bias** bias exhibited by the experiment administrator in inadvertently but subtly changing his behaviour toward participants because of knowledge of which group is control and which group is experimental; this also occurs when the researcher subconsciously shows bias in his or her evaluation of results in an effort to reach the desired conclusion (p. 34)

**explicit attitudes** attitudes of which one is aware, and that one can control (p. 98)

**expressive view of aggression** a view of aggression as a way to express anger and reduce stress (p. 206)

**external validity** the extent to which results apply to a general population (p. 31)

**extrinsic motivation** the drive to perform an action in response to an external pressure or obligation, to avoid punishment, or to achieve some outside benefit (p. 66)

**facial feedback hypothesis** a hypothesis that states that a change in our facial expressions can lead to a subsequent emotional change (p. 65)

**false consensus effect** a phenomenon that causes individuals to assume that everyone shares the same opinion they do (p. 9)

**fear-based appeal** an attempt to provoke fear in the audience in order to persuade them not to do something (p. 121)

**fearful-avoidant attachment style** the most insecure of the attachment styles, characterized by low self-esteem and low interpersonal trust (p. 231)

**field studies** studies involving data or information that is collected in naturally occurring settings (p. 27)

**foot-in-the-door technique** a compliance technique that begins with a small request that, when granted, leads to a larger request (p. 149)

**forewarning** the process of being informed ahead of time that a favoured attitude will be challenged (p. 121)

**framing heuristic** a rule that guides decision making based on the framework in which a situation or item is presented (p. 50)

**frustration** a feeling of being upset or annoyed by the inability to reach a goal or perform an activity (p. 209)

**frustration aggression theory** a theory which states that frustration precedes aggression because our motivation for aggression increases when our current behaviour is interrupted or we are prevented from reaching a goal (p. 209)

**fundamental attribution error** a more commonly known name for the correspondence bias. The scientific community now leans toward using "correspondence bias" so as not to suggest that these inferences are inherently in "error" (p. 83)

**gender prejudice** the tendency to hold a hostile attitude toward an individual because of his or her gender (p. 181)

**gender stereotypes** people's ideas about how men and women behave based on socially and culturally defined beliefs (p. 181)

**General Aggression Model (GAM)** a theory that builds on the social learning theory and provides a more integrative framework for specific theories of aggression by including situational and personal variables (p. 211)

**GRIT** "graduated and reciprocated initiatives in tension reduction," a step-by-step formula for de-escalating a conflict that involves unilateral concessions and quick reciprocation by the opposition (p. 171)

**group** two or more people who are seen as a unit and interact with one another (p. 158)

**group norms** rules or expectations regarding desirable behaviours that group members strive to follow (p. 166)

**group polarization** the tendency for an attitude or belief to become magnified within a group after members discuss an issue among themselves (p. 165)

**groupthink** a manner of thinking that happens when the desire for harmony in a decision-making group overrides a realistic evaluation of other solutions (p. 166)

**halo effect** when one positive thing is known or believed about a target person, we tend to infer that the individual is positive overall and thus has other positive features (p. 89)

**heuristics** simple rules that reduce mental effort and allow us to make decisions or judgments quickly (p. 46)

**hindsight bias** the tendency to think that one knew that something would occur all along (p. 9)

**hostile (affective) aggression** behaviour that occurs when the primary goal of an action is to make the victim suffer (p. 204)

**hostile attribution bias** bias that occurs when people assume that the intentions of another person are hostile (p. 169)

**hypothesis** a proposed explanation that can be either supported or disproven with statistics or observations (p. 23)

**illusion of control** the perception of uncontrollable events as being controllable (p. 51)

**Implicit Association Test (IAT)** a test that measures how easily we associate categories with positive or negative attitudes, including measures in categories ranging from racial and religious attitudes to attitudes about presidents. See implicit.harvard.edu/implicit/demo/. (p. 102)

**implicit attitudes** attitudes that are automatically formed and activated without our even being aware of it (p. 98)

**impression management** the process by which people either consciously or unconsciously attempt to monitor how they appear to others by regulating the information conveyed about themselves in a social interaction, and thus attitude change is more likely when counter-attitudinal behaviour occurs in public (p. 110)

**independent variable** the variable an experimenter has control over and can alter (p. 30)

**indirect aggression** an action or a behaviour that is not clearly derived from the aggressor, and where it is not obvious to the target that he or she has been the victim of aggression (p. 205)

**individualism** at the cultural level, a focus on the self as independent from others and a valuing of individual goals over the collective (p. 63)

**informational social influence** a type of influence that occurs when one turns to members of one's group to obtain accurate information (p. 145)

**informed consent** consent given when subjects are told at the beginning of a study as much information as possible about the participation in the study to determine if they would like to be involved (p. 35)

**ingratiation** a way of controlling others' impressions of us through flattery (p. 71)

**ingratiation techniques** techniques in which we get others to like us so they are more likely to comply with a request (p. 149)

**ingroup favouritism** the natural tendency to favour an ingroup versus an outgroup (p. 186)

**injunctive norms** behaviours of which people typically *approve* or *disapprove* in a given group or situation (p. 143)

**inoculation** the process of building up resistance to unwanted persuasion (p. 130)

**instinct theory** a theory in which aggression is an innate and inevitable force (p. 207)

**instrumental aggression** behaviour that occurs when the primary goal of an action is not to make the victim suffer but to attain a non-injurious goal (p. 204)

**instrumental view of aggression** a view of aggression as a way to gain social or material rewards (p. 206)

**internal validity** the ability to infer cause and effect; that the variable was manipulated was the only factor to change across conditions and so was what led to the observed effect (p. 31)

**interpersonal trust** the belief that people are generally trustworthy and dependable as opposed to the opposite and the attitude that underlies the development of attachment styles (p. 231)

**intrinsic motivation** the drive to perform an action because we enjoy it and are likely to engage in it more fully and with greater curiosity and pleasure (p. 66)

**introspection** the process of thinking about your own thoughts (p. 64)

**investment** resources that have been devoted to a relationship that cannot be retrieved (p. 242)



**jigsaw classroom technique** a teaching method that focuses on small-group activities and fosters a cooperative rather than competitive environment (p. 192)

**just-world hypothesis** the perception that people get what they deserve, based on the belief that the world is a fair and just place (p. 268)

**kin selection** the tendency of people to help their biological relatives over nonfamily members, even at great cost to themselves, thus favouring the reproductive success of one's relatives over his or her own survival (p. 258)

**limbic system** the area of the brain thought to be crucial to emotional processing and memory (p. 45)

**lowball technique** a compliance technique in which a target accepts a "low-cost" offer, only then to be told that there are additional hidden costs (p. 149)

**matched samples design** a research design in which two or more groups of individuals are identical, or matching, in terms of the third variable (p. 29)

**matching hypothesis** the hypothesis that people are more likely to form longstanding relationships with others whose social attributes match with theirs and with those who are similar in physical attractiveness (p. 237)

**mere exposure effect** the phenomenon whereby objects become better liked with exposure—we like things as they become more familiar to us (p. 100)

**mere exposure** the hypothesis that the mere repeated exposure of an individual to a stimulus is enough for an increase in favourable response to that stimulus (p. 234)

**microexpressions** involuntary expressions of facial emotion that only last a fraction of a second (p. 80)

**minority influence** a process in which a small number of people within a group guide a change in the group's attitude or behaviour (p. 148)

**modelling** a process in which one person engages in behaviour that is mimicked by another person (p. 210)

**modern (or covert) racism** negative feelings toward a group of people based on their race, manifested in more subtle forms of racism (p. 184)

**modern sexism** internalized negative feelings toward a group of people based on their gender, characterized by a denial of continued discrimination, antagonism toward women's demands, and lack of support for policies designed to help women in work and education (p. 184)

**mood congruence effect** the fact that we are more likely to remember positive information when in a positive mood, and negative information when in a negative mood (p. 53)

**mood-dependent memory** the fact that the mood that we are in when we learn information may serve as a retrieval cue when we try to remember that information (p. 54)

**name-letter effect** the tendency to show a preference for letters in our own name and prefer stimuli that contain those letters (p. 101)

**natural selection** the process whereby individuals with certain characteristics are more frequently represented in subsequent generations as the result of being better adapted for their environment (p. 6)

**naturalistic observation** research that involves watching behaviour in a real-world setting (p. 27)

**need for affiliation** the desire to establish and maintain rewarding interpersonal relationships (p. 230)

**need for cognition** the need that some individuals have to think, solve problems, and understand their world accurately (p. 85)

**negative attributional style** a style that occurs when a person explains his or her partner's behaviours in negative ways (p. 244)

**negative state relief model** a model which posits that the reason people help others is to improve their own negative mood (p. 254)

**negativity bias** the tendency for people to be more sensitive to and more likely to notice and remember negative information, which then influences the evaluation of people and situations (p. 51)

**nonverbal cues** behaviours, gestures, and expressions that convey thought or emotion without words (p. 78)

**normative social influence** a type of influence that occurs when one goes along with a group because one wants to be accepted (p. 145)

**obedience** a form of social influence in which an individual orders another person to do something (p. 150)

**observational learning** acquiring an attitude or behaviour due to the observation of others exhibiting that attitude or behaviour (p. 101)

**old-fashioned (or overt) racism** overt, oppressive acts and feelings toward a group of people based on their race (p. 184)

**old-fashioned sexism** overt sexism, characterized by the endorsement of traditional gender roles, differential treatment of men and women, and stereotypes about lesser female competence (p. 184)

**operant conditioning** a type of learning in which the frequency of a behaviour is determined by reinforcement and punishment (p. 101)

**operational definition** a definition that assigns one or more specific operational conditions to an event and then identifies how those conditions should be measured (p. 23)

**optimistic bias** the belief that bad things will happen to other people and that an individual is more likely to experience good things in life (p. 52)

**outcome-relevant involvement** the degree to which the economic or social outcome promoted in the message is important to the receiver (p. 123)

**outgroup homogeneity effect** the tendency to see outgroup members as similar to one another but ingroup members as diverse individuals (p. 186)

**overconfidence barrier** a state of having more confidence in one's judgment or control over a situation than is really justified (p. 52)

**participant bias** bias that occurs when a participant's suspicions, expectations, or assumptions about the study influence the result (p. 33)

**passionate love** a state of intense longing for union with another (p. 238)

**peer review** a process by which experts in the field review and comment on each other's work (p. 23)

**peripheral route** a type of processing that occurs when an individual lacks the ability and motivation to thoroughly listen to and evaluate a persuasive message, and is therefore influenced by external cues such as attractiveness of the speaker (p. 118)

**perseverance effect** the tendency for a schema to remain intact, even when it comes up against discrediting information (p. 43)

**persuasion** the way people communicate in order to influence other people's attitudes and behaviours (p. 118)

**placebo effect** a measurable or observable improvement in health or behaviour that is not attributed to medication or any other treatment given (p. 34)

**pluralistic ignorance** a type of norm misperception that occurs when each individual in a group privately rejects the norms of the group, but believes that others accept them (p. 143)

**post-decision dissonance** cognitive dissonance that results from having to reject one appealing choice in favour of another (p. 109)

**prefrontal cortex** the part of the brain that plays a role in higher-order thinking, including judgment, decision making, and evaluation (p. 45)

**prejudice** a negative learned attitude toward particular groups of people (p. 178)

**preoccupied attachment style** a conflicted, insecure attachment style characterized by low self-esteem and high interpersonal trust (p. 232)

**primacy effect** the phenomenon whereby the first pieces of information to which we are exposed have the most impact on our judgments (p. 87)

**prime** to activate a schema through a stimulus (p. 42)

**private conformity** a type of conformity that occurs when people truly believe the group is right; occurs even in the absence of group members (p. 145)

**proportion of similarity** an equation that divides the number of topics on which two people express similar views by the total number of topics on which they have communicated, resulting in a prediction of attraction (p. 237)

**prosocial behaviour** behaviour designed to help another person (p. 254)

**proximity** physical closeness; the smaller the physical distance, the more likely the two people will experience repeat contact, which could lead to the development of mutual attraction (p. 234)

**public conformity** a type of conformity that occurs when we feel pressured to conform to group norms. When publicly conforming, people pretend to agree with the group, but privately think the group is wrong (p. 145)

**racial prejudice** the tendency to hold a hostile attitude toward an individual because of his or her racial background (p. 181)

**racism** an institutional practice that discriminates against individuals on the basis of their race (p. 180)

**random assignment** a required technique in an experiment to be able to infer cause and effect; every participant has any equal chance of being assigned to any group in the experiment (p. 31)

**reactance** the instinctive reaction of individuals to preserve their freedom when they feel it is threatened (p. 129)

**realistic group conflict** the theory that conflict stems from competition for limited resources such as money, land, power or other resources (p. 168)

**realistic group conflict theory** the idea that when different groups are in competition for resources, they tend to close ranks, favouring ingroup members and discriminating against outgroup members (p. 187)

**recency effect** the phenomenon whereby the last pieces of information to which we are exposed have heightened impact on our judgments, relative to information received in the middle (p. 87)

**reciprocal altruism** the belief that helping others increases the likelihood that others will help us or our kin in return (p. 258)

**reciprocity** the exchange of what we receive for what we get, which can include liking those who like us back (p. 237)

**reciprocity norm** the idea that if others help us, we should help them, and that if we help them, they will help us (p. 257)

**reinforcement** an action or a process that strengthens a behaviour (p. 210)

**relative deprivation** discontent caused by the belief that we might fare badly in comparison with people in other groups (p. 187)

**reliable** consistent measurement (p. 24)

**replication** repeating a study to verify effects, usually with a different sample of participants (p. 24)

**representativeness heuristic** a rule used to estimate the likelihood of an event based on how well it fits with your expectations of a model for that event (p. 48)

**repulsion hypothesis** a hypothesis which states that similarity doesn't actually have any effect on attraction (p. 237)

**research ethics board (REB)** a committee that has been established to approve and oversee research that involves human and nonhuman animal subjects (p. 35)

**research question** the query that is the first step in the research process (p. 23)

**risky shift** the tendency for people in groups to take greater risks than if the actions were to be taken by individual members alone (p. 164)

**sample** selection of who or what will be tested in the research process (p. 24)

**schema** an automatically created cognitive framework that helps guide the way we think about and understand the society around us (p. 42)

**scientific method** an approach to thinking that involves using systematic observations, measurements, and experiments to assess information (p. 25)

**secure attachment style** the most successful of the attachment styles, characterized by high self-esteem and high interpersonal trust (p. 231)

**selective filtering** paying more attention to sensory information that fits a given schema, at the same time filtering out information that is inconsistent (p. 44)

**self-affirmation theory** the theory that we are more open to attitudinal change when we have recently been given an opportunity to affirm our core values and identity (p. 110)

**self-awareness** when attention is brought about on the self; for example, looking in a mirror, standing in front of a crowd, and listening to a recording of your voice (p. 65)

**self-concept** your mental representation or overall sense of "you" (p. 60)

**self-discrepancy theory** a theory in which our concepts of self are influenced by how close our actual selves are to the selves we would like to be (p. 64)

**self-efficacy** a person's belief in his or her ability to achieve certain goals (p. 60)

**self-esteem** a person's evaluation of his or her self-worth (p. 66)

**self-fulfilling prophecy** a prediction that causes itself to come true (p. 44)

**self-fulfilling prophecy** expecting that something will happen and acting in ways that may unintentionally elicit exactly what we expected (p. 90)

**self-handicapping** a process that involves setting up an obstacle before engaging in a task as a way to give ourselves a ready-made excuse in case we don't perform well (p. 71)

**self-monitoring** the process through which people regulate their behaviour to be perceived well by others; low self-monitors act consistently across situations, acting according to their personal views, while high self-monitors are constantly monitoring their behaviour and adjusting their reactions to fit the situation they are in (p. 72)

**self-perception theory** a theory in which, if we are unsure of the attitudes we hold, we look to our behaviour and use that to make inferences about our attitudes, much like an outside observer (p. 65)

**self-report/survey method** a form of data collection in which participants are asked to rate or describe their own behaviour or mental state (p. 27)

**self-schema** beliefs about aspects of your identity that organize the processing of information related to the self (p. 60)

**self-serving attribution** a self-protection strategy in which we are likely to believe that external factors are responsible for situations in which we perform poorly (p. 69)

**self-verification** the motivation of an individual for others to know him or her accurately, including his or her negative features (p. 81)

**self-verification theory** a theory wherein we want others to see us as we see ourselves—even when our self-concepts are negative (p. 72)

**sexism** an institutional practice that discriminates against individuals on the basis of their gender (p. 180)

**single-blind study** study in which two groups of participants are not told whether they are given the real treatment or the placebo and, therefore, do not know in which group they are (p. 34)

**situational attribution** inferring that the situation a person is in—something external to the person—caused his or her behaviour (p. 82)

**sleeper effect** the effect whereby the persuasive impact of a non-credible source increases over time; we remember the message but forget the criticisms of it (p. 120)

**social categorization** the process of dividing people into categories according to their race, gender, and other common attributes (p. 185)

**social cognitive perspective** a perspective that builds on behavioural theories and demonstrates that an individual's cognitive process influences and is influenced by behavioural associations (p. 6)

**social comparison theory** a theory wherein we compare ourselves to others in different situations because there is no given standard against which to measure our abilities and opinions (p. 70)

**social decision schemes** rules that guide how the initial distribution of views of each group member influences the final group decision (p. 164)

**social dominance orientation** seeing one's own group as naturally superior to other groups (p. 186)

**social exchange theory** an economic model of human behaviour in which people make decisions based on maximizing benefits and minimizing costs in relationships (p. 242)

**social facilitation** the enhancement of a well-learned performance when another person is present (p. 11)

**social identity theory** a theory in which we develop our identity from our group memberships (p. 62)

**social impact theory** a theory which suggests that social influence depends on the strength, immediacy, and number of source persons relative to the target person(s) (p. 146)

**social influence** the process through which other people affect an individual's thoughts or actions (p. 4)

**social interaction** relationships between two or more individuals that affect our perceptions of others and our behaviours (p. 4)

**social learning perspective** a perspective that stresses the particular power of learning through social reinforcements and punishments (p. 6)

**social learning theory** a theory that suggests that human aggression is largely learned by observing the aggressive behaviour of other people and is reinforced by consequences such as punishment or reward in the individual's environment (p. 210)

**social loafing** occurs when individuals make less of an effort when attempting to achieve a particular goal as a group than they would if they were attempting to achieve the goal on their own (p. 11)

**social norms** patterns of behaviour that are accepted as normal, and to which an individual is expected to conform, in a particular group or culture (p. 142)

**social perception** the process through which individuals form impressions of others and interpret information about them (p. 4)

**social psychology** the scientific study of the nature and causes of individual behaviour and thought in social situations (p. 4)

**social responsibility norm** the idea that we have social responsibility to help others; the extent to which this extends to outgroup members varies by culture (p. 257)

**social role** expectations for the ways in which an individual should behave in a given situation (p. 140)

**sociocultural perspective** a perspective that focuses on the relationship between social behaviour and culture (p. 6)

**source** the person or persons who deliver the message (p. 120)

**spontaneous trait inference** the process of automatically inferring traits from another person's behaviour (p. 83)

**spotlight effect** the belief that our behaviour, our appearance, and even our internal states are obvious to others (p. 72)

**stereotype** a type of schema in which we apply generalized information to an individual based on the group to which he or she belongs (p. 43)

**stereotype threat** fear or anxiety held by people in minority groups that they might conform to a negative cultural stereotype (p. 189)

**symbolic social influence** a type of influence that occurs when we change our behaviour according to the mental representation of others and our relationships with them (p. 144)

**that's-not-all technique** a compliance technique in which an initial request is followed by adding something that makes the offer more attractive (p. 150)

**theory** a general framework for understanding a concept that allows us to describe, explain, and predict behaviour (p. 22)

**theory of planned behaviour** the theory that attitudes, social norms, and the perceived control of an individual lead to behaviour (p. 105)

**third variable** any additional factor that could be responsible for an observed effect (p. 29)

**three-stage model of attribution** a model in which an observer automatically characterizes a behaviour, automatically makes a dispositional inference, and then uses conscious effort to correct for situational constraints if the observer has the cognitive capacity to do so (p. 85)

**transactional leader** a leader who believes in a ladder of authority and considers people on lower rungs to be subordinates and therefore required to follow the instructions set forth by their manager; this type of leader rewards good work and works efficiently to solve problems (p. 166)

**transformational leader** a leader who believes in inspiring his followers with energy and devotion, thereby transforming the group and its members (p. 166)

**triangular theory of love** Robert Sternberg's theory that love is made of three components: intimacy, passion, and commitment (p. 239)

**ultimate attribution error** the tendency to explain the behaviour of groups in terms of internal dispositional factors, without taking the situational constraints into consideration (p. 186)

**unconditioned response (UCR)** a response that occurs automatically in reaction to some stimulus, without learning taking place (p. 100)

**unconditioned stimulus (UCS)** a stimulus that elicits a response automatically, without learning taking place (p. 100)

**unrealistic optimism** optimism that occurs when we tend to imagine that the outcomes of situations will be better for us than for other people (p. 70)

**valence** the degree of attraction or aversion that a person feels toward a specific object, event, or idea (p. 121)

**valid** when a variable measures what it is supposed to measure (p. 24)

**variables** stimuli or characteristics that can take on different values, such as level of attraction or age (p. 23)

**what is beautiful is good effect** the phenomenon wherein beautiful things are imbued with positivity and activate positive things in the mind (p. 88)

# REFERENCES


A spirit no one can extinguish. (2011, May 17). *Edmonton Sun*. Retrieved November 12, 2011, from http://www.edmontonsun.com/2011/05/16/a-spirit-no-one-can-extinguish

A tale of two riots: Comparing the 1994 and 2011 Stanley Cup riots in Vancouver. (2011, June 16). *CBC News*. Retrieved August 12, 2011, from http://www.cbc.ca/news/canada/story/2011/06/16/f-vancouver-riot-1994-2011.html

A timeline of residential schools, the Truth and Reconciliation Commission. (2008, May 16). *CBC News*. Retrieved October 25, 2011, from http://www.cbc.ca/news/canada/story/2008/05/16/f-timeline-residential-schools.html

Aberson, C. L., Healy, M. R., & Romero, V. L. (2000). Ingroup bias and self-esteem: A meta-analysis. *Personality and Social Psychology Review, 4*, 157–173.

Aboud, F. E., & Doyle, A. B. (1996). Does talk of race foster prejudice or tolerance in children? *Canadian Journal of Behavioural Science, 28*, 161–170.

Aboud, F. E., (2003). The formation of in-group favoritism and out-group prejudice in young children: Are they distinct attitudes? *Developmental Psychology, 39*, 48–60.

Abramowitz, M. (1992, June 16). Bulls' NBA victory sparks Chicago riots. *The Washington Post*. Retrieved November 30, 2010, from http://www.washingtonpost.com/wpsrv/sports/nba/longterm/jordan/articles/riot92.htm

Acevedo, B. P., & Aron, A. (2009). Does a long-term relationship kill romantic love? *Review of General Psychology, 13*, 59–65.

Adolphs, R. (2003). Cognitive neuroscience of human social behaviour. *Nature Neuroscience, 4*, 165–178.

Adorno, T.W., Frenkel-Brunswik, E., Levinson, D. J., & Sanford, R. N. (1950). *The authoritarian personality*. New York: Harper and Row.

Aggarwal, P., & O'Brien, C. (2009). Social loafing on group projects: Structural antecedents and effect on student satisfaction. *Journal of Marketing Education, 31*, 76–85.

Ainsworth, M. D. S., Blehar, M. C., Waters, E., & Wall, S. (1978). *Patterns of attachment: A psychological study of the strange situation*. Hillsdale, NJ: Lawrence Erlbaum.

Ajzen, I., & Fishbein, M. (1977). Attitude–behavior relations: A theoretical analysis and review of empirical research. *Psychological Bulletin, 84*, 888–918.

Ajzen, I., & Fishbein, M. (Eds.). (1980). *Understanding attitudes and predicting social behaviour*. New Jersey: Prentice-Hall.

Allen, T. J., Sherman, J. W., Conrey, F. R., & Stroessner, S. J. (2009). Stereotype strength and attentional bias: Preference for confirming versus disconfirming information depends on processing capacity. *Journal of Experimental Social Psychology, 45*, 1081–1087.

Allen, V., & Levine, J. (1969). Consensus and conformity. *Journal of Experimental Social Psychology, 5*(Fall), 389–399.

Allen, V., & Levine, J. (1971). Social support and conformity: The role of independent assessment of reality. *Journal of Experimental Social Psychology, 7*, 48–58.

Alloy, L. B., & Clements, C. M. (1992). Illusion of control: Invulnerability to negative affect and depressive symptoms after laboratory and natural stressors. *Journal of Abnormal Psychology, 101*, 234–245.

Allport, G. W. (1954). *The nature of prejudice*. Reading, MA: Addison-Wesley.

Amabile, T. M., Hennessey, B. A., & Grossman, B. S. (1986). Social influences on creativity: The effects of contracted-for reward. *Journal of Personality and Social Psychology, 50*, 14–23.

Ambady, N., & Skowronski, J. J. (Eds.) (2008). *First impressions*. New York: Guilford Press.

American Civil Liberties Union. (1990). Uniform crime reports. *ACLU*. Retrieved August 8, 2010, from http://www.aclu.org/capital-punishment/case-against-death-penalty#5

Ames, D., Flynn, F. J., & Weber, E. (2004). It's the thought that counts: On perceiving how helpers decide to lend a hand. *Personality and Social Psychology Bulletin, 30*, 461–474.

Amnesty USA. (2010). *Amnesty USA*. Retrieved August 7, 2010, from http://amnestyusa.org

An, K., Hui, M. K., Leung, K. (2001). Who should be responsible? Effects of voice and compensation on responsibility attribution, perceived justice, and post-complaint behaviors across cultures. *International Journal of Conflict Management, 12*, 350–364.

Andersen, S. M., & Berk, M. S. (1998). The social-cognitive model of transference: Experiencing past relationships in the present. *Current Directions in Psychological Science, 7*, 109–115.

Andersen, S. M., & Chen, S. (2002). The relational self: An interpersonal social-cognitive theory. *Psychological Review, 109*, 619–645.

Anderson, C. A., & Carnagey, N. L. (2004). Violent evil and the general aggression model. In A. G. Miller (Ed.), *The social psychology of good and evil* (pp. 169–192). New York: Guilford Press.

Anderson, C. A., & Huesmann, L. R. (2003). Human aggression: A social-cognitive view (pp. 296–323). In M.A. Hogg & J. Cooper (Eds.) *The Handbook of Social Psychology, Revised Edition*. London: Sage Publications. (2007). Reprinted in M. A. Hogg & J. Cooper (Eds.) (pp. 259–287). The Sage Handbook of Social Psychology, London: Sage Publications.

Anderson, C. A., & Huesmann, L. R. (2003). Human aggression: A social-cognitive view. In M. A. Hogg & J. Cooper (Eds.), *The SAGE handbook of social psychology* (pp. 296–324). London: SAGE Publications Ltd.

Anderson, C. A., Benjamin, A. J., Jr., & Bartholow, B. D. (1998). Does the gun pull the trigger? Automatic priming effects of weapon pictures and weapon names. *Psychological Science, 9*, 308–314.

Anderson, C. A., Bushman, B. J., & Groom, R. W. (1997). Hot years and serious and deadly assault: Empirical test of the heat hypothesis. *Journal of Personality and Social Psychology, 73*, 1213–1223.

Anderson, C. A., Deuser, W. E., & DeNeve, K. (1995). Hot temperatures, hostile affect, hostile cognition, and arousal: Tests of a general model of affective aggression. *Personality and Social Psychology Bulletin, 21*, 434–448.

Anderson, C. A., Gentile, D. A., & Buckley, K. E. (2007). *Violent video game effects on children and adolescents: Theory, research, and public policy*. New York: Oxford University Press.

Anderson, C. A., Shibuya, A., Ihori, N., Swing, E. L., Bushman, B. J., Sakamoto, A., . . . Saleem, M. (2010). Violent video game effects on aggression, empathy, and prosocial behavior in Eastern and Western countries: A meta-analytic review. *Psychological Bulletin, 136*, 151–173.

Anderson, C. A. (1997). Effects of violent movies and trait hostility on hostile feelings and aggressive thoughts. *Aggressive Behavior, 23*, 161–178.

Anderson, J. R., & Gallup, G. G., Jr. (1999). Self-recognition in nonhuman primates: Past and future challenges. In M. Haug & R. E. Whalen (Eds.), *Animal models of human emotion and cognition* (pp. 175–194). Washington, DC: American Psychological Association.

Anthony, D. B., Holmes, J. G., & Wood, J. V. (2007). Social acceptance and self-esteem: Tuning the sociometer to interpersonal value. *Journal of Personality and Social Psychology, 92*, 1024–1039.

Antonio, A. L., Chang, M. J., Hakuta, K., Kenny, D. A., Levin, S., & Milem, J. F. (2004). Effects of racial diversity on complex thinking in college students. *Psychological Science, 15*, 507–510.

Apanovitch, A. M., McCarthy, D., & Salovey, P. (2003). Using message framing to motivate HIV testing among low-income ethnic minority women. *Health Psychology, 22*, 60–67.

Appelbaum, S. H., & Hughes, B. (1998). Ingratiation as a political tactic: Effects within the organization. *Management Decision, 36*, 85–95.

Apple co-founder Steve Jobs dies at 56. (2011, October 5). *CBC News*. Retrieved October 17, 2011, from http://www.cbc.ca/news/canada/story/2011/10/05/apple-jobs-death.html

Archer, J. (2004). Sex differences in aggression in real-world settings: A meta-analytic review. *Review of General Psychology, 8*, 291–322.

Archer, R. L., & Burleson, J. A. (1980). The effects of timing of self-disclosure on attraction and reciprocity. *Journal of Personality and Social Psychology, 38*, 120–130.

Are magnet schools perpetuating segregation? (2011, August 1). *The Huffington Post*. Retrieved October 26, 2011, from http://www.huffingtonpost.com/2011/06/01/school-segregation_n_860857.html

Argyle, M. (1987). *The psychology of happiness*. London: Methuen.

Aries, E., & Johnson, F. (1983). Close friendship in adulthood: Conversational content between same-sex friends. *Sex Roles, 9*, 83–96.

Armor, D. A., & Taylor, S. E. (2002). When predictions fail: The dilemma of unrealistic optimism. In T. Gilovich, D. Griffin, & D. Kahneman (Eds.), *Heuristics and Biases: The Psychology of Intuitive Judgment*. Cambridge, UK: Cambridge University Press.

Arndt, J., Schimel, J., Greenberg, J., & Pyszczynski, T. (2002). The intrinsic self and defensiveness: Evidence that activating the intrinsic self reduces self-handicapping and conformity. *Personality and Social Psychology Bulletin, 28*, 671–683.

Aron, A., Dutton, D. G., Aron, E. N., & Iverson, A. (1989). Experiences of falling in love. *Journal of Social and Personal Relationships, 6*, 243–257.

Aronson, E., Blaney, N., Stephan, C., Sikes, J., & Snapp, M. (1978). *The jigsaw classroom*. Beverly Hills, CA: Sage.

Asch, S. E. (1946). Forming impressions of personality. *Journal of Abnormal and Social Psychology, 41*, 258–290.

Asch, S. E. (1951). Effects of group pressure upon the modification and distortion of judgments. In H. Guetzkow (Ed.), *Groups, leadership, and men*. Pittsburgh, PA: Carnegie Press.

Asch, S. E. (1955). Opinions and social pressure. *Scientific American, 193*, 31–35.

Asch, S. E. (1956). Studies of independence and conformity: A minority of one against a unanimous majority. *Psychological Monographs*, 70.

Ash, M. G. (1992). *Kurt Lewin: Person, werk, umfeld*. Frankfurt: Peter Lang.

Ask, K., & Landström, S. (2010). Why emotions matter: Expectancy violation and affective response mediate the emotional victim effect. *Law and Human Behavior, 34*, 392–401.

Aspinwall, L.G., & Taylor, S. E. (1993). Effects of social comparison direction, threat, and self-esteem on affect, self-evaluation, and expected success. *Journal of Personality and Social Psychology, 64*, 708–722.

Assh, S. D., & Byers, E. S. (1990). Effects of behavioural exchanges and cognitions on the relationship satisfaction of dating and married persons. *Canadian Journal of Behavioural Science, 22*, 223–235.

Astin, A. W. (1998). The changing American college student: Thirty-year trends, 1966–1996. *Review of Higher Education, 21*, 115–135.

Aube, J., & Koestner, R. (1995). Gender characteristics and relationship adjustment: Another look at similarity-complementary hypothesis. *Journal of Personality, 63*, 879–903.

Avert. (2010). AIDS statistics. *Avert*. Retrieved October 11, 2010, from http://www.avert.org/usa-statistics.htm

Axsom, D., & Cooper, J. (1985). Cognitive dissonance and psychotherapy: The role of effort justification in inducing weight loss. *Journal of Experimental Social Psychology, 21*, 149–160.

Ayres, I. (1991). Fair driving: Gender and race discrimination in retail car negotiations. *Harvard Law Review, 104*, 817–872.

B.C. health-care worker wins gender discrimination suit. (2009, September 9). *CBC News*. Retrieved November 4, 2011, from http://www.cbc.ca/news/canada/british-columbia/story/2009/09/09/bc-nelson-care-aide-gender-discrimination.html

Baccus, J. R., Baldwin, M. W., & Packer, D. J. (2004). Increasing implicit self-esteem through classical conditioning. *Psychological Science, 15*, 498–502.

Back, M. D., Schmukle, S. C., & Egloff, B. (2008). Becoming friends by chance. *Psychological Science: A Journal of the American Psychological Society, 19*, 439–440.

Baddeley, A., Eysenck, M. W., & Anderson, M. C. (2009). *Memory*. New York: Psychology Press.

Bagby, R. M., Parker, J. D., Rector, N. A., & Kalemba, V. (1994). Racial prejudice in the Canadian legal system: Juror decisions in a simulated rape trial. *Law and Human Behavior, 18*, 339–350.

Bailey, D. S., & Taylor, S. P. (1991). Effects of alcohol and aggressive disposition on human physical aggression. *Journal of Research in Personality, 25*, 334–342.

Bailey, R. (2006, August 11). Don't be terrorized: You're more likely to die of a car accident, drowning, fire, or murder. *Reason.com*. Retrieved November 30, 2010, from http://reason.com/archives/2006/08/11/dont-be-terrorized

Baillargeon, R. H., Zoccolillo, M., Keenan, K., Côté, S., Pérusse, D., Wu, H. X., . . . Tremblay, R. E. (2007). Gender differences in physical aggression: A prospective population-based survey of children before and after 2 years of age. *Developmental Psychology, 43*, 13–26.

Baker-Knight, T. (1975). Don't all the girls get prettier at closing time. [Recorded by Mickey Gilley]. On *The Best of Mickey Gilley, Vol. 2*. BMI.

Baldwin, M. W., & Fehr, B. (1995). On the instability of attachment style ratings. *Personal Relationships, 2*, 247–261.

Baldwin, M. W., & Sinclair, L. (1996). Self-esteem and "if . . . then" contingencies of interpersonal acceptance. *Journal of Personality and Social Psychology, 71*, 1130–1141.

Baldwin, M. W., Granzberg, A., Pippus, L., & Pritchard, E. T. (2003). Cued activation of relational schemas: Self-evaluation and gender effects. *Canadian Journal of Behavioural Science, 35*, 153–163.

Baldwin, M. W., Keelan, J. P. R., Fehr, B., Enns,V., & Koh-Rangarajoo, E. (1996). Social cognitive conceptualization of attachment styles: Availability and accessibility effects. *Journal of Personality and Social Psychology, 71*, 94–109.

Balsam, K. F., Beauchaine, T. P., Rothblum, E. D., & Solomon, S. E. (2008). Three-year follow-up of same-sex couples who had civil unions in Vermont, same-sex couples not in civil unions, and heterosexual married couples. *Developmental Psychology, 44*, 102–116.

Bandura, A. (1962). Social learning through imitation. In M. R. Jones (Ed.), *Nebraska Symposium on Motivation*. Lincoln, NE: University of Nebraska Press.

Bandura, A. (1965). Behavioral modification through modeling procedures. In L. Krasner & L. P. Ullman (Eds.), *Research in Behavior Modification*. New York: Holt, Rinehart and Winston.

Bandura, A. (1965). Behavioral modification through modeling procedures. In L. Krasner & L. P. Ullman (Eds.), *Research in behavior modification*. New York: Holt, Rinehart & Winston.

Bandura, A. (1965). Influence of models' reinforcement contingencies on the acquisition of imitative responses. *Journal of Personality and Social Psychology, 1*, 589–595.

Bandura, A. (1973). *Aggression: Social learning analysis*. Englewood Cliffs, NJ: Prentice-Hall.

Bandura, A. (1977). Self-efficacy: Toward a unifying theory of behavioral change. *Psychological Review, 84*, 119–215.

Bandura, A. (1977). *Social learning theory*. New York: General Learning Press.

Bandura, A., Grusec, J. E., & Menlove, F. L. (1966). Observational learning as a function of symbolization and incentive set. *Child Development, 37*, 499–506.

Bandura, A., Ross, D., & Ross, S. (1961).Transmission of aggression through imitation of aggressive models. *Journal of Abnormal and Social Psychology, 63*, 575–582.

Bandura, A., Ross, D., & Ross, S. A. (1963). Imitation of film-mediated aggressive models. *Journal of Abnormal Social Psychology, 66*, 3–11.

Banks, T., & Dabbs, J. M., Jr. (1996). Salivary testosterone and cortisol in a delinquent and violent urban subculture. *The Journal of Social Psychology, 136*, 49–56.

Banse, R. (2004). Adult attachment and marital satisfaction: Evidence for dyadic configuration effects. *Journal of Social and Personal Relationships, 21*, 273–282.

Barbey, A. K., & Sloman, S. A. (2007). Base-rate respect: From ecological rationality to dual processes. *Behavioral and Brain Sciences, 30*, 241–297.

Bargh, J. A., & Williams, E. L. (2006). The automaticity of social life. *Current Directions in Psychological Science, 15*, 1–4.

Bargh, J. A., Chen, M., & Burrows, L. (1996). Automaticity of social behavior: Direct effects of trait construct and stereotype activation on action. *Journal of Personality and Social Psychology, 71*, 230–244.

Bar-Haim, Y., Ziv, T., Lamy, D., & Hodes, R. M. (2006). Nature and nurture in own-race face processing. *Psychological Science, 17*, 159–163.

Barker, R., Dembo, T., & Lewin, K. (1941). Frustration and aggression: An experiment with young children. *University of Iowa Studies in Child Welfare, 18*, 1–314.

Barnes, R. D., Ickes, W., & Kidd, R. F. (1979). Effects of the perceived intentionality and stability of another's dependency on helping behavior. *Personality and Social Psychology Bulletin, 5,* 367–372.

Barnwell, S., Borders, A., & Earleywine, M. (2006). Alcohol-aggression expectancies and dispositional aggression moderate the relationship between alcohol consumption and alcohol-related violence. *Aggressive Behavior, 32,* 517–525.

Baron, J., & Miller, J. G. (2000). Limiting the scope of moral obligations to help: A cross-cultural investigation. *Journal of Cross-Cultural Psychology, 31,* 703–725.

Baron, R. A. (1986). Distraction-conflict theory: Progress and problems. In L. Berkowitz (Ed.), *Advances in Experimental Social Psychology* (Vol. 19). Orlando, FL: Academic Press.

Baron, R. A. (1990). Countering the effects of destructive criticism: The relative efficacy of four interventions. *Journal of Applied Psychology, 75,* 235–245.

Baron, R. A. (1997). The sweet smell of . . . helping: Effects of pleasant ambient fragrance on prosocial behavior in shopping malls. *Personality and Social Psychology Bulletin, 23,* 498–503.

Baron, R. A., & Richardson, D. R. (1994). *Human Aggression* (2nd ed.). New York: Plenum.

Baron, R. S., Moore, D., & Sanders, G. S. (1978). Distraction as a source of drive in social facilitation research. *Journal of Personality and Social Psychology, 36,* 816–824.

Barth, J., Povinelli, D. J., & Cant, J. G. H. (2004). Bodily origins of self. In D. Beike, J. Lampinen, & D. Behrend (Eds.), *The self and memory* (pp. 11–44). New York: Psychology Press.

Bartholow, B. D., & Anderson, C. A. (2002). Effects of violent video games on aggressive behavior: Potential sex differences. *Journal of Experimental Social Psychology, 38,* 283–290.

Bartholow, B. D., & Heinz, A. (2006). Alcohol and aggression without consumption: Alcohol cues, aggressive thoughts, and hostile perception bias. *Psychological Science, 17,* 30–37.

Bartholow, B. D., Anderson, C. A., Carnagey, N. L., & Benjamin, A. J., Jr. (2005). Interactive effects of life experience and situational cues on aggression: The weapons priming effect in hunters and non-hunters. *Journal of Experimental Social Psychology, 41,* 48–60.

Bass, E., & Davis, L. (1988). *The courage to heal: A guide for women survivor's of child sexual abuse.* New York: Harper & Row.

Bateson, M., Nettle, D., & Roberts, G. (2006). Cues of being watched enhance cooperation in a real-world setting. *Biology Letters, 3,* 412–414.

Bateson, N. (1966, April). Familiarization, group discussion, and risk taking. *Journal of Experimental Social Psychology, 2,* 119–129.

Batson, C. D. (1991). *The altruism question: Toward a social-psychological answer.* Hillsdale, NJ: Lawrence Erlbaum Associates.

Batson, C. D., & Oleson, K. C. (1991). Current status of the empathy-altruism hypothesis. In M. S. Clark (Ed.), *Review of personality and social psychology: Vol. 12. Prosocial behavior* (pp. 62–85). Newbury Park, CA: Sage.

Batson, C. D., Duncan, B. D., Ackerman, P., Buckley, T., & Birch, K. (1981). Is empathic emotion a source of altruistic motivation? *Journal of Personality and Social Psychology, 40,* 290–302.

Batson, C. D., Dyck, I. L., Bran, J. R., Watson, J. G., Powell, A. L., McMaster, M. R., et al. (1988). Five studies testing two new egoistic alternatives to the empathy-altruism hypothesis. *Journal of Personality and Social Psychology, 55,* 52–77.

Batson, C. D., Thompson, E. R., Seuferling, G., Whitney, H., & Strongman, J. A. (1999). Moral hypocrisy: Appearing moral to oneself without being so. *Journal of Personality and Social Psychology, 77,* 525–537.

Batson, C. D. (1998). Altruism and prosocial behavior. In D. Gilbert, S. Fiske, & G. Lindzey (Eds.), *The handbook of social psychology,* (4th ed., Vol. 2, pp. 282–316).New York: McGraw-Hill.

Batson, C. D., O'Quin, K., Fultz, J., Vanderplas, M., & Isen, A. M. (1983). Influence of self-reported distress and empathy on egoistic versus altruistic motivation to help. *Journal of Personality and Social Psychology, 45,* 706–718.

Baumeister, R. F. (1988). Masochism as escape from self. *The Journal of Sex Research, 25,* 28–59.

Baumeister, R. F. (1990). Suicide as escape from self. *Psychological Review, 97,* 90–113.

Baumeister, R. F., & Leary, M. R. (1995). The need to belong: Desire for interpersonal attachments as a fundamental human motivation. *Psychological Bulletin, 117,* 497–529.

Baumeister, R. F., & Steinhilber, A. (1984). Paradoxical effects of supportive audiences on performance under pressure: The home field disadvantage in sports championships. *Journal of Personality and Social Psychology, 47,* 85–93.

Baumeister, R. F., Campbell, J. D., Krueger, J. I., & Vohs, K. D. (2003). Does high self-esteem cause better performance, interpersonal success, happiness, or healthier lifestyles? *Psychological Science in the Public Interest, 4,* 1–44.

Bayle, D. J., Henaff, M.-A., Krolak-Salmon, P. (2009). Unconsciously perceived fear in peripheral vision alerts the limbic system: A MEG study. *PLoS ONE, 4,* 1-9.

Bazerman, M. H., Beekun, R. I., & Schoorman, F. D. (1982). Performance evaluation in a dynamic context: A laboratory study of the impact of a prior commitment to the ratee. *Journal of Applied Psychology, 67,* 873–876.

Beall, P. M., & Herbert, A. M. (2008). The face wins: Stronger automatic processing of affect in facial expressions than words in a modified Stroop task. *Cognition & Emotion, 22,* 1613–1642.

Beaman, A. L., Barnes, P. J., Klentz, B., & McQuirk, B. (1978). Increasing helping rates through information dissemination: Teaching pays. *Personality and Social Psychology Bulletin, 4,* 406–411.

Beaman, A. L., Diener, E., & Klentz, B. (1979). Self-awareness and transgression in children: Two field studies. *Journal of Personality and Social Psychology, 37,* 1835–1846.

Beitchman, J. H., Mik, H. M., Ehtesham, S., Douglas, L., & Kennedy, J. L. (2004). MAOA and persistent, pervasive childhood aggression. *Molecular Psychiatry, 9,* 546–547.

Bem, D. J. (1965). An experimental analysis of self-persuasion. *Journal of Experimental Social Psychology, 1,* 199–218.

Bem, D. J. (1972). Self-perception theory. In L. Berkowitz (Ed.), *Advances in experimental social psychology* (Vol. 6, pp. 1–62). New York: Academic Press.

Bem, D. J. (1967). Self-perception: An alternative interpretation of cognitive dissonance phenomena. *Psychological Review, 74,* 183–200.

Benson, P. L., Karabenick, S. A., & Lerner, R. M. (1976). Pretty pleases: The effects of physical attractiveness, race, and sex on receiving help. *Journal of Experimental Social Psychology, 12,* 409–415.

Berg, J. H., & McQuinn, R. D. (1986). Attraction and exchange in continuing and noncontinuing dating relationships. *Journal of Personality and Social Psychology, 50,* 942–952.

Berkowitz, L. (1968). The concept of aggressive drive: Some additional considerations. In L. Berkowitz (Ed.). *Advances in Experimental Social Psychology.* New York: Academic Press.

Berkowitz, L. (1983). Aversively stimulated aggression: Some parallels and differences in research with animals and humans. *American Psychologist, 38,* 1135–1144.

Berkowitz, L. (1989). Frustration-aggression hypothesis: Examination and reformulation. *Psychological Bulletin, 106,* 59–73.

Berkowitz, L. (1993). Pain and aggression: Some findings and implications. *Motivation and Emotion, 17,* 277.

Berkowitz, L. (1998). Affective aggression: The role of stress, pain, and negative affect. *Human Aggression: Theories, Research, and Implications for Social Policy.* San Diego, CA: Academic Press.

Berkowitz, L., & Daniels, L. (1963). Responsibility and dependency. *Journal of Abnormal Social Psychology, 66,* 429–436.

Berkowitz, L., & LePage, A. (1967). Weapons as aggression-eliciting stimuli. *Journal of Personality and Social Psychology, 7,* 202–207.

Berndt, T. J. (1979). Developmental changes in conformity to peers and parents. *Developmental Psychology, 15,* 608–616.

Bernier, D. (1998). A study of coping: Successful recovery from severe burnout and other reactions to work-related stress. *Work & Stress, 12,* 50–65.

Bernstein, M., & Crosby, F. (1980). An empirical examination of relative deprivation theory. *Journal of Experimental Social Psychology, 16,* 442–456.

Berry, D. S., & Zebrowitz-McArthur, L. (1988). What's in a face? Facial maturity and the attribution of legal responsibility. *Personality and Social Psychology Bulletin, 14,* 23–33.

Berry, J. W., Poortinga, Y. H., Segall, M. H., & Dasen, P. R. (2002). *Cross-cultural psychology: Research and applications* (2nd ed.). New York, NY: Cambridge University Press.

Bertrand, M., & Mullainathan, S. (2004). Are Emily and Greg more employable than Lakisha and Jamal? A field experiment on labor market discrimination. *The American Economic Review, 94*, 991–1013.

Betancourt, H., Hardin, C., & Manzi, J. (1992). Beliefs, value orientation, and culture in attribution processes and helping behavior. *Journal of Cross-Cultural Psychology, 23*, 179–195.

Bettencourt, A. B., & Miller, N. (1996). Gender differences in aggression as a function of provocation: A meta-analysis. *Psychological Bulletin, 199*, 422–447.

Bettencourt, B. A., Charlton, K., Dorr, N., & Hume, D. L. (2001). Status differences and in-group bias: A meta-analytic examination of the effects of status stability, status legitimacy, and group permeability. *Psychological Bulletin, 127*, 520–542.

Bettencourt, B. A., Talley, A., Benjamin, A. J., & Valentine, J. (2006). Personality and aggressive behavior under provoking and neutral conditions: A meta-analytic review. *Psychological Bulletin, 132*, 751–777.

Bhatnagar, N., & Wan, F. (2008). The impact of narrative immersion and perceived self-character similarity on evaluations of product placements. *Advances in Consumer Research, 35*, 728–729.

Bierhoff, H. W., Klein, R., & Kramp, P. (1991). Evidence for the altruistic personality from data on accident research. *Journal of Personality, 59*, 263–280.

Bierhoff, H.-W. (2002). *Prosocial behaviour*. East Sussex, UK: Psychology Press.

Billedo, C. J. F. (2009). The formation of interpersonal attraction and intimate relationships on internet relay chat: An exploratory study. *Philippine Social Sciences Review, 60*, 1–32.

Bindel, J. (2010, February 19). Blame the rapist, not the victim. *The Guardian*. Retrieved August 3, 2010, from http://www.guardian.co.uk/lifeandstyle/2010/feb/19/blame-the-rapist

Bisanz, G. L., & Rule, B. G. (1989). Gender and the persuasion schema: A search for cognitive invariants. *Personality and Social Psychology Bulletin, 15*, 4–18.

Black, Latino drivers fare worse in traffic stops. (2007, April 29). Associated Press. Retrieved August 2, 2010, from http://www.msnbc.msn.com/id/18383182/

Blair, R. J. (2007). Dysfunctions of medial and lateral orbitofrontal cortex in psychopathy. *Annals of the New York Academy of Sciences, 1121*, 461–479.

Blair, R. J. R. (2001). Neuro-cognitive models of aggression, the antisocial personality disorders and psychopathy. *Journal of Neurology, Neurosurgery, and Psychiatry, 71*, 727–731.

Blanchard, F. A., Crandall, C. S., Brigham, J. C., & Vaughn, L. A. (1994). Condemning and condoning racism: A social context approach to interracial settings. *Journal of Applied Psychology, 79*, 993–997.

Blankenship, K. L., & Wegener, D. T. (2008). Opening the mind to close it: Considering a message in light of important values increases message processing and later resistance to change. *Journal of Personality and Social Psychology, 94*, 196–213.

Blatz, C. W., & Philpot, C. (2010). On the outcomes of intergroup apologies: A review. *Social and Personality Psychology Compass, 4*, 995–1007.

Blatz, C. W., Schumann, K., & Ross, M. (2009). Government apologies for historical injustices. *Political Psychology, 30*, 219–241.

Blume, E. S. (1990). *Secret Survivors: Uncovering incest and its after effects in women*. New York: John Wiley and Sons.

Bodenhausen, G. V., Kramer, G. P., & Süsser, K. (1994). Happiness and stereotypic thinking in social judgment. *Journal of Personality and Social Psychology, 66*, 621–632.

Bond, C. F., & Titus, L. J. (1983). Social facilitation: A meta-analysis of 241 studies. *Psychological Bulletin, 94*, 265–292.

Bond, M. H., & Cheung, T. S. (1983). College students' spontaneous self-concept: The effect of culture among respondents in Hong Kong, Japan, and the United States. *Journal of Cross-Cultural Psychology, 14*, 153–171.

Bond, M. H., & Dutton, D. G. (1973). The effect of interaction anticipation upon the extremity of trait ratings. *Canadian Journal of Behavioural Science, 5*, 226–233.

Bonta, J., & Andrews, D. A. (2007). *Risk-need-responsivity model for offender assessment and rehabilitation*. Ottawa, ON: Her Majesty the Queen in Right of Canada.

Bordel, S., et al. (2007). Naïve explanations of road accidents: Self-serving bias and defensive attribution. *Psihologia Resurselor Umane Revista Asociatiei de Psihologie Industriala si Organizationala, 5*, 36–47.

Bower, G. H. (1987). Commentary on mood and memory. *Behaviour Research and Therapy, 25*, 443–456.

Bowlby, J. (1969). *Attachment and loss: Vol. I: Attachment*. New York: Basic Books.

Bowlby, J. (1973). *Attachment and loss: Vol. 2: Separation: Anxiety and anger*. New York: Basic Books.

Bowlby, J. (1988). *A secure base: Parent-child attachment and healthy human development*. New York: Basic Books.

Boxer, P., Tisak, M. S., & Goldstein, S. E. (2004). Is it bad to be good? An exploration of aggressive and prosocial behavior subtypes in adolescence. *Journal of Youth and Adolescence, 33*, 91–100.

Boyce, L. A., & Herd, A. M. (2003). The relationship between gender role stereotypes and requisite military leadership characteristics. *Sex Roles, 49*, 365–378.

Boyd, R., & Richerson, P. J. (1985). *Culture and the evolutionary process*. Chicago, IL: University of Chicago Press.

Boysen, S. T., & Himes, G. T. (1999). Current issues and emergent theories in animal cognition. *Annual Reviews in Psychology, 50*, 683–705.

Bradley, P., & Charbonneau, D. (2004). Transformational leadership: Something new, something old. Military Psychology Section. *Canadian Military Journal, 5*. Retrieved October 30, 2011, from http://www.journal.dnd.ca/vo5/no1/index-eng.asp

Brandt, M. J. (2011, in press). Sexism and gender inequality across 57 societies. *Psychological Science*.

Branscombe, N. R., & Wann, D. L. (1991). The positive social and self-concept consequences of sport team identification. *Journal of Sport and Social Issues, 15*, 115–127.

Brauer, M., Judd, C. M., & Jacquelin, V. (2001). The communication of social stereotypes: The effects of group discussion and information distribution on stereotypic appraisals. *Journal of Personality and Social Psychology, 81*, 463–475.

Brehm, J. W. (1966). *A Theory of Psychological Reactance*. New York: Academic Press.

Brendl, C. M., Chattopadhyay, A., Pelham, B. W., & Carvall, M. (2005). Nameletter branding:Valence transfers when product-specific needs are active. *Journal of Consumer Research, 32*, 405–415.

Brennan, K. A., & Bosson, J. K. (1998). Attachment-style differences in attitudes toward and reactions to feedback from romantic partners: An exploration of the relational bases of self-esteem. *Personality & Social Psychology Bulletin, 24*, 699–714.

Brescoll, V. L.,& Uhlmann, E. L. (2008). Can an angry woman get ahead? Status conferral, gender, and expression of emotion in the workplace. *Psychological Science, 19*, 268–275.

Bretherton, I. (1992).The origins of attachment theory: John Bowlby and Mary Ainsworth. *Developmental Psychology, 28*, 759–775.

Brewer, M. B., & Chen, Y. R. (2007). Where (who) are collectives in collectivism? Toward conceptual clarification of individualism and collectivism. *Psychological Review, 114*, 133–151.

Brewer, M. B., & Pickett, C. L. (1999). Distinctiveness motives as a source of the social self. In T. Tyler, R. Kramer, & O. John (Eds.), *The psychology of the social self* (pp. 71–87). Hillsdale, NJ: Erlbaum.

Brickner, M. A., Harkins, S. G., & Ostrom, T. M. (1986). Effects of personal involvement: Thought provoking implications for social loafing. *Journal of Personality and Social Psychology, 51*, 763–769.

Briggs, S. R., & Cheek, J. M. (1988). On the nature of self-monitoring: Problems with assessment, problems with validity. *Journal of Personality and Social Psychology, 54*, 663–678.

Briñol, P., & Petty, R. E. (2003). Overt head movements and persuasion: A self-validation analysis. *Journal of Personality and Social Psychology, 84*, 1123–1139.

British Broadcasting Corporation. (1995). The killing screens. *Panorama Programme*.

Broemer, P. (2004). Ease of imagination moderates reactions to differently framed health messages. *European Journal of Social Psychology, 34*, 103–119.

Brown, L., & Popplewell, B. (2008, January 30). Board okays black-focused school. *Toronto Star*. Retrieved October 26, 2011, from http://www.thestar.com/article/298714

Brown, R. (1965). *Social psychology*. New York: Free Press.

Brown, R. (2000). Social identity theory: Past achievements, current problems and future challenges. *European Journal of Social Psychology, 30*, 745–778.

Brown, W. M., Cronk, L., Grochow, K., Jacobson, A., Liu, C. K., Popovic, Z., et al. (2005). Dance reveals symmetry especially in young men. *Nature, 438*, 22–29.

Brownstein, R. J., & Katzev, R. D. (1985). The relative effectiveness of three compliance techniques in eliciting donations to a cultural organization. *Journal of Applied Social Psychology, 15*, 564–574.

Bryan, C. J., Dweck, C. S., Ross, L., Kay, A. C., & Mislavsky, N. O. (2009). Political mindset: Effects of schema priming on liberal-conservative political positions. *Journal of Experimental Social Psychology, 45*, 890–895.

Bryan, J. H., & Test, M. A. (1967). Models and helping: Naturalistic studies in aiding behavior. *Journal of Personality and Social Psychology, 6*, 400–407.

Brydon-Miller, M. (1997). Participatory action research: Psychology and social change. *Journal of Social Issues, 53*, 657–666.

Buchner, J., & Huen, D. (1998). Self-advocacy: Negotiating barriers related to homophobia and heterosexism in health care settings. *International Conference on AIDS, 12*, 1137–1138.

Buehler, R., & Griffin, D. (2003). Planning, personality, and prediction: The role of future focus in optimistic time predictions. *Organizational Behavior and Human Decision Processes, 92*, 80–90.

Buehler, R., & McFarland, C. (2001). Intensity bias in affective forecasting: The role of temporal focus. *Personality and Social Psychology Bulletin, 27*, 1480–1493.

Burger, J. M. (1981). Motivational biases in the attribution of responsibility for an accident: A meta-analysis of the defensive-attribution hypothesis. *Psychological Bulletin, 90*, 496–512.

Burger, J. M. (1986). Increasing compliance by improving the deal: The that's-not-all technique. *Journal of Personality and Social Psychology, 51*, 277–283.

Burger, J. M. (2009). Replicating Milgram: Would people still obey today? *American Psychologist, 64*, 1–11.

Burger, J. M., Messian, N., Patel, S., del Prado, A., & Anderson, C. (2004). What a coincidence! The effects of incidental similarity on compliance. *Personality and Social Psychology Bulletin, 30*, 35–43.

Burger, J. M., Sanchez, J., Imberi, J. E., & Grande, L. R. (2009).The norm of reciprocity as an internalized social norm: Returning favors even when no one finds out. *Social Influence, 4*, 11–17.

Burns, R. B. (1978). The relative effectiveness of various incentives and deterrents as judged by pupils and teachers. *Educational Studies, 4*, 229–243.

Burnstein, E., & Worchel, P. (1962). Arbitrariness of frustration and its consequences for aggression in a social situation. *Journal of Personality, 30*, 528–540.

Burnstein, E., Crandall, C., & Kitayama, S. (1994). Some neo-Darwinian decision rules for altruism: Weighing cues for inclusive fitness as a function of the biological importance of the decision. *Journal of Personality and Social Psychology, 67*, 779.

Bus beheader responds to treatment: Psychiatrist. (2011, May 30). *Canadian Press.* Retrieved August 30, 2011, from http://www.cbc.ca/news/canada/manitoba/story/2011/05/30/mb-bus-beheading-vince-li.html

Bushman, B. J., & Anderson, C. A. (2001). Media violence and the American public: Scientific facts versus media misinformation. *American Psychologist, 56*, 477–489.

Bushman, B. J., & Anderson, C. A. (2002). Violent video games and hostile expectations: A test of the General Aggression Model. *Personality and Social Psychology Bulletin, 28*, 1679–1689.

Bushman, B. J., & Cantor, J. (2003). Media ratings for violence and sex: Implications for policymakers and parents. *American Psychologist, 58*, 130–141.

Bushman, B. J., & Huesmann, L. R. (2001). Effects of televised violence on aggression. In D. Singer & J. Singer (Eds.), *Handbook of Children and the Media* (pp. 223–254), Thousand Oaks, CA: Sage Publications.

Buss, D. M. (2002). Human mating strategies. *Samfundsokonomen, 4*, 47–58.

Buss, D. M. (2004). *The Evolution of Desire* (rev. ed.). New York: Basic Books.

Buss, D. M., & Barnes, M. (1986). Preferences in human mate selection. *Journal of Personality and Social Psychology, 50*, 559–570.

Buss, D. M., Larsen, R. J., Westen, D., & Semmelroth, J. (1992). Sex differences in jealousy: Evolution, physiology, and psychology. *Psychological Science, 3*, 251–255.

Butler, D., & Geis, F. L. (1990). Nonverbal affect responses to male and female leaders: Implications for leadership evaluations. *Journal of Personality and Social Psychology, 58*, 48–59.

Buunk, B. P., Oldsersma, F. L., & deDreu, C. K. W. (2001). Enhancing satisfaction through downward comparison: The role of relational discontent and individual differences in social comparison orientation. *Journal of Experimental Social Psychology, 37*, 452–467.

Byrne, D. (1961). Interpersonal attraction and attitude similarity. *Journal of Abnormal and Social Psychology, 62*, 713–715.

Byrne, D. (1971). *The attraction paradigm.* New York: Academic Press.

Byrne, D., & Nelson, D. (1965). Attraction as a linear function of proportion of positive reinforcements. *Journal of Personality and Social Psychology, 1*, 659–663.

Byrne, D., Ervin, C. R., & Lamberth, J. (1970). Continuity between the experimental study of attraction and real-life computer dating. *Journal of Personality and Social Psychology, 16*, 157–165.

Byrnes, D. A., & Kiger, G. (1990). The effect of a prejudice-reduction simulation on attitude change. *Journal of Applied Social Psychology, 20,* 341–356.

Cacioppo, J. T., & Petty, R. E. (1980). Sex differences in influenceability: Toward specifying the underlying processes. *Personality and Social Psychology Bulletin, 6*, 651–656.

Cacioppo, J. T., & Petty, R. E. (1982). The need for cognition. *Journal of Personality and Social Psychology, 42*, 116–131.

Cacioppo, J. T., Amaral, D. G., Blanchara, J. J., Cameron, J. L., Carter, C. S., Crews, D. . . . Quinn, K. J. (2007). Social neuroscience: Progress and implications for mental health. *Perspectives on Psychological Science, 2*, 99–123.

Cacioppo, J. T., Gardner, W. L., & Berntson, G. G. (1997). Beyond bipolar conceptualizations and measures: The case of attitudes and evaluative space. *Personality and Social Psychology Review, 1*, 3–25.

Cacioppo, J. T., Petty, R. E., Feinstein, J. A., Jarvis, W., & Blair, G. (1996). Dispositional differences in cognitive motivation: The life and times of individuals varying in need for cognition. *Psychological Bulletin, 119*, 197–253.

Caldwell, T. (n.d.). Media sensationalism about crime defies statistical trends toward lower crime rates. *Helium*. Retrieved July 13,2010, from http://www.helium.com/items/175618-media-sensationalism-aboutcrime-defies-statistical-trends-toward- lower-crime

Cameron, J. A., Alvarez, J. M., Ruble, D. N., & Fuligni, A. J. (2001). Children's lay theories about ingroups and outgroups: Reconceptualizing research on prejudice. *Personality and Social Psychology Review, 5*, 118–128.

Campbell, A., Muncer, S., & Gorman, B. (1993). Sex and social representations of aggression: A communal-agentic analysis. *Aggressive Behavior, 19*, 125–135.

Campbell, J. D., Trapnell, P. D., Heine, S. J., Katz, I. M., Lavallee, L. F., & Lehman, D. R. (1996). Self-concept clarity: Measurement, personality correlates, and cultural boundaries: Correction. *Journal of Personality and Social Psychology, 58*, 122–133.

Campbell, L., Simpson, J. A., Boldry, J. G., & Kashy, D. A. (2005). Perceptions of conflict and support in romantic relationships: The role of attachment anxiety. *Journal of Personality and Social Psychology, 88*, 510–531.

Campbell, L., Simpson, J. A., Boldry, J., & Kashy, D. A. (2005). Perceptions of conflict and support in romantic relationships: The role of attachment anxiety. *Journal of Personality and Social Psychology, 88*, 510–531.

Campbell, R. M., Jr., Aiken, D., & Kent, A. (2004). Beyond BIRGing and CORFing: Continuing the exploration of fan behavior. *Sport Marketing Quarterly, 13*, 151–157.

Campbell, W. K., & Sedikides, C. (1999). Self-threat magnifies the self-serving bias: A meta-analytic integration. *Review of General Psychology, 3*, 23–43.

Canada post union: Legislation quashes free collective bargaining. (2011, June 20). *Canadian Occupational Safety Magazine.* Retrieved October 30, 2011, from http://www.cos-mag.com/Legal/Legal-Stories/union-legislation-quashes-free-collective-bargaining.html

Canadian Institutes of Health Research, Natural Sciences and Engineering Research Council of Canada, and Social Sciences and Humanities Research Council of Canada. (2010, December). *Tri-Council Policy Statement: Ethical conduct for research involving humans.* Ottawa, ON: Her Majesty the Queen in Right of Canada.

Canadian Mental Health Association (2011). Violence and mental illness. Retrieved August 12, 2011, from http://www.cmha.ca/bins/content_page.asp?cid=3-108

Canadian Psychological Association. (2000). *Canadian code of ethics for psychologists* (3rd ed.). Ottawa: Author.

Canadian Union of Postal Workers. (2011, October 20). Court orders stay of proceedings in CUPW challenge to Lisa Raitt's arbitrator. Retrieved October 30, 2011, from http://www.cupw.ca/index.cfm/ci_id/13655/la_id/1.htm

Canadians behind U.S. in charitable giving. (2010, December 20). *CBC News.* Retrieved November 12, 2011, from http://www.cbc.ca/news/story/2010/12/20/con-charity-report.html?ref=rss

Cannon, C. K., & Quinsey, V. L. (1995). The likelihood of violent behaviour: Predictions, postdictions, and hindsight bias. *Canadian Journal of Behavioural Science, 27*, 92-106.

Cantor, J. R., Zillmann, D., & Einseidel, E. F. (1978). Female responses to provocation after exposure to aggressive and erotic films. *Communication Research, 5*, 395–412.

Card, N. A., Stucky, B. D., Sawalani, G. M., & Little, T. D. (2008). Direct and indirect aggression during childhood and adolescence: A meta-analytic review of gender differences, intercorrelations, and relations to maladjustment. *Child Development, 79*, 1185–1229.

Carkenord, D. M., & Bullington, J. (1993). Bringing cognitive dissonance to the classroom. *Teaching of Psychology, 20*, 41–43.

Carlson, K. B. (2009, March 1). Canadian stem cell breakthrough. *National Post.* Retrieved July 25, 2011, from http://www.nationalpost.com/news/story.html?id=1342585

Carlson, M., Charlin, V., & Miller, N. (1988). Positive mood and helping behavior: A test of six hypotheses. *Journal of Personality and Social Psychology, 55*, 211–229.

Carlson, M., Charlin, V., & Miller, N. (1988). Positive mood and helping behavior: A test of six hypotheses. *Journal of Personality and Social Psychology, 55*, 211–229.

Carnagey, N. L., & Anderson, C. A. (2005). The effects of reward and punishment in violent video games on aggressive affect, cognition, and behavior. *Psychological Science, 16*, 882–889.

Carpenter, S. (2000). Effects of cultural tightness and collectivism on self-concept and causal attributions. *Cross-Cultural Research, 34*, 38–56.

Cartwright, D. (1979). Contemporary social psychology in historical perspective. *Social Psychology Quarterly, 42*, 82–93.

Casciani, D. (2003, December 16). Racism rife in prison says watchdog. *BBC News.* Retrieved November 3, 2011, from http://news.bbc.co.uk/1/hi/uk/3322129.stm

Cash, T. F., & Derlega, V. J. (1978). The matching hypothesis: Physical attractiveness among same-sex friends. *Personality and Social Psychology Bulletin, 4*, 240–243.

Cash, T. F., Gillen, B., & Burns, D. S. (1977). Sexism and beautyism in personnel consultant decision making. *Journal of Applied Psychology, 62*, 301–310.

Causse, P. et al. (2004). Alcohol-related accident-risk perception by young drivers: Some determinants of comparative optimism. *Le Travail Humain: A Bilingual and Multidisciplinary Journal in Human Factors, 67*, 235–256.

Centers for Disease Control and Prevention. (2010). *2009 H1N1 flu ("swine flu") and you.* Retrieved May 14, 2010, from http://www.cdc.gov/h1n1flu/qa.htm

Chaiken, S. (1979). Communicator physical attractiveness and persuasion, *Journal of Personality and Social Psychology, 37*, 1387–1397.

Chaiken, S. (1980). Heuristic versus systematic information processing and the use of source versus message cues in persuasion. *Journal of Personality and Social Psychology, 39*, 752–756.

Chance, S. E., Brown, R. T., Dabbs, J. M. J., & Casey, R. (2000). Testosterone, intelligence, and behavior disorders in young boys. *Personality and Individual Differences, 28*, 437–445.

Chapple, A., Ziebland, S., & McPherson, A. (2004). Stigma, shame and blame: A qualitative study of people with lung cancer. *British Medical Journal, 328*, 1470.

Charbonneau, D., Barling, J., & Kelloway, E. K. (2001). Transformational leadership and sports performance: The mediating role of intrinsic motivation. *Journal of Applied Social Psychology*, 31, 1521–1534.

Chartrand, T. L., & Bargh, J. A. (1999). The chameleon effect: The perception–behavior link and social interaction. *Journal of Personality and Social Psychology, 76*, 893–910.

Chazan, D. (2010, March 18). Row over "torture" on French TV. *BBC News.* Retrieved November 30, 2010, from http://news.bbc.co.uk/2/hi/8573755.stm

Chemers, M. M., Hu, L., & Garcia, B. F. (2001). Academic self-efficacy and first year college student performance adjustment. *Journal of Educational Psychology, 93*, 55–64.

Chen, F. S., & Johnson, S. C. (in press). An oxytocin receptor gene variant predicts attachment anxiety in females and autism-spectrum traits in males. *Social Psychological & Personality Science.*

Chen, S. (2009, October 30). Gang rape raises question about bystanders' role. *CNN.com.* Retrieved June 3, 2010, from http://www.cnn.com/2009/CRIME/10/28/california.gang.rape.bystander/index.html

Chen, S., Boucher, H. C., & Tapias, M. P. (2006). The relational self revealed: Integrative conceptualization and implications for interpersonal life. *Psychological Bulletin, 132*, 151–179.

Cheng, C., Jose, P. E., Sheldon, K. M., Singelis, T. M., Cheung, M. W. L., Tiliouine, H., Alao, A. A., . . . Sims, C. (2011). Sociocultural differences in self-construal and subjective well-being: A test of four cultural models. *Journal of Cross Cultural Psychology, 42*, 832–855.

Childs, D. (2008, June 25). "Trust drug" oxytocin unbelievable for now. *ABC News.* Retrieved June 3, 2010, from http://abcnews.go.com/Health/MindMoodNews/story?id_5242531&page_1

Chiroro, P. M., Tredoux, C. G., Radaelli, S., & Meissner, C. A. (2008). Recognizing faces across continents: The effect of within-race variations on the own-race bias in face recognition. *Psychonomic Bulletin & Review, 15*, 1089–1092.

Choi, N. (2005). Self-efficacy and self-concept as predictors of college students' academic performance. *Psychology in the Schools, 42*, 197–205.

Chopra, A. K., & Doody, G. A. (2007). Crime rates and local newspaper coverage of schizophrenia. *The Psychiatrist, 31*, 206–208.

Christofides, E., Islam, T., & Desmarais, S. (2009). Gender stereotyping over instant messenger: The effects of gender and context. *Computers in Human Behavior, 25*, 897–901.

Cialdini, R. (1984). *Influence: Science and Practice* (5th ed.). Needham Heights, MA: Allyn & Bacon.

Cialdini, R. B. (1994). *Influence: The psychology of persuasion.* New York: Quill.

Cialdini, R. B. (2001). The science of persuasion. *Scientific American, 284*, 76–81.

Cialdini, R. B. (2003). Crafting normative messages to protect the environment. *Current Directions in Psychological Science, 12*, 105–109.

Cialdini, R. B. (2004). Crafting normative messages to protect the environment. *Current Directions in Psychological Science, 12*, 105–109.

Cialdini, R. B. (2007). *Influence: The psychology of persuasion.* New York: HarperCollins Publishers.

Cialdini, R. B. (2008). Turning persuasion from an art into a science. *Clashes of Knowledge, 1*, 199–209.

Cialdini, R. B., Borden, R. J., Thorne, R. J., Walker, M. R., Freeman, S., & Sloan, L. R. (1976). Basking in reflected glory: Three (football) field studies. *Journal of Personality and Social Psychology, 34*, 366–375.

Cialdini, R. B., Brown, S. L., Lewis, B. P., Luce, C., & Neuberg, S. L. (1997). Reinterpreting the empathy-altruism relationship: When one into one equals oneness. *Journal of Personality and Social Psychology, 73*, 481–494.

Cialdini, R. B., Kenrick, D. T., & Baumann, D. J. (1982). Mood as a determinant of prosocial behavior in children and adults. In N. Eisenberg (Ed.), *The development of prosocial behavior* (pp. 339–359). New York: Academic Press.

Cialdini, R. B., Reno, R. R., & Kallgren, C. A. (1990). A focus theory of normative conduct: Recycling the concept of norms to reduce littering in public places. *Journal of Personality and Social Psychology, 58*, 1015–1026.

Cialdini, R. B., Vincent, J. E., Lewis, S. K., Catalan, J., Wheeler, D., & Darby, B. L. (1975). A reciprocal concessions procedure for inducing compliance: The door-in-the-face technique. *Journal of Personality and Social Psychology, 31*, 206–215.

CityNews rewind: The Greyhound bus beheading. (2009, March 5). *CityTV News.* Retrieved September 2, 2011, from http://www.citytv.com/toronto/citynews/news/local/article/9113—citynews-rewind-the-greyhound-bus-beheading

Clark, J. K., Wegener, D. T., & Fabrigar, L. R. (2008). Attitude accessibility and message processing: The moderating role of message position. *Journal of Experimental Social Psychology, 44*, 354–361.

Clark, K. B., & Clark, M. P. (1947). Racial identification and preference in Negro children. Retrieved July 2, 2010, from http://i2.cdn.turner.com/cnn/2010/images/05/13/doll.study.1947.pdf

Clark, M. S. (1984). Record keeping in two types of relationships. *Journal of Personality and Social Psychology, 47*, 549–557.

Clark, M. S., & Pataki, S. (1995). Interpersonal processes influencing attraction and relationships. In A. Tesser (Ed.), *Advanced Social Psychology* (pp. 283–331). St. Louis: McGraw-Hill.

Clark, R. D., III,& Word, L. E. (1972). Why don't bystanders help? Because of ambiguity? *Journal of Personality and Social Psychology, 24,* 392–400.

Clark, S. E., & Wells, G. L. (2008). On the diagnosticity of multiple-witness identifications. *Law and Human Behavior, 32*, 406–422.

Clarke, J. N., & Everest, M. M. (2006). Cancer in the mass print media: fear, uncertainty and the medical model. *Social Science & Medicine, 62*, 2591–2600.

Clarkson, B. (2009, April 28). A blow against racism: Student strikes back after being hit, taunted—and finds himself charged with assault. *Toronto Sun*. Retrieved October 25, 2011, from http://www.torontosun.com/news/canada/2009/04/28/9272411-sun.html

Clément, M. È., & Chamberland, C. (2007). Physical violence and psychological aggression towards children: Five-year trends in practices and attitudes from two population surveys. *Child Abuse & Neglect, 31*, 1001–1011.

Cliff, J. E. (1998). Does one size fit all? Exploring the relationship between attitudes toward growth, gender, and business size. *Journal of Business Venturing, 13*, 523–542.

Cochran, J. K., & Chamlin, M. B. (2000). Deterrence and brutalization: The dual effects of executions. *Justice Quarterly, 17*, 685–706.

Cohen, B., Waugh, G., & Place, K. (1989). At the movies: An unobtrusive study of arousal-attraction. *Journal of Social Psychology, 129*, 691–693.

Cohen, D., & Nisbett, R. (1997). Field experiments examination the culture of honor: The role of institutions in perpetuating norms about violence. *Personality & Social Psychology Bulletin, 23*, 1188.

Cohen, D., Nisbett, R. E., Bowdle, B. F., & Schwartz, N. (1996). Insult, aggression, and the Southern culture of honor: An "experimental ethnography." *Journal of Personality and Social Psychology, 70*, 945–960.

Cohen, J. D. (2005). The vulcanization of the human brain: A neural perspective on interactions between cognition and emotion. *Journal of Economic Perspectives, 19*, 3–24.

Cole, T. (2001). Lying to the one you love: The use of deception in romantic relationships. *Journal of Social and Personal Relationships, 18*, 107–129.

Collins, B. E., & Guetzkow, H. (1964). *A social psychology of group processes for decision making*. New York: Wiley.

Collins, N. C., & Feeney, B. C. (2004). Working models of attachment shape perceptions of social support: Evidence from experimental and observational studies. *Journal of Personality and Social Psychology, 87*, 363–383.

Collins, N. L., & Miller, L. C. (1994). Self-disclosure and liking: A meta-analytic review. *Psychological Bulletin, 116*, 457–475.

Comer, D. (1995). A model of social loafing in real work groups. *Human Relations, 48*, 647–667.

Conflict Research Consortium. (1998). Step-by-step de-escalation (GRIT). Retrieved November 30, 2010, from http://www.colorado.edu/conflict/peace/treatment/grit.htm

Connolly, D. A. & Read, J. D. (2006). Delayed prosecutions of historic child sexual abuse: Analyses of 2064 Canadian criminal complaints. *Law and Human Behavior*, 30, 409–434.

Connolly, D. A., Price, H. L., & Read, J. D. (2006). Predicting expert social science testimony in criminal prosecutions of historic child sexual abuse. *Legal and Criminological Psychology, 11,* 55–74.

Conway, M., & Vartanian, L. R. (2000). A status account of gender stereotypes: Beyond communality and agency. *Sex Roles, 43*, 181–199.

Cooley, C. H. (1902). *Human nature and the social order*. New York: Schocken Books.

Cooper, J., & Fazio, R. H. (1984). A new look at dissonance theory. *Advances in Experimental Social Psychology, 17,* 229–265.

Cooper, W. H. (1981). Ubiquitous halo. *Psychological Bulletin, 90,* 218–244.

Corey, S. M. (1937). Professed attitudes and actual behavior. *Journal of Educational Psychology, 28*, 271–280.

Corman, S. R., Hess, A., & Justus, Z. S. (2006). Credibility in the global war on terrorism: Strategic principles and research agenda. Consortium for Strategic Communication, Arizona State University.

Correll, J., Park, B., Judd, C. M., & Wittenbrink, B. (2002). The police officer's dilemma: Using ethnicity to disambiguate potentially threatening individuals. *Journal of Personality & Social Psychology, 83*, 1314–1329.

Correll, J., Spencer, S. J., & Zanna, M. P. (2004). An affirmed self and an open mind: Self-affirmation and sensitivity to argument strength. *Journal of Experimental Social Psychology, 40,* 350–356.

Coser, L. A. (1956). *The functions of social conflict*. Glencoe, IL: Free Press.

Courage, M. L., Edison, S. C., & Howe, M. L. (2004). Variability in the early development of visual self-recognition. *Infant Behavior & Development, 27*, 509–532.

Craig, W. M., Pepler, D., & Atlas, R. (2000). Observations of bullying in the playground and in the classroom. *School Psychology International, 21*, 22–36.

Craik, F. I. M., Moroz, T. M., Moscovitch, M., Stuss, D. T., Winocur, G., Tulving, E., et al. (1999). In search of the self: A positron emission tomography study. *Psychological Science, 10*, 26–34.

Cramer, R. E., McMaster, M. R., Bartell, P. A., & Dragna, M. (1988). Subject competence and minimization of the bystander effect. *Journal of Applied Social Psychology, 18,* 1133–1148.

Crandall, C. S., Eshleman, A., & O'Brien, L. T. (2002). Social norms and the expression and suppression of prejudice: The struggle for internalization. *Journal of Personality and Social Psychology, 82*, 359–378.

Crano, W. D. (1997). Vested interest, symbolic politics, and attitude-behavior consistency. *Journal of Personality and Social Psychology, 72*, 485–491.

Crawford, J. (1998, May). *Media, stereotypes and the perpetuation of racism in Canada*. Unpublished report. University of Saskatchewan. Retrieved October 25, 2011, from http://www.usask.ca/education/coursework/802papers/crawford/jamesc.html

Crick, N. R., & Grotpeter, J. K. (1995). Relational aggression, gender, and social-psychological adjustment. *Child Development*, 66, 710–722.

Crick, N. R., & Rose, A. (2000). Toward a gender-balanced approach to the study of social-emotional development. *Toward a Feminist Developmental Psychology*. Routledge: New York, NY, 153–168.

Crick, N. R., & Dodge, K. A. (1994). A review and reformulation of social information processing mechanisms in children's social adjustment. *Psychological Bulletin, 115*, 74–101.

Crocker, J. (2002). The costs of seeking self-esteem. *Journal of Social Issues, 58*, 597–615.

Crocker, J., & Luhtanen, R. K. (2003). Level of self-esteem and contingencies of self-worth: Unique effects on academic, social, and financial problems in college freshmen. *Personality and Social Psychology Bulletin, 29*, 701–712.

Crocker, J., & Park, L. E. (2004). The costly pursuit of self-esteem. *Psychological Bulletin, 130*, 392–414.

Cropanzano, R. (Ed.). (1993). *Justice in the workplace*. Hillsdale, NJ: Erlbaum.

Crosby, F. J. (1976). A model of egoistical relative deprivation. *Psychological Review, 83*, 85–113.

Crosby, F., Bromley, S., & Saxe, L. (1980). Recent unobtrusive studies of black and white discrimination and prejudice: A literature review. *Psychological Bulletin, 87*, 546–563.

Cross, S. E., Bacon, P. L., & Morris, M. L. (2000). The relational-interdependent self-construal and relationships. *Journal of Personality and Social Psychology, 78*, 791–808.

Crowley, A. E., & Hoyer, W. D. (1994). An integrative framework for understanding two-sided persuasion. *Journal of Consumer Research, 20*, 561–574.

Crown seeks life in B.C. skinhead sentencing hearing. (1999, October 5). *CBC News*. Retrieved November 4, 2011, from http://www.cbc.ca/news/canada/story/1999/10/04/skinhead991004.html

Cruz, J. (2011, October 6). Apple stock little changed after co-founder Jobs passes away. *Bloomberg*. Retrieved October 17, 2011, from http://www.bloomberg.com/news/2011-10-06/apple-drops-in-german-floor-trading-after-steve-jobs-s-death-from-cancer.html

Cunningham, J. A., & Selby, P. L. (2007). Implications of the normative fallacy in young adult smokers aged 19-24 years. *American Journal of Public Health, 97*, 1399-1400.

Cunningham, M. R., Roberts, A. R., Barbee, A. P., Druen, P. B., & Wu, C. H. (1995). "Their ideas of beauty are, on the whole, the same as ours": Consistency and variability in the cross-cultural perception of female physical attractiveness. *Journal of Personality and Social Psychology, 68*, 261-279.

Cunningham, W. A., Johnson, M. K., Gatenby, J. C., Gore, J. C., & Banaji, M. R. (2003). Neural components of social evaluation. *Journal of Personality and Social Psychology, 85*, 639-649.

Cunningham, W. A., Johnson, M. K., Raye, C. L., Gatenby, J. C., Gore, J. C., & Banaji, M. R. (2004). Separable neural components in the processing of black and white faces. *Psychological Science, 15*, 806-813.

Cutshall, J., & Yuille, J. C. (1989). Field studied of eyewitness memory of actual crimes. In D. C. Raskin (Ed.), *Psychological methods in criminal investigation and evidence* (pp. 97-124). New York, NY: Springer Publishing Company.

D'Agostino, P. R., & Fincher-Kiefer, R. (1992). Need for cognition and the correspondence bias. *Social Cognition, 10*, 151-163.

Dabbs, J. M., Jr., & Hargrove, M. F. (1997). Age, testosterone, and behavior among female prison inmates. *Psychosomatic Medicine, 59*, 477-480.

Dabbs, J. M., Jr., & Morris, R. (1990). Testosterone, social class, and antisocial behavior in a sample of 4,462 men. *Psychological Science, 1*, 209-211.

Dabbs, J. M., Jr., Carr, T. S., Frady, R. L., & Riad, J. K. (1995). Testosterone, crime, and misbehavior among 692 male prison inmates. *Personality and Individual Differences, 18*, 627-633.

Dahl, D. W., Darke, P. R., Gorn, G. J., & Weinberg, C. B. (2005). Promiscuous or confident? Attitudinal ambivalence toward condom purchase. *Journal of Applied Social Psychology, 35*, 869-887.

Dal Cin, S., MacDonald, T. K., Fong, G. T., Zanna, M. P., & Elton, T. E. (2006). Remembering the message: Using a reminder cue to increase condom use following a safer sex intervention. *Health Psychology, 25*, 448-443.

Daly, M., & Wilson, M. (1989). Homicide and cultural evolution. *Ethology and Sociobiology, 10*, 99-110.

Dangerous offender: What the label means. (2011, August 15). *CBC News.* Retrieved August 23, 2011, from http://www.cbc.ca/news/canada/story/2010/10/21/f-dangerous-offender.html

Danzis, D. A., & Stone-Romero, E. F. (2009). Effects of helper sex, recipient attractiveness, and recipient femininity on helping behavior in organizations. *Journal of Managerial Psychology, 24*, 722-737.

Darley, J. M., & Batson, C. D. (1973). "From Jerusalem to Jericho": A study of situational and dispositional variables in helping behavior. *Journal of Personality and Social Psychology, 27*, 100-108.

Darley, J. M., & Berscheid, E. (1967). Increased liking as a result of the anticipation of personal contact. *Human Relations, 20*, 29-39.

Darley, J. M., & Gross, P. H. (1983). A hypothesis-confirming bias in labeling effects. *Journal of Personality and Social Psychology, 44*, 20-33.

Darley, J. M., & Latane, B. (1968). Bystander intervention in emergencies: Diffusion of responsibility. *Journal of Personality and Social Psychology, 8*, 377-383.

Dauvergne, M. (2007). Crime statistics in Canada, 2007. *Juristat, 28*, 1-17.

Dauvergne, M., & Brennan, S. (2011, June 7). Police-reported hate crime in Canada, 2009. *Juristat*, no. 85-002-X.

Davies, P. G., Spencer, S. J., & Steele, C. M. (2005). Clearing the air: Identity safety moderates the effects of stereotype threat on women's leadership aspirations. *Journal of Personality and Social Psychology, 88*, 276-287.

Davies, P. G., Spencer, S. J., Quinn, D. M., & Gerhardstein, R. (2002). All consuming images: How demeaning commercials that elicit stereotype threat can restrain women academically and professionally. *Personality and Social Psychology Bulletin, 28*, 1615-1628.

Davila, J., & Cobb, R. J. (2003). Predicting change in self-reported and interviewer-assessed attachment security: Tests of the individual and life-stress model. *Personality and Social Psychology Bulletin, 29*, 859-870.

Davis, D., & Follette, W. C. (2002). Rethinking the probative value of evidence: Base rates, intuitive profiling, and the "*post*diction" of behavior. *Law and Human Behavior, 26*, 133-158.

Davis, D., Shaver, P. R., & Vernon, M. L. (2004). Attachment style and subjective motivations for sex. *Personality and Social Psychology Bulletin, 30*, 1076-1090. Previously presented at Annual Meeting of the Western Psychological Association, Portland, OR, 2000.

Davis, J. H. (1973). Group decision and social interaction: A theory of social decision schemes. *Psychological Review: 80*, 97-125.

Dawes, R. M. (1990). The potential nonfalsity of the false consensus effect. In R. M. Hogarth (Ed.), *Insights in decision making:A tribute to Hillel J. Einhorn* (pp. 179-199). Chicago: University of Chicago Press.

Dawkins, R. (1976). *The selfish gene.* Oxford: Oxford University Press. de Vries, L. (2005). Opposites attract, but marry? *CBS News*. Retrieved July 5, 2010, from http://www.cbsnews.com/stories/2005/02/14/health/webmd/main674003.shtml.

de Wit, J. B. F., Das, E., & Vet, R. (2008). What works best: Objective statistics or a personal testimonial? An assessment of the persuasive effects of different types of message evidence on risk perception. *Health Psychology, 27*, 110-115.

DeBruine, L. M. (2005). Trustworthy but not lust-worthy: Context-specific effects of facial resemblance. *Proceedings of the Royal Society of Biological Sciences, 272*, 919-922.

DeBruine, L. M., Jones, B. C., Unger, L., Little, A. C., & Feinberg, D. R. (2007). Dissociating averageness and attractiveness: Attractive faces are not always average. *Journal of Experimental Psychology: Human Perception and Performance, 33*, 1420-1430.

Decety, J., & Jackson, P. L. (2006). A social-neuroscience perspective on empathy. *Current Directions in Psychological Science, 15*, 54-58.

Deci, E. L., La Guardia, J. G., Moller, A. C., Scheiner, M. J., & Ryan, R. M. (2006). On the benefits of giving as well as receiving autonomy support: Mutuality in close friendships. *Personality and Social Psychology Bulletin, 32*, 313-327.

Delplanque, S., Lavoie, M. E., Hot, P., Silvert, L., & Sequeira, H. (2004). Modulation of cognitive processing by emotional valence studied through event-related potentials in humans. *Neuroscience Letters, 356*, 1-4.

DePaulo, B. M., & Kashy, D. A. (1998). Everyday lies in close and casual relationships. *Journal of Personality and Social Psychology,74*, 63-79.

DePaulo, B. M., Lindsay, J. J., Malone, B. E., Muhlenbruck, L., Charlton, K., & Cooper, H. (2003). Cues to deception. *Psychological Bulletin, 129*, 74-118.

Destin, M., & Oyserman, D. (2010). Incentivizing education: Seeing schoolwork as an investment, not a chore. *Journal of Experimental Social Psychology, 43*, 505-512.

Deutsch, M., & Collins, M. E. (1951). *Interracial housing: A psychological evaluation of a social experiment.* Minneapolis, MN: University of Minnesota.

Devine, D. J., Clayton, L. D., Dunford, B. B., Seying, R., & Pryce, J. (2000). Jury decision making: 45 years of empirical research on deliberating groups. *Psychology, Public Policy, and Law, 7*, 622-727.

Devine, P. (1989). Stereotypes and prejudice: Their automatic and controlled components. *Journal of Personality and Social Psychology, 56*, 5-18.

Dhont, K., & Van Hiel, A. (2009). We must not be enemies: Interracial contact and the reduction of prejudice among authoritarians. *Personality and Individual Differences, 46*, 172-177.

Dickerson, C., Thibodeau, R., Aronson, E., & Miller, D. (1992). Using cognitive dissonance to encourage water conservation. *Journal of Applied Social Psychology, 22*, 841-854.

Diener, E., Fraser, S. C., Beaman, A. L., & Kelem, R. T. (1976). Effects of deindividuation variables on stealing among Halloween trick-or-treaters. *Journal of Personality and Social Psychology, 33*, 178-183.

Dijkstra, P., & Buunk, B. P. (1998). Jealousy as a function of rival characteristics: An evolutionary perspective. *Personality and Social Psychology Bulletin, 24*, 1158-1166.

Dillard, A. J., Midboe, A. M., & Klein, W. M. P. (2009). The dark side of optimism: Unrealistic optimism about problems with alcohol predicts subsequent negative event experiences. *Personality and Social Psychology Bulletin, 35*, 1540-1550.

Dion, K. K., & Dion, K. L. (1996). Cultural perspective on romantic love. *Personal Relationships, 3*, 5-17.

Dion, K. K., & Stein, S. (1978). Physical attractiveness and interpersonal influence. *Journal of Experimental Social Psychology, 14*, 97-108.

Dion, K. K., Berscheid, E., & Walster, E. (1972). What is beautiful is good. *Journal of Personality and Social Psychology, 24*, 285-290.

Dion, K. K., Pak, A. W. P., & Dion, K. L. (1990). Stereotyping physical attractiveness: A sociocultural perspective. *Journal of Cross-Cultural Psychology, 21*, 158-179.

Dion, K. L., & Dion, K. K. (1993). Individualistic and collectivistic perspectives on gender and the cultural concept of love and intimacy. *Journal of Social Issues, 49*, 53–69.

Dittman, M. (2004). What makes good people do bad things? *Monitor on Psychology, 35*, 68.

Dodge, K. A. (1986). A social information processing model of social competence in children. In M. Perlmutter (Ed.), *Minnesota Symposium on Child Psychology* (Vol. 18, pp. 77–125). Hillsdale, NJ: Erlbaum.

Dodge, K. A., Price, J. M., Bachorowski, J., & Newman, J. P. (1990). Hostile attributional tendencies in severely aggressive adolescents. *Journal of Abnormal Psychology, 99*, 385–392.

Dollard, J., Doob, L. W., Miller, N. E., Mowrer, O. H., & Sears, R. R. (1939). *Frustration and aggression*. New Haven,CT: Yale University.

Donohue, J. J., & Wolfers, J. (2006). The death penalty: No evidence for deterrence. *The Economists' Voice, 3*, 3.

Dovidio, J. F. (1984). Helping behavior and altruism: An empirical and conceptual overview. In L. Berkowitz (Ed.), *Advances in experimental social psychology* (Vol. 17, pp. 361–427). New York: Academic Press.

Dovidio, J. F., & Gaertner, S. L. (1983). Race, normative structure, and help-seeking. In B. M. DePaulo, A. Nadler, & J. D. Fisher (Eds.), *New directions in helping* (Vol. 2, pp. 285–302). New York: Academic Press.

Dovidio, J. F., & Gaertner, S. L. (2000). Aversive racism and selection decisions: 1989 and 1999. *Psychological Science, 11*, 315–319.

Dovidio, J. F., & Penner, L. A. (2007). Helping and altruism. In G. J. O. Fletcher and M. S. Clark (Eds.), *Blackwell handbook of social psychology: Interpersonal processes* (pp. 162–195). Maiden, MA: Blackwell Publishers, Ltd.

Dovidio, J. F., Gaertner, S. L., Validzic, A., Matoka, K., Johnson, B., & Frazier, S. (1997). Extending the benefits of recategorization: Evaluations, self-disclosure, and helping. *Journal of Experimental Social Psychology, 33*, 401–420.

Dovidio, J. F., Glick, P., & Rudman, L. A. (2005). *On the nature of prejudice: Fifty years after Allport*. Malden, MA: Blackwell Publishing.

Dovidio, J. F., Piliavin, J. A., Gaertner, S. L., Schroeder, D. A., & Clark, R. D., III. (1991). The arousal: Cost-reward model and the process of intervention: A review of the evidence. In M. S. Clark (Ed.), *Review of personality and social psychology: Vol. 12. Prosocial behavior* (pp. 86–118). Newbury Park, CA: Sage.

Downey, G., Freitas, A. L., Michaelis, B., & Khouri, H. (1998). The self-fulfilling prophecy in close relationships: Rejection sensitivity and rejection by romantic partners. *Journal of Personality and Social Psychology, 75*, 545–560.

Downs, C., & Lyons, P. (1991). Natural observations of the links between attractiveness and initial legal judgments. *Personality and Social Psychology Bulletin, 17*, 541–547.

Drachman, D., DeCarufel, A., & Insko, C. (1978). The extra credit effect in interpersonal attraction. *Journal of Experimental Social Psychology, 14*, 458–459.

Duff, K., & Newman, L. S. (1997). Individual differences in the spontaneous construal of behavior: Idiocentrism and the automatization of the trait inference process. *Social Cognition, 15*, 217–241.

Duncan, B. L. (1976). Differential social perception and attribution of intergroup violence: Testing the lower limits of stereotyping of blacks. *Journal of Personality and Social Psychology, 34*, 590–598.

Dunfield, K. A., & Kuhlmeier, V. A. (2010). Intention-mediated selective helping in human infants. *Psychological Science, 21*, 523–527.

Dunn, E. W., & Ashton-James, C. (2008). On emotional innumeracy: Predicted and actual affective responses to grand-scale tragedies. *Journal of Experimental Social Psychology, 44*, 692–698.

Dunn, E. W., Brackett, M. A., Ashton-James, C., Schneiderman, E., & Salovey, P. (2007). On emotionally intelligent time travel: Individual differences in affective forecasting ability. *Personality and Social Psychology Bulletin, 33*, 85–93.

Durrant, J. E., Rose-Krasnor, L., & Broberg, A. G. (2003). Physical punishment and maternal beliefs in Sweden and Canada. *Journal of Comparative Family Studies, 34*, 586–604.

Dutton, D. G. (1971). Reactions of restaurateurs to blacks and whites violating restaurant dress regulations. *Canadian Journal of Behavioural Science, 3*, 298–302.

Dutton, D. G., & Aron, A. P. (1974). Some evidence for heightened sexual attraction under conditions of high anxiety. *Journal of Personality and Social Psychology, 30*, 510–517.

Dutton, D. G., Saunders, K., Starzomski, A., & Bartholomew, K. (1994). Intimacy-anger and insecure attachment as predictors of abuse in intimate relationships. *Journal of Applied Social Psychology, 24*, 1367–1386.

Dweck, C. S. (1999). *Self-theories: Their role in motivation, personality and development.* Philadelphia, PA: The Psychology Press.

Dwyer, J. (2007, February 11). Fugitive. *The New York Times*. Retrieved August 2, 2010, from http://www.nytimes.com/2007/02/11/magazine/11Boquete.t.html

Eagly, A. H. (1978). Sex differences in influenceability. *Psychological Bulletin, 85*, 86–116.

Eagly, A. H. (1987). *Sex differences in social behavior: A social-role interpretation*. Hillsdale, NJ: Erlbaum.

Eagly, A. H., & Chaiken, S. (1993). *The Psychology of Attitudes*. Fort Worth, TX: Harcourt Brace Jovanovich.

Eagly, A. H., & Chaiken, S. (1998). Attitude structure and function. In D. T. Gilbert, S. T. Fiske, & G. Lindzey (Eds.), *The Handbook of Social Psychology* (4th ed., Vol. 1, pp. 269–322). New York: McGraw-Hill.

Eagly, A. H., & Chrvala, C. (1986). Sex differences in conformity: Status and gender role interpretations. *Psychology of Women Quarterly, 10*, 203–220.

Eagly, A. H., & Crowley, M. (1986). Gender and helping behavior: A meta-analytic review of the social psychological literature. *Psychological Bulletin, 100*, 283–308.

Eagly, A. H., & Karau, S. J. (2002). Role congruity theory of prejudice toward female leaders. *Psychological Review, 109*, 573–598.

Eagly, A. H., & Wood, W. (1991). Explaining sex differences in social behavior: A meta-analytic perspective. *Personality and Social Psychology Bulletin, 17*, 306–315.

Eagly, A. H., Ashmore, R. D., Makhijani, M. G., & Longo, L. C. (1991). What is beautiful is good, but . . . : A meta-analytic review of research on the physical attractiveness stereotype. *Psychological Bulletin, 110*, 109–128.

Eagly, A. H., Johannesen-Schmidt, M. C., & van Engen, M. L. (2003). Transformational, transactional, and laissez-faire leadership styles: A meta-analysis comparing men and women. *Psychological Bulletin, 129*, 569–591.

Edelmann, R. J., Childs, J., Harvey, S., Kellock, I., & Strain-Clark, C. (1984). The effect of embarrassment on helping. *Journal of Social Psychology, 124*, 253–254.

Edlund, J. E., & Sagarin, B. J. (2009). Sex differences in jealousy: Misinterpretation of nonsignificant results as refuting the theory. *Personal Relationships, 16*, 67–78.

Eich, E. (1995). Searching for mood dependent memory. *Psychological Science, 6*, 67–75.

Eich, E., & Macaulay, D. (2000). Are real moods required to reveal mood-congruent and mood-dependent memory? *Psychological Science, 11*, 244–248.

Eichstedt, J. A., Serbin, L. A., Poulin-Dubois, D., & Sen, M. G. (2002). Of bears and men: Infants' knowledge of conventional and metaphorical gender stereotypes. *Infant Behavior & Development, 25*, 296–310.

Eisenberg, N., & Miller, P. (1987). The relation of empathy to pro-social and related behaviors. *Psychological Bulletin, 101*, 91–119.

Eisenberg, N., Fabes, R. A., Miller, P. A., Fultz, J., Shell, R., . . . Reno, R. R. (1989). Relation of sympathy and personal distress to prosocial behavior: A multimethod study. *Journal of Personality and Social Psychology, 57*, 55–66.

Eisenberger, N. I., Lieberman, M. D., & Williams, K. D. (2003). Does rejection hurt? An fMRI study of social exclusion. *Science, 302*, 290–292.

Eisend, M. (2006). Two-sided advertising: A meta-analysis. *International Journal of Research in Marketing, 23*, 187–198.

Ekman, P. (1994). Strong evidence for universals in facial expressions: A reply to Russell's mistaken critique. *Psychological Bulletin, 115*, 268–287.

Ekman, P. (2007). *Emotions revealed: Recognizing faces and feelings to improve communication and emotional life* (2nd ed.). New York: Owl Books.

Ekman, P. (2009). *Telling lies: Clues to deceit in the marketplace, politics, and marriage* (3rd ed.). New York: W. W. Norton & Company.

Eliot, L. (2009). *Pink brain, blue brain: How small differences grow into troublesome gaps—and what we can do about it.* New York, NY: Houghton Mifflin Harcourt Publishing.

Ellison, N. B., Steinfield, C., & Lampe, C. (2007). The benefits of Facebook "friends": Social capital and college students' use of online social network sites. *Journal of Computer-Mediated Communication, 12*, 1143–1168.

Ensslen, K., & Peace, K. A. (2010). *The stranger in the alley stole my purse!: The influence of schemas and repeated recall on memory.* Poster presented at the Banff Annual Seminar in Cognitive Science (BASICS). Banff, AB, Canada.

Ensslen, K., & Peace, K. A. (2010, April). *The stranger in the alley stole my purse!: The influence of schemas and repeated recall on memory*. Poster presented at the Banff Annual Seminar in Cognitive Science. Banff, Alberta, Canada.

Erb, H., Bohner, G., Schmilzle, K., & Rank, S. (1998). Beyond conflict and discrepancy: Cognitive bias in minority and majority influence. *Personality and Social Psychology Bulletin, 24*, 620–633.

Erskine, J. A. K. (2008). Resistance can be futile: Investigating behavioural rebound. *Appetite, 50*, 415–421.

Esser, J. K. (1998). Alive and well after 25 years: A review of groupthink research. *Organizational Behavior and Human Decision Processes, 73*, 116–141.

Esses, V. M., & Hodson, G. (2006). The role of lay perceptions of ethnic prejudice in the maintenance and perpetuation of ethnic bias. *Journal of Social Issues, 62*, 453–468.

Esses, V. M., Dovidio, J. F., & Hodson, G. (2002). Public attitudes toward immigration in the United States and Canada in response to the September 11, 2001 "Attack on America." *Analysis of Social Issues and Public Policy, 2,* 69–85.

Esses, V. M., Jackson, L. M., & Armstrong, T. L. (1998). Intergroup competition and attitudes toward immigrants and immigration: An instrumental model of group conflict. *Journal of Social Issues, 54*, 699–724.

Evans, A. N., & Rooney, B. J. (2008). *Methods in psychological research*. Thousand Oaks, Calif.: Sage Publishing.

Evans, C. R., & Dion, K. L. (1991). Group cohesion and performance: A meta-analysis. *Small Group Research, 22*, 175–186.

Evans, J. A. (2002). Cautious caregivers: Gender stereotypes and the sexualization of men nurses' touch. *Journal of Advanced Nursing, 40*, 441–448.

Evans, L., & Stukas, A. A. (2007). Self-verification by women and responses of their partners around issues of appearance and weight: "Do I look fat in this?" *Journal of Social and Clinical Psychology*. *26*, 1163–1188.

Eyre, H. L. (2000). *The use of covariation information in the causal attribution of others' emotion.* Unpublished Masters' Thesis. Simon Fraser University, Burnaby, British Columbia.

Farr, R. M. (1996). *The roots of modern social psychology*. Cambridge, MA: Blackwell Publishing.

Fast, N. J., & Tiedens, L. Z. (2010). Blame contagion: The automatic transmission of self-serving attributions. *Journal of Experimental Social Psychology*, *46*, 97–106.

Fazio, R. H. (1995). Attitudes as object-evaluation associations: Determinants, consequences, and correlates of attitude accessibility. In R. E. Petty & J. A. Krosnick (Eds.), *Attitude Strength: Antecedents and Consequences* (pp. 247–282). Hillsdale, NJ: Erlbaum.

Fazio, R. H., & Olson, M. A. (2003). Attitudes: Foundations, functions, and consequences. In M. A. Hogg & J. Cooper (Eds.), *The Handbook of Social Psychology*. London: Sage, 139–160.

Fazio, R. H., & Olson, M. A. (2003). Implicit measures in social cognition research: Their meaning and use. *Annual Review of Psychology*, *54*, 297–327.

Fazio, R. H., Chen, J., McDonel, E. C., & Sherman, S. J. (1982). Attitude accessibility, attitude-behavior consistency, and the strength of the object-evaluation association. *Journal of Experimental Social Psychology, 18,* 339–357.

Fazio, R. H., Ledbetter, J. E., & Towles-Schwen, T. (2000). On the costs of accessible attitudes: Detecting that the attitude object has changed. *Journal of Personality and Social Psychology*, *78*, 197–210.

Federman, J. (Ed.). (1997). *National television violence study*. Santa Barbara: University of California, Center for Communication and Social Policy.

Feeney, J. A., & Noller, P. (1990). Attachment styles as a predictor of adult romantic relationships. *Journal of Personality and Social Psychology*, *58*, 281–291.

Fehr, B. (2006). A prototype approach to studying love. In R. J. Sternberg & K. Weis (Eds.), *The new psychology of love* (pp. 225–246). Binghamtom, NY: Vail-Ballou Press.

Fehr, E., Fischbacher, U., & Gächter, S. (2002). Strong reciprocity, human cooperation and the enforcement of social norms. *Human Nature, 13*, 1–25.

Fein, S., & Spencer, S. J. (1997). Prejudice as self-image maintenance: Affirming the self through derogating others. *Journal of Personality and Social Psychology, 73*, 31–44.

Feingold, A. (1988). Matching for attractiveness in romantic partners and same-sex friends: A meta-analysis and theoretical critique. *Psychological Bulletin*, *104*, 226–235.

Feldman, R., Weller, A., Zagoory-Sharon, O., & Levine, A. (2007). Evidence for a neuroendocrinological foundation of human affiliation: Plasma oxytocin levels across pregnancy and the postpartum period predict mother–infant bonding. *Psychological Science*, *18*, 965–970.

Festinger, L. (1954). A theory of social comparison processes. *Human Relations, 7,* 117–140.

Festinger, L. (1957). *A theory of cognitive dissonance*. Stanford, CA: Stanford University Press.

Festinger, L., & Carlsmith, J. M. (1959). Cognitive consequences of forced compliance. *Journal of Abnormal and Social Psychology, 58*, 203–210.

Festinger, L., Schachter, S., & Back, K. (1950). *Social pressures in informal groups: A study of human factors in housing*. New York: Harper.

Finger, E. C. (in press). New potential therapeutic approaches in frontotemporal dementia: Oxytocin, vasopressin, and social cognition. *Journal of Molecular Neuroscience*.

Fischer, P., & Greitemeyer, T. (2006). Music and aggression: The impact of sexual-aggressive song lyrics on aggression-related thoughts, emotions, and behavior towards the same and the opposite sex. *Personality and Social Psychology Bulletin*, *32*, 1165–1176.

Fischhoff, B. (2007). An early history of hindsight research. *Social Cognition*, *25*, 10–13.

Fisher, J. D., Fisher, W. A., Bryan, A. D., & Misovich, S. J. (2002). Information-motivation-behavioral skills model-based HIV risk behavior change intervention for inner-city high school youth. *Health Psychology, 21*, 177–186.

Fisher, R. J., & Ackerman, D. (1998). The effects of recognition and group need on volunteerism: A social norm perspective. *Journal of Consumer Research, 25*, 262–275.

Fisher, R. J., Vandenbosch, M., & Antia, K. D. (2008). An empathy-helping perspective on consumers' responses to fund-raising appeals. *Journal of Consumer Research, 35*, 1–13.

Fiske, S. T., Gilbert, D. T., & Lindzey, G. (2009). *Handbook of social psychology* (5th Ed.). Hoboken, NJ: John Wiley & Sons.

Fitzsimons, G. M., & Bargh, J. A. (2003). Thinking of you: Nonconscious pursuit of interpersonal goals associated with relationship partners. *Journal of Personality and Social Psychology, 84*, 148–164.

Flowe, H. D., & Humphries, J. E. (2011). An examination of criminal face bias in a random sample of police lineups. *Applied Cognitive Psychology, 25*, 265–273.

Flynn, F. J., & Lake, V. K. B. (2008). If you need help, just ask: Underestimating compliance with direct requests for help. *Journal of Personality and Social Psychology, 95,* 128–143.

Fontaine, P. (1998). Modern racism in Canada. *Queen's University Lecture Series*, 1–10.

Fordham, M., & Ketteridge, A. M. (1998). "Men must work and women must weep": Examining gender stereotypes in disasters. In E. Enarson & B. H. Morrow (Eds.), *The gendered terrain of disaster* (pp. 81–94). Miami, FL: Praeger Publications.

Forgas, J. P., & Williams, K. D. (Eds.) (2001). *Social influence: Direct and indirect processes*. Philadelphia, PA: Psychology Press.

Forgas, J. P., Bower, G. H., & Krantz, S. (1984). The influence of mood on perceptions of social interactions. *Journal of Experimental Social Psychology*, *20*, 497–513.

Forge, K. L., & Phemister, S. (1987). The effect of prosocial cartoons on preschool children. *Child Study Journal, 17*, 83–86.

Forrester, D. L., VanderLaan, D. P., Parker, J. L., & Vasey, P. L. (2011). Male sexual orientation and avuncularity in Canada: Implications for the kin selection hypothesis. *Journal of Cognition and Culture, 11*, 339–352.

Fortune, J. L., & Newby-Clark, I. R. (2008). My friend is embarrassing me: Exploring the guilty by association effect. *Journal of Personality and Social Psychology, 95*, 1440–1449.

Four in 10 1st marriages end in divorce: Report. (2010, October 4). *CBC News.* Retrieved July 14, 2011, from http://www.cbc.ca/news/canada/story/2010/10/04/vanier-study004.html

Fox, K. (1997). Mirror, mirror: A summary of research findings on body image. *Social Issues Research Centre*. Retrieved June 3, 2010, from http://www.sirc.org/publik/mirror.html

Frager, R. (1970). Conformity and anti-conformity in Japan. *Journal of Personality and Social Psychology, 15*, 203–210.

Fraley, R. C. (2002). Introduction to the special issue: The psychodynamics of adult attachments—bridging the gap between disparate research traditions. *Attachment and Human Development*, *4*, 131–132.

Freedman, J. (2002). *Media violence and its effect on aggression: Assessing the scientific evidence*. Toronto, ON: University of Toronto Press.

Freedman, J. L., & Fraser, S. C. (1966). Compliance without pressure: The foot-in-the-door technique. *Journal of Personality and Social Psychology*, *4*, 196–202.

Frisby, C. M. (1999, August). When bad things happen to bad people: Using social comparison theory to explain affective consequences of viewing TV talk shows. A paper presented to the Mass Communication and Society Division at the Association of Education in Journalism and Mass Communication Convention, New Orleans, LA.

Fujioka, Y., Ryan, E., Agle, M., Legaspi, M., & Toohey, R. (2009). The role of racial identity in responses to thin media ideals: Differences between Black and White college women. *Communication Research, 36*, 451–474.

Fung, H. H., & Carstensen, L. L. (2003). Sending memorable messages to the old: Age differences in preferences and memory for emotionally meaningful advertisements. *Journal of Personality and Social Psychology, 85*, 163–178.

Furnham, A. (2003). Belief in a just world: Research progress over the past decade. *Personality and Individual Differences, 34*, 795–817.

Gabriel, S., Carvallo, M., Dean, K.,Tippin, B., & Renaud, J. (2005). How I see me depends on how I see we: The role of attachment style in social comparison. *Personality and Social Psychology Bulletin, 31,* 1561–1572.

Gaertner, S. L. (1973). Helping behavior and racial discrimination among liberals and conservatives. *Journal of Personality and Social Psychology*, *25*, 335–341.

Gaertner, S. L., Dovidio, J. F., Banker, B. S., Houlette, M., Johnson, K. M., & McGlynn, E. A. (2000). Reducing intergroup conflict: From superordinate goals to decategorization, recategorization, and mutual differentiation. *Group Dynamics: Theory, Research, and Practice, 4*, 98–114.

Gaes, G. G., Kalle, R. J., & Tedeschi, J. T. (1978). Impression management in the forced compliance situation: Two studies using the bogus pipeline. *Journal of Experimental Social Psychology, 14*, 493–510.

Gagné, F. M., & Lydon, J. E. (2004). Bias and accuracy in close relationships: An integrative review. *Personality and Social Psychology Review, 8*, 322–338.

Gagné, M., & Zuckerman, M. (1999). Performance and learning goal orientations as moderators of social loafing and social facilitation. *Small Group Research, 30*, 524–541.

Gagnon, A., & Bourhis, R. Y. (1996). Discrimination in the minimal group paradigm: Social identity or self-interest? *Personality and Social Psychology Bulletin, 22*, 1289–1301.

Gallup, G. G. (1977). Chimpanzees: Self-recognition. *Science, 167*, 86–87.

Gannon, T. A., Keown, K., Polaschek, D. L. L. (2007). Increasing honest responding on cognitive distortions in child molesters: The bogus pipeline revisited. *Sexual Abuse: A Journal of Research and Treatment, 19*, 5–22.

Gansberg, M. (1964). Thirty-eight who saw murder didn't call police. *The New York Times.*

Garcia, S. M., Weaver, K., Moskowitz, G. B., & Darley, J. M. (2002). Crowded minds: The implicit bystander effect. *Journal of Personality and Social Psychology, 83,* 843–853.

Gass, R. H., & Seiter, J. S. (2003). *Persuasion, Social Influence, and Compliance Gaining* (2nd ed.). Boston, MA: Allyn & Bacon.

Gavanski, I., & Wells, G. L. (1989). Counterfactual processing of normal and exceptional events. *Journal of Experimental Social Psychology, 25*, 314–325.

Gawronski, B. (2003). Implicational schemata and the correspondence bias: On the diagnostic value of situationally constructed behavior. *Journal of Personality and Social Psychology*, *84*, 1154–1171.

Gawronski, B. (2009). Ten frequently asked questions about implicit measures and their frequently supposed, but not entirely correct answers. *Canadian Psychology, 50*, 141–150.

Gawronski, B., & Bodenhausen, G. V. (2006). Associative and propositional processes in evaluation: An integrative implicit and explicit attitude change. *Psychological Bulletin, 132*, 692–731.

Gawronski, B., Peters, K. R., Brochu, P. M., & Strack, F. (2008). Understanding the relations between different forms of racial prejudice: A cognitive consistency perspective. *Personality and Social Psychology Bulletin, 34*, 648–665.

Geary, D. C., Vigil, J., & Byrd-Craven, J. (2004). Evolution of human mate choice. *The Journal of Sex Research*, *41*, 27–42.

Geen, R. G., & Donnerstein, E. (Eds.) (1998). *Human aggression: Theories, research, and implications for social policy*. San Diego, CA: Academic Press.

Geist, M. (2007, October 2). Radiohead's pay-as-you-can. Retrieved August 13, 2011, from http://www.michaelgeist.ca/content/view/2273/85/

George, D., Carroll, P., Kersnick, R., & Calderon, K. (1998). Gender-related patterns of helping among friends. *Psychology of Women Quarterly, 22*, 685–704.

George, J. M., & Brief, A. P. (1992). Feeling good-doing good: A conceptual analysis of the mood at work-organizational spontaneity relationship. *Psychological Bulletin, 112*, 310–329.

Gerard, H. B., Wilhelmy, R. A., & Conolley, E. S. (1968). Conformity and group size. *Journal of Personality and Social Psychology*, *8*, 79–82.

Gergen, K. J. (1973). Social psychology as history. *Journal of Personality and Social Psychology*, *26*, 309–320.

Gerrard, M., Gibbons, F. X., & Bushman, B. J. (1996). The relation between perceived vulnerability to HIV and precautionary sexual behavior. *Psychological Bulletin, 119,* 390–409.

Gershoff, A. D., Mukherjee, A., & Mukhopadhyay, A. (2008). What's not to like? Preference asymmetry in the false consensus effect. *Journal of Consumer Research*, *35*, 119–125.

Gerstenfeld, P. B., Grant, D. R., & Chang, C. P. (2003). Hate online: A content analysis of extremist websites. *Analyses of Social Issues and Public Policy*, *3*, 29–44.

Gibbs, J. L., Ellison, N. B., & Heino, R. D. (2006). Self-presentation in online personals: The role of anticipated future interaction, self-disclosure, and perceived success in internet dating. *Communication Research, 33*, 152–177.

Gibson, B. (2008). Can evaluative conditioning change attitudes toward mature brands: New evidence from the Implicit Association Test. *Journal of Consumer Research, 35*, 178–188.

Gibson, B., & Maurer, J. (2000). Cigarette smoking in the movies: The influence of product placement on attitudes toward smoking and smokers. *Journal of Applied Social Psychology, 30*, 1457–1473.

Gigerenzer, G. (2004a). Dread risk, September 11, and fatal traffic accidents. *Psychological Science*, *15*, 286–287.

Gigerenzer, G. (2004b). Fast and frugal heuristics: The tools of bounded rationality. In D. Koehler & N. Harvey (Eds.), *Blackwell handbook of judgment and decision making* (pp. 62–88). Oxford, UK: Blackwell.

Gilbert, D. (2006). *Stumbling on Happiness*. New York: Random House.

Gilbert, D. T., & Ebert, J. E. J. (2002). Decisions and revisions: The affective forecasting of escapable outcomes. Unpublished manuscript, Harvard University.

Gilbert, D. T., Pinel, E. C., Wilson, T. D., Blumberg, S. J., & Wheatley, T. (1998). Immune neglect: A source of durability bias in affective forecasting. *Journal of Personality and Social Psychology*, *75*, 617–638.

Gilbert, D., & Malone, P. (1995). The correspondence bias. *Psychological Bulletin*, *117*, 21–38.

Gilbert, D., Pelham, B., & Krull, D. (1988). On cognitive busyness: When person perceivers meet persons perceived. *Journal of Personality and Social Psychology*, *54*, 733–740.

Giles, L. C., Glonek, G. F., Luszcz, M. A., & Andrews, G. R. (2005). Effect of social networks on 10-year survival in very old Australians: The Australian longitudinal study of aging. *Journal of Epidemiology and Community Health*, *59*, 574–579.

Gillath, O., Mikulincer, M., Fitzsimons, G. M., Shaver, P. R., Schachner, D. A., & Bargh, J. A. (2006). Automatic activation of attachment-related goals. *Personality and Social Psychology Bulletin, 32*, 1375–1388.

Gilovich, T. (1990). Differential construal and the false consensus effect. *Journal of Personality and Social Psychology*, *59*, 623.

Gilovich, T., Medvec, V. H., & Savistsky, K. (2000). The spotlight effect in social judgment: An egocentric bias in estimates of the salience of one's own actions and appearance. *Journal of Personality and Social Psychology*, *78*, 211–222.

Gilovich, T., Vallone, R., & Tversky, A. (1985). The hot hand in basketball: On the misperception of random sequences. *Cognitive Psychology*, *17*, 295–314.

Glenn, A. L., & Raine, A. (2009). Psychopathy and instrumental aggression: Evolutionary, neurobiological, and legal perspectives. *International Journal of Law & Psychiatry*, *32*, 253–258.

Glick, P., & Fiske, S. T. (2001). An ambivalent alliance: Hostile and benevolent sexism as complementary justifications of gender inequality. *American Psychologist, 56,* 109–118.

Glick, P., Fiske, S. T., Mladinic, A., Saiz, J. L., Abrams, D., Masser, B., et al. (2000). Beyond prejudice as simple antipathy: Hostile and benevolent sexism across cultures. *Journal of Personality and Social Psychology*, *79,* 763–775.

Goffman, E. (1952). On cooking the mark out: Some aspects of adaptation to failure. *Psychiatry*, *15*, 451–463.

Golby, A. J., Gabrieli, J. D. E., Chiao, J. Y., & Eberhardt, J. L. (2001). Differential responses in the fusiform region to same-race and other-race faces. *Nature Neuroscience*, *4*, 845–850.

González, Y. S., Moreno, D. S., & Schneider, B. H. (2004). Friendship expectations of early adolescents in Cuba and Canada. *Journal of Cross-Cultural Psychology, 35*, 436–445.

Goodwin, R., & Findlay, C. (1997). "We were just fated together" . . . Chinese love and the concept of yuan in England and Hong Kong. *Personal Relationships*, *4*, 85–92.

Goodyear-Grant, E., & Croskill, J. (2011). Gender affinity effects in vote choice in Westminister systems: Assessing "flexible" voters in Canada. *Politics & Gender,* *7*, 223–250.

Gopnik, A., Meltzoff, A. N., & Kuhl, P. K. (1999). *The scientist in the crib: What early learning tells us about the mind*. New York: HarperCollins.

Gordijn, E. H., De Vries, N. K., & de Dreu, C. K. W. (2002). Minority influence on focal and related attitudes: Change in size, attribution, and information processing. *Personality and Social Psychology Bulletin, 28*, 1315–1326.

Gordon, I., Zagoory-Sharon, O., Leckman, J., & Feldman, R. (2010). Oxytocin and the development of parenting in humans. *Biological Psychiatry*, *68*, 377–382.

Gore, K., Tobiasen, M., & Kayson,W. (1997). Effects of sex of caller, implied sexual orientation of caller, and urgency on altruistic response using the wrong number technique. *Psychological Reports*, *80*, 927–930.

Gosling, S. (2008). *Snoop: What your stuff says about you.* New York: Basic Books.

Gottman, J. M. (1994). *Why marriages succeed or fail . . . and how you can make yours last*. New York: Simon & Schuster.

Gottman, J. M., Levenson, R. W., Swanson, C., Swanson, K., Tyson, R., & Yoshimoto, D. (2003). Observing gay, lesbian and heterosexual couples' relationships: Mathematical modeling of conflict interaction. *Journal of Homosexuality*, *45*, 65–91.

Grabe, M. E., & Kamhawi, A. S. (2006). Hard wired for negative news? Gender differences in processing broadcast news. *Communication Research*, *33*, 346–369.

Graham, K., Bernards, S., Osgood, D. W., & Wells, S. (2006). Bad nights or bad bars? Multi-level analysis of environmental predictors of aggression in late-night large-capacity bars and clubs. *Addiction, 101*, 1569–1580.

Graham, K., West, P., & Wells, S. (2000). Evaluating theories of alcohol-related aggression using observations of young adults in bars. *Addiction, 95*, 847–863.

Graham, S. (2001, August 10). Parkinson's patents feel the placebo effect. *Scientific American*. Retrieved June 3, 2010, from http://www.scientificamerican.com/article.cfm?id_parkinsons-patients-feel

Gray, J. D., & Silver, R. C. (1990). Opposite sides of the same coin: Former spouses' divergent perspectives in coping with their divorce. *Journal of Personality and Social Psychology, 59*, 1180–1191.

Green, M. J., & Phillips, M. L. (2004). Social threat perception and the evolution of paranoia. *Neuroscience and Biobehavioral Reviews, 28*, 333–342.

Greenwald, A. G., Banaji, M. R., Rudman, L. A., Farnham, S.D., Nosek, B. A., & Rosier, M. (2000). Prologue to a unified theory of attitudes, stereotypes, and self-concept. In J. Forgas (Ed.), *The role of affect in social cognition* (pp. 308–330). Cambridge, UK: Cambridge University Press.

Greenwald, A. G., McGhee, D. E., & Schwartz, J. L. K. (1998). Measuring individual differences in implicit cognition: The Implicit Association Test. *Journal of Personality and Social Psychology, 74,* 1464–1480.

Greenwald, A.G., Oakes, M. A., & Hoffman, H. (2003). Targets of discrimination: Effects of race on responses to weapons holders. *Journal of Experimental Social Psychology*, *39*, 399–405.

Grekul, J., Krahn, H., & Odynak, D. (2004). Sterilizing the "feeble-minded": Eugenics in Alberta, Canada, 1929–1972. *Journal of Historical Sociology, 17*, 358–384.

Greyhound bus killer found not criminally responsible. (2009, March 5). *CBC News.* Retrieved August 30, 2011, from http://www.cbc.ca/news/canada/manitoba/story/2009/03/05/mb-li-verdict.html

Griskevicius, V., Goldstein, N. J., Mortensen, C. R., Cialdini, R. B., & Kenrick, D. T. (2006). Going along versus going alone: When fundamental motives facilitate strategic (non)conformity. *Journal of Personality and Social Psychology, 91*, 281–294.

Groff, B. D., Baron, R. S., & Moore, D. L. (1983). Distraction, attentional conflict, and drivelike behavior. *Journal of Experimental Social Psychology, 19*, 359–380.

Guadagno, R. E., & Cialdini, R. B. (2002). Online persuasion: An examination of gender differences in computer-mediated interpersonal influence. *Group Dynamics: Theory Research and Practice*, *6*, 38–51.

Gueguen, N., & De Gail, M. (2003). The effect of smiling on helping behavior: Smiling and Good Samaritan behavior. *Communication Reports, 16,* 133–140.

Guimond, S., Chatard, A., Martinot, D., Crisp, R. J., & Redersdorff, S. (2006). Social comparison, self-stereotyping, and gender differences in self-construals. *Journal of Personality and Social Psychology, 90*, 221–242.

Gupta, U., & Singh, P. (1982). Exploratory study of love and liking and type of marriages. *Indian Journal of Applied Psychology*, *19*, 92–97.

Gurwitz, S., & Marcus, M. (1978). Effects of anticipated interaction, sex and homosexual stereotypes on first impressions. *Journal of Applied Social Psychology*, *8*, 47–56.

Gusnard, D. A., Akbudak, E., Shulman, G. L., & Raichle, M. E. (2001). Medial prefrontal cortex and referential mental activity: Relation to a default mode of brain function. *Proceedings of the National Academy of Sciences*, *98*, 4259–4264.

Hadjikhani, N., Hoge, R., Snyder, J., & de Gelder, B. (2008). Pointing with the eyes: The role of gaze in communicating danger. *Brain Cognition, 68*, 1–8.

Hafer, C. L. (2000). Do innocent victims threaten the belief in a just world? Evidence from a modified Stroop task. *Journal of Personality and Social Psychology, 79*, 165–173.

Hafer, C. L., & Bègue, L. (2005). Experimental research on just-world theory: Problems, developments, and future challenges. *Psychological Bulletin, 131*, 128–167.

Hafer, C. L., Reynolds, K. L., & Obertynski, M. A. (1996). Message comprehensibility and persuasion: Effects of complex language in counterattitudinal appeals to laypeople. *Social Cognition, 14*, 317–337.

Halberstadt, J., & Rhodes, G. (2000). The attractiveness of nonface averages: Implications for an evolutionary explanation of the attractiveness of average faces. *Psychological Science, 11*, 285–289.

Halberstadt, J., & Rhodes, G. (2003). It's not just average faces that are attractive: Computer-manipulated averageness makes birds, fish, and automobiles attractive. *Psychonomic Bulletin and Review, 10*, 149–156.

Halliday, J. (2011, November 8). "Gang recruitment" videos: MPs back call for police to have blocking power. *The Guardian.* Retrieved November 13, 2011, from http://www.guardian.co.uk/media/2011/nov/08/social-media-block-videos-gangs

Halligan, S., Cooper, P., Healy, S., & Murray, L. (2008). The attribution of hostile intent in mothers, fathers, and their children. *Journal of Abnormal Child Psychology*, *35*, 594–604.

Hamermesh, D. S., & Biddle, J. E. (1994). Beauty and the labor market. *American Economic Review, 84*, 1174–1194.

Hamermesh, D. S., & Parker, A. (2005). Beauty in the classroom: Instructors' pulchritude and putative pedagogical productivity. *Economics of Education Review*, *24*, 369–376.

Hampson, R. (2010). "A 'watershed' case in school bullying?" *USA Today*. Retrieved July 31, 2010, from http://www.usatoday.com/news/nation/2010-04-04-bullying_N.htm

Hancock, J. T., Curry, L., Goorha, S., & Woodworth, M. T. (2008). On lying and being lied to: A linguistic analysis of deception. *Discourse Processes*, *45*, 1–23.

Hancock, J. T., Toma, C., & Ellison, N. (2007). The truth about lying in online dating profiles. *Proceedings of the ACM Conference on Human Factors in Computing Systems* (CHI 2007), 449–452.

Hancock, J. T., Woodworth, M., & Goorha, S. (2010). See no evil: The effect of communication medium and motivation on deception detection. *Group Decision and Negotiation, 19,* 327–336.

Haney, C., & Zimbardo, P. G. (1998). The past and future of U.S. prison policy: Twenty-five years after the Stanford Prison Experiment. *American Psychologist*, *53*, 709–727.

Harari, H., & McDavid, J. W. (1973). Name stereotypes and teachers' expectations. *Journal of Educational Psychology, 65*, 222–225.

Hardin, C. D., & Higgins, E. T. (1996). Shared reality: How social verification makes the subjective objective. In R. M. Sorrentino, & E. T. Higgins (Eds.), *Handbook of motivation and cognition: The interpersonal context* (Vol. 3, pp. 28–84). New York: Guilford Press.

Harlow, H. (1958). The nature of love. *American Psychologist,13*, 673–685.

Harmon-Jones, E., & Allen, J. J. B. (2001). The role of affect in the mere exposure effect: Evidence from psychophysiological and individual differences approaches. *Personality and Social Psychology Bulletin, 27*, 889–898.

Harrell, W. A. (1978). Physical attractiveness, self-disclosure, and helping behavior. *Journal of Social Psychology, 104,* 15–17.

Harris, M. B. (1994). Gender of subject and target as mediators of aggression. *Journal of Applied Social Psychology*, *24*, 453–471.

Harris, P. R., Griffin, D. W., & Murray, S. (2008). Testing the limits of optimistic bias: Event and person moderators in a multilevel framework. *Journal of Personality and Social Psychology, 95*, 1225–1237.

Harsch, E. (2007). Conflict resources: From 'curse' to blessing. *Africa Renewal*, *20*, 17.

Hartup, W. W., & Stevens, N. (1997). Friendships and adaptation in the life course. *Psychological Bulletin*, *121*, 355–370.

Harvey, M. D., & Enzle, M. E. (1981). A cognitive model of social norms for understanding the transgression-helping effect. *Journal of Personality and Social Psychology, 41*, 866–875.

Hassin, R., & Trope, Y. (2000). Facing faces: Studies on the cognitive aspects of physiognomy. *Journal of Personality and Social Psychology*, *78*, 837–852.

Hastings, P. D., Rubin, K. H., & DeRose, L. (2005). Links among gender, inhibition, and parental socialization in the development of prosocial behavior. *Merrill-Palmer Quarterly, 51*, 467–493.

Hatfield, E. (1988). The passionate love scale. In C. M. Davis, W. L. Yarber, & S. L. Davis (Eds.), *Sexuality-related measures: A compendium*. Bloomington, IN.

Hatfield, E., & Sprecher, S. (1986). *Mirror, mirror . . .* New York: State University of New York Press.

Hatfield, E., & Sprecher, S. (1986). Measuring passionate love in intimate relations. *Journal of Adolescence*, *9*, 383–410.

Havas, D. A., Glenberg, A. M., Gutowski, K. A., Lucarelli, M. J., & Davidson, R. J. (2010). Cosmetic use of botulinum toxin-a affects processing of emotional language. *Psychological Science*, *21*, 895–900.

Hays, R. B. (1985). A longitudinal study of friendship development. *Journal of Personality and Social Psychology*, *48*, 909–924.

Hazlewood, J. D., & Olson, J. M. (1986). Covariation information, causal questioning, and interpersonal behavior. *Journal of Experimental Social Psychology, 22*, 276–291.

Health Canada (2010). Major findings from the Canadian Alcohol and Drug Use Monitoring Survey (CADUMS) 2010. Retrieved October 10, 2011, from http://www.hc-sc.gc.ca/hc-ps/drugs-drogues/stat/index-eng.php.

Heatherton, T. F., & Baumeister, R. F. (1991). Binge eating as escape from self-awareness. *Psychological Bulletin, 110*, 86–108.

Heatherton, T. F., Wyland, C. L., Macrae, C. N., Demos, K. E., Denny, B. T., & Kelley, W. M. (2006). Medial prefrontal activity differentiates self from close others. *Social Cognitive and Affective Neuroscience (SCAN), 1*, 18–25.

Heaton, J. A. (2011). 10 Canadian supermodels. *Fashionism.ca.* Retrieved October 3, 2011, from http://fashionism.ca/Galleries/Articles/canadian_models.htm

Heider, F. (1958). *The psychology of interpersonal relations.* Hillsdale, NJ: Erlbaum.

Heilman, M. E. (2001). Description and prescription: How gender stereotypes prevent women's ascent up the organizational ladder. *Journal of Social Issues*, *57*, 657–674.

Heim, C., Young, L. J., Newport, D. J., Mletzko, T., Miller, A. H., & Nemeroff, C. B. (2009). Lower CSF oxytocin concentrations in women with a history of childhood abuse. *Molecular Psychiatry, 14*, 954–958.

Heine, S. J., & Lehman, D. R. (1995). Cultural variation in unrealistic optimism: Does the West feel more invulnerable than the East? *Journal of Personality and Social Psychology, 68*, 595–607.

Heine, S. J., & Lehman, D. R. (1997). Culture, dissonance, and self-affirmation. *Personality and Social Psychology Bulletin*, *23*, 389–400.


Heine, S. J., & Lehman, D. R. (1997). Culture, dissonance, and self-affirmation. *Personality and Social Psychology Bulletin, 23*, 389–400.


Heine, S. J., & Lehman, D. R. (1997). The cultural construction of self-enhancement: An examination of group-serving biases. *Journal of Personality and Social Psychology, 72*, 1268–1283.

Heine, S. J., Lehman, D. R., Peng, K., & Greenholtz, J. (2002). What's wrong with cross-cultural comparisons of subjective Likert scales?: The reference-group effect. *Journal of Personality and Social Psychology, 82*, 903–918.

Henkel, L., & Mather, M. (2007).Memory attributions for choices: How beliefs shape our memories. *Journal of Memory and Language*, *57*, 163–176.

Herek, G. M. (2009). Hate crimes and stigma-related experiences among sexual minority adults in the United States: Prevalence estimates from a national probability sample. *Journal of Interpersonal Violence*, *24*, 54–74.

Hewitt, P. L., Flett, G. L., & Ediger, E. (1995). Perfectionism traits and perfectionistic self-presentation in eating disorder attitudes, characteristics, and symptoms. *International Journal of Eating Disorders, 18*, 317–326.

Higgins, E. T. (1987). Self-discrepancy: A theory relating self and affect. *Psychological Review, 94*, 319–340.

Higgins, E. T., & Bryant, S. L. (1982). Consensus information and fundamental attribution error: The role of development and in-group versus out-group knowledge. *Journal of Personality and Social Psychology, 43*, 889–900.

Higgins, E. T., & King, G. (1981). Accessibility of social constructs: Information-processing consequences of individual and contextual variability. In N. Cantor & J. Kihlstrom (Eds.), *Personality, cognition, and social interaction*. Hillsdale, NJ: Erlbaum.

Higgins, E. T., Rholes, W. S., & Jones, C. R. (1977). Category accessibility and impression formation. *Journal of Experimental Social Psychology, 13*, 141–154.

Higgins, N. C., & Bhatt, G. (2001). Culture moderates the self-serving bias: Etic and emic features of causal attributions in India and in Canada. *Social Behavior and Personality, 29*, 49–62.

Higgins, N. C., St. Amand, M. D., & Poole, G. D. (1997). The controllability of negative life experiences mediates unrealistic optimism. *Social Indicators Research, 42*, 299–323.

Hirono, N. (2000). Left frontotemporal hypoperfusion is associated with aggression in patients with dementia. *Archives of Neurology*, *57*, 861–866.

Hirsh, J. B., & Inzlicht, M. (2008). The devil you know: Neuroticism predicts neural response to uncertainty. *Psychological Science, 19*, 962–967.

Hjalmarsson, R. (2009). Does capitol punishment have a "local" deterrent effect on homicides? *American Law and Economics Review, 11*, 310–334.

Hockey riots throughout Canadian history. (2011, June 16). *The Globe and Mail.* Retrieved October 26, 2011, from http://m.theglobeandmail.com/news/national/british-columbia/hockey-riots-throughout-canadian-history/article2064096/

Hodgson, J. F. (2001). Police violence in Canada and the USA: Analysis and management. *Policing: An International Journal of Police Strategies & Management, 24*, 520–551.

Hodson, G. (2008). Interracial prison contact: The pros for (socially dominant) cons. *British Journal of Social Psychology, 47*, 325–351.

Hodson, G., & Costello, K. (2007). Interpersonal disgust, ideological orientations, and dehumanization as predictors of intergroup attitudes. *Psychological Science, 18*, 691–698.

Hodson, G., & Sorrentino, R. M. (1997). Groupthink and uncertainty orientation: Personality differences in reactivity to the group situation. *Group Dynamics, 1*, 144–155.

Hodson, G., Dovidio, J. R., & Esses, V. M. (2003). Ingroup identification as a moderator of positive-negative asymmetry in social discrimination. *European Journal of Social Psychology, 33*, 215–233.

Hoffman, E., McCabe, K. A., & Smith, V. L. (1998). Behavioral foundations of reciprocity: Experimental economics and evolutionary psychology. *Economic Inquiry, 36*, 335–352.

Hoffman, H., Janssen, E., & Turner, S. L. (2004). Classical conditioning of sexual arousal in women and men: Effects of varying awareness and biological relevance of the conditioned stimulus. *Archives of Sexual Behaviour, 33*, 43–53.

Hofmann, W., Gawronski, B., Gschwendner, T., Le, H., & Schmitt, M. (2005). A meta-analysis on the correlation between the implicit association test and explicit self-report measures. *Personality and Social Psychology Bulletin, 31*, 1369–1385.

Hogan, J., & Holland, B. (2003). Using theory to evaluate personality and job-performance relations: A socioanalytic perspective. *Journal of Applied Psychology, 88*, 100–112.

Høigaard, R., Säfvenbom, R., & Tønnessen, F. E. (2006). The relationship between group cohesion, group norms, and perceived social loafing in soccer teams. *Small Group Research, 37*, 217–232.

Holder, M. D., & Coleman, B. (2009). The contribution of social relationships to children's happiness. *Journal of Happiness Studies, 10*, 329–349.

Holland, R. W., Verplanken, B., & van Knippenberg, A. (2003). From repetition to conviction: Attitude accessibility as a determinant of attitude certainty. *Journal of Experimental Social Psychology, 39*, 594–601.

Hollands, G. J., Prestwich, A., & Marteau, T. M. (2011). Using aversive images to enhance healthy food choices and implicit attitudes: An experimental test of evaluative conditioning. *Health Psychology, 30*, 195–203.

Holmes, J. G. (2000). Social relationships: The nature and function of relational schemas. *European Journal of Social Psychology, 30*, 447–495.

Holt-Lundstad, J., Birmingham, W., & Jones, B. Q. (2008). Is there something unique about marriage? The relative impact of marital status, relationship quality, and network social support on ambulatory blood pressure and mental health. *Annals of Behavioral Medicine, 35*, 239–244.

Holt-Lunstad J., Smith T. B., & Layton J. B. (2010). Social relationships and mortality risk: A meta-analytic review. *Public Library of Science Medicine, 7*(7).

Honey, P. L., & Coulombe, C. D. (2009). Effects of context and relative rank on mate choice and affiliation ratings. *Evolutionary Psychology, 7*, 449–462.

Hoorens, V., Smits, T., & Sheppard, J. A. (2008). Comparative optimism in the spontaneous generation of future life events. *British Journal of Social Psychology, 47*, 441–451.

Hornstein, H. (1976). *Cruelty and kindness: A new look at aggression and altruism*. Englewood Cliffs, NJ: Prentice Hall.

Hoshino-Browne, E., & Kunda, Z. (2000, August). *Activation and application processes of Asian stereotypes in realistic interaction*. Paper presented at the 108th Annual Convention of the American Psychological Association, Washington, DC.

Hoshino-Browne, E., Zanna, A. S., Spencer, S. J., Zanna, M. P., Kitayama, S., & Lackenbauer, S. (2005). On the cultural guises of cognitive dissonance: The case of Easterners and Westerners. *Journal of Personality and Social Psychology, 89*, 294–310.

Hovland, C. I., Irving, L. J., & Kelly, H. H. (1953). *Communication and Persuasion: Psychological Studies of Opinion Change*. New Haven, CT: Yale University Press.

Hovland, C. I., Lumsdale, A. A., & Sheffield, F. D. (1949). *Experiments on mass communication: Studies in social psychology in World War II (Vol. 3)*. Princeton, NJ: Princeton University Press.

Hovland, C. I., & Weiss, W. (1951). The influence of source credibility on communication Effectiveness. *Public Opinion Quarterly, 15*, 635–650.

Huang, X., & Van de Vliert, E. (2003). Where intrinsic job satisfaction fails to work: National moderators of intrinsic motivation. *Journal of Organizational Behavior, 24*, 159–179.

Huesmann, L. R., Moise-Titus, J., Podolski, C. L., & Eron, L. (2003). Longitudinal relations between children's exposure to TV violence and their aggressive and violent behavior in young adulthood: 1977–1992. *Developmental Psychology, 39*, 201–221.

Hugenberg, K., & Bodenhausen, G. V. (2003). Facing prejudice: Implicit prejudice and the perception of facial threat. *Psychological Science, 14*, 640–643.

Hughes, S. M., Harrison, M. A., & Gallup G. G., Jr. (2002). The sound of symmetry: Voice as a marker of developmental stability. *Evolution and Human Behavior, 23*, 173–180.

Hull, J. G., & Young, R. D. (1983). The self-awareness-reducing effects of alcohol consumption: Evidence and implications. In J. Suls & A. G. Greenwald (Eds.), *Psychological Perspectives on the Self* (Vol. 2). Hillsdale, NJ: Erlbaum.

Husted, V., Madey, S. F., & Gilovich, T. (1995). When less is more: Counterfactual thinking and satisfaction among Olympic medalists. *Journal of Personality and Social Psychology, 69*, 603–610.

Huston, T. L., & Vangelisti, A. L. (1991). Socioemotional behavior and satisfaction in marital relationships: A longitudinal study. *Journal of Personality and Social Psychology, 61*, 721–733.

Hynie, M., MacDonald, T. K., & Marques, S. (2006). Self-conscious emotions and self-regulation in the promotion of condom use. *Personality and Social Psychology Bulletin, 32*, 1059–1071.

Iacoboni, M. (2009). Imitation, empathy, and mirror neurons. *Annual Review of Psychology, 60*, 653–670.

Iacoboni, M., Woods, R. P., Brass, M., Bekkering, H., Mazziotta, J. C., Rizzolatti, G. (1999). Cortical mechanisms of human imitation. *Science, 286*, 2526–2528.

Ickes, W. J., & Simpson, J. A. (2004). Motivational aspects of empathic accuracy. In M. B. Brewer & M. Hewstone (Eds.), *Emotion and Motivation: Perspectives on Social Psychology*. Malden, MA: Blackwell Publishing.

Imhoff, R. (2009). What motivates nonconformity? Uniqueness seeking blocks majority influence. *Personality and Social Psychology Bulletin, 35*, 309–320.

Ingham, A. G., Levinger, G., Graves, J., & Peckham, V. (1974). The Ringelmann effect: Studies of group size and group performance. *Journal of Experimental Social Psychology, 10*, 371–384.

Isen, A. M., Clark, M., & Schwartz, M. (1976). Duration of the effect of good mood on helping: "Footprints in the sands of time." *Journal of Personality and Social Psychology, 34*, 385–393.

Isen, A. M., Shalker, T. E., Clark, M., & Karp, L. (1978). Affect, accessibility of material in memory, and behavior. *Journal of Personality and Social Psychology, 36*, 1–12.

Isen, A. M., & Levin, P. F. (1972). The effect of feeling good on helping: Cookies and kindness. *Journal of Personality and Social Psychology, 21*, 384–388.

Isenberg, D. J. (1986). Group polarization: A critical review and meta-analysis. *Journal of Personality and Social Psychology, 50*, 1141–1151.

Ito, T. A., Larsen, J. T., Smith, N. K., & Cacioppo, J. T. (1998). Negative information weighs more heavily on the brain: The negativity bias in evaluative categorizations. *Journal of Personality and Social Psychology, 75*, 887–900.

Ito, T. A., Thompson, E., & Cacioppo, J. T. (2004). Tracking the timecourse of social perception: The effects of racial cues on event-related brain potentials. *Personality and Social Psychology Bulletin, 30*, 1267–1280.

Iyengar, S. S., & Lepper, M. R. (2000). When choice is demotivating: Can one desire too much of a good thing? *Journal of Personality and Social Psychology, 79*, 995–1006.

Izard, C. E. (1990). Facial expressions and the regulation of emotions. *Journal of Personality and Social Psychology, 58*, 487–498.

Jack Layton remembered as "courageous." (2011, August 22). *CBC News.* Retrieved October 31, 2011, from http://www.cbc.ca/news/politics/story/2011/08/22/layton-obituary.html

Jackman, M. R., & Jackman, R. (1983). *Class awareness in the United States.* Berkeley: University of California Press.

Jacobi, L., & Cash, T. F. (1994). In pursuit of the perfect appearance: Discrepancies among self-ideal percepts of multiple physical attributes. *Journal of Applied Social Psychology, 24*, 379–396.

Janis, I. L. (1982). *Groupthink* (2nd ed.). Boston: Houghton Mifflin.

Janis, I. L., & Feshbach, S. (1953). Effects of fear-arousing communications. *The Journal of Abnormal and Social Psychology, 48*, 78–92.

Janiszewski, C., & Warlop, L. (1993). The influence of classical conditioning procedures on subsequent attention to the conditioned brand. *The Journal of Consumer Research, 20*, 171–189.

Jeannerod, M. (2003). The mechanism of self-recognition in humans. *Behavioural Brain Research, 142*, 1–15.

Jehl, D. (1999). "Arab honor's price: A woman's blood." *New York Times,* 1–7.

Jehl, D. (1999, June 20). For shame: A special report; Arab honor's price: A woman's blood. *The New York Times*. June 20, 1999.

Jelenec, P., & Steffens, M. C. (2002). Implicit attitudes toward elderly women and men. *Current Research in Social Psychology, 7*, 275–293.

Jia, L., Karpen, S. C., & Hirt, E. R. (2011, in press). Beyond anti-Muslim sentiment: Opposing the Ground Zero mosque as a means to pursuing a stronger America. *Psychological Science*.

Jiang, L., Dahl, D., Chattopadhyay, A., & Hoegg, J.-A. (2009). The persuasive role of incidental similarity in attitudes and purchase intentions in a sales context. *Advances in Consumer Research, 36*, 598–599.

Jiaquan, X., Kochanek, K. D., Murphy, S. L., & Tejada-Vera, B. (2010). Deaths: Final data for 2007. *National Vital Statistics Reports, 58*.

Johnson, D. E., Erez, A., Kiker, D. S., & Motowidlo, S. J. (2002). Liking and attributions of motives on relationship between a ratee's reputation and helpful behaviors. *Journal of Applied Psychology, 87*, 808–815.

Johnson, R. C., Danko, G. P. Darvill, T. J., Bochner, S., Bowers, J. K., Huang, Y. H., et al. (1989). Cross cultural assessment of altruism and its correlates. *Personality and Individual Differences, 10*, 855–868.

Johnson, R. D., & Downing, L. L. (1979). Deindividuation and valance of cues: Effects on prosocial and antisocial behavior. *Journal of Personality and Social Psychology, 37*, 1532–1538.

Jones, C. R., Olson, M.A., & Fazio, R. H. (2010). Evaluative conditioning: The "how" question. In M. P. Zanna & J. M. Olson (Eds.), *Advances in Experimental Social Psychology* (Vol. 43). San Diego: Academic Press.

Jones, E. E., & Davis, K. E. (1965). From acts to dispositions: The attribution process in social psychology. In L. Berkowitz (Ed.), *Advances in Experimental Social Psychology* (Vol. 2, pp. 219–266). New York: Academic Press.

Jones, E. E., & Harris, V. A. (1967). The attribution of attitudes. *Journal of Experimental Social Psychology, 3*, 1–24.

Jones, E. E., & Nisbett, R. E. (1971). *The actor and the observer: Divergent perceptions of the causes of behavior*. New York: General Learning Press.

Jones, E., & Sigall, H. (1971). The bogus pipeline: A new paradigm for measuring affect and attitude. *Psychological Bulletin, 76*, 349–364.

Jones, J. T., & Cunningham, J. D. (1996). Attachment styles and other predictors of relationship satisfaction in dating couples. *Personal Relationships, 3*, 387–399.

Jones, J. T., Pelham, B. W., Carvallo, M., & Mirenberg, M. C. (2004). How do I love thee? Let me count the Js: Implicit egotism and interpersonal attraction. *Journal of Personality and Social Psychology, 87*, 665–683.

Josephson, W. L. (1995). *Television violence: A review of the effects on children of different ages*. Ottawa: National Clearinghouse on Family Violence, Health Canada.

Judd, C. M., Blair, I. V., & Chapleau, K. M. (2004). Automatic stereotypes versus automatic prejudice: Sorting out the possibilities in the Payne (2002) weapon paradigm. *Journal of Experimental Social Psychology, 40*, 75–81.

Judge, T. A., Erez, A., & Bono, J. E. (1998). The power of being positive: The relation between positive self-concept and job performance. *Human Performance, 11*, 167–187.

Jury convicts man of murder in death at Belle Isle bridge. (1996). Associated Press. *The Blade*: Toledo, Ohio.

Jussim, L. (1986). Self-fulfilling prophecies: A theoretical and integrative view. *Psychological Review, 93*, 429–445.

Jussim, L., & Harber, K. D. (2005). Teacher expectations and self-fulfilling prophecies: Knowns and unknowns, resolved and unresolved controversies. *Personality and Social Psychology Review, 9*, 131–155.

Jussim, L., & Harber, K. D. (2005). Teacher expectations and self-fulfilling prophecies: Knowns and unknowns, resolved and unresolved controversies. *Personality and Psychology Review*, *9*, 131–155.

Jussim, L., Eccles, J., & Madon, S. (1996). Social perception, social stereotypes, and teacher expectations: Accuracy and the quest for the powerful self-fulfilling prophecy. *Advances in Experimental Social Psychology, 28*, 281–388.

Kabay, M. E. (2001). *Anonymity and pseudonymity in cyberspace: Deindividuation, incivility and lawlessness versus freedom and privacy*. Paper presented at the Annual Conference of the European Institute for Computer Anti-Virus Research (EICAR). Munich, Germany.

Kahneman, D., & Tversky, A. (1973). On the psychology of prediction. *Psychological Review*, *80*, 237–251.

Kalven, H., & Zeisel, H. (1966). *The American jury*. Boston, MA: Little, Brown.

Karau, S. J., & Williams, K. D. (1993). Social loafing: A meta-analytic review and theoretical integration. *Journal of Personality and Social Psychology, 65*, 681–706.

Karau, S. J., & Williams, K. D. (1997). The effects of group cohesiveness on social loafing and social compensation. *Group Dynamics: Theory, Research, and Practice, 1*, 156–168.

Kataoka, H. C., Latham, G. P., & Whyte, G. (1997). The relative resistance of the situational, patterned behavior, and conventional structured interviews to anchoring effects. *Human Performance, 10*, 47–63.

Katz, D. (1979). Floyd H. Allport (1890–1978). *American Psychologist, 34*, 351–353.

Katz, D., & Braly, K. (1933). Racial stereotypes of one hundred college students. *Journal of Abnormal and Social Psychology*, *28*, 280–290.

Katz, P. A., Sohn, M., & Zalk, S. R. (1975). Perceptual concomitants of racial attitudes in urban grade-school children. *Developmental Psychology*, *11*, 135–144.

Kawakami, K., Phills, C. E., Steele, J. R., & Dovidio, J. F. (2007). (Close) distance makes the heart grow fonder: Improving implicit racial attitudes and interracial interactions through approach behaviors. *Journal of Personality and Social Psychology, 92*, 957–971.

Keelan, J. P. R., Dion, K. L., & Dion, K. K. (1994). Attachment style and heterosexual relationships among young adults: A short-term panel study. *Journal of Social and Personal Relationships*, *11*, 201–214.

Keillor, J. M., Barrett, A. M., Crucian, G. P., Kortenkamp, S., & Heilman, K. M. (2002). Emotional experience and perception in the absence of facial feedback. *Journal of the International Neuropsychological Society, 8*, 130–135.

Kellerman, A. L. (1993). Gun ownership as a risk factor for homicide in the home. *New England Journal of Medicine*, *329*, 1084–1091.

Kelley, H. H. (1950). The warm-cold variable in first impressions of persons. *Journal of Personality*, *18*, 431–439.

Kelley, H. H. (1972). Attribution in social interaction. In E. E. Jones, D. E. Kanouse, H. H. Kelley, R. E. Nisbett, S. Valins, & B. Weiner (Eds.), *Attribution: Perceiving the causes of behavior* (pp. 1–26). Morristown, NJ: General Learning Press.

Kelley, H. H., & Michela, J. L. (1980). Attribution theory and research. *Annual Review of Psychology*, *31*, 457–501.

Kelley, K., & Byrne, D. (1976). Attraction and altruism: With a little help from my friends. *Journal of Research in Personality, 10*, 59–68.

Kelley, W. M., Macrae, C. N., Wyland, C. L., Caglar, S., Inati, S., Heatherton, T. F. (2002). Finding the self? An event-related fMRI study. *Journal of Cognitive Neuroscience, 14*, 785–794.

Kelly, D. J., Quinn, P. C., Slater, A. M., Lee, K., Ge, L., & Pascalis, O. (2007). The other-race effect develops during infancy: Evidence of perceptual narrowing. *Psychological Science, 18*, 1084–1089.

Keltner, D., & Robinson, R. J. (1997). Defending the status quo: Power and bias in social conflict. *Personality and Social Psychology Bulletin*, *23*, 1066–1077.

Kennedy, M., & Boswell, R. (2011, August 23). Canada mourns "incredible loss" of Jack Layton. *Vancouver Sun*. Retrieved October 31, 2011, from http://www.vancouversun.com/news/Jack+Layton+dead+after+bout+with+cancer/5288307/story.html

Kenny, D. A. (1994). *Interpersonal perception: A social relations analysis*. New York: Guilford.

Kenny, D. A. (2000). *PERSON: A general model for understanding interpersonal perception*. Unpublished manuscript, University of Connecticut.

Kenny, D. A., & Acitelli, L. K. (2001). Accuracy and bias in perceptions of the partner in close relationships. *Journal of Personality and Social Psychology, 80*, 438–439.

Kenrick, D. T., Neuberg, S. L., Zierk, K. L., & Krones, J. M. (1994). Evolution and social cognition: Contrast effects as a function of sex, dominance, and physical attractiveness. *Personality and Social Psychology Bulletin*, *20*, 210–217.

Kenrick, D. T., Sadalla, E. K., Groth, G.,& Trost, M. R. (1990). Evolution, traits, and the stages of human courtship: Qualifying the parental investment model [Special issue: Biological foundations of personality: Evolution, behavioral genetics, and psycho- physiology]. *Journal of Personality*, *58*, 97–116.

Kernis, M. H. (2003). Toward a conceptualization of optimal self-esteem. *Psychological Inquiry*, *14*, 1–26.

Kerr, N. L., MacCoun, R. J., & Kramer, G. P. (1996). Bias in judgment: Comparing individuals and groups. *Psychological Review, 103*, 687–719.

Kesic, D., Thomas, S. D. M., & Ogloff, J. R. P. (2010). Mental illness among police fatalities in Victoria 1982–2007: Case linkage study. *Australian and New Zealand Journal of Psychiatry, 44*, 463–468.

Key, J. P. (1997). Research design in occupational education. Oklahoma State University. Retrieved June 3, 2010, from http://www.okstate.edu/ag/agedcm4h/academic/aged5980a/5980/newpage110.htm

Khan, S. (2002, September 12). Don't shackle us to 9/11. *The Globe and Mail.* Retrieved October 26, 2011, from http://www.ctv.ca/special/sept11/hubs/muslim/khan.html

Khanlou, N., & Peter, E. (2005). Participatory action research: Considerations for ethical review. *Social Science & Medicine, 60*, 2333–2340.

Kichuk, S. L., & Wiesner, W. H. (1998). Work teams: Selecting members for optimal performance. *Canadian Psychology, 39*, 23–32.

Kielburger, C., & Kielburger, M. (2011, October 25). Shame on China? Shame on us. *The Huffington Post.* Retrieved November 29, 2011, from http://www.huffingtonpost.com/mobileweb/1969/12/31/china-toddler-run-over_n_1028315.html

Kiene, S. M., Barta, W. D., Zelenski, J. M., & Cothran, D. L. (2005). Why are you bringing up condoms *now*? The effect of message content on framing effects of condom use messages. *Health Psychology, 24*, 321–326.

Kim, H. S., Sherman, D. K., Mojaverian, T., Sasaki, J. Y., Park, J., Suh, E. M., & Taylor, S. E. (in press). Gene-culture interaction: Oxytocin receptor polymorphism (OXTR) and emotion regulation. *Social Psychological & Personality Science*.

Kim, H., & Markus, H. R. (1999). Deviance or uniqueness, harmony or conformity? A cultural analysis. *Journal of Personality and Social Psychology, 77*, 785–800.

Kim, H., & Markus, H. R. (1999). Deviance or uniqueness, harmony or conformity? A cultural analysis. *Journal of Personality and Social Psychology, 77*, 785–800.

Kimura, T. (2007, May 9). Mother's Day: Companies cash in on marketing to Mom. *CBC News*. Retrieved October 3, 2011, from http://www.cbc.ca/news/background/consumers/mothersday.html

King, G, McDougall, J., DeWitt, D., Hong, S., Miller, L., Offord, D., . . . LaPorta, J. (2005). Pathways to children's academic performance and prosocial behaviour: Roles of physical health status, environmental, family, and child factors. *International Journal of Disability, Development and Education, 52*, 313–344.

Kirsch, S. (2006). Cartoon violence and aggression in youth. *Aggressive and Violent Behavior, 11*, 547–557.

Kirsh, S. J. (2012). *Children, adolescents, and media violence: A critical look at the research* (2nd Ed.). London: Sage Publications Inc.

Kitayama, S., & Uchida, Y. (2005). Interdependent agency: An alternative system for action. In R. M. Sorrentino & D. Cohen (Eds.), *Cultural and social behaviour: The Ontario symposium* (pp. 137–164). Mahwah, NJ: Erlbaum.

Kitayama, S., Snibbe, A. C., Markus, H. R., & Suzuki, T. (2004). Is there any "free" choice? Self and dissonance in two cultures. *Psychological Science, 15*, 527–533.

Kitayama, S., Takagi, H., & Matsumoto, H. (1995). Casual attribution of success and failure: Cultural psychology of the Japanese self. *Japanese Psychological Review, 38*, 247–280.

Klein, J., & Dawar, N. (2004). Corporate social responsibility and consumers' attributions and brand evaluations in a product-harm crisis. *International Journal of Research in Marketing, 21*, 203–217.

Kleinke, C. L. (1977). Effects of dress on compliance to requests in a field setting. *Journal of Social Psychology, 101*, 223–224.

Klohnen, E. C. & Bera, S. (1998). Behavioral and experiential patterns of avoidantly and securely attachment women across adulthood: A 31-year longitudinal perspective. *Journal of Personality and Social Psychology, 74*, 211–223.

Klohnen, E. C., & Luo, S. (2003). Interpersonal attraction and personality: What is attractive—self similarity, ideal similarity, complementarity, or attachment security? *Journal of Personality and Social Psychology, 85*, 709–722.

Klucharev, V. A., Hytonen, K., Rijpkema, M., Smidts, A., & Fernandez, G. (2009). Reinforcement learning signal predicts social conformity. *Neuron, 61*, 140–151.

Knafo, A., & Plomin, R. (2006). Parental discipline and affection in children's prosocial behavior: Genetic and environmental links. *Journal of Personality and Social Psychology, 90*, 147–164.

Knapp, M., & Hall, J. A. (2006). *Nonverbal communication in human interaction*. Belmont, CA: Thomson Wadsworth.

Knutson, K. M., Mah, L., Manly, C. F., & Grafman, J. (2007). Neural correlates of automatic beliefs about gender and race. *Human Brain Mapping, 28*, 915–930.

Ko, S. J., Judd, C. M., & Blair, I. (2006). What the voice reveals: Within- and between-category stereotyping on the basis of voice. *Personality and Social Psychology Bulletin, 32*, 806–819.

Koestner, R., Losier, G. F., Worren, N. M., Baker, L., Vallerand, R. J. (1995). False consensus effects for the 1992 Canadian Referendum. *Canadian Journal of Behavioural Science, 27*, 214–225.

Kohler, P., Manhart, L., & Lafferty, W. (2008). Abstinence-only and comprehensive sex education and the initiation of sexual activity and teen pregnancy. *Journal of Adolescent Health, 42*, 344–351.

Korchmaros, J. D., & Kenny, D. A. (2001). Emotional closeness as a mediator of the effect of genetic relatedness on altruism. *Psychological Science, 12*, 262–265.

Kozlowski, S. W. J., Kirsch, M. P., & Chao, G. T. (1986). Job knowledge, ratee familiarity, conceptual similarity, and halo error: An exploration. *Journal of Applied Psychology, 71*, 45–49.

Krämer, N. C., & Winter, S. (2008). Impression management 2.0: The relationship between self-esteem, extraversion, self-efficacy, and self-presentation within social networking sites. *Journal of Media Psychology, 20*, 106–116.

Kraus, M. W., & Chen, S. (2009). Striving to be known by significant others: Automatic activation of self-verification goals in relationship contexts. *Journal of Personality and Social Psychology, 97*, 58–73.

Kraut, R., Kiesler, S., Boneva, B., Cummings, J., Helgeson, V., & Crawford, A. (2003). Internet paradox revisited. In J. Turow and A. Kavanaugh (Eds.), *The wired homestead: An MIT press sourcebook on the internet and the family* (pp. 347–383). Cambridge, MA: Massachusetts Institute of Technology Press.

Kraut, R., Patterson, M., Lundmark, V., Kiesler, S., Mukophadhyay, T., & Scherlis, W. (1998). Internet paradox: A social technology that reduces social involvement and psychological well-being? *American Psychologist, 53*, 1017–1031.

Kriesberg, L. (2003, September). De-escalating gestures. *Beyond Intractibility Version IV.* Retrieved December 1, 2010, from http://www.beyondintractability.org/essay/disarming_behavior

Kristof, N., (2010). Celebrate: Save a mother. *The New York Times*. Retrieved July 17, 2010, from http://www.nytimes.com/2010/05/09/opinion/09kristof.html?_r_2

Krosnick, J. A., & Alwin, D. F. (1989). Aging and susceptibility to attitude change. *Journal of Personality and Social Psychology*, 57, 416–425.

Krueger, J. (2011, October 18). Toddler incident in China shows "volunteer's dilemma." *CNN News*. Retrieved November 12, 2011, from http://www.cnn.com/2011/10/18/opinion/kreuger-china-incident/index.html

Krueger, J., & Clement, R. W. (1994). The truly false consensus effect: An ineradicable and egocentric bias in social perception. *Journal of Personality and Social Psychology, 67*, 596–610.

Kruger, J. (1999). Lake Wobegon be gone! The "below-average effect" and the egocentric nature of comparative ability judgments. *Journal of Personality and Social Psychology, 77*, 221–232.

Kruglanski, A. W., & Webster, D. M. (1996). Motivated closing of the mind: "Seizing" and "freezing." *Psychological Review, 103*, 263–283.

Krull, D. S., Loy, M. H. M., Lin, J., Wang, C. F., Chen, S., & Zhao, X. (1999). The fundamental fundamental attribution error: Correspondence bias in individualist and collectivist cultures. Personality *and Social Psychology Bulletin, 25*, 1208–1219.

Kuhn, M. H., & McPartland, T. S. (1954). An empirical investigation of selfattitude. *American Sociological Review, 19*, 68–76.

Kump, L. (2010, December 5). Teaching the teachers. *Forbes*. Retrieved July 17, 2010, from http://www.forbes.com/free_forbes/2005/1212/115.html

Kunda, Z. (1999). *Social cognition: Making sense of people*. Cambridge, MA: The MIT Press.

Kunda, Z., & Oleson, K. C. (1997). When exceptions prove the rule: How extremity of deviance determines the impact of deviant examples on stereotypes. *Journal of Personality and Social Psychology, 72*, 965–979.

Kunda, Z., & Spencer, S. J. (2003). When do stereotypes come to mind and when do they color judgment? A goal-based theoretical framework for stereotype activation and application. *Psychological Bulletin, 129*, 522–544.

Kurdek, L. A. (1991). Sexuality in homosexual and heterosexual couples. In K. McKinney & S. Sprecher (Eds.), *Sexuality in Close Relationships* (pp. 177–191). Hillsdale, NJ: Erlbaum.

Kurdek, L. A. (2004). Are gay and lesbian cohabiting couples really different from heterosexual married couples? *Journal of Marriage and Family, 66*, 880–900.

La Guardia, J. G., Ryan, R. M., Couchman, C. E., & Deci, E. L. (2000). Within-person variability in security of attachment: A self-determination theory perspective on attachment, need fulfillment, and well-being. *Journal of Personality and Social Psychology, 79*, 367–384.

Ladouceur, R., & Sévigny, S. (2005). Structural characteristics of video lotteries: Effects of a stopping device on illusion of control and gambling persistence. *Journal of Gambling Studies, 21*, 117–131.

Laird, J. D. (1974). Self-attribution and emotion: The effects of expressive behavior on the quality of emotional experience. *Journal of Personality and Social Psychology, 29*, 475–486.

Laird, J. D. (2007). *Feelings: The perception of self. Series in affective science*. New York: Oxford University Press.

Lambert, A. J., Payne, B. K., Jacoby, L. L., Shaffer, L. M., Chasteen, A. L., & Khan, S. R. (2003). Stereotypes as dominant responses: On the "social facilitation" of prejudice in anticipated public contexts. *Journal of Personality and Social Psychology, 84*, 277–295.

Landry, R., Amara, N., & Laamary, M. (2001). Utilization of social science research knowledge in Canada. *Research Policy, 30*, 333–349.

Langer, E. J. (1975). The illusion of control. *Journal of Personality and Social Psychology, 32*, 311–328.

Langer, E. J. (1982). The illusion of control. In D. Kahneman, P. Slovic, & A. Tversky (Eds.), *Judgment Under Uncertainty: Heuristics and Biases*. New York: Cambridge University Press.

Langer, E. J., Blank, A., & Chanowitz, B. (1978). The mindfulness of ostensibly thoughtful action. The role of "placebic" information in interpersonal interaction. *Journal of Personality and Social Psychology, 36*, 635–642.

Langlois, J. H., & Roggman, L. A. (1990). Attractive faces are only average. *Psychological Science, 1*, 115–121.

Langlois, J. H., Ritter, J. M., Roggman, L. A., & Vaughn, L. S. (1991). Facial diversity and infant preferences for attractive faces. *Developmental Psychology, 27*, 79–84.

Langton, N., Robbins, S. P., & Judge, T. A. (2010). *Organizational behaviour: Concepts, controversies, applications* (5th Cdn. ed.). Don Mills, ON: Pearson Education Canada.

LaPiere, R. T. (1934). Attitudes versus actions. *Social Forces, 13*, 230–237.

Laroche, M., Kim, C., & Zhou, L. (1996). Brand familiarity and confidence as determinants of purchase intention: An empirical test in a multiple brand context. *Journal of Business Research, 37*, 115–120.

Larson, J. R. Jr., Foster-Fishman, P. G., & Keys, C. B. (1994). Information sharing in decision-making groups. *Journal of Personality and Social Psychology, 67*, 446–461.

Lashinsky, A. (2008). Google wins again. *Fortune Magazine*. Retrieved October 11, 2010, from http://money.cnn.com/2008/01/18/news/companies/google.fortune/index.htm

*Laskis v. Osler, Hoskin & Harcourt LLP*. (2011, January 28). Filed in the United States District Court (New York), 11 CIV 0585.

Latane, B. (1981). The psychology of social impact. *American Psychologist, 36*, 343–356.

Latane, B., & Darley, J. (1969). Bystander "apathy." *American Scientist, 57*, 244–268.

Latane, B., & Darley, J. M. (1968). Group inhibition of bystander intervention in emergencies. *Journal of Personality and Social Psychology, 10*, 215–221.

Latane, B., Williams, K., & Harkins, S. (1979). Many hands make light the work: The causes and consequences of social loafing. *Journal of Personality and Social Psychology, 37*, 822–832.

Latham, G. P., & Sue-Chan, C. (1998). Selecting employees in the 21st century: Predicting the contribution of I-O psychology to Canada. *Canadian Psychology, 39*, 14–22.

Lau, G. P., Kay, A. C., & Spencer, S. J. (2008). Loving those who justify inequality: The effects of system threat on attraction to women who embody benevolent sexist ideals. *Psychological Science, 19*, 20–21.

Laursen, B., & Hartup, W. W. (2002). The origins of reciprocity and social exchange in friendships. *New Directions for Child and Adolescent Development, Spring 2002*, 27–40.

Lawrence, E., Bunde, M., Barry, R. A., Brock, R. L., Sullivan, K. T., Pasch, L. A., et al. (2008). Partner support and marital satisfaction: Support amount, adequacy, provision, and solicitation. *Personal Relationships, 15*, 445–463.

Leach, C. W., Spears, R., Branscombe, N. R., & Doosje, B. (2003). Malicious pleasure: Schadenfreude at the suffering of another group. *Journal of Personality and Social Psychology, 84*, 932–943.

Leary, M. R. (1998). The social and psychological importance of self-esteem. In R. M. Kowalski & M. R. Leary (Eds.), *The Social Psychology of Emotional and Behavioral Problems: Interfaces of Social and Clinical Psychology* (pp. 197–221). Washington, DC: American Psychological Association.

Leary, M. R. (2004). *The Curse of the Self: Self-Awareness, Egotism, and the Quality of Human Life*. New York: Oxford University Press.

Leary, M. R. (2007). Motivational and emotional aspects of the self. *Annual Review of Psychology, 58*, 317–344.

LeDoux, J. (2002). *The synaptic self: How our brains become who we are.* New York: Penguin.

Lee, A., & Aaker, J. (2004). Bringing the frame into focus: The influence of regulatory fit on processing fluency and persuasion. *Journal of Personality and Social Psychology, 86*, 205–218.

Lee, C. M., Geisner, I. M., Lewis, M. A., Neighbors, C., & Larimer, M. E. (2007). Social motives and the interaction between descriptive and injunctive norms in college student drinking. *Journal of Studies on Alcohol and Drugs, 68*, 714–721.

Lee, J., Carman, T., & Duggan, E. (2011, November 2). Richmond plane crash rescuers share a common bond: Heroes from the Richmond plane crash tell their story. *Vancouver Sun*. Retrieved November 9, 2011, from http://www.vancouversun.com/news/Richmond+plane+crash+rescuers+share+common+bond/5635210/story.html

Lee, K., Carswell, J. J., & Allen, N. J. (2000). A meta-analytic review of occupational commitment: Relations with person- and work-related variables. *Journal of Applied Psychology, 85*, 799–811.

Lennox, R. D., & Wolfe, R. N. (1984). Revision of the Self-Monitoring Scale. *Journal of Personality and Social Psychology, 46*, 1349–1364.

Leonard, C. (2010, June 25). Panera Co. to open more pay-what-you-wish eateries. *Associated Press*. Retrieved August 16, 2010, from http://www.google.com/hostednews/ap/article/ALeqM5g__EQOG9DhU1YwC4Fo4s5QREdbgD9GIE6682

Leonardi, A., & Gonida, E. (2007). Predicting academic self-handicapping in different age groups: The role of personal achievement goals and social goals. *British Journal of Educational Psychology, 77*, 595–611.

Lepper, M. R., Greene, D., & Nisbett, R. E. (1973). Undermining children's intrinsic interest with extrinsic rewards: A test of the "overjustification" hypothesis. *Journal of Personality and Social Psychology, 28*, 129–137.

Lerman, R. (2002). *Marriage and the economic well-being of families with children: A review of the literature*. Washington, DC: The Urban Institute and American University.

Lerner, J. S., Gonzalez, R. M., Small, D. A., & Fischhoff, B. (2003). Effects of fear and anger on perceived risks of terrorism. A national field experiment. *Psychological Science, 14*, 144–150.

Lerner, M. J. (1980). *The belief in a just world: A fundamental delusion*. New York: Plenum Press.

Lerner, M. J., & Miller, D. T. (1978). Just world research and the attribution process: Looking back and ahead. *Psychological Bulletin, 85*, 1030–1051.

LeRoy, S., Gabel, T., & Veldhius, N. (2003). Comparing charitable giving in Canada & the United States: Canada's generosity gap. *Fraser Forum, December 2003*, 9–15.

Leschied, A. W., Cummings, A., Van Brunschot, M., Cunningham, A., & Saunders, A. (2000). *Female adolescent aggression: A review of the literature and the correlates of aggression*. Gatineau, QC: Canadian Minister of Public Health Works and Government Services.

Leventhal, H., Singer, R., & Jones, S. (1965). Effects of fear and specificity of recommendation upon attitudes and behavior, *Journal of Personality and Social Psychology, 2*, 20–29.

Levin, I. P., & Gaeth, G. J. (1988). Framing of attribute information before and after consuming the product. *Journal of Consumer Research, 15*, 374–378.

Levine, M., Prosser, A., Evans, D., & Reicher, S. (2005). Identity and emergency intervention: How social group membership and inclusiveness of group boundaries shapes helping behavior. *Personality and Social Psychology Bulletin, 31*, 443–453.

Levine, M., Prosser, A., Evans, D., & Reicher, S. (2005). Identity and emergency intervention: How social group membership and inclusiveness of group boundaries shape helping behavior. *Personality and Social Psychology Bulletin, 31*, 443–453.

Levine, R. V. (2003). Measuring helping behavior across cultures. In W. J. Lonner, D. L. Dinnel, S. A. Hayes, & D. N. Sattler (Eds.), *Online Readings in Psychology and Culture* (Unit 15, Chapter 9), (http://www.wwu.edu/_culture), Center for Cross-Cultural Research, Western Washington University, Bellingham, Washington.

Levine, R. V. (2003). *The power of persuasion: How we're bought and sold.* Hoboken, NJ: John Wiley & Sons.

Levine, R. V., Martinez, T. S., Brase, G., & Sorenson, K. (1994). Helping in 36 U.S. cities. *Journal of Personality and Social Psychology, 67*, 69–82.

Levine, R. V., & Norenzayan, A. (1999). The pace of life in 31 countries. *Journal of Cross Cultural Psychology, 30*, 178–205.

Levy, K. N., & Kelly, K. M. (2010). Sex differences in jealousy: A contribution from attachment theory. *Psychological Science, 21*, 168–173.

Lewandowski, G. W., Jr., Aron, A., Bassis, S., & Kunak, J. (2006). Losing a self-expanding relationship: Implications for the self-concept. *Personal Relationships, 13*, 317–331.

Lewin, K. (1948). *Resolving social conflicts: Selected papers on group dynamics*. New York: Harper.

Lewin, K., Lippitt, R., & White, R. W. (1939). Patterns of aggressive behavior in experimentally created "social climates." *The Journal of Social Psychology, 10*, 271–299.

Lewis, J. (1983). *Something hidden: A biography of Wilder Penfield*. Halifax, NS: Goodread Biographies.

Liberman, N., & Chaiken, S. (2009). When values matter: Expressing values in behavioral intentions for the near vs. distant future. *Journal of Experimental Social Psychology, 45*, 35–43.

Lieberman, J. D. (2002). Head over the heart or heart over the head CEST and extralegal heuristics in juror decision making. *Journal of Applied Social Psychology, 32*, 2526–2553.

Lieberman, M., Ochsner, K., Gilbert, D., & Schacter, D. (2001). Do amnesiacs exhibit cognitive dissonance reduction?: The role of explicit memory and attention in attitude change. *Psychological Science, 12*, 135–140.

Lightdale, J. R., & Prentice, D. A. (1994). Rethinking sex differences in aggression: Aggressive behavior in the absence of social roles. *Personality and Social Psychology Bulletin, 20*, 34–44.

Lilienfeld, S. O., Ammirati, R., & Landfield, K. (2009). Giving debiasing away: Can psychological research on correcting cognitive errors promote human welfare? *Perspectives on Psychological Science, 4*, 390–398.

Lindgaard, G., Fernandes, G., Dudek, C., & Brown, J. (2006). Attention web designers: You have 50 milliseconds to make a good first impression! *Behaviour & Information Technology, 25*, 115–126.

Lindskold, S., & Han, G. (1988). GRIT as a foundation for integrative bargaining. *Personality and Social Psychology Bulletin, 14*, 335–345.

Livingston, I., Doyle, J., & Mangan, D. (2010,April 25). Stabbed hero dies as more than 20 people stroll past him. *The New York Post*. Retrieved from http://www.nypost.com/p/news/local/queens/passers_by_let_good_sam_die_5SGkf5XDP5ooudVuEd8fbI

Lochhead, C., & Tipper, J. (2008, Autumn). A profile of recently divorced or separated mothers and fathers. *Transition*, 7–10.

Loftus, E. F. (2005). Planting misinformation in the human mind: A 30-year investigation of the malleability of memory. *Learning & Memory, 12*, 361–366.

Loftus, E. F., & Davis, D. (2006). Recovered memories. *Annual Review of Clinical Psychology, 2*, 469–498.

Lopez, R., & Marx, J. (2003). The money song. In *Avenue Q: The musical*. New York: RCA Victor.

Lorenz, K. (1963/2002). *On aggression*. London, UK: Routledge Classics.

Loza, W., & Clements, P. (1991). Incarcerated alcoholics' and rapists' attributions of blame for criminal acts. *Canadian Journal of Behavioural Science, 23*, 76–83.

Luszczynska, A., Cao, D. S., Mallach, N., Pietron, K., Mazurkiewicz, M., & Schwarzer, R. (2010). Intentions, planning, and self-efficacy predict physical activity in Chinese and Polish adolescents: Two moderated mediation analyses. *International Journal of Clinical and Health Psychology, 10*, 265–278.

Lyons, A., & Kashima, Y. (2003). How are stereotypes maintained through communication?: The influence of stereotype sharedness. *Journal of Personality and Social Psychology, 85*, 989–1005.

Lyubomirsky, S., King, L., & Diener, E. (2005). The benefits of frequent positive affect: Does happiness lead to success? *Psychological Bulletin, 131*, 803–855.

Ma, Z., Wang, X., Jaeger, A., Anderson, T., Wang, Y., & Saunders, D. (2002). Individual perception, bargaining behavior, and negotiation outcomes: A comparison across two countries. *International Journal of Cross Cultural Management, 2*, 171–184.

Macauley, A. C., Commanda, L. E., Freeman, W. L., Gibson, N., McCabe, M. L., Robbins, C. M., & Twohig, P. L. (1999). Participatory research maximises community and lay involvement. *British Medical Journal, 319*, 774–778.

MacCoun, R. J., & Kerr, N. L. (1988). Asymmetric influence in mock jury deliberation: Jurors' bias for leniency. *Journal of Personality and Social Psychology, 54*, 21–33.

MacDonald, G., & Leary, M. R. (2005). Why does social exclusion hurt? The relationship between social and physical pain. *Psychological Bulletin, 131*, 202–223.

MacDonald, T. K., & Hynie, M. (2008). Ambivalence and unprotected sex: Failing to predict sexual activity is associated with decreased condom use. *Journal of Applied Social Psychology, 38*, 1092–1107.

MacDonald, T. K., & Martineau, A. M. (2002). Self-esteem, mood, and intentions to use condoms: When does low self-esteem lead to risky health behaviors? *Journal of Experimental Social Psychology, 38*, 299–306.

MacDonald, T. K., Fong, G. T., Zanna, M. P., & Martineau, A. M. (2000). Alcohol myopia and condom use: Can alcohol intoxication be associated with more prudent behavior? *Journal of Personality and Social Psychology, 78*, 605–619.

MacDonald, T. K., MacDonald, G., Zanna, M. P., & Fong, G. T. (2000). Alcohol, sexual arousal, and intentions to use condoms in young men: Applying alcohol myopia theory to risky sexual behavior. *Health Psychology, 19*, 290–298.

MacDonald, T. K., Zanna, M. P., & Fong, G. T. (1995). Decision making in altered states: Effects of alcohol on attitudes towards drinking and driving. *Journal of Personality and Social Psychology, 68*, 973–985.

MacDonald, T. K., Zanna, M. P., & Fong, G. T. (1996). Why common sense goes out the window: Effects of alcohol on intentions to use condoms. *Personality and Social Psychology Bulletin, 22*, 763–775.

MacGeorge, E. L. (2003). Gender differences in attributions and emotions in helping contexts. *Sex Roles, 48*, 175–182.

Mackay, N., & Barrowclough, C. (2005). Accident and emergency staff's perceptions of deliberate self-harm: Attributions, emotions and willingness to help. *British Journal of Clinical Psychology, 44*, 255–267.

Mackie, D. M., & Queller, S. (2000). The impact of group membership on persuasion: Revisiting "who says what to whom with what effect?" In D. J. Terry & M. A. Hogg (Eds.), *Attitudes, behavior, and social context: The role of norms and group membership* (pp. 135–155). Mahwah, NJ: Lawrence Erlbaum.

Mackie, D. M., Worth, L. T., & Asuncion, A. G. (1990). Processing of persuasive in-group messages. *Journal of Personality and Social Psychology, 58*, 812–822.

MacKinnon, S. P., Hall, S., & MacIntyre, P. D. (2007). Origins of the stuttering stereotype: Stereotype formation through anchoring-adjustment. *Journal of Fluency Disorders, 32*, 297–309.

MacLin, M. K., & Herrera, V. (2006). The criminal stereotype. *North American Journal of Psychology, 8*, 197–208.

MacLin, M. K., Downs, C., MacLin, O. H., & Caspers, H. M. (2009). The effect of defendant facial expression on mock juror decision-making: The power of remorse. *North American Journal of Psychology, 11*, 323–332.

Macmillan, M. (1997). *Freud evaluated: The completed arc*. New York: MIT Press.

Macrae, C. N., Bodenhausen, G. V., Milne, A. B., & Jetten, J. (1994). Out of mind but back in sight: Stereotypes on the rebound. *Journal of Personality and Social Psychology*, *67*, 808–881.

Madell, D. E., & Muncer, S. J. (2007). Control over social interactions: An important reason for young people's use of the Internet and mobile phones for communication? *CyberPsychology & Behavior*, *10*, 137–140.

Madon, S., Guyll, M., Spoth, R., & Willard, J. (2004). Self-fulfilling prophecies: The synergistic accumulative effect of parents' beliefs on children's drinking behaviour. *Psychological Science, 15*, 837–845.

Maehr, M. L. (1974). Culture and achievement motivation. *American Psychologist, 29*, 887–896.

Maharaj, R. (2008). Corporate governance, groupthink and bullies in the boardroom. *International Journal of Disclosure and Governance, 5*, 68–92.

Maio, G. R., & Olson, J. M. (1995). Involvement and persuasion: Evidence for different types of involvement. *Canadian Journal of Behavioural Science, 27*, 64–78.

Maisto, M. (2010, October 19). Apple Mac sales up 58 percent, thanks to iPad, iPhone. *eWeek. com.* Retrieved August 23, 2011, from http://www.eweek.com/c/a/Desktops-and- Notebooks/Apple-Mac-Sales-Up-58-Percent-Thanks-to-iPad-iPhone-601805/

Mandel, D. R., & Dhami, M. K. (2005). "What I did" versus "what I might have done": Effect of factual versus counterfactual thinking on blame, guilt, and shame in prisoners. *Journal of Experimental Social Psychology, 41*, 627–635.

Mandel, D. R., Hilton, D. J., & Catellani, P. (Eds.) (2005). *The psychology of counterfactual thinking*. New York, NY: Routledge.

Mann, S., Vrij, A., & Bull, R. (2004). Detecting true lies: Police officers' ability to detect suspects' lies. *Journal of Applied Psychology*, *89*, 137–149.

Mantovani, F. (2001). Cyber attraction: The emergence of computer-mediated communication in the development of interpersonal relationships. In L. Anolli, R. Ciceri, & G. Riva (Eds.), *Say not to say: New perspectives on miscommunication* (pp. 236–252). Amsterdam, The Netherlands: IOS Press.

Marangoni, C., Garcia, S., Ickes, W., & Teng, G. (1995). Empathic accuracy in a clinically relevant setting. *Journal of Personality and Social Psychology, 68*, 854–869.

Mares, M. L., & Woodard, E. (2005). Positive effects of television on children's social interactions: A meta-analysis. *Media Psychology, 7*, 301–322.

Marks, G., & Miller, N. (1987). Ten years of research on the false consensus effect: An empirical and theoretical review. *Psychological Bulletin*, *102*, 72–90.

Markus, H. (1977). Self schemata and processing information about the self. *Journal of Personality and Social Psychology, 35*, 63–78.

Markus, H. R. (2008). Pride, prejudice, and ambivalence: Toward a unified theory of race and ethnicity. *American Psychologist, 63*, 651–670.

Markus, H., & Kitayama, S. (1991). Culture and the self: Implications for cognition, emotion, and motivation. *Psychological Review, 98*, 224–253.

Markus, H., & Nurius, P. (1986). Possible selves. *American Psychologist*, *41*, 954–969.

Marlow, L. A., Waller, J., & Wardle, J. (2010). Variation in blame attributions across different cancer types. *Cancer Epidemiology, Biomarkers, & Prevention*, *19*, 1799–1805.

Marsh, H. W., & Craven, R. G. (2006). Reciprocal effects of self-concept and performance from a multidimensional perspective: Beyond seductive pleasure and unidimensional perspectives. *Perspectives on Psychological Science, 1*, 133–163.

Marshall, G., & Zimbardo, P. G. (1979). The affective consequence of inadequately explained physiological arousal. *Journal of Personality and Social Psychology*, *37*, 970–988.

Maslach, C. (1979). The emotional consequences of arousal without reason. In C. E. Izard (Ed.), *Emotions in Personality and Psychopathology* (pp. 565–590). New York: Plenum.

Mather, M., & Johnson, M. K. (2000). Choice-supportive source monitoring: Do our decisions seem better to us as we age? *Psychology and Aging, 15*, 596–606.

Mather, M., Shafir, E., & Johnson, M. K. (2000). Remembering chosen and assigned options. *Memory & Cognition*, *31*, 422–433.

Matheson, K., & Dursun, S. (2001). Social identity precursors to the hostile media phenomenon: Partisan perceptions of coverage of the Bosnian conflict. *Group Processes Intergroup Relations, 4*, 116–125.

Mazur, A., & Booth, A. (1998). Testosterone and dominance in men. *Behavioral and Brain Sciences, 21*, 353–397.

McAdams, D. P. (1989). *Intimacy: The need to be close*. New York: Doubleday.

McArthur, L. Z. & Berry, D. S. (1987). Cross-cultural agreement in perceptions of babyfaced adults. *Journal of Cross-Cultural Psychology, 18*, 165–192.

McCarthy, A., Lee, K., Itakura, S., & Muir, D. W. (2006). Cultural display rules drive eye gaze during thinking. *Journal of Cross Cultural Psychology, 37*, 717–722.

McConahay, J. B. (1986). Modern racism, ambivalence, and the Modern Racism Scale. In J. F. Dovidio & S. L. Gaertner (Eds.), *Prejudice, discrimination, and racism* (pp. 91–125). Orlando, FL: Academic Press.

McCrea, S. M. (2008). Self-handicapping, excuse making, and counterfactual thinking: Consequences for self-esteem and future motivation. *Journal of Personality and Social Psychology, 95*, 274–292.

McFadden, R. (1974). A model's dying screams are ignored at the site of Kitty Genovese's murder. *The New York Times*.

McGovern, L. P., Ditzian, J. L., & Taylor, S. P. (1975). The effect of one positive reinforcement on helping behavior. *Bulletin of the Psychonomics Society, 5*, 421–423.

McGuire, A. M. (1994). Helping behaviors in the natural environment: Dimensions and correlates of helping. *Personality and Social Psychology Bulletin*, *20*, 45–56.

McGuire, W. J. (1964). Inducing resistance to persuasion. In L. Berkowitz (ed.) *Advances in experimental social psychology* (Vol. 1, pp.192–229). New York: McGraw-Hill.

McGuire, W. J., & Papageorgis, D. (1961). The relative efficacy of various types of prior belief-defense in producing immunity against persuasion. *The Journal of Abnormal and Social Psychology*, *62*, 327–337.

McIntyre, M. (2009, March 4). Accused decapitator Vince Li trial: Not guilty! *NowPublic.* Retrieved August 30, 2011, from http://www.nowpublic.com/world/march-04-2009-accused-decapitator-vince-li-trial-not-guilty

McKenna, K. Y. A., Green, A., & Gleason, M. (2002). Relationship formation on the Internet: What's the big attraction? *Journal of Social Issues*, *58*,9–31.

McKimmie, B. M., Newton, C. J., Terry, D. J., & Schuller, R. A. (2004). Jurors' responses to expert witness testimony: The effects of gender stereotypes. *Group Processes & Intergroup Relations, 7*, 131–143.

McKinley, J. (2009, June 26). New border fear: Violence by a rogue militia. *The New York Times*. Retrieved December 1, 2010, from http://www.nytimes.com/2009/06/27/us/27arizona.html

McLean, T. (2011, May 16). Donations pour in for Slave Lake fire victims. *Edmonton Sun*. Retrieved November 12, 2011, from http://www.edmontonsun.com/2011/05/16/donations-pour-in-for-slave-lake-fire-victims

McNeill, D., Cassell, J., & McCullough, K. E. (1994). Communicative effects of speech-mismatched gestures. *Research on Language & Social Interaction, 27*, 223–237.

McPherson, M., Smith-Lovin, L., & Cook, J. M. (2001). Birds of a feather: Homophily in social networks. *Annual Review of Sociology*, *27*, 415–444.

Mead, G. H. (1934). *Mind, self, and society*. Chicago, IL: University of Chicago Press.

Meagher, E. (2004, September 1). Are antidrug ads backfiring? *Psychology Today*. Retrieved July 15, 2010, from http://www.psychologytoday.com/articles/200411/are-antidrug-ads-backfiring

Medvec, V. H., & Savitsky, K. (1997). When doing better means feeling worse: The effects of categorical cutoff points on counterfactual thinking and satisfaction. *Journal of Personality and Social Psychology*, *72*, 1284–1296.

Meissner, C. A., & Brigham, J. C. (2001). Thirty years of investigating the own-race bias in memory for faces: A meta-analytic review. *Psychology, Public Policy, & Law*, *7*, 3–35.

Melloy, K. (2010, June 29). Iceland's prime minister marries female partner. *Edge Boston*. Retrieved July 28, 2010, from http://www.edgeboston.com/index.php?ch_news&sc_&sc2_news&sc3_&id_107412

Merkle, E. R., & Richardson, R. A. (2000). Digital dating and virtual relating: Conceptualizing computer mediated romantic relationships. *Family Relations, 49*, 187–192.

Merton, R. K. (1948). The self-fulfilling prophecy. *Antioch Review, 8*, 193–210.

Merton, R. K., & Kitt, A. S. (1950). Contributions to the theory of reference group behaviour. In R. K. Merton & P. F. Lazarsfeld (Eds.), *Studies in the scope and method of "The American Soldier"* (pp. 40–106). Glencoe, IL: The Free Press.

Meston, C. M., & Frohlich, P. F. (2003). Love at first fright: Partner salience moderates roller-coaster-induced excitation transfer. *Archives of Sexual Behavior, 32*, 537–544.

Meyerowitz, B. E., & Chaiken, S. (1987).The effect of message framing on breast self-examination attitudes, intentions, and behavior. *Journal of Personality and Social Psychology, 52,* 500–510.

Mickelson, K. D., Kessler, R. C., & Shaver, P. R. (1997). Adult attachment in a nationally representative sample. *Journal of Personality and Social Psychology, 73*, 1092–1106.

Milgram, S. (1963). Behavioral study of obedience. *Journal of Abnormal and Social Psychology, 67*, 371–378.

Milgram, S. (1965). Liberating effects of group pressure. *Journal of Personality and Social Psychology, 1*, 127–134.

Miller, B. L., Seeley, W. W., Mychack, P., Rosen, H. J., Mena, I., & Boone, K. (2001). Neuroanatomy of the self: Evidence from patients with frontotemporal dementia. *Neurology, 57*, 817–821.

Miller, C. (2009). Social psychology, mood, and helping: Mixed results for virtue ethics. *Journal of Ethics,13*, 145–173.

Miller, C. (2009). Yes we did! Basking in reflected glory and cutting off reflected failure in the 2008 presidential election. *Analyses of Social Issues and Public Policy, 9*, 283–296.

Miller, D. T., & Ross, M. (1975). Self-serving biases in the attribution of causality: Fact or fiction? *Psychological Bulletin, 82*, 213–225.

Miller, J. G. (1984). Culture and the development of everyday social explanation. *Journal of Personality and Social Psychology, 46*, 961–978.

Miller, L. C., Putcha-Bhagavatula, A., & Pederson, W. C. (2002). Men's and women's mating preferences: Distinct evolutionary mechanisms? *Current Directions in Psychological Science, 11*, 88–93.

Miller, N., & Marks, G. (1982). Assumed similarity between self and other: Effect of expectation of future interaction with that other. *Social Psychology Quarterly, 45*, 100–105.

Miller, P. J. E., & Rempel, J. K. (2004). Trust and partner-enhancing attributions in close relationships. *Personality and Social Psychology Bulletin, 30*, 695–705.

Mishna, F., Saini, M., & Solomon, S. (2009). Ongoing and online: Children and youth's perceptions of cyber bullying. *Children and Youth Services Review, 31*, 1222–1228.

Mitchell, J. R. (2010, May 5). *Transformational leadership*. Presentation for the Town Hall Meeting of the Infrastructure and Environment Group of DND. Sussex Circle, Inc. Retrieved October 30, 2011, from http://www.sussexcircle.com/pdf/049-MitchellTransformLeadership.pdf

Mitchell, T. L., Haw, R. M., Pfeifer, J. E., & Meissner, C. A. (2005). Racial bias in mock juror decision-making: A meta-analytic review of defendant treatment. *Law and Human Behavior, 29*, 621–637.

Mnookin, R. (2010). *Bargaining with the devil: When to negotiate, when to fight*. New York: Simon & Schuster.

Mojab, S., & Hassanpour, A. (2003). The politics and culture of "honour killing": The murder of Fadime Sahindal. *Atlantis, 28*, 56–69.

Moll, J., Krueger, F., Zahn, R., Pardini, M., de Oliveira-Souza, R., & Grafman, J. (2006). Human fronto-mesolimbic networks guide decisions about charitable donation. *Proceedings of the National Academy of Sciences, 103*, 15623–15628.

Monin, B., & Norton, M. I. (2003). Perceptions of a fluid consensus: Uniqueness bias, false consensus, false polarization, and pluralistic ignorance in a water conservation crisis. *Personality and Social Psychology Bulletin, 29*, 559–567.

Monteith, M. J. (1993). Self-regulation of prejudiced responses: Implications for progress in prejudice reduction efforts. *Journal of Personality and Social Psychology, 65*, 469–485.

Moreland, R. L., & Beach, S. (1992). Exposure effects in the classroom: The development of affinity among students. *Journal of Experimental Social Psychology, 28*, 255–276.

Moreland, R. L., & Zajonc, R. B. (1982). Exposure effects in person perception: Familiarity, similarity, and attraction. *Journal of Experimental Social Psychology, 18*, 395–415.

Morell, V. (1993) Evidence found for a possible 'aggression gene.' *Science, 260*(5115), 1722–1723.

Moretti, M. M., & Higgins, E. T. (1999). Own versus other standpoints in self-regulation: Developmental antecedents and functional consequences. *Review of General Psychology, 3*, 188–223.

Morgan, G. S., Mullen, E., & Skitka, L. J. (in press). When values and attributions collide: Liberals' and conservatives' values motivate attributions for alleged misdeeds. *Personality and Social Psychology Bulletin.*

Moriarty, T. (1975). Crime, commitment, and the responsive bystander: Two field experiments. *Journal of Personality and Social Psychology, 59*, 50–60.

Morita, T., Itakura, S., Saito, D. N., Nakashita, S., Harada, T., Kochiyama, T., et al. (2008).The role of the right prefrontal cortex in self-evaluation of the face: A functional magnetic resonance imaging study. *Journal of Cognitive Neuroscience, 20*, 342–355.

Morling, B., & Lamoreaux, M. (2008). Measuring culture outside the head: A meta-analysis of cultural products. *Personality and Social Psychology Review*, 12, 199–221.

Morris, M. W., & Peng, K. (1994). Culture and cause: American and Chinese attributions for social and physical events. *Journal of Personality and Social Psychology, 67*, 949–971.

Morrow-Howell, N., Lott, L.,& Ozawa, M. (1990). The impact of race on volunteer helping relationships among the elderly. *Social Work, 35*, 395–402.

Morton, F. L., & Allen, A. (2001). Feminists and the courts: Measuring success in interest group litigation in Canada. *Canadian Journal of Political Science, 34*, 55–84.

Morwitz, V. G., & Pluzinski, C. (1996). Do polls reflect opinion or do opinions reflect polls? The impact of political polling on voters' expectations, preferences, and behavior. *Journal of Consumer Research, 23*, 53–67.

Moscovici, S., & Zavalloni, M. (1969). The group as a polarizer of attitudes. *Journal of Personality and Social Psychology, 12*, 125–135.

Moskalenko, S., & Heine, S. J. (2003). Watching your troubles away: Television viewing as a stimulus for subjective self-awareness. *Personality and Social Psychology Bulletin, 29*, 76–85.

Mueller, C. M., & Dweck, C. S. (1998). Praise for intelligence can undermine children's motivation and performance. *Journal of Personality and Social Psychology, 75*, 33–52.

Mullen, B., Migdal, M. J., & Rozell, D. (2003). Self-awareness, deindividuation, and social identity: Unraveling theoretical paradoxes by filling empirical lacunae. *Personality and Social Psychology Bulletin, 29*, 1071–1081.

Muller, R. T., Sicoli, L. A., & Lemieux, K. E. (2000). Relationship between attachment style and posttraumatic stress symptomology among adults who report the experience of childhood abuse. *Journal of Traumatic Stress, 13*, 321–332.

Murdock, N., Edwards, C., & Murdock, T. B. (2010). Therapists' attributions for client premature termination: Are they self-serving? *Psychotherapy: Theory, Research and Practice, 47*, 221–234.

Murphy, K. R., & Balzer, W. K. (1986). Systematic distortions in memory-based behavior ratings and performance evaluation: Consequences for rating accuracy. *Journal of Applied Psychology, 71*, 39–44.

Murray, S. L., Holmes, J. G., & Griffin, D. W. (1996). The self-fulfilling nature of positive illusions in romantic relationships: Love is not blind, but prescient. *Interpersonal Relations and Group Processes, 71*, 1155–1180.

Murstein, B. & Christy, P. (1976). Physical attractiveness and marriage adjustment in middle-aged couples. *Journal of Personality and Social Psychology, 34*, 537–542.

Musch, J. (2003). Personality differences in hindsight bias. *Memory, 11*, 473–489.

Mustanski, B. (2010, March 22). New study suggests bans on gay marriage hurt mental health of LGB people. *Psychology Today*. Retrieved December 1, 2010, from http://www.psychologytoday.com/blog/the-sexual-continuum/201003/new-study-suggests-bans-gay-marriagehurt-mental-health-lgb-people

Myers, D. G. (2000). The funds, friends, and faith of happy people. *American Psychologist, 55*, 56–57.

Myers, J., Madathil, J., & Tingle, L. (2005). Marriage satisfaction and wellness in India and the United Status: A preliminary comparison of arranged marriage and marriages of choice. *Journal of Counseling and Development, 83*, 183–190.

Myers, T., Godin, G., Lambert, J., Calzavara, L., & Locker, D. (1996). Sexual risk and HIV-testing behaviour by gay and bisexual men in Canada. *AIDS Care, 8*, 297–310.

Nadler, A., & Fisher, J. D. (1974). The effects of the level of the donor's resources on the recipient's perception of his subsequent self-help behavior. *Personality and Social Psychology Bulletin, 1*, 390–392.

Nadler, A., Fisher, J. D., & Itzhak, S. B. (1983).With a little help from my friend: Effect of single or multiple act aid as a function of donor and task characteristics. *Journal of Personality and Social Psychology, 44*, 310–321.

Nadler, A., Fisher, J. D., & Streufert, S. (1974). The donor's dilemma: Recipient's reactions to aid from friend or foe. *Journal of Applied Social Psychology, 4*, 275–285.

Nairn, A., & Fine, C. (2008). Who's messing with my mind? The implications of dual-process models for the ethics of advertising to children. *International Journal of Advertising, 27*, 447–470.

National Commission for the Protection of Human Subjects of Biomedical and Behavioral Research. (1974). Ethical principles and guidelines for the protection of human subjects in research. *The Belmont Report*. Retrieved June 2, 2010, from http://ohsr.od.nih.gov/guidelines/belmont.html

National Fire Protection Association. (2008). *The U.S. fire problem*. Retrieved May 4, 201, from http://www.nfpa.org/itemDetail.asp?categoryID_953&itemID_23071&URL_Research%20&%20Reports/Fire%20statistics/The%20U.S.%20fire%20problem&cookie%5Ftest_1

National Retail Foundation (2011, April 28). This Mother's Day, Mom's getting pampered, according to NRF survey. Retrieved October 3, 2011, from http://www.nrf.com/modules.php?name=News&op=viewlive&sp_id=1114

Nauert, R. (2010, May 19). Good looks sway court decisions. *PsychCentral*. Retrieved October 11, 2010, from http://psychcentral.com/news/2010/05/18/good-looks-sway-court- decisions/13906.html

Naumann, L. P., Vazire, S., Rentfrow, P. J., & Gosling, S. D. (2009). Personality judgments based on physical appearance. *Personality and Social Psychology Bulletin, 35*, 1661–1671.

Nelson, A., & Robinson, B. W. (2006). *Gender in Canada* (3rd ed.). Toronto, ON: Pearson Prentice Hall.

Nelson,J.(2003).Reality TV a mood lifter. *Chicago Tribune*. Retrieved July 13, 2010, from http://articles.chicagotribune.com/2003-09-17/features/0309170317_1_reality-television-writer-and-senior-editor-reality-tv

Nelson, L. D., & Simmons, J. (2007). Moniker maladies: When names sabotage success. *Psychological Science, 18*, 1106–1112.

Nemeth, R. J., & Belli, R. F. (2006). The influence of schematic knowledge on contradictory versus additive misinformation: False memory for typical and atypical items. *Applied Cognitive Psychology, 20*, 563–573.

Neuman, W. L. (2008). *Understanding research*. Toronto, ON: Pearson.

Newcomb, T. M. (1961). *The acquaintance process*. New York: Holt, Rinehart and Winston.

Newman, L. S. (1993). How individuals interpret behavior: Idiocentrism and spontaneous trait inference. *Social Cognition, 11*, 243–269.

Newsom, J. T. (1999). Another side to caregiving: Negative reactions to being helped. *Current Directions in Psychological Science, 8*, 183–187.

Ng, B., Kumar, S., Ranclaud, M., & Robinson, E. (2001). Ward crowding and incidents of violence on an acute psychiatric inpatient unit. *Psychiatric Services, 52*, 521–525.

Nickerson, R. S. (1998). Confirmation bias: A ubiquitous phenomenon in many guises. *Review of General Psychology, 2*, 175–220.

Nisbett, R. E., & Cohen, D. (1996). *Culture of honor: The psychology of violence in the South*. Denver, CO: Westview Press.

Nisbett, R. E., & Wilson, T. D. (1977). The halo effect: Evidence for unconscious alteration of judgments. *Journal of Personality and Social Psychology, 35*, 250–256.

Nisbett, R. E., Fong, G. T., Lehman, D. R., & Cheng, P. W. (1987). Teaching reasoning. *Science, 238*, 625–631.

Nisbett, R. E., Peng, K., Choi, I., & Norenzayan, A. (2001). Culture and systems of thought: Holistic versus analytic cognition. *Psychological Review, 108*, 291–310.

Noar, S. M., Harrington, N. G., & Aldrich, R. S. (1987). The role of message tailoring in the development of persuasive health communication messages. *Communication, 33*, 387–435.

Noel, J. G., Wann, D. L., & Branscombe, N. R. (1995). Peripheral ingroup membership status and public negativity toward outgroups. *Journal of Personality and Social Psychology, 68*, 127–137.

Noguchi, K., Gohm, C., Dalsky, D., & Sakamoto, S. (2006) Cultural differences related to positive and negative valence. *Asian Journal of Social Psychology, 10*, 68–76.

Norem, J. K., & Cantor, N. (1986).Defensive pessimism: Harnessing anxiety as motivation. *Journal of Personality and Social Psychology, 51*, 1208-1217.

Norris, J. M., & Wylie, A. M. (1995). Gender stereotyping of the managerial role among students in Canada and the United States. *Group & Organization Management, 20*, 167–182.

Norris, P., & Inglehart, R. (2000). Cultural barriers to women's leadership: A worldwide comparison. *International Political Science Association*. Retrieved October 30, 2011, from http://www.hks.harvard.edu/fs/pnorris/Acrobat/IPSA%202000%20Cultural%20Barriers%20to%20Women's%20Leadership.pdf

North, A. C., Linley, A., & Hargreaves, D. J. (2000). Social loafing in a co-operative classroom task. *Educational Psychology, 20*, 389–392.

North, A. C., Tarrant, M., & Hargreaves, D. J. (2004).The effects of music on helping behavior: A field study. *Environment and Behavior, 36*, 266–275.

North, R. J., & Swann, W. B. (2009). Self-verification 360 degrees: Illuminating the light and dark sides. *Self and Identity, 8*, 131–146.

Nosek, B. A. (2007). Implicit-explicit reactions. *Current Directions in Psychological Science, 16*, 65–69.

Novotny, P., Colligan, R. C., Szydlo, D. W., Clark, M. M., Rausch, S., Wampfler, J., et al. (2010). A pessimistic explanatory style is prognostic for poor lung cancer survival. *Journal of Thoracic Oncology, 5*, 326–332.

Nunes, K. L., Firestone, P., & Baldwin, M. W. (2007). Indirect assessment of cognitions of child sexual abusers with the implicit association test. *Criminal Justice and Behavior, 34*, 454–475.

Nurses get $2.3 million in compensation for gender discrimination. (2011, October 30). *Montreal Gazette*. Retrieved November 4, 2011, from http://www.montrealgazette.com/health/Nurses+million+compensation+gender+discrimination/5630518/story.html

O'Connor, S. C., & Rosenblood, L. K. (1996). Affiliation motivation in everyday experience: A theoretical comparison. *Journal of Personality and Social Psychology, 70*, 513–522.

O'Keefe, D. J., & Jensen, J. D. (2007). The relative persuasiveness of gainframed and loss-framed messages for encouraging disease prevention behaviors: A meta-analytic review. *Journal of Health Communication, 12*, 623–644

O'Toole, M. (2010, April 28). 79-year-old subway robbery victim: 'My instinct, fight and chase them. So I chase them'. *National Post*. Retrieved from http://network.nationalpost.com/NP/blogs/toronto/archive/2010/04/28/79-year-old-subway-robbery-victim-my-instinct-fight-and-chase-them-so-i-chase-them.aspx

O'Toole, M. (2010, May 21). Two men arrested in subway mugging of 79-year-old. National Post. Retrieved November 29, 2011, from http://news.nationalpost.com/2010/05/21/two-men-arrested-in-subway-mugging-of-79-year-old/

Ohman, A., Lundqvist, D., & Karolinska, F. E. (2001).The face in the crowd revisited: A threat advantage with schematic stimuli. *Journal of Personality and Social Psychology, 80*, 381–396.

Olson, I. R., & Marshuetz, C. (2005). Facial attractiveness is appraised in a glance. *Emotion, 5*, 498–502.

Olweus, R., Mattsson, A., Schalling, D., & Low, H. (1988). Circulating testosterone levels and aggression in adolescent males: A causal analysis. *Psychosomatic Medicine, 50*, 261–272.

Omoto, A. M., & Snyder, M. (1995). Sustained helping without obligation: Motivation, longevity of service, and perceived attitude change among AIDS volunteers. *Journal of Personality and Social Psychology, 68*, 671–686.

Orue, I., Bushman, B. J., Calvete, E., Thomaes, S., Orobio de Castro, B., & Hutteman, R. (2011). Monkey see, monkey do, monkey hurt: Longitudinal effects of exposure to violence on children's aggressive behaviour. *Social Psychological & Personality Science, 2*, 432–437.

Osbeck, L. M., Moghaddam, F. M., & Perreault, S. (1997). Similarity and attraction among majority and minority groups in a multicultural context. *International Journal of Intercultural Relations, 1*, 113–123.

Osgood, C. E. (1962). *An alternative war or surrender*. Urbana, IL: University of Illinois Press.

Osnos, E. (2011, October 18). China's bystander effect, Letter from China. *The New Yorker*. Retrieved November 12, 2011, from http://www.newyorker.com/online/blogs/evanosnos/2011/10/chinas-bystander-effect.html

Ostrov, J. M., Gentile, D. A., & Crick, N. R. (2006). Media exposure, aggression and prosocial behavior during early childhood: A longitudinal study. *Social Development, 15*, 612–627.

Otten, S., & Wentura, D. (1999). About the impact of automaticity in the Minimal Group Paradigm: Evidence from an affective priming task. *European Journal of Social Psychology, 29*, 1049–1071.

Oyserman, D., Coon, H. M., & Kemmelmeier, M. (2002). Rethinking individualism and collectivism: Evaluation of theoretical assumptions and meta-analyses. *Psychological Bulletin, 128*, 3–72.

Packer, D. J. (2008). Identifying systematic disobedience in Milgram's obedience experiments. *Perspectives on Psychological Science, 3*, 301–304.

Packer, D. J. (2009). Avoiding groupthink: Whereas weakly identified members remain silent, strongly identified members dissent about collective problems. *Psychological Science, 20*, 546–548.

Pajares, F. (1996). Self-efficacy beliefs in achievement settings. *Review of Educational Research, 66*, 543–578.

Palmer, E., & McDowell, C. (1981). Children's understanding of nutritional information presented in breakfast cereal commercials. *Journal of Broadcasting, 25*, 295.

Paloucek, K. J. (2011, May). Shania Twain tries to overcome a career-paralyzing emotional barrier—all on TV. *Channel Guide Magazine*. Retrieved August 16, 2011, from http://channelguidemag.zap2it.com/articles/why-not-shania-twain-own-0511.php

Park, P., Brydon-Miller, M., Hall, B., & Jackson, T. (1993). *Voices of change: Participatory action research in the United States and Canada*. Westport, CT: Bergin & Garvey.

Parker, S. K., Bindel, U. K., & Strauss, K. (2010). Making things happen: A model of proactive motivation. *Journal of Management, 36*, 827–856.

Patel, A. (2011, September 11). 9/11 ten years later: Muslim women, organizations work to fight discrimination. *The Huffington Post Canada*. Retrieved October 26, 2011, from http://www.huffingtonpost.ca/2011/09/11/911-muslim-women-discrimination_n_957305.html

Pavlov, I. P. (1927). *Conditioned reflexes: An investigation of the physiological activity of the cerebral cortex*. Oxford, UK: Oxford University Press.

Payne, B. K. (2001). Prejudice and perception: The role of automatic and controlled processes in misperceiving a weapon. *Journal of Personality and Social Psychology, 81*, 181–192.

Peace, K. A., & Brower, K. L. (2011). *The effect of bogus arousal feedback and valence on CBCA scores for lying and truth-telling*. Manuscript in preparation.

Peace, K. A., & Porter, S. (2011). Remembrance of lies past: A comparison of the features and consistency of truthful and fabricated trauma narratives. *Applied Cognitive Psychology, 25*, 414–423.

Peace, K. A., & Sinclair, S. M. (in press). Cold-blooded lie catchers?: An investigation of psychopathy, emotional processing, and deception detection. *Legal and Criminological Psychology*.

Peace, K. A., Brower, K. L., & Rocchio, A. (2011, June). *Is truth stranger than fiction? Bizarre details, fantasy proneness, and credibility assessment of eyewitness testimony*. Poster presented at the Bi-annual Society for Applied Research in Memory and Cognition (SARMAC) Conference. New York City, NY.

Peace, K. A., Brower, K. L., & Shudra, R. D. (in press). Fact or fiction?: Discriminating true and false allegations of victimization. In A. N. Hutcherson (Ed.), *Psychology of victimization* (pp. 1–79). Hauppauge, NY: Nova Science Publishers.

Peach, J. M., Yoshida, E., Spencer, S. J., Zanna, M. P., & Steele, J. R. (2011). Recognizing discrimination explicitly while denying it implicitly: Implicit social identity protection. *Journal of Experimental Social Psychology, 47*, 283–292.



Pechmann, C., & Shih, C. F. (1999), Smoking scenes in movies and antismoking advertisements before movies: Effects on youth. *Journal of Marketing, 63*, 1–13.

Pennebaker, J. W., Dyer, M. A., Caulkins, R. S., Litowitz, D. L., Ackerman, P. L., Anderson, D. B., et al. (1979). Don't the girls get prettier at closing time: A country and western application to psychology. *Personality and Social Psychology Bulletin, 5*, 122–125.

Penner, L. A., Dertke, M. C.,& Achenbach, C. J. (1973). The "flash" system: A field study of altruism. *Journal of Applied Social Psychology, 3*, 362–370.

Penner, L. A., Dovidio, J. F., Piliavin, J. A., & Schroeder, D. A. (2005). Prosocial behavior: Multilevel perspectives. *Annual Review of Psychology, 56*, 14.1–14.28.

Peplau, L. A., & Fingerhut, A. W. (2007).The close relationships of lesbians and gay men. *Annual Review of Psychology, 58*, 405–424.

Pepler, D. & Sedighdeilami, F. (1998). *Aggressive girls in Canada*. Ottawa: Applied Research Branch, Strategic Policy, Human Resources Development Canada.

Perlini, A. H., & Hansen, S. D. (2001). Moderating effects of need for cognition on attractiveness stereotyping. *Social Behavior and Personality, 29*, 313–322.

Perlini, A. H., Bertolissi, S., & Lind, D. L. (1999). The effects of women's age and physical appearance on evaluations of attractiveness and social desirability. *Journal of Social Psychology, 139*, 343–354.

Perlow, L., & Weeks, J. (2002). Who's helping whom? Layers of culture and workplace behavior. *Journal of Organizational Behavior, 23*, 345–361.

Perlow, L., & Weeks, J. (2002). Who's helping whom? Layers of culture and workplace behavior. *Journal of Organizational Behavior, 23*, 345–361.

Peruche, B. M., & Plant, E. A. (2006). Racial bias in perceptions of athleticism: The role of motivation in the elimination of bias. *Social Cognition, 24*, 438–452.

Pettigrew, T. F. (1979). The ultimate attribution error: Extending Allport's cognitive analysis of prejudice. *Personality and Social Psychology Bulletin, 5*, 461–476.

Pettigrew, T. F. (1998). Intergroup contact theory. *Annual Review of Psychology, 49*, 65–85.

Pettigrew, T. F., & Tropp, L. R. (2000). Does intergroup contact reduce prejudice: Recent meta-analytic findings. In S. Oskamp (Ed.), *Reducing prejudice and discrimination* (pp. 93–114). Mahwah, NJ: Lawrence Erlbaum Associates.

Pettigrew, T., & Tropp, L. (2006). A meta-analytic test of intergroup contact theory. *Journal of Personality and Social Psychology, 90*, 751–783.

Petty, R. E., & Cacioppo, J. T. (1977). Forewarning, cognitive responding, and resistance to persuasion. *Journal of Personality and Social Psychology, 35*, 645–655.

Petty, R. E., & Cacioppo, J. T. (1981). *Attitudes and persuasion: Classic and contemporary approaches*. Dubuque, IA: William C. Brown.

Petty, R. E., & Cacioppo, J. T. (1984). The effects of involvement on responses to argument quantity and quality: Central and peripheral routes to persuasion. *Journal of Personality and Social Psychology, 46*, 69–81.

Petty, R. E., & Cacioppo, J. T. (1986). *Communication and persuasion: Central and peripheral routes to attitude change*. New York: Springer-Verlag.

Petty, R. E., & Wegener, D. T. (1999). The elaboration likelihood model: Current status and controversies. In S. Chaiken & Y. Trope (Eds.), *Dual-process theories in social psychology* (pp. 41–72). New York: Guilford Press.

Petty, R. E., Cacioppo, J. T., & Goldman, R. (1981). Personal involvement as a determinant of argument-based persuasion. *Journal of Personality and Social Psychology, 41*, 847–885.

Petty, R. E., Wells, G. L., & Brock, T. C. (1976). Distraction can enhance or reduce yielding to propaganda: Thought disruption versus effort justification. *Journal of Personality and Social Psychology, 34*, 874–884.

Pew Research Center. (2009, September 9). Muslims widely seen as facing discrimination: Views of religious similarities and differences. *Pew Research Center Publications*. Retrieved December 1, 2010, from http://pewresearch.org/pubs/1336/perceptions-of-islam-religioussimilarities-differences

Philpot, C. R., & Hornsey, M. J. (2008). What happens when groups say sorry: The effect of intergroup apologies on their recipients. *Personality and Social Psychology Bulletin, 34*, 474–489.

Picard, A. (2009, October 19). Reader questions on H1N1 answered. *The Globe and Mail*. Retrieved August 12, 2011, from http://www.theglobeandmail.com/life/health/new-health/conditions/cold-and-flu/h1n1-swine-flu/reader-questions-on-h1n1-answered/article1329448/page1/.

Pierce, T., & Lydon, J. (1998). Priming relational schemas: Effects of contextually activated and chronically accessible interpersonal expectations on responses to a stressful event. *Journal of Personality and Social Psychology, 75*, 1441–1448.

Piliavin, J. A. (2003). Doing well by doing good: Benefits for the benefactor. In C. L. M. Keyes & J. Haidt (Eds.), *Flourishing: Positive Personality and the Life Well Lived* (pp. 227–247).Washington, DC: American Psychological Association.

Piliavin, J. A., & Unger, R. K. (1985) The helpful but helpless female: Myth or reality? In V. O'Leary, R. K. Unger, & B. S. Wallston (Eds.), *Women, Gender and Social Psychology* (pp.149–186) Hillsdale, NJ: Erlbaum.

Pilkington, N. W., & Lydon, J. E. (1997). The relative effect of attitude similarity and attitude dissimilarity on interpersonal attraction: Investigating the moderating roles of prejudice and group membership. *Personality and Social Psychology Bulletin, 23*, 107–122.

Piwinger, M., & Ebert, H. (2001). Impression Management: Wie aus Niemand Jemand wird. In G. Bentele (Ed.), *Kommunikationsmanagement: Strategien, Wissen, Lösungen*. Neuwied, Germany: Luchterhand.

Plant, E. A., Peruche, B. M., & Butz, D. A. (2005). Eliminating automatic racial bias: Making race non-diagnostic for responses to criminal suspects. *Journal of Experimental Social Psychology, 41*, 141–156.

Plant, E.A., & Devine, P. G. (1998). Internal and external motivation to respond without prejudice. *Journal of Personality and Social Psychology, 75*, 811–832.

Police arrest man in Pa. subway hammer attack. *MSNBC*. (2008, September 10). Associated Press. Retrieved November 30, 2010, from http://www.msnbc.msn.com/id/26638199/

Police: People watched gang rape of teen and did nothing to help. (2009, October 27). *The Huffington Post*. Retrieved December 2, 2011 from http://www.huffingtonpost.com/2009/10/27/police-people-watched-gan_n_334975.html

Pollard, M. S., & Wu, Z. (1998). Divergence of marriage patterns in Quebec and elsewhere in Canada. *Population Development and Review, 24*, 329–356.

Pomerleau, A., Bolduc, D., Malcuit, G., & Cossette, L. (1990). Pink or blue: Environmental gender stereotypes in the first two years of life. *Sex Roles, 22*, 359–367.

Pornari, C. D., & Wood, J. (2010). Peer and cyber aggression in secondary school students: The role of moral disengagement, hostile attribution bias, and outcome expectancies. *Aggressive Behavior, 36*, 81–94.

Pornpitakpan, C. (2004). The persuasiveness of source credibility: A critical review of five decades of evidence. *Journal of Applied Social Psychology, 34*, 243–281.

Porter, M., & Haslam, N. (2005). Predisplacement and postdisplacement factors associated with mental health of refugees and internally displaced persons: A meta-analysis. *Journal of the American Medical Association, 294*, 602–612.

Porter, S., & Peace, K. A. (2007). The scars of memory: A prospective, longitudinal investigation of the consistency of traumatic and positive emotional memories in adulthood. *Psychological Science, 18*, 435–441.

Porter, S., & ten Brinke, L. (2009). Dangerous decisions: A theoretical framework for understanding how judges assess credibility in the courtroom. *Legal and Criminological Psychology, 14*, 119–134.

Porter, S., McCabe, S., Woodworth, M., & Peace, K. A. (2007). "Genius is 1% inspiration and 99% perspiration" . . . or is it? An investigation of the effects of motivation and feedback on deception detection. *Legal and Criminological Psychology, 12*, 297–309.

Porter, S., Peace, K. A., Douglas, R. L., Doucette, N. L. (in press). Recovered memory evidence in the courtroom: Facts and fallacies. In J. Ziskin, S. Anderer, and D. Faust (Eds.), *Coping with Psychiatric and Psychological Testimony*. Oxford University Press.

Postmes, T., Spears, R., & Cihangir, S. (2001). Quality of decision making and group norms. *Journal of Personality and Social Psychology, 80*, 918–930.

Postmes, T., Spears, R., & Lea, M. (1999). Social identity, group norms, and "deindividuation": Lessons from computer-mediated communication for social influence in the group. In N. Ellemers, R. Spears, & B. Doosje (Eds.), *Social Identity: Context, Commitment, Content*. Oxford: Blackwell.

Poteat, V. P. (2007). Peer group socialization of homophobic attitudes and behavior during adolescence. *Child Development, 78*, 1830–1842.

Poteat, V. P., Espelage, D. L., & Green, H. D., Jr. (2007). The socialization of dominance: Peer group contextual effects on homophobic and dominance attitudes. *Journal of Personality and Social Psychology, 92*, 1040–1050.

Pratto, F., Sidanius, J., Stallworth, L. M., & Malle, B. F. (1994). Social dominance orientation: A personality variable predicting social and political attitudes. *Journal of Personality and Social Psychology, 67*, 741–763.

Pretty, G. H., & Seligman, C. (1984). Affect and the overjustification effect. *Journal of Personality and Social Psychology, 46*, 1241–1253.

Provine, R. R. (2005).Yawning. *American Scientist, 93*, 532–539.

Public Health Agency of Canada (2010, January 28). Bi-weekly and cumulative number of deaths due to Pandemic (H1N1) 2009, by province/territory, Canada. Retrieved August 12, 2011, from http://www.phac-aspc.gc.ca/alert-alerte/h1n1/wave-vague2-eng.php

Purdon, C., Rowa, K., Antony, M. M. (2005). Thought suppression and its effects on thought frequency, appraisal and mood state in individuals with obsessive-compulsive disorder. *Behaviour Research and Therapy, 43*, 93–108.

Quinn, J. M., & Wood, W. (2004). Forewarnings of influence appeals: Inducing resistance and acceptance. In E. S. Knowles & J. A. Linn (Eds.), *Resistance and persuasion* (pp. 193–214). Mahwah, NJ: Lawrence Erlbaum.

Quinn, P. C., Kelly, D. J., Lee, K., Pascalis, O., & Slater, A. M. (2008). Preference for attractive faces in human infants extends beyond conspecifics. *Developmental Science, 11*, 76–83.

Raghunathan, R., & Trope, Y. (2002). Walking the tightrope between feeling good and being accurate: Mood as a resource in processing persuasive messages. *Journal of Personality and Social Psychology, 83*, 510–525.

Ramachandran, V. S. (2006). Mirror neurons and imitation learning as the driving force behind "the great leap forward" in human evolution. *The Third Culture*. Retrieved September 20, 2010, from http://www.edge.org/3rd_culture/ramachandran/ramachandran_p1.html

Rapoport, A. (1960). *Fights, games, and debates*. Ann Arbor, MI: University of Michigan Press.

Raver, J. L., Ehrhart, M. G., & Chadwick, I. C. (2011, in press). The emergence of team helping norms: Foundations within members' attributes and behavior. *Journal of Organizational Behavior*.

RCMP faces $1M payout on discrimination case. (2008, April 17). *CBC News*. Retrieved October 25, 2011, from http://www.cbc.ca/news/canada/saskatchewan/story/2008/04/17/rcmp-discrimination.html

RCMP, Greyhound, feds sued over McLean beheading. (2011, February 16). *Winnipeg Free Press*. Retrieved on August 30, 2011, from http://www.winnipegfreepress.com/breakingnews/Greyhound-RCMP-government-sued-ovre-McLean-beheading-116345794.html

Read, J. D., & Desmarais, S. L. (2009). Lay knowledge of eyewitness issues: A Canadian evaluation. *Applied Cognitive Psychology, 23*, 301–326.

Read, J. D., Connolly, D. A., & Welsh, A. (2006) An archival analysis of actual cases of historic child sexual abuse: A comparison of jury and bench trials. *Law and Human Behavior, 30, 259–285*.

Record number of women elected. (2011, May 3). *CBC News*. Retrieved November 18, 2011, from http://www.cbc.ca/news/politics/canadavotes2011/story/2011/05/03/cv-election-women.html#

Reddy, R. D. (1980). Individual philanthropy and giving behavior. In D. H. Smith & J. Macaulay (Eds.), *Participation in social and political activities* (pp. 370–399). San Francisco, CA: Jossey-Bass.

Regoeczi, W. C. (2003). When context matters: A multilevel analysis of household and neighbourhood crowding on aggression and withdrawal. *Journal of Environmental Psychology, 23*, 457–470.

Reis, H. T., & Aron, A. (2008). Love: What is it, why does it matter, and how does it operate? *Perspectives on Psychological Science, 3*, 80–86.

Reisenzein, R. (1983). The Schachter theory of emotion: Two decades later. *Psychological Bulletin, 94*, 239–264.

Rentfrow, P. J., & Gosling, S. D. (2006). Message in a ballad: The role of music preferences in interpersonal perception. *Psychological Science, 17*, 236–242.

Restaurant shift turns into nightmare. (2005, November 10). *ABC News Primetime*. Retrieved November 30, 2010, from http://abcnews.go.com/Primetime/story?id_1297922&page_1

Rhee, E., Uleman, J. S., Lee, H. K., & Roman, R. J. (1995). Spontaneous self-concepts and ethnic identities in individualistic and collectivistic cultures. *Journal of Personality and Social Psychology, 69*, 142–152.

Rhodes, G. (2006). The evolution of facial attractiveness. *Annual Review of Psychology*, *57*, 199–266.

Ricci, L. A., Rasakham, K., Grimes, J. M., & Melloni, R. H., Jr. (2006). Serotonin-1A receptor activity and expression modulate adolescent anabolic/androgenic steroid-induced aggression in hamsters. *Pharmacology, Biochemistry and Behavior, 85*, 1–11.

Ridge, S. R. & Feeney, J. A. (1998). Relationship history and relationship attitudes in gay males and lesbians: Attachment style and gender differences. *Australian & New Zealand Journal of Psychiatry*, *32*, 848–860.

Riek, B. M., Mania, E. W., & Gaertner, S. L. (2006). Intergroup threat and outgroup attitudes: A meta-analytic review. *Personality and Social Psychological Review, 10*, 336–353.

Ringelmann, M. (1913). Recherches sur les moteurs animes: Travail de l'homme. *Annales de l'Institut National Agronomique*, 2e serie, tom XIII, 1–40.

Rizzolatti, G., & Craighero, L. (2004). The mirror-neuron system. *Annual Review of Neuroscience*, *27*, 169–192.

Roberts, R. (2010, April 26). Subway riders refuse to intervene as thugs rob man, 79. *National Post.* Retrieved from http://network.nationalpost.com/NP/blogs/toronto/archive/2010/04/26/subway-riders-refuse-to-intervene-as-thugs-rob-man-79.aspx

Roberts, W. L. (1999). The socialization of emotional expression: Relations with prosocial behaviour and competence in five samples. *Canadian Journal of Behavioural Science, 31*, 72–85.

Roberts-Moore, J. (2002). Establishing recognition of past injustices: Uses of archival records in documenting the experience of Japanese Canadians during the Second World War. *Archivaria, 53*, 64–75.

Robinson, B. M., & Elias, L. J. (2005). Novel stimuli are negative stimuli: Evidence that negative affect is reduced in the mere exposure effect. *Perceptual and Motor Skills, 100*, 365–372.

Robinson, L. A. (1999). The relationships between attachment style and romantic attachment, autonomy and equality in lesbian relationships. *Australian Journal of Psychology*, *51*, 137–137.

Robinson, W. (2007). Operational definitions. *The University of Tennessee Knoxville*. Retrieved June 3, 2010 from http://web.utk.edu/_wrobinso/540_lec_opdefs.html

Roese, N. J. (1997). Counterfactual thinking and marketing: Introduction to the special issue. *Psychology and Marketing*, *17*, 277–280.

Roese, N. J., & Jamieson, D. W. (1993). Twenty years of bogus pipeline research: A critical review and meta-analysis. *Psychological Bulletin, 114*, 363–375.

Roese, N. J., & Olson, J. M. (1994). Attitude importance as a function of repeated attitude expression. *Journal of Experimental Social Psychology, 30*, 39-51

Rogers, C. R. (1959). A theory of therapy, personality, and interpersonal relationships, as developed in the client-centered framework. In S. Koch (Ed.), *Psychology: A study of science* (pp. 184–256). New York, NY: McGraw Hill.

Romano, E., Tremblay, R. E., Boulerice, B., & Swisher, R. (2005). Multilevel correlates of childhood physical aggression and prosocial behaviour. *Journal of Abnormal Child Psychology, 33*, 565–578.

Ronquillo, J., Denson, T., Lickel, B., Lu, Z-L., Nandy, A., & Maddox, K. B. (2007). The effects of skin tone on race -related amygdala activity: An fMRI investigation. *Social Cognitive and Affective Neuroscience, 2*, 39–44.

Rosenbaum, M. E. (1986).The repulsion hypothesis: on the non-development of relationships. *Journal of Personality and Social Psychology*, *50*, 29–36.

Rosenberg, M. (1965). *Society and adolescent self-image*. Princeton, NJ: Princeton University Press.

Rosenquist, J. N., Murabito, J., Fowler, J. H., & Christakis, N. A. (2010). The spread of alcohol consumption behavior in a large social network. *Annals of Internal Medicine*, *152*, 426–433.

Rosenthal, R., & Jacobson, L. (1968). *Pygmalion in the classroom*. New York: Holt, Rinehart and Winston.

Ross, L. (1977). The intuitive psychologist and his shortcomings: Distortions in the attribution process. In L. Berkowitz (Ed.), *Advances in experimental social psychology* (Vol. 10). New York: Academic Press.

Ross, L., & Nisbett, R. E. (1991) *The person and the situation*. New York: McGraw-Hill.

Ross, L., Amabile, T. M., & Steinmetz, J. L. (1977). Social roles, social control, and biases in social perception. *Journal of Personality and Social Psychology*, *35*, 485–494.

Ross, L., Greene, D., & House, P. (1977). The false consensus effect: An egocentric bias in social perception and attribution processes. *Journal of Experimental Social Psychology*, *13*, 279–301.

Ross, L., Lepper, M. R., & Hubbard, M. (1975). Perseverance in self-perception and social perception: Biased attributional processes in the debriefing paradigm. *Journal of Personality and Social Psychology*, *32*, 880–892.

Roszell, P., Kennedy, D., & Grabb, E. (1989). Physical attractiveness and income attainment among Canadians. *Journal of Psychology: Interdisciplinary and Applied, 123*, 547–559.

Roth, M. (2010, December 26). Looking across the racial divide: How eyewitness testimony can cause problems. *Pittsburgh Post-Gazette.* Retrieved November 2, 2011, from http://www.post-gazette.com/pg/10360/1113570-115.stm

Rozin, P., & Royzman, E. B. (2001). Negativity bias, negativity dominance, and contagion. *Personality and Social Psychology Review*, *5*, 296–320.

Rubin, K. H., & Thompson, A. (2002). *The friendship factor: Helping our children navigate their social world - and why it matters for their success and happiness*. New York: Penguin Group.

Ruder, M., & Bless, H. (2003). Mood and the reliance on the ease of retrieval heuristic. *Journal of Personality and Social Psychology, 85*, 20–32.

Rudman, L. A. (2004). Sources of implicit attitudes. *Current Directions in Psychological Science*, *13*, 80–83.

Rudman, L. A., Ashmore, R. D., & Gary, M. L. (2001). "Unlearning" automatic biases: The malleability of implicit stereotypes and prejudice. *Journal of Personality and Social Psychology*, *81*, 856–868.

Rudman, L. A., Phelan, J. E., & Heppen, J. (2007). Developmental sources of implicit attitudes. *Personality and Social Psychology Bulletin, 33*, 1700–1713.

Rusbult, C. E. (1991). Commentary on Johnson's "Commitment to personal relationships": What's interesting, and what's new? In W. H. Jones & D. W. Perlman (Eds.), *Advances in Personal Relationships* (Vol. 3, pp. 151–169). London: Kingsley.

Rusbult, C. E., & Zembrodt, I. M. (1983). Responses to dissatisfaction in romantic involvements: A multidimensional scaling analysis. *Journal of Experimental Social Psychology*, *43*, 1230–1242.

Ruvolo, A. P., Fabin, L.A., & Ruvolo, C. M. (2001). Relationship experiences and change in attachment characteristics of young adults: The role of relationship breakups and conflict avoidance. *Personal Relationships*, *8*, 265–281.

Ryan, C. S., & Bogart, L. M. (1997). Development of new group members' in-group and out-group stereotypes: Changes in perceived group variability and ethnocentrism. *Journal of Personality and Social Psychology, 73*, 719–732.

Rye, B. J., Greatrix, S. A., & Enright, C. S. (2006). The case of the guilty victim: The effects of gender of victim and gender of perpetrator on attributions of blame and responsibility. *Sex Roles, 54*, 639–649.

Sacks, O. (2007, September). The abyss: Music and amnesia. *The New Yorker.* Retrieved July 8, 2010, from http://www.newyorker.com/reporting/2007/09/24/070924fa_fact_sacks?currentPage_1

Saladin, M., Saper, Z., & Breen, L. (1988). Perceived attractiveness and attributions of criminality: What is beautiful is not criminal. *Canadian Journal of Criminology, 30*, 251–259.

Salmivalli, C., & Voeten, M. (2004). Connections between attitudes, group norms, and behaviour in bullying situations. International Journal of Behavioral Development, 28, 246–258.

Salwen, K., & Salwen, H. (2010). *The power of half: One family's decision to stop taking and start giving back*. Boston: Houghton Mifflin Harcourt.

Sandys, M., & Dillehay, R. C. (1995). First-ballot votes, predeliberation dispositions, and final verdicts in jury trials. *Law and Human Behavior, 19*, 175–195.

Sangrigoli, S., Pallier, C., Argenti, A. M., Ventureyra, V. A. G., & de Schonen, S. (2005). Reversibility of the other-race effect in face recognition during childhood. *Psychological Science, 16*, 440–444.

Santor, D. A., Messervey, D., & Kusumakar, V. (2000). Measuring peer pressure, popularity, and conformity in adolescent boys and girls: Predicting school performance, sexual attitudes, and substance use. *Journal of Youth and Adolescence, 29*, 163–182.

Santos, A., Meyer-Lindenberg, A., Deruelle, C. (2010). Absence of racial, but not gender, stereotyping in Williams syndrome children. *Current Biology*, *20*, R307–R308.

Saucier, D. A., Miller, C. T., & Doucet, N. (2005). Differences in helping whites and blacks: A meta-analysis. *Personality and Social Psychology Review, 9*, 2–16.

Schachter, S., & Singer, J., (1962) Cognitive, social, and physiological determinants of emotional state. *Psychological Review, 69*, 379–399.

Schaller, M. (2008). Evolutionary bases of first impressions. In N. Ambady & J. J. Skowronski (Eds.), *First impressions* (pp. 15–34). New York, NY: Guilford Press.

Schaller, M., & Cialdini, R. B. (1988).The economics of empathic helping: Support for a mood management motive. *Journal of Experimental Social Psychology, 24*, 163–181.

Scharfe, E., & Bartholomew, K. (1994). Reliability and stability of adult attachment patterns. *Personal Relationships, 1*, 2–43.

Schiller, D., Freeman, J. B., Mitchell, J. P., Uleman, J. S., & Phelps, E. A. (2009). A neural mechanism of first impressions. *Nature Neuroscience, 12*, 508–514.

Schimmack, U. (2005). Attentional interference effects of emotional pictures: Threat, negativity, or arousal? *Emotion, 5*, 55–66.

Schnall, S., Roper, J., & Fessler, D. M. T. (2010). Elevation leads to altruistic behavior, above and beyond general positive affect. *Psychological Science, 21*, 315–320.

Schoenborn "not criminally responsible" for murders: Father was insane when he killed 3 children, judge finds. (2010, February 22). *CBC News.* Retrieved October 17, 2011, from http://www.cbc.ca/news/canada/british-columbia/story/2010/02/22/bc-schoenborn-verdict.html

Schoenborn, C. A. (2004). Marital status and health: United States, 1999–2002. *Advance Data, 351*.

Schrammel, J., Köffel, C., & Tscheligi, M. (2009). How much do you tell? Information disclosure behaviour on different types of online communities. ACM *Computing & Technology, June 2009*, 275–284.

Schuller, R. A., & Hastings, P. A. (1996). Trials of battered women who kill: The impact of alternative forms of expert evidence. *Law and Human Behavior, 20*, 167–187.

Schuller, R. A., & Jenkins, G. (2007). Expert evidence pertaining to battered women: Limitations and reconceptualizations. In M. Costanzo, D. Krauss, & K. Pezdek (Eds.), *Expert psychological testimony for the courts* (pp. 203–225). Mahwah, NJ: Lawrence Erlbaum Associates.

Schuller, R. A., & Vidmar, N. (1992). Battered woman syndrome evidence in the courtroom: A review of the literature. *Law and Human Behavior, 16*, 273–291.

Schuller, R. A., Terry, D., & McKimmie, B. (2005). The impact of expert testimony on jurors' decisions: Gender of the expert and testimony complexity. *Journal of Applied Social Psychology, 35*, 1266–1280.

Schumacher, J. A., & Smith Slep, A. M. (2004). Attitudes and dating aggression: A cognitive dissonance approach. *Prevention Science, 5*, 231–243.

Schunk, D. H. (1995). Self-efficacy and education and instruction. In J. E. Maddux (Ed.), *Self-efficacy, adaptation, and adjustment: Theory, research, and application* (pp. 281–303). New York: Plenum Press.

Schwarz, N. (1990). Feelings as information: Informational and motivational functions of affective states. In E. T. Higgins & R. M. Sorrentino (Eds.), *Handbook of motivation and cognition* (pp. 527–561). New York: Guilford Press.

Schwarz, N., & Bohner, G. (2001).The construction of attitudes. In A. Tesser & N. Schwarz (Eds.), *Intrapersonal Processes (Blackwell Handbook of Social Psychology)* (pp. 436–457). Oxford, UK: Blackwell.

Scott, K., & Straus, M. (2007). Denial, minimization, partner blaming, and intimate aggression in dating relationships. *Journal of Interpersonal Violence, 22*, 851–871.

Scourfield, J., John, B., Martin, N., & McGuffin, P. (2004). The development of prosocial behaviour in children and adolescents: A twin study. *Journal of Child Psychology and Psychiatry, 45*, 927–935.

Sebastian, C., Burnett, S., & Blakemore, S. J. (2008). Development of the self-concept during adolescence. *Trends in Cognitive Science, 12*, 441–446.

Sedikides, G., & Gregg, A. P. (2003). Portraits of the self. In M. A. Hogg & J. Cooper (Eds.), *Sage handbook of social psychology* (pp. 110–138). London: Sage.

Segerstrom S. C., & Sephton S. E. (2010). Optimistic expectancies and cell-mediated immunity: The role of positive affect. *Psychological Science, 21*, 448–455.

Seinen, I., & Schram, A. (2006). Social status and group norms: Indirect reciprocity in a experiment. *European Economic Review, 50*, 581–602.

Seiter, J. S. (2007). Ingratiation and gratuity: The effect of complimenting customers on tipping behavior in restaurants. *Journal of Applied Social Psychology, 37*, 478–485.

Serbin, L. A., Poulin-Dubois, D., & Eichstedt, J. A. (2002). Infants' responses to gender-inconsistent events. *Infancy, 3*, 531–542.

Serbin, L. A., Poulin-Dubois, D., Colburne, K. A., Sen, M. G., & Eichstedt, J. A. (2001). Gender stereotyping in infancy: Visual preferences for and knowledge of gender-stereotyped toys in second year. *International Journal of Behavioral Development, 25*, 7–15.

Seto, M. C., Maric, A., & Barbaree, H. E. (2001). The role of pornography in the etiology of sexual aggression. *Aggression and Violent Behavior, 6*, 35–53.

Sev'er, A., & Yurdakul, G. (2001). Culture of honor, culture of change: A feminist analysis of honor killings in rural turkey. *Violence Against Women, 7*, 964–998.

Sexual assault on campus. (2010, April 12). *The Ubyssey*. Retrieved November 12, 2011, from http://ubyssey.ca/features/sexual-assault-on-campus/

Seyle, D. C., & Swann, W. B. (2007). Being oneself in the workplace: Self-verification and identity in organizational contexts. In C. A. Bartel, S. Blader, & A.Wrzesniewski (Eds.), *Identity and the modern organization* (pp. 201–222). Mahwah, NJ: Lawrence Erlbaum Associates.

Shadd, A. (1989). Institutionalized racism and Canadian history: Notes of a Black Canadian. In O. McKague (Ed.), *Racism in Canada* (pp. 1–5). Saskatoon, SK: Fifth House Publishers.

Shaver, P. R., & Hazan, C. (1993). Adult romantic attachment: Theory and evidence. In D. Perlman & W. Jones (Eds.), *Advances in personal relationships* (Vol. 4, pp. 29–70). London: Kingsley.

Shaw, M. E. (1981). *Group Dynamics: The Psychology of Small Group Behavior*. New York: McGraw-Hill.

Sheeran, P., Abraham, C., & Orbell, S. (1999). Psychosocial correlates of heterosexual condom use: A meta-analysis. *Psychological Bulletin, 125*, 90–132.

Sheldon, K. M. (2005). Positive value change during college: Normative trends and individual differences. *Journal of Research in Personality, 39*, 209–223.

Shellenbarger, S. (2009). Father's day: Why men are hard-wired to cuddle their babies. *The Wall Street Journal Blogs*. Retrieved December 1, 2010, from http://blogs.wsj.com/juggle/2009/06/19/fathers-day-whymen-are-hard-wired-to-cuddle-their-babies/

Shenfeld, H. (2011, May 3). Shania Twain: My divorce was the wake-up call I needed. *People Magazine.* Retrieved August 16, 2011, from http://www.people.com/people/article/0,20486696,00.html

Sheridan, M. (2009, May 31). Kidnappers swoop on China's girls. *The Times.* Retrieved December 1, 2010, from http://www.timesonline.co.uk/tol/news/world/asia/article6396010.ece

Sherif, M. (1937). An experimental approach to the study of attitudes. *Sociometry, 1*, 90–98.

Sherif, M. (1966). The psychology of social norms. Oxford, UK: Harper Torchbooks.

Sherif, M., & Sherif, C. W. (1956). *An outline of social psychology*. New York: Harper.

Sherif, M., Harvey, O. J., White, B. J., Hood, W. R., & Sherif, C. W. (1961/1988). *The Robbers Cave experiment: Intergroup conflict and cooperation*. Middletown, CT: Wesleyan University Press.

Sherif, M., Harvey, O. J., White, J., Hood, W. R., & Sherif, C. W. (1954). *Intergroup conflict and cooperation: The Robbers Cave experiment.* Norman, OK: University Book Exchange.

Sherman, J. W., Gawronski, B., Gonsalkorale, K., Hugenberg, K., Allen, T. J., & Groom, C. J. (2008). The self-regulation of automatic associations and behavioral impulses. *Psychological Review, 115*, 314–335.

Sherman, J. W., Kruschke, J. K., Sherman, S. J., Percy, E. J., Petrocelli, J. V., & Conrey, F. R. (2009). Attentional processes in stereotype formation: A common model for category accentuation and illusory correlation. *Journal of Personality and Social Psychology, 96*, 305–323.

Shiue, Y. C., Chiu, C. M., & Chang, C. C. (2010). Exploring and mitigating social loafing in online communities. *Computers in Human Behavior, 26*, 768–777.

Shocking online content being used to recruit youth: RCMP. (2011, June 7). *Sun News.* Retrieved November 2, 2011, from http://www.sunnewsnetwork.ca/sunnews/sciencetech/archives/2011/06/20110607-102712.html

Shotland, R. L., & Heinold, W. D. (1985). Bystander response to arterial bleeding: Helping skills, the decision-making process, and differentiating the helping response. *Journal of Personality and Social Psychology, 49*, 347–356.

Shotland, R. L., & Johnson, M. P. (1978). Bystander behavior and kinesics: The interaction between the helper and victim. *Environmental Psychology and Nonverbal Behavior, 2*, 181–190.

Shotland, R. L., & Stebbins, C. A. (1983). Emergency and cost as determinants of helping behavior and the slow accumulation of social psychological knowledge. *Social Psychology Quarterly, 46*, 36–46.

Shotland, R. L., & Straw, M. K. (1976). Bystander response to an assault: When a man attacks a woman. *Journal of Personality and Social Psychology, 34*, 990–999.

Shrout, P. E., Herman, C. M., & Bolger, N. (2006). The costs and benefits of practical and emotional support on adjustment: A daily diary study of couples experiencing acute stress. *Personal Relationships, 13*, 115–134.

Sidanius, J. & Pratto, F. (1999). *Social dominance: An intergroup theory of social hierarchy and oppression*. New York: Cambridge University Press.

Simourd, D. J., & Mamuza, J. M. (2000). The hostile interpretations questionnaire: Psychometric properties and construct validity. *Criminal Justice and Behavior, 27*, 645–663.

Simplicio, M. D., Massey-Chase, R., Cowen, P. J., & Harmer, C. J. (2009). Oxytocin enhances processing of positive versus negative emotional information in healthy male volunteers. *Journal of Pharmacology, 23*, 241–248.

Simpson, B., & Willer, R. (2008). Altruism and indirect reciprocity: The interaction of person and situation in prosocial behavior. *Social Psychology Quarterly, 71*, 37–52.

Simpson, J. A., Campbell, B., & Berscheid, E. (1986). The association between romantic love and marriage: Kephart (1967). Twice revisited. *Personality and Social Psychology Bulletin, 12*, 363–372.

Sinclair, R. C., & Mark, M. M. (1995). The effects of mood state on judgemental accuracy: Processing strategy as a mechanism. *Cognition & Emotion, 9*, 417–438.

Singh, D. (1993). Adaptive significance of female physical attractiveness: Role of waist-to-hip ratio. *Journal of Personality and Social Psychology, 65*, 293–307.

Sintay, L., & Ibanga, I. (June 10, 2009). Recession causes increase in teen dating violence. *Good Morning America*. Retrieved June 3, 2010, from http://abcnews.go.com/GMA/story?id_7798098&page_1

Sissons, M. (1981). Race, sex, and helping behavior. *British Journal of Social Psychology, 20*, 285–292.

Sistrunk, F., & McDavid, J. W. (1971). Sex variable in conforming behavior. *Journal of Personality and Social Psychology, 17*, 200–207.

Skinner, B. F. (1938). *The behavior of organisms: An experimental analysis*. Oxford, UK: Appleton-Century.

Skitka, L. J. (1999). Ideological and attributional boundaries on public compassion: Reactions to individuals and communities affected by a natural disaster. *Personality and Social Psychology Bulletin, 25*, 793–792.

Skitka, L. J., Mullen, E., Griffin, T., Hutchinson, S., & Chamberlin, B. (2002). Dispositions, ideological scripts, or motivated correction? Understanding ideological differences in attributions for social problems. *Journal of Personality and Social Psychology, 83*, 470–487.

Skitka, L. J., Saunders, B., Morgan, G. S., & Wisneski, D. (2009).Dark clouds and silver linings: Socio-psychological responses to September 11, 2001. In M. J. Morgan (Ed.), *The day that changed everything? Looking at the impact of 9-11* (Vol. 3, pp. 63–80). New York: Palgrave MacMillan.

Slater, M. D. (1997). Persuasion processes across receiver goals and message genres. *Communication Theory, 7*, 125–148.

Slave Lake donations buried in Calgary dump. (2011, August 10). *CBC News*. Retrieved November 12, 2011, from http://www.cbc.ca/news/canada/calgary/story/2011/08/10/calgary-slave-lake-donations-dumped.html

Slotter, E. B., Gardner, W. L., & Finkel, E. J. (2009).Who am I without you? The influence of romantic breakup on the self-concept. *Personality and Social Psychology Bulletin, 36*, 147.

Slovic, P., & Fischhoff, B. (1977). On the psychology of experimental surprises. *Journal of Experimental Psychology: Human Perception and Performance, 3*, 544–551.

Smeaton, G., Byrne, D., & Murnen, S. K. (1989). The repulsion hypothesis revisited: Similarity irrelevance or dissimilarity bias? *Journal of Personality and Social Psychology, 56*, 54–59.

Smith, B. N., Kerr, N. A., Markus, M. J., & Stasson, M. F. (2001). Individual differences in social loafing: Need for cognition as a motivator in collective performance. *Group Dynamics, 5*, 150–158.

Smith, K. D., Keating, J. P., & Stotland, E. (1989). Altruism reconsidered: The effect of denying feedback on a victim's status to empathic witnesses. *Journal of Personality and Social Psychology, 57*, 641–650.

Smith, M. (2005). The politics of same-sex marriage in Canada and the United States. *Political Science & Politics*, (April), 225–228.

Smith, P. B., & Bond, M. H. (1993). *Social psychology across cultures*. Hemel Hempstead: Harvester Wheatsheaf.

Smith, P. B., Bond, M. H., & Kağitçibaşi, C. (2006). *Understanding social psychology across cultures*. London: Sage Publications.

Snyder, M. (1974). *Self-monitoring scale*. Retrieved August 13, 2010 from http://pubpages.unh.edu/_ckb/SELFMON2.html

Snyder, M. (1979). Self-monitoring processes. In L. Berkowitz (Ed.), *Advances in experimental social psychology* (Vol. 12, pp. 85–126). Orlando, FL: Academic Press.

Snyder, M., & Swann, W. B. (1978). Hypothesis-testing processes in social interaction. *Journal of Personality and Social Psychology, 36*, 1202–1212.

Snyder, M., Berscheid, E., & Glick, P. (1985). Focusing on the exterior and the interior: Two investigations of the initiation of personal relationships. *Journal of Personality and Social Psychology, 48*, 1427–1439.

Snyder, M., Omoto, A. M., & Crain, A. L. (1999). Punished for their good deeds: Stigmatization of AIDS volunteers. *American Behavioral Scientist, 42*, 1175–1192.

Social Psychology Network. (2010). *2010 action teaching award winner*. Retrieved August 12, 2010, from http://www.socialpsychology.org/action/2010winner.html

Society for the Psychological Study of Social Issues. (2010). About SPSSI. *SPSSI*. Retrieved August 12, 2010, from http://www.spssi.org/indexcfm?fuseaction_Page.viewPage&pageId_479

Soldat, A. S., & Sinclair, R. C. (2001). Colors, smiles, and frowns: External affective cues can directly affect responses to persuasive communications in a mood-like manner without affecting mood. *Social Cognition, 19*, 469–490.

Solomon Asch Center for Study of Ethnopolitical Conflict. (2000). *About Solomon Asch*. Retrieved May 2, 2010, from http://www.brynmawr.edu/aschcenter/about/solomon.htm

Soma, K. K., Scotti, M. A. L., Newman, A. E. M., Charlier, T. D., & Demas, G. E. (2008). Novel mechanisms for neuroendocrine regulation of aggression. *Frontiers in Neuroendocrinology, 29*, 476-489.

Sommers, S. R., & Ellsworth, P. C. (2000). Race in the courtroom: Perceptions of guilt and dispositional attributions. *Personality and Social Psychology Bulletin, 26*, 1367–1379.

Sorrentino, R. M., Bobocel, D. R., Gitta, M. Z., Olson, J. M., & Hewitt, E. C. (1988). Uncertainty orientation and persuasion: Individual differences in effects of personal relevance on social judgments. *Journal of Personality and Social Psychology, 55*, 357–371.

Sparrow, B., & Wegner, D. M. (2006). Unpriming: The deactivation of thoughts through expression. *Journal of Personality and Social Psychology, 91*, 1009–1019.

Spencer, S. J., Fein, S., Wolfe, C.T., Fong, C., & Dunn, M. A. (1998). Automatic activation of stereotypes: The role of self-image threat. *Personality and Social Psychology Bulletin, 24*, 1139–1152.

Spencer, S. J., Steele, C. M., & Quinn, D. (1999). Stereotype threat and women's math performance. *Journal of Experimental Social Psychology, 35*, 4–28.

Sprafkin, J. N., Liebert, R. M., & Poulos, R. W. (1975). Effects of a prosocial televised example on children's helping. *Journal of Experimental Child Psychology, 20*, 119–126.

Sprecher, S., & Schwartz, P. (1994). Equity balance in the exchange of contributions in close relationships. In M. L. Lerner & G. Mikula (Eds.), *Entitlement and the Affectional Bond: Justice in Close Relationships* (pp. 11–41). New York: Plenum Press.

Squire, L. R. (1992). Memory and the hippocampus: A synthesis from findings with rats, monkeys, and humans. *Psychological Review, 99*, 195–231.

Staples, D. (2011, August 5). Edmonton is hardly Canada's murder capital. *Edmonton Journal*. Retrieved September 19, 2011, from http://www.edmontonjournal.com/news/Edmonton+hardly+Canada+murder+capital/5208616/story.html

Stasser, G., Kerr, N. L., & Bray, R. M. (1981). The social psychology of jury deliberations: Structure, process, and product. In N. L. Kerr & R. M. Bray (Eds.), *The Psychology of the Courtroom*. New York: Academic Press.

Statistics Canada. (2010a). Homicide in Canada, 2009. *The Daily,* October 26.

Statistics Canada. (2010b). Leading causes of death, 2007. *The Daily,* November 30.

Steele, C. M. (1988).The psychology of self-affirmation: Sustaining the integrity of the self. In L. Berkowitz (Ed.), *Advances in experimental social psychology, Vol. 21: Social psychological studies of the self: Perspectives and programs.* (pp. 261–302). San Diego, CA: Academic Press.

Steele, C. M., & Aronson, J. (1995). Stereotype threat and the intellectual test performance of African-Americans. *Journal of Personality and Social Psychology, 69,* 797–811.

Steele, C. M., & Josephs, R. A. (1990). Alcohol myopia: Its prized and dangerous effects. *American Psychologist, 45,* 921–933.

Steele, C. M., Spencer, S. J., & Aronson, J. (2002). Contending with group image: The psychology of stereotype and social identity threat. In M. P. Zanna (Ed.), *Advances in experimental social psychology* (pp. 379–440). San Diego, CA: Academic Press.

Steele, J. R., Reisz, L., Williams, A., & Kawakami, K. (2007). Women in mathematics: Examining the hidden barriers that gender stereotypes can impose. In R. J. Burke & M. C. Mattis (Eds.), *Women and minorities in science, technology, engineering and mathematics: Upping the numbers* (pp. 159–183). Cheltenham, UK: Edward Elgar Publishing Limited.

Steele, J., Choi, Y. S., & Ambady, N. (2004). Stereotyping, prejudice, and discrimination: The effect of group-based expectations on moral functioning. In T. A. Thorkildsen and H. J. Walberg (Eds.), *Nurturing morality* (pp. 77–97). New York, NY: Kluwer Academic Press.

Stel, M., & Vonk, R. (2010). Mimicry in social interaction: Benefits for mimickers, mimickees, and their interaction. *British Journal of Psychology, 101,* 311–323.

Stel, M., van Baaren, R. B., & Vonk, R. (2007). Effects of mimicking: Acting prosocially by being emotionally moved. *European Journal of Social Psychology, 38,* 965–976.

Stelzl, M., Janes, L., & Seligman, C. (2008). Champ or chump: Strategic utilization of dual social identities of others. *European Journal of Social Psychology, 38,* 128–138.

Stephan, W. G., & Vogt, W. P. (Eds.) (2004). *Programs for improving intergroup relations: Theory, practice, and research.* New York: Teachers College Press.

Sternberg, R. J. (1986). A triangular theory of love. *Psychological Review, 93,* 119–135.

Sternberg, R. J. (1987). Liking versus loving: A comparative evaluation of theories. *Psychological Bulletin, 102,* 331–345.

Sternberg, R. J. (1997). *Thinking styles.* New York: Cambridge University Press.

Stewart D. D. & Stasser G., (1995). Expert role assignment and information sampling during collective recall and decision making. *Journal of Personality and Social Psychology, 69,* 619–628.

Stewart, S., Stinnett, H., & Rosenfeld, L. B. (2000). Sex differences in desired characteristics of short-term and long-term relationship partners. *Journal of Social and Personal Relationships, 17,* 843–853.

Stewart-Williams, S. (2007). Altruism among kin vs. non kin: Effects of cost of help and reciprocal exchange. *Evolution and Human Behavior, 28,* 193–198.

Stinson, D. A., Cameron, J. J., Wood, J. V., Gaucher, D., & Holmes, J. G. (2009). Deconstructing the "reign of error": Interpersonal warmth explains the self-fulfilling prophecy of anticipated acceptance. *Personality and Social Psychology Bulletin, 35,* 1165–1178.

Stone, L., & Boyle, T. (2011, October 18). Elderly woman breaks hip at Niagara hospital, told by staff to call ambulance. *The Star.* Retrieved on November 9, 2011, from http://www.thestar.com/news/canada/article/1071790—elderly-woman-breaks-hip-at-niagara-hospital-told-by-staff-to-call-ambulance

Stoner, J. A. F. (1961). A comparison of individual and group decisions involving risk. Unpublished master's thesis. Massachusetts Institute of Technology.

Strack, F., Martin, L. L., & Stepper, S. (1988). Inhibiting and facilitating conditions of the human smile: A nonobtrusive test of the facial feedback hypothesis. *Journal of Personality and Social Psychology, 54,* 768–777.

Stürmer, S., Snyder, M., & Omoto, A. M. (2005). Prosocial emotions and helping: The moderating role of group membership. *Journal of Personality and Social Psychology, 88,* 532–546.

Sullivan, P. (2010, September 10). Preparing children to be safe at college. *The New York Times.* Retrieved December 1, 2010, from http://www.nytimes.com/2010/09/11/your-money/11wealth.html

Sulsky, L. M., & Keown, J. L. (1998). Performance appraisal in the changing world of work: Implications for the meaning and measurement of work performance. *Canadian Psychology, 39,* 52–59.

Sung, H. (2009, June 9). Money is the biggest cause of stress for half of Canadians, women more stressed than men except with work. *Synovate Research.* Retrieved October 10, 2011, from http://www.synovate.com/news/article/2009/06/money-is-biggest-cause-of-stress-for-half-of-canadians-women-more-stressed-than-men-except-with-work.html

Sunstein, C. (2001). Echo chambers: Bush v. Gore, impeachment, and beyond. Princeton Digital Books Plus.

Sunstein, C. R. (2002). The law of group polarization. *The Journal of Political Philosophy, 10,* 175–195.

Swann, W. B. Jr., Hixon, J. G., & De La Ronde, C. (1992). Embracing the bitter "truth": Negative self-concepts and marital commitment. *Psychological Science, 3,* 118–121.

Swann, W. B., Jr., Stein-Seroussi, A., & Giesler, B. (1992).Why people self-verify. *Journal of Personality and Social Psychology, 62,* 392–401.

Swann,W. B., & Read, S. J. (1981). Self-verification processes: How we sustain our self-conceptions. *Journal of Experimental Social Psychology, 17,* 351–372.

Swim, J. K., & Sanna, L. J. (1996). He's skilled, she's lucky: A meta-analysis of observers' attributions for women's and men's successes and failures. *Personality and Social Psychology Bulletin, 22,* 507–519.

Swim, J. K., Aikin, K. J., Hall, W. S., & Hunter, B. A. (1995). Sexism and racism: Old-fashioned and modern prejudices. *Journal of Personality and Social Psychology, 68,* 199–214.

Szpunar, K. K., Schellenberg, G., & Pliner, P. (2004). Liking and memory for musical stimuli as a function of exposure. *Journal of Experimental Psychology: Learning, Memory, and Cognition, 30,* 370–381.

Szymanski, D. M., Kashubeck-West, S., & Meyer, J. (2008). Internalized heterosexism: Measurement, psychosocial correlates, and research directions. *The Counseling Psychologist, 38,* 525–574.

Tafarodi, R. W., Marshall, T. C., & Katsura, H. (2004). Standing out in Canada and Japan. *Journal of Personality, 72,* 785–814.

Tajfel, H., & Billig, M. (1974). Familiarity and categorization in intergroup behavior. *Journal of Experimental Social Psychology, 10,* 159–170.

Tajfel, H., & Turner, J. C. (1986). An integrative theory of intergroup conflict. In S. Worchel & W. Austin (Eds.), *Psychology of intergroup relations* (pp. 2–24). Chicago, IL: Nelson-Hall.

Tajfel, H., & Turner, J. C. (1986). The social identity theory of inter-group behavior. In S. Worchel & W. Austin (Eds.), *Psychology of intergroup relations.* Chigago, IL: Nelson-Hall.

Tan, D. T. Y., & Singh, R. (1995). Attitudes and attraction: A developmental study of the similarity–attraction and dissimilarity–repulsion hypotheses. *Personality and Social Psychology Bulletin, 21,* 975–986.

Tanaka, J. W., Kiefer, M., & Bukach, C. M. (2004). A holistic account of the own-race effect in face recognition: Evidence from a cross-cultural study. *Cognition, 93,* B1–B9.

Tang, K. L. (1998). Rape law reform in Canada: The success and limits of legislation. *International Journal of Offender Therapy and Comparative Criminology, 42,* 258–270.

Tapper, K., & Boulton, M. J. (2005). Victim and peer group responses to different forms of aggression among primary school children. *Aggressive Behavior, 31,* 238–253.

Tapper, K., & Boulton, M. J. (2004). Sex differences in levels of physical, verbal and indirect aggression amongst primary school children and their associations with beliefs about aggression. *Aggressive Behavior, 30,* 123–145.

Tashiro, T., & Frazier, P. (2003). "I'll never be in a relationship like that again": Personal growth following romantic relationship breakups. *Personal Relationships, 10,* 113–128.

Tasso, A., Monaci, M. G., Trentin, R., & Rosabianca, A. (2005). Frame effects in persuasive messages against smoking. *Proceedings of the XXVII Annual Conference of the Cognitive Science Society,* Stresa, Italy, pp. 2162–2165.

Tavris, C., & Aronson, E. (2007). *Mistakes were made (but not by me): Why we justify foolish beliefs, bad decisions, and hurtful acts.* New York: Houghton Mifflin Harcourt.

Taylor, D. M., & Usborne, E. (2010). When I know who "we" are, I can be "me": The primary role of cultural identity clarity for psychological well-being. *Transcultural Psychiatry, 47*, 93–111.

Taylor, S. E., & Brown, J. D. (1988). Illusion and well-being: A social psychological perspective on mental health. *Psychological Bulletin, 103*, 193–210.

Taylor, T. S., & Hosch, H. M. (2004). An examination of jury verdicts for evidence of a similarity-leniency effect, an out-group punitiveness effect, or a black sheep effect. *Law and Human Behavior, 28*, 587–598.

Tennen, H., & Affleck, G. (1993). The puzzles of self-esteem: A clinical perspective. In R. F. Baumeister (Ed.), *Self-esteem: The puzzle of low self-regard* (pp. 241–262). New York: Plenum Press.

Tesser, A. (1988). Toward a self-evaluation maintenance model of social behavior. In L. Berkowitz (Ed.), *Advances in Experimental Social Psychology* (Vol. 21, pp. 181–227). New York: Academic Press.

Tetlock, P. E. (2005). *Expert political judgment: How good is it? How can we know?* Princeton, NJ: Princeton University Press.

Tews, M. J., Stafford, K., & Zhu, J. (2009). Beauty revisited: The impact of attractiveness, ability, and personality in the assessment of employment suitability. *International Journal of Selection and Assessment, 17*, 92–100.

Thaler, R. H., & Sunstein, C. R. (2008). *Nudge: Improving decisions about health, wealth, and happiness*. New Haven, CT: Yale University Press.

The bystander effect: Why people in crowds may be less likely to help. (2011, October 22). *CBC News*. Retrieved November 12, 2011, from http://www.cbc.ca/news/canada/story/2011/10/22/f-bystander-effect.html

The Mark Twitchell case. (2011). *Edmonton Journal*. Retrieved November 13, 2011, from http://www.edmontonjournal.com/news/twitchell-case/index.html

The murder of Reena Virk and trials of Kelly Ellard. (2009, June 12). *CBC News*. Retrieved September 19, 2011, from http://www.cbc.ca/news/canada/story/2009/04/14/f-virk-timeline.html

The story behind Mother's Day—and why it's so important. (2011, May 7). *The Vancouver Sun*. Retrieved October 3, 2011, from http://www.vancouversun.com/life/story+behind+Mother+important/4744865/story.html

Thibaut, J. W., & Kelley, H. H. (1952). *The social psychology of groups*. New York: John Wiley & Sons.

Thibaut, J. W., & Kelley, H. H. (1959). *The social psychology of groups*. New York: John Wiley & Sons.

Thompson, L. (1998). *The mind and heart of the negotiator*. Upper Saddle River, NJ: Prentice-Hall.

Thompson, S. (2010, September). *Policing Vancouver's mentally ill: The disturbing truth*. Vancouver, BC: Vancouver Police Department.

Thompson, S. C. (1999). Illusions of control: How we overestimate our personal influence. *Current Directions in Psychological Science, 8*, 187–190.

Thompson, S. C., Anderson, K., Freedman, D., & Swan, J. (1996). Illusions of safety in a risky world: A study of college students' condom use. *Journal of Applied Social Psychology, 26*, 189–210.

Thorndike, E. L. (1935). Measurements of the influence of recency. *The American Journal of Psychology, 47*, 294–300.

Toi, M., & Batson, C. D. (1982). More evidence that empathy is a source of altruistic motivation. *Journal of Personality and Social Psychology, 43*, 281–292.

Tolman, C. W. (1965). Emotional behaviour and social facilitation of feeding in domestic chicks. *Animal Behaviour, 13*, 493–496.

Toma, C., & Hancock, J. T. (2010). Looks and lies: The role of physical attractiveness in online dating self-presentation and deception. *Communication Research, 37*, 335–351.

Toma, C., & Hancock, J. T. (in press). What lies beneath: The linguistic traces of deception in online dating profiles. *Journal of Communication*.

Tomaszczyk, J. C., Fernandes, M. A., & MacLeod, C. M. (2008). Personal relevance modulates the positivity bias in recall of emotional pictures in older adults. *Psychonomic Bulletin & Review, 15*, 191–196.

Tomaszczyk, J. C., Fernandes, M. A., & MacLeod, C. M. (2008). Personal relevance modulates the positivity bias in recall of emotional pictures in older adults. *Psychonomic Bulletin & Review, 15*, 191–196.

Toobin, J. (1996). *The run of his life: The people v. O. J. Simpson*. New York: Random House.

Tooby, J., & Cosmides, L. (1988). The evolution of war and its cognitive foundations. Technical report, Institute for Evolutionary Studies. Palo Alto, CA.

Toscos, T., Faber, A., An, S., & Gandhi, M. (2006). Chick clique: Persuasive technology to motivate teenage girls to exercise. *Extended Abstracts on Human Factors in Computing Systems*, 1873–1878.

Towles-Schwen, T., & Fazio, R. H. (2001). On the origins of racial attitudes: Correlates of childhood experiences. *Personality and Social Psychology Bulletin, 27*, 162–175.

Tracy, J. L., & Matsumoto, D. (2008). The spontaneous display of pride and shame: Evidence for biologically innate nonverbal displays. *Proceedings of the National Academy of Sciences, 105*, 11655–11660.

Tracy, J. L., & Robins, R. W. (2008). The nonverbal expression of pride: Evidence for cross-cultural recognition. *Journal of Personality and Social Psychology, 94*, 516–530.

Tracy, J. L., Robins, R. W., & Schriber, R. A. (2009). Development of a FACS-verified set of basic and self-conscious emotion expressions. *Emotion, 9*, 554-559.

Trafimow, D., Triandis, H. C., & Goto, S. G. (1991). Some tests of the distinction between the private self and the collective self. *Journal of Personality and Social Psychology, 60*, 649–655.

Tragedy in Taber. (2004, April 27). *CBC News*. Retrieved September 19, 2011, from http://www.cbc.ca/news/background/taber/

Transport Canada. (2007). *Canadian motor vehicle traffic collision statistics, 2007*. Ottawa: Canadian Council of Motor Transport Administration.

Tremblay, R. E., & Nagin, D. S. (2005). The developmental origins of physical aggression in humans. In R. E. Tremblay, W. W. Hartnup, and J. Archer (Eds.), *Developmental origins of aggression* (pp. 83-106). New York, NY: Guilford Press.

Trenholm, C., Devaney, B., Fortson, K., Quay, L., Wheeler, J., & Clark, M. (2007). *Impacts of four Title V, Section 510 abstinence education programs*. Princeton, NJ: Mathematica Policy Research.

Triplet, R. G. (1992). Discriminatory biases in the perception of illness: The application of availability and representativeness heuristics to the AIDS crisis. *Basic and Applied Social Psychology, 13*, 303–322.

Triplett, N. (1898).The dynamogenic factors in pacemaking and competition. *American Journal of Psychology, 9*, 507–533.

Trope, Y., & Liberman, A. (1996). Social hypothesis testing: Cognitive and motivational mechanisms. In E. T. Higgins & A. W. Kruglanski (Eds.), *Social psychology: Handbook of basic principles*. New York: Guilford Press.

Tsang, J. A. (2006). Gratitude and prosocial behaviour: An experimental test of gratitude. *Cognition and Emotion, 20*, 138–148.

Tversky, A., & Kahneman, D. (1973). Availability: A heuristic for judging frequency and probability. *Cognitive Psychology, 5*, 207–232.

Tversky, A., & Kahneman, D. (1974). Judgment under uncertainty: Heuristics and biases. *Science, 185*, 1124–1131.

Tversky, A., & Kahneman, D. (1982). Evidential impact of base rates. In D. Kahneman, P. Slovic, & A. Tversky (Eds.), *Judgment under uncertainty: Heuristics and biases*. Cambridge, MA: Cambridge University Press.

Tynes, B., & Markoe, S. (2010). The role of color-blind racial attitudes in reactions to racial discrimination in social network sites. *Journal of Diversity in Higher Education, 3*, 1-13.

Tyson, P. D. (1998). Physiological arousal, reactive aggression, and the induction of an incompatible relaxation response. *Aggression and Violent Behavior, 3*, 143–158.

Uleman, J. S. (1989). A framework for thinking intentionally about unintended thoughts. In J. S. Uleman & J. A. Bargh (Eds.), *Unintended thought* (pp. 425–449). New York: Guilford Press.

Uleman, J. S., Newman, L. S., & Moskowitz, G. B. (1996). People as flexible interpreters: Evidence and issues from spontaneous trait inference. In M. P. Zanna (Ed.), *Advances in experimental social psychology* (Vol. 28, pp. 211–279). San Diego, CA: Academic Press.

Uleman, J. S., Saribay, S. A., & Gonzalez, C. M. (2008). Spontaneous inferences, implicit impressions, and implicit theories. *Annual Review of Psychology, 59*, 329–360.

Ungar, S., & Sev'er, A. (1989). "Say it ain't so, Ben": Attributions for a fallen hero. *Social Psychology Quarterly, 52*, 207–212.

United Nations. (2010). *Violence against women*. Retrieved July 28, 2010, from http://www.unifem.org/gender_issues/violence_against_women/

University of Gothenburg. (2010, February 22). Cyberbullying: A growing problem. *ScienceDaily*. Retrieved September 28, 2010, from http://www.sciencedaily.com/releases/2010/02/100222104939.htm

Unkelbach, C., Forgas, J. P., & Denson, T. (2007). The turban effect: The influence of Muslim headgear and induced affect on aggressive responses in the shooter bias paradigm. *Journal of Experimental Social Psychology, 43*, 513–528.

Usborne, E., & Taylor, D. M. (2010). The role of cultural identity clarity for self-concept clarity, self-esteem, and subjective well-being. *Personality and Social Psychology Bulletin, 36*, 883–897.

Utne, M. K., & Kidd, R. F. (1980). Equity and attribution. In G. Mikula (Ed.), *Justice and social interaction* (pp. 63–93).New York: Springer-Verlag.

Valins, S. (1966). Cognitive effects of false heart-rate feedback. *Journal of Personality and Social Psychology, 4*, 400–408.

Vaillancourt, T., & Hymel, S. (2004). The social context of children's aggression. In M. M. Moretti, C. L. Odgers, & M. A. Jackson (Eds.), *Girls and aggression: Contributing factors and intervention principles* (pp. 57–74). New York, NY: Kluwer Academic.

Vaish, A., Grossmann, T., & Woodward, A. (2008). Not all emotions are created equal: The negativity bias in social-emotional development. *Psychological Bulletin, 134*, 383-403.

Vallone, R. P., Ross, L., & Lepper, M. R. (1985). The hostile media phenomenon: Biased perception and perceptions of media bias in coverage of the Beirut massacre. *Journal of Personality and Social Psychology, 49*, 577–585.

van Baaren, R. B., Holland, R.W., Kawakami, K., & van Knippenberg, A. (2004). Mimicry and prosocial behavior. *Psychological Science, 15*, 71–74.

van Baaren, R. B., Horgan, T. G., Chartrand, T. L., & Dijkmans, M. (2004). The forest, the trees, and the chameleon: Context dependence and mimicry. *Journal of Personality and Social Psychology, 86*, 453–459.

van Honk, J., & Schutter, D. (2007).Testosterone reduces conscious detection of signals serving social correction implications for antisocial behavior. *Psychological Science, 18*, 663–667.

Van Yperen, N. W., & Buunk, B. P. (1994). Social comparison and social exchange in marital relationships. In M. J. Lerner & G. Mikula (Eds.), *Entitlement and the Affectional Bond: Justice in Close Relationships* (pp. 89–115). New York: Plenum Press.

Van Yperen, N., & Buunk, B. (1990). A longitudinal study of equity and satisfaction in intimate relationships. *European Journal of Social Psychology, 20*, 287–309.

VanderStoep, S. W., & Shaughnessy, J. J. (1997, April). Taking a course in research methods improves reasoning about real-life events. *Teaching of Psychology, 24*, 122–124.

Varma, A., Toh, S. M., & Pichler, S. (2006). Ingratiation in job applications: Impact on selection decisions. *Journal of Managerial Psychology, 21*, 200–210.

Vasey, P. L., & VanderLaan, D. P. (2010). An adaptive cognitive dissociation between willingness to help kin and nonkin in Samoan Fa' afafine. *Psychological Science, 21*, 292–97.

Vasey, P. L., Pocock, D. S., & VanderLaan, D. P. (2007). Kin selection and male androphilia in Samoan fa'afafine. *Evolution and Human Behavior, 28*, 159–167.

Veldhuizen, S., Urbanoski, K., & Cairney, J. (2007). Geographical variation in the prevalence of problematic substance use in Canada. *Canadian Journal of Psychiatry, 52*, 426–433.

Vescio, T. K., Gervais, S., Snyder, M., & Hoover, A. (2005). Power and the creation of patronizing environments: The stereotype-based behaviors of the powerful and their effects on female performance in masculine domains. *Journal of Personality and Social Psychology, 88*, 658–672.

Vidmar, N., & Dittenhoffer, T. (1981). Informed public opinion and death penalty attitudes. *Canadian Journal of Criminology, 23*, 43–48.

Vince Li not criminally responsible for beheading. (2009, March 5). *CTV News*. Retrieved September 2, 2011, from http://www.ctv.ca/CTVNews/Canada/20090304/bus_verdict_090305/

Violent crime in 15-year decline: Report. (2009, October 6). *CBC News*. Retrieved September 19, 2011, from http://www.cbc.ca/news/canada/story/2009/10/06/vital-signs-violent-crime-community-report380.html

Visser, P. S., & Krosnick, J. A. (1998). Development of attitude strength over the life cycle: Surge and decline. *Journal of Personality and Social Psychology, 6*, 1389–1410.

Visser, P. S., Krosnick, J. A., & Simmons, J. P. (2003). Distinguishing the cognitive and behavioral consequences of attitude and certainty: A new approach to testing the common-factor hypothesis. *Journal of Experimental Social Psychology, 39*, 118–141.

Vitale, J. E., Newman, J. P., Serin, R. C., & Bolt, D. M. (2005). Hostile attributions in incarcerated adult male offenders: An exploration of diverse pathways. *Aggressive Behavior, 31*, 99–115.

Vittengl, J. R., & Holt, C. S. (2000). Getting acquainted: The relationship of self-disclosure and social attraction to positive affect. *Journal of Social and Personal Relationships, 17*, 53–66.

Vivian J. E., & Berkowitz N. H. (1992). Anticipated bias from an outgroup: An attributional analysis. *European Journal of Social Psychology, 22*, 414–424.

Volkman, K. (2010, May 20). Panera chairman: Pay-what-you-can cafe "test of humanity." *St. Louis Business Journal*. Retrieved December 1, 2010, from http://stlouis.bizjournals.com/stlouis/stories/2010/05/17/daily52.html

von Schneidemesser, L. (1996). Soda or pop? *Journal of English Linguistics, 24*, 270–287.

Vonk, R. (2002). Self-serving interpretations of flattery: Why ingratiation works. *Journal of Personality and Social Psychology, 82*, 515–526.

Vrij, A. (2008). *Detecting lies and deceit: Pitfalls and opportunities*. Chichester, UK: John Wiley & Sons Ltd.

Vrij, A., Evans, H., Akehurst, L., & Mann, S. (2004). Rapid judgments in assessing verbal and nonverbal cues: Their potential for deception researchers and lie detection. *Applied Cognitive Psychology, 18*, 283–296.

Vrij, A., Granhag, P. A., & Porter, S. (2010). Pitfalls and opportunities in nonverbal and verbal lie detection. *Psychological Science in the Public Interest, 11*, 89–121.

Wade, A., & Beran, T. (2011). Cyberbullying: The new era of bullying. *Canadian Journal of School Psychology, 26*, 44–61.

Wagner, J. A., III. (1995). Studies of individualism-collectivism: Effects on cooperation in groups. *Academy of Management Journal, 38*, 152–172.

Wahl, O. E., Wood, A., & Richards, R. (2002). Newspaper coverage of mental illness: Is it changing? *Psychiatric Rehabilitation Skills, 6*, 9–31.

Walker, J. W. (1997). *Race, rights and the law in the Supreme Court of Canada*. Osgoode, ON: Osgoode Society for Canadian Legal History and Wilfrid Laurier University Press.

Walker, J. W. (2006). *Responding to racism in Canada: Problems and policies in historical perspective.* Paper presented to the Ontario Human Rights Commission.

Wallace, H. M., Baumeister, R. F., & Vohs, K. D. (2005). Audience support and choking under pressure: A home disadvantage? *Journal of Sports Sciences, 23*, 429–438.

Wallach, M. A., Kogan, N., & Bem, D. J. (1962). Group influence on individual risk taking. *Journal of Abnormal and Social Psychology, 65*, 75–86.

Wallop, H., & Cockcroft, L. (2007, October 9). Oasis, Jamiroquai to follow Radiohead. *Telegraph.co.uk*. Retrieved December 1, 2010, from http://www.telegraph.co.uk/news/uknews/1565638/Oasis-Jamiroquai-tofollow-Radiohead.html

Walster, E. G., Walster, W., & Traupmann, J. (1978). Equity and premarital sex. *Journal of Personality and Social Psychology, 37*, 82–92.

Walster, E., Walster, G. W., Berscheid, E., & Dion, K. (1971). Physical attractiveness and dating choice: A test of the matching hypothesis. *Journal of Experimental Social Psychology, 7*, 173–189.

Walton, P. (2003, July 18). Aune's story stuns police. *Nanaimo Daily News*.

Wang, Z., Walther, J. B., & Hancock, J. T. (2010). Social identification and interpersonal communication in computer-mediated communication: What you do versus who you are in virtual groups. *Human Communication Research, 35*, 59–85.

Ward, A., Ramsay, R., & Treasure, J. (2000). Attachment research in eating disorders. *British Journal of Medical Psychology, 73*, 35–51.

Ward, T., Hudson, S. M., & Marshall, W. L. (1996). Attachment style in sex offenders: A preliminary study. *The Journal of Sex Research, 33*, 17–20.

Watkins, L. M., & Johnston, L. (2000). Screening job applicants: The impact of physical attractiveness and application quality. *International Journal of Selection and Assessment, 8*, 76–84.

Watkins, L. M., & Johnston, L. (2000). Screening job applicants: The impact of physical attractiveness and application quality. *International Journal of Selection and Assessment, 8*, 76–84.

Watson, D. C. (2011). Gossip and the self. *Journal of Applied Social Psychology, 41*, 1818–1833.

Watt, S. E., & Larkin, C. (2010). Prejudiced people perceive more community support for their views: The role of own, media, and peer attitudes in perceived consensus. *Journal of Applied Social Psychology, 40*, 710–731.

Wayland, M. (2009). Today's swine flu headlines. *NBC San Diego*. Retrieved May 14, 2010, from http://www.nbcsandiego.com/news/localbeat/New-Today-on-Swine-Flu.html

Webb, E. J., Campbell, D. T., Schwartz, R. D., & Sechrest, L. (1966). *Unobtrusive measures: Nonreactive measures in the social sciences*. Chicago, IL: Rand McNally.

Weber, R., & Crocker, J. (1983). Cognitive processes in the revision of stereotypic beliefs. *Journal of Personality and Social Psychology, 45*, 961–977.

Wegener, D. T., & Petty, R. E. (1994). Mood management across affective states: The hedonic contingency hypothesis. *Journal of Personality and Social Psychology, 66*, 1034–1048.

Wegener, D. T., Petty, R. E., Smoak, N. D., & Fabrigar, L. R. (2004). Multiple routes to resisting attitude change. In E. S. Knowles & J. A. Linn (Eds.), *Resistance and persuasion* (pp. 13–38). Mahwah, NJ: Lawrence Erlbaum.

Wei, R., Chia, S. C., & Lo, V. H. (2011). Third-person effect and hostile media perception influences on voter attitudes toward polls in the 2008 U.S. presidential election. *International Journal of Public Opinion Research, 23*, 169–190.

Weinstein, N. D. (1982). Unrealistic optimism about susceptibility to health problems. *Journal of Behavioral Medicine, 5*, 441–460.

Wenzlaff, R. M., & Wegner, D. M. (2000). Thought suppression. *Annual Review of Psychology, 51*, 59–91.

Werner, C. M., Stoll, R., Birch, P., & White, P. H. (2002). Clinical validation and cognitive elaboration: Signs encourage sustained recycling. *Basic and Applied Social Psychology, 24*, 185–203.

Wessel, E., Drevland, G. C. B., Eilertsen, D. E., & Magnussen, S. (2006). Credibility of the emotional witness: A study of ratings by court judges. *Law and Human Behavior, 30*, 221–230.

Westcoast Coalition for Human Dignity. (2003). Facing hate in Canada. Retrieved November 3, 2011, from http://www.crr.ca/divers-files/en/pub/faSh/ePubFaShFacHateCan.pdf

Whittlesea, B. W. A., & Price, J. R. (2001). Implicit/explicit memory versus analytic/nonanalytic processing: Rethinking the mere exposure effect. *Memory & Cognition, 29*, 234-246.

Whitty, M. T. (2008). Revealing the "real" me, searching for the "actual" you: Presentations of self on an internet dating site. *Computers in Human Behavior, 24*, 1707–1723.

Whyte, G. (1998). Recasting Janis's groupthink model: The key role of collective efficacy in decision fiascoes. *Organizational Behavior and Human Decision Processes, 73*, 185–209.

Widmeyer, W. N., & Loy, J. W. (1988). When you're hot, you're hot: Warm-cold effects in first impressions of persons and teaching effectiveness. *Journal of Educational Psychology, 80*, 118–121.

Wiebe, L. (2011, June 24). Fans react as Jets name made official. *Winnipeg Free Press*. Retrieved October 31, 2011, from http://www.winnipegfreepress.com/special/nhl/Fans-react-as-Jets-name-made-official-124524584.html

Wilbert, C. (2008, October 8). As economy worsens, so does stress. *WebMD*. Retrieved December 1, 2010 from http://www.webmd.com/balance/stress-management/news/20081008/as-economyworsens-so-does-stress

Wilder, D. A. (1993). The role of anxiety in facilitating stereotypic judgments of out-group behavior. In D. M. Mackie & D. L. Hamilton (Eds.), *Affect, cognition, and stereotyping* (pp. 87–109). San Diego, CA: Academic Press.

Wilke, H., & Lanzetta, J. T. (1970). The obligation to help: The effects of amount of prior help on subsequent helping behavior. *Journal of Experimental Social Psychology, 6*, 488–493.

Williams, K. D., Nida, S. A., Baca, L. D., & Latane, B. (1989). Social loafing and swimming: Effects of identifiability on individual and relay performance of intercollegiate swimmers. *Basic and Applied Social Psychology, 10*, 73–81.

Williams, T. M., Zabrack, M. L., & Joy, L. A. (1982). The portrayal of aggression on North American television. *Journal of Applied Social Psychology, 12*, 360-380.

Willis, J., & Todorov, A. (2006). First impressions: Making up your mind after a 100-ms exposure to a face. *Psychological Science, 17*, 592–598.

Wilson, D. W. (1978). Helping behavior and physical attractiveness. *The Journal of Social Psychology, 104*, 313–314.

Wilson, D. W., & Kahn, A. (1975). Rewards, costs, and sex differences in helping behavior. *Psychological Reports, 36*, 31–34.

Wilson, S. J., & Lipsey, M. W. (2006). The effects of school-based social information processing interventions on aggressive behavior: Part I Universal Programs. *Campbell Systematic Reviews, 5*.

Wilson, T. D. (1990). Self-persuasion via self-reflection. In J. M. Olson & M. P. Zanna (Eds.), *Self-inference processes: The Ontario Symposium* (Vol. 6, pp. 43–67). Hillsdale, NJ: Erlbaum.

Wilson, T. D., & Gilbert, D. T. (2005). Affective forecasting: Knowing what to want. *Current Directions in Psychological Science, 14*, 131–134.

Wilson, T. D., & Schooler, J. W. (2008). Thinking too much: Introspection can reduce the quality of preferences and decisions. In R. H. Fazio & R. E. Petty (Eds.), *Attitudes: Their structure, function, and consequences* (pp. 299–317). New York: Psychology Press.

Winkielman, P., Halberstadt, J., Fazendeiro,T., & Catty, S. (2006). Prototypes are attractive because they are easy on the eye. *Psychological Science, 17*, 799–806.

Wohl, M. J. A., Hornsey, M. J., & Bennett, S. H. (2011, in press). Why group apologies succeed and fail: Intergroup forgiveness and the role of primary and secondary emotions. *Journal of Personality and Social Psychology*.

Wojcieszak, M. (2008). False consensus goes online: Impact of ideologically homogeneous groups on false consensus. *Public Opinion Quarterly, 72*, 781–791.

Wong, J. (2011, May 31). Why educational apartheid is not the answer to curbing dropout rates for specific racial and ethnic groups. *Toronto Life*. Retrieved October 26, 2011, from http://www.torontolife.com/daily/informer/from-print-edition-informer/2011/05/31/why-educational-apartheid-is-not-the-answer-to-curbing-dropout-rates-for-specific-racial-and-ethnic-groups/

Wong, J., (2010, September 28). What evil lurks: Sexual assault is a serious problem at universities, and our schools are overlooking the solution. *Toronto Life*. Retrieved November 12, 2011, from http://www.torontolife.com/daily/informer/from-print-edition-informer/2010/09/28/what-evil-lurks-sexual-assault-is-a-serious-problem-at-universities-and-our-schools-are-overlooking-the-solution/2/

Wood, W. (1986). Access to attitude-relevant information in memory as a determinant of attitude-behavior consistency. *Journal of Experimental Social Psychology, 22*, 328–338.

Wood, W., & Stagner, B. (1994). Why are some people easier to influence than others? In S. Shavitt & T. C. Brock (Eds.), *Persuasion* (pp. 149–174). Boston: Allyn & Bacon.

Wood, W., Lundgren, S., Ouellette, J. A., Busceme, S., & Blackstone, T. (1994). *Psychological Bulletin, 115*, 323–345.

Woodworth, M., & Porter, S. (2002). In cold blood: characteristics of criminal homicides as a function of psychopathy. *Journal of Abnormal Psychology, 111*, 436–445.

Worchel, S., Lee, J., & Adewole, A. (1975). Effects of supply and demand on ratings of object value. *Journal of Personality and Social Psychology, 32*, 906–914.

Word, C. O., Zanna, M. P., & Cooper, J. (1974). The nonverbal mediation of self-fulfilling prophecies in interracial interaction. *Journal of Experimental Social Psychology, 10*, 109–120.

Xiaohe, X., and Whyte, M. K. (1990). Love matches and arranged marriages: A Chinese replication. *Journal of Marriage and the Family, 52*, 709–722.

Yeates, K. O., Bigler, E. D., Dennis, M., Gerhardt, C. A., Rubin, K. H., Stancin, T., . . . Vannatta, K. (2007). Social outcomes in childhood brain disorder: A heuristic integration of social neuroscience and developmental psychology. *Psychological Bulletin, 133*, 535–556.

Yee, N., Ducheneaut, N., Yao, M., & Nelson, L. (2011). Do men heal more when in drag?: Conflicting identity cues between user and avatar. *CHI'11: Proceedings of the 2011 Annual Conference on Human Factors in Computing Systems*.

Young, R. K., Kennedy, A. H., Newhouse, A., Browne, P., & Theissen, D. (1993). The effects of names on perception of intelligence, popularity, and competence. *Journal of Applied Social Psychology, 23*, 21.

Yzerbyt, V., Corneille, O., & Estrada, C. (2001). The interplay of subjective essentialism and entitativity in the formation of stereotypes. *Personality and Social Psychology Review*, *5*, 141–155.

Zaccaro, S. J. (2007). Trait-based perspectives of leadership. *American Psychologist*, *62*, 6–16.

Zajonc, R. B. (1965). Social facilitation. *Science*, *149*, 269–274.

Zajonc, R. B. (1968). Attitudinal effects of mere exposure. *Journal of Personality and Social Psychology*, *9*, 1–27.

Zajonc, R. B. (1993). Brain temperature and subjective emotional experience. In M. Lewis & J. M. Haviland (Eds.), *Handbook of emotions* (pp. 209–220). New York: Guilford.

Zajonc, R. B., & Rajecki, D. W. (1969). Exposure and affect: A field experiment. *Psychonomic Science, 17*, 216–217.

Zajonc, R. B., Heingartner, A., & Herman, E. M. (1969). Social enhancement and impairment of performance in the cockroach. *Journal of Personality and Social Psychology, 13*, 83–92.

Zajonc, R. B., Heingartner, A., & Herman, E. M. (1969). Social enhancement and impairment of performance in the cockroach. *Journal of Personality and Social Psychology, 13*, 83–92.

Zak, P. J. (2008, June). The neurobiology of trust. *Scientific American*.

Zak, P. J., Kurzban, R., & Matzner, W. T. (2005). Oxytocin is associated with human trustworthiness. *Hormones and Behavior*, *48*, 522–527. Retrieved June 4, 2010, from http://www.sas.upenn.edu/psych/PLEEP/pdfs/2005%20Zak%20Kurzban%20&%20Matzner&20H%20&%20B.pdf

Zanbaka, C., Goolkasian, P., & Hodges, L. F. (2006, April). Can a virtual cat persuade you? The role of gender and realism in speaker persuasiveness. *Conference on Human Factors in Computing Systems*, 1–10.

Zanna, M. P., & Pack, S. J. (1975). On the self-fulfilling nature of apparent sex differences in behavior. *Journal of Experimental Social Psychology*, *11*, 583–591.

Zanna, M. P., & Rempel, J. K. (1988). Attitudes: A new look at an old concept. In D. Bartal & A. W. Kruglanski (Eds.), *The social psychology of knowledge* (pp. 315–334).Cambridge, UK: Cambridge University Press.

Zárate, M. A., Garcia, B., Garza, A. A., & Hitlan, R. (2004). Cultural threat and perceived realistic group conflict as predictors of attitudes towards Mexican immigrants. *Journal of Experimental Social Psychology, 40*, 99–105.

Zelek, B., & Phillips, S. P. (2003). Gender and power: Nurses and doctors in Canada. *International Journal for Equity in Health, 2*, 1–5.

Zillmann, D. (1971). Excitation transfer in communication-mediated aggressive behavior. *Journal of Experimental Social Psychology*, *7*, 419–434.

Zillmann, D. (1983). Transfer of excitation in emotional behavior. In J. T. Cacipoppo & R. E. Petty (Eds.), *Social Psychophysiology: A Sourcebook*. New York: Guildford Press.

Zillmann, D. (1996). Sequential dependencies in emotional experience and behavior. In R. D. Kavanaugh, B. Zimmerberg, & S. Fein (Eds.) *Emotion: Interdisciplinary Perspectives*, Mahwah, NJ: Lawrence Erlbaum.

Zimbardo, P. (2007). *The Lucifer effect: Understanding how good people turn evil*. New York: Random House, Inc.

Zimbardo, P. G. (1969). The human choice: Individuation, reason, and order versus deindividuation, impulse, and chaos. *Nebraska Symposium on Motivation*, *17*, 237–307.

Zimbardo, P. G. (1971). One final act of rebellion. *The Stanford Prison Experiment*. Retrieved June 3, 2010, from http://www.prisonexp.org/psychology/36

Zimbardo, P. G. (1971). The power and pathology of imprisonment. *Congressional Record*. (Serial No. 15, 1971-10-25). Hearings before Subcommittee No. 3, of the Committee on the Judiciary, House of Representatives, Ninety-Second Congress, *First Session on Corrections, Part II, Prisons, Prison Reform and Prisoner's Rights: California*. Washington, DC: U.S. Government Printing Office.

Zimbardo, P. G. (1970). The human choice: Individuation, reason, and order versus deindividuation, impulse, and chaos. In W. J. Arnold & D. Levine (Eds.), *1969 Nebraska Symposium on Motivation* (pp. 237–307). Lincoln, NE: University of Nebraska Press.

Zimmerman, B. J., Bandura, A., & Martinez-Pons, M. (1992). Self-motivation for academic attainment: The role of self-efficacy beliefs and personal goal setting. *American Educational Research Journal*, *29*, 663–676.

Zuckerman, E., & Jost, J. T. (2001). What makes you think you're so popular? Self-evaluation maintenance and the subjective side of the "friendship paradox." *Social Psychology Quarterly*, *64*, 207–233.

Zuwerink, J. R., & Devine, P. G. (1996). Attitude importance and resistance to persuasion: It's not just the thought that counts. *Journal of Personality and Social Psychology*, *70*, 931–944.

# CREDITS

## PHOTO CREDITS

**CHAPTER 01** **2** Jupiterimages/Thinkstock; **4t & 16tl** Toronto Star/GetStock.com; **4b** Digital Vision/Thinkstock; **5l** © David J. Green/Alamy; **5c** Mike Flippo/Shutterstock; **5r** Ariel Skelley/Getty Images; **6b & 16tr** © Daniel Laflor/istockphoto; **6t** istockphoto/Thinkstock; **7tl** LattaPictures/istockphoto; **7tr** Jason Stitt/Shutterstock; **7bl** Supri Suharjoto/Shutterstock; **7br** Comstock/Thinkstock; **8** Image Source/Getty Images; **10** Pierre Bourgault/Demotix/Corbis; **11t** © Eliza Snow/istockphoto; **11b** Jupiterimages/Thinkstock; **12l** Svemir/Shutterstock; **12r** © Nozomi Stall/Dreamstime.com; **13** Jupiter Images/Thinkstock; **14 & 16br** AP images; **15** © INTERFOTO/Alamy

**CHAPTER 02** **18** istockphoto/Thinkstock; **20t** kated/Shutterstock; **20b** THE CANADIAN PRESS/Andrew Vaughan; **21t** Michael Blann/Thinkstock; **21b & 36tl** JupiterImages/Thinkstock; **22t & 36cl**; © Kurt Paris/istockphoto; **22b** JupiterImages/Thinkstock; **23t** Loren Rodgers/Shutterstock; **23b** oliveromg/Shutterstock; **24t** stockbyte/Thinkstock; **24b** Jason Merritt/Getty Images; **25** Shutterstock; **26** © Abdussadik/Dreamstime.com; **27 & 36bl** istockphoto/Thinkstock; **29 & 36tr** Digital Vision/Thinkstock; **31 & 36cr** Philip G. Zimbardo, Inc.; **32** Itana/Shutterstock; **33** Koksharov Dmitry/Shutterstock; **34 & 36br** iStockphoto/Thinkstock; **35** iStockphoto/Thinkstock

**CHAPTER 03** **40 & 56t** istockphoto/Thinkstock; **43c** © Nuno Silva/istockphoto; **43tl, tr, bl, br** © Charles Islander/istockphoto; **44** Michael Biann/Thinkstock; **45** © MedicalRF.com/Alamy; **46** Steve Mason/Thinkstock and "Used with the permission of the Bank of Canada".; **47tl** © Abimages/Dreamstime.com; **47tr** Romanchuck Dimitry/Shutterstock; **47b** Comstock/Thinkstock; **49t & 56b** David S. Holloway/Getty Images; **49b** Frederick M. Brown/Getty Images; **50** istockphoto/Thinkstock; **51 & 56c** Robert Koene/Thinkstock; **52** © Monkey Business Images/Dreamstime.com; **53** The Canadian Press/AP Photo/David J. Phillip; **54** Tracy Whiteside/Shutterstock; **55t** © Mlenny Photography/istockphoto; **55b** Canadian Cancer Society/Advertising Agency: DDB Canada/Photographer: Ron Baxter Smith

**CHAPTER 04** **58** Fer Gregory/Shutterstock; **60 & 74t** George Pimentel/WireImage/Getty Images; **61** Ellen Nolan; **62t** © Pictorial Press Ltd/Alamy; **62b** James Balog/Getty Images; **63l** Edyta Pawlowska/Shutterstock; **63r** East/Shutterstock; **64** The Canadian Press/Olivier Douliery/ABACAUSA.COM; **67** istockphoto/Thinkstock; **68t** Imagesource/Getty Images; **68b** © hartphotography1/istockphoto; **70** © Moviestore collection Ltd/Alamy; **72 & 74b** The Canadian Press/Michael Yarish/TM and Copyright © 20th Century Fox Film Corp. All rights reserved, Courtesy: Everett Collection; **73t & 74c** istockphoto/Thinkstock; **73b** © Stígur Karlsson/istockphoto

**CHAPTER 05** **76** Charles Sykes-AP/The Canadian Press; **78 & 92t** © Troels Graugaard/istockphoto; **79c** Alex Staroseltsev/Shutterstock; **79tr** Jupiter Images/Thinkstock; **79br** © YanLev/istockphoto; **79b** © Halina Yakushevich/Dreamstime.com; **79bl** © OSTILL/istockphoto; **79tl** Gorich/Shutterstock; **79tc** © hugo chang/istockphoto; **80 & 92c** istockphoto/Thinkstock; **81** Jupiter Images/Thinkstock; **85 & 92b** The Canadian Press/AP Photo/Seth Wenig; **86** BananaStock/Thinkstock; **87** William Perugini/Shutterstock; **88** © Aleksandar Bracinac/istockphoto; **89** © Rex Features [2005] all rights reserved"/The Canadian Press; **90** Jo Ann Snover/Shutterstock; **91** Hermera/Thinkstock

**CHAPTER 06** **96** THE CANADIAN PRESS/Winnipeg Free Press—James Turner; **98 & 112t** © Christopher Pattberg/istockphoto; **99t** Petr Student/Shutterstock; **99c** © Olivier Le Queinec/Dreamstime.com; **99b** © Ashestosky/Dreamstime.com; **100** © Chris Ryan/Alamy; **101** © First Light/Alamy; **102l** © Mark Bowden/istockphoto; **102r** © Jeffrey Zavitski/istockphoto; **104 & 112b** Lasse Kristensen/Shutterstock; **105** © Charlieaja/Dreamstime.com; **106** March of Dimes Canada; **107 & 112c** Shutterstock; **108** istockphoto/Thinkstock; **109** Stockbyte/Thinkstock; **110** The Granger Collection, NYC—All rights reserved.; **111** Rock the Vote Canada

**CHAPTER 07** **116** © Kati1313/Dreamstime.com; **118** © Angela Gyorfy/istockphoto; **119t & 132tl** Jupiterimages/Thinkstock; **119b** Digital Vision/Thinkstock; **120** The Canadian Press/Tom Hanson; **121** Artpose Adam Borkowski/Shutterstock; **122** © archives/istockphoto; **123** Photo provided courtesy of Molson Canada 2005; **124t** Stephen Coburn/Shutterstock; **124b** © NYC images/Alamy; **125** © Ssuaphoto/Dreamstime.com; **126c** Le Do/Shutterstock; **126t, tr, br, bl, tl** Kuzmin Andrey/Shutterstock; **127t & 132bl** istockphoto/Thinkstock; **127b** © Ruslan Kotliarevskyi/istockphoto; **128 & 132tr** Maria R. T. Deseo; **129** Vladimir Sazonov/Shutterstock; **130 & 132br** © Stevanovicigor/Dreamstime.com; **131bl** © Ispace/Dreamstime.com; **131br** © Grgk/Dreamstime.com

**CHAPTER 08** **138** Stockbyte/Thinkstock; **140** erics/Shutterstock; **141tl** Cynthia Farmer/Shutterstock; **141c** Photodisc/Thinkstock; **141bl** The Canadian Press Images/Francis Vachon; **141br** Derek Gordon/Shutterstock; **142bl** still/Shutterstock; **142br & 154tl** © Queerstock, Inc./Alamy; **143** Make-A-Wish Foundation of Canada; **144** Digital Vision/Thinkstock; **145l** Pixland/Thinkstock; **145r** Photos.com/Thinkstock; **147 & 154bl** AP Photo/dapd/Berthold Stadler/The Canadian Press; **148** © Piotr Marcinski/Dreamstime.com; **150 & 154tr** Tungphoto/Shutterstock; **151** Hemera/Thinkstock; **153 & 154br** Associated Press

**CHAPTER 09** **156** Digital Vision/Thinkstock; **158t & 172tl** istockphoto/Thinkstock; **158b** istockphoto/Thinkstock; **159** AP Photo/Bernat Armague/The Canadian Press; **160l** © Sean Locke/istockphoto; **160r** Trae Patton/NBC/NBCU Photo Bank via AP Images/The Canadian Press/© NBC [2010] all rights reserved"; **161** Claus Mikosch/Shutterstock; **162 & 172cl** © Leontura/istockphoto; **163** Ryan McVay/Thinkstock; **164** istockphoto/Thinkstock; **165** STILLFX/Shutterstock; **166t** NASA/courtesy of nasaimages.org; **166b & 172bl** © Rich Legg/istockphoto; **167** THE CANADIAN PRESS/Ryan Remiorz; **168** CP PHOTO/Jonathan Hayward; **169** © Moviestore collection Ltd/Alamy; **171 & 172br** istockphoto/Thinkstock

**CHAPTER 10** **176** Comstock/Thinkstock; **179** Library Archives Canada; **181 & 194tl** Illustrator Taylor Callery; **182** Olgysha/Shutterstock; **183 & 183tc** © Jason Horowitz/Alamy; **184** Digital Vision/Thinkstock; **185 & 194bl** © monkeybusinessimages/istockphoto; **186** Jupiterimages/Thinkstock; **187** © Photo_Alto/istockphoto; **188** Cheryl Casey/Shutterstock; **189t** © zhang bo/istockphoto; **189b** Digital Vision/Thinkstock; **190tl** © Chris Fertnig/istockphoto; **190tc** Photodisc/Thinkstock; **190tr & 194br** Umit Erdem/Shutterstock; **190br & 194tr** © Blend Images/Alamy; **191** istockphoto/Thinkstock

**CHAPTER 11** **202** oliveromg/Shutterstock; **204 & 220tl** istockphoto/Thinkstock; **205tl** Zurijeta/Shutterstock; **205tr** pzAxe/Shutterstock; **205bl** prodakszyn/Shutterstockl **205br** Franz Pfluegl/Shutterstock; **206** © Courtney Perry/Dallas Morning News/Corbis; **207 & 220bl** Tom Brakefield/Thinkstock; **209** KMazur/WireImage/Getty Images; **210** Toby Burrows/Thinkstock; **211** Albert Bandura; **212** Stockbyte/Thinkstock; **214t** Ryan McVay/Getty Images; **214b** John Lehmann/The Globe and Mail/The Canadian Press; **216 & 220tr** Don Bendickson/Shutterstock; **218 & 220br** BananaStock/Thinkstock; **219** Yuri Arcurs/Shutterstock

**CHAPTER 12** **228** AVAVA/Shutterstock; **231 & 246tl** Hemera/Thinkstock; **232tl** Photodisc/Thinkstock; **232tr** Piotr Marcinski/Shutterstock; **232bl** Barbara Penoyar/Thinkstock; **232br** © Martin Norris Studio

Photography/Alamy; **233 & 246cl** BananaStock/Thinkstock; **234** Jupiterimages/Thinkstock; **236bl** istockphoto/Thinkstock; **236br** Jupiterimages/Thinkstock; **238** BananaStock/Thinkstock; **239 & 246bl** © AF archive/Alamy; **240t** Olga Sapegina/Shutterstock; **240b** Ajay Bhaskar/Shutterstock; **242 & 246tr** BananaStock/Thinkstock; **243** Hemera Technologies; **244 & 246br** © Sirimo/istockphoto; **245** Jupiterimages/Thinkstock

**CHAPTER 13** **252** © Steve Debenport; **254 & 270tl** Keith Brofsky/Thinkstock; **255** Siri Stafford/Thinkstock; **256** AP Photo/Potomac News, Peter Cihelka; **257 & 270bl** Jupiter Images/Thinkstock; **259** Lucky Business/Shutterstock; **260** The New York Times Photo Archives; **262** Hemera Technologies/Thinkstock; **263** istockphoto/Thinkstock; **264** Jupiter Images/Thinkstock; **265 & 270tr** © Johner Images/Alamy; **266 & 270br** © AF archive/Alamy; **267l** © Catherine Yeulet/istockphoto; **267r** Brand X Pictures/Thinkstock; **269** istockphoto/Thinkstock

**READINGS AND APPLIED SOCIAL PSYCHOLOGY** **38–39, 134–137, 196–201, 222–227, 248–251, 221–273 background** © Olga Gabay/istockphoto; **94** Digital Vision/Thinkstock; **95** Digital Vision/Thinkstock; **114** Digital Vision/Thinkstock; **115** © trekandshoot/Dreamstime.com; **174** Junial Enterprises/Shutterstock; **175** CP PHOTO/Frank Gunn; **195–201 background** Comstock Images/Thinkstock.

## LITERARY CREDITS

**CHAPTER 03** **47** Dauvergne, M. (2007). Crime statistics in Canada, 2007. *Juristat, 28*, 1-17; Statistics Canada. (2010); **48** Blackwell Publishing, Ltd. (UK) G Gigerenzer; Koehler D; N Harvey; Fast and frugal heruristics: The tools of bounded rationality, in D. Koehler & N. Harvey (Eds.) Blackwell handbook of judgement and decision making (pp. 62-88)

**CHAPTER 06** **98** J.T Cacioppo and W.L. Gardner and G.G. Berntson (1997) Beyond bipolar conceptualizations and measures. The case of attitudes and evaluative space. Personality and Social Psychology Review; 1, 3-25; **103** Adapted from: Jelenec, P., & Steffens, M. C. (2002). Implicit attitudes toward elderly women and men. Current Research in Social Psychology, 7, 275-293; **107** D M Carkenord; J Bullington , Teaching of Psychology (20) pp. 41-43, copyright © 1993 (Sage Publications) Reprinted by Permission of SAGE Publications.

**CHAPTER 08** **152** From the book "Obedience to Authority" by Stanley Milgram, Harper & Row, 1974

**CHAPTER 11** **213** B J Bushman; C A Anderson 2002 violent video games and hostile expectations: A test of the General Aggression model Personality and social psychology Bulletin 28, 1679-1689 SAGE Publishing

**CHAPTER 12** **241** American Psychological Association (APA) Sources: Sternberg, R. J. (1986). A triangular theory of love. Psychological Review, 93(2), 119-135

**READINGS** **38–39** 1Henrich, J., Heine, S. J. & Norenzayan, A. Behav. Brain Sci. doi:10.1017/S0140525X0999152X (2010). 2 Henrich, J., Heine, S. J. & Norenzayan, A. Behav. Brain Sci. doi: 10.1017/S0140525X10000725 (2010). 3Arnett, J. Am. Psychol. 63, 602-614 (2008). NATURE, Vol. 466, Page 29 Copyright 2010 Macmillan Publishers Limited; **134–137** Indecent Influence: The Positive Effects of Obscenity on Persuasion, Cory R. Scherer, Brad J. Sagarin, SOCIAL INFLUENCE Vol. 1, Issue 2, Pages 138-146. Copyright 2006 Psychology Press Ltd., reprinted with permission of the publisher (Taylor & Francis Ltd, http://www.tandf.co.uk/journals); **196–201** NEWSWEEK, September 4, 2009, Copyright 2009 Harman Newsweek LLC; **222–257** Facial Structure Is a Reliable Cue of Aggressive Behavior JUSTIN M. CARRÉ, 1 CHERYL M. MCCORMICK, and CATHERINE J. MONDLOCH1, 1*Department of Psychology and 2Centre for Neuroscience, Brock University;* **248–251** Reproduced with permission. Copyright © (2010) Scientific American, a division of Nature America, Inc. All rights reserved; **272–273** PSYCHOLOGICAL SCIENCE, Vol. 21, Pages 381-383 Copyright 2010 Association for Psychological Science "The Smell of Virtue: Clean Scents promote Reciprocity and Charity" By KATIE LILJENQUIST, CHEN-BO ZHONG and ADAM D. GALINSKY Feb 4, 2010.

# INDEX

## C



## D

## U



## V



## W



## Y



## Z